CONFLICT AND CONSENSUS
IN MODERN AMERICAN HISTORY

CONFLICT AND CONSENSUS IN MODERN AMERICAN HISTORY

THIRD EDITION

Edited with Introductions by

Allen F. Davis

Temple University

Harold D. Woodman

Purdue University

D. C. HEATH AND COMPANY

Lexington, Massachusetts Toronto London

For Gregory and Paul
and Allan and David

PREFACE

We are pleased that the reception to our book has warranted the publication of a third edition. In this new edition we have retained the basic organization as well as the emphasis on the themes of conflict and consensus. We continue to believe that the presentation of conflicting views within the context of general interpretations allows the beginning student to deepen his understanding of particular periods in American history at the same time that it provides him with the basis for interpreting the broad sweep of his country's history.

In this edition, as in the others, we have avoided presenting only two extreme positions on each problem raised. Such an either/or approach could force the student into making an artificial choice or into the equally erroneous belief that truth is always to be found midway between two extremes. We have, therefore, in every case included at least three selections dealing with the same problem in an attempt to illustrate the subtleties of interpretation.

Our main concern has not been with historiography, although we do direct interested students to relevant historiographical discussions. The beginning student is not especially interested in the shifting interpretations of historical data, nor should he be at this stage. He should be interested in learning what happened and why it happened, in learning how it is possible for two historians to examine the same evidence and then arrive at different conclusions. We have, therefore, concentrated not on the evolution of historical writing but on the historical problems themselves. We hope to leave the student with a heightened understanding of the problems of interpretation of the various periods in American history and also to provide the ammunition for thoughtful and spirited discussions. For those who wish to pursue any matter further, we have provided brief, annotated bibliographies at the end of each problem.

In this edition we have added a number of new problems and dropped a few that appeared in the previous editions. We have also made a number of substitutions in the remaining problems. Changes have been dictated by our desire to make the book more useful in the introductory course, to include some of the good work that has appeared since the first and second editions, and to incorporate the changing approaches to the themes of conflict and consensus. We have been aided in making these changes by the thoughtful suggestions of many teachers who have used the other editions. Our title change (from *Conflict or Consensus* to *Conflict and Consensus*) reflects the changing approaches to the study of American history in recent years.

For this edition we also offer an expanded introduction that is designed to help the beginning student to understand why historians disagree. It has been our experience that students are often confused rather than enlightened when they are presented with conflicting interpretations of the same events. We have therefore provided a very brief introduction to historical methods that could, if the instructor so desired, serve as the basis for discussions during the first or second meetings of class.

ALLEN F. DAVIS
HAROLD D. WOODMAN

ACKNOWLEDGMENTS

The editing of this book has put us in the debt of many. We wish to thank the various publishers and authors for permission to reprint copyrighted material. Former instructors in our introductory course in American history at the University of Missouri will recognize many of the ideas in this book; we are grateful for their aid and recognize that in a real sense they have been collaborators. We would also like to thank the many teachers and students who have made useful comments on the earlier editions of this book. We would especially note the invaluable aid of the following: Richard S. Kirkendall, John Lankford, Walter V. Scholes, and Selwyn Troen of the University of Missouri, Columbia; Robert L. Branyan and Lawrence H. Larsen of the University of Missouri, Kansas City; Thomas C. Barrow of Clark University; Franklin Mitchell of the University of Southern California; Lyle Dorsett of the University of Colorado; James F. Watts of the City College of the City University of New York; Alonzo Hamby of Ohio University; John Burnham of Ohio State University; J. Stanley Lemons of Rhode Island College; Herbert Ershkowitz, Robert Miller, and Howard Ohline of Temple University. We would also like to thank Susan Ellmaker and Linda Harris, graduate students at Temple University, for their part in improving this edition. Ida Mae Wolff of Columbia, Missouri patiently and efficiently typed the manuscript.

Finally, we want to express a special debt to our wives, Roberta Davis and Leonora Woodman, who offered aid and encouragement at every step in the preparation of this book.

CONTENTS

Introduction: History and Historians   xiii

1 BUSINESS IN AN INDUSTRIAL AGE

Industrialism Under Way, *Samuel P. Hays*   5
The Robber Barons, *Matthew Josephson*   16
Industrial Statesmen, *Allan Nevins*   34

2 FARMERS IN AN INDUSTRIAL AGE

The Farmers' Grievances, *John D. Hicks*   50
Populism: Nostalgic Agrarianism, *Richard Hofstadter*   65
Populism: Realistic Radicalism, *Norman Pollack*   76

3 WORKINGMEN IN AN INDUSTRIAL AGE

American Labor Violence, *Philip Taft* and *Philip Ross*   90
A Harmony of Beliefs, *Edward C. Kirkland*   109
Labor and Capitalism in America, *Selig Perlman*   122
The Worker's Search for Power, *Herbert G. Gutman*   133

4 MIGRANTS TO AN URBAN AMERICA

The Uprooted, *Oscar Handlin*   154
The Making of a Negro Ghetto, *Allan H. Spear*   170
Race: Thinking May Make It So, *Edward C. Banfield*   184
Violence in the Cities, *Richard C. Wade*   200

5 THE PROGRESSIVE MOVEMENT

Progressivism: Anti-Business Reform, *Russell Nye*   219

Progressivism: Middle-Class Disillusionment, *George Mowry*   229
A Condition of Excitement, *Eric Goldman*   241
The Triumph of Conservatism, *Gabriel Kolko*   247

6 THE NEW DEAL

Conservative Reform Movement, *Frank Freidel*   271
The Third American Revolution, *Carl N. Degler*   287
Middle-Class America Refurbished, *Howard Zinn*   304

7 THE UNITED STATES AS A WORLD POWER

The American Approach to Foreign Policy, *John Spanier*   325
An Appraisal of American Foreign Policy, *William G. Carleton*   338
No More Vietnams?, *Ronald Steel*   347
Militarism and Imperialism, *Paul A. Baran* and *Paul M. Sweezy*   356
The Limits of Consensus, *Gabriel Kolko*   370

8 THE AGE OF ANXIETY AND PROTEST

The Emerging Republican Majority, *Kevin Phillips*   394
The Artificial Majority, *Theodore J. Lowi*   409
The Radical Right: The Dispossessed, *Daniel Bell*   416
Young Men of the 1950's: A Generation of Bureaucrats,
    William H. Whyte, Jr.   431
The New Radicals of the 1960's, *Paul Jacobs* and *Saul Landau*   443
Crisis in the New Left, *Larry David Nachman*   451
The Future of the Civil Rights Movement, *Bayard Rustin*   464
Black Radicalism, *Vincent Harding*   476

9 THE AMERICAN CHARACTER

Abundance and the Formation of Character, *David M. Potter*   501
The Other America, *Michael Harrington*   512
The Significance of the Frontier in American History,
    Frederick Jackson Turner   527
From Morality to Morale, *David Riesman*   547

INTRODUCTION: HISTORY AND HISTORIANS

Most students are introduced to the study of history by being immersed, usually by way of a fat textbook, in a vast sea of names, dates, events, and statistics. Each student's skill is then tested by an examination that requires him to show how much of this data he remembers; the more he remembers, the higher his grade. From this experience a number of conclusions seem obvious: the study of history is the study of "facts" about the past; the more "facts" you know, the better you are as a student of history; the professional historian, be he teacher or textbook writer, is simply one who brings together a very large number of "facts."

Of course, only the most naive of students fails to see that the data of history, the "facts," are presented in an organized manner. Textbooks tell not only what happened, but also why it happened. Thus, for example, the student learns that Puritans began coming from England to the Massachusetts Bay colony in the New World in 1630, but he also learns why they came when he reads of the conflicts between the Puritans and the established church in England. Similarly, he reads of the steady trek of people westward during the nineteenth century, but at the same time he learns details that explain this movement of people—the availability of fertile lands in the West, the discovery of gold in California, the improvement of roads and other transportation facilities.

But the beginning student, even as he comes to recognize that his teacher and his textbook are explaining as well as describing events in the past, still has no reason to alter his notions as to what history is all about. He is still working in the realm of "fact." The "fact" of the movement of people into Ohio is explained by the "fact" that fertile land was available there. He may learn more details about the event—how many people went to Ohio, when they arrived, where they settled—and about the explanation—the cost of land in Ohio, the availability of credit, the exhaustion of soils in the eastern states. Or he may be introduced to a fuller explanation when he reads that some people came to Ohio to escape their creditors or to seek adventure or to speculate in land. In either case, he is simply learning more "facts." An advanced course in American history in high school differs from the sixth-grade course in American history in that it gives more detail; the older student must remember more "facts."

A student who has been introduced to history in this way, may end up confused when he discovers in a book such as this that historians often disagree sharply with one another. To be sure, each historian presents his material in the familiar way; he tells what happened and why it happened by presenting a mass of historical data. But the student soon discovers that two or three or more historians dealing with the same event may come to quite different conclusions about it. Sometimes two historians will use two very different sets of "facts" in describing an event and this leads them to different conclusions. But at other times the same "facts" are given different meanings by different historians and their conclusions therefore differ.

The common-sense reaction to this state of affairs is to conclude that one historian is right while the other is wrong. But common sense will take the student no further than this. Presumably, the historian who is wrong will have his "facts" wrong. But this is seldom the case. The student finds that both historians argue reasonably—and persuasively. And the "facts"—the names, dates, events, figures—usually turn out to be correct. Moreover, to complicate matters, he often finds that the contending historians more or less agree on the facts; that is, they use much the same data to come to different conclusions. To argue that both are right when both say different things seems irrational and, in any case, such an approach is often unacceptable to a teacher who expects his students to take a position. The only way out for the baffled student is to choose one point of view for reasons he cannot fully explain. History, which had seemed to be a cut-and-dried matter of memorizing "facts," now becomes a matter of choosing one good interpretation from among many. Historical truth becomes a matter of personal preference to be chosen like a brand-name item in a supermarket.

This position is hardly satisfying. And when his teacher informs him that the controversy over historical interpretations is what lends excitement to the study of history, he can only respond that he feels more confusion than excitement. He cannot help but feel that two diametrically opposed points of view about an event cannot both be right; yet he lacks the ability to decide between them.

Obviously, there is no easy solution to this problem. Indeed, if there were, the problem would not be a problem at all because historians would not differ in their interpretations. Historians do not disagree in order to provide the raw material for "problems" books such as this one; they disagree because each historian views the past from a particular perspective. Once the student grasps this, he has taken the first step toward being able to evaluate the work of various historians. But before he can take this first step, the student must consider a problem he has more or less taken for granted. He must ask himself what history really is.

The word "history" has several meanings. In its broadest sense, it denotes the whole of the human past. More restricted is the notion that history is the *recorded* past, that is, that part of human life which has left some sort of record such as folk-tales, artifacts, or written documents. Finally, history may be defined as that which historians write about the past.

Of course, the three meanings are related. The historian writing about the past bases his story on the remains of the past, on the artifacts and documents left by people. Obviously he cannot know everything for the simple reason that not every event, every happening, was fully and completely recorded. And the further back he goes in time, the fewer are the records that remain. In this sense, then, the historian can only approximate history in the first meaning above, that is, history as the entire human past.

But this does not say enough. If the historian cannot know everything because not everything was recorded, neither does he use all the records that are available to him. Rather, the historian *selects* from the total those records he deems most significant. Moreover, to complicate matters a bit more, the historian also recreates parts of the past for which he has no recorded evidence. Like a detective, he pieces together evidence to fill in the gaps in the available records.

The historian is able to select evidence and to create evidence by using some theory or idea of human motivation and behavior. Sometimes this appears to be easy, requiring very little sophistication and subtlety. Thus, for example, the historian investigating America's entry into World War I would probably find that the sinking of American merchant ships on the high seas by German submarines was relevant to his discussion. At the same time, he would most likely not use evidence that President Woodrow Wilson's wife bought a new hat during the first months of 1917. The choice as to which fact to use is based on a theory—admittedly, in this case a rather crude theory, but a theory nonetheless. It would go something like this: National leaders contemplating war are more likely to be influenced by belligerent acts against their countries than by the hat-buying habits of their wives.

The choice, of course, is not always so obvious. But, before pursuing the problem further, it is important to note that a choice must be made. The historian does not just present the facts; he presents *some* facts and not others. He chooses those facts that seem significant and rejects the others. This is one of the reasons why historians disagree. They have different views or different theories concerning human behavior and therefore find different kinds of information significant.

Perhaps it might appear that it is the subject matter being investigated rather than any theory held by the historian that dictates which facts are significant. But this is not really so. With a little imagination—and poetic license—one could conceive of a psychological explanation for Wilson's actions that would include mounting frustration and anger fed in part, at least, by his strong disapproval of his wife's silly new hat. In this case the purchase by his wife of a new hat would be a relevant fact in explaining Wilson's decision to ask Congress for a declaration of war. If the reader finds this outlandish, it is only because his notion of presidential motivation does not include this kind of personal reaction as an influence in determining matters of state.

If the choices were always as simple as choosing between German submarines and Mrs. Wilson's new hat, the problem would be easily resolved. But usually the choices are not so easy to make. The historian investigating United States entry into World War I will find in addition to German submarine warfare a whole series of other facts that could be relevant to the event under study. For instance, he will find that the British government had a propaganda machine at work in the United States that did its best to win public support for the British cause. He will discover that American bankers had made large loans to the British, loans that would not be repaid in the event of a British defeat. He will read of the interception of the "Zimmerman Note," in which the German foreign secretary ordered the German minister in Mexico, in the event of war, to suggest an alliance between Germany and Mexico whereby Mexico, with German support, could win back territory taken from Mexico by the United States in the Mexican War. He will also find among many American political leaders a deep concern over the balance of power in Europe, a balance that would be destroyed—to America's disadvantage—if the Germans were able to defeat the French and the British and thereby emerge as the sole major power in Europe.

What then is the historian investigating America's entry into World War I to make of these facts? He could simply conclude that America entered the war for several reasons and then list the facts he has discovered. By doing so he would be making two important assumptions: 1) Those facts he puts on his list—in this case, German submarine warfare, British propaganda, American loans, the Zimmerman Note, and concern over the balance of power—are the main reasons, while those he does not list are not important; and 2) those things he puts on his list are of equal importance in explaining the U.S. role. But another historian might argue that the list is incomplete in that it does not take into account the generally pro-British views of Woodrow Wilson, views that stemmed from the President's background and education. The result will be a disagreement between the two historians. Moreover, because the second historian raises the question of Wilson's views, he will find a number of relevant facts that the first historian would ignore. He will concern himself with Wilson's education, the influence of his teachers, the books he read, and the books he wrote. In short, although both historians are dealing with the same subject—America's entry into World War I—they will come to different conclusions and use different facts to support their points of view. The facts selected, and those ignored, will depend not on the problem being studied but on the point of view of the historian.

Similarly, a third historian might maintain that the various items on the list should not be given equal weight, that one of the reasons listed, say bankers' loans, was most important and that the others seemed to be significant only because of the overwhelming power of the bankers to influence American policy. The theory here would be that economic matters are the key to human motivation and that a small number of wealthy bankers have a disproportionate ability to influence government. Again, the third historian will disagree with the first two and he will find relevant certain facts that the others will not—for example, bankers' opinions, the lobbying activities of bankers, financial and political connections between bankers and politicians, and the like.

In the examples given, historians disagree and use different facts or give different emphasis to the same facts because they begin from different premises; in other words, they have different theories of human motivation. But there is still another realm of disagreement which, although it often appears similar to that just discussed, in fact stems from something rather different. Historians sometimes disagree because they are not really discussing the same thing. Often they are merely considering different levels of cause and effect. A few examples will illustrate this point.

The simplest level of analysis of cause and effect is to recognize what may be called proximate cause. "I was late for class," you explain, "because I overslept." Or, to use an historical example, "The Civil War began because South Carolina shore batteries under the command of General Beauregard opened fire on the federal garrison at Fort Sumter on April 12, 1861." Neither statement can be faulted on the grounds that it is inaccurate, but at the same time neither is sufficient as an explanation of the event being considered. The next question is obvious: Why did you oversleep, or why did relations between one state and the federal government reach the point where differences had to be settled by war? To this you may answer that you were out very late last night at a party, and the historian may respond that the authorities in South Carolina concluded that the election of Abraham Lincoln and his subsequent actions in threatening to supply the federal garrison at Fort Sumter were a clear menace to the well-being of South Carolina.

We have now dug more deeply into the problems, but the answers may still not be sufficient to satisfy us. Again we ask the question why and the answer takes us more deeply into the causes of the events under consideration. As we probe further, of course, the answers become more difficult and more complex. The problems discussed earlier—a theory of motivation and the selection of facts—begin to become increasingly important, and disagreements among historians will begin to emerge. But the potential for another kind of disagreement also arises. The further back or the deeper the historian goes, the more factors there are to be considered and the more tenuous the connection between cause and effect becomes. Historians may disagree about the point at which to begin their analysis, that is, about the location of a point beyond which the causal connection becomes so tenuous as to be meaningless. You might argue that the ultimate cause of your being late to class was the fact that you were born, but obviously this goes back too far to be meaningful. That you were born is, of course, a necessary factor—unless that had happened, you could not have been late—but it is not a sufficient factor; it does not really tell enough to explain your behavior today. Similarly, we could trace the cause of the Civil War back to the discovery of America, but again, this is a necessary but not a sufficient cause.

The point at which causes are both necessary and sufficient is not self-evident. In part, the point is determined by the theoretical stance of the historian. If he decides that slavery is the key to understanding the coming of the Civil War, the point will be located somewhere along the continuum of the history of slavery in the United States. But even those historians who agree that slavery is the key to the war will not necessarily agree at what point slavery becomes both necessary and sufficient. The historian who believes that slavery was a constant irritant driving the North and South apart might begin his discussion with the introduction of blacks into Virginia in 1619. He would find relevant the antislavery attitudes of Northerners during the colonial period, the conflict over slavery in the Constitutional Convention, the Missouri Compromise, the militant abolitionist movement of the 1830's, and the Compromise of 1850. But another historian might argue that the slavery issue did not become really significant until it was associated with the settlement of the western lands. He would probably begin his discussion with the Missouri Compromise and the facts he would find most relevant would be those that illustrated the fear many people had of the expansion of slavery into the new western lands.

Ostensibly, both historians would be discussing the role of slavery in the coming of the Civil War, but actually they would be discussing two different things. For the first historian, the expansion of slavery to the West would be only part of a longer and more complex story; for the second, slavery and the West would be the whole story. Sometimes the same facts would be used by both, with each giving them different weight and significance, but at other times, one of the historians would find some facts relevant which the other would not.

The reader should now be in a position to understand something of the sources of disagreement among historians. Historians arrive at different conclusions because they have different notions about human motivation and different ideas about what constitutes necessary and sufficient cause. Historical facts as such have no intrinsic meaning; they take on meaning and significance only when they are organized and presented by a historian with a particular point of view. The well-used phrase, "let the facts speak for themselves," therefore has no real meaning. The facts do *not* speak for themselves; the historian uses the facts in a particular way and therefore he, and not the facts, is doing the speaking.

By shifting our analysis from the historian's conclusions to his assumptions (from which the conclusions flow), we are in a better position to evaluate his work. To be sure, we still cannot "solve" the problem of disagreement; that is, we cannot, merely by understanding the theoretical stance of the historian, eliminate all disagreement. If the state of our knowledge were such that it provided us with a model of unquestioned validity that completely explained human behavior, we could employ this model to explain our data, our historical facts. Any analysis that began by assuming a different model or explanation would therefore be wrong.[1]

But since we do not have such a complete and foolproof explanation, disagreements are destined to remain. For the reader who has been patient enough to follow the argument to this point, the conclusions stated here may appear somewhat dismal and unrewarding. In convincing him that evaluating a historical interpretation is not like picking an item off a supermarket shelf, have we done more than move him to another store with a different stock on its shelves? If there are many explanatory models to choose from, and if no one of them is complete, foolproof, and guaranteed true, then it would appear that we are simply in another store with different merchandise on display.

Such a conclusion is unwarranted. In the first place, the student who is able to understand the premises from which a historian begins will be able to comprehend the way the historian works and the process by which he fashions his interpretation. Moreover, this understanding will enable him to evaluate the work of historians. For at this stage the student is no longer simply memorizing details; nor is he attempting to evaluate a historical essay by trying to discover whether each of the facts presented is true. He can now ask more important questions of the material before him: Is the premise from which the historian begins an adequate explanation for human behavior? Do the facts he presents really flow from his premises and support his conclusions? Are there other data the historian has ignored that would tend to undermine his argument and throw doubt on the adequacy of his premises?

As he attempts to answer these questions, the student begins to learn history by thinking and acting like a historian. And as he does, he begins to accumulate knowledge and understanding and insight in much the same ways that historians do. Historians are constantly discovering new information;

---

[1] It should be noted in passing that even if we had such a theory, there would be much room for disagreement because we would often lack the required data. Some essential information would be lost through deliberate or accidental destruction. Other information might leave no record. Records of births, deaths, income, and so forth are now required by law, but in earlier days these records were not kept or were kept only sporadically. And telephone and personal conversations might leave no concrete record even though they could have a profound influence on behavior.

diaries, letters, business records, and family Bibles are always being found in attics, basements, and even in remote corners of large research libraries. Historians are also gaining new insights from the research of social scientists such as economists, political scientists, sociologists, and psychologists. Investigations by these scholars into such problems as mass hysteria, the influence of propaganda on behavior, the effects of the money supply on economic change, the relationship between voting patterns and race and ethnic origin, and the psychological effects of racism all provide insights that may be of value to historians investigating the past. Historians are also mastering and using new techniques. For example, the computer now permits the historian to handle huge masses of data quickly and accurately.

Historians also learn from one another. For example, when one historian discovers the existence of certain political, social, and economic relationships in a given city at a certain time, he provides other historians studying other cities, either at the same or different times, with what may be important and enlightening insights. International comparisons of similar events and institutions can also reveal important features that will be invisible or obscure when these events and institutions are viewed from the perspective of a single nation's history. Finally, historians are influenced by the events and occurrences of their own time. During World War II, for instance, historians reexamined the causes and consequences of World War I, just as the war in Vietnam is now providing new perspectives for the Cold War years. The civil rights movement of the 1960's inspired a number of historians to reinterpret the role of the abolitionists in the events leading up to the Civil War and to give more attention to slavery, race, and prejudice in American life. Similarly, the riots and urban violence of recent years are causing historians to examine the riots and violence of other periods.

At first it may seem frustrating to realize that there is no one easy answer to the problems historians raise and that "truth" is but an elusive yet intriguing goal in a never-ending quest. But when the student realizes this, he has *begun* his education. And at that point, he will find the study of history to be a significant, exhilarating, and useful part of his education. For coming to grips with conflicting interpretations of the past is more than an interesting classroom game; it is part of a larger process of coming to terms with the world around us. Every day we are asked to evaluate articles in newspapers and magazines or reports of events provided by friends or radio commentators. A knowledge of history provides a background for interpreting these accounts; but more than that, the past and the present are so interconnected that one's interpretation of the American Revolution, slavery, the progressive movement, or American foreign policy after World War II are intimately related to one's views toward civil rights and domestic and foreign policy today.

The discussion thus far has emphasized the element of disagreement among historians and has attempted to show the beginning student how these disagreements arise and how he should deal with them. But if disagreements arise because historians often start their analyses from different perspectives, it does not follow that there is no agreement at all among historians. On the contrary, groups of historians have tended to assume similar theoretical postures, and the result has been the emergence of "schools" of historical writing. All differences among members of a particular school do not disappear, but their approaches remain similar enough to differentiate them from members of other schools.

Identifying schools and placing historians in them is seldom easy and is always somewhat arbitrary. The reasons are obvious enough: The amount and complexity of works about America's past are so great that it is possible to identify a large number of schools. Moreover, since few historians begin with an explicit ideology or philosophy of history, their work may fit into a number of possible schools. Finally, most good historians do not cling dogmatically to a particular approach. As their research and writing proceeds, as they learn more, or as contemporary events alter their perspectives, their interpretations tend to change.

In organizing this book we have chosen two recurrent and important schools, or interpretive themes, in the writings on American history: conflict and consensus. Admittedly, the choice, in one sense at least, is arbitrary; we could have chosen from a number of other unifying themes. On the other hand, the choice has not been completely arbitrary in that these themes—conflict and consensus—expressed either explicitly or implicitly, may be found in virtually all major interpretations of our country's past. The student who reads the following pages and attempts to evaluate the arguments presented will be faced with two real and meaningful ways to understand the American past and, indeed, to judge the contemporary American scene.

Stripped to its essentials, the task of the historian is to deal with change. And nowhere does the historian find change more manifest than when he studies the United States. Almost in the twinkling of an eye a vast, scarcely populated continent was transformed into a major industrial power of phenomenal complexity. Overnight, virgin forests became fertile farms, Indian trails became roads, highways, and railroads, and empty spaces became bustling cities. Matching this transformation of the physical face of the continent were equally momentous changes in politics, social relations, ideas, and attitudes. For most Americans, constant and rapid change was inevitable if only because it was so obvious. "Ten years in America are like a century in Spain," wrote the German immigrant Francis Lieber soon after his arrival in the United States early in the nineteenth century. "The United States really changes in some respects more within ten years than a country like Spain has within a hundred."

But who could argue that Europe was static and unchanging? True enough, Europe had little in the way of trackless wildernesses to be discovered, settled, and transformed; and true also, Europe was crowded with the remnants of what might appear to be an unchanging past—cathedrals and monuments, aristocratic and royal institutions, and ways of doing things that seemed to have existed time out of mind. But at the same time, Europe periodically exploded into change. Indeed, time after time, Americans saw Europe swept by rebellion and war as one group after another sought, often successfully, to revolutionize European lives and institutions.

Generations of American historians have tried to describe and to explain the vast alterations that have taken place on the North American continent. As they did so, many kept one eye on the changes in European institutions and sought to compare and to contrast the nature of changes in the Old World with those of the New. But even as they read the historical documents, often in the light of European history and experience, the historians themselves were living through vast and rapid changes taking place around them in the United States.

The writings by American historians have been varied and rich. But from this variety two rather distinct traditions have emerged, each of which has sought to provide an explanation for the course of American history.

One tradition or point of view holds that the key to American history, like that of Europe, is conflict. Historians who adhere to this point of view speak in terms of revolution and class and sectional conflict. They stress the differences among Americans—class differences, social differences, political differences. Their emphasis is on fundamental conflicts: democrats versus aristocrats, debtors versus creditors, workers versus businessmen, North versus South, farmers versus railroads, blacks versus whites. Change, they argue, is a function of this never-ending conflict; it arises from the efforts of particular groups and classes to impose their hegemony over American society, or at least to increase their influence over that society.

The other tradition stresses the uniqueness of the American experience by finding a basic consensus in American society. According to this tradition, all Americans of whatever class or station shared what was essentially a common outlook. To be sure, Americans did not all live alike nor did they always agree with one another. But their disagreements, especially when compared with the dissensions that divided European society, were not fundamental. Consensus historians do not ignore class and sectional differences nor do they deny conflicts between groups such as workers and employers. But they do deny that these conflicts were basic. Americans, they argue, achieved a consensus on fundamentals; if they disagreed, their disagreements were minor differences within an underlying consensus. Change then is the result of a fundamental agreement that change is required and does not arise from a struggle for power.

Although both these themes can be found in the earliest writings on American history, they became dominant interpretive themes only during the twentieth century. The theme of conflict was central to the writings of what Richard Hofstadter has called the "Progressive Historians": Frederick Jackson Turner, Charles A. Beard, and Vernon L. Parrington. Growing up in the midst of the nation's rapid industrialization and living in a time of growing protest against the problems created by that industrialization, these historians saw the past in terms of bitter conflict. Their influence, as the reader of the following pages will discover, was profound. The theme of consensus was in part a reaction to what was considered to be the overstatements of the conflict school and in part a reaction to the world of the 1950's. At that time, European wars and revolutionary conflicts seemed strangely alien to American society, as did historical interpretations cast in the European mold. Looking at the past, these historians discovered that America had always been different from Europe; Americans had, for the most part, been spared the bitter conflicts that plagued Europe. Like the conflict historians of an earlier generation, the new consensus historians had a great influence on American historical thought.

But the consensus historians were not without their critics. John Higham argued that they were "homogenizing" American history; he accused them of "carrying out a massive grading operation to smooth over America's social convulsions." He and other critics did not simply call for a return to the history of the progressive historians. They argued that the pendulum had swung too far; the past in the books and articles of the consensus historians had become bland and meaningless.

In recent years, conflict has been rediscovered. Sometimes it has been in the older categories posed by the progressive historians, but more often it appears in the form of a new set of dualities. A group of radical historians, the "new left," has entered the lists. But if the new left is united in its radical stance, it is not united in its evaluation of the themes of conflict and consensus: leftist historians, like their liberal and conservative colleagues, find themselves in both camps.

And so the lines that divide the conflict from the consensus historians are not as sharp as they once were and many contemporary historians are drawing from both in their analyses of America's past. Nevertheless, the differences persist and will continue to do so. In the readings that follow, the student is introduced to the two traditions and their variations through the words of their most able exponents.

SUGGESTIONS FOR FURTHER READING

The literature on the philosophy and practice of history comes from the pens of both philosophers and practicing historians. A few recent volumes have been written specifically for the beginning student; an example is Walter T. K. Nugent, *Creative History* (Philadelphia, 1967). More sophisticated but eminently readable

* Available in paperback edition.

are E. H. Carr, *What Is History? (New York, 1964), Louis Gottschalk, *Understanding History (New York, 1963), Allan Nevins, *The Gateway to History (Garden City, New York, 1962), and Marc Bloch, *The Historian's Craft (New York, 1953). A splendid anthology prefaced by an illuminating introduction is Hans Meyerhoff, ed., *The Philosophy of History in Our Time (Garden City, New York, 1959). Another good collection of readings on the philosophy of history is Patrick Gardiner, ed., Theories of History (New York, 1959). The books listed have bibliographies that will take the interested student as far as he might wish to go in the field.

Students wishing to pursue the historiography (that is, the history of historical writing) of the conflict-consensus theme should begin with the progressive historians. Charles A. Beard was a prolific writer, but the best approach to him is through Charles and Mary Beard, The Rise of American Civilization (New York, 1927, 1930), a lively and interesting interpretation of the whole course of American history, with an emphasis on class and economic conflict. Beard's *An Economic Interpretation of the Constitution (New York, 1913, 1935) must be read by any serious student. Vernon Parrington's three-volume *Main Currents in American Thought (New York, 1927, 1930) complements Beard's work and deals with the relationship of literature and ideas to society and social movements. Frederick Jackson Turner's essays may be found in *The Frontier in American History (New York, 1920) and *The Significance of Sections in American History (New York, 1932). There are many discussions of the work and influence of these historians; the reader can do no better than to begin with Richard Hofstadter, *The Progressive Historians (New York, 1968), the work of a perceptive and sensitive critic. This book's great value is enhanced by an outstanding "bibliographical essay" that will lead the student deep into the literature on the subject.

Any serious student of the consensus historians must read and study Louis Hartz, *The Liberal Tradition in America (New York, 1955) and the key works of Daniel J. Boorstin: *The Genius of American Politics (Chicago, 1953), *The Americans: The Colonial Experience (New York, 1958), and *The Americans: The National Experience (New York, 1965). A perceptive discussion of these books as well as of the entire consensus school along with good bibliographical information may be found in the Hofstadter volume cited above. An important and provocative critique of the consensus approach is John Higham, "The Cult of the American Consensus," Commentary, XXVII (February 1959), pp. 93–100. See also, J. Rogers Hollingsworth, "Consensus and Continuity in Recent American Historical Writing," South Atlantic Quarterly, LXI (Winter 1962), pp. 40–50, and Gene Wise, "Political 'Reality' in Recent American Scholarship: Progressives versus Symbolists," American Quarterly, XXIX, Part 2 (Summer 1967), pp. 303–328.

A good introduction to the work of the "new left" in much of its variety is Barton J. Bernstein, ed., *Towards a New Past: Dissenting Essays in American History (New York, 1968). A critical evaluation of the work of this group, which can also serve as an introductory bibliography, is Irwin Unger, "The 'New Left' and American History: Some Recent Trends in United States Historiography," American Historical Review, LXXVII (July 1967), pp. 1237–1263.

CONFLICT AND CONSENSUS
IN MODERN AMERICAN HISTORY

1
BUSINESS IN AN INDUSTRIAL AGE

Although most historians and economists agree that America's industrial revolution—or, to use W. W. Rostow's striking phrase, "the take-off into sustained growth"—had begun in the pre-Civil War days, the postwar years were marked by great industrial development. Older industries expanded and new industries—oil, electricity, and the automobile, to name three of the most significant—grew into giants by the early decades of the twentieth century. Thus, if industrialism was not new in the post-Civil War years, it certainly became more pervasive during this time. Industry, mainly concentrated in the Northeast before the Civil War, rapidly spread to the West after the civil conflict. Heavy industry gradually became more important in terms of the value of its products, and large scale production came to dominate American industry.

The results were profound. Large scale production required heavy capital expenditures and skilled leadership. A huge working class and a large middle class of professionals congregated in rapidly growing industrial urban centers. Smaller firms found it increasingly difficult to compete with the larger, more influential and richer firms.

As production figures soared and more goods and services became available, serious problems began to appear. A relatively few men, the leaders of the new industrial empires, seemed to be dominating American life. Critics complained of corruption and venality in public and private life and traced the cause to the materialism of the business classes. "Society, in these states, is canker'd, crude, superstitious, and rotten," charged Walt Whitman in his "Democratic Vistas." He decried the "depravity of the business classes" and the "corruption, bribery, falsehood, maladministration" in government on all levels. In 1873 Mark Twain and Charles D. Warner published a long and rambling novel in which they described corruption and decay behind the glittering facade of progress, a novel aptly entitled, The Gilded Age.

For such critics, the period was one of conflict. Rapacious business leaders, often termed "robber barons," supported by a corrupt government, enriched themselves at the expense of less fortunate businessmen and of the public at large. The results were high prices, shoddy merchandise, poor service, and the rule of a business elite which ignored the well-being of the people.

Others deny that this is an accurate portrayal of the age of industrial expansion. Business leaders are termed "industrial statesmen" and they are given credit for solid accomplishments, by those who hold this view. These men are seen as innovators, organizers, and risk takers. They invested their money and their talents in the organization of modern enterprise, always seeking new methods to expand production, to lower costs, and to make more goods and services available to the people. Although these men were motivated by a desire for wealth and power, the net result of their efforts was substantial progress for the entire nation. In a word, then, there was no basic

3

conflict between the aims and methods of the business community and the needs and desires of the entire nation.

These differing views are illustrated in the selections which follow. Samuel P. Hays describes some of the economic changes of the era. While not denying that these changes "took place in an atmosphere of speculation, waste, and disorder" Hays finds that "the desire to create wealth possessed all Americans." The benefits and the problems of industrialism affected everyone and all had to seek ways to adjust. For Hays, then, industrialism required the development of a new consensus among the American people.

The next two selections deal in detail with John D. Rockefeller and the Standard Oil Company he organized and led. For Matthew Josephson, industrialists such as Rockefeller were "robber barons." Granting the ability and energy of men such as Rockefeller, Josephson finds them often to have been ruthless exploiters who brought hardship and difficulty to many. Any positive contributions they made were merely inadvertent by-products of their greedy and predatory quest for wealth and power. Allan Nevins, going over much the same ground, gives another emphasis. Without ignoring many of the negative features of Rockefeller's activities, Nevins concludes that on balance Rockefeller made an important contribution: "Innovator, thinker, planner, bold entrepreneur, he was above all an organizer—one of the master organizers of the era."

Interpretations of the Gilded Age inevitably touch on the question of morality. Are business leaders to be condemned for their moral lapses, for their greed, violence, and unfair tactics? If so, can we attack them on these grounds and find other classes in society less guilty? Or must we realize that people in the past cannot be judged by present-day moral standards?

Perhaps the moral question is not the most important question to ask. Perhaps we would do better to judge the industrialists by their contribution to the economic growth and well-being of the nation. This approach suggests a wide range of questions. Did big business give leadership to the great industrial expansion? Or did these men, through their activities, impede the full development of the economy? Did they by their unrestrained activities create more problems than they solved? If they made contributions, what specifically were they? If they did not, how specifically did they hinder progress?

Industrialism Under Way

Samuel P. Hays

To the uncritical observer, the record of industrialism has been written in the production statistics, the accomplishments of inventor-heroes, and the rising standard of living of the American people. Even more significant, however, were the less obvious and the less concrete changes: the expansion of economic relationships from personal contacts within a village community to impersonal forces in the nation and the entire world; the standardization of life accompanying the standardization of goods and of methods of production; increasing specialization in occupations with the resulting dependence of people upon each other to satisfy their wants; a feeling of insecurity as men faced vast and rapidly changing economic forces that they could not control; the decline of interest in non-material affairs and the rise of the acquisition of material wealth as the major goal in life. These intangible innovations deeply affected the American people; here lay the real human drama of the new age.

The Transportation and Communications Revolution

In the United States in the nineteenth century many factors favored industrial growth. Abundant resources, high in quality and exploitable with relatively small amounts of labor and capital, lay waiting to be developed. Industry could draw a large and cheap labor supply from a reservoir of peasants in Europe who eagerly responded when they learned of American economic opportunities. Domestic capital, derived from earlier mercantile enterprise, provided funds essential for the nation's internal development; European capital augmented domestic savings especially in mining, railroads, and banks. Enterprisers in the United States, moreover, faced few political barriers to economic exchange; the Constitution prohibited states from imposing restrictions on interstate commerce and thereby promoted combination of the factors of production over a vast and varied geographical area. Finally, pre-industrial America had developed a capable group of entrepreneurs; though experienced chiefly in organizing commerce, they were eager to take advantage of every opportunity to expand their operations. The American people displayed a vigorous spirit of enterprise notably in the North, which boasted of its "Yankee ingenuity."

A nationwide transportation system constructed between 1820 and 1915 enabled Americans to exploit fully these latent factors of economic growth. The success of the Erie Canal in New York and the development of the steamboat set off a craze of canal building in the 1820's and initiated a revolution in transportation and communication. Railroads, first constructed in the 1830's, soon surpassed the canals in importance. Although slowed momentarily by the Civil War, railroad expansion proceeded with great rapidity between 1868 and the depression of 1893. Construction was limited to the area east of the Mississippi prior to the Civil War but expanded to the Pacific Coast in the 1870's and 1880's. In the industrial Northeast new mileage produced an extremely dense and complex network. By 1915, when the railroads boasted some 250,000 miles of track, not an important community in the country lay outside this extensive system.

Railroad mileage grew rapidly because Americans in all walks of life visualized the economic progress that cheap transportation could set in motion. Merchants in thriving communities and in communities which hoped to thrive endeavored to reach wider markets by extending their transportation facilities. Before the Civil War, merchants of each of the major Atlantic seaports—New York, Boston, Philadelphia, and Baltimore—promoted competitive railroad building to tap the interior Ohio Valley. The search for markets generated hundreds of similar projects throughout the country. Frequently they were financed through bond and stock subscriptions raised either from merchants themselves or from the general public in campaigns which local commercial associations promoted. Farmers eagerly joined in the crusade; they, too, contributed personal savings and often mortgaged their farms to raise funds to speed construction. Whole communities, realizing that the key to economic growth lay in transportation, participated in the mania. When the town of Ithaca, New York, for example, bonded itself for funds to construct a railroad, the local editor exclaimed, "There is no reason why the direct route from San Francisco to New York may not be through Ithaca." Such enthusiasts visualized new industry, new jobs, better markets, and rising property values that canals and railroads would create. Although these visions were often unrealistic, transportation promoters were not inclined to discourage them.

Cheap, rapid transportation brought all sectors of the economy into close contact with one another; factors of production could be combined far more readily than before. Previously, for example, high shipment costs often prohibited the combination of iron ore and coal located scarcely ten miles apart; but now the economic distance between such resources was phenomenally reduced. Canals and steamboats lowered river-transport costs to less than a tenth of land travel. Initially railroads did not lower rates further between points served by waterways; but they were faster than steamboats, were free from ice and low-water barriers, and penetrated to areas which water carriers could not possibly reach.

These efficiencies stimulated economic growth not only by reducing the cost of production but even more significantly by creating a national market; the transportation and communications revolution destroyed barriers to distribution and permitted producers to sell to consumers throughout the nation. For example, the local blacksmith's plowshares, kettles, pots, and pans before the transportation revolution cost less than similar items manufactured fifty miles away and subject to high shipping charges. Manufacturers were excluded from every distant market, but within their own locality enjoyed a monopoly. Railroads in particular now eliminated these exclusive markets; they opened every part of the country to the products of modern industry and by stimulating mass consumption greatly encouraged the growth of mass production.

No less important in accelerating the tempo of economic life was rapid nationwide communication. The telegraph was first successfully operated in 1844 by Samuel F. B. Morse (1791–1872), a New England artist turned inventor. Widely used during the Civil War, it co-ordinated the myriad transactions of a growing economy as effectively as it had aided military operations. While the telegraph speeded communications over longer distances, the telephone, patented by Alexander Graham Bell (1847–1922) in 1876, replaced messengers in the mushrooming urban centers and speeded the complex administrative processes necessary for large-scale industrial management. The modern press, though less spectacular, was equally vital in co-ordinating the intricate functions of the new economy. Technical innovations, such as the rotary press (1875), enormously increased the output and lowered the cost of newspaper production. Nationwide advertising, which appeared first in the religious journals, the most widely circulated magazines of the day, brought producer and consumer together with a speed previously impossible. The new communication supplemented the new transportation in creating the highly integrated and complex human relationships inherent in modern industrialism.

Railroad construction in the latter half of the nineteenth century served as the most important direct stimulant to production. Lumber mills, quarries, ironworks, and carriage factories found a rapidly growing market in railways. The railroad-construction labor force reached 200,000 in the boom of the 1880's. The new roads, moreover, were major users of both domestic and foreign capital. The close correspondence between the ups and downs of new construction and nationwide economic fluctuations in the post-Civil War era provided evidence of the all-pervasive impact of the railroad on the entire economy. A loss of confidence in railroads affected the money market so as to trigger the depressions of 1873, 1884, and 1893.

The rapidly expanding iron and steel industry, stimulated enormously by the railroads, became the foundation of industrial America. Far outstripping the domestic supply, the need for iron and steel constantly encouraged expansion of American mills. By 1850 railroads had become the leading industrial market for iron, and by 1875 railroad construction, reconstruction, and maintenance consumed over half of the iron produced in the United States. The demand for railroad iron, moreover, brought about the all-important technological shift from charcoal to coke in iron production. Before the introduction of the steam locomotive, rural blacksmiths, who purchased most of the iron, preferred a charcoal-manufactured product which they could work more easily than iron smelted with coal. Coal-smelted iron was quite satisfactory for structural shapes, rails, and locomotives. Coke-produced iron, moreover, permitted a mass production of iron previously not practical. The heavy cost of transporting wood for charcoal limited the size of the area from which fuel could be feasibly drawn, and consequently the size of the blast furnace. But the enormous coal fields of western Pennsylvania presented no such limitations; in a relatively small geographical area they provided the fuel essential for large-scale production. Once the new railroad market appeared, therefore, coke replaced charcoal, and huge blast furnaces and rolling mills grew rapidly in the new capital of the iron industry at Pittsburgh.

A number of farsighted entrepreneurs, most notably Andrew Carnegie (1835–1919), a Scotch immigrant who rose from bobbin-boy to steel magnate in seventeen years, rapidly expanded iron and steel production both in size and technique. The Carnegie steelworks catered to the railroad industry. Carnegie, who was widely known for his ability as a salesman, cultivated the personal friendship of railroad executives and obtained heavy orders for rails, bridge steel, and other structural shapes. He led the way in organizing a vertically integrated iron and steel business. By combining in one organization the major elements of the industry he rapidly reduced the costs of production. After bringing into his enterprise Henry Clay Frick, who owned immense deposits of coking coal in western Pennsylvania, Carnegie acquired a heavy interest in the rich Lake Superior iron-ore area and purchased a fleet of carriers to bring the ore across the Great Lakes to Lake Erie ports.

Railroads, then, both lowered the cost of transportation and stimulated the economy directly by their use of labor, capital, and iron. They also created the mass markets that made mass production possible. When markets were local and limited in size, there was no incentive for businessmen to produce in larger amounts to realize the resultant savings in costs. But the unlimited possibilities of the new mass markets stimulated entrepreneurs to explore and develop mass-production techniques. In the iron and steel industry, for example, the size and scope of production increased rapidly: the average daily output of a blast furnace increased from no more than 45 tons before the Civil War to more than 400 tons in the early twentieth century. Mass production was introduced in many other fields as well, notably lumbering, flour milling, meat packing, and textile manufacturing. For example, larger and more efficient saws were adopted in the lumber industry, and in the milling industry the rolling process, first used extensively in Minneapolis, increased both the output and the quality of flour.

Mass production also depended upon improved techniques, of which standardization of parts and processes was especially significant. Repetitive production of a standard item, independent of the vagaries of the individual craftsman, was the heart of the technical revolution. Each product had to be assembled from a given number of parts, any one of which could be replaced by an identical part. This method of manufacture was developed first in the production of guns in the early nineteenth century by Eli Whitney (1765–1825), a New Englander who earlier had invented the cotton gin (1793) while studying law in Georgia. Others soon applied the principle of interchangeable parts to clocks, sewing machines, typewriters, and many other items. The success of this innovation depended on exact measurement, provided by the vernier caliper, which was first made in the United States in 1851. Subsequent improvements of this device made it possible in the twentieth century to measure one ten-thousandth of an inch. At first limited to the mass production of parts, standardization soon invaded the process of assembling parts into finished products. Frederick Taylor (1856–1915), for example, undertook extensive time-and-motion studies to provide the basic data for standardizing assembly methods in factories. Coming from a well-to-do Philadelphia family, Taylor gave up the study of law at Harvard to become an apprentice machinist at the age of nineteen. Fourteen years later, after rising from laborer to chief engineer of the Midvale Steel Company, he organized his own firm to sell to manufacturers the idea of "scientific management," which involved techniques to promote efficiency not only in the shop but also in the office and in the accounting and sales departments. New assembly methods were first used dramatically by Henry Ford (1863–1947), who established the assembly line, or "progressive line production," in the automobile industry in 1914.

The rapid growth of the American economy depended also on an increasing specialization and division of labor. Relatively independent jacks-of-all-trades (village blacksmiths, for example) gave way to many interdependent individuals skilled in particular economic activities. Most striking was the separation of labor and management functions, which arose slowly in agriculture but rapidly in industry. Specialized managers and specialized wage earners replaced semi-independent artisans; manual laborers no longer organized production or sold finished products. Specialized retailing replaced the general store; the jobber concentrated increasingly on a particular line of goods; investment bankers who floated stocks and bonds became separated from commercial bankers who made loans to business. The sole link among these specialists lay in the price-and-market system in which impersonal monetary values governed the relationships between buyers and sellers of labor, commodities, and credit. Those at the core of this price-and-market network, such as capitalists and business managers, possessed great power to manipulate it, while farmers and wage earners, far less capable of influencing large economic affairs, were more frequently manipulated by others. Thus, the closely knit economy of specialists gave rise to a division between dominant and subordinate, central and peripheral, economic roles.

A simpler distribution system, involving fewer middlemen and more direct buying and selling, replaced the innumerable traders formerly required. Previously manufacturers had sold almost exclusively to jobbers who stocked the goods of many different makers and forwarded them in turn to wholesalers. This system was defective for manufacturers: jobbers hesitated to push any particular line of goods, but manufacturers were eager to exploit the possibilities of a national market by rapidly expanding sales of their own goods. Manufacturers took over more and more of the process of distribution. In 1896, for example, the Pittsburgh Plate Glass Company, dissatisfied with the practices of its jobbers, established a chain of warehouses throughout the country to distribute its own products. Such firms, bypassing jobbers, sold directly to regional wholesalers and often to retailers as well as to industrial and institutional buyers. They developed active sales departments, spent increasing sums for advertising, and registered brand names at the Patent Office in order to distinguish their products from other standard, mass-produced items. Traveling salesmen now represented the producer, and Rural Free Delivery (1896) and Parcel Post (1913) enabled manufacturers to sell to farmers without middlemen. Such innovations in mass retailing as the Sears-Roebuck and Montgomery Ward mail-order houses, the chains, and the department store, which often purchased directly from manufacturers, also contributed to a simpler and more efficient distribution system.

Changes in grain marketing dramatically illustrated the manner in which distribution became more efficient. Marketing facilities in Chicago, the new center of the grain trade, could not handle the immense amounts of wheat which railroads poured into the city from the Middle West in the 1850's and 1860's. A revolution in grain handling resulted. Wheat, formerly transported in bags and carried from railroad to lake vessel on human shoulders, now was shipped bulk in freight cars, dumped into endless chain-buckets, carried to the top of huge elevators, and dropped into ships. The savings in labor and the consequent decline in distribution costs were enormous. The entire system of transporting grain from the Middle West to European markets became equally streamlined. Thus there developed a unified national grain-marketing system in which Chicago commodity merchants played a key role. . . .

Waste, Speculation, Dishonesty

The economic growth of the post-Civil War era took place in an atmosphere of speculation, waste, and disorder. Americans, convinced that their natural resources were unlimited, took little care to save or renew them. Confident that the value of property would rise in the course of rapid growth, every property holder became a speculator, fondly hoping to make a capital gain, to sell at a figure far above the purchase price. Each enterpriser rushed to obtain his share of the markets and productive possibilities suddenly created. It was a field day for the promoter, the individual who visualized opportunities not in continuous profits from a stable enterprise but in the original profits of creating a new enterprise. Charles R. Flint (1850–1934), for example, widely known as the "father of the trusts," organized a score of industrial consolidations, including the United States Rubber Company and the predecessor of the International Business Machines Corporation. Landowners promoted towns that would, they said, outshine El Dorado; townspeople promoted transportation that would, they said, make their village the hub of the universe; and investment bankers promoted business consolidations that would, they said, establish one corporation as the emperor of business. Optimism as to the unlimited future persuaded enterprisers on every hand to pay dearly those who would set economic activity in motion.

The desire to create wealth possessed all Americans. It was not only rich men or great corporation presidents who exploited resources or speculated in property. The farmer who purchased one hundred and sixty acres from a railroad or obtained it free from the government under the Homestead Act (1862) hoped as eagerly for an increase in values as did the land agent who acquired fifty thousand acres of fine timber. Far more important than differences in the size of their holdings was the common desire of all to profit from the rising price of land. Frequently the man with less property complained of the speculative propensities of the "large corporations," but such arguments usually arose from jealousy rather than from a fundamental difference in attitude. The man of small means, moreover, exploited natural resources as eagerly as did the corporate owners; neither looked upon soil, forests, or minerals as limited, and neither wished to pay the increasing costs of more prudent resource management. Only a small number grew rich from profits from the rise in values, but few failed to grasp the opportunity when it came their way.

Not many enterprisers felt compelled to behave so as to retain the confidence and trust of their associates and the public. The rush to secure as large a share as possible of the new markets gave rise to sharp competitive practices. The Standard Oil Company, for example, received from railroads not only rebates on its shipments, a common practice, but a percentage of the shipping charges paid by its competitors as well. Such practices, soon condemned as "unfair," were often illegal. Both large and small entrepreneurs constantly sought ways of evading the spirit of hampering laws. Tempted by unregulated stock exchanges and by the reservoirs of capital in the new corporate form of business organization, many directors could not resist manipulating securities for personal gain at the expense of stockholders. The notorious Jim Fisk and Jay Gould, after joining with Daniel Drew to fleece the Erie Railroad, almost cornered the New York gold supply for their own personal profit. Such men did not hesitate to bribe whole legislatures to obtain laws essential to carry out their aims. The New York lawmakers responded readily to the interests of Fisk, Gould, and Drew, and on the national level the Grant administration seemed extraordinarily close to the operations of a great number of economic freebooters. These were only extreme examples of the instability in both public and private relations fostered by the rush to take advantage of the new opportunities to create wealth. . . .

The Response to Industrialism

The unifying theme of American history between 1885 and 1914, so many historians have argued, was a popular attack against corporate wealth. Through their state and federal governments, according to this interpretation, the discontented sought to curb corporations and thereby to promote greater economic opportunity for all. This analysis accepts, uncritically, the popular ideas of the Populist-Progressive Era. It is a far too simple explanation.

Industrialism did create disparities in wealth and class divisions beyond our comprehension today. But the social, economic, and political movements of those thirty years reveal something more fundamental and more varied than an attempt by the dispossessed to curb the wealthy. They comprised a reaction not against the corporation alone but also against industrialism and the many ways in which it affected the lives of Americans. The people of that era sought to do much more than simply to control corporations; they attempted to cope with industrial change in all its ramifications. True, they centered their fire on the business leader, but he was a symbol of change which they could conveniently attack, rather than the essence of change itself. A simple interpretation of the discontented poor struggling against the happy rich does violence to the complexity of industrial innovation and to the variety of human striving that occurred in response to it.

In a number of instances, as we have observed in the preceding pages, Americans responded to industrialism in ways far different from those described by many historians. Reforms frequently arose from the well-to-do themselves; the social justice movement, for example, grew up among those who had sufficient leisure to be concerned with education, parks, and the working conditions of women and children. On the other hand, the "people" often opposed the measures which, according to historians, were designed to curb corporate influence. Urban immigrants, for example, resenting the attack on the city political machine, opposed urban civic reforms. In the political upheaval of the 1890's, the industrial workingman refused to join the down-trodden farmer in capturing the Democratic party, and, in one of the greatest political transformations of modern American history, flocked to the Republican party, which was supposedly under corporate domination. It is not surprising that historians, while studying the agrarian revolt in detail, have failed to examine carefully this industrial-urban feature of the political unrest of the early 1890's. To do so would require an admission that rural-urban conflicts were as strong, if not stronger, than the hostility toward corporate wealth.

Although industrial innovation was the common American experience between 1885 and 1914, not all were aware of, or concerned with, the same facets of this change. Manufacturers, merchants, farmers, and workers were most disturbed by the new, impersonal price-and-market economy. The individual enterpriser now felt engulfed by a tidal wave of world-wide influences which he could scarcely understand, let alone control. Those concerned with personal values, on the other hand—religious leaders, women active in public affairs, the new middle class, and the rising group of intellectuals excitedly searching for knowledge about human life—were most impressed with the materialistic bent of industrial society and its hostility to the human spirit. For the millions of people torn from accustomed rural patterns of culture and thrust into a strange, urban environment, the meaning of industrialism lay in a feeling of uprootedness, in the disintegration of old ways of life and the loss of familiar surroundings. Those left behind on the farms experienced the new forces through the expansion of urban culture and its threat to the nation's agrarian traditions. They feared that metropolitan influences would reach out and drastically change the life they knew. Finally, those in the South and West lived under the shadow of a far more highly developed area, which, they felt, deliberately imposed restraints upon the economic growth of their regions.

Industrialism increased the desire for material gain among all Americans; but economic motivation does not wholly explain the behavior of the American people during these years. Industrialism was less important in changing the motives of Americans than in profoundly altering the environment, the setting within which men and women strove for many different goals. Whether one was most concerned with the life of the spirit, with social institutions, or with economic gain, he had to come to terms with the vastly new society brought about by industrialism. The way in which Americans made this adjustment varied according to the positive goals they wished to achieve.

Those with a major concern for economic gain took collective action to influence the price-and-market system and to obtain a larger share of the increased wealth. Those most interested in the life of the free, independent, human spirit feared collective economic action and tried to promote the conditions that would enhance self-reliance, responsibility, and qualities of personal character. Migrants from rural to urban areas sought to create and maintain new ways of group living which would give meaning to their lives in a rapidly moving and impersonal society. Farmers fought back against the cities, often blindly and bitterly, temporarily imposing their patterns of life on the urban areas, but in the long run to no avail. And the South and the West appealed to the federal government for aid in economic growth and for laws to restrict the policies of northeastern corporations and thereby to foster a freer climate in which industry in their section could grow.

Through politics the American people enlisted the aid of public agencies to help solve their problems. Less important in itself, politics was primarily the means whereby people tried to realize their goals in economic, social, intellectual, and religious life. Into the political arena, therefore, were focused all the impulses of these eventful years; and political institutions, as a result, could not remain uninfluenced by industrial change. Political parties' and legislative action became the instruments of both industrial growth and the adjustment to industrial innovation. When many found partisan politics ineffective for their purposes, they fashioned new methods of political action.

Industrialism also thrust Americans irrevocably onto the world scene. Some reached out to seek material gain abroad, others to implement an expanded program of national security, and still others as cultural evangelists to spread the American "way of life" to those whom they considered backward. At the same time, the communications revolution drew events abroad closer to the experience of the American people. In the face of such momentous changes, how should Americans respond? Some, arguing that the nation was invincible, demanded that the United States vigorously assert its military might and economic interest. But others believed that foreign policy should strengthen the ties with other peoples rather than divide us from them, and especially that the nation's leaders should explore every possible way of solving disputes peacefully.

Two world wars, the Great Depression of 1929, and a world balancing on the brink of war and self-destruction have blunted our present awareness of the consequences of the events between 1885 and 1914. These later happenings, like industrialism itself, have drastically altered the lives of Americans and forced upon them new types of adjustments. Yet most of the characteristic reactions of the Populist-Progressive Era remain with us today. Occupational groups still seek organization as the answer to their problems, and the struggle among powerful economic groups is an increasingly important fact in the formation of private and public economic policy. Those concerned with personal values and the freedom of individual expression continue to cope with hostile influences, although the threat in more recent years has come as much from the drive for national security as from industrial growth. Cultural and sectional adjustments are often submerged today; yet rural-urban, native-foreign, and sectional differences continue to give rise to major conflicts among the American people. As the twentieth century proceeded, the nation became ever more tightly involved in international life, and the constant threat of being drawn into world war loomed even more ominously. Yet as early as 1914, many of the later responses to this profound change had already clearly appeared. In foreign as well as in domestic affairs, therefore, the decade of the 1890's was a dividing point in American history, separating the old from the new and setting a pattern for much of the future.

The Robber Barons

Matthew Josephson

In John D. Rockefeller, economists and historians have often seen the classic example of the modern monopolist of industry. It is true that he worked with an indomitable will, and a faith in his star à la Napoleon, to organize his industry under his own dictatorship. He was moreover a great innovator. Though not the first to attempt the plan of the pool—there were pools even in the time of Cicero—his South Improvement Company was the most impressive instance in history of such an organism. But when others had reached the stage of the pool, he was building the solid framework of a monopoly.

Rockefeller's problems were far more difficult than those for instance of Carnegie, who quickly won special economies through constructing a very costly, well-integrated, technically superior plant upon a favored site. In the oil-refining business, a small still could be thrown up in the '70's for manufacturing kerosene or lubricating oil at a tenth the cost of the Edgar Thomson steel works. The petroleum market was mercurial compared to iron, steel and even coal; there were thousands of petty capitalists competing for advantage in it. Hence the tactics of Rockefeller, the bold architecture of the industrial edifice he reared, have always aroused the liveliest interest, and he himself appeals to us for many reasons as the greatest of the American industrialists. In no small degree this interest is owing to the legend of "Machiavellian" guile and relentlessness which has always clung to this prince of oil.

After the dissolution of the South Improvement Company, Rockefeller and Flagler had come to a conference of the irate diggers of petroleum with mild proposals of peaceful coöperation, under the heading of the "Pittsburgh Plan." The two elements in the trade, those who produced the raw material from the earth and those who refined it, were to combine forces harmoniously.

From The Robber Barons, copyright, 1934, renewed, 1962, by Matthew Josephson, pp. 264–284, 394–396. Reprinted by permission of Harcourt Brace Jovanovich, Inc.

"You misunderstand us," Rockefeller and Flagler said. "Let us see what combination will do."

There was much suspicion. One of Titusville's independent refiners (one of those whom Standard Oil tried to erase from the scene) made a rather warlike speech against the plan, and he recalls that Rockefeller, who had been softly swinging back and forth in a rocking chair, his hands over his face, through the conference, suddenly stopped rocking, lowered his hands and looked straight at his enemy. His glance was fairly terrifying.

You never saw such eyes. He took me all in, saw just how much fight he could expect from me, and then up went his hands and back and forth went his chair.

At this very moment, Rockefeller was arranging anew the secret rebates with the leading railroads of the country, which had been so loudly decried in 1872. Upon the refined oil he shipped from Cleveland he received a rebate of 50 cents a barrel, giving him an advantage of 25 percent over his competitors. Once more the railroads continued a form of espionage for his company. But all arrangements were now effected in a more complete secrecy.

Equally secret was the campaign Rockefeller pursued to amalgamate with his own company the strongest refineries in the country. According to Miss Tarbell's "History," he now constantly "bent over a map of the refining interests of the country," or hurried from one secret conference to another, at Cleveland, New York, or at Saratoga, "the Mecca of schemers," where long hours of nocturnal debate in a certain pavilion brought into his plan the refineries of Pittsburgh and Philadelphia. Look at what combination has done in one city, Cleveland, he would say. The plan now was for all the chosen ones to become the nucleus of a private company which should gradually acquire control of all the refineries everywhere, become the only shippers, and have the mastery of the railroads in the matter of freight rates. Those who came in were promised wealth beyond their dreams. The remarkable economies and profits of the Standard were exposed to their eyes. "We mean to secure the entire refining business of the world," they were told. They were urged to dissemble their actions. Contracts were entered into with the peculiar secret rites which Mr. Rockefeller habitually preferred. They were signed late at night at his Euclid Avenue home in Cleveland. The participants were besought not to tell even their wives about the new arrangements, to conceal the gains they made, not to drive fast horses or put on style, or buy new bonnets, or do anything to let people suspect there were unusual profits in oil-refining, since that might invite competition.

In this campaign perhaps fifteen of the strongest firms in the country, embracing four-fifths of the refining trade, were brought into alliance with the Standard Oil Company by 1875–78. Among them were individuals who had opposed Rockefeller most strenuously a season before: the ablest of these,

J. J. Vandergrift and John Archbold of the Pennsylvania oil regions, Charles Pratt and Henry Rogers of New York, entering the family of Standard Oil as partners by exchange of stock. They continued under their own corporate identity as "Acme Oil Company," or "Pratt & Rogers," but shared the same freight advantages as Standard Oil, used the same sources of information and surveillance, the common organization of agents and dealers in the distributing field.

"I wanted able men with me," Rockefeller said later. "I tried to make friends with these men. I admitted their ability and the value of their enterprise. I worked to convince them that it would be better for both to cooperate."

In the meantime a campaign no less elaborate and bold was pursued to eliminate from the field those firms whose existence was considered superfluous. Rockefeller did not "confiscate" his opponents outright. In the interests of his great consolidation he measured the value of their properties without sentiment, and gave his terms. Thus a plant which had cost $40,000 might in the future, after his own plans had matured, be worth little more than $15,000, or 37½ cents on the dollar. Such an offer he would make and this only. The victim, as the case might be, would surrender if timid, or attempt resistance in trade, or practice blackmail upon him, or fight him to the finish and have resort to the highest courts.

Where a "deal" across the table could not be effected, Rockefeller might try a variety of methods of expropriation. With his measured spirit, with his organized might, he tested men and things. There were men and women of all sorts who passed under his implacable rod, and their tale, gathered together reverently by Miss Tarbell, has contributed to the legend of the "white devil" who came to rule over American industry.

A certain widow, a Mrs. Backus of Cleveland, who had inherited an oil-refinery, had appealed to Mr. Rockefeller to preserve her, "the mother of fatherless children." And he had promised "with tears in his eyes that he would stand by her." But in the end he offered her only $79,000 for a property which had cost $200,000. The whole story of the defenseless widow and her orphans, the stern command, the confiscation of two-thirds of her property, when it came out made a deep stir and moved many hearts.

In another instance a manufacturer of improved lubricating oils set himself up innocently in Cleveland, and became a client of the Standard Oil for his whole supply of residuum oils. The Rockefeller company encouraged him at first, and sold him 85 barrels a day according to a contract. He prospered for three years, then suddenly when the monopoly was well launched in 1874, his supply was cut down to 12 barrels a day, the price was increased on some pretense, and the shipping cost over the railroads similarly increased. It became impossible to supply his trade. He offered to buy of Rockefeller 5,000 barrels and store it so that he might assure himself of a future supply. This was refused.

"*I saw readily what that meant,*" *the man Morehouse related to the Hepburn Committee in 1879. "That meant squeeze you out—Buy out your works. . . . They paid $15,000 for what cost me $41,000. He [Rockefeller] said that he had facilities for freighting and that the coal-oil business belonged to them; and any concern that would start in that business, they had sufficient money to lay aside a fund and wipe them out—these are the words.*"

In the field of retail distribution, Rockefeller sought to create a great marketing machine delivering directly from the Standard Oil's tank wagons to stores in towns and villages throughout the United States. But in the laudable endeavor to wipe out wasteful wholesalers or middlemen, he would meet with resistance again, as in the producing fields. Where unexpectedly stout resistance from competing marketing agencies was met, the Standard Oil would simply apply harsher weapons. To cut off the supplies of the rebel dealer, the secret aid of the railroads and the espionage of their freight agents would be invoked again and again. A message such as the following would pass between Standard Oil officials:

We are glad to know you are on such good terms with the railroad people that Mr. Clem [handling independent oil] gains nothing by marking his shipments by numbers instead of by names.

Or again:

Wilkerson and Company received car of oil Monday 13th—70 barrels which we suspect slipped through at the usual fifth class rate—in fact we might say we know it did—paying only $41.50 freight from here. Charges $57.40. Please turn another screw.

The process of "Turning the Screw" has been well described by Henry D. Lloyd. One example is that of a merchant in Nashville, Tennessee, who refused to come to terms and buy from Standard Oil; he first found that all his shipments were reported secretly to the enemy; then by a mysterious coincidence his freight rates on shipments of all kinds were raised 50 percent, then doubled, even tripled, and he felt himself under fire from all parts of the field. He attempted to move his merchandise by a great roundabout route, using the Baltimore & Ohio and several other connecting roads, but was soon "tracked down," his shipments lost, spoiled. The documents show that the independent oil-dealers' clients were menaced·in every way by the Standard Oil marketing agency; it threatened to open competing grocery stores, to sell oats, meat, sugar, coffee at lower prices. "If you do not buy our oil we will start a grocery store and sell goods at cost and put you out of business."

By this means, opponents in the country at large were soon "mopped up"; small refiners and small wholesalers who attempted to exploit a given district were routed at the appearance of the familiar red-and-green tank wagons, which were equal to charging drastically reduced rates for oil in one town, and twice as much in an adjacent town where the nuisance of competition no longer existed. There were, to be sure, embittered protests from the victims, but the marketing methods of Standard Oil were magnificently efficient and centralized; waste and delay were overcome; immense savings were brought directly to the refining monopoly.

But where the Standard Oil could not carry on its expansion by peaceful means, it was ready with violence; its faithful servants knew even how to apply the modern weapon of dynamite.

In Buffalo, the Vacuum Oil Company, one of the "dummy" creatures of the Standard Oil system, became disturbed one day by the advent of a vigorous competitor who built a sizable refinery and located it favorably upon the water front. The offices of Vacuum conducted at first a furtive campaign of intimidation. Then emboldened or more desperate, they approached the chief mechanic of the enemy refinery, holding whispered conferences with him in a rowboat on Lake Erie. He was asked to "do something." He was urged to "go back to Buffalo and construct the machinery so it would bust up . . . or smash up," to fix the pipes and stills "so they cannot make a good oil. . . . And then if you would give them a little scare, they not knowing anything about the business. You know how . . . ." In return the foreman would have a life annuity which he might enjoy in another part of the country.

So in due time a small explosion took place in the independent plant, as Lloyd and Miss Tarbell tell the tale, from the records of the trial held several years later, in 1887. The mechanic, though on the payrolls of the Vacuum Oil Company, led a cursed existence, forever wandering without home or country, until in complete hysteria he returned to make a clean breast of the whole affair. The criminal suit against high officials of the Standard Oil monopoly included Henry Rogers and John Archbold, but the evil was laid by them to the "overenthusiasm" of underlings. Evidence of conspiracy was not found by the court, but heavy damages were awarded to the plaintiff, who thereafter plainly dreaded to reënter the dangerous business.

These and many other anecdotes, multiplied, varied or even distorted, spread through the Oil Regions of Pennsylvania and elsewhere through the country (as ogre-tales are fed to children), and were accumulated to make a strange picture of Mr. Rockefeller, the baron of oil. Miss Tarbell in her "History," written in her "muck-raking" days, has dwelt upon them with love. She has recorded them in rending tones with a heart bleeding for the petty capitalists for whom alone "life ran swift and ruddy and joyous" before the "great villain" arrived, and with his "big hand reached out from nobody knew where to steal their conquest and throttle their future."

But if truth must be told, the smaller capitalists, in the producing field especially, were themselves not lacking in predatory or greedy qualities; as Miss Tarbell herself admits, they were capable of hurrying away from church on Sundays to tap enemy tanks or set fire to their stores of oil. What they lacked, as the Beards have commented, was the discipline to maintain a producers' combination equal in strength to that of the refiners. The other factors in the industry engaged in individualistic marketing or refining ventures were very possibly "mossbacks," as one of the Standard Oil chieftains growled, "left in the lurch by progress."

The campaigns for consolidation, once launched, permitted Rockefeller little rest, and engaged his generalship on many fronts at once. In a curious interview given while he was in Europe, cited by Flynn, he himself exclaimed:

How often I had not an unbroken night's sleep, worrying about how it was all coming out. . . . Work by day and worry by night, week in and week out, month after month. If I had foreseen the future I doubt whether I would have had the courage to go on.

With unblinking vigilance he conducted throughout his company an eternal war against waste. We have spoken of his unequaled efficiency and power of organization. There is a famous note to his barrel factory in his careful bookkeeper's hand which has been cited with amused contempt by his critics, to show how attention to small details absorbed his soul. It reads:

Last month you reported on hand, 1,119 bungs. 10,000 were sent you beginning this month. You have used 9,527 this month. You report 1,092 on hand. What has become of the other 500?

It is not a laughing matter, this affair of 500 barrel bungs, worth at the most a dollar or two in all. Rockefeller's hatred of waste told him that in a large-scale industry the rescued pennies multiplied a million times or more represented enormous potential gains. This was to be true of all the great industrial leaders after Rockefeller's time; the spirit regarded as parsimony is a large-visioned conception of technical efficiency in handling big machines. Thus the feeding of horses, the making of his own glue, hoops, barrels, all was carefully supervised and constantly reduced in cost. Barrels were cut $1.25 apiece, saving $4,000,000 a year, cans were reduced 15 cents, saving $5,000,000 a year, and so forth. In absorbing the services of J. J. Vandergrift, in 1872, Rockefeller had acquired as an ally to his enterprise a combination of small pipe lines called the United Pipe Lines. His lieutenants then constructed more pipes; and by 1876 he controlled almost half the existing pipe lines, some running 80 to 100 miles, to the railroad terminals and shipping points. At this time the largest pipe-line interest in competition with Standard Oil's was the Empire Transportation Company, headed by Colonel Joseph Potts, but dominated by the officers of the Pennsylvania Railroad, which held an option over the entire property.

Himself an aggressive entrepreneur, Potts soon found that he must expand or suffer extinction. To the alarm of the Rockefeller organization, he purchased several big refineries in New York and proceeded to pipe crude oil from the oil fields and over the railroad to seaboard. Rockefeller vehemently petitioned the railroad to withdraw from his domain. Refused at an interview, he promised that he would take his own measures, and left his adversaries with expressions of sanctimonious regret, the form in which his most deadly threats were usually offered.

It was war, a war of rates. He moved with lightning speed. At once the other railroads, Erie and New York Central, were ordered to stand by, lowering their freight rates for him while he slashed the price of refined oil in every market which Potts reached.

But Potts, a stubborn Presbyterian, fought back harder than anyone Rockefeller had ever encountered. He replied in kind by further price cuts; he then began to build large refineries at the coast ports, lined up independent oil-producers behind him, and reserves in quantities of tank cars, in barges, ships, dock facilities. During the bitter conflict, with which, as Flynn relates, the hills and fields of Pennsylvania resounded, both sides, and the railroads supporting them as well, suffered heavy wounds. Yet Rockefeller would not desist, since Standard Oil's whole system of organization was endangered.

In the midst of this furious engagement a great blow fell upon the enemies of John D. Rockefeller, as if given by the hand of God to whom he constantly prayed. During the summer of 1877 the workers of the Baltimore & Ohio Railroad struck against wage cuts and their strike spread quickly to adjacent railroads, raging with especial violence in the Pennsylvania system. The most destructive labor war the nation had ever known was now seen in Baltimore and Pittsburgh, with militant mobs fighting armed troops and setting in flames property of great value in revenge for the many deaths they suffered. During this storm which the railroad barons had sown by cutting wages 20 percent and doubling the length of freight trains, the Pennsylvania interests quickly came to terms with Standard Oil, so that they might be free to turn and crush the rebellious workers. The entire business of Empire Transportation was sold out to the oil combination at their own terms, while Potts was called off. In Philadelphia, Rockefeller and his partners, quietly jubilant, received the sword of the weeping Potts.

The oil industry as a whole was impressed with the victory of Standard Oil over a railroad ring which had seemed invincible in the past. In a movement of fear many other interests hastened to make terms with Rockefeller. By the end of 1878 he controlled all the existing pipe-line systems; through a new freight pool he directed traffic or quantities of supplies to the various regions or cities as he pleased.

By 1876 this industry had assumed tremendous proportions. Of the annual output of nearly 10,000,000 barrels, the Standard Oil Company controlled approximately 80 percent, while exports of petroleum products to the value of $32,000,000 passed through their hands. But in 1877 the great Brad-ford oil field was opened with a wild boom, the uproarious coal-oil scenes of '59 were enacted anew, crowds rushed to the new fields, acreage values boomed, oil gushed out in an uncontrollable flood—half again as much oil as existed before came forth almost overnight. The markets grew demoralized again, just when Rockefeller seemed to have completed his conquest of the old Oil Regions.

What was he to do? In the two years that followed he directed his orga-nization at the high tension of an ordnance department in wartime, so that piping, refining and marketing capacity might be expanded in time, and the almost untenable supply handled without faltering. With utmost energy a huge building program was carried on and further millions were staked on the hazardous business. Then, holding down the unruly producers, he imposed harsh terms through his pipe lines, refusing storage, forcing them to sell the oil they drilled "for immediate shipment" at the depressed prices of 64 to 69 cents a barrel, or have it run into the ground.

The overproduction could not be stopped. The oil men raged at the great machine which held them in bonds. Once more the independents gath-ered all their forces together to form a protective combination of their own. They founded the Parliament of Petroleum. They raised funds to construct an immense "free" pipe line running over the mountains to the seaboard, and ridding them at last of the railroads which hemmed them in. The new Tide-water Pipe Line would break Standard's control over railroad rates and bring crude oil to the sea.

Rockefeller's agents now lobbied in the state legislature of Pennsylvania to have the proposed pipe line banned. Failing of this his emissaries were thrown out over the state to buy up right of way in the path of the enemy's advance. But the Tidewater's engineers moved with equal speed and secrecy, eluded the defense which Rockefeller threw in their way and by April, 1879, completed their difficult project.

From successive stations, the great pumps were to drive oil over the very top of the Alleghenies, and down to Williamsport, touching the Reading Railroad, which had joined forces with the independents. Amid picturesque celebration—while the spies of the Standard Oil looked on incredulously—the valves were opened, the oil ran over the mountain and down toward the sea! Rockefeller was checkmated—but to whom would the producers and their free pipe line sell the crude oil at the seaboard? They had no inkling, though they berated him, of the extent of his control at the outlet.

The opposition to the Rockefeller "conspiracy" now rose to its climax of enthusiasm. The hundreds of petty oil men who fought to remain "inde-pendent" and keep their sacred right to flood the market or "hold up" con-sumers at their own pleasure, won sympathy everywhere; and with the aid of local politicians in New York and Pennsylvania they also had their day in court. Their tumult had grown so violent that at long last the lawmakers of

Pennsylvania moved to prosecute the monopolists for "conspiracy in restraint of trade." Writs were served and on April 29, 1879, a local Grand Jury indicted John D. Rockefeller, William Rockefeller, J. A. Bostwick, Henry Flagler, Daniel O'Day, J. J. Vandergrift and other chieftains of Standard Oil for criminal conspiracy, to "secure a monopoly of the oil industry, to oppress other refiners, to injure the carrying trade, to extort unreasonable railroad rates, to fraudulently control prices," etc. Simultaneously in New York State, the legislature appointed a committee of investigation of railroads, headed by the young lawyer A. Barton Hepburn. Forced to look at all the facts which were brought out by the Hepburn Committee, the nation was shocked. The railroad interests, as archconspirators, were at once under heavy fire. But no one understood the scope and meaning of the new phase reached in industrial life at this stage, save perhaps Mr. Chauncey Depew, who in a moment of illumination exclaimed on behalf of the railroad interests he so gallantly championed: "Every manufacturer in the state of New York existed by violence and lived by discrimination. . . . By secret rates and by deceiving their competitors as to what their rates were and by evading all laws of trade these manufacturers exist." This was God's truth and certainly true of all the other states in the Union. And of course under the prevailing circumstances there was nothing to be done, save recommend certain "regulative" laws.

With Rockefeller, there had arisen the great industrial combination in colossal and "sinister" form; he was the mighty bourgeois who was to expropriate all the petty bourgeois and his name was to be the rallying cry of parties and uprisings. The outlook for monopoly seemed dark, yet the trial, in the name of a democratic sovereignty which held "sacred" the property of the "conspirators," whatever the means by which they may have preëmpted or confiscated such property—was to be simply a comedy, and was to be enacted again and again. Before the bar of justice, Rockefeller and his brilliant lieutenants would appear, saying, "I refuse to answer on the advice of counsel." A Henry Rogers, a Flagler, would use every shift which such philosophers of the law as Joseph Choate or Samuel C. T. Dodd might counsel. They would "refuse to incriminate themselves" or evade reply on a point of technicality, or lie pointblank. Or, as in the case of the terribly cynical Archbold, they would simply jest, they would make mock of their bewildered prosecutors.

It was Rockefeller who made the most profound impression upon the public. He seemed distinguished in person; with his tall stooping figure, his long well-shaped head, his even jaw. His long, fine nose, his small birdlike eyes set wide apart, with the narrowed lids drooping a little, and the innumerable tiny wrinkles, made up a remarkable physiognomy. But his mouth was a slit, like a shark's. Rockefeller, impeccably dressed and groomed, thoroughly composed, pretendedly anxious to please, foiled his accusers with ease. Every legal subterfuge was used by him with supreme skill. Certain of his denials were legally truthful, as Flynn points out, since stockownership concerning which he was questioned was often entrusted temporarily (in time for such trials) to mere clerks or bookkeepers in his employ.

But the moment came when he was asked specifically about his connection with the notorious refiners' pool of 1872.

"Was there a Southern Improvement Company?"

"I have heard of such a company."

"Were you not in it?"

"I was not."

His hearers were amazed at the apparent perjury he made pointblank with even voice and an inscrutable movement of the eyes. But no! He had been only a director of the *South Improvement Company*, and not of the "Southern Improvement Company," as the prosecutor had named it by mistake.

If Rockefeller was embittered by the cruel fame he won, he never showed it. The silence he preserved toward all reproaches or questions may have been a matter of clever policy; yet it suggested at bottom a supreme contempt for his critics and accusers alike.

"We do not talk much—we saw wood!"

There were times when his movements were hampered, times when he dared not enter the State of Pennsylvania though the authorities there called for him impatiently; times when it was equally convenient to remain almost in hiding at his New York headquarters in Pearl Street, while the world at large howled against him. Yet he moved with unequaled agility and force against all serious attacks upon his industrial barony.

The menace of the Tidewater Pipe Line which cut through his network of railroads and refineries he must crush at all costs. This was far more important than any impeachment of his character. Fertile in expedients at a crisis, he could also be infinitely patient. It used to be said: "To Mr. Rockefeller a day is as a year, and a year as a day. He can wait, but he never gives up." Now when he perceived that the Tidewater's line to the sea was a reality, he besieged it from all sides. On the one hand he offered to buy all the oil it ran, a tempting offer which would have made the affair most profitable to the stockholders. Rebuffed here he proceeded to use the inventions of his rivals and build a long pipe line of his own to the sea. Night and day his engineers and gangs labored in the mountains, to connect the Bradford fields with the Standard Oil terminal at Bayonne. Then before the walls of Bayonne, where lay his great coastal refineries and storage tanks, his pipe line was stopped by an interested railroad from which he would have removed his freight business. The Town Council of Bayonne was induced to be friendly and grant a franchise; the Mayor who resisted for a time was suddenly won over; and in all secrecy, because of the need of haste to prevent a blocking franchise by the railroad, his gangs assembled. There were 300 men ready in the night of September 22, 1879, with all materials, tools, wagons gathered, waiting for the signal—the swift passage of an ordinance by the Town Council and its signing by the Mayor. Then with mad speed the trench across the city was dug, the pipes laid, jointed and covered, before the dawn. The National Transit Company was completed as the largest pipe-line system in the field.

His own line of communications was now secured against the enemy. But he also pursued a campaign of secret stock purchase for control, gaining a minority interest in the Tidewater company, creating dissensions within, damaging its credit, detaching its officials, instigating suits for receivership, serving writs, injunctions, and more writs, until the managers seemed to struggle for their very sanity. Day by day these blows fell mysteriously, until in 1882 the adversary surrendered and effected the best agreement possible under the circumstances. By this a minor part of the oil-transporting business was apportioned to itself and it yielded up its independence after four years of fighting an unresting, infinitely armed master. All the pipe lines were now amalgamated under Standard Oil control; the great railroads, notably the Pennsylvania, were forced by agreement and in return for a stipulated yearly ransom to retire from the business of oil transportation forever. John D. Rockefeller at the age of forty-four had accomplished his ambition—he was supreme in the oil industry, "the symbol of the American monopolist."

Up to 1881 the forty-odd companies controlled by Rockefeller and his partners formed a kind of *entente cordiale* bound by interchange of stock. This form of union being found inadequate or impermanent, the counsel of the Standard Oil Company, Samuel C. T. Dodd, came forward with his idea of the Trust. By a secret agreement of 1882, all the existing thirty-seven stockholders in the divers enterprises of refining, piping, buying or selling oil conveyed their shares "in trust" to nine Trustees: John and William Rockefeller, O. H. Payne, Charles Pratt, Henry Flagler, John Archbold, W. G. Warden, Jabez Bostwick and Benjamin Brewster. The various stockholders then received "trust certificates" in denominations of $100 in return for the shares they had deposited; while the Trustees, controlling two-thirds of all the shares, became the direct stockholders of all the companies in the system, empowered to serve as directors thereof, holding in their hands final control of all the properties. The Trustees could dissolve any corporations within the system and organize new ones in each state, such as the Standard Oil of New Jersey, or the Standard Oil of New York. Nor could any outsiders or newly arrived stockholders have any voice in the affairs of the various companies. The Trustees formed a kind of supreme council giving a centralized direction to their industry. Such was the first great Trust; thus was evolved the harmonious management of huge aggregations of capital, and the technique for large-scale industry.

Dodd, the resourceful philosopher of monopoly, defended his beautiful legal structure of the "Standard Oil Trust" both in a pamphlet of 1888 and in an argument before a Congressional committee of that year. It was but the outcome of a crying need for centralized control of the oil business, he argued. Out of disastrous conditions had come "coöperation and association among the refiners, resulting eventually in the Standard Oil Trust [which] enabled the refiners so coöperating to reduce the price of petroleum products, and thus benefit the public to a very marked degree." In these arguments, learned economists of the time, such as Professor Hadley, supported Dodd. The Trust, as perfected monopoly, pointed the way to the future organization of all industry, and abolished "ruinous competition."

From their headquarters in the small old-fashioned building at 140 Pearl Street the supreme council of an economic empire sat together in conference like princes of the Roman Church. Here in utmost privacy confidential news brought by agents or informers throughout the world was discussed, and business policies determined. The management and responsibility was skillfully divided among committees: there was a committee on Crude Oil, a committee on Marketing, on Transportation, and numerous other departments. By these new processes markets or developments everywhere in everybody's business were followed or acted upon.

Every day the astute leaders rounded together by Rockefeller lunched together in Pearl Street, and later in a large and famous office building known as 26 Broadway. No one questioned the pre-eminence of John D. Rockefeller, though Charles Pratt usually sat at the head of the table. The aggressive Archbold was closest to John D. Rockefeller. His brother William Rockefeller, an amiable mediocrity, but immensely rich as well, and long trained in the use of money, depended most upon Henry H. Rogers. Rogers took a more dominant place in the management with the passing years. He is described by Thomas Lawson as "one of the most distinguished-looking men of the time, a great actor, a great fighter, an intriguer, an implacable foe."

These, together with Brewster, Barstow, J. H. Alexander and Bostwick, were the leaders who carried on their industrial operations throughout the world like a band of conspiratorial revolutionists. But "there was not a lazy bone nor a stupid head" in the whole organization, as Miss Tarbell has said. Behind them were the active captains, lieutenants, followers and workers, all laboring with the pride, the loyalty, the discipline and the enthusiasm born of the knowledge that "they can do no better for themselves" anywhere than under the "collar" of the Standard Oil. Freed of all moral scruples, curiously informed of everything, they were prompted by a sense of the world's realities which differed strangely from that of the man in the street. They were a major staff engaged in an eternal fight; now they scrapped unprofitable plants, acquiring and locating others; or now they gathered themselves for tremendous mobilizing feats during emergencies in trade. They found ways of effecting enormous economies; and always their profits mounted to grotesque figures: in 1879, on an invested capital of $3,500,000, dividends of $3,150,000 were paid; the value of the congeries of oil companies was then estimated at $55,000,000. Profits were overwhelmingly reinvested in new "capital goods" and with the formation of the Trust capitalization was set at $70,000,000. By 1886 net earnings had risen to $15,000,000 per annum.

"Hide the profits and say nothing!" was the slogan here. To the public prices had been reduced, it was claimed. But after 1875, and more notably after 1881, despite the fluctuations of crude oil a firm tendency set in for the markets of refined oil products. Upon the charts of prices the rugged hills and valleys of oil markets turn into a nearly level plain between 1881 and 1891. Though raw materials declined greatly in value, and volume increased, the margin of profit was consistently controlled by the monopoly; for the services of gathering and transporting oil, the price was not lowered in twenty years, despite the superb technology possessed by the Standard Oil. Questioned on this, that "frank pirate" Rogers replied, laughing: "We are not in business for our health, but are out for the dollar."

While the policy of the monopoly, as economists have shown, might be for many reasons to avoid maximum price levels—such as invited the entrance of competition in the field—it was clearly directed toward keeping the profit margin stable during a rising trend in consumption 'and falling "curve" in production cost. Similarly in perfecting its technology the Trust was guided by purely pecuniary motives, as Veblen points out, and it remains always a matter of doubt if the mightier industrial combinations improved their service to society at large in the highest possible degree. As often as not it happened that technical improvements were actually long delayed until, after a decade or more, as in the case of Van Syckel's pipe line of 1865, their commercial value was proved beyond a doubt. It was only after rivals, in desperation, contrived the pumping of oil in a two-hundred-mile-long pipe line that Rockefeller followed suit. So it was with the development of various by-products, the introduction of tank cars, etc.

The end in sight was always, as Veblen said, increase of ownership, and of course pecuniary gain rather than technical progress in the shape of improved workmanship or increased service to the community. These latter effects were also obtained. But to a surprising degree they seem accidental by-products of the long-drawn-out struggles, the revolutionary upheavals whence the great industrial coalitions sprang.

The greatest service of the industrial baron to business enterprise seemed to lie elsewhere, as Veblen contended. "The heroic role of the captain of industry is that of a deliverer from an excess of business management." It is a "sweeping retirement of business men as a class from service . . . a casting out of business men by the chief of business men."

John D. Rockefeller said that he wanted in his organization "only the big ones, those who have already proved they can do a big business. As for the others, unfortunately they will have to die."

The obscure tumult in the Oil Regions in 1872, the subsequent exposures of the railroad rebate and the oil monopoly in 1879, made a lively though unclear impression upon the public mind. Now the more imaginative among the mass of consumers felt fear course through them at the thought of secret combinations ranged against them, the loud demagogue was roused from his slumbers, the reformer set off upon his querulous and futile searches. But among the alert entrepreneurs of all the money marts an entirely different response must have been perceptible. With envious lust the progress of the larger, more compact industrial organizations, like that of Carnegie Brothers & Company, or the associations formed by a Rockefeller, was now studied. Ah-ha! there was the way to profits in these confused and parlous times. How quickly and abundantly those fellows accumulated cash and power! "I was surprised," confessed William Vanderbilt before a committee of New York legislators in 1878, "at the amount of ready cash they were able to provide." He referred to the oil-refiners' combination. In the twinkling of an eye they had put down 3,000,000 to buy out Colonel Potts' pipe-line company. And in the following year Vanderbilt, commenting to the Hepburn Committee at Albany on the shrewdness of the Standard Oil ring, said:

> There is no question about it but these men are smarter than I am a great deal. . . . I never came in contact with any class of men as smart and alert as they are in their business. They would never have got into the position they now are. And one man could hardly have been able to do it; it is a combination of men.

The storms of public indignation, as we have seen, vented themselves chiefly upon the railroad heads who "discriminated against the little fellow" by the rebate and freight pool. But far from being frightened at such protests the money-changers hastened to throw their gold at the feet of him who promised them crushing, monopolistic advantages. So Villard, in 1881, by whispering his plans to conquer all the Northwest overnight, attracted instantly a powerful following of capitalists to his "blind pool." So the lawyers or undertakers who came forward with plans for secret trade associations or pools in salt, beef, sugar or whiskey, were heard with intense excitement by men who yesterday were busy ambushing or waylaying each other in the daily routine of their business.

They would say to each other, as in the Salt Association, formed earliest of all, "In union there is strength. . . ." Or, "Organized we have prospered; unorganized not." "Our combination has not been strong enough; the market is demoralized." And others would murmur fearsomely: "But we will be prosecuted for 'restraint of trade.' There are state laws in Maryland, Tennessee and elsewhere which hold that 'monopolies are odious.' There is the common law against trade conspiracy. . . ."

Then a bolder voice among the plotters would say: "How much did you make last year? Not a cent? Are you making anything now? Well, what do you propose to do? Sit here and lose what capital you have got in the business? There is only one way to make any money in a business like the—business and that is to have a pool."

Thus the trail would be blazed. The industrialists, like the railroad barons before them, came together in furtive conferences, much mistrusting each other, but lamenting together the bad times and owning to the folly of competition among themselves; while those who made pools, as they heard by rumor, in oil or salt flourished. After much bickering and jockeying, the lawyers would draw up binding agreements by which the amount of output would be fixed, quotas and territories would be assigned to each member, and business orders proportionally allotted, with fines levied upon those who broke the rules. These planning agreements the members of the pool would promise faithfully to live by.

The first pools, crude experiments in a "federalism" of industry, were as inept as the first weak devices for union among laborers. Their tactics and results differed widely. By 1880, certain pools such as the salt pool had got the margin of profit much higher by "pegging" the market price of a barrel of salt at about double what it was formerly, and holding steadily to this level. Their procedure usually avoided raising the market price too high. This would beget fresh competition. However, they kept prices "moderately" firm, although supply might actually be abundant. The essential object in view was "to increase the margins between the cost of materials and the price of the finished product," and this was effected, according to Ripley, "in almost every case."

A variety of economies were gained by pooling, depending upon the firmness of the association. Railroads were forced to give rebates; inefficient or badly located plants were closed down; excess sales forces and labor were reduced, a "war chest" was accumulated and competitors were driven out. To intruders the cost of necessary machinery might be made more burdensome. Thus in connection with the Wire Nail Pool, independents declared to government investigators:

We found the market in which we could buy machines [to manufacture nails] was very limited, most of the machine manufacturers having entered into an agreement with the combination to stop making them for outside parties.

In some cases the pool might, as in the case of salt in 1881, decide to "slaughter the market" for a reason, giving the coup de grâce to overstocked competitors in some areas, then resume the even tenor of their ways. Or they would sell low in one section which was pestered by competition, and recoup off the general market. The pools, in short, claimed to represent the party of "modernity," of progress by specializing machinery, buying raw materials cheaper, utilizing more by-products, research units, export development, advertising and selling in common. While "not wishing to take the position of posing before the public as benefactors to any extent," yet they claimed that industry was more stabilized, prices were seldom raised inordinately, and labor was paid higher wages—though here one famous manufacturer, John Gates, admitted that this was done on demand, in periods of affluence, when it was seen they had high profits and desired to avoid labor troubles. Generally they assumed a marvelous command over the labor situation—here was one of their surest gains. The workman became truly their commodity; for in time of a strike, orders could be shifted to other factories in a different section of the country and these kept running full blast.

In other cases, it was also notable that a technique of central control, extremely rigid and absolute, was developed. Immediately upon formation of the Distilling & Cattle Feeding Association, as Ripley relates, prices were cut sharply to force competitors into the pool, rivals were bought up or forced out, sometimes by negotiation and sometimes by intimidation or violence. Then by 1889, from twelve to twenty whiskey distilleries were operated on behalf of eighty-three plants previously existing, great savings were effected, and profits were steady and high enough to "accumulate a surplus for purpose of contest with outsiders." Thus the "whiskey ring," as Henry Lloyd wrote at the time, regulated the liquor traffic as no government could up to then or ever since effectively do, decreeing where and how much liquor should be made, and enforcing their decree, controlling alcohol, hence the sciences, medicine, even the arts and poetry. By February, 1888, only two large independents out of eighty distilleries resisted the combination. These were in Chicago, and one of them in April of that year published in the Chicago Tribune the fact that they had caught a spy of the combination in their works; later, tampering with the valves of their vats was discovered; then offers of large bribes if they would sell out their plants. In December, according to Lloyd's account, this distillery became the scene of an awful explosion:

All the buildings in the neighborhood were shaken and many panes of glass were broken. . . . There were 15,000 barrels of whiskey stored under the roof that was torn open, and if these had been ignited a terrible fire would have been added to the effect of the explosion. A package of dynamite which had failed to explode, though the fuse had been lighted, was found on the premises by the Chicago police. . . .

In the meantime, the years of depression after 1893 had wrought no less signal changes in the nature of the Standard Oil Company. This industrial empire, which continued to conquer markets and sources of supply in Russia and China as well as at the frontiers of the two Americas, was in no way checked by the period of general hardship. Nor had prohibitive laws, or condemnation of the company in certain regions such as the State of Ohio, hampered its progress in any degree. The order of dissolution in Ohio had simply been resisted by every legal subterfuge conceivable to its counsels; and then after seven years the Standard Oil had simply sloughed off its skin, and appeared as a New Jersey holding corporation.

But after 1893 the Standard Oil Company had a dual character. It was no longer simply an industrial monopoly, composed of men who simply owned and managed their oil business; it became, in great part, a reservoir of money, a house of investment bankers or absentee owners. So rapid has been the increase in annual profits, from $15,000,000 per annum in 1886 to $45,000,000 in 1899, that there was always more cash than could be used as capital in the oil and kindred trades. It became inevitable that the Standard Oil men make reinvestments regularly and extensively in new enterprises which were to be carried on under their absentee ownership. By a coincidence these developments came at a time when John D. Rockefeller announced his "retirement" from active business.

Moody in his "Masters of Capital" relates:

The Rockefellers were not the type of investors who were satisfied with five or six percent. . . . They meant to make, if possible, as large profits in the investment of their surplus cash as they had been accustomed to make in their own line of business. But to make money at so rapid a pace called for the same shrewd, superior business methods. . . . To discerning men it was clear that ultimately these other enterprises into which the Standard Oil put its funds must be controlled or dominated by Standard Oil. William Rockefeller had anticipated this development to some extent years before when he had become active in the financial management of the Chicago, Milwaukee and St. Paul Railroad. But it was not until after the panic of 1893 that he and his associates began to reach out aggressively to control the destinies of many corporations.

John D. Rockefeller at this time possessed a fortune that has been estimated at two hundred millions; his brother William owned probably half as much, while his associates who usually moved in conjunction with him or his brother, Rogers, Flagler, Harkness, Payne, and various others combined now to form a capital of a size probably unprecedented in history. Soon the money markets felt the entrance of the Standard Oil "gang" in strange ways, as they began buying and selling pieces of capital, industries, men and material. This omnipotent group had brought a "new order of things" into the world of high finance. They had introduced into Wall Street operations, according to Henry Clews, "the same quiet, unostentatious, but resistless measures that they have always employed heretofore in their corporate affairs." Where a Gould might sometimes face the chance of failure, or a Commodore Vanderbilt have to fight for his life, Clews continued wonderingly, these men seemed to have removed the element of chance:

Their resources are so vast that they need only to concentrate on any given property in order to do with it what they please . . . that they have thus concentrated . . . is a fact well known. . . . They are the greatest operators the world has ever seen, and the beauty of their method is the quiet and lack of ostentation . . . no gallery plays . . . no scare heads in the newspapers . . . no wild scramble or excitement. With them the process is gradual, thorough, and steady, with never a waver or break.

In the conduct of these far-flung undertakings the Standard Oil family had always the loyal coöperation of the captains and lieutenants who wore their "collar" so contentedly, and who sent confidential news every day from all parts of the world. The "master mind" in these investment operations nowadays would seem to have been Henry Rogers; while important alliances . . . were effected with Stillman, the astute commander of the National City Bank, and Harriman, the rising giant of railroads.

After the headquarters of Standard Oil had been removed from Pearl Street to the high building at 26 Broadway, the active leaders of The System, as Thomas W. Lawson termed it, would go upstairs every day at eleven o'clock, to the fifteenth floor, and gather together around a large table. It was the high council of a dynasty of money, and men everywhere now spoke with bated breath of the commands which went forth from this council, and of the power and relentlessness of The System. In his romantic history, "Frenzied Finance," the stock-market plunger Lawson seems to blubber at the stupendous holdings of the Standard Oil "gang" toward 1900—"its countless miles of railroads . . . in every state and city in America, and its never-ending twistings of snaky pipe lines . . . its manufactories in the East, its colleges in the South, and its churches in the North." The guarded headquarters of Standard Oil aroused and have always aroused an awe which Lawson accurately reflects:

At the lower end of the greatest thoroughfare in the greatest city of the New World is a huge structure of plain gray-stone. Solid as a prison, towering as a steeple, its cold and forbidding facade. . . . Men point to its stern portals, glance quickly up at the rows of unwinking windows, nudge each other, and hurry onward, as the Spaniards used to do when going by the offices of the Inquisition. The building is No. 26 Broadway.

Industrial Statesmen

Allan Nevins[*]

It was a massive and stirring chapter of American history which was written by McCormick, Carnegie, Morgan, Duke, Armour, James J. Hill, Harriman, and the other towering figures of industry and commerce in the late nineteenth century; and reasons exist for placing Rockefeller, the richest, the longest-lived, the most attacked, and the most famous, at the head of the group. No other, not even Carnegie, gained such a double preëminence: foremost in business, foremost in philanthropy, in his era. We have called this chronicle a study in power, and it is clear that his special power was organizing power. Behind this organizing genius, which has analogies with Richelieu's or Bismarck's, lay a combination of traits not the less interesting because of their simplicity, conspicuity, and harmony.

All observers must be struck, in studying his career, by his singlemindedness; his sharpness of insight; his cool disdain of emotional factors; his instinct for the future—that ability to "see around the corner" which Archbold lauded; his breadth of ambition; and his skill (which to opponents sometimes seemed merciless) in finding novel weapons to attain his ends—his strategic ingenuity, in short.

His singlemindedness, which differentiates him so sharply from Carnegie or Morgan, and reminds us of Cecil Rhodes, was part and parcel of an intense concentration. In his early days, as he put it, he was "all business"; he remained virtually all business until he retired to distribute his fortune, when he was all the retired giver and nothing else. In his active business years he played no games; was indifferent to theatre or concert-chamber; cared nothing for literature or art. A consistent Republican, he left party activity to others; a stern prohibitionist, he did no crusading; a financial supporter of

[*] crappy liberal of a historian.

many activities, he held personally aloof from causes. The church alone gave him any considerable diversion from his central pursuit. His concentration was made easier by his detached, unpassionate nature; "the most unemotional man I have ever known," testified Jerome Greene. To him Dr. Johnson's injunction to clear the mind of cant was always unnecessary. Outside home and congregation, friends and associates, where an unexpected warmth welled to the surface, he was an impassive analyst, precise, logical, and penetrating. He foresaw problems and opportunities long before most men, and his uninterrupted rise showed how quickly he pierced to the heart of every situation.

His chill, clear insight was allied with a primal urge of ambition. Since from boyhood he was determined to get into business for himself, he methodically obtained a training for large enterprises. He chose a lucrative, expanding line of affairs—a commission house—to perfect his experience and gain capital. It was the experience he most valued; but the profits were large enough to lift him above complete reliance on investment bankers. He meant to be always, in his own phrase, "on the progressive side of things"; and at twenty-two he found a progressive side-venture, oil. Within two years his analytical mind was convinced that petroleum had a solid future. Repeated oil-strikes, culminating in Pithole, demonstrated an amplitude of raw materials; America and Europe furnished proofs of an irresistible demand for better illuminants and lubricants. The alert, precise, farsighted young Clevelander cast the chrysalis of the commission house behind him to rise on wings; he would be a manufacturer.

At least instinctively, his foresight transcended the special field he chose. The age of big business was now opening. Within fifteen years of Appomattox, it was to burgeon in the packing houses of Chicago and the flour mills of Minneapolis; the car-shops of Pullman and the wagon-plant of Studebaker; the steel-mills of Pittsburgh and Bethlehem; the farm-implement works of McCormick, Oliver, and Ames. And the big unit, irresistibly, was to begin replacing little units. The village flourmills withered under the competition of Washburn and Pillsbury; the custom shoemaker surrendered to the huge Lynn factory; the small distiller was crushed out of existence by Peoria and Baltimore; local butchers began to feel the impact of Nelson Morris and Swift. Railroad systems (themselves an example of the large snake swallowing all the small ones) created a truly national market, national units of production were the inevitable result. When Rockefeller & Andrews began work, an age of mass operations was opening. With his piercing vision Rockefeller saw the possibilities of economy, efficiency, and profit in large-scale manufacturing. He was not interested in making a quick fortune and then stepping aside; not interested in a moderately successful business yielding a moderate income down the years. Gearing his ambition to the main trends of the age, he pushed his undertaking indomitably forward to the largest possible result.

The young manufacturer stepped into an arena of grim, implacable warfare. Refiners battled against refiners, for the industry was over-expanded; in a self-choking growth of small plants, many resorted to price-slashing, espionage, rebate-snatching, and other unhappy devices to keep alive. Producers battled against producers, and the producing interest against the refining interest. The well-owners tried to organize, and tried again, and yet again—always failing, but always believing that *their* organization was righteous, while a refiners' organization was wicked. The teamster interest fought the pipe line interest. Railroads fought canals. Railroad system fought railroad system, the wars of the Pennsylvania, New York Central, Erie, and Baltimore & Ohio inevitably involving the oil traffic. The chief refining centers fought each other: Pittsburgh was the enemy of the Regions, Philadelphia and New York the enemy of Pittsburgh, and Cleveland the enemy of them all. The business and political morals of the age were shocking: it was the period of Gould and Drew, Boss Tweed and Boss Shepherd, Grantism in Washington and Reconstruction in the South. With a few shining exceptions, the men who forged ahead in business were almost of necessity stern, ruthless battlers.

In the omnipresent business warfare Rockefeller fought after his own fashion, which was that of a cool, subtle strategist, relentlessly intent on his goals. Deeply shocked by his early experience with the chaos of the oil industry, disillusioned by his contacts with the irrepressibly speculative producers, convinced that much law-making on industry fitted only a bygone age, he resolved to organize the refining industry to furnish stability, economy, solvency, and if possible high profits. He would form an alliance of the chief companies, who would impose a centralized control. Dissenters who attacked the great aggregation would be trampled under without pity; coöperative firms would be absorbed on generous terms. This was "our plan." We must not forget that Rockefeller was just beginning his thirties when drawn into the South Improvement scheme; still in his early thirties when made head of the National Refiners' Association. Obviously, he had not only vision but traits of command. The Association tried to work out a plan of combination with the producers, and found them unable to keep their agreements. When the trial failed, young Rockefeller turned to the building of a refiners' combination so complete that it would possess a virtual monopoly, and to the creation of a central direction so trusted and efficient that he could be sure of compliance with his and his associates' policies.

Monopoly was and is a hateful thing. Rockefeller's aim, when pushed to almost complete monopoly, was and is repugnant to believers in social and economic freedom and was certain to involve him in opprobrium. We must be sufficiently objective, however, to keep in mind a basic fact: that in industry after industry at this time the chaos and cruelty of over-competition bred a resort to monopoly as the natural cure. To every element in the oil industry by 1870—transport interests, producing interests, refining interests, marketing interests—the excesses of competition seemed absolutely insufferable; they caused constant confusion, turmoil, loss, and bankruptcy; the little men and the big alike were harried by anxiety, tortured by peril, and not infrequently crushed.

So it was in the salt business, the anthracite business, the sugar business, the tobacco business, the meat business, and many others. At a later date Rockefeller, like Duke, Havemeyer, Armour, and the other authors of combinations, was accused of being motivated by a sadistic desire to destroy rivals, and by an avaricious appetite for inordinate profits. It is true that Rockefeller thought the little men wasteful, inefficient, irresponsible; it is true that he wanted high returns. But his Trust, and dozens of the other trusts which sprang up between 1870 and 1900, were not primarily an expression of Lawless Mammonism. They were primarily a spasmodic, inevitable response to the uncertainties, wastes, and cruelties of unbridled competition.

Once Rockefeller had set this goal in "our plan," he perceived just how to reach it. He established a practical control of Cleveland, the most strategic point, in 1872–73; he then moved to a practical control of all refining in 1873–79. At thirty-nine he and his associates were masters of American oil manufacturing. They saw that they must take control of the pipe lines, which were supplanting the railroads in moving crude oil; a few lightning strategic moves, and the pipes had become one of the main sources of Standard income. As oil production moved into Ohio and Indiana, they saw that they must make sure of their sources of oil—and make certain that no formidable competitors rose on these new floods. Buying wide acreages in the Lima field, building the large Whiting refinery, using the South Penn Company to extend their holdings in West Virginia, Rockefeller and his partners raised their production of crude oil from zero to a great fraction of the American total.

Meanwhile, Rockefeller had perfectly understood that demand must be continuously maintained at high level if the refineries were to operate continuously at anything like capacity. He had therefore taken efficient steps to construct a complex marketing organization, and to maintain customer demand by recognized trade names and high standards of service.

The oil business was thus vertically integrated from the well-head to the consumers of the multiple oil products; mass production of raw materials, mass manufacturing, and mass distribution were meshed in a mechanism of unexampled power and efficiency. Under Rockefeller, integration had taken place downward from manufacturing and marketing to crude oil production; later, when powerful new oil companies arose, it was usually to take place upward from production to distribution. But the vital fact is that Rockefeller and his group saw the importance of vertical integration when it was still a novelty in business; they set a pattern which was quickly followed by Duke in tobacco, and by other leaders, and which in time became a norm for much of American industry. This was constructive pioneering of a high quality.

Constructive, too, were many of the innovations for which the Standard was responsible. Its precise, scientific cost-accounting system; its tremendously thorough use of byproducts; its superiority in making cans, barrels, and tank cars; its energy in bringing pipes to every well, and in the rapid building of tankage facilities for sudden floods of crude oil; its development of the Frasch process for utilizing Lima production, as later it devised another special process for using California oil—all this had a creative quality. Bulk terminal stations to handle bulk shipments were few and primitive until the Standard emerged; it made them models of their kind. Singer, Colt, McCormick and others established great export fabrics, but no foreign business was reared with more enterprise, care, and solidity than that of the Standard; a business which withstood Russian assaults and gave the United States, in the long era when it was a debtor nation, a strong continuous resource in the balance of trade. Reviewing all this, we can understand Rockefeller's remark to W. T. Halliday, long president of the Standard of Ohio, that while "caretakers" in business are useful, "builders" are far more important. "They are relatively few. Yet they are the lifeblood of an organization, and you can never overpay a builder."

It is obvious that a great part of Rockefeller's success first in business and then in philanthropy is to be credited not to his personal efforts, but to the extraordinarily able and devoted groups of associates who labored with him. In business, Flagler, Harkness, Payne, H. H. Rogers, Charles and Charles M. Pratt, Archbold, Warden, Lockhart, the Bedfords, McGregor, Folger, and by no means least, William Rockefeller, were but the more outstanding men in a staff which, we may repeat, was perhaps the most brilliant that American business has yet known. Yet strong as it was, it was not more remarkable than the group which helped Rockefeller disburse his fortune in ways beneficial to mankind: Frederick T. Gates, Simon and Abraham Flexner, Wallace Buttrick, Drs. Herter, Prudden, and Biggs, Seaman A. Knapp, William H. Baldwin, George E. Vincent, Jerome Greene, Raymond B. Fosdick, and perhaps above all his son, John D. Rockefeller, Jr., who in time became one of the most respected of all Americans. In the history of philanthropic planning and administration that group, too, would be difficult indeed to match. Writing in the *Random Reminiscences* of the Standard Oil combination, Rockefeller remarked that its starting-point was "not so much the consolidation of the firms in which we had a personal interest, but the coming together of the men who had the combined brainpower to do the work." Much that was credited to him individually was really the result of "combined brainpower."

In giving full credit to the talents and energies of these two groups, however, we little diminish the stature of Rockefeller himself. Men of preëminent capacity do not place themselves under the guidance of a bungler or weakling; strength is attracted to strength, and when we find a full-panoplied staff harmoniously at work, we may be sure that in the background stands some powerful figure. Had young Rockefeller lacked vision, he would not have seen that Flagler possessed just the gifts to supplement his own;

had the magnate been less alert and perceptive, he would not have divined that Gates was just the lieutenant needed to help him in his benefactions: Rockefeller knew how to furnish his co-workers tools and give them a sense of mutual loyalty. As a strong associate, A. P. Coombe, once said: "When a man goes to work for Standard Oil, he has a rebirth. He gets a new father and mother and new brothers and sisters." It is significant that, ruggedly^v powerful as Rockefeller's chief associates in business were, they never challenged his primacy; that, quarrelsome as some of them were, nobody ever quarreled with *him*. It is significant also that his associates in philanthropy, men far better educated than he was, never once complained of a major decision of his, and never once had to reproach him for meddlesomeness after a grant was made.

That the debit side of the ledger has a heavy account is undeniable. The combination of which Rockefeller was captain was one of the most hard-hitting entities in a hard-hitting business world. Its methods were often as questionable as its central aim of monopoly. It made small competitors, as we have noted, "sick," it forced them to "sweat," it stifled them without compunction. It used, like nearly every other concern that could do so, the rebate. For a time it took not merely rebates but a drawback payment secretly exacted from competitors by the railroads, as cruel a device as business history records. Though the period in which this drawback was pocketed was short, it left an ineffaceable stain on the history of the Trust. Like various competitors in the oil business, but more systematically and effectively, the Standard resorted to espionage. With a duplicity that all must find repugnant, it sometimes employed dummy companies. It often "cut to kill," as Miss Tarbell wrote, reducing prices in a given locality until competition was destroyed, and then restoring high charges. That it drew excessive profits from the oil consumers is proved by the size of the fortunes which its heads accumulated. All this, and the long battle with state and Federal opponents of monopoly, entailed forty years of obloquy, most of it visited on Rockefeller's head.

All the while Rockefeller remained a fervent Christian, unhesitant in his devotion to the church and its ethical principles. How, some critics asked, could he play such a double role? The answer is that to him it did not appear a double role. From a chaotic industry he was building an efficient industrial empire for what seemed to him the good not only of its heads but of the general public. If he relaxed his general methods of warfare (he was not blamable for some extreme acts of Carley, Pierce, and O'Day) a multitude of small competitors would smash his empire and plunge the oil business back to chaos. He always believed in what William McKinley called "benevolent assimilation"; he preferred to buy out rivals on decent terms, and to employ the ablest competitors as helpers. It was when his terms were refused that he ruthlessly crushed the "outsiders." And he did so because, as John T. Flynn writes, "he had that quality of the great commander engaged on large enterprises of surveying the necessities of his task with high intelligence, and appraising the suffering of his victims in its proper proportion to the scene." It seemed to him better that a limited number of small businesses should die than that the whole industry should go through a constant process of half-dying, reviving, and again half-dying.

γ Obviously, any comprehensive judgment on Rockefeller's business career must be subjective and dependent on the economic assumptions brought to the judgment-bar. Did the deadweight the Standard Oil hung upon business ethics (for though it would be hard to prove that it depressed the current code, it certainly did nothing to raise it) outweigh the great constructive innovations of the combination, and the example set by its efficiency and order? Were the exterminative ravages of the Standard among its rivals greater than the exterminative ravages of over-competition before it rose to power? These are but two of the many questions whose answer depends upon variable assumptions. One fact, however, is certain: that the oldtime black-and-white antithesis between monopoly and "perfect competition" is as dead as the view that industrial concentration can or should be destroyed. Imperfect competition is the rule in modern industrialized nations; the best competition is that which Joseph A. Schumpeter called the Process of Creative Destruction, an industrial mutation which "incessantly revolutionizes the industrial structure from within, incessantly destroying the old one and incessantly creating a new one." Both the Standard's type of monopoly, and the types of oligopoly exposed by the Temporary National Economic Commission inquiry, are in the long run intolerable; but they are not so intolerable as the "perfect competition" contemplated by the makers of the Sherman Act would be.

Once the fortune was acquired, Rockefeller's use of it was in most respects exemplary; he was as great an innovator and organizer in philanthropy as he had been in business. The unexampled scale of his gifts, running to some $550,000,000, was not their most striking feature. What made them arresting was the skill with which he and his experts planned them. The various foundations which he, his son, and their aides set up, governed by able men working in almost complete independence, became models for large-scale philanthropy in America and other lands. Their objects, administrative mechanisms, methods, and spirit, have been widely copied. Foundations had existed long before, but not any like these. Some of their principles, moreover, had stamped his thoughtful, conscientious giving from the days when he was comparatively poor. His emphasis on ameliorative work at the sources of misery or evil, his use of money to stimulate self-help and giving by others, and his desire to establish continuing activities, remained fundamental in his distribution of the fortune.

In important respects, events outran Rockefeller's vision and planning. The ultimate growth of the oil industry was unquestionably far greater than he had anticipated, his organization of that industry went faster and further than he had expected, and his fortune greatly exceeded his initial dreams. In

1870 he doubtless had a vision of the domain of oil as equaling that of an-thracite or copper; he could not have foreseen the gigantic business that by 1910 had tapped seas of petroleum from Pennsylvania to California, affected every home and machine shop, started a revolution in transportation, and become a spectacular part of world commerce. Initially, in all probability, he had counted on a milder type of monopoly, on more persuasion and less force, than became necessary. The riotous individualism of the industry; the spread of production west and south and the tendency of independent refiners to follow it; the iron-fisted quality of associates like Archbold, O'Day, and Camden; the necessity of taking hurried precautions, keeping emergency pace with new developments, and making safety-first the rule—all this made for a sterner and more autocratic type of monopoly than he had wished. He would have said with Lincoln that to a great extent events controlled him, not he events. But it was the final magnitude of his fortune that proved most unexpected and astonishing.

The size of that fortune, as we have said, was an historical accident. In no true sense of the word did he, Carnegie, and Henry Ford earn the huge accumulations which came to them. Only the special economic, legal, and fiscal situation of the United States 1865–1917 rendered it possible to make and keep so much money. Recognizing this fact, Rockefeller always regarded himself as a trustee rather than an owner. His statement at the University of Chicago that "God gave me money," sometimes quoted as a piece of sancti-monious arrogance, was actually uttered in a spirit of complete humility. He devoutly believed that Providence had made him a trustee for these hundreds of millions, not to be kept but to be wisely disbursed. He meant to see that the gold was used to do the utmost possible good. It is for the meticulous care, the administrative ability, and the general sagacity which he and his staff applied to the laborious work of distribution that gratitude is really due them.

And though the United States has resolved that such aggregations of wealth shall henceforth be regarded as unjust, anti-social, and dangerous, in this instance fate did not serve the nation ill. The fortune fell into the hands of a man who had proved his possession of strong liberal impulses; who even as a youth earning a few dollars a week, his necessities poorly met, had given a substantial part of his meagre wage to charity. Few indeed are those who make the sacrifices recorded in Ledger A. He had given from the outset without regard to religion, race, party, or section; he had increased his giving as his means grew. The fortune went to a man who had proved a remarkable capac-ity for gearing his effort to the creative impulses of his time, who knew how to find and keep expert assistants, and who was so devoid of egotism that, having once devoted his funds to an object, he cut himself off from all further control of the money. Much as the United States prides itself on efficiency, waste has always been a large element in its life. Waste is perhaps the saddest feature of the world of today: waste of life, energy, and wealth. It may be called a happy accident that one individual was enabled to show how much in education, health, scientific advancement, and human welfare could be bought by a single half billion of dollars studiously and imaginatively applied.

We may well decide, in our final view, that the extremes of praise and blame heaped upon Rockefeller were both unwarranted. His enemies during his years of power abused him as one of the archcriminals of the age; his admirers during his later years of philanthropy lauded him as one of the world's chief benefactors. Neither estimate possessed historical truth. We may well decide also that, viewed critically, he was not a very attractive personage. Much as his intimates admired him, to the world at large he seemed—and seems—deficient in humanly likable qualities. But that he was one of the most powerful leaders of his time there can be no doubt. Innovator, thinker, planner, bold entrepreneur, he was above all an organizer—one of the master organizers of the era. Taking the most confused, muddled, and anarchic of American industries, he organized it with a completeness, efficiency, and constructive talent that amazed beholders and affected all business activities. Turning to the vague field of philanthropy, he organized a series of undertakings that became models for all givers who followed him. By virtue of this organizing power, backed by keenness of mind, tenacity of purpose, and firmness of character, he looms up as one of the most impressive figures of the century which his lifetime spanned.

SUGGESTIONS FOR FURTHER READING

Samuel P. Hays, *The Response to Industrialism (Chicago, 1957) deserves to be read in its entirety. This thoughtful book is relevant not only to the discussion here but to the chapters on labor, the farmers, and the Progressives. Gustavus Myers, History of the Great American Fortunes (New York, 1907) is a blistering attack on the businessmen. Henry Demarest Lloyd, *Wealth against Commonwealth (New York, 1894) is sharply critical of John D. Rockefeller as is Ida M. Tarbell, The History of Standard Oil Company (New York, 1904; abridged version in paperback). Allan Nevins' views are spelled out in detail in his long biography of Rockefeller, a portion of which is reprinted here: John D. Rockefeller: The Heroic Age of American Enterprise, 2 vols. (New York, 1940) and Study in Power: John D. Rockefeller, Industrialist and Philanthropist, 2 vols. (New York, 1953). Like Nevins, Ralph W. and Muriel E. Hidy, Pioneering in Big Business, 1882–1911: History of Standard Oil Company (New Jersey) (New York, 1955) stress the importance of Rockefeller in organizing the oil business. Louis M. Hacker, The Triumph of American Capitalism (New York, 1940) places the contributions of the post-Civil War industrialists in the context of earlier economic history; although often critical of them, Hacker concludes by praising their accomplishments.

Josephson's discussion of Rockefeller is taken from his long study of *The Robber Barons (New York, 1934), an entertaining and insightful analysis of all the major business leaders of the time. As famous (or infamous) as Rockefeller was J. P. Morgan. Two very different pictures of the great banker may be found in Frederick Lewis Allen, *The Great Pierpont Morgan* (New York, 1949) and Lewis Corey, *The House of Morgan* (New York, 1930).

Useful interpretive surveys of the vast literature on the subject may be found in Edward C. Kirkland, "The Robber Barons Revisited," *American Historical Review*, LXVI (October 1960), pp. 68–73; Hal Bridges, "The Robber Baron Concept in American History," *Business History Review*, XXXII (Spring 1958), pp. 1–13; Thomas C. Cochran, "The Legend of the Robber Barons," *The Pennsylvania Magazine of History and Biography*, LXXIV (July 1950), pp. 307–21; Gabriel Kolko, "The Premises of Business Revisionism," *Business History Review*, XXXIII (Autumn 1959), pp. 330–44.

* Available in paperback edition.

2
FARMERS IN AN INDUSTRIAL AGE

"Those who labor in the earth are the chosen people of God," wrote Thomas Jefferson. Virtue resides in the hearts of the agriculturists, he explained. "Corruption of morals in the mass of cultivators is a phenomenon of which no age nor nation has furnished an example." To this day many Americans have the vague feeling that farming is the most natural, the most virtuous occupation, that somehow those who work the land are especially important to the survival of American democracy.

Yet farmers are rarely mentioned in American history except in discussions of farmers' problems. And, indeed, over the years the American farmer has had many serious problems. In the colonial period, when most of the nation's citizens tilled the soil, the small farmers along the frontier bore the brunt of the Indian raids and lamented the lack of adequate protection for their families and lands. They complained that they were under-represented in the assemblies, over-taxed, and given too few of the bridges and roads they demanded. Occasionally, when they felt that their problems had gone unheeded too long, they rebelled against colonial authorities.

Independence did not end the small farmers' difficulties. Shays's Rebellion in Massachusetts, the Whiskey Rebellion in Pennsylvania, both put down quickly, represented the unhappiness and the discontent of some farmers.

Working the land may have seemed an ideal occupation to those living in the cities, but many farmers knew better. The everyday struggle to eke out a living from the soil, often without the cooperation of the elements, was hard and frequently frustrating. Nor did the passage of time solve the farmers' problems; more often new problems were added to the old.

From the colonial period to the early nineteenth century, most of those who worked the land were subsistence farmers, that is, they produced the greatest part of what they ate and wore. A few had a cash crop—potash or grain (often distilled into whiskey) or cotton or tobacco, depending on the area—but most sold very little of what they raised. With the rise of industrialism in the mid-nineteenth century, and the improvement of transportation, first through the canal and then the railroad, subsistence farming gave way in many areas to commercial farming. Farmers concentrated on cash crops, wheat or cotton or pork, and used the proceeds to buy the food and clothing and the other items they needed. With the rise of commercial farming, the farmer lost his economic independence. He became increasingly dependent on the bankers, who lent him money to buy more land and machinery needed to increase production, and upon the railroad, which was often the only way he could get his crop to market. Moreover, his income, and hence his well-being, depended upon the vicissitudes of the world-wide market for his crop.

The spread of commercial farming and the expansion of industrialism, especially in the years after the Civil War, raised the standard of living of many farmers, who were able to purchase some of the luxuries enjoyed by the city-dweller. Often, however, the price of higher living standards was great. Many went deeply in debt as they sought to increase production through the purchase of new lands and machinery. As production rose, prices went down; efforts to increase income through further increases in production compounded the problem. Fluctuations of the business cycle, as well as the natural disasters of droughts, floods, hail, and wind added to the farmers' woes. Increasingly in the years after the Civil War, the farmer felt victimized, and often he blamed the railroad or the banker for his plight. To improve his situation he attempted to organize. He joined the Patrons of Husbandry, more commonly known as the Grange. At first primarily a social organization, inevitably the Grange became involved in politics in several mid-western states and successfully pressured for laws regulating railroads. Most of the laws proved inadequate and the farmers continued to agitate, joining societies like the Agricultural Wheel in Arkansas, the Farmers' Union in Louisiana, and the Farmers' Alliances in various other states. All of this organizing came to a climax in 1892 when many farmers bolted the two regular parties and formed the Peoples' or Populist Party.

The Populists regarded their movement as a struggle against what they termed "the interests," a massive conspiracy of bankers, railroads, and big businessmen which sought to exploit the farmers. Their only defense, they concluded, was organization and struggle. For many of their opponents, the movement was fraught with danger, for it smacked of revolution. Some historians have accepted this evaluation and concluded that the farmers' movements represented a fundamental class conflict in American society. Other scholars disagree. They insist that the farmers were not revolutionary, but, like other Americans at the time, were merely seeking a bigger slice of the economic pie. Some historians add that the Populists were suffering from their inability to adapt to changing economic conditions and longed to turn back the clock, to return to the age of subsistence agriculture, the small family farm, and the pastoral village. Examples of these evaluations are presented in the following selections.

In the first selection, John D. Hicks spells out the farmers' grievances against the railroads, big business, bankers, and middlemen. The picture that emerges is one of sharp class conflict, with agrarians—West and South—arrayed against Eastern capitalists. Richard Hofstadter, in the next selection, finds the Populists unable to understand the problems they faced. Instead of attempting to adapt to the modern world, they looked backward to what seemed to be better days; instead of realistically assessing their problems, they viewed themselves as victims of a conspiracy. But the conspiracy, according to Hofstadter, was a product of their imagination. Norman Pollack, on the other hand, sees the conflict between farmers and businessmen as real and important. He insists that the Populists were realistic radicals who looked not to the past but to a future when the businessmen would no longer be able to exploit farmers and workers.

There can be no doubt that the farmer's life was often difficult and that his complaints were real and justified. But did the farmer's problems stem from fundamental differences in American society? Was he a victim, as he claimed, of the businessmen and bankers who controlled the country? Did his efforts to organize to improve his condition signal class war between farmer and businessman? Or were the farmers simply the victims of overproduction which drove their prices down? If so, then perhaps their complaints and their organizational efforts, despite the rhetoric involved, were merely efforts to adapt to the new industrial age.

The Farmers' Grievances

John D. Hicks

In the spring of 1887 a North Carolina farm journal stated with rare accuracy what many farmers in all sections of the United States had been thinking for some time.

> There is something radically wrong in our industrial system. There is a screw loose. The wheels have dropped out of balance. The railroads have never been so prosperous, and yet agriculture languishes. The banks have never done a better or more profitable business, and yet agriculture languishes. Manufacturing enterprises never made more money or were in a more flourishing condition, and yet agriculture languishes. Towns and cities flourish and "boom" and grow and "boom," and yet agriculture languishes. Salaries and fees were never so temptingly high and desirable, and yet agriculture languishes.

Nor was this situation imputed to America alone. Once in an unguarded burst of rhetoric a high priest of the Alliance movement pointed out that similar conditions prevailed in all thickly populated agricultural countries, "high tariff and low tariff; monarchies, empires, and republics; single gold standard, silver standard or double standard." It was true indeed that the blessings of civilization had not fallen upon all mankind with equal bounty. To the upper and middle classes more had been given than to the lower; to the city dweller far more than to his country kinsman. The farmer had good reason to believe, as he did believe, that he worked longer hours, under more adverse conditions, and with smaller compensation for his labor than any other man on earth.

For this condition of affairs the farmer did not blame himself. Individual farmers might be lacking in industry and frugality, but farmers as a class were

From John D. Hicks, The Populist Revolt. University of Minnesota Press, Minneapolis. © 1931 by University of Minnesota; renewed 1959 by John D. Hicks.

devoted to these virtues. Those who gave up the struggle to win wealth out of the land and went to the cities so generally succeeded in the new environment that a steady migration from farm to city set in. Why should the same man fail as a farmer and succeed as a city laborer? More and more the conviction settled down upon the farmer that he was the victim of "some extrinsic baleful influence." Someone was "walking off with the surplus" that society as a whole was clearly building up and that in part at least should be his. He was accustomed to regard himself as the "bone and sinew of the nation" and as the producer of "the largest share of its wealth." Why should his burdens be "heavier every year and his gains . . . more meager?" Why should he be face to face with a condition of abject servility? Not himself, certainly, but someone else was to blame.

The farmer never doubted that his lack of prosperity was directly traceable to the low prices he received for the commodities he had to sell. The period from 1870 to 1897 was one of steadily declining prices. As one writer put it, the farmer's task had been at the beginning of this era "to make two spears of grass grow where one grew before. He solved that. Now he is struggling hopelessly with the question how to get as much for two spears of grass as he used to get for one." Accurate statistics showing what the farmer really received for his crops are almost impossible to obtain, but the figures given by the Department of Agriculture for three major crops, given in the table below, will at least reveal the general downward trend of prices.

AVERAGE MARKET PRICES OF THREE CROPS, 1870–1897

Years	Wheat (per bushel)	Corn (per bushel)	Cotton (per pound)
1870–1873	106.7	43.1	15.1
1874–1877	94.4	40.9	11.1
1878–1881	100.6	43.1	9.5
1882–1885	80.2	39.8	9.1
1886–1889	74.8	35.9	8.3
1890–1893	70.9	41.7	7.8
1894–1897	63.3	29.7	5.8

These prices are subject to certain corrections. They are as of December 1, whereas the average farmer had to sell long before that time, often on a glutted market that beat down the price to a much lower figure. They make no allowance, either, for commissions to dealers, for necessary warehouse charges, nor for deductions made when the produce could not be regarded as strictly first class. They fail to show, also, the difference in prices received along the frontier, where the distance to market was great, and in the eastern states, where the market was near at hand. In 1889, for example, corn was sold in Kansas for as low a price as ten cents a bushel and was commonly burned in lieu of coal. In 1890 a farmer in Gosper County, Nebraska, it was said, shot his hogs because he could neither sell nor give them away.

So low did the scale of prices drop that in certain sections of the country it was easy enough to prove, statistically at least, that farming was carried on only at an actual loss. It was generally agreed that seven or eight cents of the price received for each pound of cotton went to cover the cost of production; by the later eighties, moreover, many cotton growers were finding it necessary to market their crops for less than they had been getting. The average price per bushel received by northwestern wheat growers dropped as low as from forty-two to forty-eight cents, whereas the cost of raising a bushel of wheat was variously estimated at from forty-five to sixty-seven cents. Statisticians held that it cost about twenty-one cents to produce a bushel of corn, but the western farmer sometimes had to take less than half that sum. Quoth one agitator:

We were told two years ago to go to work and raise a big crop, that was all we needed. We went to work and plowed and planted; the rains fell, the sun shone, nature smiled, and we raised the big crop that they told us to; and what came of it? Eight cent corn, ten cent oats, two cent beef and no price at all for butter and eggs—that's what came of it. Then the politicians said that we suffered from over-production.

Not politicians only but many others who studied the question held that overproduction was the root of the evil. Too many acres were being tilled, with the result that too many bushels of grain, too many bales of cotton, too many tons of hay, too many pounds of beef were being thrown upon the market each year. As the population increased, the number of consumers had advanced correspondingly, but the increase in production had gone on even more rapidly. It was a fact that the per capita output of most commodities had risen with each successive year. The markets of the world were literally broken down. With the supply so far in excess of the demand, prices could not possibly be maintained at their former levels.

*   *   *

But the farmers and their defenders refused to place much stock in the overproduction theory. Admitting that the output from the farm had increased perhaps even more rapidly than population, they could still argue that this in itself was not sufficient to account for the low prices and the consequent agricultural depression. They pointed out that, with the general improvement of conditions among the masses, consumption had greatly increased. Possibly the demand attendant upon this fact alone would be nearly, if not quite, sufficient to offset the greater yearly output. There would be, moreover, even heavier consumption were it possible for those who needed and wanted more of the products of the farm to buy to the full extent of their ability to consume. In spite of all the advances of the nineteenth century the world was not yet free from want. "The makers of clothes were underfed; the makers of food were underclad." Farmers used corn for fuel in the West because the prices they were offered for it were so low, while at the same moment thousands of people elsewhere faced hunger and even starvation because the price of flour was so high. Why should the Kansas farmer have to sell his corn for eight or ten cents a bushel when the New York broker could and did demand upwards of a dollar for it? Were there not certain "artificial barriers to consumption?" Were there not "certain influences at work, like thieves in the night," to rob the farmers of the fruits of their toil?

Many of the farmers thought that there were; and they were not always uncertain as to the identity of those who stood in the way of agricultural prosperity. Western farmers blamed many of their troubles upon the railroads, by means of which all western crops must be sent to market. There was no choice but to use these roads, and as the frontier advanced farther and farther into the West, the length of the haul to market increased correspondingly. Sometimes western wheat or corn was carried a thousand, perhaps even two thousand, miles before it could reach a suitable place for export or consumption. For these long hauls the railroads naturally exacted high rates, admittedly charging "all the traffic would bear." The farmers of Kansas and Nebraska and Iowa complained that it cost a bushel of corn to send another bushel of corn to market, and it was commonly believed that the net profit of the carrier was greater than the net profit of the grower. The farmers of Minnesota and Dakota were accustomed to pay half the value of their wheat to get it as far towards its final destination as Chicago. Small wonder that the farmer held the railroads at least partly responsible for his distress! He believed that if he could only get his fair share of the price for which his produce eventually sold he would be prosperous enough. "How long," a Minnesota editor queried, "even with these cheap and wonderfully productive lands, can . . . any agricultural community pay such enormous tribute to corporate organization in times like these, without final exhaustion?"

Local freight rates were particularly high. The railroads figured, not without reason, that large shipments cost them less per bushel to haul than small shipments. The greater the volume of traffic the less the cost of carrying any portion of that traffic. Accordingly, on through routes and long hauls where there was a large and dependable flow of freight the rates were comparatively low—the lower because for such runs there was usually ample competition. Rates from Chicago to New York, for example, were low in comparison with rates for similar distances from western points to Chicago, while between local points west of Chicago the rates were even more disproportionate. Sometimes the western local rate would be four times as great as that charged for the same distance and the same commodity in the East. The rates on wheat from Fargo to Duluth were nearly double those from Minneapolis to Chicago —a distance twice as great. It cost as much as twenty-five cents a bushel to transport grain from many Minnesota towns to St. Paul or Minneapolis, while for less than as much more it could be transported all the way to the seaboard. Indeed, evidence was at hand to show that wheat could actually be sent from Chicago to Liverpool for less than from certain points in Dakota to the Twin Cities. Iowa farmers complained that it cost them about as much to ship in corn from an adjoining county for feeding purposes as it would have cost to ship the same corn to Chicago; and yet the Iowa rates seemed low to the farmers of Nebraska, who claimed that they paid an average of fifty percent more for the same service than their neighbors across the Missouri River.

Undoubtedly it cost the railroads more to haul the sparse freight of the West than it cost them to haul the plentiful freight of the East. Railway officials pointed out that western traffic was nearly all in one direction. During one season of the year for every car of wheat hauled out an empty car had to be hauled in, while the rest of the time about ninety percent of the traffic went from Chicago westward. They asserted that the new roads were often in thinly settled regions and were operated at a loss even with the highest rates. James J. Hill maintained that the roads were reducing rates as fast as they could, and to prove it he even declared himself "willing that the state make any rates it see fit," provided the state would "guarantee the roads six percent on their actual cost and a fund for maintenance, renewal and other necessary expenditures." President Dillon of the Union Pacific deplored the ingratitude of the farmers who grumbled about high rates. "What would it cost," he asked, "for a man to carry a ton of wheat one mile? What would it cost for a horse to do the same? The railway does it at a cost of less than a cent." Moreover, he thought that unreasonable rates could never long survive, for if a railroad should attempt anything of the sort competition would come immediately to the farmers' aid, and a parallel and competing line would be built to drive the charges down.

But critics of the railroads saw little that was convincing in these arguments. As for the regulation of rates by competition, it might apply on through routes, providing the roads had no agreement among themselves to prevent it, but competition could scarcely affect the charges for local hauls for the simple reason that the average western community depended exclusively upon a single road. Only rarely did the shipper have a choice of two or more railway companies with which to deal, and even when he had this choice there was not invariably competition. The roads reached agreements among themselves; more than that, they consolidated. "The number of separate railroad companies operating distinct roads in Minnesota was as high as twenty, three years ago," wrote the railway commissioner of that state in 1881. "Now the number is reduced to substantially one-third that number." Nor did Minnesota differ particularly in this respect from any other frontier state. Throughout the eighties as the number of miles of railroad increased, the number of railroad companies tended to decrease. Communities that prided themselves upon a new "parallel and competing line" were apt to discover "some fine morning that enough of its stock had been purchased by the older lines to give them control." Thus fortified by monopoly, the railroads, as the farmer saw it, could collect whatever rates they chose.

*   *   *

It was commonly believed also that the practice of stock-watering had much to do with the making of high rates. The exact extent to which the railroads watered their stock, or to which a particular railroad watered its stock, would be a difficult matter to determine, but that the practice did exist in varying degrees seems not to be open to question. A writer in Poor's *Manual* for 1884 stated that the entire four billion dollars at which the railways of the United States were capitalized represented nothing but so much "water." So sweeping a statement seems rather questionable, but the belief was general that railroad companies got their actual funds for investment from bond issues and passed out stocks to the shareholders for nothing. The roads, indeed, did not deny the existence of a certain amount of stock-watering. They argued that their property was quite as likely to increase in value as any other property—farm lands, for example—and that they were justified in increasing their capital stock to the full extent that any increase in value had taken place. Some of their apologists held also that the value of the road was determined by its earning power rather than by the amount actually invested in the enterprise. It followed, therefore, that new capital stock should be issued as fast as the earnings of the road showed that the old valuation had been outgrown.

But to those who suffered from the high rates all these arguments seemed like so many confessions of robbery. The governor of Colorado, considering especially the sins of the Denver and Rio Grande, declared it "incredible that the legitimate course of business can be healthfully promoted by any such inflated capitalization. There must be humbug, if not downright rascality, behind such a pretentious array of figures." The *Kansas Alliance* saw in the prevalent custom of stock-watering an evil "almost beyond comprehension." It placed the total amount of railway overcapitalization at a sum far in excess of the national debt and described these inflated securities as "an ever present incubus upon the labor and land of the nation." Jerry Simpson of Kansas figured that the 8,000 miles of road in his state cost only about $100,000,000, whereas they were actually capitalized at $300,000,000 and bonded for $300,000,000 more. "We who use the roads," he argued, "are really paying interest on $600,000,000 instead of on $100,000,000 as we ought to." Such statements could be multiplied indefinitely. The unprosperous farmers of the frontier saw nothing to condone in the practice of stock-watering. Honest capitalization of railroad property would, they felt, make possible a material reduction in rates. And, in spite of the assertion of one who defended the practice of stock-watering that a citizen who questioned "the right of a corporation to capitalize its properties at any sum whatever committed an 'impertinence,' " the farmers had no notion that the matter was none of their business.

High rates due to overcapitalization and other causes were not, however, the sole cause of dissatisfaction with the railways. It was commonly asserted that the transportation companies discriminated definitely against the small shipper and in favor of his larger competitors. The local grain merchant without elevator facilities or the farmer desirous of shipping his own grain invariably had greater and graver difficulties with the roads than did the large elevator companies. These latter, the farmers contended, were favored by "inside rates," by rebates, and by preferential treatment with regard to cars.

* * *

The indictment against the railroads was the stronger in view of their political activities. It is not unfair to say that normally the railroads—sometimes a single road—dominated the political situation in every western state. In Kansas the Santa Fe was all-powerful; in Nebraska the Burlington and the Union Pacific shared the control of the state; everywhere the political power of one or more of the roads was a recognized fact. Railway influence was exerted in practically every important nominating convention to insure that no one hostile to the railways should be named for office. Railway lobbyists were on hand whenever a legislature met to see that measures unfavorable to the roads were quietly eliminated. Railway taxation, a particularly tender question, was always watched with the greatest solicitude and, from the standpoint of the prevention of high taxes, usually with the greatest of success. How much bribery and corruption and intrigue the railroads used to secure the ends they desired will never be known. For a long time, however, by fair means or foul, their wishes in most localities were closely akin to law. Beyond a doubt whole legislatures were sometimes bought and sold.

* * *

But from the standpoint of the western pioneer the crowning infamy of the railroads was their theft, as it appeared to him, of his lands. Free lands, or at least cheap lands, had been his ever since America was. Now this "priceless heritage" was gone, disposed of in no small part to the railroads. To them the national government had donated an area "larger than the territory occupied by the great German empire," land which, it was easy enough to see, should have been preserved for the future needs of the people. For this land the railroads charged the hapless emigrant from "three to ten prices" and by a pernicious credit system forced him into a condition of well-nigh perpetual "bondage." "Only a little while ago," ran one complaint, "the people owned this princely domain. Now they are *starving for land*—starving for an opportunity to labor—starving for the right to create from the soil a subsistence for their wives and little children." To the western farmers of this generation the importance of the disappearance of free lands was not a hidden secret to be unlocked only by the researches of some future historian. It was an acutely oppressive reality. The significance of the mad rush to Oklahoma in 1889 was by no means lost upon those who observed the phenomenon. "These men want *free land*," wrote one discerning editor. "They want *free land*—the land that Congress squandered . . . the land that should have formed the sacred patrimony of unborn generations." Senator Peffer of Kansas understood the situation perfectly. "Formerly the man who lost his farm could go west," he said, "now there is no longer any west to go to. Now they have to fight for their homes instead of making new." And in no small measure, he might have added, the fight was to be directed against the railroads.

Complaints against the railways, while most violent in the West, were by no means confined to that section. Practically every charge made by the western farmers had its counterpart elsewhere. In the South particularly the sins that the roads were held to have committed differed in degree, perhaps, but not much in kind, from the sins of the western roads. Southern railroads, like western railroads, were accused of levying "freight and fares at their pleasure to the oppression of the citizens" and of making their rates according to the principle, "take as much out of the pockets of the farmers as we can without actually taking it all." Southerners believed, in fact, that the general decline in freight rates that had accompanied the development of the railroads throughout the country was less in the South than anywhere else and that their section was for this reason worse plagued by high rates than any other.

*   *   *

These common grievances of South and West against the railroads promised to supply a binding tie of no small consequence between the sections. Whether they were westerners or southerners, the orators of revolt who touched upon the railway question spoke a common language. Moreover, the common vocabulary was not used merely when the malpractices of the railroads were being enumerated. Any eastern agitator might indeed have listed many of the same oppressions as typical of his part of the country. But the aggrieved easterner at least suffered from the persecutions of other easterners, whereas the southerner or the westerner was convinced that he suffered from a grievance caused by outsiders. In both sections the description of railway oppression was incomplete without a vivid characterization of the wicked eastern capitalist who cared nothing for the region through which he ran his roads and whose chief aim was plunder. This deep-seated antagonism for a common absentee enemy was a matter of the utmost importance when the time came for bringing on joint political action by West and South. . . .

*   *   *

If the farmer had little part in fixing the price at which his produce sold, he had no part at all in fixing the price of the commodities for which his earnings were spent. Neither did competition among manufacturers and dealers do much in the way of price-fixing, for the age of "big business," of trusts, combines, pools, and monopolies, had come. These trusts, as the farmers saw it, joined with the railroads, and if necessary with the politicians, "to hold the people's hands and pick their pockets." They "bought raw material at their own price, sold the finished product at any figure they wished to ask, and rewarded labor as they saw fit." Through their machinations "the farmer and the workingman generally" were "overtaxed right and left."

One western editor professed to understand how all this had come about. The price-fixing plutocracy, he argued, was but the "logical result of the individual freedom which we have always considered the pride of our system." The American ideal of the "very greatest degree of liberty" and the "very least legal restraint" had been of inestimable benefit to the makers of the trusts. Acting on the theory that individual enterprise should be permitted unlimited scope, they had gone their way without let or hindrance, putting weaker competitors out of business and acquiring monopolistic privileges for themselves. At length the corporation "had absorbed the liberties of the community and usurped the power of the agency that created it." Through its operation "individualism" had congealed into "privilege."

The number of "these unnatural and unnecessary financial monsters" was assumed to be legion. An agitated Iowan denounced the beef trust as "the most menacing" as well as the most gigantic of "about 400 trusts in existence." A Missouri editor took for his example the "plow trust. As soon as it was perfected the price of plows went up 100 percent . . . who suffers? . . . Who, indeed, but the farmer?" Senator Plumb of Kansas held that the people of his state were being robbed annually of $40,000,000 by the produce trust. Southern farmers complained of a fertilizer trust, a jute-bagging trust, a cottonseed oil trust. Trusts indeed there were: trusts that furnished the farmer with the clothing he had to wear; trusts that furnished him with the machines he had to use; trusts that furnished him with the fuel he had to burn; trusts that furnished him with the materials of which he built his house, his barns, his fences. To all these he paid a substantial tribute. Some of them, like the manufacturers of farm machinery, had learned the trick of installment selling, and to such the average farmer owed a perpetual debt.

*   *   *

It was the grinding burden of debt, however, that aroused the farmers, both southern and western, to action. The widespread dependence upon crop liens in the South and farm mortgages in the West has already been described. In the South as long as the price of cotton continued high and in the West as long as the flow of eastern capital remained uninterrupted, the grievances against the railroads, the middlemen, and the tariff-protected trusts merely smouldered. But when the bottom dropped out of the cotton market and the western boom collapsed, then the weight of debt was keenly felt and frenzied agitation began. The eastern capitalists were somehow to blame. They had conspired together to defraud the farmers—"to levy tribute upon the productive energies of West and South." They had made of the one-time American freeman "but a tenant at will, or a dependent upon the tender mercies of soulless corporations and of absentee landlords." . . .

As one hard season succeeded another the empty-handed farmer found his back debts and unpaid interest becoming an intolerable burden. In the West after the crisis of 1887 interest rates, already high, rose still higher. Farmers who needed money to renew their loans, to meet partial payments on their land, or to tide them over to another season were told, truly enough, that money was very scarce. The flow of eastern capital to the West had virtually ceased. The various mortgage companies that had been doing such a thriving business a few months before had now either gone bankrupt or had made drastic retrenchments. Rates of seven or eight percent on real estate were now regarded as extremely low; and on chattels ten or twelve percent was considered very liberal, from eighteen to twenty-four percent was not uncommon, and forty percent or above was not unknown. Naturally the number of real estate mortgages placed dropped off precipitately. Instead of the six thousand, worth nearly $5,500,000, that had been placed in Nebraska during the years 1884 to 1887, there were in the three years following 1887 only five hundred such mortgages, worth only about $650,000, while only one out of four of the farm mortgages held on South Dakota land in 1892 had been contracted prior to 1887. When the farmer could no longer obtain money on his real estate, he usually mortgaged his chattels, with the result that in many localities nearly everything that could carry a mortgage was required to do so. In Nebraska during the early nineties the number of these badges of "dependence and slavery" recorded by the state auditor averaged over half a million annually. In Dakota many families were kept from leaving for the East only by the fact that their horses and wagons were mortgaged and could therefore not be taken beyond the state boundaries.

Whether at the old rates, which were bad, or at the new, which were worse, altogether too often the western farmer was mortgaged literally for all he was worth, and too often the entire fruits of his labor, meager enough after hard times set in, were required to meet impending obligations. Profits that the farmer felt should have been his passed at once to someone else. The conviction grew on him that there was something essentially wicked and vicious about the system that made this possible. Too late he observed that the money he had borrowed was not worth to him what he had contracted to pay for it. As one embittered farmer-editor wrote,

There are three great crops raised in Nebraska. One is a crop of corn, one a crop of freight rates, and one a crop of interest. One is produced by farmers who by sweat and toil farm the land. The other two are produced by men who sit in their offices and behind their bank counters and farm the farmers. The corn is less than half a crop. The freight rates will produce a full average. The interest crop, however, is the one that fully illustrates the boundless resources and prosperity of Nebraska. When corn fails the interest yield is largely increased.

What was the fair thing under such circumstances? Should the farmer bear the entire load of adversity, or should the mortgage-holder help? Opinions varied, but certain extremists claimed that at the very least the interest should be scaled down. If railroads were permitted to reorganize, reduce their interest rates, and save their property when they got into financial straits, why should the farmer be denied a similar right?

The only reorganization to which the farmer had recourse, as a rule, was through foreclosure proceedings, by which ordinarily he could expect nothing less than the loss of all his property. Usually the mortgagor was highly protected by the terms of the mortgage and could foreclose whenever an interest payment was defaulted, whether the principal was due or not. In the late eighties and the early nineties foreclosures came thick and fast. Kansas doubtless suffered most on this account, for from 1889 to 1893 over eleven thousand farm mortgages were foreclosed in this state, and in some counties as much as ninety percent of the farm lands passed into the ownership of the loan companies. It was estimated by one alarmist that "land equal to a tract thirty miles wide and ninety miles long had been foreclosed and bought in by the loan companies of Kansas in a year." Available statistics would seem to bear out this assertion, but the unreliability of such figures is notorious. Many farmers and speculators, some of them perfectly solvent, deliberately invited foreclosure because they found after the slump that their land was mortgaged for more than it was worth. On the other hand, many cases of genuine bankruptcy were settled out of court and without record. But whatever the unreliability of statistics the fact remains that in Kansas and neighboring states the number of farmers who lost their lands because of the hard times and crop failures was very large.

In the South the crop-lien system constituted the chief mortgage evil and the chief grievance, but a considerable amount of real and personal property was also pledged for debt. Census statistics, here also somewhat unreliable because of the numerous informal and unrecorded agreements, show that in Georgia about one-fifth of the taxable acres were under mortgage, and a special investigation for the same state seemed to prove that a high proportion of the mortgage debt was incurred to meet current expenditures rather than to acquire more land or to make permanent improvements. Similar conditions existed throughout the cotton South. Chattel mortgages were also freely given, especially by tenants, but frequently also by small proprietors. Interest rates were as impossibly high as in the West, and foreclosures almost as inevitable. Evidence of foreclosures on chattels could be found in the "pitiful heaps of . . . rubbish" that "commonly disfigured the court house squares." Foreclosures on land, or their equivalent, were numerous, serving alike to accelerate the process of breaking down the old plantations and of building up the new "merchant-owned 'bonanzas.'" Many small farmers lapsed into tenantry; indeed, during the eighties the trend was unmistakably in the direction of "concentration of agricultural land in the hands of merchants, loan agents, and a few of the financially strongest farmers."

Taxation added a heavy burden to the load of the farmer. Others might conceal their property. The merchant might underestimate the value of his stock, the householder might neglect to list a substantial part of his personal property, the holder of taxable securities might keep his ownership a secret, but the farmer could not hide his land. If it was perhaps an exaggeration to declare that the farmers "represent but one-fourth of the nation's wealth and they pay three-fourths of the taxes," it was probably true enough that land bore the chief brunt of taxation, both in the South and in the West. Tax-dodging, especially on the part of the railroads and other large corporations, was notorious. Some North Carolina railroads had been granted special exemptions from taxation as far back as the 1830's, and they still found them useful. In Georgia the railroads paid a state tax but not a county tax. Nearly everywhere they received special treatment at the hands of assessors, state boards of equalization, or even by the law itself. Western land-grant railroads avoided paying taxes on their huge holdings by delaying to patent them until they could be sold. Then the farmer-purchaser paid the taxes. Meantime the cost of state and local government had risen everywhere, although most disproportionately in the West, where the boom was on. In the boom territory public building and improvement projects out of all proportion to the capacity of the people to pay had been undertaken, and railways, street-car companies, and other such enterprises had been subsidized by the issuing of state or local bonds, the interest and principal of which had to be met by taxation. For all this unwise spending the farmers had to pay the greater part. The declaration of one Kansas farmer that his taxes were doubled in order "to pay the interest on boodler bonds and jobs voted by nontaxpayers to railroad schemes and frauds and follies which are of no benefit to the farmer" was not without a large element of truth. The farmer was convinced that he was the helpless victim of unfair, unreasonable, and discriminatory taxation. Here was another reason why he was "gradually but steadily becoming poorer and poorer every year."

Beset on every hand by demands for funds—funds with which to meet his obligations to the bankers, the loan companies, or the tax collectors and funds with which to maintain his credit with the merchants so that he might not lack the all-essential seed to plant another crop or the few necessities of life that he and his family could not contrive either to produce for themselves or to go without—the farmer naturally enough raised the battle cry of "more money." He came to believe that, after all, his chief grievance was against the system of money and banking, which now virtually denied him credit and which in the past had only plunged him deeper and deeper into debt. There must be something more fundamentally wrong than the misdeeds of railroads and trusts and tax assessors. Why should dollars grow dearer and dearer and scarcer and scarcer? Why, indeed, unless because of the manipulations of those to whom such a condition would bring profit?

Much agitation by Greenbackers and by free-silverites and much experience in the marketing of crops had made clear even to the most obtuse, at least of the debtors, that the value of a dollar was greater than it once had been. It would buy two bushels of grain where formerly it would buy only one. It would buy twelve pounds of cotton where formerly it would buy but six. The orthodox retort of the creditor to such a statement was that too much grain and cotton were being produced—the overproduction theory. But, replied the debtor, was this the whole truth? Did not the amount of money in circulation have something to do with the situation? Currency reformers were wont to point out that at the close of the Civil War the United States had nearly two billions of dollars in circulation. Now the population had doubled and the volume of business had probably trebled, but the number of dollars in circulation had actually declined! Was not each dollar overworked? Had it not attained on this account a fictitious value?

The Appreciating Dollar, 1865 – 1895

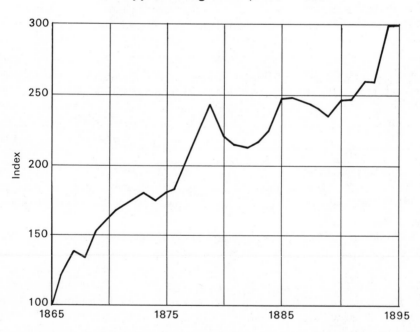

Whatever the explanation, it was clear enough that the dollar, expressed in any other terms than itself, had appreciated steadily in value ever since the Civil War. The depreciated greenback currency, in which all ordinary business was transacted until 1879, reached by that year a full parity with gold. But the purchasing power of the dollar still continued its upward course. For this phenomenon the quantity theory may be—probably is—an insufficient explanation, but in the face of the figures from which the accompanying chart has been drawn, the fact of continuous appreciation can hardly be denied.

For those farmers who were free from debt and were neither investors nor borrowers such a condition might have had little meaning. The greater purchasing power of the dollar meant fewer dollars for their crops, but it meant also fewer dollars spent for labor and supplies. Conceivably, the same degree of prosperity could be maintained on the smaller income. But in the West and in the South the number of debt-free farmers was small indeed, and for the debtor the rising value of the dollar was a serious matter. The man who gave a long-term mortgage on his real estate was in the best position to appreciate how serious it was. Did he borrow a thousand dollars on his land for a five-year term, then he must pay back at the end of the allotted time a thousand dollars. But it might well be that, whereas at the time he had contracted the loan a thousand dollars meant a thousand bushels of wheat or ten thousand pounds of cotton, at the time he must pay it the thousand dollars meant fifteen hundred bushels of wheat or fifteen thousand pounds of cotton. Interest, expressed likewise in terms of produce, had mounted similarly year by year so that the loss to the borrower was even greater than the increase in the value of the principal. What it cost the debtor to borrow under such circumstances has been well expressed by Arnett in the [following] table . . . , which is based on statistics taken from the census of 1890.

DEBT APPRECIATION, 1865–1890

Average Five-year Debt Contracted in	Appreciation (in terms of dollar's purchasing power)
1865–1869	35.2
1870–1874	19.7
1875–1879	4.5
1880–1884	11.7
1885–1890	11.6

Add to this the unreasonably high interest rates usually exacted and the commissions and deductions that were rarely omitted and the plight of the debtor farmer becomes painfully clear. He was paying what would have amounted to about a twenty or twenty-five percent rate of interest on a nonappreciating dollar.

It was, moreover, far from comforting to reflect that in such a transaction what was one man's loss was another's gain. Nor was it surprising that the harassed debtor imputed to the creditor, to whose advantage the system worked, a deliberate attempt to cause the dollar to soar to ever greater and greater heights. Had not the creditor class ranged itself solidly behind the

Resumption Act of 1875, by which the greenback dollar had been brought to a parity with gold? Was not the same class responsible for the "crime of 1873," which had demonetized silver and by just so much had detracted from the quantity of the circulating medium? Was there not, indeed, a nefarious conspiracy of creditors—eastern creditors, perhaps with English allies—to increase their profits at the expense of the debtors—western and southern—by a studied manipulation of the value of the dollar? "We feel," said Senator Allen of Nebraska, "that, through the operation of a shrinking volume of money, which has been caused by Eastern votes and influences for purely selfish purposes, the East has placed its hands on the throat of the West and refused to afford us that measure of justice which we, as citizens of a common country, are entitled to receive." And the grievance of the West against the East was also the grievance of the South.

Nor was this grievance confined to resentment against the steadily mounting value of the dollar. There was in addition an undeniable and apparently unreasonable fluctuation in its purchasing power during any given year. At the time of crop movements, when the farmers wished to sell—indeed, had to sell, in most cases—the dollar was dear and prices were correspondingly depressed. When, on the other hand, the crop had been marketed and the farmers' produce had passed to other hands, the dollar fell in value and prices mounted rapidly. Wall Street speculators and others bought heavily when prices were low and sold later when prices were high at handsome profits—profits which, the farmers firmly believed, should have gone to the original producer.

*   *   *

Such were the grievances of which the farmers complained. They suffered, or at least they thought they suffered, from the railroads, from the trusts and the middlemen, from the money-lenders and the bankers, and from the muddled currency. These problems were not particularly new. Always the farmer had had to struggle with the problem of transportation. He had never known a time when the price of the things he had to buy was not as much too high as the price of the things he had to sell was too low. He had had his troubles with banks and bankers. But those earlier days were the days of cheap lands, and when things went wrong the disgruntled could seek solace in a move to the West. There was a chance to make a new start. Broader acres, more fertile fields, would surely bring the desired results. And with the restless ever moving to the West, the more stable elements of society left behind made pleasing progress. Now with the lands all taken and the frontier gone, this safety valve was closed. The frontier was turned back upon itself. The restless and discontented voiced their sentiments more and fled from them less. Hence arose the veritable chorus of denunciation directed against those individuals and those corporations who considered only their own advantage without regard to the effect their actions might have upon the farmer and his interests.

Populism: Nostalgic Agrarianism

Richard Hofstadter

The Two Nations

For a generation after the Civil War, a time of great economic exploitation and waste, grave social corruption and ugliness, the dominant note in American political life was complacency. Although dissenting minorities were always present, they were submerged by the overwhelming realities of industrial growth and continental settlement. The agitation of the Populists, which brought back to American public life a capacity for effective political indignation, marks the beginning of the end of this epoch. In the short run the Populists did not get what they wanted, but they released the flow of protest and criticism that swept through American political affairs from the 1890's to the beginning of the first World War.

Where contemporary intellectuals gave the Populists a perfunctory and disdainful hearing, later historians have freely recognized their achievements and frequently overlooked their limitations. Modern liberals, finding the Populists' grievances valid, their programs suggestive, their motives creditable, have usually spoken of the Populist episode in the spirit of Vachel Lindsay's bombastic rhetoric:

> Prairie avenger, mountain lion,
> Bryan, Bryan, Bryan, Bryan,
> Gigantic troubadour, speaking like a siege gun,
> Smashing Plymouth Rock with his boulders from the West.

There is indeed much that is good and usable in our Populist past. While the Populist tradition had defects that have been too much neglected,

Reprinted by permission of Alfred A. Knopf, Inc. from The Age of Reform *by Richard Hofstadter. Copyright © 1955 by Richard Hofstadter.*

it does not follow that the virtues claimed for it are all fictitious. Populism was the first modern political movement of practical importance in the United States to insist that the federal government has some responsibility for the common weal; indeed, it was the first such movement to attack seriously the problems created by industrialism. The complaints and demands and prophetic denunciations of the Populists stirred the latent liberalism in many Americans and startled many conservatives into a new flexibility. Most of the "radical" reforms in the Populist program proved in later years to be either harmless or useful. In at least one important area of American life a few Populist leaders in the South attempted something profoundly radical and humane—to build a popular movement that would cut across the old barriers of race—until persistent use of the Negro bogy distracted their following. To discuss the broad ideology of the Populists does them some injustice, for it was in their concrete programs that they added most constructively to our political life, and in their more general picture of the world that they were most credulous and vulnerable. Moreover, any account of the fallibility of Populist thinking that does not acknowledge the stress and suffering out of which that thinking emerged will be seriously remiss. But anyone who enlarges our portrait of the Populist tradition is likely to bring out some unseen blemishes. In the books that have been written about the Populist movement, only passing mention has been made of its significant provincialism; little has been said of its relations with nativism and nationalism; nothing has been said of its tincture of anti-Semitism.

The Populist impulse expressed itself in a set of notions that represent what I have called the "soft" side of agrarianism. These notions, which appeared with regularity in the political literature, must be examined if we are to re-create for ourselves the Populist spirit. To extract them from the full context of the polemical writings in which they appeared is undoubtedly to oversimplify them; even to name them in any language that comes readily to the historian of ideas is perhaps to suggest that they had a formality and coherence that in reality they clearly lacked. But since it is less feasible to have no labels than to have somewhat too facile ones, we may enumerate the dominant themes in Populist ideology as these: the idea of a golden age; the concept of natural harmonies; the dualistic version of social struggles; the conspiracy theory of history; and the doctrine of the primacy of money. The last of these I will touch upon in connection with the free-silver issue. Here I propose to analyze the others, and to show how they were nurtured by the traditions of the agrarian myth.

The utopia of the Populists was in the past, not the future. According to the agrarian myth, the health of the state was proportionate to the degree to which it was dominated by the agricultural class, and this assumption pointed to the superiority of an earlier age. The Populists looked backward with longing to the lost agrarian Eden, to the republican America of the early years of the nineteenth century in which there were few millionaires and, as they saw it, no beggars, when the laborer had excellent prospects and the farmer had abundance, when statesmen still responded to the mood of the people and there was no such thing as the money power. What they meant— though they did not express themselves in such terms—was that they would like to restore the conditions prevailing before the development of industrialism and the commercialization of agriculture. It should not be surprising that they inherited the traditions of Jacksonian democracy, that they revived the old Jacksonian cry: "Equal Rights for All, Special Privileges for None," or that most of the slogans of 1896 echoed the battle cries of 1836. General James B. Weaver, the Populist candidate for the presidency in 1892, was an old Democrat and Free-Soiler, born during the days of Jackson's battle with the United States Bank, who drifted into the Greenback movement after a short spell as a Republican, and from there to Populism. His book, A Call to Action, published in 1892, drew up an indictment of the business corporation which reads like a Jacksonian polemic. Even in those hopeful early days of the People's Party, Weaver projected no grandiose plans for the future, but lamented the course of recent history, the growth of economic oppression, and the emergence of great contrasts of wealth and poverty, and called upon his readers to do "All in [their] power to arrest the alarming tendencies of our times."

Nature, as the agrarian tradition had it, was beneficent. The United States was abundantly endowed with rich land and rich resources, and the "natural" consequence of such an endowment should be the prosperity of the people. If the people failed to enjoy prosperity, it must be because of a harsh and arbitrary intrusion of human greed and error. "Hard times, then," said one popular writer, "as well as the bankruptcies, enforced idleness, starvation, and the crime, misery, and moral degradation growing out of conditions like the present, being unnatural, not in accordance with, or the result of any natural law, must be attributed to that kind of unwise and pernicious legislation which history proves to have produced similar results in all ages of the world. It is the mission of the age to correct these errors in human legislation, to adopt and establish policies and systems, in accord with, rather than in opposition to divine law." In assuming a lush natural order whose workings were being deranged by human laws, Populist writers were again drawing on the Jacksonian tradition, whose spokesmen also had pleaded for a proper obedience to "natural" laws as a prerequisite of social justice.

Somewhat akin to the notion of the beneficence of nature was the idea of a natural harmony of interests among the productive classes. To the Populist mind there was no fundamental conflict between the farmer and the worker, between the toiling people and the small businessman. While there might be corrupt individuals in any group, the underlying interests of the productive majority were the same; predatory behavior existed only because it was initiated and underwritten by a small parasitic minority in the highest places of power. As opposed to the idea that society consists of a number of different and frequently clashing interests—the social pluralism expressed, for instance, by Madison in the *Federalist*—the Populists adhered, less formally to be sure, but quite persistently, to a kind of social dualism: although they knew perfectly well that society was composed of a number of classes, for all practical purposes only one simple division need be considered. There were two nations. "It is a struggle," said Sockless Jerry Simpson, "between the robbers and the robbed." "There are but two sides in the conflict that is being waged in this country today," declared a Populist manifesto. "On the one side are the allied hosts of monopolies, the money power, great trusts and railroad corporations, who seek the enactment of laws to benefit them and impoverish the people. On the other are the farmers, laborers, merchants, and all other people who produce wealth and bear the burdens of taxation. . . . Between these two there is no middle ground." "On the one side," said Bryan in his famous speech against the repeal of the Sherman Silver Purchase Act, "stand the corporate interests of the United States, the moneyed interests, aggregated wealth and capital, imperious, arrogant, compassionless. . . . On the other side stand an unnumbered throng, those who gave to the Democratic party a name and for whom it has assumed to speak." The people versus the interests, the public versus the plutocrats, the toiling multitude versus the money power—in various phrases this central antagonism was expressed. From this simple social classification it seemed to follow that once the techniques of misleading the people were exposed, victory over the money power ought to be easily accomplished, for in sheer numbers the people were overwhelming. "There is no power on earth that can defeat us," said General Weaver during the optimistic days of the campaign of 1892. "It is a fight between labor and capital, and labor is in the vast majority."

The problems that faced the Populists assumed a delusive simplicity: the victory over injustice, the solution for all social ills, was concentrated in the crusade against a single, relatively small but immensely strong interest, the money power. "With the destruction of the money power," said Senator Peffer, "the death knell of gambling in grain and other commodities will be sounded; for the business of the worst men on earth will have been broken up, and the mainstay of the gamblers removed. It will be an easy matter, after the greater spoilsmen have been shorn of their power, to clip the wings of the little ones. Once get rid of the men who hold the country by the throat, the parasites can be easily removed." Since the old political parties were the primary means by which the people were kept wandering in the wilderness, the People's Party advocates insisted, only a new and independent political party could do this essential job. As the silver question became more prominent and the idea of a third party faded, the need for a monolithic solution became transmuted into another form: there was only one *issue* upon which the money power could really be beaten and this was the money issue. "When we have restored the money of the Constitution," said Bryan in his Cross of

Gold speech, "all other necessary reforms will be possible; but . . . until this is done there is no other reform that can be accomplished."

While the conditions of victory were thus made to appear simple, they did not always appear easy, and it would be misleading to imply that the tone of Populistic thinking was uniformly optimistic. Often, indeed, a deep-lying vein of anxiety showed through. The very sharpness of the struggle, as the Populists experienced it, the alleged absence of compromise solutions and of intermediate groups in the body politic, the brutality and desperation that were imputed to the plutocracy—all these suggested that failure of the people to win the final contest peacefully could result only in a total victory for the plutocrats and total extinction of democratic institutions, possibly after a period of bloodshed and anarchy. "We are nearing a serious crisis," declared Weaver. "If the present strained relations between wealth owners and wealth producers continue much longer they will ripen into frightful disaster. This universal discontent must be quickly interpreted and its causes removed." "We meet," said the Populist platform of 1892,

in the midst of a nation brought to the verge of moral, political, and material ruin. Corruption dominates the ballot-box, the Legislatures, the Congress, and touches even the ermine of the bench. The people are demoralized. . . . The newspapers are largely subsidized or muzzled, public opinion silenced, business prostrated, homes covered with mortgages, labor impoverished, and the land concentrating in the hands of the capitalists. The urban workmen are denied the right to organize for self-protection, imported pauperized labor beats down their wages, a hireling standing army, unrecognized by our laws, is established to shoot them down, and they are rapidly degenerating into European conditions. The fruits of the toil of millions are boldly stolen to build up colossal fortunes for a few, unprecedented in the history of mankind; and the possessors of these, in turn, despise the Republic and endanger liberty.

Such conditions foreboded "the destruction of civilization, or the establishment of an absolute despotism." . . .

History as Conspiracy

There was . . . a widespread Populist idea that all American history since the Civil War could be understood as a sustained conspiracy of the international money power.

The pervasiveness of this way of looking at things may be attributed to the common feeling that farmers and workers were not simply oppressed but oppressed deliberately, consciously, continuously, and with wanton malice by "the interests." It would of course be misleading to imply that the Populists stand alone in thinking of the events of their time as the results of a conspiracy. This kind of thinking frequently occurs when political and social antagonisms are sharp. Certain audiences are especially susceptible to it—particularly, I believe, those who have attained only a low level of education, whose access to information is poor, and who are so completely shut out from access to the centers of power that they feel themselves completely deprived of self-defense and subjected to unlimited manipulation by those who wield power. There are, moreover, certain types of popular movements of dissent that offer special opportunities to agitators with paranoid tendencies, who are able to make a vocational asset out of their psychic disturbances. Such persons have an opportunity to impose their own style of thought upon the movements they lead. It would of course be misleading to imply that there are no such things as conspiracies in history. Anything that partakes of political strategy may need, for a time at least, an element of secrecy, and is thus vulnerable to being dubbed conspiratorial. Corruption itself has the character of conspiracy. In this sense the Crédit Mobilier was a conspiracy, as was the Teapot Dome affair. If we tend to be too condescending to the Populists at this point, it may be necessary to remind ourselves that they had seen so much bribery and corruption, particularly on the part of the railroads, that they had before them a convincing model of the management of affairs through conspiratorial behavior. Indeed, what makes conspiracy theories so widely acceptable is that they usually contain a germ of truth. But there is a great difference between locating conspiracies *in* history and saying that history *is*, in effect, a conspiracy, between singling out those conspiratorial acts that do on occasion occur and weaving a vast fabric of social explanation out of nothing but skeins of evil plots.

When conspiracies do not exist it is necessary for those who think in this fashion to invent them. Among the most celebrated instances in modern history are the forgery of the Protocols of the Elders of Zion and the grandiose fabrication under Stalin's regime of the Trotzkyite-Bukharinite-Zinovievite center. These inventions were cynical. In the history of American political controversy there is a tradition of conspiratorial accusations which seem to have been sincerely believed. Jefferson appears really to have believed, at one time, that the Federalists were conspiring to re-establish monarchy. Some Federalists believed that the Jeffersonians were conspiring to subvert Christianity. The movement to annex Texas and the war with Mexico were alleged by many Northerners to be a slaveholders' conspiracy. The early Republican leaders, including Lincoln, charged that there was a conspiracy on the part of Stephen A. Douglas to make slavery a nationwide institution. Such pre-Civil War parties as the Know-Nothing and Anti-Masonic movements were based almost entirely upon conspiratorial ideology. The Nye Committee, years ago, tried to prove that our entry into the first World War was the work of a conspiracy of bankers and munitions-makers. And now not only our entry into the second World War, but the entire history of the past twenty years or so is being given the color of conspiracy by the cranks and political fakirs of our own age.

Nevertheless, when these qualifications have been taken into account, it remains true that Populist thought showed an unusually strong tendency to account for relatively impersonal events in highly personal terms. An overwhelming sense of grievance does not find satisfactory expression in impersonal explanations, except among those with a well-developed tradition of intellectualism. It is the city, after all, that is the home of intellectual complexity. The farmer lived in isolation from the great world in which his fate was actually decided. He was accused of being unusually suspicious, and certainly his situation, trying as it was, made thinking in impersonal terms difficult. Perhaps the rural middle-class leaders of Populism (this was a movement of farmers, but it was not led by farmers) had more to do than the farmer himself with the cast of Populist thinking. At any rate, Populist thought often carries one into a world in which the simple virtues and unmitigated villainies of a rural melodrama have been projected on a national and even an international scale. In Populist thought the farmer is not a speculating businessman, victimized by the risk economy of which he is a part, but rather a wounded yeoman, preyed upon by those who are alien to the life of folkish virtue. A villain was needed, marked with the unmistakable stigmata of the villains of melodrama, and the more remote he was from the familiar scene, the more plausibly his villainies could be exaggerated.

It was not enough to say that a conspiracy of the money power against the common people was going on. It had been going on ever since the Civil War. It was not enough to say that it stemmed from Wall Street. It was international: it stemmed from Lombard Street. In his preamble to the People's Party platform of 1892, a succinct, official expression of Populist views, Ignatius Donnelly asserted: "A vast conspiracy against mankind has been organized on two continents, and it is rapidly taking possession of the world. If not met and overthrown at once it forebodes terrible social convulsions, the destruction of civilization, or the establishment of an absolute despotism." A manifesto of 1895, signed by fifteen outstanding leaders of the People's Party, declared: "As early as 1865–66 a conspiracy was entered into between the gold gamblers of Europe and America. . . . For nearly thirty years these conspirators have kept the people quarreling over less important matters while they have pursued with unrelenting zeal their one central purpose. . . . Every device of treachery, every resource of statecraft, and every artifice known to the secret cabals of the international gold ring are being made use of to deal a blow to the prosperity of the people and the financial and commercial independence of the country."

The financial argument behind the conspiracy theory was simple enough. Those who owned bonds wanted to be paid not in a common currency but in gold, which was at a premium; those who lived by lending money wanted as high a premium as possible to be put on their commodity by increasing its scarcity. The panics, depressions, and bankruptcies caused by their policies only added to their wealth; such catastrophes offered opportunities to engross the wealth of others through business consolidations and foreclosures. Hence the interests actually relished and encouraged hard times. The Greenbackers had long since popularized this argument, insisting that an adequate legal-tender currency would break the monopoly of the "Shylocks." Their demand for $50 of circulating medium per capita, still in the air when the People's Party arose, was rapidly replaced by the less "radical" demand for free coinage of silver. But what both the Greenbackers and free-silverites held in common was the idea that the contraction of currency was a deliberate squeeze, the result of a long-range plot of the "Anglo-American Gold Trust." Wherever one turns in the Populist literature of the nineties one can find this conspiracy theory expressed. It is in the Populist newspapers, the proceedings of the silver conventions, the immense pamphlet literature broadcast by the American Bimetallic League, the Congressional debates over money; it is elaborated in such popular books as Mrs. S. E. V. Emery's *Seven Financial Conspiracies which have Enslaved the American People* or Gordon Clark's *Shylock: as Banker, Bondholder, Corruptionist, Conspirator.*

Mrs. Emery's book, first published in 1887, and dedicated to "the enslaved people of a dying republic," achieved great circulation, especially among the Kansas Populists. According to Mrs. Emery, the United States had been an economic Garden of Eden in the period before the Civil War. The fall of man had dated from the war itself, when "the money kings of Wall Street" determined that they could take advantage of the wartime necessities of their fellow men by manipulating the currency. "Controlling it, they could inflate or depress the business of the country at pleasure, they could send the warm life current through the channels of trade, dispensing peace, happiness, and prosperity, or they could check its flow, and completely paralyze the industries of the country." With this great power for good in their hands, the Wall Street men preferred to do evil. Lincoln's war policy of issuing greenbacks presented them with the dire threat of an adequate supply of currency. So the Shylocks gathered in convention and "perfected" a conspiracy to create a demand for their gold. The remainder of the book was a recital of a series of seven measures passed between 1862 and 1875 which were alleged to be a part of this continuing conspiracy, the total effect of which was to contract the currency of the country further and further until finally it squeezed the industry of the country like a hoop of steel.

Mrs. Emery's rhetoric left no doubt of the sustained purposefulness of this scheme—described as "villainous robbery," and as having been "secured through the most soulless strategy." She was most explicit about the so-called "crime of 1873," the demonetization of silver, giving a fairly full statement of the standard greenback-silverite myth concerning that event. As they had it, an agent of the Bank of England, Ernest Seyd by name, had come to the United States in 1872 with $500,000 with which he had bought enough support in Congress to secure the passage of the demonetization measure. This measure was supposed to have greatly increased the value of American four percent bonds held by British capitalists by making it necessary to pay them in gold only. To it Mrs. Emery attributed the panic of 1873, its bankruptcies, and its train of human disasters: "Murder, insanity, suicide, divorce, drunkenness and all forms of immorality and crime have increased from that day to this in the most appalling ratio."

"Coin" Harvey, the author of the most popular single document of the whole currency controversy, *Coin's Financial School*, also published a novel, *A Tale of Two Nations*, in which the conspiracy theory of history was incorporated into a melodramatic tale. In this story the powerful English banker Baron Rothe plans to bring about the demonetization of silver in the United States, in part for his own aggrandizement but also to prevent the power of the United States from outstripping that of England. He persuades an American Senator (probably John Sherman, the *bête noire* of the silverites) to co-operate in using British gold in a campaign against silver. To be sure that the work is successful, he also sends to the United States a relative and ally, one Rogasner, who stalks through the story like the villains in the plays of Dion Boucicault, muttering to himself such remarks as "I am here to destroy the United States—Cornwallis could not have done more. For the wrongs and insults, for the glory of my own country, I will bury the knife deep into the heart of this nation." Against the plausibly drawn background of the corruption of the Grant administration, Rogasner proceeds to buy up the American Congress and suborn American professors of economics to testify for gold. He also falls in love with a proud American beauty, but his designs on her are foiled because she loves a handsome young silver Congressman from Nebraska who bears a striking resemblance to William Jennings Bryan!

One feature of the Populist conspiracy theory that has been generally overlooked is its frequent link with a kind of rhetorical anti-Semitism. The slight current of anti-Semitism that existed in the United States before the 1890's had been associated with problems of money and credit. During the closing years of the century it grew noticeably. While the jocose and rather heavy-handed anti-Semitism that can be found in Henry Adams's letters of the 1890's shows that this prejudice existed outside Populist literature, it was chiefly Populist writers who expressed that identification of the Jew with the usurer and the "international gold ring" which was the central theme of the American anti-Semitism of the age. The omnipresent symbol of Shylock can hardly be taken in itself as evidence of anti-Semitism, but the frequent references to the House of Rothschild make it clear that for many silverites the Jew was an organic part of the conspiracy theory of history. Coin Harvey's Baron Rothe was clearly meant to be Rothschild; his Rogasner (Ernest Seyd?) was a dark figure out of the coarsest anti-Semitic tradition. "You are very wise in your way," Rogasner is told at the climax of the tale, "the commercial way, inbred through generations. The politic, scheming, devious way, inbred through generations also." One of the cartoons in the effectively illustrated *Coin's Financial School* showed a map of the world dominated by the tentacles of an octopus at the site of the British Isles, labeled: "Rothschilds." In Populist demonology, anti-Semitism and Anglophobia went hand in hand.

The note of anti-Semitism was often sounded openly in the campaign for silver. A representative of the New Jersey Grange, for instance, did not hesitate to warn the members of the Second National Silver Convention of 1892 to watch out for political candidates who represented "Wall Street, and the Jews of Europe." Mary E. Lease described Grover Cleveland as "the agent of Jewish bankers and British gold." Donnelly represented the leader of the governing Council of plutocrats in *Caesar's Column*, one Prince Cabano, as a powerful Jew, born Jacob Isaacs; one of the triumvirate who lead the Brotherhood of Destruction is also an exiled Russian Jew, who flees from the apocalyptic carnage with a hundred million dollars which he intends to use to "revive the ancient splendors of the Jewish race, in the midst of the ruins of the world." One of the more elaborate documents of the conspiracy school traced the power of the Rothschilds over America to a transaction between Hugh McCulloch, Secretary of the Treasury under Lincoln and Johnson, and Baron James Rothschild. "The most direful part of this business between Rothschild and the United States Treasury was not the loss of money, even by hundreds of millions. It was the resignation of the country itself INTO THE HANDS OF ENGLAND, as England had long been resigned into the hands of HER JEWS."

Such rhetoric, which became common currency in the movement, later passed beyond Populism into the larger stream of political protest. By the time the campaign of 1896 arrived, an Associated Press reporter noticed as "one of the striking things" about the Populist convention at St. Louis "the extraordinary hatred of the Jewish race. It is not possible to go into any hotel in the city without hearing the most bitter denunciation of the Jews as a class and of the particular Jews who happen to have prospered in the world." This report may have been somewhat overdone, but the identification of the silver cause with anti-Semitism did become close enough for Bryan to have to pause in the midst of his campaign to explain to the Jewish Democrats of Chicago that in denouncing the policies of the Rothschilds he and his silver friends were "not attacking a race; we are attacking greed and avarice which know no race or religion."

It would be easy to misstate the character of Populist anti-Semitism or to exaggerate its intensity. For Populist anti-Semitism was entirely verbal. It was a mode of expression, a rhetorical style, not a tactic or a program. It did not lead to exclusion laws, much less to riots or pogroms. There were, after all, relatively few Jews in the United States in the late 1880's and early 1890's, most of them remote from the areas of Populist strength. It is one thing, however, to say that this prejudice did not go beyond a certain symbolic usage, quite another to say that a people's choice of symbols is of no significance. Populist anti-Semitism does have its importance—chiefly as a symptom of a certain ominous credulity in the Populist mind. It is not too much to say that the Greenback-Populist tradition activated most of what we have of modern popular anti-Semitism in the United States. From Thaddeus Stevens and Coin Harvey to Father Coughlin, and from Brooks and Henry Adams to Ezra Pound, there has been a curiously persistent linkage between anti-Semitism and money and credit obsessions. A full history of modern anti-Semitism in the United States would reveal, I believe, its substantial Populist lineage, but it may be sufficient to point out here that neither the informal connection between Bryan and the Klan in the twenties nor Thomas E. Watson's conduct in the Leo Frank case were altogether fortuitous. And Henry Ford's notorious anti-Semitism of the 1920's, along with his hatred of "Wall Street," were the foibles of a Michigan farm boy who had been liberally exposed to Populist notions.

Populism: Realistic Radicalism

Norman Pollack

Did Populism accept industrialism and social change, basing its protest on what it believed to be the realities of the 1890's? Or did it seek instead to restore pre-industrial society, comprehending neither the major trends of its age nor the solutions necessary to cope with these altered circumstances? Was Populism therefore a progressive or retrogressive, a forward- or backward-looking, social force? The disparity noted above is nowhere better seen than in the conclusion reached by historians on these questions. Whatever their personal view of the movement, itself important because Populism has had its critics as well as supporters, and whatever their field of specialization, historians agree in regarding it, in the words of Professor John D. Hicks, as "beginning the last phase of a long and perhaps losing struggle—the struggle to save agricultural America from the devouring jaws of industrial America."

That this retrogressive framework can be supported through the examples of numerous industrial revolutions is undeniable; clearly, agrarians often aligned with conservative groups in the vain attempt to turn back history. Nor do the results appear different when agrarian movements acted alone and in a radical direction, for they seemed generally incapable of combining with industrial labor to promote a society both democratic *and* industrial. Thus, whether radical or conservative, agrarianism in a world perspective takes on the shape of a retrogressive social force. It would, however, be a serious mistake merely to assume that all industrial transformations follow the same pattern. I submit that while the generalization is not without foundation, the American experience proves a notable exception. For three reasons, this difference has not been sufficiently appreciated: The belief that agrarianism must act retrogressively, deduced usually from situations of abrupt transition from feudalism to capitalism, is no longer questioned; Americanists have followed suit, accepting this view and then confining their research to more specific problems; and most important, the actual evidence on the agrarian response to industrialism has not hitherto been presented. . . .

Proponents of this framework adopt the following line of reasoning: Populism did not adjust to industrialism; hence, the movement occupied an untenable historical position. And because it looked backward, its long-range solutions were, by definition, unrealistic. This meant that by not comprehending the basis for its discontent, Populism was forced to search for simplistic explanations and, ultimately, scapegoats. The result is a cumulatively deteriorating position; as protest becomes more emotional, it bears less resemblance to reality. The final image is that of a movement of opportunists, crackpots, and anti-Semites, whose perception of the world conforms to the dictates of a conspiracy theory of history. The over-all consequence of this image is that Populism has been denied its traditional place as a democratic social force. Rather, its significance for American history is altered so greatly that it has come to stand as the source for later proto-fascist groups, McCarthyism, anti-Semitism, xenophobia, and anti-intellectualism. One senses the proportions of this denigration process when it is seen that the very term "populistic" has passed into the working vocabulary of many intellectuals as an epithet, signifying the traits just enumerated.

The final dissociation of this image from previous scholarship occurs over the question of social conditions during the 1890's. Earlier writers never challenged the fact of hard times. Rather, they took Populist protest seriously as a direct response to economic grievances. It would be well to recall the situation facing Populism, as found in Hicks and other standard accounts: the serious decline in farm prices during the period 1870–1897; the railroad rate structure and, perhaps as important, railroad land and tax policies; high mortgage indebtedness within a financial context of contracting currency; actual dispossession from the land; adverse marketing arrangements, particularly the power of elevator companies to fix prices and establish grading standards; and consumption in a monopolistic framework.

The new image of Populism, by emphasizing irrationality, shifts the responsibility for discontent away from society and to Populism itself: The movement was more rhetorical than radical; hence, its protest was grossly exaggerated. Following this through, proponents of this view held that Populism was not a trustworthy barometer for reflecting actual conditions. The result was that the extent of oppression became increasingly minimized, and finally glossed over. And because the basis for discontent was almost totally denied, Populism then became subject to the charge of double irrationality: Not only was it retrogressive, but it responded to nonexistent grievances. Meanwhile, the society which gave birth to the protest was forgotten or exonerated. . . .

I propose, then, the following historical definition of midwestern Populism: While primarily an agrarian movement, it also contained significant support from industrial labor, social reformers, and intellectuals. The interaction between these groups was expressed not in terms of pre-industrial producer values, but of a common ideology stemming from a shared critique of existing conditions. In a word, Populism regarded itself as a class movement, reasoning that farmers and workers were assuming the same material position in society. Thus, it accepted industrialism but opposed its capitalistic form, seeking instead a more equitable distribution of wealth. But Populism went further in its criticism: Industrial capitalism not only impoverished the individual, it alienated and degraded him. The threat was not only subsistence living, but the destruction of human faculties. According to Populism, there was an inverse relation between industrialism and freedom, because the machine was being made to exploit rather than serve man. Is Populism, then, a socialist movement? Here labels become unimportant; it was far more radical than is generally assumed. Had Populism succeeded, it could have fundamentally altered American society in a socialist direction. Clearly, Populism was a progressive social force.

Populism had a peculiar notion of freedom: Man was free only when society encouraged the fullest possible development of human potentiality. Addressing the mammoth Tattersall rally, which climaxed the 1894 People's party campaign in Chicago, Henry Demarest Lloyd declared: "The people's party is more than the organized discontent of the people. It is the organized aspiration of the people for a fuller, nobler, richer, kindlier life for every man, woman, and child in the ranks of humanity." Seeking to enhance human self-fulfillment, it could not be a temporary phenomenon: "The people's party is not a passing cloud on the political sky. It is not a transient gust of popular discontent caused by bad crops or hard times." Rather, "It is an uprising of principle, and the millions who have espoused these principles will not stop until they have become incorporated into the constitution of the government and the framework of society." Thus, the goal of Populism was "the hope of realizing and incarnating in the lives of the common people the fullness of the divinity of humanity."

Here, then, was a standard for judging industrial America in the 1890's: Did it promote "the divinity of humanity," or merely produce dehumanized and impoverished men? While human rights is an abstraction admirably suited to campaign rhetoric, the theme recurs with sufficient frequency and intensity to indicate that Populists took it seriously. As Hamlin Garland stated to James B. Weaver, in the midst of the latter's 1892 presidential campaign: "Don't confine the fight to any one thing money or land. Let's make the fight for *human liberty* and for the rights of man." Ignatius Donnelly, in a circular prepared for party members in the 1896 campaign, defined the task at hand as "the preservation of humanity in the highest estate of which it is capable on earth." And Senator Allen of Nebraska similarly held that Populism "rests on the cause of labor and the brotherhood of man."

Populists further clarified their conception of human rights by distinguishing it from property rights. Governor Lorenzo D. Lewelling of Kansas, in a major speech, reminded his Kansas City audience that "we have so much regard for the rights of property that we have forgotten the liberties of the individual." A Broken Bow, Nebraska, paper saw the conflict as that of the "rights of man" and the "rights of capital." And one in Nelson, Nebraska, characterized it as between "the wealthy and powerful classes who want the control of the government to plunder the people" and "the people" themselves, who are "contending for equality before the law and the rights of man."

More concretely, human rights are a sham unless predicated upon an equitable distribution of wealth. An editorial in the Lincoln, Nebraska, *Farmers' Alliance* expressed the view in these words: "The people's party has sprung into existence not to make the black man free, but to emancipate all men; not to secure political freedom to a class, but to gain for all *industrial* freedom, without which there can be no political freedom; no lasting people's government." Making "industrial freedom" the precondition for political freedom, it further asserted that the People's party "stands upon the declaration that 'all men are created equal,' having equal right to live, labor and enjoy the fruits of their labor. It teaches that none should have power to enjoy without labor." On the contrary, Populism "demands equal opportunities and exact justice in business for each individual and proposes to abolish all monopolistic privileges and power." Thus, the perspective is refined still further: Monopoly poses the principal threat to human rights. Significantly, the editorial immediately added that the People's party "is the first party that has comprehended the great question of injustice and proposed an adequate remedy for the evils of society." Its closing sentence reveals that, while opposing monopoly, Populism accepted industrialism: Populists "shall make of this nation an industrial democracy in which each citizen shall have an equal interest."

At the same Tattersall rally where Lloyd spoke, Clarence Darrow also called for a more democratic industrial system: "We of the People's party believe that the men who created our wonderful industrial system have the right to enjoy the institution which they have created." A Columbus, Nebraska, paper voiced the same sentiment: "The people do not want to tear up the railroads nor pull down the factories." Instead, "they want to build up and make better everything." And social protest became necessary to secure these conditions, for "even a worm will writhe and struggle when stepped upon, and surely, if Americans cannot be anything higher, they can be a nation of worms." As the Populist organ in Wahoo, Nebraska, simply observed: "There should be no want." Thus, industrial America could, but did not,

provide greater material benefits for the total society. The technological potential was present for overcoming poverty, the results otherwise. A correspondent to Lloyd summarized this feeling when he wrote: "The whole ideal
of our civilization is wrong."

But privation was not inevitable; measures could be taken to create a
more equitable distribution of wealth. Here the essential rationality of Populism becomes clear: Man could rationally control his society, particularly by
harnessing the productive forces already in existence. But this could not occur
under the existing form of social organization, for industrial capitalism was
not responsive to human needs. Society, in a word, had to be changed. And
while the means selected were moderate—working through the political system—this should not obscure the radical conception Populists maintained of
politics. The same Columbus paper defined politics as the ability to control
"the distribution of wealth." Politics no longer meant seeking office, still less
preserving the status quo. Rather, this paper added, "Politics can cause this
country to bloom and blossom like the rose; it can make our people, generally
speaking, prosperous, happy and contented, or it can stagnate every kind of
enterprise, reduce the masses to want and misery and cause our people to
become restless, desperate and blood-thirsty."

Frank Doster, a Populist leader in Kansas, spelled out in detail this demand for political action to achieve the benefits of technology. Speaking at
Topeka on Labor Day of 1894, Doster pointed out that although "steam, electricity, compressed air, are utilized to do the work of man," the expected gains
failed to materialize. These productive forces, which are "the common property of all," have not benefited the total society because they "have been
made the monopoly of the few." Through this monopoly structure they "have
been turned aside from the beneficent ends for which designed, to serve the
selfish purposes of avarice and greed." Moreover, Populism was, according to
Doster, the only major political force which sought to control economic concentration in the interests of the larger society: "In the face of the power
exerted by the monopolists of these tremendous engines of industry and
commerce the republican and democratic parties stand paralyzed—hypnotized,
as it were, unable to control it or give direction and shape for common good."
Here the traditional charge is reversed; a Populist holds that the major parties
have been overwhelmed by these rapid changes. "The failure to adapt the
legislation of the country to the strange conditions which this new life has
forced upon us is the cause in greater part of our industrial ills." The statement suggests the attempt to confront, not retreat from, the new situation.
Accordingly, Doster closed with a presentation of "two political formulae,"
serving as the "philosophic bases" for reliance upon governmental action:
Government must "do that for the individual which he can not successfully
do for himself, and which other individuals will not do for him upon just and
equitable terms." And more comprehensively, "the industrial system of a na-

tion, like its political system, should be a government of and for and by the people alone."

Stepping back momentarily to view Populist thought in a wider ideological spectrum, one immediately recognizes its challenge to what are generally considered the prevailing ideologies of the period—the success myth, social Darwinism, and laissez faire. Governor Lewelling's Kansas City speech clearly states the Populist case for paternalism: "It is the business of the Government to make it possible for me to live and sustain the life of my family." Further, "It is the duty of government to protect the weak, because the strong are able to protect themselves." This is totally at variance with the success-myth faith in individual self-help through character development, industry, and perseverance. An article in the *Farmers' Alliance* suggests why Populists could not subscribe to the success myth: It contradicted their actual experiences, denied their grievances, and led to markedly different conclusions regarding the operation of the economic system. Hence, "No effort of the people, no degree of economy, no amount of industry in their several avocations could have averted these results. The people are as powerless as though they were actually in a state of bondage." A change in the nature of society, not a reliance on individual self-help, was necessary: "While the cause exists the evils *must* and *will* remain."

But Populism rejected the success myth, and indeed laissez faire and social Darwinism, for a more basic reason. Unbridled individualism, it contended, destroyed rather than promoted the general welfare. Its own counter-formulation, simply, was that cooperation and mutual help, not competition and self-help, led to true individualism.

An editorial in the *Farmers' Alliance* stated the argument as follows: "The plutocracy of to-day is the logical result of the individual freedom which we have always considered the pride of our system." In fact, "The theory of our government has been and is that the individual should possess the very greatest degree of liberty consistent, not with the greatest good of the greatest number, but with the very least legal restraint compatible with law and order. Individual enterprise was allowed unlimited scope." Thus, individualism creates monopoly capitalism, where "the corporation has absorbed the community." Instead, the reverse must take place: "The community must now absorb the corporation—must merge itself into it. Society must enlarge itself to the breadth of humanity." The editorial closed with an unmistakable repudiation of these other value systems: "A stage must be reached in which each will be for all and all for each. The welfare of the individual must be the object and end of all effort." And three years later, this paper (under its new name, *Alliance-Independent*) succinctly noted that "a reigning plutocracy with the masses enslaved, is the natural development and end of individualism." It remained for the Topeka *Advocate* to add a final, somewhat ironic, comment: "The horror of 'paternalism' hangs like a black pall over the buried hopes of the helpless poor."

Populism was even more unsparing in its criticism of social Darwinism, especially the latter's sanction of competition and survival of the fittest. Governor Lewelling, again in the Kansas City speech, warned that unless the government exerted greater control over industrial capitalism there would be "a state of barbarism and everywhere we slay, and the slayer in turn is slain and so on the great theatre of life is one vast conspiracy all creatures from the worm to the man in turn rob their fellows." For him, social Darwinism meant "the law of natural selection the survival of the fittest—Not the survival of the fittest, but the survival of the strongest." Lewelling concluded: "It is time that man should rise above it."

George H. Gibson, in a letter to the *Alliance-Independent* (he later became its editor), expressed a similar view of competition. Arguing that the type of social reform represented by Jane Addams was futile, he observed: "Uplifting the masses is all right, but it would be much better to put a stop to the beastly struggle which crowds them down." Nor did Gibson reason abstractly; he denied the wisdom of competition by what was daily taking place in American society. "There are tens of thousands in this city [Chicago] all the time out of work, fighting for positions and the low wages which enable capitalists to rake off dividends for idle and scheming stockholders." Writing later to Henry D. Lloyd, Gibson outlined his counter-proposal to competition: "We must put together our property, labor, economic wisdom, knowledge, varying talents, Christianizing or democratizing what we have and are . . . We feel that it is wrong to continue the selfish struggle, even with charitable or philanthropic intent, as many noble souls are doing."

Using for his standard "political and economic equality," a Walnut Grove, Minnesota, editor judged competitive society in these terms: "The calamities that have heretofore and that now are upon us—as a nation—are but the measure or indicator of the extent that this standard has been departed from in the practice of the competitive system." Nor did Populists admire those who were presumably the fittest. Ignatius Donnelly characterized them as follows: "Shallow-pated, sordid, unintellectual, they stand there, grabbing and grinning, while their brethren march past them to destruction." The Columbus, Nebraska, paper was less charitable, describing "the so-called great men" as "moral cowards and public plunderers" who have "reversed the code of morals and stand up like hypocrites of olden times and thank god they are not like other men are." And it opposed these men, again not on abstract grounds, but because it regarded competition as destroying all but the victors: "They have the power to impoverish the farmers, make millions of good men tramps; to reduce their employees to silent slaves; to ruin great cities; to plunge a happy and prosperous nation into sorrow and bankruptcy."

These criticisms do not, however, reflect a conspiracy theory of history;

Populists were concerned with the consequences of power, not the personalities or motivations of successful men. Referring to Rockefeller, Henry D. Lloyd noted that personal questions are extraneous because "the main point is the simple issue of monopoly." Even if "they are angels," he continued, the problem remains critical so long as they "have obtained the power of controlling the markets." Lloyd argued somewhat earlier in this same fashion against Carnegie, "I have no sort of feeling" against the man, but he is nonetheless "one of the worst representatives of our mercenary system of ordering industry which is perverting it from the supply of demand and the production and distribution of the wealth in nature for the use of all men, and making it an instrument of personal aggrandisement and cannibalistic selfishness."

Nor did Populism concede the more attractive side of social Darwinism, the latter's belief that society evolved into progressively higher stages. Technological progress was one matter—its translation into material well-being quite another. "While we think, brag of it, how far we are ahead of any former civilization," wrote a Minnesota state senator to Donnelly, "I for one am disgusted of the bragging and boasting and simply believe it is not true." Surely, through improvements in communications, "we are making history a little faster than when those elements were lacking in the world's affairs." But, he added, "I disdain to call it progress when, considering what it eventually . . . will lead to." This position is exceedingly interesting, for it starts from the recognition that technology provides the means for the liberation of man: "I have heard it asserted that the printing Press, telegraph, etc. have educated the masses, that the direful relapse will not come again as in the past." Yet, he then reaches a decidedly unexpected conclusion. While it can serve man, technology can also be used to insure a greater domination over man. In a word, progress is not only meaningless for a defective society; it actually becomes harmful by intensifying these defects. For Populism, then, progress was not an unmixed blessing: "Bosh, our would be masters have a corner on the whole outfit of the inventions, and they are now just as much employed to the destruction of human rights as formerly in the absence of those inventions the people's ignorance was used as a means."

Yet, Populism denied not the idea of progress but its realization in existing society. Optimistic in reforming zeal, Populism was still essentially pessimistic in its awareness of the ensuing obstacles. Not surprisingly, the result was an ambivalence with pessimism the overriding factor. A letter to Bryan after the 1896 election stated that an "appeal to reason may elevate the human race to a point we dream not of." But the same letter tempered this optimistic outburst with a sobering reminder: "A social system which permits puny children to toil in grimy factories and foul sweatshops while brawny men walk the streets vainly begging for work . . . is damnable!" How, then, could the net balance be otherwise than on the pessimistic side when Populists continually asked themselves such questions as this: "And for what object has this tremendous slaughter of the human family and this unparalleled suffering of the living been inflicted upon mankind?"

SUGGESTIONS FOR FURTHER READING

John D. Hicks, *The Populist Revolt (Minneapolis, 1931) deserves to be read in its entirety. Broader in scope and sympathetic to the farmers is Fred A. Shannon's outstanding work, *The Farmers' Last Frontier: Agriculture, 1860–1897 (New York, 1945). Excellent introductions to Southern Populism are C. Vann Woodward, *The Origins of the New South, 1877–1913 (Baton Rouge, 1951) and Sheldon Hackney, From Populism to Progressivism in Alabama, 1890–1920 (Princeton, 1969).

Especially useful examples of the vast literature dealing with farmers' problems are Allan G. Bogue, *Money at Interest: The Farm Mortgage on the Middle Border (Ithaca, New York, 1955), Bogue, *From Prairie to Cornbelt: Farming on the Illinois and Iowa Prairies in the Nineteenth Century (Chicago, 1963), Paul W. Gates, Fifty Million Acres: Conflicts over Kansas Land Policy, 1854–1890 (Ithaca, New York, 1954), and Theodore Saloutos and John D. Hicks, *Twentieth Century Populism (Lincoln, Nebraska, 1951).

In the 1950's Richard Hofstadter's *The Age of Reform (a portion of which is reprinted here) began a reexamination of the Populists. He and others charged the Populists with some degree of responsibility for the anti-Semitism, isolationism, and anti-intellectualism in American life. C. Vann Woodward discusses some of this anti-Populist literature in "The Populist Heritage and the Intellectual," American Scholar, XXIX (Winter 1959–60), pp. 55–72, also reprinted in Woodward, *The Burden of Southern History (Baton Rouge, 1960). The attack on the Populists has also produced a vigorous defense. In addition to the book by Norman Pollack (reprinted here in part), see Walter T. K. Nugent, The Tolerant Populists (Chicago, 1963).

* Available in paperback edition.

3
WORKINGMEN IN AN INDUSTRIAL AGE

The ultimate effect of the industrialization of the United States would be added opportunities, increased wages, more and better goods and services, and improved working conditions. But behind the statistics of economic growth and rising standards of living were serious problems brought by the rapid and often chaotic economic and social changes. Workers often found themselves crowded into urban slums that were marked by unspeakable filth and grossly inadequate public services. In the shops and factories hours were usually long, conditions dangerous and unhealthy, and wages woefully low. Periodic economic crises threw people out of work and gave employers a powerful weapon to force down the wages and lengthen the working hours of those who remained employed.

To protect themselves, workingmen would often unite, sometimes in trade unions but usually in less formal and structured organizations. When organized and determined workers used the strike in their struggle against organized and equally determined employers, the result was bitter and, at times, even violent. Striking workers were often greeted at plant gates by armed guards hired by factory owners intent upon dispersing the pickets and maintaining production with unorganized labor. Workers regularly armed themselves, equally resolved to keep the struck factory closed by preventing "scabs" from entering the shops. When these two determined and armed groups met, the result was invariably a bloody clash.

Historians, of course, cannot ignore the many instances of conflict and every labor history bristles with accounts of violent struggles between labor and management. From this many scholars conclude that there is no tradition of consensus in this aspect of American history.

Yet others argue that conflict is not the basic underlying feature in American labor history. Without attempting to ignore the conflicts, they point to other aspects of the American labor movement. They argue that only a few American unionists have been radicals and that never has the trade-union movement followed a program designed to overthrow the existing social and economic system. Those unions which have adopted a radical or revolutionary program have always been in the distinct minority and the major portion of organized labor has consistently repudiated the radical sections of the movement.

In a word, then, these historians point to consensus as the basic theme in American labor history. Labor and management, they argue, have often disagreed over wages and working conditions and these disagreements often led to strikes and conflicts, but behind these disagreements there existed an underlying unity based upon an acceptance of the sanctity of private property as well as the most important features of American democratic government.

Just as those historians who emphasize consensus cannot ignore the violent conflicts which often characterized labor-management relations, those who stress conflict cannot ignore the fact that the major portions of the

American labor movement have not been radical and revolutionary. Still they continue to insist that conflict is the basic theme. Some argue that although the labor movement is not socialistic, it has always adopted goals which would fundamentally alter our social and economic system even if they would not completely destroy it. Others argue that the American labor movement will soon become socialistic, like its European counterparts.

Some of the problems involved in interpreting American labor history can be seen in the selections which follow. In the first selection, Philip Taft and Philip Ross begin by pointing out that "the United States has had the bloodiest and most violent labor history of any industrial nation in the world." They note that this violence has persisted until relatively recent times despite the fact that American workers have never adopted an ideology that has advocated violence as a tactic. Labor violence has diminished in recent years, they conclude, because the "conditions that gave rise to past labor violence have been eliminated," but they add that "a restoration of these conditions" would bring renewed violence in labor-management relations.

In the next selection, Edward Kirkland argues that an emphasis on labor violence is "misleading" in that it obscures the fact that there was a "harmony of interests" between labor and capital. Selig Perlman arrives at similar conclusions, but he approaches the problem from a broader vantage point. Looking for a general theory of the American labor movement, he finds trade unions in the United States, for the most part, rejecting class-conscious radicalism and adopting instead an emphasis on what he calls job consciousness. American workers are concerned with wages and working conditions, not with the overthrow of private property, and this, he concludes, is the only policy possible in America. Like Perlman, Herbert G. Gutman views the working-class movement within the context of the whole of American society. He concludes that the reaction to the "worker's search for power" was not uniform throughout the country. In the smaller towns, middle-class and professional people were much more sympathetic to the workers' demands than they were in the large cities.

It is clear that one approach to the evaluation of the labor movement, including the many instances of strikes and violence, rests upon an assessment of the nature of the divisions between worker and employer. Do the activities of organized labor reflect fundamental class conflict in American society? Are the aims and interests of each group so different and opposed that sharp and bitter conflict has been and will continue to be inevitable? Or do workers and employers in the United States accept the fundamentals of the system? Are workers interested in no more than increasing their share of the nation's wealth?

But perhaps these questions pose the question too starkly. If it be granted that American labor is not radical or socialistic, does it follow that workingmen have simply accepted the ideas and outlook of the employers? Is it not more realistic to speak of a mutual accommodation between labor and capital than of a capitulation on the part of labor? If so, what is the nature of this accommodation?

What of the future? Radicals place great emphasis on the role of the working class in the overthrow of private property, in the replacement of capitalism by socialism. Does the history of American labor point in this direction?

American Labor Violence

Philip Taft
and Philip Ross

The United States has had the bloodiest and most violent labor history of any industrial nation in the world. Labor violence was not confined to certain industries, geographic areas, or specific groups in the labor force, although it has been more frequent in some industries than in others. There have been few sections and scarcely any industries in which violence has not erupted at some time, and even more serious confrontations have on occasion followed. Native and foreign workers, whites and blacks have at times sought to prevent strike replacements from taking their jobs, and at other times have themselves been the object of attack. With few exceptions, labor violence in the United States arose in specific situations, usually during a labor dispute. The precipitating causes have been attempts by pickets and sympathizers to prevent a plant on strike from being reopened with strikebreakers, or attempts of company guards, police, or even by National Guardsmen to prevent such interference. At different times employers and workers have played the roles of aggressors and victims. Union violence was directed at limited objectives; the prevention of the entrance of strikebreakers or raw materials to a struck plant, or interference with finished products leaving the premises. While the number seriously injured and killed was high in some of the more serious encounters, labor violence rarely spilled over to other segments of the community.

Strikers, no matter how violent they might be, would virtually always seek to win the sympathy of the community to their side, and therefore

From *Philip Taft and Philip Ross, "American Labor Violence: Its Causes, Character, and Outcome,"* in *Hugh Davis Graham and Ted Robert Gurr, A Report Submitted to the National Commission on the Causes and Prevention of Violence by the Task Force on Historical and Comparative Perspectives (1969).*

attacks or even incitements against those not connected [with] or aiding the employer would be carefully avoided. Such conduct was especially common in the organized strikes, those which were called and directed by a labor organization. Strike violence can therefore be differentiated from violence that is stimulated by general discontent and a feeling of injustice. Moreover, the unions were normally anxious to avoid violence and limit its impact because, simultaneously with the strike, the organization might also be operating under a contract and negotiating with other employers in an attempt to solve differences and promote common interests. Unions seek and must have at least the grudging cooperation of employers. No major labor organization in American history ever advocated violence as a policy, even though the labor organizations recognized that it might be a fact of industrial life.

Trade unions from the beginning of their existence stressed their desire for peaceful relations with employers. However, minority groups within the labor movement or without direct attachment to it advocated the use of violence against established institutions and also against leaders in government, industry, and society. The union leader might hope to avoid violence, but recognized that in the stress of a labor dispute it might be beyond the ability of the union to prevent clashes of varying seriousness. They might erupt spontaneously without plan or purpose in response to an incident on the picket line or provocation. Those who saw in violence a creative force regarded the problem differently; they had no objectives of immediate gain; they were not concerned with public opinion. They were revolutionaries for whom the radical transformation of the economic and social system was the only and all-consuming passion.

The most virulent form of industrial violence occurred in situations in which efforts were made to destroy a functioning union or to deny to a union recognition.

The Influence of Ideology

There is only a solitary example in American labor history of the advocacy of violence as a method of political and economic change. In the 1880's a branch of anarchism emerged that claimed a connection with organized and unorganized labor and advocated individual terror and revolution by force. The principle of "propaganda by the deed," first promulgated at the anarchist congress in Berne, Switzerland, in 1876, was based upon the assumption that peaceful appeals were inadequate to rouse the masses. This view could be interpreted as a call upon workers to create their own independent institutions, such as trade unions, mutual aid societies, and producer and consumer cooperatives. However, almost from the beginning this doctrine was interpreted to mean engaging in insurrectionary and putschist activities, and in terror directed against the individual. Emphasis upon individual force gained added strength from the terroristic acts of members of the People's Will, an organization of Russian revolutionaries who carried out campaigns of violence against persons, culminating in the assassination of Czar Alexander II in 1881.

Not all anarchists approved these tactics. Many thought that social problems could be solved only by addressing oneself to the removal of evils, by changing institutions and the minds of men. In addition, the reaction against acts of terror, the arrests and imprisonment of militants, weakened the movement by depriving it of some of its more vigorous and courageous elements. Nevertheless, the London congress of 1881, which established the International Working People's Association as the center for the national anarchist federations, came out in favor of "propaganda by the deed" as a creative method for carrying on warfare against capitalist society and its leaders.

Social revolutionary views were not widely accepted in the United States during the 1880's, but the difference between the moderates and the militants, which divided the European movement, was also in evidence here. As early as 1875 education and defense organizations (*Lehr und Wehr Vereine*) were organized in Chicago, and they soon spread to other cities. Members met regularly and drilled with arms. It was the issue of using arms which was largely responsible for the split in the Socialist Labor Party in 1880, and the more militant social revolutionaries gradually approached the anarchist position on politics and violence.

An attempt to unite the scattered groups of social revolutionaries was made by the Chicago conference of 1881 and was unsuccessful. The meeting adopted a resolution recognizing "the armed organizations of workingmen who stand ready with the gun to resist encroachment upon their rights, and recommend the formation of like organizations in all States." This was only a prelude to the convention held in Pittsburgh in 1883, dominated by Johann Most, a German-born revolutionary who had served prison terms in a number of countries. Most had come to the United States in December 1882, and transferred his journal, *Freiheit*, to New York. Through the spoken and written word he became the leader of the anarchists in the United States and the leading figure of the predominantly immigrant revolutionaries.

In typically Socialist fashion, the congress explained the causes of the evils afflicting modern society. Since all institutions are aligned against him, the worker has a right to arm himself for self-defense and offense. The congress noted that no ruling class ever surrendered its privileges and urged organization for planning and carrying out rebellion. Capitalists will not leave the field except by force. These ideas had some influence among a limited number of workers, largely immigrants. Most himself did not favor trade unions, regarding them as compromising organizations, and even refused to support the 8-hour movement in the 1880's. Anarchists, however, were active in union organizations and some regarded them as the ideal type of workmen's societies. Albert Parsons, August Spies, and Samuel Fielden, all of them defendants in the Haymarket Trial, had close connections with a part of the Chicago labor movement.

The anarchists were not all of the same view, but many of them, including Most, not only advocated the formation of armed societies, but published materials on the making of explosives. *Revolutionary War Science* (*Revolutionäre Kriegswissenschaft*) is a treatise on the use of arms and the making of what we would call "Molotov cocktails." There is little evidence that these suggestions were ever taken seriously by many workers, and the anarchist movement's greatest influence in the United States was in the 1880's. Even at the height of their influence the anarchists had few supporters. Whatever violence took place in the United States cannot be traced to the thinking of Most or any of his coworkers. In fact, even then it was widely believed that the armed societies were engaging in playing a game, and that they represented little danger to the community. It is quite certain that violence in labor disputes was seldom inspired by the doctrine of "propaganda by the deed," whose self-defeating nature convinced many of its exponents of its fallacy. In this regard, experience was a more potent force than moral considerations. Governments reacted to these terrorist methods with savage repression. One of the few incidents of anarchist violence in the United States was an attack by Alexander Berkman on Henry Frick during the Homestead strike. The boomerang effect of this action was to transform the hated Frick into a folk hero when, though wounded, he fought off his attacker. The assassination of William McKinley by the anarchist Czolgosz is another example. Most did not repudiate the tactic, but laid down conditions for its use that were critical of Berkman's conduct.

In France, Italy, and Spain anarchist-inspired violence was savagely repressed, as were the few attempts in Germany and Austria.

The Industrial Workers of the World (IWW)

Unlike the other national federations such as the Knights of Labor, the American Federation of Labor, and the Congress of Industrial Organizations, the IWW advocated direct action and sabotage. These doctrines were never clearly defined, but did not include violence against isolated individuals. Pamphlets on sabotage by Andre Tridon, Walker C. Smith, and Elizabeth Gurley Flynn were published, but Haywood and the lawyers for the defense at the Federal trial for espionage in Chicago in 1918 denied that sabotage meant destruction of property. Instead Haywood claimed it meant slowing down on the job when the employer refused to make concessions.

It is of some interest that IWW activity was virtually free of violence. The free-speech fight was a form of passive resistance in which members mounted soapboxes and filled the jails. The IWW did not conduct a large number of strikes, and aside from the one in McKee's Rock[s], Pa., a spontaneous strike which the IWW entered after it was called, the IWW strikes were peaceful.

The two bloodiest episodes in the life of the IWW were in Everett and Centralia, Wash., each connected with the attempt to organize lumber workers. The Everett confrontation started when the Lumber Workers Industrial Union No. 500 opened a hall in Everett in the spring of 1916, in an effort to recruit members. Street meetings were prevented and the sheriff deported the speakers and other members of the IWW to Seattle on a bus. It is of some interest to note that a speaker who advocated violence at a meeting at the IWW hall in Everett was later exposed as a private detective. For a time the deportations were stopped, but they were resumed in October 1916. An estimated 300 to 400 members were deported by the sheriff and vigilantes from Everett. On October 30, 1916, 41 IWW men left Seattle by boat. They were met by the sheriff and a posse, seized, and made to run the gauntlet between two rows of vigilantes who beat their prisoners with clubs.

On November 5, 1916, the IWW in Seattle chartered a boat, the Verona, and placed an additional 39 men on another vessel. The chartered boat set out for Everett. Having been informed of the attempt of the IWW to land peacefully, the sheriff and about 200 armed men met the chartered vessel at the dock. The sheriff sought to speak to the leaders. When none came forward and the passengers sought to land, a signal to fire into the disembarking men was given by the sheriff. Five members of the IWW and two vigilantes were killed, and 31 members of the IWW and 19 vigilantes were wounded by gunfire. The Verona and the other vessel carrying members of the IWW returned to Seattle without unloading at Everett. Almost 300 were arrested, and 74 were charged with first-degree murder. The acquittal of the first defendant led to the dismissal of the case against the others.

Another tragedy occurred in Centralia, Wash., a lumber town of almost 20,000 inhabitants. Several times the IWW sought to open a hall in that community, but in 1916 the members were expelled by a citizens' committee, and 2 years later the IWW hall was wrecked during a Red Cross parade. With dogged persistence the IWW opened another hall. When threats were made to wreck it, the IWW issued a leaflet pleading for avoidance of raids upon it. During the Armistice Day parade in 1919, members of the IWW were barricaded in their hall and when the hall was attacked, opened fire. Three members of the American Legion were killed, and a fourth died from gunshot wounds inflicted by Wesley Everest, himself a war veteran. Everest was lynched that night by a citizen mob. Eleven members of the IWW were tried for murder. One was released, two were acquitted and seven were convicted of second degree murder. A labor jury from Seattle that had been attending the trial claimed that the men fired in self-defense and should have been acquitted. It is not necessary to attempt to redetermine the verdict to recognize that the IWW in Everett and Centralia was the victim, and the violence was a response to attacks made upon its members for exercising their constitutional rights.

A number of States, beginning with Minnesota in 1917, passed criminal syndicalist laws that forbade the advocacy of force and violence as a means of social change. On the basis of the theory that the IWW advocated force and violence to bring about industrial changes, several hundred men were tried, and 31 men served in the penitentiary in Idaho, 52 in Washington, and 133 in California. These convictions were not based upon acts of violence committed by those tried.

The Practice of Violence in the 1870's and 1880's

Repudiation of theories did not eliminate the practice of violence from the American labor scene. The pervasiveness of violence in American labor disputes appears paradoxical because the great majority of American workers have never supported views or ideologies that justified the use of force as a means of reform or basic social change, nor have American workers normally engaged in the kind of political activity that calls for demonstrations or for physical confrontation with opponents. Through most of its history, organized labor in the United States has depended largely upon economic organizations —unions—for advancement through collective bargaining, and upon pressure politics and cooperation with the old parties for achieving its political aims. Yet we are continually confronted with examples of violent confrontations between labor and management. Does industrial violence reveal a common characteristic with basic causes and persistent patterns of behavior, or is it a series of incidents linked only by violence? Labor violence has appeared under many conditions, and only an examination of the events themselves can reveal their nature and meaning.

The Strikes and Riots of 1877. The unexpected strikes and riots which swept over the United States in 1877 with almost cyclonic force began in Martinsburg, W. Va., after the Baltimore [and] Ohio Railroad had announced its second wage cut in a relatively short period. The men left their trains and drove back those who sought to replace them. Governor Henry W. Mathews called upon President Rutherford B. Hayes for Federal assistance, and the latter, despite his reluctance, directed troops to be sent. Federal troops had a calming influence on the rioters in Martinsburg, but 2 days later, on July 20, Governor John Lee Carroll of Maryland informed the President that an assemblage of rioters ". . . has taken possession of the Baltimore [and] Ohio Railroad depot" in Baltimore, had set fire to it, and "driven off the firemen who attempted to extinguish the same, and it is impossible to disperse the rioters." Governor Carroll also asked for Federal aid.

Order was restored immediately by Federal troops, but Governor Carroll then appealed for help in putting down a disturbance at Cumberland. Requests also were made for troops to be sent to Philadelphia, where the authorities feared [an] outbreak of rioting. The most serious trouble spot, however, was Pittsburgh, where the attempt to introduce "double headers" was the cause of one of the more serious disturbances of the year. The changes might have been accepted if they had not followed cuts in pay and loss of jobs—both caused by declining business. Open resistance began, and when a company of militia sought to quell the disturbance it was forced to retreat before the mob and take refuge in a railroad roundhouse where it was under constant attack. A citizens' posse and Federal troops restored order.

Railroads in Pennsylvania, New York, and New Jersey suffered almost complete disruption. The Erie, New York Central, the Delaware Lackawanna Western, and the Canada Southern operating in Ohio, Pennsylvania, and New York States were struck on July 24, idling about 100,000 workers. Federal and State troops were used to suppress rioting, and sometimes the State police were themselves the cause of violence. After 13 persons were killed and 43 wounded in a clash between militia and citizens in Reading, Pa., for example, a coroner's jury blamed the troops for an unjustified assault upon peaceful citizens.

*   *   *

In summary, a recent student tells us:

In 1877 the disorders swept through the major rail centers of the nation: Baltimore, Philadelphia, Pittsburgh, Buffalo, Cleveland, Toledo, Columbus, Cincinnati, Louisville, Indianapolis, Chicago, St. Louis, Kansas City, and Omaha, to name only the more important. Outside this central area there were brief flare-ups in New York City and Albany in the Northeast, in Little Rock, New Orleans, and Galveston in the South, and in San Francisco on the Pacific Slope. About two-thirds of the country's total rail mileage lay within the strike-affected area, and in those zones strikers halted most freight trains and delayed many passenger and mail trains.

The Report of the Committee to Investigate the Railroad Riots in July, 1877, issued by the Pennsylvania Legislature, limits itself to events within that State. Nevertheless, it alludes to factors which were present in virtually every other community in which rioting took place. The report states that the riots

. . . were the protests of laborers against the system by which his wages were arbitrarily fixed and lowered by his employer without consultation with him, and without his consent . . . . The immediate cause of the first strike . . . that at Pittsburgh, July 19th, was the order by the Pennsylvania Railroad Company to run "double headers" . . . . This order of itself, had there been no previous reductions of wages or dismissals of men on account of the depression in business, *would probably have caused no strike, but following so soon after the second reduction . . . and the feeling of uneasiness and dissatisfaction existing among the laboring men of the country generally, caused by the want of labor and the low price thereof as compared with a few years previous, all together combined to set in motion this strike . . . . Each strike was independent of those on other roads, each having a local cause particularly its own. As before stated, there was a sort of epidemic of strikes running through the laboring classes of the country, more particularly those in the employ of large corporations, caused by the great depression of business which followed the panic of 1873, by means whereof many men were thrown out of work, and the wages of those who get work were reduced.*

The riots of 1877 mirrored deeply felt grievances generated by several years of unemployment and wage cuts. All the rioting cannot be attributed to striking workmen and their sympathizers. Railroads, urban transportation systems, and trucking are among the industries that are almost completely exposed to attack during a labor dispute. They operate in the open, and it is difficult to prevent attacks by strikers and sympathizers upon working personnel and property. The strikes and riots of 1877 were, however, a violent protest against deteriorating conditions and the suffering and misery endured during a great depression. The widespread and ferocious reaction has no parallel in our history, but there are others of lesser magnitude that were important in shaping labor-management relations.

*   *   *

Labor Violence in the 1890's

Not all violence was inspired by employers. While employer obduracy might lead to rejection of recognition, such conduct was in itself legally permissible. Had workers passively accepted such decisions, the level of violence in American labor disputes would have been reduced. Workers were, however, unwilling to watch their jobs forfeited to a local or imported strikebreaker. Employers could shut down their plants and attempt "to starve" their employees out of the union. Such a policy might have worked, but employers cognizant of their rights and costs frequently refused to follow such a self-denying tactic. As a consequence violence initiated from the labor side was also prevalent. In the 1890's violent outbreaks occurred in the North, South, and West, in small communities and metropolitan cities, testifying to the common attitudes of Americans in every part of the United States. While workers might react against the denial of what they regarded as their rights, the outcome of their violent behavior seldom changed the course of events. Serious violence erupted in several major strikes of the 1890's, the question of union recognition being a factor in all of them. As will be noted below, the Homestead strike, which was a defensive action in behalf of an existing and recognized union, and the Pullman strike, which was called in behalf of other workers denied recognition, also failed. Violence in the Coeur d'Alene copper area eventually led to the destruction of the Western Federation of Miners in that district. Violence was effective in the Illinois coalfields only because the community and the Governor of the State were hostile to the efforts of two coal producers to evade the terms of a contract acceptable to the great majority of producers in Illinois.

Although steel workers in Pennsylvania and copper miners in Idaho had different ethnic origins and worked under dissimilar conditions, each reacted with equal ferocity to the attempts of their employers to undermine their unions.

Homestead. In Homestead, Pa., the domineering head of the Carnegie Steel Co., Henry C. Frick, used a difference over wages and a contract expiration date as an excuse for breaking with the union. When the union called a strike against the demands of Frick, the latter was ready to bring in a bargeload of Pinkerton operatives to guard his plant from the harassment of union pickets. Frick's plan became known, and the guards were met by several hundred steel workers. In the battle to land the guards from the barges, two Pinkertons and two strikers were killed. Another attempt to land also ended in failure. Eventually the Pinkertons were forced to surrender and some were severely mauled by strikers and sympathizers. At the plea of the sheriff, the Governor ordered 7,000 troops to Homestead. Leaders were arrested, but juries refused to convict.

While the violence was temporarily successful in holding off the landing attempted on July 4, it was unable to change the outcome of the contest between the union and Frick. Under the cover of the protection given to him by the National Guard, he was able to open his mills. Furnaces were lit on July 15, and the company announced that applications for work would be received until July 21. The following day a large force of nonunion men entered the plant. Ultimately the union was defeated, and according to a leading student of the steel industry of another generation, John A. Fitch, the union never recovered from its defeat in Homestead. The steel workers were fearful of Frick's attempt to break the union. The hiring of several hundred Pinkertons and their stealthy efforts to land convinced the strikers that a serious movement to destroy their organization was on the way, and the use of the hated Pinkertons sharpened their anger. An investigation by the U.S. Senate noted: "Every man who testified, including the proprietors of the detective agencies, admitted that the workmen are strongly prejudiced against the so-called Pinkertons and their presence at a strike serves to unduly inflame the passions of the strikers."

Coeur d'Alene. Organization of the metal miners in the Coeur d'Alene region in Idaho was followed by the mine operators' establishment of an association after the miner's union had successfully won a wage increase. A lockout was called several months after the miners' success, and every mine in the area was closed down. An offer of lower wages was rejected. The strikers were not passive. Strikebreakers were urged to leave or were forcibly expelled; court injunctions against violence were ignored. In July 1892 the situation deteriorated. A union miner was killed by guards, and it brought an attack by armed miners upon the barracks housing guards employed by the Frisco mill. It was dynamited, and one employee was killed and 20 wounded. An attack on the Gem mill followed and although five strikers were killed and more wounded, the mill surrendered. The guards gave up their weapons and were ordered out of the county. Armed with Winchesters, the armed strikers marched on Wardner, where they forced the Bunker Hill mine to discharge its nonunion contingent.

At the request of the Governor, who sent the entire National Guard, Federal troops were sent to restore order. The commanding general ordered all union men arrested and lodged in a hastily built stockade or bullpen. The commander of the State militia removed local officials sympathetic to the strikers and replaced them with others favorable to his orders. Trains were searched and suspects removed. Active union men were ordered dismissed from their jobs. The district was treated like a military zone, and companies were prohibited from employing union men. About 30 men were charged with conspiracy, and four were convicted, but subsequently released by the U.S. Supreme Court. Nevertheless, the miners were able to win recognition from all but the largest of the mining companies, which set the stage for a more spectacular encounter 7 years later.

*   *   *

The Pullman Strike. Railroad strikes have been among the more violent types of labor dispute. Normally, railroad workers are not more aggressive than other workers. However, railroads cover large open areas and their operations are always open to the rock thrower or the militant picket who may take it upon himself to discourage strikebreaking. A sympathy strike by the newly organized American Railway Union with the workers in the Pullman shops led to a widespread suspension of railroad service in 1894. What stands out in this bitter clash is the sympathy that the losing struggle generated among thousands of railroad workers. The refusal of the Pullman Co. to discuss the restoration of a wage cut with its employees was interpreted as an example of corporate arrogance. Like 1877, 1894 was a depression year, and many workers were without a job or income.

The strike started in May, and the American Railway Union, meeting in convention the following month, sought to bring about a settlement of the differences. When the American Railway Union imposed its boycott upon Pullman equipment, its action was challenged by the General Manager's Association, made up of the executives of the 24 railroads entering Chicago. Special guards were engaged, Federal marshals were appointed to keep the trains moving, and if an employee refused to handle Pullman equipment he was discharged. Attempts to operate with strikebreakers led to fearful resistance. Rioting was widespread, and at the request of the railroads and advice of Attorney General Richard Olney, Federal troops were sent to Chicago, over the protests of Governor John B. Altgeld. Every road west of Chicago felt the impact of the strike. Clashes between strikers and strikebreakers brought out Federal or State troops in Nebraska, Iowa, Colorado, Oklahoma, and California. Although the loss of life and property was not as serious as during the disturbances of 1877, the Pullman strike affected a wider area. An estimated 34 people were killed and undetermined millions of dollars were lost in the rioting connected with this conflict. President Grover Cleveland claimed "that within the states of North Dakota, Montana, Idaho, Colorado, Washington, Wyoming, California, and the territories of Utah and New Mexico it was impracticable to enforce federal law by the ordinary course of judicial procedure. For this reason," he revealed, "military forces were being used."

The immediate cause of the violence was the. determination of the General Manager's Association to defeat the sympathy strike. When the boycott of Pullman cars was announced, the association declared that the employees of the railroads had no right to punish the carriers nor impose hardships upon the traveling public. The association declared "it to be the lawful right and duty of said railway companies to protect against said boycott, to resist the same in the interest of their existing contracts, and for the benefit of the traveling public, and that we will act unitedly to that end." The extension of support by the union brought forth the support of the carriers for the Pullman Co. It is however, as has been noted, extremely difficult to avoid disorders in a strike in an industry whose operations are carried on over an open and extensive area. Any occurrence can attract hundreds and even thousands of people who because of sympathy or search for excitement or loot can expand a simple incident into a large-scale riot. The chief inciters to violence were not known, and the police and the officers of the railroads did not agree on whether union members or city toughs were the chief promoters of the turmoil.

The Federal Government hired marshals in numerous railroad centers to protect the property of the carriers. Attorney General Richard Olney stated that the extra funds expended for this purpose by the Federal Government amounted to at least $400,000.

The responsibility for violence rests largely on the behavior of George Pullman. His attitude was similar to those held by many industrialists. He was unwilling to allow his workers the slightest influence upon the decisions of the company which greatly affected their welfare. Like other firms, the Pullman Co. was suffering losses of business as a result of the depression, and it may not have been able to meet the demands of its employees. It could, however, have conferred in good faith and explained its position instead of following a policy of peremptory rejection and dismissal of those who had asked for a reconsideration of a wage cut. Pullman's attitude, shared by many industrialists, tells us something about the cause of violence in labor disputes. Arrogant, intransigent, unwilling to meet with their employees, owners depended upon their own or the Government's power to suppress protest. Behind the powerful shield they could ignore the periodic outbreaks by their labor force; they knew that these seldom were strong enough to gain victory.

*   *   *

The 10 Years Between 1900 and 1910

The first decade of the 20th century witnessed expansion of union membership, which increased opportunities for conflicts with employers. As in previous periods, strikes were on occasion marked by violence. The prospect of violence was heightened by rising employer resistance to union objectives. The signs of this new employer response consisted of the founding of many employer associations, the beginning of the open-shop campaign, and the use of Citizen Alliances as assault troops on union picket lines.

Pennsylvania Anthracite Coalfields. Violence in Illinois and in the Coeur d'Alene was carried out primarily by native or Americanized workers. Through the 1870's the Pennsylvania anthracite area was dominated by English-speaking workers: Americans, English, Scotch, Irish, and Welsh were the principal sources of labor. By 1900, large numbers of Eastern and Southern Europeans had come into the area, and the English-speaking ratio in the population had dropped from 94 percent in 1880 to 52 percent in 1900. With the destruction of the Knights of Labor and the Amalgamated Association of Anthracite Miners, no offset to the companies' power existed. Absence of checkweighmen, the existence of the company store, and the complete domination of the area by the coal companies were unrestrained evils. Nothing better demonstrates the abuse of power than an attack in 1897 upon miners who had struck against the high prices at the company store and were peacefully marching from Hazleton to Latimer. The sheriff and a force of deputies met the marchers on the road and ordered them to disperse. When they failed to obey instantly, the sheriff ordered his deputies to fire on the unresisting paraders. Eighteen were killed and 40 seriously wounded. Many of the killed and wounded were shot in the back. The sheriff and several deputies were tried for murder but were acquitted.

In 1900, the United Mine Workers of America was able to challenge successfully the anthracite coal operators. Although the union had only about 7 percent of the miners in the area in the organization, it called a strike in September of 1900. There was only one serious clash between strikers and guards, which led to the death of a strikebreaker. Immediately 2,400 troops were sent into the area by the Governor. The strike was settled on terms not unfavorable to the union, and the single violent encounter played no role in the outcome. Peace in the anthracite mines was brought about by political pressure but also by the skillful leadership of John Mitchell, the president of the United Mine Workers. Mitchell had always deplored the use of violent methods and constantly pleaded for negotiations as a peaceful means of settling labor disputes. He further recognized the importance of retaining public sentiment on the strikers' side, and he was determined to prevent the use of widespread prejudice against the Southern European immigrant worker to defeat them. This strike was, however, only a skirmish; the anthracite workers were to face a more serious trial 2 years later.

When negotiations between the operators and the union broke down in April 1902, it appeared that the strike would be more violent than the preceding one. A more aggressive spirit was evident among the men, and the companies appeared to be equally determined to scotch further progress of the union. Hundreds of commissions for iron and coal police to guard mining property were issued, and the companies decided to recruit strikebreakers and operate during the strike. An attack on a colliery at Old Forge on July 1 resulted in the killing of a striker; another was killed at Duryea the next day. Shootings and assaults became more common as the strike dragged on, and at the end of July the Governor ordered two regiments to Shenandoah, where the town was literally taken over by rioters. In this community a merchant suspected of supplying ammunition to deputies was beaten to death, and deputies and strikebreakers were assaulted. On August 18, troops were sent to Carbon County after a coal and iron policeman killed a striker. Trestles and bridges were dynamited and nonstrikers assaulted. The Governor, in September, sent troops into the three anthracite counties. Violence did not abate. On September 28, a striker was killed, and later in the day, 700 strikers assaulted and wrecked the Mount Carmel office of the Lehigh Valley Coal Co. and seized the roads leading to the colliery. In a summary of violence at the end of September, the New York Tribune claimed that in the disturbances arising out of the strike, 14 had been killed, 16 shot from ambush, 42 others severely injured, and 67 aggravated assaults had occurred; 1 house and 4 bridges were dynamited, 16 houses, 10 buildings, 3 washrooms around mines, and 3 stockades were burned; 6 trains were wrecked and there were 9 attempted wrecks, 7 trains attacked, and students in 14 schools went on strike against teachers whose fathers or brothers were working during the strike.

Despite the extent of violence, it is doubtful whether it had any decisive effect on the outcome of the strike. In insisting that the strikers were prevented from working because of union intimidation, the operators claimed that the mines would be opened and fully manned if adequate protection were granted. The Governor of Pennsylvania sent the entire National Guard of the State into the anthracite area, but their presence did not increase the output of coal. This demonstration that the tieup was not the result of coercion but of the determination of the miners to bargain through a union ended the impasse.

What made the union victory possible was the conciliatory attitude of Mitchell. Firm on essentials, he was ready to compromise on details. Careful not to antagonize public opinion, he emphasized the justice of the miners' cause, the right of men to bargain collectively over the terms of employment. Although considerable violence developed during the second anthracite strike, none of it had the spectacular features of some of the battles in the Rocky Mountain area (see below). Mitchell and his subordinates always pleaded for peaceful behavior, and while the advice was often honored in the breach, neither he nor any other leaders could be attacked for advocating destruction of property or assaults upon persons which, had they done so, would have given employers a powerful argument with which to sway public sentiment.

The Colorado Labor War. The use of force to settle differences was more common in the Western mining camps at the turn of the century than in Eastern manufacturing or even mining communities. In the West there was a tendency for violence to erupt on a larger scale. In 1894 Colorado's Governor, David M. Waite, ordered the dispersal of an army of company-employed deputies in a mining-labor dispute. Only the intervention of the troops prevented a battle between strikers and deputies.

Later, in 1901, after a successful walkout, the union miners deported a group of strikebreakers who had taken their jobs during the strike. The tendency for each side to resort to force to settle differences led to a gradual escalation of the level of violence, which reached a point where the Western Federation of Miners faced the combined power of the Mine Operator's Association, aided by the State government and a private employer's group, the militant Citizen's Alliance. It was an unequal struggle in which men were killed and maimed; union miners imprisoned in the bullpen; union halls, newspapers, and cooperatives sacked; and many strikers deported. There is no episode in American labor history in which violence was as systematically used by employers as in the Colorado labor war of 1903 and 1904. The miners fought back with a ferocity born of desperation, but their use of rifles and dynamite did not prevent their utter defeat.

*   *   *

Summary and Conclusions

The United States has experienced more frequent and bloody labor violence than any other industrial nation. Its incidence and severity have, however, been sharply reduced in the last quarter of a century. The reduction is even more noteworthy when the larger number of union members, strikes, and labor-management agreements are considered. The magnitude of past violence is but partially revealed by available statistics. One writer estimated that in the bloody period between January 1, 1902, and September 30, 1904, 198 persons were killed and 1,966 injured in strikes and lockouts. Our own independent count, which grossly understates the casualties, records over 700 deaths and several thousands of serious injuries in labor disputes. In addition, we have been able to identify over 160 occasions on which State and Federal troops have intervened in labor disputes.

The most common cause of past violent labor disputes was the denial of the right to organize through refusal to recognize the union, frequently associated with the discharge of union leaders. Knowledge of workers' resentment at their inability to join unions encouraged employers to take defensive measures during strikes and lockouts. These measures often included the hiring of guards who, by their provocative behavior, often created the very conditions they had been engaged to minimize.

The melancholy record shows that no section of the United States was free from industrial violence, that its origin and nature were not due to the influence of the immigrant or the frontier, nor did it reflect a darker side of the American character. Labor violence was caused by the attitudes taken by labor and management in response to unresolved disputes. The virtual absence at present of violence in the coal and copper mines, breeding grounds for the more dramatic and tragic episodes, are eloquent testimony that labor violence from the 1870's to the 1930's was essentially shaped by prevailing attitudes on the relations between employer and employee. Once these were changed, a change accomplished partly by legal compulsion, violence was sharply reduced.

Employer Violence. Employers and unions were both guilty of violence. Employer violence frequently had the cover of law. No employer was legally bound to recognize the union of his employees. He has and always had the right to defend his property and maintain free access to the labor and commodity markets. In anticipation of trouble, the employer could call on the community police force, and depending upon size and financial ability, supplement them with protective auxiliaries of his own. Such actions usually had public support, for the employer was exercising a recognized right to self-defense, despite widespread recognition by many public leaders in and out of Government of the desirability, need, and justice of collective bargaining. In the absence of the authority and effective sanctions of protective labor legislation, many employers fought unionism with every weapon at their command, in the certainty that their hostility was both lawful and proper.

Union Violence. Facing inflexible opposition, union leaders and their members frequently found that nothing, neither peaceful persuasion nor the intervention of heads of government, could move the employer towards recognition. Frustration and desperation impelled pickets to react to strikebreakers with anger. Many violent outbreaks followed efforts of strikers to restrain the entry of strikebreakers and raw materials into the struck plant. Such conduct, obviously illegal, opened the opportunity for forceful police measures. In the long run, the employers' side was better equipped for success. The use of force by pickets was illegal on its face, but the action[s] of the police and company guards were in vindication of the employers' rights.

The effect of labor violence was almost always harmful to the union. There is little evidence that violence succeeded in gaining advantages for strikers. Not only does the rollcall of lost strikes confirm such a view, but the use of employer agents, disguised as union members or union officials for advocating violence within the union, testifies to the advantage such practices gave the employer. There were a few situations, in areas made vulnerable by their openness such as a strike in municipal transportation or involving teamsters, where violence was effective in gaining a favorable settlement. Even here, however, such as in the Teamsters' strike in Chicago in 1905, the violence often failed. The most sensational campaigns of the Western Federation of Miners to bring their opponents to heel by the use of force were unsuccessful, and the union was virtually driven out of its stronghold. The campaign of dynamiting of the Iron Workers' Union ended in the conviction of the McNamaras. Subsequent convictions of a number of union leaders, including its president, who were convicted of transporting dynamite and of conspiracy in the Federal courts, almost wrecked the union. The campaign of violence carried on by the molders against the members of the antiunion National Founders Association failed to change the latter's policy.

The right to organize was not retained in Homestead, or won in Pullman, the Colorado metal mines, Coeur d'Alene, or in the steel mills in 1919, although the sacrifice by union members, especially the rank and file members, was great. In fact, the victories gained by violent strikes are rather few, for the use of violence tends to bring about a hardening of attitudes and a weakening of the forces of peace and conciliation. A community might be sympathetic to the demands of strikers, but as soon as violent confrontations took place, the possibility was high that interest would shift from concern for the acceptance of union demands to the stopping of the violence.

It is the violent encounters that have provided organized labor with its lists of martyrs, men and women who gave their lives in defense of the union and collective bargaining. The role of martyrdom is not for us to assay, and may be useful in welding the solidarity of the group. The blood of the martyr may be the seed of the church, but in labor disputes it is doubtful if the sacrifices have been worth the results obtained. The evidence against the effectiveness of violence as a means of gaining concessions by labor in the United States is too overwhelming to be a matter of dispute.

Except for contemporary examples, we have not dealt with the numerous minor disturbances, some of them fairly serious, that were settled by the use of the normal police force. We have also generally avoided the many instances in which organizers and active unionists were denied their right to remain in communities or were the victims of local vigilante groups. We know that union organizers could not enter the closed coal towns, and that labor speakers could neither hire a hall nor speak in a public square in many communities. A number of coal counties in Kentucky and West Virginia built what amounted to an iron wall against the invasion of union organizers. The situation became worse during strikes. In the 1919 steel strike, the mayor of Duquesne, Pa., announced that "Jesus Christ could not hold a meeting in Duquesne," let alone the secretary-treasurer of the American Federation of Labor.

*   *   *

Persistence of Violence. We are, however, confronted with a paradox in that violence in labor disputes persisted even though it seldom achieved fruitful results. With few exceptions, labor violence was the result of isolated and usually unplanned acts on a picket line, or occurred during a prohibited parade or demonstration protesting employer obduracy or police brutality. It might also start by attempts of pickets to prevent the transportation of strikebreakers or goods, and a clash would follow police intervention. Where the employer refused to deal with the union, the possibility of eventual violence was always high. The desire of the American worker for union representation took place in the teeth of employer opposition that was able to impose heavy sanctions for union activity. The reproduction of conditions in which violence is spawned inevitably was followed by outbreaks of violence. Violence could be successfully repressed by superior force but it could not be eliminated until its causes were removed.

The Reduction in Violence. The elimination in 1933 of the most important single cause of violence, refusal to recognize the union for purposes of collective bargaining, came about at the time when union membership was lower than it had been for 15 years. The first step taken was the adoption of section (7)(a) in the National Industrial Recovery Act, which guaranteed workers in industries operating under codes of fair competition the right to organize and bargain collectively through their own representatives. This provision was only partially effective in protecting the right to organize, but it was a significant beginning. Its successor, the National Labor Relations Act, with its amendments, has now been on the books for 33 years, and it is 31 years since it has been upheld by the Supreme Court. The sharp decline in the level of industrial violence is one of the great achievements of the National Labor Relations Board.

It may have been a fortunate coincidence that the labor laws guaranteeing the right to organize were enacted at the time the character of business management was changing. The professional business executive, who has increasingly come to dominate management, is not inclined to regard his business in the same sense as the head of a family-developed firm. He is more flexible in his thinking and more responsive to social and political changes. It may not be an accident that some of the bitterest contemporary labor disputes —Kohler and Perfect Circle, for example—took place in family-held businesses. The professional business leader is more detached, more pragmatic in his reactions, and knows that American business has sufficient resilience to adapt itself to free collective bargaining. The performance of American industry since the end of World War II demonstrates that union organization and collective bargaining are not incompatible with satisfactory profits and a high rate of technological change.

*   *   *

Has widescale violence been permanently erased from American industry? The reduction in violence in labor disputes has been accompanied by sharp increases in violent behavior in other areas of American life. This is no accident. The conditions that gave rise to past labor violence have been eliminated and a restoration of these conditions would lead to a reversion in conduct. Any tampering with the complex mechanism that governs our contemporary labor policy is an invitation towards unharnessing of the forces of violence and hate that we have successfully mastered.

Labor and Other Forms of Violence. Can one draw more general conclusions from the labor experience, or are they peculiar to the problems of workers seeking to establish unions in industry? On many occasions the union operated in a hostile community, while minorities carry on their protests in their own friendly neighborhoods. Nevertheless, in both situations the reaction of the majority is likely to be decisive. There have been times where public sentiment was so strongly on the labor side that no matter what violence it committed, it ran no risk of estranging local public sentiment. Such was the case in Virden and in the far more questionable situation in Herrin. Usually, however, violence led to the alienation of public opinion and sometimes to a shift in public sentiment to approval of severe actions against the strike. The evidence is clear that the absence of violence committed by unions would not have retrieved many lost strikes. However, it appears highly probable that the advocacy or the practice of organized and systematic violence on the union side would have prevented the enactment of the New Deal labor legislation.

There is no evidence that majorities will supinely accept violence by minorities. The fact that rioters are fighting for a just cause or reacting to oppression has not, in the case of labor, led to the condoning of violence by the public. The desirability of collective bargaining had, prior to the 1930's, been endorsed by a number of public bodies and all 20th-century Presidents of the United States. Such views were also sponsored by leading students in the field, legislators, clergymen, and others. Such approval did not save labor from severe repression.

It appears to us that it is a gross confusion of the problem to emphasize the creative character of violence as a guide to the behavior of minorities suffering from serious inequities and injustice. Creative violence obviously refers to the successful revolutions in England, the United States, France, and Russia. It appears to us that such a view is completely irrelevant if it is not vicious and highly misleading. We are concerned not with revolutionary uprisings, which such a view implies, but [with] how a minority can achieve belated justice. Although we believe that minorities can obtain little through violence, we are also convinced, on the basis of labor experience, that violence will continue unless attention is paid to the removal of grievances.

In some respects the violence in the ghettos resembles the kind that surrounded labor disputes; it arises without prior planning and out of isolated instances that may not repeat themselves. It is also highly probable that violence of this kind will be unproductive or even counterproductive, in that it will antagonize many who would normally support the claims of minorities for equal justice and opportunity. Yet the labor analogy with racial minorities can be pushed too far. Labor's grievances were specific and could be met by single or groups of employers with concessions. The adverse effects of granting these concessions were small, injured few people, and employers could generally pass on any added costs to consumers. On the other hand, to the extent that the grievances of minorities are of a general nature and the meeting of their demands impinges upon the privileges of wide sections of the community, the resolution of their disputes is apt to be met with greater opposition.

A Harmony of Beliefs

Edward C. Kirkland

Hazards and Charms of Political Action

Labor had always had an alternative to boycotts and strikes—politics. There was much to recommend it. Some issues—prison-made goods, immigration restriction, child labor—could only be handled by legislation, if at all. Economic pressure against employers could not repeal statutes hampering labor organizations or strike the blinders from the eyes of judges. Politics was a means of action as useful in a falling as in a rising market. It did not call for the men to leave their tools and machines; it simply asked them to go to the ballot box and vote their interests. This had the consecration of being the democratic and the American way. The auguries of success were favorable. As employers were all too well aware, there were more workers than there were managers, and, besides, the former could call on reformers sympathetic to labor's cause. From Massachusetts, where an old pillar of anti-slavery, Wendell Phillips, maintained the momentum of agitation in behalf of labor, to Illinois, where the members of Hull House, a Chicago settlement house, conducted investigations and drew up legislation, such outsiders lent aid.

As in the case of economic pressure, resort to political action involved decisions by the union as to when to act and as to the methods employed. Through logic and pressing necessity, labor came quickly to see that it must aid in the defense of its oppressed members before the courts, especially since judicial decisions concerned larger issues than the fate of individuals at the bar. Such occasional stabs at political action did not involve complex organization; appeals could be made for funds through existing labor journals and through correspondence. Legislation was a more subtle matter, for the simple constitutional right of petition required the maintenance of a lobby. Among other things, this was expensive. Though the National Labor Union demanded a lobby, it was not until the mid-eighties that Powderly was proposing that the Knights set up a lobby in every state capital and in Washington to push labor bills and keep tabs on legislators.

But lobbies faced much the same difficulty as strike pickets; somehow they were more "educative" and "persuasive" when they represented strength and could promise rewards and threaten reprisals. One way to achieve this effectiveness was to vote for trade union members who ran for public office; a second was to vote for the friends and punish the enemies of labor, no matter on what ticket they were running, a procedure quaintly termed non-partisanship. The Knights adopted both these measures. In 1886 the General Assembly resolved: "We will hold responsible at the ballot box all members of Congress who neglect or refuse to vote in compliance" with the Knights' demands. Thirdly labor could go it alone by establishing its own political party or combine with others to do so. The National Labor Union had done this in 1870–1872. At the end of the seventies the Knights of Labor were half way in the Greenback-Labor Party and seemed likely to repeat the commitment in 1886, but the next year Powderly reverted to his fundamental non-partisan stand.

The leaders of the American Federation of Labor and its constituent unions were generally non-political, though they were less vacillating than Powderly and more forceful verbally. In 1885 P. J. McGuire of the Carpenters was expressing his disillusionment with labor legislation. Such laws Democrats and Republicans made to fool the workers, not to be enforced. "We have come to the conclusion that wherever we can help ourselves we will do it, without asking the aid of the Government, and if we want to make a law we will make it in our own trades unions and try to enforce it through them by contracts with our employers." Years later, Samuel Gompers summarized what history had taught him: "An independent labor and progressive movement was inaugurated by the National Labor Union and David Davis of Illinois was nominated for the Presidency in 1872. The National Labor Union never held another convention. It had spent its force; it had nominated a candidate for president."

It required conviction, courage and parliamentary skill for Gompers to keep the Federation on the non-political course, for the Socialist-Labor Party, boring from within the union ranks, sought direct representation at the Federation's meetings and, in the mid-nineties, presented an eleven-point political program introduced with a preamble proposing, as in Great Britain, "the principle of independent labor politics as an auxiliary to their economic action." The depression of 1893 and the hard knocks union organization had taken, as at Homestead, gave the Socialists their chance. In the main battle Gompers put down the insurgents, but at the Denver Convention of 1894 he lost the presidency of the Federation for the only time during his life as labor leader. In Socialist eyes the defeat of their program committed the Federation to an "opportunistic political line." Such episodes also convinced believers in pure and simple trade unionism that association with reformers was not a one-way street.

While such evidence would seem to demonstrate that the conspicuous national organizations were moving from political to industrial weapons, other labor groupings provide evidence for a contrary conclusion. Since the structure of American political action was not corporate but geographical, political activity by organized labor naturally clustered about organizations on a geographical basis, state or urban aggregations. Since urban labor unions were apt to embrace more foreign or Socialist members, their influence helped to push central labor unions along the path of politics. Thus in New York City the call for the establishment of the Central Labor Union was issued in 1881 by a member of a Socialist local assembly of the Knights of Labor, and the Central's Declaration of Principles re-echoed Socialist slogans about the class struggle and the desirability of political action. Its constitution included the precautionary provisions that the union should have no permanent president lest he "sell out the union to any political party" and no public official or lawyer could be a delegate to the union. By 1886 the Central Labor Union was debating in an abstract fashion whether labor should take independent political action or try to swing its followers from party to party in a balance-of-power policy.

A famous boycott case in New York City in which the judge sentenced the boycotters to Sing Sing for "extortion" (they had collected $1,000 from the employer through arbitration) gave urgency to a program of participation in politics and seemed to reenforce the necessity of independent political action. Through a series of accommodations, the Central Labor Union nominated the single tax reformer, Henry George, for mayor. The Democrats under Tammany Hall nominated Abram S. Hewitt, the philanthropist employer, and the Republicans, young Theodore Roosevelt. The excitement of the campaign and the criticalness of the issue so infected the high command of labor that Terence Powderly and Samuel Gompers spoke and worked for Henry George. Hewitt won, George was second, Roosevelt third. On their roles as participants, both Powderly and Gompers had sober second thoughts. The former wrote of 1887, "I am glad I didn't talk [for George] this year," and the latter characterized the 1886 campaign as "this curious determination to disregard experience."

The New York campaign of 1886 did not have to surmount all the customary handicaps to labor's political action. The George candidacy had a campaign chest, an ad hoc journal, a roster of speakers and a force of volunteer workers. But it collided with some powerful advantages of the established parties. This was a period of intense political loyalties, partly inherited from the Civil War days; the habit of independent voting was not widespread. Nor were all political issues aligned along the axis of the labor-capital controversy. Workers were citizens and party members before they were workers. Politics, like religion, was a divisive factor and astute labor leaders tried to keep it out of the labor organizations. That was why lawyers were not allowed in the Knights of Labor. This was a period when politics became a business, the period of the machine. Neither a successful lobby nor a third party could be improvised; politics required full-time, sophisticated attention, and labor leaders in politics were part-time amateurs who lacked know-how and staying power. Curiously enough their political ideology reflected that of the employers. Politics was dishonest, a dirty business. The labor union cause, like private business enterprise, became a sort of holy grail, above or beyond politics. Furthermore, like their business counterparts, some union leaders thought government action was really futile and wrong. P. J. McGuire affirmed, "I believe the Government had better keep its hands off private business as much as possible."

Labor Legislation

Although labor legislation in extent and enforcement fell short of the expectations of the more hopeful, the record was not one of absolute failure. At the end of the century an agent of the Industrial Commission surveyed the status of protective legislation. Just over half the states had legislation prohibiting the labor of children in factories; the age limitation was ordinarily fourteen but some additional years were added if the children lacked education. The states which did not have child labor laws were generally in the trans-Mississippi West or in the South. Nearly every Eastern state had passed legislation regulating the hours of labor for women and minors of both sexes in factories and mercantile establishments. The general limitation was to ten hours a day and sixty hours a week, though Massachusetts had a fifty-eight hour week and Wisconsin a forty-eight. About half the states had factory acts, so called after the great English factory act of 1831, enforcing certain standards of safety and sanitation in factories and sometimes other establishments. There were almost no factory acts in the South or beyond the Mississippi. In the chief industrial states of the East and Midwest there were generally laws providing for the licensing, inspection and, in Pennsylvania, the prohibition of sweatshops. Such establishments usually produced clothing, artificial flowers, and cigars in tenements or houses. Practically all the states "in which mines of any character are located" had mining laws providing for mining inspectors to see that operators obeyed provisions for escape shafts, ventilation, safety lamps, and for care in carrying and hoisting products and personnel and in handling explosives. Laws on the statute books were not self-enforcing and much of this legislation perforce dealt with definitions and details of administration.

That the trans-Mississippi West in general stood aloof from this movement was due to its agricultural preoccupations; that the South did so was due, in part, to its desire to establish industries and not handicap their advance. In truth, the cutthroat competition among states for industrial growth was one reason for the general slowness in passing this legislation and laxness in enforcing it. The difficulty of securing uniform legislation, where the central government had limited powers within a federal system, exasperated both employers and employees, and, among other things, explained the latter's disillusionment with political activity.

Some ascribed the movement for legislation to employers or to government officials, such as commissioners of statistics for labor, who had come to look upon themselves as the guardians of labor's interests. Others, like McNeill of Massachusetts, felt that the "initiative" for such legislation came "in every instance" from labor men. More commonly the state of mind of the community was felt to be responsible. "I do not believe Massachusetts would have accomplished what she has done in the way of factory legislation unless there had been enough sense of justice in the leisure class and the educated class to uphold the work of the workingman, and not only uphold it but aid it actively." As usual Gompers had the common sense of the matter: "What is everybody's business is nobody's business, and organized labor makes it its business and then has the sympathy of the general public to come in and aid."

The Value of Labor

Whether wrung at first instance from employers or realized at second hand in legislation, the program of organized labor took off from certain assumptions. Perhaps these are best summarized in the bald assertion of the Grand Secretary of the Knights of Labor: "We know we have produced the wealth." The theory that labor was the source of all value was as commonplace with the Federation of Labor as it was with the Knights. It followed that unions were concerned with attaining an acknowledgment of labor's nobility and dignity by community and employer. The reason the Central Labor Union of New York advocated in 1882 an annual Labor Day distinct from other national holidays was that labor alone had no day which it could call its own. Though at least one employer thought this holiday hardly attained its lofty objectives ("drunken rabble, harvest for saloon keepers"), its implied tribute to work certainly ought to have won popular sympathy in a generation which worshipped work and suspected leisure. It did. In 1893 the committee of the Senate investigating Homestead casually remarked in an obiter dictum: "It should not be forgotten that labor is the source of all wealth."

Even wider approval might have been forthcoming if labor's thoughts about its own value had been somewhat less exclusive and somewhat less oblivious of other factors in the productive process. Labor on the whole grudgingly allowed capital a place. After all, capital was "the fruit of labor" and interest "may probably be right." Labor's blind spot was management.

"Do not let the man who has no money hire capital to build the factory and to buy the raw material, and pay interest on that money, and then hire money to pay his labor, and make a profit above all that, and hire a superintendent at a good salary to manage the business, and be himself one of the lords of the land—so-called." Paradoxically Gompers preferred the capitalist with an inherited status to the self-made man. It was the fortunes of this latter group—Jay Gould was usually the example—that seemed to be made by some dishonesty or magic; they could not be accounted for by "the natural increase of capital." Parasitic employers should "go into a workshop and earn an honest living instead of undertaking to make money from nothing, absolutely nothing."

The Wages System

No specific phase of labor union policy was more interpenetrated by the theory that labor created all wealth than was wages; for "the wage question is the labor question." At first organized labor hoped to avoid the complexities, injustice, and industrial strife engendered by the wages system. They would abolish it. In his own Moulders' Union and in the National Labor Union William Sylvis became the prophet of producers' cooperation. The moulders would build and operate their own factories and divide all the returns, be they profits or wages. Ultimately such cooperation would end poverty and elevate the workers spiritually and morally. This did not mean that producers' cooperation had solely an idealistic motive; in periods of business depression or after strikes had failed, producers' cooperatives served the practical end of putting people to work.

From time to time the Knights of Labor were enthusiastic over cooperation. In 1885 its Grand Secretary, for instance, was rather impatient with his unions' concern with wages. This was a mere short-time matter "while we remain wage workers." Instead the Knights desired to solve the problem of just distribution "by going into business for ourselves, contributing our own money, and starting a business of our own." Uriah Stephens, like Sylvis, was a zealot for cooperation, and Terence V. Powderly in his first annual address to the General Assembly in 1880 summoned the Knights to abolish the wage system and embark upon a crusade for cooperation "which will eventually make every man his own master—every man his own employer; a system which will give the laborer a fair proportion of the products of his toil. . . . There is no good reason why labor cannot, through cooperation, own and operate mines, factories and railroads." There were always some among the Knights who dragged their feet on this issue; and by the end of the eighties the Order was retreating on this front as on most others.

Though, as a central organization, the Knights of Labor undertook but one cooperative enterprise, a coal mine, its constituent assemblies or trades embarked upon several experiments. Their number in the mid-eighties may have reached 135. They were most numerous in mining, coopering, and shoe-making, occupations in which individual skill continued to play a considerable part. Most cooperative ventures were small, the average amount of investment per establishment being $10,000. Most cooperatives failed, and those that did not assumed an organizational form far from flawless. The original investors among the workingmen became a directoral élite interested in profits; they employed other workers at wages, sometimes low ones, and they cut the price of their products to compete with unionized rivals. Surveying these failures and deviations, one observer came to the conclusion that they were due to the effort "to get rid of the *entrepreneur* or manager." In spite of labor's blind spot on this score, managerial talent was necessary and it was rare.

Few experiments by organized labor have stirred so much interest as pro-ducers' cooperation and won so much approval, particularly among intellec-tuals. At one extreme E. L. Godkin of the *Nation* beat the drum for cooperation with the zeal of a Sylvis or a Stephens, and for much the same reasons. At the other extreme a group of reformers like R. T. Ely and E. W. Bemis, for whom Godkin would have had only contempt, undertook a study of cooperative enterprises on a regional basis. According to R. T. Ely, who wrote an introduction for the essays published by the *Johns Hopkins Studies in Historical and Political Science*, the investigators found more significant examples of cooperation in the United States than in England and demon-strated that one of

the prime conditions of success of cooperation is moral integrity of the coopera-tors. The cause of failure is more frequently ethical than intellectual weakness. This is true of all popular movements and for the mass of men. . . . Christ uttered a scientific truth, confirmed by every careful and intelligent observation of economic phenomena when he said, "Seek ye first the kingdom of God and His righteousness, and all these things [economic goods] shall be added unto you."

The practical men heading the A.F. of L. who had to face the day-to-day problems of labor while expecting that "ultimately" after the passage of ages workers would become their own capitalists and their own employers, in general accepted the wage system and sought to make the best of it rather than to escape to utopia on the installment plan. Since they still adhered to the labor theory of value, they naturally thought labor should have a "prior" claim to the results of the wealth-producing process and that wages should not be determined by profits or dividends. Employers who could not make a profit and pay workers their rightful share should be driven out of industry by the stern rule of the survival of the fittest. As to the proper share for workers, labor leaders were apt to resort to generalities: it should be "just" and "reasonable" and "fair." Since these terms, however useful as slogans, were not self-defining, labor leaders advanced equivalents: a "living" wage, a "decent" wage, enough "to live comfortably." To objectives, so stated, few could take exception; they were, however, a sort of time bomb planted beneath the wage policy of employers. Organized labor, for instance, was not greatly interested in real wages. Their conclusion that cheap goods meant cheap labor revealed a distaste for tying wages to the cost of living. "I believe in high wages and high prices for commodities. . . . When a man has good wages he can save something even if prices are high." Organized labor looked forward to a wage level which would give them a surplus above mere living.

Another complaint of employers was that the unions hoped to set all workers' wages at a uniform standard and thus hampered the paying of wages based on differences in skill and industry. Although Gompers acknowledged that he preferred time to piecework for its "excellence and perfection," he nonetheless felt that superior workers should and would get higher wages. All the union insisted upon was the "life-line" of a minimum wage. Actually the search for definitively just wages has the static quality of most formulas. The economy was dynamic; labor's wage theory was fluid and pragmatic. Said Gompers: "I know we are living under the wage system, and so long as that lasts, it is our purpose to secure a continually larger share for labor, for the wealth producers. Whether the time shall come, as this constantly increasing share to labor goes on, when profits shall be entirely eliminated, and the full product of labor, the net result of production, go to the laborer . . . I am perfectly willing that the future shall determine and work out."

The Eight-Hour Day

While labor's wage policy was for more and more, its policy on hours was for less and less. On this question, to an exceptional degree in labor history, the unions operated on the basis of a thought-out creed, which, coming early in the period, resembled a theological doctrine. In the sixties, Ira Stewart, a self-educated machinist of Boston, began propagandizing the advantages of the eight-hour day. This was daring, for two decades later at least one manufacturer thought "ten hours a day is about right for a day's labor." Stewart's visionary concept went further than a minor improvement in the status quo. He felt that the workers, having attained greater leisure, would look around and see how others spent it—even the exhibitionist expenditures of the rich had utility—and thus develop their own cultural and social interests. As a result of their uplifted status, they would demand higher wages. As Stewart's wife, an able woman, put it in a jingle:

> Whether you work by the piece or work by the day
> Decreasing the hours increases your pay.

When workers had wants and the means to satisfy them, there would be an end to the underconsumption responsible for unemployment and for business depression. The shortening of the work day need not reduce production, for improved methods and machinery would compensate.

While these happy outcomes might appeal to employers, Steward's further inference that eventually his system would so erode profits that the glory of the cooperative commonwealth would come in could hardly reassure them. Quite clearly Stewart's ideas, like those of Henry George and Edward Bellamy, involved a new order of society. Luckily they had the advantage of combining a short-range objective and a long-range cure-all. The latter, like most panaceas, was almost too easy and automatic. Since the shortened day fitted in with reformist optimism, with the efforts of practical men to cope with the unemployment of depression, and with the natural human desire to cut down hours of labor, the eight-hour program in one gloss or another colored the thinking of labor organizations for decades. Originally workers expected to realize the program through agitation and legislation. The diversity of state jurisdictions and the consequent fear in each state lest producers in another get an advantage pointed to the desirability of Congressional legislation. Nearly everyone agreed, however, that the Constitution had given the central government no power directly to regulate hours in private industry.

Within the limited area of its own workers, Federal legislation was possible. In 1868 a Federal statute declared, "That eight hours shall constitute a day's work for all laborers, workmen, and mechanics now employed . . . by or on behalf of the government of the United States." For this measure it is hard to unearth any immediate political explanation. The National Labor Union under William Sylvis had made the eight-hour day an important part of its program, and on its behalf Sylvis and others lobbied with the President and with Congress. A Senator also acknowledged that the "experiment" had "been discussed before the country." Perhaps a stronger wave than usual in the ebb tide of Civil War reform carried the measure to safety on the beach. However murky the background, the act naturally aroused expectations, for the phrasing was explicit and it covered wage earners in private establishments working under government contracts. These factors, along with the example of the nation as a "model employer," could have had great weight. Actually administrative officials and the courts made the act a nullity. They held it was directive and not mandatory, that wages would have to be reduced with a reduction of hours. Workers had little choice but to continue under previous stipulations.

This experience, along with their general hesitancy about politics, turned organized labor to the alternative weapon of economic pressure. It had always been their chief means against private employers. General campaigns for the eight-hour day, as contrasted with sporadic demands in particular establishments or occupations, were waged on an urban basis, for instance in New York City in 1872, but the national movement for the same purpose waited until the mid-eighties. Even then there was an atmosphere of the accidental about the drive. That stumbling forerunner of the A.F. of L., the Federation of Organized Trades and Labor Unions, in order to recoup its waning strength resolved in 1884, "that eight hours shall constitute a legal day's labor from and after May 1, 1886, and that we recommend to labor organizations throughout this jurisdiction that they so direct their laws as to conform to this resolution by the time named." Persuasion or the threat of action or a general strike might bring employers to compliance.

The resolution did not necessarily enlist the support of the larger and rival Knights of Labor. Although the course of Powderly and other leaders was certainly equivocal, the membership of the Knights, according to the evidence, was enthusiastic for the eight-hour drive. Thus, as it turned out, there was a widespread rank-and-file support for action. Politicians and even a portion of the press gave approval. The momentum thus generated carried furthest in metropolitan areas. Even before the date set workers were striking for and securing a shorter day's work. Chicago, with 80,000 participants and strikers, mounted the biggest drive. Then the Haymarket episode, as we have seen, shattered the movement. In the nineties the American Federation of Labor attempted to put together again the pieces of the eight-hour philosophy but in a different frame. Such constituent unions as were eager for a reduction of hours and well-heeled enough to undertake a strike were to be backed by the Federation and financially supported by it. A series of galloping strikes would thus attain eight hours for organized workers. This tactic met with both success and failure, but by the end of the century the Federation discarded even this effort. Though the movement had shortened hours, it had not attained, except in special instances, the eight-hour optimum. To Gompers the issue in 1901 was still a "burning" one, and for reasons which Ira Stewart would have commended.

A Harmony of Beliefs

We have noted that the philosophy of labor frequently resembled that of managers and employers. A belief in natural law and in practical measures are cases in point. Also labor tended to accept the values of the society about it and wished simply to share in them more generously. Nor was there much divergence in group attitudes over the fundamentals of the economic order or the features currently attending its hasty and disturbing development. For labor as for capital, production was a goal; the former relished the fact that "we are producing wealth to-day at a greater ratio than ever in the history of mankind."

One means to this end was machinery, and labor, instead of smashing machines, admired the inventive genius which created them and advocated their introduction. The eight-hour day program was postulated upon the introduction of machinery which would, in spite of fewer hours, maintain production. Labor's complaint was that it did not get its share of the advantages of machinery. The solution, most often commended for its ideology and ingenuity, was the one the International Typographical Union followed when the Mergenthaler linotype machine threatened in 1887 and after to destroy the old-fashioned type-setting by hand. The president of the International Union shrewdly observed, "Those familiar with the productiveness of machines are agreed that hand work cannot begin to compete with them, and it is therefore futile to attempt to stay the tide of their introduction." The union accepted the machine. However, by its insistence that they be operated by already skilled operatives it prevented extensive technological unemployment and it used the productiveness of the machines to facilitate a shorter working day. The union also insisted on a minimum wage. For the industrial picture as a whole Gompers was explicit: "In the great race for the production of wealth we do not want to go back to the primitive methods; no sane man wants that."

The collective action of the labor union was, according to its leaders, an evolution in response to circumstance. Were they able to apply a similarly benevolent judgment to parallel developments—the business combination, big business, the trust? Hostility to the trust on the part of the Knights smacked more of agrarian than industrial criticism. Gompers was unwilling to embark upon a "general proposition." "We view the trust from the standpoint that they are our employers, and the employer who is fair to us, whether an individual, or a collection of individuals, an aggregation of individuals in the form of a corporation or a trust, matters little to us so long as we obtain the fair conditions." The general opinion of labor leaders added up to a tentative willingness to tolerate combinations, for the latter seemed to hold out the promise of more stable wages, a better guarantee of continuous work, and also an easier way to establish common conditions of labor than by dealing with hosts of small competitors. On the asserted lowering of prices by big business, Gompers pointed out labor was not greatly interested in this accomplishment—"I am not a cheap man, anyway"—and that prices tended to decline largely because of mechanization. He did fear that trusts had a tendency and ability "to prevent the will of the people by buying up legislators." As for trust policy, the government had better leave combinations alone, for the "State is not capable of preventing development or natural concentration of industry." Instead of regulating business, the Interstate Commerce Act and the Sherman Anti-Trust Act had been turned against labor to deprive it "of the benefit of organized effort."

When anti-business statutes were dismissed as "panaceas" by labor's spokesmen, it was unlikely that its high command would be enthusiastic over proposals seriously challenging an owner's right to manage his property. The cooperative enthusiasms of the Knights contained no threat of confiscation nor idea of government direction. Within the A.F. of L. an energetic socialist minority differed from the officers on the fundamental issue of private enterprise. In the nineties this faction sponsored a program calling for the municipal ownership of public utilities, the nationalization of telegraphs, telephones, railroads and mines, and the "collective ownership by the people of all means of production and distribution." Against this last proposal, article 10, Gompers and his allies fought with skill, determination and success. After the failure of the A.F. of L. to endorse public ownership, socialist influence fell off. Perhaps no point illustrated better the tolerance of the unions for private enterprise than the consistent refusal of their leaders to count among its failures the panics and depressions of these years. "I think that panics come, not through those men's [employers'] idiocy or incompetency, but are attributable to causes not generally understood."

Since the expressed thought of the leaders of organized labor was at bottom conservative and empirical and becoming more so and treasured the same scheme of values as did ownership-management, it would seem that the latter group might well vouchsafe the dearly-sought recognition the former strove for. Increasingly it did. Every great labor crisis, which in theory should have closed the ranks of employers, produced at least one capitalist of purest ray serene with courage and insight enough to look beyond doctrinaire partisanship. After the great railroad strikes of the seventies, culminating in the destructive Pittsburgh rioting of 1877, Congress investigated the alarming situation. The chairman of the committee was Abram S. Hewitt, a Representative and a noted ironmaster. In 1878 Hewitt was observing in an address,

A new power has entered into the industrial world, which must be recognized. . . . It must be heard. Its just demands must be heeded. . . . The great result achieved is that capital is ready to discuss. It is not to be disguised that till labor presented itself in such an attitude as to compel a hearing capital was unwilling to listen; but now it does listen. The results already attained are full of encouragement.

Again after Haymarket, when the air quivered with hysteria, Andrew Carnegie cut down the danger of revolution to pygmy size, and concluded: "The right of the working-men to combine and to form trades-unions is no less sacred than the right of the manufacturer to enter into associations and conferences with his fellows, and it must be sooner or later conceded. . . . My experience has been that trades-unions upon the whole are beneficial both to labor and to capital." Carnegie went so far as to doubt the wisdom of the conventional belief that an employer should hire strikebreakers. And in the labor disturbances of the 1890's, Marcus Alonzo Hanna derided the philanthropic façade of the town of Pullman and exploded: "A man who won't meet his men half-way is a God-damn fool!" The suspicion that Hanna only inferentially advocated union recognition soon vanished when he became the chief participant in the efforts of the National Civic Federation, whose members included labor leaders and capitalists, to abate industrial conflict by persuasion and mediation. And it was practical men in "the upper" and "lower classes," not economists, who led the way to the acceptance of unionism. At least that would seem to be the gravamen of an address delivered in 1888 to his fellow economists by their president, Francis A. Walker.

In truth, it is as misleading to write the history of labor between 1860 and 1900 in terms of labor upheavals or uprisings as it is to detect in every local breakdown of orderly development the pattern of a general strike or any other form of proto-revolutionary action. This was a period when the immense productive powers of the country were in transition from one system to another. The great problem was adjustment. Some turbulence was bound to attend the search for answers to the questions of what was fair and just and to the even more searching query of what was feasible and possible. That labor did not crystallize into a permanent party of discontent, nor come to regard itself as a group apart from the community with no responsibility for the common welfare, was a tribute to the discernment, foresight and flexibility of both labor and capital.

Labor and Capitalism
in America

Selig Perlman

The most distinctive characteristic of the development of the labor movement in America has not been, as in Germany, a slow but certain shedding
of the philosophy originally imparted by an intellectual leadership. No intellectuals, in the true sense of the word, presided at its birth. The main feature
of its development has been rather a perpetual struggle to keep the organization from going to pieces for want of inner cohesiveness. For, it has had to
cope with two disruptive tendencies: First, American labor has always been
prone, though far more in the past than now, to identify itself in outlook, interest, and action, with the great lower middle class, the farmers, the small
manufacturers and business men, in a word, with the "producing classes" and
their periodic "anti-monopoly" campaigns. Second, and here is a tendency of
a rising rather than diminishing potency, the American employer has, in general, been able to keep his employees contented with the conditions, determined by himself, on which they individually accepted employment. Both
these tendencies have seriously hindered the efforts of trade unionism towards
stability and solidarity. The first tendency proved inimical because the organized wage earners would periodically be drawn into the whirlpool of politics
under the banner of the "anti-monopoly" parties, so, under the American system of party politics, invariably suffering dissension, and ultimately disintegration. The second of the tendencies mentioned has balked unionism because
the employer, wielding the initiative, has been able successfully to carry his
own individualistic competitive spirit into the ranks of his employees. Moreover, both factors making for disintegration go back to a common cause. For

whether the labor organization has succumbed to the lure of a political reform movement aiming to shield the "small man" and the "man on the make," and has broken up in political dissension; or whether it has failed to get started because the individual laborer has accepted the incentive of a bonus wage and of a better opportunity for advancement within the framework of a non-union bargain, the ultimate explanation, at all events, lies in the basic conditions of life in the American community—economic, political, ethnic, mental, and spiritual. Some of these are a heritage from the past, others of more recent origin, but all are closely interwoven with the present and the future of American labor.

The Basic Characteristics of the American Community

1. The Strength of the Institution of Private Property. A labor movement must, from its very nature, be an organized campaign against the rights of private property, even where it stops short of embracing a radical program seeking the elimination, gradual or abrupt, "constitutional" or violent, of the private entrepreneur. When this campaign takes the political and legislative route, it leads to the denial of the employer's right to absolute control of his productive property. It demands and secures regulatory restrictions which, under American constitutional practice, are within the province of the "police power" vested in the states and granted by specific authority to Congress; only they must, in every case, square with "public purpose," as that term is interpreted in the last analysis by the United States Supreme Court. When the same campaign follows the economic route, the route of unionism, strikes, boycotts, and union "working rules," the restrictions on the rights of property are usually even more thoroughgoing and far-reaching, since unions are less amenable to judicial control than are legislatures and Congress. A third form of the labor movement seeks to promote cooperative production and distribution, neither of which is practiced appreciably in this country. This co-operative movement sets out to beat private capitalism by the methods of private business: greater efficiency and superior competitive power. To the advocates of the rights of private property, this third mode of the labor movement is the least offensive.

Because the labor movement in any form is a campaign against the absolute rights of private property, the extent to which the institution of private property is intrenched in the community in which a labor movement operates is of overwhelming importance to it. . . .

The enormous strength of private property in America, at once obvious to any observer, goes back to the all-important fact that, by and large, this country was occupied and settled by laboring pioneers, creating property for themselves as they went along and holding it in small parcels. This was the way not only of agriculture but also of the mechanical trades and of the larger scale industries. Thus the harmony between the self-interest of the individual pursuing his private economic aim and the general public interest proved a real and lasting harmony in the American colonies and states. This Adam Smith saw in 1776, his eye on the frugal and industrious class of masters of workshops still on the threshold of their elevation by the industrial revolution yet to come. Every addition to the total of the privately held wealth was at the same time an addition to the productive equipment in the community, which meant a fuller satisfaction of its wants and a higher level of the general welfare. Moreover, being held in small parcels, wealth was generally accessible to whomever would pay the price in industry, frugality, and ingenuity. Furthermore, this condition had not been destroyed even with the coming in of modern "big business," combinations, mergers, and "trusts." For, too often does the grandeur of business on its modern gigantic scale, the magnitude of billion dollar corporations completely hide from one's view those other millions of small businesses. These, here and now, may be forced to struggle hard for existence, perhaps only to fail in the end. But failing, still others will take their place and continue to form a social layer firm enough to safeguard against even a possible revolutionary explosion from below. The earnestness with which judges will rush to stand between legislatures and menaced property rights; the rigor of their application of the injunction to keep unionists and strikers from interfering with those rights in their own way; the ease with which a typically American middle-class community may work itself up, or be worked up, into an anti-radical hysteria, when Soviet missionaries or syndicalist agitators are rumored to be abroad in the land; and the flocking to the election polls of millions to vote for the "safe" candidate—all are of one piece, and are to be explained by the way in which the American community originated and grew.

This social and economic conservatism, bred in the American community from the beginning, has been tested repeatedly by sections of the American labor movement, now wittingly, now unwittingly, and invariably the test has evoked the same and identical reaction. It began in 1829, when the Workingman's Party of New York, moved by the desire to frighten employers lest they add to the recently won ten-hour day, officially endorsed the crude communistic "Equal Division" program of Thomas Skidmore. A whole generation had to pass before the recollection of this brief indiscretion had faded from the public memory and ceased to plague the labor movement. Another such test of the public mind was the unplanned, but virtual anarchy of the destructive great railway strikes of 1877, from Baltimore to San Francisco. It was then that the judiciary, watching the paralysis which had seized the democratically chosen sheriffs and governors, and remembering well the Commune of Paris of 1871, resolved to insure society against a labor revolution by dint of the injunction, the outlawing of the boycott, and like measures. Nine years later, the Chicago "Anarchists," with a full-blown program of revolutionary syndicalism in all but the name itself, were made to feel the ferocious self-defense of a gigantically growing and self-satisfied community against those who would import the methods of the class struggle of Russia and of Spain. Still later, in the Pullman strike of 1894, the labor movement saw how the courts, the Federal Executive, and the ruling forces in the country could be counted on to act as one in crushing any real or fancied industrial rebellion. The treatment of the Industrial Workers of the World in the Western States, the anti-"Red" hysteria of 1919 and 1920, and the great godsend which the syndicalist past of William Z. Foster proved to the employers in defeating the great steel strike in 1919, which he led, are of too recent occurrence to necessitate detailed discussion. The state of Kansas, a representative American farming and middle-class community, furnishes perhaps the most telling illustration of the typical American reaction to industrial radicalism. That state, which was in 1912 a stamping ground for Roosevelt progressivism, just as it had been the heart of the "Populism" of the nineties, showed no hesitancy, in 1919, when the coal miners' strike had endangered the comfort of its citizenry, at enacting a law depriving of the right to strike, labor in public utilities and in other industries supplying food, fuel, and clothing, which the law classed as public utilities for that purpose.

Briefly, if the century-long experience of American labor as an organized movement holds any great lesson at all, that lesson is that under no circumstances can labor here afford to arouse the fears of the great middle class for the safety of private property as a basic institution. Labor needs the support of public opinion, meaning the middle class, both rural and urban, in order to make headway with its program of curtailing, by legislation and by trade unionism, the abuses which attend the employer's unrestricted exercise of his property rights. But any suspicion that labor might harbor a design to do away altogether with private property, instead of merely regulating its use, immediately throws the public into an alliance with the anti-union employers. . . .

2. *The Lack of a Class Consciousness in American Labor.* The overshadowing problem of the American labor movement has always been the problem of staying organized. No other labor movement has ever had to contend with the fragility so characteristic of American labor organizations. In the main, this fragility of the organization has come from the lack of class cohesiveness in American labor. . . .

The cause of this lack of psychological cohesiveness in American labor is the absence, by and large, of a completely "settled" wage earning class. Sons of wage earners will automatically follow their fathers' occupations in the mining districts, which, because of their isolation, are little worlds in themselves. The Negroes in industry are, of course, a hereditary wage earning group. And apparently such a class has developed also in the textile centers. To be sure, the great mass of the wage earners in American industry today, unless they have come from the farm intending to return there with a part of their wages saved, will die wage earners. However, many of these do not stay in a given industry for life, but keep moving from industry to industry and from locality to locality, in search for better working conditions. Moreover, the bright son of a mechanic and factory hand, whether of native or immigrant parentage, need not despair, with the training which the public schools give him free of charge and with whatever else he may pick up, of finding his way to this or that one of the thousand and one selling "lines" which pay on the commission basis; or, if his ambition and his luck go hand in hand, of attaining to some one of the equally numerous kinds of small businesses, or, finally, of the many minor supervisory positions in the large manufacturing establishments, which are constantly on the lookout for persons in the ranks suitable for promotion. It is, therefore, a mistake to assume that, with the exhaustion of the supply of free public land, the wage earner who is above the average in ambition and ability, or at least his children, if they are equally endowed (and the children's opportunities color the parents' attitude no less than do their own), have become cooped up for good in the class of factory operatives. For today, the alternative opportunities to being a lowly factory hand are certainly more varied and entail less hardship than the old opportunity of "homesteading" in the West and "growing up with the country."

But, in a sense, the opportunity of the "West" has never ceased. In this vast country, several historical industrial stages are found existing side by side, though in demarcated areas. There is, therefore, the opportunity to migrate from older to newer and less developed sections, in which a person without much or any inherited property may still find the race for economic independence a free and open race. The difference between a section in the United States which is still underdeveloped economically and a similar one in a European country, is the difference between a navigable stream with some obstacles in its bed still waiting to be removed, and a stagnant pool without an outlet. In the former, opportunities are plentiful, multipliable by effort, and only waiting to be exploited; in the latter, the few extant opportunities are jealously monopolized by their incumbents.

If the characteristically American fluidity of economic society has preserved and created opportunities for the non-propertied individual of not much more than average ability, those with a higher ability and a gift for leadership have found their upward progression smoother still. Participation in political life in America has never been reserved to the upper classes, as until recently in England, nor to those with a higher education, as in France, but is open to all who can master the game. In the past, before the trade unions became stabilized, capable of holding both their leaders and their membership, considerable leadership material drained away from labor into politics. However, at that time industry had not yet come to appreciate the "political" talent of handling men as a valuable business asset. But in the present era of "personnel management" and "industrial relations" departments, of "Welfare capitalism," and of efficiency by "inducement" and "leadership," there is room for that sort of talent, at least in the largest establishments. For the present, businessmen look to college trained men to fill these positions. But it is not at all precluded that what otherwise might have been union leadership talent, is being drawn into this sort of activity.

Another cause of the lack of "class-consciousness" in American labor was the free gift of the ballot which came to labor at an early date as a by-product of the Jeffersonian democratic movement. In other countries, where the labor movement started while the workingmen were still denied the franchise, there was in the last analysis no need of a theory of "surplus value" to convince them that they were a class apart and should therefore be "class conscious." There ran a line like a red thread between the laboring class and the other classes. Not so, where that line is only an economic one. Such a line becomes blurred by the constant process of "osmosis" between one economic class and another, by fluctuations in relative bargaining power of employer and employee with changes in the business cycle, and by other changing conditions.

Next to the abundant economic opportunities available to wage earners in this country, and to their children, immigration has been the factor most guilty of the incohesiveness of American labor. To workers employed in a given industry, a new wave of immigrants, generally of a new nationality, meant a competitive menace to be fought off and to be kept out of that industry. For, by the worker's job consciousness, the strongest animosity was felt not for the employer who had initiated or stimulated the new immigrant wave, but for the immigrants who came and took the jobs away. When immigrants of a particular nationality acquired higher standards and began rebuilding the unions which they destroyed at their coming, then a new nationality would arrive to do unto the former what these had done unto the original membership. The restriction of immigration by the quota system has at last done away with this phenomenon, which formerly used to occur and recur with an inevitable regularity.

American labor remains the most heterogeneous laboring class in existence—ethnically, linguistically, religiously, and culturally. With a working class of such a composition, to make socialism or communism the official "ism" of the movement, would mean, even if the other conditions permitted it, deliberately driving the Catholics, who are perhaps in the majority in the American Federation of Labor, out of the labor movement, since with them an irreconcilable opposition to socialism is a matter of religious principle. Consequently the only acceptable "consciousness" for American labor as a whole is a "job consciousness," with a "limited" objective of "wage and job control"; which not at all hinders American unionism from being the most "hard hitting" unionism in any country. Individual unions may, however, adopt whatever "consciousness" they wish. Also the solidarity of American labor is a solidarity with a quickly diminishing potency as one passes from the craft group,—which looks upon the jobs in the craft as its common property for which it is ready to fight long and bitterly,—to the widening concentric circles of the related crafts, the industry, the American Federation of Labor, and the world labor movement. . . .

. . . The future builders of the American Federation of Labor, like Strasser and Gompers of the Cigar Makers and McGuire of the Carpenters, studied the labor question both theoretically and experimentally. They studied Marx and the other European socialists, but they were also constantly testing to see what appeals were "taking" with the workingmen so that they came in as permanent members, and what appeals had only an ephemeral effect. It was in this unusual school, in which theory was mixed with direct experience, that they discovered that the union card was the only real bond that held wage earners together, not politics, whether "greenback" or socialist. They found that a labor movement became proof against disintegration only when it was built around the job. These discoveries did not at first estrange them from socialism as a program for the future. But as time went on and they became engrossed in their "job unionism," which eschewed politics and every other quick social panacea; as they watched their organizations grow from nothing to something like the large and stable British "Amalgamated" unions, from which the International Cigar Makers' Union, reorganized by Strasser and Gompers, copied its comprehensive benefit features and centralized financial management; and as they observed with pride how their organizations, small though they still were, held together and grew steadily, in defiance of the alternating tides in business conditions so fatal to the labor organizations which had preceded theirs; then the original socialistic class-consciousness of these "philosophers-organizers" gradually paled if not shriveled, and in its place flourished a robust trade unionist "job and wage consciousness."

It was indeed a new species of trade unionism that was thus evolved. It differed from the trade unionism that the native American labor movement had evolved earlier, in that it grasped the idea, supremely correct for American conditions, that the economic front was the only front on which the labor army could stay united. From this it followed that when a business depression or a powerful combination of employers made the chances for advance on that front unlikely for the time being, the correct strategy was not, as the unions before them had done, to shift the main strength to the political front, because that front seemed weakly held by the enemy. On the contrary, this unionism reasoned that, during depression, labor's strategy should be thoroughly to dig in on the same economic front, awaiting the next opportunity, which was certain to come, for advancing further; in the meantime using every device, like benefit features, to keep the membership from dropping out. For the American labor movement, which, during the first half century of its existence, had been doing exactly the opposite, that is, abandoning trade unionism for the lure and excitement of "anti-monopoly" politics, this discovery was as pivotal a discovery as that by the Rochdale pioneers was for the world co-operative movement. But this discovery, it should not be forgotten, could neither have been hit upon nor later exalted into the cardinal principle of the American labor movement, if the class-consciousness of these "philosopher-organizers" had not, from the beginning, rendered them immune against being swept off their feet by the "producer consciousness" of the individualistic panaceas of the native American labor movement, and thus kept them at their "study-experiment" in their own trade unions. In this circuitous way, therefore, the class-conscious International of Marx was the cause of the least class-conscious labor movement in the world today.

In the evolution of the psychology of the American wage earner, the fruition of this "job and wage conscious" unionism and its eventual mastery of the whole field meant a final and complete rupture with the old "producing classes" point of view, which saw the road to economic democracy in a restoration to the individual, or to intimately associated groups of individuals, of access to economic opportunity in land, marketing, and credit; this opportunity once restored, competition alone would suffice to preserve it all around. This philosophy, as already noted, had issued from the typically American premise of an existing abundance of opportunity for every industrious person, an abundance, however, which conspiring monopolists have artificially converted into scarcity. The predominance of the "anti-monopoly" point of view in the American labor movement down to this time actually denoted a mental subordination of the wage earner to the farmer, a labor movement in the grip of a rural ideology. In contrast, the ideology of the American Federation of Labor was both an urban and a wage earner's ideology. It was based on a consciousness of limited job opportunities, a situation which required that the individual, both in his own interest and in that of a group to which he immediately belonged, should not be permitted to occupy any job opportunity except on the condition of observing the "common rule" laid down by his union. The safest way to assure this group control over opportunity, though also a way so ideal that only a union as favored as the printers' was able to actualize it entirely, was for the union, without displacing the employer as the owner of his business and risk taker, to become the virtual owner and administrator of the jobs. Where such an outright "ownership" of the jobs was impossible, the union would seek, by collective bargaining with the employers, to establish "rights" in the jobs, both for the individual and for the whole group, by incorporating, in the trade agreement, regulations applying to overtime, to the "equal turn," to priority and seniority in employment, to apprenticeship, to the introduction and utilization of machinery, and so forth. Thus the industrial democracy envisaged by this unionism descended from Marxism was not a democracy of individualistic producers exchanging products under free competition, with the monopolist banished, but a highly integrated democracy of unionized workers and of associated employer-managers, jointly conducting an industrial government with "laws" mandatory upon the individual.

How far the unionism of the American Federation of Labor had traveled from the "anti-monopoly" philosophy of the old American labor movement was clearly revealed in its attitude on the "trust" question. Early in the present century, while almost the whole nation was insisting that the government should break up the trusts, or at least regulate them with most stringent legislation, many going so far as to demand price fixing by government, the American Federation of Labor declared unequivocally that the "trusts" were an inevitable economic development before which the law was completely helpless, but the power of which could be controlled by another economic power, the organized trade union movement. Is it, therefore, a mere coincidence that the German trade unions, thirty years later, facing the "trustified" Germany of today, should equally have despaired of the political state as an instrument for curbing the "trusts," and should, like the American unionists in the late nineties, have seen that the main road to industrial democracy lies within the economic sphere?

Stable Unionism at Work

The American Federation of Labor entered upon a triumphant possession of the field of organized labor about 1890, with the virtual disappearance of its rival, the Knights of Labor. It survived in the struggle with the Knights because it was the product of continuous experimentation ever since the early seventies, when Gompers' "Ten Philosophers" first developed their "theory-practice" method of self-instruction. This experimentation by the trade unions went on through alternating periods of depression and prosperity, avoiding the most serious political excitements, like the "Populist" in the early nineties; but going through with the mistaken attempt to copy the British Trades Union Congress in their first federation, the Federation of Organized Trades and Labor Unions of the United States and Canada, 1881–1886. And all the while the trade union organizations were being hammered into shape in the struggles with employers, and especially in the life and death struggle with the Knights of Labor. The resultant unionism had therefore the merit that it "fitted" both the external environment and the American workman's psychology. For otherwise, beset on all sides, without and within the labor movement, it could neither have survived, nor attained a stability thitherto unknown in American labor history. The unionism of the American Federation of Labor "fitted," first, because it recognized the virtually inalterable conservatism of the American community as regards private property and private initiative in economic life. It, too, accordingly arrayed itself on the same side, demanding only that the employers should concede the union's right to control the jobs through "recognition" embodied in the trade agreement; and in this attitude it remained unperturbed in the face of all the charges by socialist intellectuals of treason to labor or even of corruption.

This unionism "fitted," secondly, because it grasped the definite limitations of the political instrument under the American Constitution and under

American conditions of political life. It therefore used the political weapon only sparingly and with great circumspection. It went into politics primarily to gain freedom from adverse interference by judicial authority in its economic struggles;—it did not wish to repeat former experiences when trade unions standing sponsor for a labor party found themselves dragged down to the ground by internecine political strife. The American Federation of Labor made itself felt politically by exercising pressure on the old parties; but it kept politics at arm's length from its own cherished trade union organization. It must be acknowledged, however, that the American movement, led by leaders risen from the ranks, could withstand the political temptation with so much greater ease than the European movements, because it saw little to choose between an autocratic capitalist management of industry and a bureaucratic one by "experts" appointed by the state.

Thirdly, the unionism of the Federation was a fit unionism to survive because it was under no delusion as to the true psychology of the workingman in general and of the American workingman in particular. It knew that producers' co-operation was a beautiful but a really harmful dream, since it only caused labor to fritter away its spiritual and material resources by shouldering itself with an impossible task of winning in the unequal competition between the capitalist-managed business undertakings, which marched like an army, and co-operatively managed ones, which were governed more by debating clubs.

This unionism was also without illusions with regard to the actual extent of labor solidarity. It knew that where wage earners were held together by the feeling that their jobs came out of a common job reservoir, as did those in the same or in closely related crafts, their fighting solidarity left nothing to be desired; provided that their unity was safeguarded by vigilantly uprooting "dual" unions as so many noxious weeds and by enforcing a military discipline against "outlaw" actions within the union itself. The leaders of this unionism also knew, however, that they had to go slow in pressing on to greater solidarity. Where conditions made cooperation between different craft groups urgent, it was best obtained through free co-operation in "departments" of unions in the same industry, each union reserving the right to decide for itself in every situation whether to co-operate or not. Thus, as with allied sovereign states, solidarity in action remained dependent on the sense of honor of each ally instead of on compulsion. . . .

This "stable unionism," from the nineties to the present, has undergone many vicissitudes: alternating prosperity and depression; employers' belligerency in many industries and conciliatoriness in others; the heaping up of legal disabilities by court decisions, and the "removal" of these disabilities by legislation under friendly administrations. This unionism entered upon a new day in the emergency of the World War period, when it phenomenally expanded in thitherto barred industries, the membership skyrocketing up to 4,000,000. Then followed an "open shop" and wage deflation campaign of equally unheard of intensity, in which most of the wartime gains were lost. Nevertheless, unionism has emerged as a permanent national force, though no more than a minority interest in the American community. As a minority interest, viewed askance by the majority, unionism has been under the necessity, if its influence and numbers were not to diminish but to grow, of exercising constant care lest by radical action on its part, the middle-class public should be thrown into an alliance with the reactionaries. For this necessary caution, unionism has been attacked as passionately from the "left," as the "open shop" employers and conservative interests have, for the opposite reason, assailed it from the "right."

The Worker's Search
for Power

Herbert G. Gutman

Until very recent times, the worker has never seemed quite so glamorous or important as his counterpart, the entrepreneur. This is especially true of the Gilded Age, where attention focuses more readily and with greater delight upon Jim Fisk or Commodore Vanderbilt or John D. Rockefeller than on the men whose labor built their fortunes to dizzying heights. Furthermore, those studies devoted to labor in this period have devoted too much attention to too little. Excessive interest in the Haymarket riot, the "Molly Maguires," the great strikes of 1877, the Homestead lockout, the Pullman strike, and close attention to the violence and disorder attending them has obscured the deeper and more important currents of which these things were only symptoms. Close attention has also focused on the small craft unions, the Knights of Labor, and the early Socialists, thus excluding the great mass of workers who belonged to none of these groups, and creating an uneven picture of labor in the Gilded Age. Surely it is time to broaden the approach into a study of labor in the society of the time as a whole.

Labor history in the Gilded Age had little to do with those matters traditionally and excessively emphasized by scholars. Too few workers belonged to trade unions to make them that important; it is that simple. There is a fundamental distinction between the wage-earners as a social class and the small minority of the working population that belonged to labor organizations. The full story of the wage-earner in that era is much more than the

Excerpts from Herbert G. Gutman, "The Worker's Search for Power: Labor in the Gilded Age," in H. Wayne Morgan, ed., The Gilded Age: A Reappraisal (Syracuse, N.Y.: Syracuse University Press, 1963), pp. 38–56, 67–68, © 1963 by Syracuse University Press, are reprinted by permission of Syracuse University Press.

tale of struggling craft unions and the exhortations of committed trade-unionists and assorted reformers and radicals. The dramatic events that rise up out of that generation's labor history mask significant underlying developments. Finally, the national perspective emphasized by so many labor historians often blurs and misrepresents those issues important to large segments of the postbellum working population and to other economic and social groups who had contact with the wage-earner. Most of the available literature about labor in the Gilded Age is excessively thin and suffers from serious and fundamental deficiencies. There are huge gaps in our knowledge of the entire period. Little of the secondary literature is concerned with the workers themselves, their communities, and the day-to-day occurrences that shaped their outlook. The narrow institutional development of trade unions has been emphasized more than the way the social and economic structure and the ideology of a rapidly industrializing society affected workers and employers. Excessive concern with craft workers has meant the serious neglect of the impact of a new way of life, industrial capitalism, upon large segments of the population.

A rather stereotyped conception of labor and of industrial relations in the Gilded Age has gained widespread credence. Final and conclusive generalizations about labor abound. A labor economist describes industrial conflict in the 1870's in an authoritative fashion:

During the depression from 1873 to 1879, employers sought to eliminate trade unions by a systematic policy of lock outs, blacklists, labor espionage, and legal prosecution. The widespread use of blacklists and Pinkerton labor spies caused labor to organize more or less secretly, and undoubtedly helped bring on the violence that characterized labor strife during this period. [Emphasis added.]

A labor historian asserts, "Employers *everywhere* seemed determined to rid themselves of 'restrictions upon free enterprise' by smashing unions." The "*typical* [labor] organization during the seventies," writes another scholar, "was secret for protection against intrusion by outsiders." Such seemingly final judgments are very questionable. How *systematic* were lockouts, blacklists, and legal prosecutions? How *widespread* was the use of labor spies and private detectives? Was the secret union the *typical* form of labor organization? Did violence *characterize* industrial relations?

It is widely believed that the industrialist exercised a great deal of power and had almost unlimited freedom of choice when dealing with his workers after the Civil War. Part of this belief reflects the weakness or absence of trade unions. Another justification for this interpretation, however, is somewhat more shaky. It is the assumption that industrialism generated new kinds of economic power which, in turn, *immediately* affected the social structure and the ideology of that time. The supposition that "interests" rapidly reshaped "ideas" is entirely too simple and therefore misleading. "The social pyramid," Joseph Schumpeter pointed out, "is never made of a single substance, is never seamless." There is no single *Zeitgeist*, except in the sense of a construct. The economic interpretation of history "would at once become untenable and unrealistic . . . if its formulation failed to consider that the manner in which production shapes social life is essentially influenced by the fact that human protagonists have always been shaped by past situations." Too often, the study of industrial development and industrial relations in the Gilded Age has neglected these pertinent strictures.

Careful study of a number of small industrial communities in this era suggests that the relationships between "interest" and "ideology" was very complex and subtle. In this period, industrial capitalism was relatively new as a total way of life and therefore was not fully institutionalized. Much of the history of industrialism at that time is the story of the painful process by which an old way of life was discarded for a new one. The central issue was the rejection or modification of an old set of "rules" and "commands" which no longer fit the new industrial context. Since so much was new, traditional stereotypes about the popular sanctioning of the rules and values of industrial society either demand severe qualification or entirely fall by the wayside. Among questionable commonly held generalizations are those that insist that the worker was isolated from the rest of society; that the employer had an easy time and a relatively free hand in imposing the new disciplines; that the spirit of the times, the ethic of the Gilded Age, worked to the advantage of the owner of industrial property; that workers found little if any sympathy from nonworkers; that the quest for wealth obliterated nonpecuniary values; and that industrialists swept aside countless obstacles with great ease. The usual picture of these years portrays the absolute power of the employer over his workers and emphasizes his ability to manipulate a sympathetic public opinion as well as various political, legal, and social institutions to his advantage.

The story is not so simple, however, as intensive examination of numerous strikes and lockouts shows. The new way of life was more popular and more quickly sanctioned in large cities than in small towns dominated by one or two industries. Put another way, the social environment in the large American city after the Civil War was more often hostile toward workers than was that in the smaller industrial towns. Employers in large cities had more freedom of choice than their counterparts in small towns where local conditions of one kind or another often hampered the employer's decision-making power. The ideology of many nonworkers in these small towns was not entirely hospitable toward industrial, as opposed to traditional, business enterprise. Strikes and lockouts in large cities seldom lasted as long as similar disputes outside of these urban centers. In the large city, there was almost no sympathy for the city worker from the middle and upper classes. At the same time, a good deal of pro-labor and anti-industrial sentiment (the two are not necessarily the same) flowed from similar occupational groups in the small towns. It is a commonplace that the small-town employer of factory labor often reached out of his local environment for aid of one kind or another in solving industrial disputes, but insufficient attention has been given to those elements in the contemporary social structure and ideology which shaped such decisions.

Though the direct economic relationships in large cities and in small towns and outlying industrial regions were essentially similar, the social structure in each of these areas was profoundly different. Here is the crucial clue to these distinct patterns of thought and behavior. Private enterprise was central to the economy of the small industrial town as well as to that of the large metropolitan city, but it functioned in a different social environment. The social structure and ideology of a given time are not derived only from economic institutions. In the Gilded Age, a time of rapid economic and social transformation and a time when industrial capitalism was still young and relatively new to the United States, parts of an ideology that were alien to the new industrialism retained a powerful hold on the minds of many who lived outside the large cities.

Men and their thoughts were different in the large cities. "The modern town," John Hobson wrote of the large nineteenth-century cities, "is a result of the desire to produce and distribute most economically the largest aggregate of material goods: economy of work, not convenience of life, is the object." In such an environment, "anti-social feelings" were exhibited "at every point by the competition of workers with one another, the antagonism between employers and employed, between sellers and buyers, factory and factory, shop and shop." Persons dealt with each other less as human beings and more as "things." The *Chicago Times*, for example, argued that "political economy" was "in reality the autocrat of the age" and occupied "the position once held by the Caesars and the Popes." According to the *New York Times*, the "antagonistic . . . position between employers and the employed on the subject of work and wages" was "unavoidable. . . . The object of trade is to get as much as you may and give as little as you can." The *Chicago Tribune* celebrated the coming of the centennial in 1876 by observing, "Suddenly acquired wealth, decked in all the colors of the rainbow, flaunts its robe before the eyes of Labor, and laughs with contempt at honest poverty." The country, "great in all the material powers of a vast empire," was entering "upon the second century weak and poor in social morality as compared with one hundred years ago."

More than economic considerations shaped the status of the working population in large cities after the Civil War, for the social structure there unavoidably widened the distance between the various social and economic classes. Home and job often were far apart. A man's fellow workers often differed from his friends and neighbors. Face-to-face relationships became less meaningful as the city grew larger and as production became more diverse and more specialized. "It has always been difficult for well-to-do people of the upper and middle classes," wrote Samuel Lane Loomis, a Protestant minister, in the 1880's, "to sympathize and to understand the needs of their poorer neighbors." The large city, both impersonal and confining, made it even harder. Loomis was convinced that "a great and growing gulf" lay "between the working-class and those above them." A Massachusetts clergyman saw a similar void between the social classes and complained: "I once knew a wealthy manufacturer who personally visited and looked after the comforts of his invalid operatives. I know of no such case now." All in all, the fabric of human relationships was cloaked in a kind of shadowed anonymity that became more and more characteristic of urban life.

Social contact was more direct in the smaller post-Civil War industrial towns and regions. The *Cooper's New Monthly*, a reform trade-union journal, insisted that while "money" was the "sole measure of gentility and respectability" in large cities "a more democratic feeling" prevailed in small towns. "The most happy and contented workingmen in the country," wrote the *Iron Molder's Journal*, "are those residing in small towns and villages. . . . We want more towns and villages and less cities." Except for certain parts of New England [and] the mid-Atlantic states, the post-Civil War industrial towns and regions were relatively new to that kind of enterprise. The men and women who lived and worked in these areas in the Gilded Age usually had known another way of life and doggedly contrasted the present with the past. They grasped the realities of the new industrialism for a simple reason: the nineteenth-century notion of enterprise came quickly to these regions after the Civil War, but the social distance between the various economic classes that characterized the large city came much more slowly and hardly paralleled industrial developments. In the midst of the new industrial enterprise with its new set of commands, therefore, men often clung to an older ("agrarian") set of values. They often judged the economic and social behavior of local industrialists by these older and more humane values. The social structure of the large city differed from that of the small industrial town because of the more direct human relationships among the residents of the smaller towns. Although many of these persons were not personally involved in the industrial process, they always felt its presence. Life may have been more difficult and less cosmopolitan in these small towns, but it was also less complicated. This life was not romantic, for it frequently meant company-owned houses and stores as well as conflicts between workers and employers over rights that were taken for granted in agricultural communities and large cities. Yet, the nonurban industrial environment had in it a kind of compelling simplicity. Its inhabitants lived and worked together, and a certain sense of community threaded their everyday lives. Men knew each other well, and the anonymity that veiled so much of urban life was not nearly so severe. There was of course more than enough economic hardship and plain despair in these towns, but the impersonal social environment of the large city in the Gilded Age was almost entirely lacking.

The first year of the 1873 depression suggests sharply the differences between the large urban center and the small industrial town. There is no question about the severity of the economic crisis. Its consequences were felt throughout the entire industrial sector, and production, employment, and income fell sharply everywhere. The dollar value of business failures in 1873 was greater than in any other single year between 1857 and 1893. The deflation in the iron and steel industry was especially severe: 266 of the nation's 666 iron furnaces were out of blast by January 1, 1874, and more than 50 percent of the rail mills were silent. A New York philanthropic organization figured that 25 percent of the city's workers, nearly 100,000 persons, were unemployed in the winter months of 1873–74. "The simple fact is that a great many laboring men are out of work," wrote the New York Graphic. "It is not the fault of merchants and manufacturers that they refuse to employ four men when they can but one, and decline to pay four dollars for work which they can buy for two and a half." Gloom and pessimism settled over the entire country, and the most optimistic predicted only that the panic would end in the late spring months of 1874. James Swank, the secretary of the American Iron and Steel Association, found the country suffering "from a calamity which may be likened to a famine or a flood." "The nation," he sourly observed, "is to have a period of enforced rest from industrial development. Let the causes be what they may, the fact that we are resting is patent to all men."

A number of serious labor difficulties occurred in small industrial towns and outlying industrial regions during the first year of the depression, revealing much about the social structure of these areas. Although each of these incidents had its own unique character, a common set of problems shaped all of them. The depression generated difficulties for employers everywhere. Demand fell away and industrialists necessarily cut production as well as costs in order to sell off accumulated inventory and retain a hold on shrinking markets. This general contraction caused harsh industrial conflict in many parts of the country. "No sooner does a depression in trade set in," observed David A. Harris, the conservative head of the Sons of Vulcan, a national craft union for puddlers and boilermen, "than all expressions of friendship to the toiler are forgotten." The New York Times insisted that the depression would "bring wages down for all time," and it advised employers to dismiss workers who struck against wage reductions. This was not the time for the "insane imitations of the miserable class warfare and jealousy of Europe." The Chicago Times found that strikers were "idiots" and "criminals," while its sister newspaper, the Chicago Evening Journal, said the economic crisis was not "an unmixed evil" because labor would finally learn "the folly and danger of trade organizations, strikes, and combinations . . . against capital." Iron Age was similarly sanguine. "We are sorry for those who suffer," it explained, "but if the power of the trade unions for mischief is weakened . . . the country will have gained far more than it loses from the partial depression of industry." After employers withdrew "every concession" made to the unions and "forced wages down to the lowest rates, . . . simple workingmen" would learn they

were misled by "demagogues and unprincipled agitators." Trade unions "crip-
pled the productive power of capital" and retarded the operation of "beneficent natural laws of progress and development." James Swank was somewhat
more generous. Prices had fallen, and it was "neither right nor practicable for
all the loss to be borne by the employers." "Some of it," he explained, "must
be shared by the workingmen. . . . We must hereafter be contented with
lower wages for our labor and be more thankful for the opportunity to labor
at all."

In cutting costs in 1873 and 1874, many employers faced difficult problems, but a central trouble emerged when they found that certain aspects of
the social structure and ideology in small industrial towns hindered their
freedom of action. It proved relatively easy for them to announce a wage cut
or to refuse publicly to negotiate with a local trade union, but it often proved
quite difficult to enforce such decisions easily and quickly. In instance after
instance, and for reasons that varied from region to region, employers reached
outside of their local environment to help assert their local authority.

Industrialists used various methods to strengthen their local positions
with their workers. The state militia brought order to a town or region swept
by industrial conflict. Troops were used in railroad strikes in Indiana, Ohio,
and Pennsylvania; in a dispute involving iron heaters and rollers in Newport,
Kentucky; in a strike of Colorado ore diggers; in two strikes of Illinois coal
miners; and in a strike of Michigan ore workers. At the same time, other employers aggravated racial and nationality problems among workers by intro-
ducing new ethnic groups in their towns as a way of ending strikes, forcing
men to work under new contracts, and destroying local trade unions. Negroes
were used in coal disputes. Danish, Norwegian, and Swedish immigrants were
brought into mines in Illinois, and into the Shenango Valley and the northern anthracite region of Pennsylvania. Germans went to coal mines in northern Ohio along with Italian workers. Some Italians also were used in western
Pennsylvania as coal miners and in western and northern New York as railroad workers. A number of employers imposed their authority in other ways.
Regional, not local, blacklists were tried in the Illinois coal fields, on certain
railroads, in the Ohio Valley iron towns, and in the iron mills of eastern
Pennsylvania. Mine operators in Pennsylvania's Shenango Valley and Tioga
coal region used state laws that allowed them to evict discontented workers
from company-owned houses in mid-winter.

In good part, the social structure in these small towns and the ideology
of many of their residents, who were neither workers nor employers, shaped
the behavior of those employers who reached outside their local environments
in order to win industrial disputes. The story is different for every town, but
has certain similarities. The strikes and lockouts had little meaning in and of
themselves, and it is of passing interest to learn whether the employers or the
workers gained a victory. The incidents assume broader significance as they
shed light on the distribution of power in these towns and on those important

social and economic relationships which shaped the attitudes and actions of workers and employers.

One neglected aspect of the small industrial town after the Civil War is its political structure. Because workers made up a large proportion of the electorate and often participated actively in local politics, they were able at times to influence local and regional affairs in a manner not open to wage-earners in the larger cities. There is no evidence in 1874 that workers held elected or appointed offices in large cities. In that year, nevertheless, the post-master of Whistler, Alabama, was a member of the Iron Molder's International Union. George Kinghorn, a leading trade-unionist in the southern Illinois coal fields, was postmaster of West Belleville, Illinois. A local labor party swept an election in Evansville, Indiana. Joliet, Illinois, had three workers on its city council. A prominent official of the local union of iron heaters and rollers sat on the city council in Newport, Kentucky. Coal and ore miners ran for the state legislature in Carthage, Missouri, in Clay County, Indiana, and in Belleville, Illinois. The residents of Virginia City, a town famous to western mythology, sent the president of the local union of miners to the national Congress. In other instances, town officials and other officeholders who were not wage-earners sympathized with the problems and difficulties of local workers or displayed an unusual degree of objectivity during local industrial disputes.

It was the same with many local newspapers in these towns, for they often stood apart from the industrial entrepreneur and subjected his behavior to searching criticisms. Editorials in these journals defended *local* workers and demanded redress for their grievances. Certain of these newspapers were entirely independent in their outlook, and others warmly endorsed local trade-union activities.

The small businessmen and shopkeepers, the lawyers and professional people, and the other nonindustrial members of the middle class were a small but vital element in these industrial towns. Unlike the urban middle class they had direct and everyday contact with the new industrialism and with the problems and the outlook of workers and employers. Many had risen from a lower station in life and intimately knew the meaning of hardship and toil. They could judge the troubles and complaints of both workers and employers by personal experience and by what happened around them and did not have to rely on secondary accounts. While they invariably accepted the concepts of private property and free entrepreneurship, their judgments about the *social* behavior of industrialists often drew upon noneconomic considerations and values. They saw no necessary contradiction between private enterprise and gain on the one hand, and decent, humane social relations between workers and employers on the other. In a number of industrial conflicts, segments of the local middle class sided with the workers in their communities. A Maryland weekly newspaper complained in 1876, "In the changes of the last thirty years not the least unfortunate is the separation of personal relations between employers and employees." At the same time that most metropolitan newspapers sang paeans of joy for the industrial entrepreneur and the new way of life, the *Youngstown Miner and Manufacturer* thought it completely wrong that the "Vanderbilts, Stewarts, and Astors bear, in proportion to their resources, infinitely less of the burden incident to society than the poorest worker." The *Ironton Register* defended dismissed iron strikers as "upright and esteemed . . . citizens" who had been sacrificed "to the cold demands on business." The *Portsmouth Times* boasted, "We have very little of the cod-fish aristocracy, and industrious laborers are looked upon here with as much respect as any class of people."

Detailed illustrations of the difficulties certain employers faced when they sought to enforce crucial economic decisions in small towns reveal a great deal about the social structure of these areas and the outlook of many residents. These illustrations also tell something of the obstacles industrialists often encountered in their efforts to deal with workers.

In 1873 when the depression called a temporary halt to the expansion of the Illinois mining industry, Braidwood, Illinois, was less than a dozen years old. Coal mining and Braidwood had grown together, and by 1873, 6,000 persons lived in the town. Except for the supervisors and the small businessmen and shopkeepers, most of the residents were coal miners and their families. Braidwood had no "agricultural neighborhood to give it support" and "without its coal-shafts" it would have had "no reasonable apology for existing." The town had three coal companies, but the Chicago, Wilmington, and Vermillion Coal Company was by far the largest, and its president, James Monroe Walker, also headed the Chicago, Burlington, and Quincy Railroad. This firm operated five shafts and employed 900 men, more than half the resident miners. Most of the owners did not live in the town: Walker, for example, resided in Chicago. The miners were a mixed lot, and unlike most other small industrial towns in this era Braidwood had an ethnically diverse population. About half the miners came from Ireland. Another 25 percent were English, Welsh, and Scotch. A smaller number were Swedes, Italians, and Germans, and still others came from France and Belgium and even from Poland and Russia. There were also native-born miners. "The town of Braidwood," a contemporary noted, "is . . . nearly akin to Babel as regards the confusion of tongues."

Although they came from diverse backgrounds, the miners were a surprisingly cohesive social community. A trade union started in 1872 was strong enough to extract a reasonable wage agreement from the three coal firms. A hostile observer complained that nearly all the voters were miners and that a majority of the aldermen and justices of the peace "are or have been miners."

The depression cut the demand for coal and created serious problems for the operators. By March, 1874, at least 25 percent of the miners were unemployed, and the town was "dull beyond all precedent." In late May the operators, led by the Chicago, Wilmington, and Vermillion firm, cut the rate for digging coal from $1.25 to $1.10 a ton and reduced the price for "pushing" coal from the work wall to the shaft nearly in half. They announced that the mines would close on June 1 unless the men accepted the new contract for a full year. The miners' efforts at compromise and suggestions of arbitration were summarily rejected, and the mines closed. The general superintendent of the largest company displayed "a haughty indifference as to whether the mines 'run' or not" and would not listen to the miners' bitter complaints that they could not have received "worse treatment in the old country" and that the "Wilmington fellows" were "right up and down monopolists." Instead, the Chicago, Wilmington, and Vermillion company contacted private labor contracting agencies in Chicago and recruited a large number of unskilled laborers, most of whom were Scandinavian immigrants and were not miners. Three days after the strike began, 65 Chicago workers arrived. More came two weeks later, and from then on a small number arrived daily until the end of July when the number increased sharply. At the same time, anticipating trouble in putting the new men to work, the operators brought special armed Chicago Pinkerton police to the town.

Difficulties plagued the operators from the start. The miners realized they had to check the owners' strategy in order to gain a victory. As soon as new workers arrived, committees of miners explained the difficulty to them. "We ask the skilled miners not to work," the leader of the strikers explained. "As to green hands, we are glad to see them go to work for we know they are . . . a positive detriment to the company." All but three of the first 65 new workers agreed to return to Chicago, and since they lacked funds the miners and other local residents paid their rail fare and cheered them as they boarded a Chicago-bound train. By mid-July one shaft that usually employed 200 men had no more than ten workers. At the end of July, only 102 men worked in the mines, and not one of them was a resident miner. The disaffected miners also met the challenge of the Pinkerton men. The miners appointed a 72-man committee to prevent violence and to protect company property. The mayor and the sheriff swore in twelve of these men as special deputies, and, with one exception (when the wives of certain miners chased and struck Allan Pinkerton), the miners behaved in a quiet and orderly manner.

Time and again, Braidwood's tiny middle class—the businessmen, the storekeepers, and the public officials—strengthened the striking miners. According to one reporter, they "all back[ed] the miners." They denied complaints by the owners that the miners were irresponsible and violent. One citizen condemned the coal companies for creating "excitement so as to crush the miners" and declared that "public sympathy" was "entirely" with the workers. The Chicago Tribune reporter found that "Braidwood is with the strikers root and branch." The attitude of the local publicly elected officials, for example, is of great interest. The operators wanted Pinkerton and his men appointed "special deputies" and made "merchant police" with power to arrest persons trespassing on company properties, but the mayor and the sheriff turned them down and deputized the strikers. Mayor Goodrich forbade parading in the streets by the Pinkerton men, and the sheriff ordered them to surrender their rifles and muskets. The sheriff did not want "a lot of strangers dragooning a quiet town with deadly weapons in their hands," and he said he feared the miners "a good deal less than . . . the Chicago watchmen."

The operators faced other troubles. Local judges and police officials enforced the law more rigorously against them and their men than against the resident miners. In one instance, two new workers who got into a fight one Sunday were arrested for violating the Sabbath law and fined $50 and court costs. Unable to pay the fine, they were put to work on the town streets. One of them, jailed for hitting an elderly woman with a club, was fined $100 and court costs. A company watchman was arrested four times, twice for "insulting townspeople." Frustrated in these and other ways by the miners and the townspeople, the operators finally turned for help to the state government, and E. L. Higgins, the adjutant general and head of the state militia, went to Braidwood to see if troops were needed. Higgins openly supported the mine owners. He tried to prevent union men from talking with new workers, and although he asked the mayor to meet him in the office of the Chicago, Wilmington, and Vermillion firm, he "never went to see the officers of the city . . . to gain an unprejudiced account of the strike." "If this is what the military forces and officers are kept for," one miner observed, "it is high time . . . such men [were] struck off the State Government payroll and placed where they belong." Mayor Goodrich reminded Higgins that neither the Braidwood nor the Will County authorities had asked for state interference. In a bitter letter to the Chicago Times, Goodrich wondered whether Higgins had come "in his official capacity or as an agent of the coal company," and firmly insisted that "the citizens of this city were not aware that martial law had been proclaimed or an embargo placed upon their speech."

Unable fully to exercise their authority in the town and worried about the possibility of losing the fall trade, the operators confessed their failure and surrendered to the strikers fourteen weeks after the conflict had started. The final agreement pleased the miners, and they were especially amused when the Chicago, Wilmington, and Vermillion company agreed to send all the new workers back to Chicago. A spokesman for the operators, however, bitterly assailed the Braidwood mayor and other public officials for their failure to understand the meaning of "peace, order, and freedom." Surely the operators had further cause for complaint in 1877 when Daniel McLaughlin, the president of the miners' union, was elected mayor of Braidwood, other miners were chosen aldermen, and one was chosen police magistrate.

Manufacturers in the small industrial iron towns of the Ohio Valley such as Ironton and Portsmouth, Ohio, and Newport and Covington, Kentucky, had troubles similar to those of the Braidwood coal operators in 1873 and 1874. Several thousand men and fifteen iron mills were involved in a dispute over wages that lasted for several months. The mill owners who belonged to the Ohio Valley Iron Association cut the wages of skilled iron heaters and roller men 20 percent on December 1, 1873. After the workers complained that the manufacturers were taking "undue advantage" of them "owing to the present financial trouble," their wages were cut another 10 percent. The valley mill owners worked out a common policy; they decided to close all the mills for a month or so in December and then reopen them under the new scale. Hard times would bring them new workers.

Although the mill owners in large cities such as St. Louis, Indianapolis, and Cincinnati found it easy to bring in new workers from the outside, it was another story in the small towns. They could hire new hands in Pittsburgh, Philadelphia, and other eastern cities, but the social environment in Covington, Portsmouth, Newport, and Ironton made it difficult for them to hold on to these men. The locked-out workers found sympathy from other townspeople. In such an environment they were a relatively homogeneous group and made up a large part of the total population of the town. When workers agitated in small towns, paraded the streets, or engaged in one or another kind of collective activity, their behavior hardly went unnoticed.

The difficulties faced by the small-town iron manufacturers beset especially Alexander Swift, owner of the Swift Iron and Steel Works in Newport, Kentucky. Although his workers suffered from almost indescribable poverty after the factory closed, they would not surrender. When Swift reopened his mill, he had it guarded by armed "special policemen." Some of the new workers left the town after they learned of the conflict, and the "police" accompanied the rest to and from their work. The old workers made Newport uncomfortable for the new hands. There was no violence at first, but many strikers and their wives, especially the English and Welsh workers, gathered near the mill and in the streets where they howled at the "black sheep" as they went to and from work. The Newport workers exerted pressure on them in "the hundred ways peculiar to workingmen's demonstrations." Swift was embittered, for at the end of January only a few men worked in his mill.

Swift was not alone in his troubles; mill owners in Covington, Ironton, and Portsmouth were in similar difficulty. Early in February, therefore, the Ohio Valley Iron Association announced that unless the men returned to work on or before February 20 they would lose their jobs and never again be hired in the valley iron mills. When most of the workers refused to return, they were fired. New workers were quickly brought to the towns, and Swift demanded special police protection for them from the Newport City Council, but it assigned only regular police to guard them. Crowds jeered the new men, and there were several fights. A large number of new workers again left Newport. Swift appealed to the police to ban street demonstrations by the workers and their families, but his plea was rejected. "We never went any further with those fellows," a striker explained, "than calling them 'black sheep' and 'little lambs.' . . . When they'd be going to work in the morning with the policemen on each side of them, we'd cry 'Ba-a-a-a.' " Swift armed his new workers with pistols. When the strikers and their supporters gathered to jeer these men, one of the new workers shot wildly into the crowd and killed a young butcher's helper. The enraged crowd chased Swift's men out of the city, and Swift, after blaming the shooting on the failure of the Newport authorities to guard his men properly, closed the mill.

These events did not go unnoticed in the Ohio Valley. The *Portsmouth Times* leveled a barrage of criticism at Swift and the other manufacturers. It asked whether or not they had a "right" to circulate the names of strikers in the same manner as "the name of a thief is sent from one police station to another." Such action was "cowardly . . . intimidation," and the *Times* asked: "Does not continued and faithful service deserve better treatment at the hands of men whose fortunes have been made by these workmen they would brand with the mark of CAIN? . . . Is this to be the reward for men who have grown gray in the service of these velvet-lined aristocrats? . . . Out on such hypocrisy!" After the shooting in Newport, the *Times* turned on Swift and called him a "bloodletter." Violence was wrong, the *Times* admitted, "wrong in theory and practice," but it nevertheless advised the striking iron workers: "If the gathered up assassins from the slums and alleys of the corrupt cities of the East are brought here to do deeds of lawlessness and violence, the stronger the opposition at the beginning the sooner they will be taught that the city of Portsmouth has no need of them."

Immune from such criticism, Swift continued to try to break down the strength of the Newport workers. In the end he succeeded. He realized that the only way to weaken the strikers was to suppress their power of public demonstration and therefore urged the Newport mayor to enforce local ordinances against dangerous and "riotous" crowds, asked the Kentucky governor to send state militia, and even demanded federal troops. Although the mayor banned "all unusual and unnecessary assemblages" in the streets, Swift still asked for state troops, and on March 5, the Kentucky governor ordered twenty-five members of the Lexington division of the state militia to Newport. The arrival of the militia weakened the strikers and created a favorable environment for Swift and his plans. Street demonstrations were banned. The police were ordered to arrest "all persons using threatening or provoking language." When a number of unskilled strikers offered to return at the lower wage, Swift turned them away. He also rejected efforts by a member of the city council to effect a compromise with the old workers. A week after the troops arrived and three and a half months after the start of the lockout, Swift fully controlled the local situation. New men worked in his factory, and the strikers admitted defeat.

The use of troops, however, was bitterly condemned in the Ohio Valley. A reporter for the *Cincinnati Enquirer* found that the "general opinion" in Newport was that Swift's maneuver was "little else than a clever piece of acting intended to kindle public sentiment against the strikers and . . . gain

the assistance of the law in breaking up a strike." A Newport judge assailed
the Kentucky governor, and a local poet sang of the abuse of state power:

> Sing a song of sixpence
>   Stomachs full of rye,
> Five-and-twenty volunteers,
>   With fingers in one pie;
> When the pie is opened
>   For money they will sing,
> Isn't that a pretty dish
>   For the City Council Ring?

There was less drama in the other Ohio Valley iron towns than in Newport, but the manufacturers in Portsmouth, Ironton, and Covington faced
similar trouble. The old workers persuaded many new hands to leave the
region. "A few men who try to work," wrote an Ironton observer, "are 'bah-d'
at from the cross streets as they go to and from the shops. To have a lot of
boys follow one up with cries of 'bah, black sheep' is a torment few workmen
can endure." When fourteen Philadelphia workers arrived in Ironton and
learned of the troubles for the first time, they left the city. Strikers paid their
return rail fare. In Portsmouth, the same happened, and the departing workers publicly declared, "A nobler, truer, better class of men never lived than
the Portsmouth boys . . . standing out for their rights." Nonstrikers in these
towns also acted contrary to the manufacturers' interests. Each week the
Portsmouth Times attacked the mill owners. "We are not living under a
monarchy," the *Times* insisted, and the "arbitrary actions" of the employers
were not as "unalterable as the edicts of the Medes and Persians." A Covington justice of the peace illustrated something of the hostility felt toward the
companies. Three strikers were arrested for molesting new hands, but he freed
one of them and fined the other men a dollar each and court costs. A new
worker, however, was fined twenty dollars for disorderly conduct and for carrying a deadly weapon. He also had to post a $500 bond as a guarantee that
he would keep the peace.

In the end, except in Newport where Swift had successfully neutralized
the power of the workers, a compromise wage settlement was finally worked
out. Certain of the mills succeeded in bringing in new men, but some manufacturers withdrew the blacklist and rehired their striking workers. Commenting on the entire dispute, a friend of the Ohio Valley iron manufacturers
bitterly complained: "Things of this sort make one ask whether we are really
as free a people as we pretend to be." Convinced that the workers had too
much power and that the manufacturers were not fully free entrepreneurs,
this devotee of classical laissez faire doctrine sadly concluded: "If any indi-

vidual cannot dispose of his labor when and at what price he pleases, he is living under a despotism, no matter what form the government assumes."

*   *   *

There is much to say about the attitude toward labor that existed in large cities, but over all opinion lay a popular belief that iron laws governed not only the economy but life itself, and that he who tampered with them through social experiments or reforms imperiled the whole structure. The *Chicago Times* was honest if perhaps callous in saying: "Whatever cheapens production, whatever will lessen the cost of growing wheat, digging gold, washing dishes, building steam engines, is of value. . . . The age is not one which enquires when looking at a piece of lace whether the woman who wove it is a saint or a courtesan." It came at last almost to a kind of inhumanity, as one manufacturer who used dogs as well as men in his operation discovered. The employer liked the dogs better than the men. "They never go on strike for higher wages, have no labor unions, never get intoxicated and disorderly, never absent themselves from work without good cause, obey orders without growling, and are very reliable."

The contrast between urban and rural views of labor and its fullest role in society and life is clear. In recent years, many have stressed "entrepreneurship" in nineteenth-century America without distinguishing between entrepreneurs in commerce and trade and entrepreneurs in industrial manufacturing. Reflecting the stresses and strains in the thought and social attitudes of a generation passing from the old agricultural way of life to the new industrial America, many men could justify the business ethic in its own sphere without sustaining it in operation in society at large or in human relationships. It was one thing to apply brute force in the market place, and quite another to talk blithely of "iron laws" in operation when men's lives and well-being were at stake.

Not all men had such second thoughts about the social fabric which industrialism and commercialism were weaving, but in the older areas of the country, still susceptible to the cries of an ancient conscience, the spirits of free enterprise and free action were neither dead nor mutually exclusive. As the story shows clearly, many elements of labor kept their freedom of action and bargaining even during strikes. And the worker was not without shrewdness in his appeal to public opinion. There is a certain irony in realizing that rural, or at least small-town America, supposedly alien and antagonistic toward the city and its ways, remained in this period a stronghold of freedom for the worker seeking his economic and social rights.

But perhaps this is not so strange after all, for rural America, whatever its narrowness and faults, had always preached individualism and personal freedom. It was the city, whose very impersonality would one day make it a kind of frontier of anonymity, which often preached personal restriction and the law of the economic and social jungle. As industrialism triumphed, the businessman's powers increased, yet it is significant that in this generation of genuine freedom of action, he was often hindered and always suspect in vast areas of the nation which cheered his efforts toward wealth even while often frustrating his methods.

Facile generalizations are easy to make and not always sound, but surely the evidence warrants a new view of labor in the Gilded Age. The standard stereotypes and textbook clichés about its impotence and division before the iron hand of oppressive capitalism do not fit the facts. Its story is far different when surveyed in depth, carrying in it overtones of great complexity. And it is not without haunting and instructive reminders that even in an age often dominated by lusts for power, men did not forget or abandon old and honored concepts of human dignity and worth.

SUGGESTIONS FOR FURTHER READING

Selig Perlman was a student of John R. Commons of the University of Wisconsin and his point of view reflects that of the so-called Wisconsin School. Other studies from this group are the four-volume *History of Labor in the United States* by Commons and others (New York, 1918–35); and Philip Taft's massive two-volume history of the A. F. of L.: *The A. F. of L. in the Time of Gompers* (New York, 1957); *The A. F. of L. from the Death of Gompers to the Merger* (New York, 1959). The influence of the Wisconsin school may be seen in a recent survey history of *American Labor* by the British historian, Henry Pelling (Chicago, 1960), and also, of course, in the essay by Taft and Ross printed above.

Strongly opposed to the Wisconsin group is Philip S. Foner whose Marxist interpretation of the *History of the Labor Movement in the United States* (four volumes to date; New York, 1947–1965) emphasizes class struggle and conflict. Violent labor conflict can be seen in studies of specific strikes: Almont Lindsay, *The Pullman Strike* (Chicago, 1942) and Henry David, *History of the Haymarket Affair* (New York, 1936). Louis Adamic's theme is expressed in the title of his book, *Dynamite, The Story of Class Violence in America* (New York, 1931).

In recent years many labor historians have tried to break away from the study of organized labor and/or individual strikes and have emphasized instead the history of workers (rather than unions) in the context of social change in the United States. Herbert G. Gutman's article is a part of this new trend. See also his "Protestantism and the American Labor Movement: The Christian Spirit in the Gilded Age," *American Historical Review, LXXII* (October 1966), 74–101. Problems of social mobility among the workers are dealt with by Stephan Thernstrom, *Poverty and Progress: Social Mobility in a Nineteenth Century City* (Cambridge, Mass., 1964).

* Available in paperback edition.

4
MIGRANTS TO AN URBAN AMERICA

The history of modern America is in many ways a history of urbanism. "The United States was born in the country, but has moved to the city," Richard Hofstadter has written. Of course, there were cities in America from the very beginning of the nation's history; Philadelphia, with a population of about 25,000 in 1776, was one of the largest cities in the British Empire. But in the early years of the new republic, the urban population was small. In 1790 there were only twenty-four towns in the United States with a population of 2,500 or more (the census definition of an urban place); the 201,655 urban residents in that year accounted for only about five percent of the total population.

Throughout the nineteenth century, the urban population grew rapidly. By 1860 about twenty percent of the population resided in cities and forty years later about four Americans in ten were urban dwellers. When the census of 1920 revealed that more than half the American population lived in cities, one scholar noted that "The city of today is responsible for most of what is good, and for most of what is bad, in our national life and ideals." For better or for worse, the United States was an urban nation.

Rapid urbanization did not bring universal approval from the nation's intellectual and cultural leaders. Some, such as Frederick C. Howe, saw the city as "The Hope of Democracy" and pictured the metropolis as the center of culture, business, and opportunity. But many, recalling Thomas Jefferson's warnings, distrusted the city, seeing it as a source of corruption and sin which threatened American democracy.

Of course, there was much to distrust about city life. Cities were undeniably corrupt and filthy and often the scenes of violence and crime. Even more frightening, they seemed strangely alien with their hordes of immigrants from the farms and cities of Europe. During the century after 1820, 38 million Europeans came to America; between 1902 and 1914 well over half a million immigrants arrived every year. Most of the latter came from southern and eastern Europe and settled in the cities.

Americans had always prided themselves on being a mixture of many races and nationalities and had viewed their country as a haven for the oppressed. As early as 1782, the naturalized New Yorker, Crèvecoeur, had written: "He is an American who leaving behind him all his ancient prejudices and manners, receives new ones from the new mode of life he has embraced. . . . Here individuals of all nations are melted into a new race of men. . . ." Despite the image of the melting pot, however, newly arrived immigrants were often greeted with suspicion. In the early nineteenth century, Irish and German immigrants faced resentment that occasionally boiled over into riots and violence. Antagonism towards newcomers increased as millions of eastern and southern European immigrants flocked to America during the late nineteenth and early twentieth centuries. Many Americans—including second-generation immigrants—began to question the concept of open immigration and called for restrictions.

The melting pot did not seem to be working. Contrary to expectations, the immigrants did not become Americanized overnight. They organized their own communities and their own national societies and held desperately to their old ways. The problems in the cities seemed to be the result of the arrival of millions of alien people who were unable and unwilling to adopt American ways.

But immigrants continued to come, lured by the hope of a better life in the New World. Often they were bitterly disappointed, finding instead crowded tenements, poor jobs, and violence in the teeming streets; they lived days of struggle and nights of loneliness in an alien land. Yet, for many, America was the land of opportunity; or at least it was better than the old country. One German wrote home: "No one can give orders to anybody here, one is as good as another, no one takes off his hat to another as you have to do in Germany."

Most newcomers to America's growing cities were not foreigners, however, but native Americans who left their rural villages and farms to seek a new life and, they hoped, new opportunities in the cities. They too faced the problem of adjusting to new living and working conditions. Urban migrants, whatever their nationality, suffered the hardships associated with cities that had grown too fast to provide adequate housing, streets, sewers, police protection, and transportation. One group of native migrants, the blacks, suffered additionally from racism.

There can be no doubt that the great migration to American cities in the nineteenth and twentieth centuries produced tensions and conflicts that often erupted into bloody violence. For many historians, this is the proper emphasis to give to the experience. But other historians have argued that despite the conflict, the newcomers were usually integrated into American society. The cities, they argue, offered new opportunities; the bewildered newcomers of one year became the solid citizens of the next. Still other historians, even if they accept the view that the melting pot was effective, maintain that there is one conspicuous exception. Black Americans, they argue, were prevented from seizing the opportunities available to other migrants. While antagonism against foreigners and rural whites faded, racism remained an all but insurmountable obstacle blocking the progress of the blacks.

In the following selections the reader is introduced to some of the ways in which the problems of urban migration have been evaluated. In the first selection, Oscar Handlin discusses the alienation of the immigrants both from their native land and from the new world which they had entered. His stress is on conflict rather than on assimilation. He would not deny that many succeeded in America, but success, when it came, was costly in human terms.

Allan H. Spear, in the next selection, deals with the special problems of the black. His analysis of the creation of the black ghetto in Chicago leads him to conclude that the experience of the blacks was unique. Unlike other migrants, black Americans were prevented from assimilating into American urban society. In the next selection, Edward C. Banfield takes a contrary view. Although he does not deny the existence of racism, he maintains that class rather than race is the basis for the black's difficulties: "Today the Negro's main disadvantage is the same as the Puerto Rican's and Mexican's: namely, that he is the most recent unskilled, and hence relatively low-income, migrant to reach the city from a backward rural area."

In the final selection, Richard C. Wade surveys urban violence in broad historical perspective, arguing that while violence has always characterized American urban life, its causes over the years have been largely mitigated with the result that "the level of large-scale disorder and violence is less ominous today than it has been during much of the past." The one major exception to this generalization is the violence associated with racial antagonism. Denying that race conflict is mainly class conflict, Wade argues that racism created the ghetto, limited opportunities for the blacks, and left the nation with "a growingly alienated and embittered group" in its midst.

In judging the urban experience in America should we emphasize the violence, the riots, the crime, and the corruption, or should we stress the cultural and economic achievements of our cities? Should we stress the urban melting pot, where many ethnically diverse people came together and found an opportunity to improve themselves, or should we emphasize the alienation, the pathos, and the conflict? Is discrimination against the blacks simply the result of their being the last group to enter the cities? Or is racism a special problem that other migrants never had to face?

The Uprooted

Oscar Handlin

Letters bring the low voices across the sea. The unfamiliar pens grope for the proper words. When you ask somebody to write for you, you must go and treat him. Therefore you try yourself. In the store are printed forms. Sometimes they will do to transmit information. But you wish through this lifeless paper to do more than send news. With painful effort and at the sacrifice of precious time, you express the solidarity you still feel with those who stayed behind. The sheet is then the symbol of the ties that continue to bind.

Ceremonial salutations, *to my dearest* . . . to every him and her who filled the days of the old life and whom I will never see again. By this letter I kiss you. To the aged parents who bred and nurtured, who took trouble over, shed tears for me and now have none to comfort them; to the brother who shared my tasks and bed; to my comrades of the fields; to all the kin who joined in festivals; to the whole visible communion, the oneness, of the village that I have forfeited by emigration; to each I send my greetings. And with my greetings go wishes that you may have the sweet years of life, of health and happiness, alas elusive there and here.

They are wanderers to the wide world and often yearn toward the far direction whence they have come. Why even the birds who fly away from their native places still hasten to go back. Can ever a man feel really happy condemned to live away from where he was born? Though by leaving he has cut himself off and knows he never will return, yet he hopes, by reaching backward, still to belong in the homeland.

It is to that end that the husband and wife and older children gather to assist in the composition; it is to that end that they assemble to read the reply. Little enough occurs to them that is worth recording, certainly not the

From The Uprooted by Oscar Handlin, pp. 259–285. Copyright 1951 by Oscar Handlin. Reprinted by permission of Atlantic-Little, Brown and Co.

monotonous struggle of getting settled. Instead their lines go to reminiscence, to the freshening of memories, to the commemoration of anniversaries. Later, when the art spreads and photographs are available at low cost, these are exchanged with great frequency.

Other acts of solidarity also absorbed the attention of the immigrants. Vivid recollections of the suffering they had left behind spurred them on in the effort to set aside from their own inadequate earnings enough to aid the ones who had not come. By 1860 the Irish alone were sending back four or five million dollars a year; a half-century later, the total remitted by all groups was well over one hundred and forty million for a twelve-month period. Often, in addition, some unusual disaster evoked a special sympathetic response—the church burned down, or famine appeared, or war. Such contributions recognized the continued connectedness with the old place. In time, that was further strengthened by involvement in nationalistic movements which established a political interest in the affairs of the Old Country, an interest the peasants had not had while they were there.

As the passing years widened the distance, the land the immigrants had left acquired charm and beauty. Present problems blurred those they had left unsolved behind; and in the haze of memory it seemed to these people they had formerly been free of present dissatisfactions. It was as if the Old World became a great mirror into which they looked to see right all that was wrong with the New. The landscape was prettier, the neighbors more friendly, and religion more efficacious; in the frequent crises when they reached the limits of their capacities, the wistful reflection came: *This would not have happened there.*

The real contacts were, however, disappointing. The requests—that back there a mass be said, or a wise one consulted, or a religious medal be sent over—those were gestures full of hope. But the responses were inadequate; like all else they shrank in the crossing. The immigrants wrote, but the replies, when they came, were dull, even trite in their mechanical phrases, or so it seemed to those who somehow expected these messages to evoke the emotions that had gone into their own painfully composed letters. Too often the eagerly attended envelopes proved to be only empty husks, the inner contents valueless. After the long wait before the postman came, the sheets of garbled writing were inevitably below expectations. There was a trying sameness to the complaints of hard times, to the repetitious petty quarrels; and before long there was impatience with the directness with which the formal greeting led into the everlasting requests for aid.

This last was a sore point with the immigrants. The friends and relatives who had stayed behind could not get it out of their heads that in America the streets were paved with gold. *Send me for a coat . . . . There is a piece of land here and if only you would send, we could buy it . . . . Our daughter could be married, but we have not enough for a dowry . . . . We are ashamed, everyone else gets . . . much more frequently than we.* Implicit in these solicitations was the judgment that the going-away had been a desertion, that unfulfilled obligations still remained, and that the village could claim assistance as a right from its departed members.

From the United States it seemed there was no comprehension, back there, of the difficulties of settlement. It was exasperating by sacrifices to scrape together the remittances and to receive in return a catalogue of new needs, as if there were not needs enough in the New World too. The immigrants never shook off the sense of obligation to help; but they did come to regard their Old Countrymen as the kind of people who depended on help. The trouble with the Europeans was, they could not stand on their own feet.

The cousin green off the boat earned the same negative appraisal. Though he be a product of the homeland, yet here he cut a pitiable figure; awkward manners, rude clothes, and a thoroughgoing ineptitude in the new situation were his most prominent characteristics. The older settler found the welcome almost frozen on his lips in the face of such backwardness.

In every real contact the grandeur of the village faded; it did not match the immigrants' vision of it and it did not stand up in a comparison with America. When the picture came, the assembled family looked at it beneath the light. This was indeed the church, but it had not been remembered so; and the depressing contrast took some of the joy out of remembering.

The photograph did not lie. There it was, a low building set against the dusty road, weather-beaten and making a candid display of its ill-repair. But the recollections did not lie either. As if it had been yesterday that they passed through those doors, they could recall the sense of spaciousness and elevation that sight of the structure had always aroused.

Both impressions were true, but irreconcilable. The mental image and the paper representation did not jibe because the one had been formed out of the standards and values of the Old Country, while the other was viewed in the light of the standards and values of the New. And it was the same with every other retrospective contact. Eagerly the immigrants continued to look back across the Atlantic in search of the satisfactions of fellowship. But the search was not rewarded. Having become Americans, they were no longer villagers. Though they might willingly assume the former obligations and recognize the former responsibilities, they could not recapture the former points of view or hold to the former judgments. They had seen too much, experienced too much to be again members of the community. It was a vain mission on which they continued to dispatch the letters; these people, once separated, would never belong again.

Their home now was a country in which they had not been born. Their place in society they had established for themselves through the hardships of crossing and settlement. The process had changed them, had altered the most intimate aspects of their lives. Every effort to cling to inherited ways of acting and thinking had led into a subtle adjustment by which those ways were given a new American form. No longer Europeans, could the immigrants then say that they belonged in America? The answer depended upon the conceptions held by other citizens of the United States of the character of the nation and of the role of the newcomers within it.

In the early nineteenth century, those already established on this side of the ocean regarded immigration as a positive good. When travel by sea became safe after the general peace of 1815 and the first fresh arrivals trickled in, there was a general disposition to welcome the movement. The favorable attitude persisted even when the tide mounted to the flood levels of the 1840's and 1850's. The man off the boat was then accepted without question or condition.

The approval of unlimited additions to the original population came easily to Americans who were conscious of the youth of their country. Standing at the edge of an immense continent, they were moved by the challenge of empty land almost endless in its extension. Here was room enough, and more, for all who would bend their energies to its exploitation. The shortage was of labor and not of acres; every pair of extra hands increased the value of the abundant resources and widened opportunities for everyone.

The youth of the nation also justified the indiscriminate admission of whatever foreigners came to these shores. There was high faith in the destiny of the Republic, assurance that its future history would justify the Revolution and the separation from Great Britain. The society and the culture that would emerge in this territory would surpass those of the Old World because they would not slavishly imitate the outmoded forms and the anachronistic traditions that constricted men in Europe. The United States would move in new directions of its own because its people were a new people.

There was consequently a vigorous insistence that this country was not simply an English colony become independent. It was a nation unique in its origins, produced by the mixture of many different types out of which had come an altogether fresh amalgam, the American. The ebullient citizens who believed and argued that their language, their literature, their art, and their polity were distinctive and original also believed and argued that their population had not been derived from a single source but had rather acquired its peculiar characteristics from the blending of a variety of strains.

There was confidence that the process would continue. The national type had not been fixed by its given antecedents; it was emerging from the experience of life on a new continent. Since the quality of men was determined not by the conditions surrounding their birth, but by the environment within which they passed their lives, it was pointless to select among them. All would come with minds and spirits fresh for new impressions; and being in America would make Americans of them. Therefore it was best to admit freely everyone who wished to make a home here. The United States would then be a great smelting pot, great enough so that there was room for all who voluntarily entered; and the nation that would ultimately be cast from that crucible would be all the richer for the diversity of the elements that went into the molten mixture.

The legislation of most of the nineteenth century reflected this receptive attitude. The United States made no effort actively to induce anyone to immigrate, but neither did it put any bars in the way of their coming. Occasional laws in the four decades after 1819 set up shipping regulations in the hope of improving the conditions of the passage. In practice, the provisions that specified the minimum quantities of food and the maximum number of passengers each vessel could carry were easily evaded. Yet the intent of those statutes was to protect the travelers and to remove harsh conditions that might discourage the newcomers.

Nor were state laws any more restrictive in design. The seaports, troubled by the burdens of poor relief, secured the enactment of measures to safeguard their treasuries against such charges. Sometimes the form was a bond to guarantee that the immigrant would not become at once dependent upon public support; sometimes it was a small tax applied to defray the costs of charity. In either case there was no desire to limit entry into the country; and none of these steps had any discernible effect upon the volume of admissions.

Once landed, the newcomer found himself equal in condition to the natives. Within a short period he could be naturalized and acquire all the privileges of a citizen. In some places, indeed, he could vote before the oath in court so transformed his status. In the eyes of society, even earlier than in the eyes of the law, he was an American.

It was not necessary that the immigrants should read deeply in the writings of political and social theorists to understand this conception of America. The idea was fully and clearly expressed in practice. The sense of being welcome gave people who had elsewhere been counted superfluous the assurance that their struggles to build a new life would be regarded with sympathy by their new neighbors. On such a foundation they could proceed to settle down in their own ways, make their own adjustments to the new conditions.

Significantly, the newcomers were not compelled to conform to existing patterns of action or to accept existing standards. They felt free to criticize many aspects of the life they discovered in the New World, the excessive concern with material goods and the inadequate attention to religion, the pushiness and restlessness of the people, the transitory quality of family relationships. The boldness of such judgments testified to the voluntary nature of immigrant adjustment. The strangers did not swallow America in one gulp; through their own associations and their own exertions they discovered how to live in the new place and still be themselves.

Until the 1880's the diverse groups in the United States got in each other's way only on very unusual occasions; generally rapid expansion made room for the unrestrained activity of all. Indeed the newcomers themselves did not then become issues; nor was there then any inclination to question the desirability of continuing the traditional open policy. But the second generation was an unstable element in the situation; as it grew in prominence, it created troublesome problems precisely because it had not a fixed place in the society. Standing between the culture of its parents and the culture of the older America, it bared the inadequacies of the assumption that the fusion of the multitude of strains in the melting pot would come about as a matter of course. The moments of revelation, though still rare, were profoundly shocking.

The discovery came most commonly in matters related to employment. However the native wage earner may have judged the effects of the immigrants upon the economy in general, he knew that these people did not directly compete with him for his job. But the children of the immigrants were Americans who were not content with the places that went to foreigners. On the labor market the offspring of the newcomers jostled the sons of well-established families. There was still no lack of space in a productive system that grew at an ever-accelerating pace. But the ambitious youngster every now and then hit upon the advertisement, No Irish need apply! The hurt would affect him, but also his father. It would disclose to these immigrants, and to many who came later, the limits of their belonging to America.

In politics also there were occasions on which the activities of the new citizens met the hostility of the old. If the consequences then were more striking, it was because there was less room for competition in the contest for political control. There were times when groups of men, unable to attain their own ends through government and unable to understand their own failure, sought to settle the blame on the foreign-born in their midst. In the 1850's, for instance, agitation of the slavery question and of a host of reform proposals put an intolerable strain upon the existing party structure. Years of compromise had produced no durable solution; instead they had given rise to grave forebodings of the calamitous Civil War that impended.

At the point of crisis, the stranger who stood in the way of attainment of some particular objective became the butt of attack. Abolitionists and reformers who found the conservative Irish arrayed against them at the polls, proslavery politicians who made much of the radicalism of some of the German leaders, and temperance advocates who regarded an alien hankering after alcohol as the main obstruction on the way to universal abstinence—such people were the backbone of the Know-Nothing Party that leaped to sudden prominence in the election of 1854. The oddly assorted elements that entered this political coalition had little in common; it took them only two years to come to know each other better, and once they did the party fell apart. Nothing positive had drawn such men together; they were attracted to each other rather by the fears that troubled them all. Incapable for the moment of confronting the real divisions within their society, many Americans achieved a temporary unity by cohering against the outsider in their midst.

The Know-Nothing movement disappeared as rapidly as it had appeared. In that respect it traced a course later followed by similar movements that flashed across the political horizon—the A.P.A. of the 1890's and the anti-German agitation of the First World War. These brief lapses in relationships that were generally peaceful had no enduring effects upon legislation or upon the attitudes of the mass of the native-born.

But even very brief glimpses of the hatred that might be generated against them disturbed the immigrants. The memory of charges violently made lingered long after the charges themselves were no longer a threat. They left behind a persistent uneasiness. The foreign-born could not forget that their rights as citizens had once been challenged. Could they help but wonder how fully they belonged in the United States? Occasional street fights among the boys that pitted group against group, from time to time more serious riots in which the unruly elements in the town attacked the aliens, and the more frequent slurs from press and platform kept alive that doubt.

Yet until the 1880's confidence outweighed the doubt. So long as those native to the country retained the faith that America would continue to grow from the addition of variety to its culture, the newcomers retained the hope, despite the difficulties of settlement and the discouragement of sporadic acts of hostility, that there would be here a home for the homeless of Europe.

As the nineteenth century moved into its last quarter, a note of petulance crept into the comments of some Americans who thought about this aspect of the development of their culture. It was a long time now that the melting pot had been simmering, but the end product seemed no closer than before. The experience of life in the United States had not broken down the separateness of the elements mixed into it; each seemed to retain its own identity. Almost a half-century after the great immigration of Irish and Germans, these people had not become indistinguishable from other Americans; they were still recognizably Irish and German. Yet even then, newer waves of newcomers were beating against the Atlantic shore. Was there any prospect that all these multitudes would ever be assimilated, would ever be Americanized?

A generation earlier such questions would not have been asked. Americans of the first half of the century had assumed that any man who subjected himself to the American environment was being Americanized. Since the New World was ultimately to be occupied by a New Man, no mere derivative of any extant stock, but different from and superior to all, there had been no fixed standards of national character against which to measure the behavior of newcomers. The nationality of the new Republic had been supposed fluid, only just evolving; there had been room for infinite variation because diversity rather than uniformity had been normal.

The expression of doubts that some parts of the population might not become fully American implied the existence of a settled criterion of what was

American. There had been a time when the society had recognized no distinction among citizens but that between the native and the foreign-born, and that distinction had carried no imputation of superiority or inferiority. Now there were attempts to distinguish among the natives between those who really belonged and those who did not, to separate out those who were born in the United States but whose immigrant parentage cut them off from the truly indigenous folk.

It was difficult to draw the line, however. The census differentiated after 1880 between natives and native-born of foreign parents. But that was an inadequate line of division; it provided no means of social recognition and offered no basis on which the true Americans could draw together, identify themselves as such.

Through these years there was a half-conscious quest among some Americans for a term that would describe those whose ancestors were in the United States before the great migrations. Where the New Englanders were, they called themselves Yankees, a word that often came to mean non-Irish or non-Canadian. But Yankee was simply a local designation and did not take in the whole of the old stock. In any case, there was no satisfaction to such a title. Its holders were one group among many, without any distinctive claim to Americanism, cut off from other desirable peoples prominent in the country's past. Only the discovery of common antecedents could eliminate the separations among the really American.

But to find a common denominator, it was necessary to go back a long way. Actually no single discovery was completely satisfactory. Some writers, in time, referred to the civilization of the United States as Anglo-Saxon. By projecting its origins back to early Britain, they implied that their own culture was always English in derivation, and made foreigners of the descendants of Irishmen and Germans, to say nothing of the later arrivals. Other men preferred a variant and achieved the same exclusion by referring to themselves as "the English-speaking people," a title which assumed there was a unity and uniqueness to the clan which settled the home island, the Dominions, and the United States. Still others relied upon a somewhat broader appellation. They talked of themselves as Teutonic and argued that what was distinctively American originated in the forests of Germany; in this view, only the folk whose ancestors had experienced the freedom of tribal self-government and the liberation of the Protestant Reformation were fully American.

These terms had absolutely no historical justification. They nevertheless achieved a wide currency in the thinking of the last decades of the nineteenth century. Whatever particular phrase might serve the purpose of a particular author or speaker, all expressed the conviction that some hereditary element had given form to American culture. The conclusion was inescapable: to be Americanized, the immigrants must conform to the American way of life completely defined in advance of their landing.

There were two counts to the indictment that the immigrants were not so conforming. They were, first, accused of their poverty. Many benevolent citizens, distressed by the miserable conditions in the districts inhabited by the laboring people, were reluctant to believe that such social flaws were indigenous to the New World. It was tempting, rather, to ascribe them to the defects of the newcomers, to improvidence, slovenliness, and ignorance rather than to inability to earn a living wage.

Indeed to those whose homes were uptown the ghettos were altogether alien territory associated with filth and vice and crime. It did not seem possible that men could lead a decent existence in such quarters. The good vicar on a philanthropic tour was shocked by the moral dangers of the dark unlighted hallway. His mind rushed to the defense of the respectable young girl: *Whatever her wishes may be, she can do nothing—shame prevents her from crying out.* The intention of the reformer was to improve housing, but the summation nevertheless was, *You cannot make an American citizen out of a slum.*

The newcomers were also accused of congregating together in their own groups and of an unwillingness to mix with outsiders. The foreign-born flocked to the great cities and stubbornly refused to spread out as farmers over the countryside; that alone was offensive to a society which still retained an ideal of rusticity. But even the Germans in Wisconsin and the Scandinavians in Minnesota held aloofly to themselves. Everywhere, the strangers persisted in their strangeness and willfully stood apart from American life. A prominent educator sounded the warning: *Our task is to break up their settlements, to assimilate and amalgamate these people and to implant in them the Anglo-Saxon conception of righteousness, law, and order.*

It was no simple matter to meet this challenge. The older residents were quick to criticize the separateness of the immigrant but hesitant when he made a move to narrow the distance. The householders of Fifth Avenue or Beacon Street or Nob Hill could readily perceive the evils of the slums but they were not inclined to welcome as a neighbor the former denizen of the East Side or the North End or the Latin Quarter who had acquired the means to get away. Among Protestants there was much concern over the growth of Catholic, Jewish, and Orthodox religious organizations, but there was no eagerness at all to provoke a mass conversion that might crowd the earlier churches with a host of poor foreigners. When the population of its neighborhood changed, the parish was less likely to try to attract the newcomers than to close or sell its building and move to some other section.

Indeed there was a fundamental ambiguity to the thinking of those who talked about "assimilation" in these years. They had arrived at their own view that American culture was fixed, formed from its origins, by shutting out the great mass of immigrants who were not English or at least not Teutonic. Now it was expected that those excluded people would alter themselves to earn their portion in Americanism. That process could only come about by increasing the contacts between the older and the newer inhabitants, by sharing jobs, churches, residences. Yet in practice, the man who thought himself an Anglo-Saxon found proximity to the other folk just come to the United States uncomfortable and distasteful and, in his own life, sought to increase rather than to lessen the gap between his position and theirs.

There was an escape from the horns of this unpleasant dilemma. It was tempting to resolve the difficulty by arguing that the differences between Americans on the one hand and Italians or Jews or Poles on the other were so deep as to admit of no conciliation. If these other stocks were cut off by their own innate nature, by the qualities of their heredity, then the original breed was justified both in asserting the fixity of its own character and in holding off from contact with the aliens.

Those who wished to support that position drew upon a sizable fund of racialist ideas that seeped deep into the thinking of many Americans toward the end of the nineteenth century. From a variety of sources there had been accumulated a body of doctrine that proclaimed the division of humanity into distinct, biologically separate races.

In the bitter years of controversy that were the prelude to the Civil War, there were Southerners who had felt the urgency of a similar justification. The abolitionists had raised the issue of the moral rightness of slavery, had pronounced it sinful to hold a fellow man in bondage. Sensitive to the criticism but bound in practice to his property, the plantation owner was attracted by the notion that the blacks were not his fellow men. Perhaps, as George Fitzhugh told him, the Negroes were not really human at all, but another order of beings, condemned by their natures to a servile status.

During the tragic reconstruction that followed the peace the argument acquired additional gravity. The formal, legal marks of subordination were gone; it was the more important to hold the colored people in submission by other means. Furthermore the section was now under the control of a national authority, dominated by Northern men; the vanquished faced the task of convincing the victors of the essential propriety of the losing cause.

For years after the end of the war, Southerners directed a stream of discussion across the Mason-Dixon line. Through their writing and talking ran an unvarying theme—the Negro was inherently inferior, did not need or deserve, could not use or be trusted with, the rights of humans. It did not matter how many auditors or readers were persuaded; the very agitation of the question familiarized Americans with the conception of race.

Eastward from the Pacific Coast came a similar gospel, also the product of local exigencies. Out of the dislocating effects of depression in 1873 and of the petering-out of the mining economy, there had developed in California a violently anti-Chinese movement. Those who regarded the Oriental as the source of all the state's difficulties were not content with what discriminatory measures the legislature could enact. They wished no less than the total exclusion of the Chinese.

Satisfaction of that demand could come only from the Federal Congress; and to get Congress to act, it was necessary to persuade representatives from every section of the reality of the menace. The attack upon the little brown rice-eaters, congenitally filthy and immoral, had the same consequences as the Southern charges against the Negro; it made current the notion of in-eradicable race differences.

A third problem brought the prestige of many influential names to the support of the idea. The War with Spain had given the United States substantial new overseas possessions, government of which posed troublesome problems. In the traditional pattern of American expansion, additional lands were treated as territories, held in a transitional stage until the time when they would become states. But their residents were citizens, endowed with all the rights of residents of the older part of the Union.

Substantial bodies of opinion opposed the extension of such treatment to the newly acquired islands. The proponents of navalism and of an aggressive imperialism, businessmen interested in the possibilities of profitable investments, and Protestant clergymen attracted by the possibility of converting large numbers of Catholics and heathen preferred to have the conquered areas colonies rather than territories, preferred to have the inhabitants subjects rather than citizens protected by the Constitution. To persuade the nation that such a departure from past policy was appropriate, the imperialists argued that the conquered peoples were incapable of self-government; their own racial inferiority justified a position of permanent subordination.

By 1900, the debates over the Negro, the Chinese, and the Filipino had familiarized Americans with the conception of permanent biological differences among humans. References to the "realities of race" by then had taken on a commonplace, almost casual quality. Early that year, for instance, a distinguished senator, well known for his progressive temperament and scholarly attainments, spoke exultantly of the opportunities in the Philippines and in China's limitless markets. *We will not renounce our part in the mission of our race, trustee of the civilization of the world. God has not been preparing the English-Speaking and Teutonic People for one thousand years for nothing. He has made us the master organizers to establish system where chaos reigns. He has marked the American People as the chosen nation to finally lead in the regeneration of the world.*

These ideas were unsystematic; as yet they were only the unconnected defenses of specific positions. But there were not lacking men to give these rude conceptions a formal structure, to work them up into a scientific creed.

Sociology toward the end of the century, in the United States, was only just emerging as a discipline of independent stature. The certitude with which its practitioners delivered their generalizations covered its fundamental immaturity of outlook. The American social scientists approached their subject through the analysis of specific disorders: criminality, intemperance, poverty, and disease. Everywhere they looked they found immigrants some-

how involved in these problems. In explaining such faults in the social
order, the scholar had a choice of alternatives: these were the pathological
manifestations of some blemish, either in the nature of the newcomers or in
the nature of the whole society. It was tempting to accept the explanation that
put the blame on the outsiders.

From the writings of the Europeans Gobineau, Drumont, and Cham-
berlain, the sociologists had accepted the dictum that social characteristics
depended upon racial differences. A succession of books now demonstrated
that flaws in the biological constitution of various groups of immigrants were
responsible for every evil that beset the country—for pauperism, for the low
birth rate of natives, for economic depressions, for class divisions, for prostitution and homosexuality, and for the appearance of city slums.

Furthermore, the social scientists of this period were not content with
academic analysis. They were convinced their conclusions must be capable
of practical application and often became involved in the reform movements
which, by planning, hoped to set right the evils of the times. The sociologist
eager to ameliorate the lot of his fellow men by altering the conditions of
their lives found the newcomers intractable, slow to change, obstacles in the
road to progress. Since few among these thinkers were disposed to accept the
possibility they might themselves be in error, they could only conclude the
foreigners were incapable of improvement. From opposite ends of the country, two college presidents united in the judgment that the immigrants were
*beaten men from beaten races, biologically incapable of rising, either now or
through their descendants, above the mentality of a twelve-year-old child.*

The only apparent solution was in eugenics, the control of the composition of the population through selection of proper stocks based on proper
heredity. A famous social scientist expressed it as his considered opinion that
*race differences are established in the very blood. Races may change their
religions, their form of government, and their languages, but underneath they
may continue the PHYSICAL, MENTAL, and MORAL CAPACITIES and
INCAPACITIES which determine the REAL CHARACTER of their RE-
LIGION, GOVERNMENT, and LITERATURE.* Surface conformity would
only conceal the insidious subtle characteristics that divided the native from
the foreign-born.

The fear of everything alien instilled by the First World War brought to
fullest flower the seeds of racist thinking. Three enormously popular books
by an anthropologist, a eugenicist, and a historian revealed to hundreds of
thousands of horrified Nordics how their great race had been contaminated
by contact with lesser breeds, dwarfed in stature, twisted in mentality, and
ruthless in the pursuit of their own self-interest.

These ideas passed commonly in the language of the time. No doubt
many Americans who spoke in the bitter terms of race used the words in a
figurative sense or in some other way qualified their acceptance of the harsh
doctrine. After all, they still recognized the validity of the American tradition

of equal and open opportunities, of the Christian tradition of the brotherhood of man. Yet, if they were sometimes troubled by the contradiction, nevertheless enough of them believed fully the racist conceptions so that five million could become members of the Ku Klux Klan in the early 1920's.

Well, a man who was sixty then had seen much that was new in his lifetime; and though he had not moved from the town of his birth, still his whole world had wandered away and left him, in a sense, a stranger in his native place. He too knew the pain of unfamiliarity, the moments of contrast between what was and what had been. Often he turned the corner of some critical event and confronted the effects of an industrial economy, of an urban society, of unsettled institutions, and of disorderly personal relationships. And, as he fought the fear of the unknown future, he too yearned for the security of belonging, for the assurance that change had not singled out him alone but had come to the whole community as a meaningful progression out of the past.

It was fretfully hard, through the instability of things, to recognize the signs of kinship. In anxious dread of isolation the people scanned each other in the vain quest for some portentous mark that would tell them who belonged together. Frustrated, some created a sense of community, drew an inner group around themselves by setting the others aside as outsiders. The excluded became the evidence of the insiders' belonging. It was not only, or not so much, because they hated the Catholic or Jew that the silent men marched in hoods, but because by distinguishing themselves from the foreigner they could at last discover their common identity, feel themselves part of a meaningful body.

The activities of the Klan were an immediate threat to the immigrants and were resisted as such. But there was also a wider import to the movement. This was evidence, at last become visible, that the newcomers were among the excluded. The judgment at which the proponents of assimilation had only hinted, about which the racist thinkers had written obliquely, the Klan brought to the open. The hurt came from the fact that the mouthings of the Kleagle were not eccentricities, but only extreme statements of beliefs long on the margin of acceptance by many Americans. To the foreign-born this was demonstration of what they already suspected, that they would remain as alienated from the New World as they had become from the Old.

Much earlier the pressure of their separateness had begun to disturb the immigrants. As soon as the conception of Americanization had acquired the connotation of conformity with existing patterns, the whole way of group life of the newcomers was questioned. Their adjustment had depended upon their ability as individuals in a free society to adapt themselves to their environment through what forms they chose. The demand by their critics that the adjustment take a predetermined course seemed to question their right, as they were, to a place in American society.

Not that these people concerned themselves with theories of nationalism, but in practice the hostility of the "natives" provoked unsettling doubts about the propriety of the most innocent actions. The peasant who had become a Polish Falcon or a Son of Italy, in his own view, was acting as an American; this was not a step he could have taken at home. To subscribe to a newspaper was the act of a citizen of the New World, not of the Old, even if the journal was one of the thousand published by 1920 in languages other than English. When the immigrants heard their societies and their press described as un-American they could only conclude that they had somehow become involved in an existence that belonged neither in the old land nor in the new.

Yet the road of conformity was also barred to them. There were matters in which they wished to be like others, undistinguished from anyone else, but they never hit upon the means of becoming so. There was no pride in the surname, which in Europe had been little used, and many a new arrival was willing enough to make a change, suitable to the new country. But August Björkegren was not much better off when he called himself Burke, nor [was] the Blumberg who became Kelly. The Lithuanians and Slovenes who moved into the Pennsylvania mining fields often endowed themselves with nomenclature of the older settlers, of the Irish and Italians there before them. In truth, these people found it difficult to know what were the "American" forms they were expected to take on.

What they did know was that they had not succeeded, that they had not established themselves to the extent that they could expect to be treated as if they belonged where they were.

If he was an alien, and poor, and in many ways helpless, still he was human, and it rankled when his dignity as a person was disregarded. He felt an undertone of acrimony in every contact with an official. Men in uniform always found him unworthy of respect; the bullying police made capital of his fear of the law; the postmen made sport of the foreign writing on his letters; the streetcar conductors laughed at his groping requests for directions. Always he was patronized as an object of charity, or almost so.

His particular enemies were the officials charged with his special oversight. When misfortune drove him to seek assistance or when government regulations brought them to inspect his home, he encountered the social workers, made ruthless in the disregard of his sentiments by the certainty of their own benevolent intentions. Confident of their personal and social superiority and armed with the ideology of the sociologists who had trained them, the emissaries of the public and private agencies were bent on improving the immigrant to a point at which he would no longer recognize himself.

The man who had dealings with the social workers was often sullen and uncooperative; he disliked the necessity of becoming a case, of revealing his dependence to strangers. He was also suspicious, feared there would be no understanding of his own way of life or of his problems; and he was resentful, because the powerful outsiders were judging him by superficial standards of their own. The starched young gentleman from the settlement house took stock from the middle of the kitchen. Were there framed pictures on the walls? Was there a piano, books? He made a note for the report: *This family is not yet Americanized; they are still eating Italian food.*

The services are valuable, but taking them is degrading. It is a fine thing to learn the language of the country; but one must be treated as a child to do so. *We keep saying all the time, This is a desk, this is a door. I know it is a desk and a door. What for keep saying it all the time? My teacher is a very nice young lady, very young. She does not understand what I want to talk about or know about.*

The most anguished conflicts come from the refusal of the immigrants to see the logic of their poverty. In the office it seems reasonable enough: people incapable of supporting themselves would be better off with someone to take care of them. It is more efficient to institutionalize the destitute than to allow them, with the aid of charity, to mismanage their homes. But the ignorant poor insist on clinging to their families, threaten suicide at the mention of the Society's refuge, or even of the hospital. What help the woman gets, she is still not satisfied. Back comes the ungrateful letter. *I don't ask you to put me in a poorhouse where I have to cry for my children. I don't ask you to put them in a home and eat somebody else's bread. I can't live here without them. I am so sick for them. I could live at home and spare good eats for them. What good did you give me to send me to the poorhouse? You only want people to live like you but I will not listen to you no more.*

A few dedicated social workers, mostly women, learned to understand the values in the immigrants' own lives. In some states, as the second generation became prominent in politics, government agencies came to co-operate with and protect the newcomers. But these were rare exceptions. They scarcely softened the rule experience everywhere taught the foreign-born, that they were expected to do what they could not do—to live like others.

For the children it was not so difficult. They at least were natives and could learn how to conform; to them the settlement house was not always a threat, but sometimes an opportunity. Indeed they could adopt entire[ly] the assumption that national character was long since fixed, only seek for their own group a special place within it. Some justified their Americanism by discovery of a colonial past; within the educated second generation there began a tortuous quest for eighteenth-century antecedents that might give them a portion in American civilization in its narrower connotation. Others sought to gain a sense of participation by separating themselves from later or lower elements in the population; they became involved in agitation against the Orientals, the Negroes, and the newest immigrants, as if thus to draw closer to the truly native. Either course implied a rejection of their parents who had themselves once been green off the boat and could boast of no New World antecedents.

The old folk knew then they would not come to belong, not through their own experience nor through their offspring. The only adjustment they had been able to make to life in the United States had been one that involved the separateness of their group, one that increased their awareness of the differences between themselves and the rest of the society. In that adjustment they had always suffered from the consciousness they were strangers. The demand that they assimilate, that they surrender their separateness, condemned them always to be outsiders. In practice, the free structure of American life permitted them with few restraints to go their own way, but under the shadow of a consciousness that they would never belong. They had thus completed their alienation from the culture to which they had come, as from that which they had left.

The Making
of a Negro Ghetto

Allan H. Spear

The problems of class conflict, industrial strife, and corrupt politics that confronted Chicago's reformers at the turn of the century were complicated by the city's great ethnic diversity. Since the Civil War, the emerging metropolis had attracted peoples from every part of the world. By 1890, 77.9 percent of its population was foreign born or of foreign parentage. The Germans, Irish, and Scandinavians were still the largest ethnic groups in the city, but after 1880, increasing numbers of Poles, Lithuanians, Czechs, Italians, and Eastern European Jews entered the city, concentrating in Chicago's perennial area of first settlement—the near West Side. There, cultural alienation complicated the problems of poverty. Facing the baffling complexities of urban life and an alien culture, these new groups strove against difficult odds to maintain their own ethnic integrity. Although various immigrant groups met the problems of American life in diverse ways, all attempted, through the creation of community institutions or the preservation of a traditional family structure, to maintain enough of their heritage to provide identity and a sense of belonging.

There were, then, many Chicagos by the end of the century. The reformers faced not merely the problem of an exploited working class, but of numerous worker enclaves, each clinging proudly to its own traditions. The newcomers' ignorance of American economic and political life made them particularly susceptible to the blandishments of unscrupulous employers and political bosses. A few of the reformers, such as Jane Addams and Graham Taylor, attempted to bring the immigrants into the mainstream of the city's life while at the same time respecting and even encouraging their cultural diversity. But many old-stock Chicagoans—and this included many of the sons and daughters of the earlier immigrants—were hostile, or at best patronizing, toward the ways of the newcomers.

Of Chicago's many ethnic groups, none had a longer local history than the Negroes. According to tradition, the first permanent settler on the site of Chicago was a black trader from Santo Domingo, Jean Baptiste Pointe de Saible, who built a cabin on the mouth of the Chicago River in about 1790. The beginning of Negro community life in the city can be traced to the late 1840's, when a small stream of fugitive slaves from the South and free Negroes from the East formed the core of a small Negro settlement. Soon there were enough Negroes in Chicago to organize an African Methodist Episcopal church, and within a decade several more churches and a number of social and civic clubs were flourishing. By 1860, almost a thousand Negroes lived in Chicago. A small leadership group, headed by a well-to-do tailor, John Jones, participated in antislavery activities and articulated the grievances of a people who already found themselves the victims of segregation and discrimination.

Despite the presence of an active antislavery movement, Negroes in antebellum Chicago were severely circumscribed. Residents of downstate Illinois frequently characterized Chicago as a "sinkhole of abolition" and a "nigger-loving town"; yet the sympathy that many white Chicagoans expressed for the Southern slaves was not often extended to the local Negroes. To be sure, the antislavery press, on occasion, noted approvingly the orderliness and respectability of the city's Negro community, but little was done to improve the status of the group. Chicago's Negroes could not vote, nor could they testify in court against whites. State law forbade intermarriage between the races. Segregation was maintained in the schools, places of public accommodation, and transportation. Chicago's abolitionists regarded these conditions as side issues and manifested little interest in them.

Between 1870 and 1890, the Chicago Negro community grew from less than four thousand to almost fifteen thousand and developed a well delineated class structure and numerous religious and secular organizations. After the fire of 1871, the community became more concentrated geographically. Most Negroes lived on the South Side, but were still well interspersed with whites. Although a majority of the city's Negroes worked as domestic and personal servants, a small business and professional class provided community leadership. St. Clair Drake and Horace Cayton described the Chicago Negro community of this period as

a small, compact, but rapidly growing community divided into three broad social groups. The "respectables"—churchgoing, poor or moderately prosperous, and often unrestrained in their worship—were looked down upon somewhat by the "refined" people, who, because of their education and breeding, could not sanction the less decorous behavior of their racial brothers. Both of these groups were censorious of the "riffraff," the "sinners"—unchurched and undisciplined.

During the postwar years, the formal pattern of segregation that had characterized race relations in antebellum Chicago broke down. By 1870, Negroes could vote. In 1874, the school system was desegregated. A decade later, after the federal civil rights bill was nullified by the United States Supreme Court, the Illinois legislature enacted a law prohibiting discrimination in public places. Despite these advances, however, the status of Negroes in Chicago remained ambiguous. They continued to face discrimination in housing, employment, and, even in the face of the civil rights law, public accommodations. But they were not confined to a ghetto. Most Negroes, although concentrated in certain sections of the city, lived in mixed neighborhoods. Negro businessmen and professional men frequently catered to a white market and enjoyed social, as well as economic, contacts with the white community. And although Negro churches and social clubs proliferated, there were still few separate civic institutions. Local Negro leaders were firmly committed to the ideal of an integrated community in which hospitals, social agencies, and public accommodations would be open to all without discrimination.

From the beginning, the experience of Chicago's Negroes had been, in significant ways, separate from the mainstream of the city's history. No other ethnic group had been legally circumscribed; no white minority had been forced to fight for legal recognition of citizenship rights. In 1890, despite the improvement in the Negroes' status since 1865, many of their problems were still unique. In a chiefly industrial city, they worked principally in domestic and service trades, almost untouched by labor organization and industrial strife. The political and economic turmoil of the late nineteenth century seemed to have little effect on the city's Negroes. No Jane Addams or Graham Taylor sought to bring them within the reform coalition that was attempting to change the life of the city. Generally ignored by white Chicagoans, Negroes were viewed neither as a threat to the city's well-being nor as an integral part of the city's social structure. Most responsible whites probably held the view quoted by Ray Stannard Baker: "We have helped the Negro to liberty; we have helped to educate him to stand on his own feet. Now let's see what he can do for himself. After all, he must survive or perish by his own efforts."

Still, the story of Chicago's Negroes in the late nineteenth and early twentieth centuries is interwoven with the general history of the city. As their numbers increased between 1890 and 1910, Negroes became ever more conspicuous, and the indifference with which they had been regarded in the nineteenth century changed to hostility. Labor strife, ethnic tension, political corruption, and inefficiency—the problems of greatest concern to white Chicagoans—all helped determine the status of the city's Negroes. So too did the rise of racist doctrines that many old-stock Chicagoans applied indiscriminately to Negroes and the "new" immigrants. The virulently anti-Negro works of Thomas Dixon, the Chautauqua addresses of South Carolina's Senator Benjamin Tillman, as well as the anti-immigrant propaganda of Prescott Hall,

Henry Pratt Fairchild, and Madison Grant epitomized an age of race chauvinism in which Anglo-Americans strove to preserve a mythical racial purity.

The profound changes that took place in the Chicago Negro community between the 1890's and 1920 had both internal and external dimensions. On the one hand, they were the result of the mounting hostility of white Chicagoans. Whites grew anxious as a growing Negro population sought more and better housing; they feared job competition in an era of industrial strife when employers frequently used Negroes as strikebreakers; and they viewed Negro voters as pawns of a corrupt political machine. All of these fears were accentuated by the rise of a racist ideology that reinforced traditional anti-Negro prejudices. On the other hand, Negroes were not passive objects in the developments of the early twentieth century. Their response to discrimination and segregation, the decisions their leaders made, and the community activities in which they engaged all helped to shape the emerging Negro ghetto. The rise of Chicago's black ghetto belongs to both urban history and Negro history; it was the result of the interplay between certain trends in the development of the city and major currents in Negro life and thought.

*   *   *

Between 1890 and 1915, the Negro population of Chicago grew from less than fifteen thousand to over fifty thousand. Although this growth was overshadowed by the massive influx of Negroes during and after World War I, this was nevertheless a significant increase. By the eve of World War I, although Negroes were still a minor element in the city's population, they were far more conspicuous than they had been a generation earlier. The population increase was accompanied by the concentration of Negroes into ever more constricted sections of the city. In the late nineteenth century, while most Negroes lived in certain sections of the South Side, they lived interspersed among whites; there were few all-Negro blocks. By 1915, on the other hand, the physical ghetto had taken shape; a large, almost all-Negro enclave on the South Side, with a similar offshoot on the West Side, housed most of Chicago's Negroes.

Migration was the major factor in the growth of the Negro community, and most migrants were coming from outside of the state. Over 80 percent of Chicago's Negro population in 1900 was born in states other than Illinois. The largest portion of these migrants originated in the border states and in the Upper South: Kentucky, and Missouri, in particular, had sent large groups of Negroes to Chicago. The states of the Deep South were, as yet, a secondary source of Chicago's Negro population; only 17 percent had come from these states as opposed to 43 percent from the Upper South. The states located directly south of Chicago supplied a larger segment of the population than the southeastern states, but there were sizable groups born in Virginia and Georgia.

From the beginning of Chicago's history, most Negroes had lived on the South Side. As early as 1850, 82 percent of the Negro population lived in an area bounded by the Chicago River on the north, Sixteenth Street on the south, the South Branch of the river on the west, and Lake Michigan on the east. The famous South Side black belt was emerging—a narrow finger of land, wedged between the railroad yards and industrial plants just west of Wentworth Avenue and the fashionable homes east of Wabash Avenue. By 1900, the black belt stretched from the downtown business district as far south as Thirty-ninth Street. But there were also sizable Negro enclaves, usually of a few square blocks each, in several other sections of the city. The Thirteenth Ward Negro community stretched along West Lake Street from

TABLE I   NEGRO POPULATION OF CHICAGO 1850–1930

| | | | | Percent Increase | |
| | | | | --- | --- |
Date	Total Population	Negro Population	Percent Negro	Total Population	Negro Population
1850	29,963	323	1.1	. . .	. . .
1860	109,260	955	0.9	265	196
1870	293,977	3,691	1.2	174	286
1880	503,185	6,480	1.1	68	75
1890	1,099,850	14,271	1.3	119	120
1900	1,698,575	30,150	1.9	54	111
1910	2,185,283	44,103	2.0	29	46
1920	2,701,705	109,453	4.1	24	148
1930	3,376,438	233,903	6.9	25	114

SOURCE: *U.S. Census Reports, 1850–1930.*

Ashland to Western. The Eighteenth Ward Negroes lived in the old immigrant neighborhood on the Near West Side near Hull House. On the Near North Side, Negroes had begun to settle in the Italian Seventeenth Ward. And on the South Side, beyond the black belt, communities of upper- and middle-class Negroes had emerged in Hyde Park, Woodlawn, Englewood, and Morgan Park.

Despite this concentration of Negroes in enclaves, the Negro population of the city was still relatively well distributed in 1900. Nineteen of the city's thirty-five wards had a Negro population of at least .5 percent of the total population of the ward and fourteen wards were at least 1 percent Negro. Only two wards had a Negro population of more than 10 percent. In 1898, just over a quarter of Chicago's Negroes lived in precincts that were more than 50 percent Negro, and over 30 percent lived in precincts that were at least 95 percent white. As late as 1910, Negroes were less highly segregated from native whites than were Italian immigrants.

The decade 1900 to 1910 saw several significant changes in the population pattern of Negroes in Chicago. The growth rate, which had far outpaced the white growth rate in the 1890's, declined from 111 percent to 46 percent, and the proportion of Negroes in the population increased from 1.9 percent to only 2 percent. Yet despite this stabilization, the Negro population was still composed largely of migrants. Over 77 percent of Chicago's Negroes were born outside of Illinois. This represents only a slight drop from 1900 and was almost five times as great as the corresponding figure for white Chicagoans. Only three major Negro communities in the country—Los Angeles, Denver, and Oklahoma City, all young Western cities with highly mobile populations—had higher proportions of out-of-state migrants than Chicago. Even such burgeoning industrial centers as Detroit, Pittsburgh, and Cleveland had a lower percentage of Negroes born in other states.

The concentration of Negroes in enclaves was clearly increasing throughout this period. By 1910, over 30 percent lived in predominantly Negro sections of the city and over 60 percent in areas that were more than 20 percent Negro. Whereas in 1900 nineteen of thirty-five wards had been over .5 percent Negro, this figure was reduced to thirteen in 1910. Furthermore, the second and third wards, which included the heart of the black belt, were now 25 percent Negro, while in 1900 only one ward had even approached that figure.

Negro residential patterns for 1910 can be seen most clearly through the use of census tract data. Of 431 census tracts in the city, Negroes could be found in all but ninety-four; eighty-eight were at least 1 percent Negro. Four tracts were over 50 percent Negro, but no tract was more than 61 percent Negro. Despite greater concentration, therefore, there were still few all-Negro neighborhoods in Chicago.

The eight or nine neighborhoods that had been distinguishable as areas of Negro settlement in 1900 remained the core of the Chicago Negro community in 1910. The principal South Side black belt was slowly expanding to accommodate the growing population. Not only did Negroes push steadily southward, but the narrow strip of land that made up the black belt began to widen as Negroes moved into the comfortable neighborhood east of State Street. By the end of the decade, Negroes could be found as far east as Cottage Grove Avenue.

Statistical data, then, reveal several definite trends in the pattern of Negro population in Chicago in the early twentieth century. The growth rate between 1900 and 1910 had decreased from the previous decade, but was still 50 percent greater than that of whites. Most of the population increase was the result of migration, particularly from the nearby border states. Negroes could be found throughout much of the city and the Negro neighborhoods were by no means exclusively black. But the concentration of Negroes in two enclaves on the South and West Sides was increasing. As the population grew, Negroes were not spreading throughout the city but were becoming confined to a clearly delineated area of Negro settlement.

The increasing physical separation of Chicago's Negroes was but one reflection of a growing pattern of segregation and discrimination in early twentieth-century Chicago. As the Negro community grew and opportunities for interracial conflict increased, so a pattern of discrimination and segregation became ever more pervasive. And perhaps the most critical aspect of interracial conflict came as the result of Negro attempts to secure adequate housing.

The South Side black belt could expand in only two directions in the early twentieth century—south and east. To the north lay the business district, which was moving south; in fact, commercial and light industrial concerns were pushing Negroes out of the area between Twelfth and Twenty-second Streets. West of Wentworth Avenue was a district of low-income immigrant homes, interspersed with railroad yards and light industry; the lack of adequate housing made this area undesirable for Negro expansion. East of State Street, on the other hand, was a neighborhood suitable for Negro residential requirements. This area, bounded by Twelfth and Thirty-ninth Streets, State Street and Lake Michigan, had, in the 1880's and early 1890's, included the most fashionable streets in the city—Prairie and Calumet Avenues. But by 1900, the wealthy residents were moving to the North Side, leaving behind them comfortable, if aging, homes. South of Thirty-ninth Street was an even more desirable residential area—Kenwood and Hyde Park —and across Washington Park from the southern extremity of the black belt were the new and attractive communities of Woodlawn and Englewood. In these areas, between 1900 and 1915, the lines were drawn in the struggle for housing that would subsequently lead to full-scale racial war. If no major battle was fought before 1915, there were at least several preliminary skirmishes that set the pattern for future, and more serious, confrontations.

Negro expansion did not always mean conflict, nor did it mean that a neighborhood would shortly become exclusively black. In 1910, not more than a dozen blocks on the South Side were entirely Negro, and in many mixed areas Negroes and whites lived together harmoniously. But as Negroes became more numerous east of State and south of Fifty-first, friction increased and white hostility grew. When a Negro family moved into a previously all-white neighborhood, the neighbors frequently protested, tried to buy the property, and then, if unsuccessful, resorted to violence to drive out the interlopers. In many cases, the residents organized to urge real estate agents and property owners to sell and rent to whites only. The whites often succeeded in keeping Negroes out, at least temporarily. When their efforts failed, they gradually moved out, leaving the neighborhood predominantly, although rarely exclusively, Negro.

Such incidents occurred with only minor variations throughout the prewar period. In 1900, three Negro families brought about "a nervous prostration epidemic" on Vernon Avenue. Five years later, an attempt to oust Negroes from a Forrestville Avenue building landed in court. In 1911, a committee of Champlain Avenue residents dealt with a Negro family in the neighborhood by the "judicious use of a wagon load of bricks"; the *Record-*

Herald described the affair as "something as nearly approaching the operations of the Ku Klux Klan as Chicago has seen in many years." Englewood residents, two years later, did not have to go quite so far; the objectionable party, this time a white man with a Negro wife, agreed to sell his property to a hastily organized "neighborhood improvement association." A Negro who moved into a home on Forrestville Avenue in 1915, on the other hand, termed an offer of this type "blackmail," but after several days of intimidation, he too submitted and sold his property.

Perhaps the most serious incident, and the one which provides the most insight into the nature of the housing conflict, occurred in Hyde Park—Chicago's most persistent racial trouble spot—in 1909. A separate town until 1892, Hyde Park was still an area of pleasant, tree-shaded streets, large, comfortable homes, and a vigorous cultural life centered on the campus of the new but thriving University of Chicago. Negroes were no strangers to the community: for many years a few families, mostly house servants and hotel employees who worked in the neighborhood, had clustered on Lake Avenue near Fifty-fifth Street, on the eastern edge of Hyde Park. Now this community began to expand and Negroes occupied homes in nearby white blocks.

White Hyde Parkers responded to the Negro "invasion" with a concerted drive to keep Negroes out of white areas. The Hyde Park Improvement Protective Club was organized in the autumn of 1908; headed by a prominent attorney, Francis Harper, it soon boasted 350 members, "including some of the wealthiest dwellers on the South Side." In the summer of 1909, the Club issued a manifesto: Negro residents of Hyde Park must confine themselves to the "so-called Districts," real estate agents must refuse to sell property in white blocks to Negroes, and landlords must hire only white janitors. To implement this policy, the Club appointed a committee to purchase property owned by Negroes in white blocks and to offer bonuses to Negro renters who would surrender their leases. Moreover, the Club threatened to blacklist any real estate firm that defied its edict. "The districts which are now white," said Harper, "must remain white. There will be no compromise."

Despite the efforts of the Negro residents of Hyde Park to counter the activities with indignation meetings and boycotts, the white campaign continued. The neighborhood newspaper supported the Improvement Club, and Harper maintained that he had "received hosts of letters commending the course of the organization." When the Club was unable to persuade a Negro family to move voluntarily, the neighbors used more direct tactics: vandals broke into a Negro home on Greenwood Avenue one night and broke all the windows; the family left the next day. In September, the Club announced a boycott of merchants who sold goods to Negroes living in white neighborhoods. It urged separate playgrounds and tennis courts for Negroes in Washington Park, and, in its annual report, advocated segregation of the public schools. "It is only a question of time," a Club spokesman predicted, "when there will be separate schools for Negroes throughout Illinois." The group operated more quietly after 1909, but it had achieved its major goal. The little Negro community on Lake Avenue dwindled in size and the rest of Hyde Park remained white for forty years.

The Hyde Park episode well illustrates the intensification of anti-Negro feeling in the early twentieth century. This feeling could even create strong sentiment among whites for a return to formalized segregation—separate schools and recreation facilities. Some white Chicagoans spoke of the necessity for a residential segregation ordinance. The incident also provided an early example of techniques that were to become increasingly important as whites continually tried to stem the tide of Negro residential "invasion": the neighborhood improvement association, the community newspaper, the boycott, and in the last resort, violence. Furthermore, the episode was significant because it occurred in a middle- and upper-class community, and its victims were middle- and upper-class Negroes attempting to find comfortable homes among people of their own economic status. The housing problem for Negroes was not restricted to the poor; even the affluent were blocked in their quest for a decent place to live.

The unwillingness of whites to tolerate Negroes as neighbors had far-reaching results. Because Negroes were so limited in their choice of housing, they were forced to pay higher rents in those buildings that were open to them. Real estate agents frequently converted buildings in marginal neighborhoods from white to Negro and demanded rents 10 to 15 percent higher than they had previously received. Sophonisba Breckinridge of Hull House estimated that a Negro family "pays $12.50 for the same accommodations the Jew in the Ghetto received for $9 and the immigrant for $8." One realty company inserted two advertisements for the same apartment in a daily newspaper: one read, "seven rooms, $25"; the other, "seven rooms for colored people, $37.50." High rents often forced Negro families to take in lodgers. A 1912 survey of 1,775 South Side Negroes reported that 542, or 31 percent, lived as lodgers in the homes of others.

Living conditions in much of the black belt closely resembled conditions in the West Side ghetto or in the Stockyards district. Although Negroes could find some decent homes on the fringes of the Negro section, the core of the black belt was a festering slum. Here was an area of one- and two-story frame houses (unlike the older Eastern cities Chicago had, as yet, few large tenements), usually dilapidated with boarded-up porches and rickety wooden walks. Most of the buildings contained two flats and, although less crowded than houses in the Jewish, Polish, and Bohemian slums, they were usually in worse repair. The 1912 survey revealed that in a four-block area in the black belt, only 26 percent of the dwellings were in good repair—as compared to 71 percent in a similar sampling in a Polish neighborhood, 57 percent among Bohemians, and 54 percent in the ethnically mixed Stockyards district. "Colored tenants," the survey reported, "found it impossible to persuade their landlords either to make the necessary repairs or to release them from their contracts; . . . it was so hard to find better places in which to live that they were forced to make the repairs themselves, which they could rarely afford to do, or to endure the conditions as best they might."

White real estate agents, insensitive to class differences among Negroes, made no attempt to uphold standards in middle-class Negro neighborhoods as they did in comparable white districts. They persistently rented flats in "respectable" Negro neighborhoods to members of the "sporting element," thus forcing middle-class Negroes to move continually in search of decent areas to live and rear families. As a result, neighborhood stability was at best temporary. The streets east of State, which had become the mecca of the Negro middle class in the late 1890's, began to decline by 1905. A few years later the district was characterized by "men and women half clothed hanging out of a window," "rag-time piano playing . . . far into the night," and "shooting and cutting scrapes."

Municipal policy regarding vice further complicated the situation. City authorities, holding that the suppression of prostitution was impossible, tried to confine it to certain well-defined areas where it could be closely watched. The police frequently moved the vice district so as to keep it away from commercial and white residential areas. Invariably they located it in or near the black belt, often in Negro residential neighborhoods. The chief of police declared that so long as prostitutes confined their activities to the district between Wentworth and Wabash, they would not be apprehended. Neighborhood stability, then, was threatened not only by the influx of Negro "shadies," but by the presence of an officially sanctioned vice district catering primarily to whites.

Periodic attempts to clean up the red-light district received little support from Negro leaders who believed that such campaigns would merely drive the undesirables deeper into Negro residential neighborhoods. When legal prostitution was finally abolished in 1912, these fears were fully realized; vice in Chicago continued to be centered in the black belt. Fannie Barrier Williams, a prominent Negro civic leader, summed up the plight of the middle- and upper-class Negro: "The huddling together of the good and the bad, compelling the decent element of the colored people to witness the brazen display of vice of all kinds in front of their homes and in the faces of their children, are trying conditions under which to remain socially clean and respectable."

The pattern of Negro housing, then, was shaped by white hostility and indifference: limited in their choice of homes, Negroes were forced to pay higher rents for inferior dwellings and were frequently surrounded by prostitutes, panderers, and other undesirable elements. This, together with the poverty of the majority of Chicago Negroes, produced in the black belt the conditions of slum-living characteristic of American cities by the end of the nineteenth century.

The most striking feature of Negro housing, however, was not the existence of slum conditions, but the difficulty of escaping the slum. Euro-

pean immigrants needed only to prosper to be able to move to a more desirable neighborhood. Negroes, on the other hand, suffered from both economic
deprivation and systematic racial discrimination. "The problem of the Chicago
Negro," wrote Sophonisba Breckinridge,

is quite different from the white man and even that of the immigrants. With the
Negro the housing dilemma was found to be an acute problem, not only among
the poor, as in the case of the Polish, Jewish, or Italian immigrants, but also
among the well-to-do. . . . Thus, even in the North, where the city administration
does not recognize a "Ghetto" or "pale," the real estate agents who register and
commercialize what they suppose to be a universal race prejudice are able to enforce one in practice.

The development of a physical ghetto in Chicago, then, was not the
result chiefly of poverty; nor did Negroes cluster out of choice. The ghetto
was primarily the product of white hostility. Attempts on the part of Negroes
to seek housing in predominantly white sections of the city met with resistance
from the residents and from real estate dealers. Some Negroes, in fact, who
had formerly lived in white neighborhoods, were pushed back into the black
districts. As the Chicago Negro population grew, Negroes had no alternative
but to settle in well-delineated Negro areas. And with increasing pressure for
Negro housing, property owners in the black belt found it profitable to force
out white tenants and convert previously mixed blocks into all-Negro blocks.
The geographical dimensions of Black Chicago in the early twentieth century
underwent no dramatic shift similar, for instance, to Negro New York, where
the center of Negro life moved to previously all-white Harlem in less than a
decade. Negroes in Chicago were not establishing new communities. But to
meet the needs of a growing population, in the face of mounting white resistance, Negro neighborhoods were becoming more exclusively Negro as they
slowly expanded their boundaries.

*   *   *

As white hostility almost closed the housing market to Negroes and
created a physical ghetto, it also limited the opportunities for Negroes to
secure desirable jobs and gain access to public facilities. Chicago Negroes in
the early twentieth century were confined to the domestic and personal service
trades and were unable to gain even a foothold in industry and commerce. In
1900, almost 65 percent of the Negro men and over 80 percent of the Negro
women worked as domestic and personal servants, while only 8.3 percent of
the men and 11.9 percent of the women were engaged in manufacturing (and
most of the women so employed worked in their own homes as dressmakers
and seamstresses). In 1910 the basic pattern remained the same. Over 45
percent of the employed Negro men worked in just four occupations—as
porters, servants, waiters, and janitors—and over 63 percent of the women
were domestic servants or laundresses. In both 1900 and 1910, more Negroes

were engaged in the professions than their numbers would warrant, but these were concentrated in professions that required relatively little formal training —music, the theater, and the clergy. Relatively few Negroes could be found in the legal, medical, and teaching professions. A large portion of those Negroes employed in manufacturing, trade, and transportation were unskilled laborers.

Negroes entered occupations that were not desirable enough to be contested by whites. When white workers sought jobs in trades dominated by Negroes, they were usually able to drive the Negroes out. In the nineteenth century, for instance, many Negroes had worked as barbers and coachmen, but by the early twentieth century, whites had replaced most of them in these capacities. Hence Negroes "were constantly driven to lower kinds of occupations which are gradually being discarded by the white man." These jobs were generally low-paying, carried the stigma of servility, and offered few opportunities for advancement. Porters in hotels, stores, and railroads, and janitors in apartment buildings and business houses had no chance to move up to better positions because these concerns hired Negroes in no other capacities. Among the service trade employees, only waiters could look forward to promotions; the job of headwaiter, which paid as much as one hundred dollars a month, was perhaps the most lucrative to which Negroes could aspire. Negro women were particularly limited in their search for desirable positions. Clerical work was practically closed to them and only a few could qualify as school teachers. Negro domestics often received less than white women for the same work, and they could rarely rise to the position of head servant in large households—a place traditionally held by a Swedish woman.

Several factors combined to keep Negroes out of industry and trade— especially the skilled and semiskilled jobs. First, most employers were simply disposed against hiring Negroes so long as an adequate supply of white labor was available—and with open immigration from Europe there was seldom a labor shortage. These employers feared that their white employees would object to working with Negroes, and many believed that Negro workers were less efficient. Secondly, many Negroes with skills had acquired them in the South and were often unable to meet Northern standards. Moreover, they were seldom able to acquire skills in the North: apprentice programs were usually open to whites only, and Negroes had little desire to learn a trade so long as its job prospects remained uncertain. Finally, the refusal of most trade unions to admit black workers on an equal basis kept Negroes out of many trades. Some unions completely excluded Negroes through clauses in their constitutions; others admitted Negroes, but then either segregated them in separate, subordinate locals, excluded them from specific projects, or simply made no effort to find jobs for them.

*   *   *

Most observers—both Negro and white—agreed that the status of Negroes in Chicago was deteriorating, and some saw parallels between developments in Chicago and the hardening of Jim Crow patterns in the South. Two white commentators noted that "in the face of increasing manifestations of race prejudice, the Negro has come to acquiesce silently as various civil rights are withheld him in the old 'free North.' " A Negro columnist, in 1914, took an even more pessimistic position. He noted that "Afro-American people in increasing numbers are refused the accommodations of public places . . . in . . . violation of the laws of the state of Illinois," that "discrimination is manifesting itself more and more in the courts of Chicago," and that "the police department is especially filled with the wicked and unlawful determination to degrade Afro-Americans and fix upon them the badge of inferiority." He concluded that Negroes "are more and more being reduced to a fixed status of social and political inferiority."

To compare the evolution of the Negro's status in Chicago with the crystallization of the caste system in the South during the same period was an exaggeration. Discrimination in Chicago remained unofficial, informal, and uncertain; the Negro's status did not become fixed. Nevertheless, as Negroes became more numerous and conspicuous, white hostility increased and Negroes encountered an ever more pervasive pattern of exclusion. Edward E. Wilson, a Negro attorney, noted that the growth of the Negro community "brought [Negroes] into contact with whites who hardly knew that there were a thousand Colored people in Chicago." Moreover, "Colored children have appeared in numbers in many schools," and "Colored men have pushed their way into many employments." "All these things," he concluded, "have a tendency to cause the whites to resort to jim crow tactics."

By 1915, Negroes had become a special group in the social structure of prewar Chicago. They could not be classified as merely another of Chicago's many ethnic groups. The systematic proscription they suffered in housing and jobs, the discrimination they often—although not always—experienced in public accommodations and even municipal services, the violence of which they were frequently victims, set them apart from the mainstream of Chicago life in significant ways. They were forced to work out their destiny within the context of an increasingly biracial society.

*   *   *

The Chicago experience, therefore, tends to refute any attempt to compare Northern Negroes with European immigrants. Unlike the Irish, Poles, Jews, or Italians, Negroes banded together not to enjoy a common linguistic, cultural, and religious tradition, but because a systematic pattern of discrimination left them no alternative. Negroes were tied together less by a common cultural heritage than by a common set of grievances. Even those who made a major effort to emphasize the positive aspects of separate Negro development were hard-pressed. The Garveyites, for instance, were forced to glorify an African past that had no relationship to the historical experience of

American Negroes. Racial solidarity was a response rather than a positive force. It was an attempt to preserve self-respect and foster self-reliance in the face of continual humiliations and rebuffs from white society.

The persistence of the Chicago Negro ghetto, then, has been not merely the result of continued immigration from the South, but the product of a special historical experience. From its inception, the Negro ghetto was unique among the city's ethnic enclaves. It grew in response to an implacable white hostility that has not basically changed. In this sense it has been Chicago's only true ghetto, less the product of voluntary development within than of external pressures from without. Like the Jewries of medieval Europe, Black Chicago has offered no escape. Irishmen, Poles, Jews, or Italians, as they acquired the means, had an alternative: they could move their enclaves to more comfortable environs or, as individuals, leave the enclaves and become members of the community at large. Negroes—forever marked by their color —could only hope for success within a rigidly delineated and severely restricted ghetto society. No physical wall has encircled the black belt. But an almost equally impervious wall of hostility and discrimination has isolated Negroes from the mainstream of Chicago life. Under such conditions, Negroes have tried, often against impossible odds, to make the best of their circumstances by creating a meaningful life of their own. But they have done so, not out of choice, but because white society has left them no alternative.

Race: Thinking May Make It So

Edward C. Banfield

The most conspicuous fact of life in the city is racial division. A hundred times a day there are confrontations between black and white, and almost every day an explosion turns part of some city into a battleground. The residential suburbs are mostly white—often "lily-white"; the central cities, especially their older, more deteriorated parts, and above all their slums, are predominantly or entirely black. Many observers see little reason to hope for improvement. The city, they say, has always exploited, humiliated, and degraded its immigrant groups. But whereas all the others eventually have been able to escape their oppressors by joining them, the Negro, marked as he is by skin color, can never do so. For him, in this view, the city is degradation without hope. "The dark ghettoes," writes Kenneth B. Clark, "are social, political, educational, and—above all—economic colonies. Their inhabitants are subject peoples, victims of the greed, cruelty, insensitivity, guilt, and fear of their masters."

The view to be developed here is altogether different from this one. The existence of ethnic and racial prejudice both past and present is a fact too painfully evident to require assertion. Being subject to prejudice, however, it is clear in retrospect, was not the main disadvantage of the Irish, Jews, Italians, and others. Nor is it the *main* one of the Negro—not to mention the Puerto Rican and the Mexican—today. The other minority groups once lived in the oldest parts of the inner city—and the Negro lives in them now —not so much because they were looked down on (although, of course, they were) as because they had low incomes. It was because they were *poor* that they had to come to the city, and being poor they could not afford good housing on the outskirts of the city or in the suburbs, nor could they afford to commute to the factories, stores, and offices where they worked. Similarly, the neighborhoods in which the other groups lived were often squalid and vicious—as the Negro slum is now—not because they were subject people, victimized and degraded by the city (although there was an element of that, too), but because every wave of immigration brought many whose culture was lower-class.

Today the Negro's *main* disadvantage is the same as the Puerto Rican's and Mexican's: namely, that he is the most recent unskilled, and hence relatively low-income, migrant to reach the city from a backward rural area. The city is not the end of his journey but the start of it. He came to it not because he was lured by a cruel and greedy master but because he was attracted by job, housing, school, and other opportunities that, bad as they were, were nevertheless better by far than any he had known before. Like earlier immigrants, the Negro has reason to expect that his children will have increases of opportunity even greater than his. If he lives in a neighborhood that is all-black, the reason is not white prejudice simply, and in some instances it may not be that at all. This physical separation may arise from various causes—his having a low income, his being part of a wave of migration that inundated all of the cheap housing then available (had more been available, more migrants might well have come to take it), his having cultural characteristics that make him an undesirable neighbor, his inclination to live among his own kind. The example of Orientals, groups whose mean income and education are now higher than those of the white Protestant and possibly of the Jew, proves that acceptance and upward mobility need not depend upon the absence of distinguishing physical characteristics.

The misfortune, amounting to a tragedy, is not that Negroes got to the city but that they got there so late and then in such great numbers in so short a time. It is likely that had they moved to the city in large numbers in the decades between the Civil War and the First World War, most Negroes would long since have entered the middle class. Those who *did* come north in this period did enter it soon: Philadelphia and Cleveland, for example, had predominantly middle-class Negro communities before the turn of the century. Unfortunately, however, mob violence against them in the cities and job discrimination in favor of European immigrants kept most away. There would doubtless be slums in the central cities today even if there had been a large-scale movement of Negroes three or four generations ago, but the slums would not be all-black and they would not be surrounded by all-white suburbs. Therefore, one very serious danger—that of economic and class-cultural problems being mistaken for racial ones—would not exist.

Almost everything said about the problems of the Negro tends to exaggerate the purely racial aspects of the situation. (The same is true of what is said of the Puerto Rican, the Mexican, and other groups, but discussion here will be limited to the Negro.) "Purely racial" factors mean, first, prejudice on racial grounds (not only prejudice against but also prejudice for— that is, racial pride) and, second, whatever cultural characteristics pertain to a racial group qua racial group. The importance of these factors is exaggerated implicitly by any statement about the Negro that fails—as almost all do—to take account of the many other (nonracial or contingently racial) factors that are at work along with the purely racial ones. These nonracial factors include, especially, income, class, education, and place of origin (rural or urban, Southern or not). No doubt the effect of these factors on the Negro has been increased by the operation of racial ones in the background: for example, the lack of education that in large measure accounts for the Negro's handicaps is itself to be explained largely by racial discrimination past and present. (On the other hand, there are groups—rural Southern whites, for example—whose handicaps are much like the Negro's and must be explained entirely by non-racial factors.) In any case, there is no a priori reason to assume (as is too often done) that the causes operating in the evolution of a problem over time ("historical" causes) must be identical with those operating to perpetuate that problem at any given time ("continuing" causes). The concern here is with the continuing causes of the Negro's problems, which, it will be argued, are seldom purely racial and very often have little or nothing to do with race. In short, what will here be called the Statistical Negro—that is, the Negro when all nonracial factors have been controlled for—is a very different fellow from what will be called the Census Negro. In some respects the Statistical Negro is indistinguishable from the white, and in all respects the differences between him and the white are smaller than those between the Census Negro and the white.

For example, the Census Negro has a birthrate about one-third higher than does the white. If, however, women who have lived on Southern farms are left out of account, the Negro birthrate does not differ significantly from that of the white. If, in addition, women with less than a high school education are omitted, the Negro rate is actually a little lower than the white.

The school dropout rate among Census Negro adolescents is almost twice that among whites. But when the occupation of parents is controlled for, this difference is much reduced, and with children of white-collar parents it almost disappears.

At all educational levels the Census Negro earns less than the white. On the average, however, he has achieved less well in school (in the schools of the Northeast he is 3.3 years behind the white in achievement by grade 12; moreover, many Negroes attend schools having a "social promotion" policy by which children are promoted whether they have learned anything or not). It is likely that if differences in the educational achievement of graduates were fully taken into account, racial prejudice would be found to have much less significance for earnings differences than otherwise appears; indeed, it may be that the Statistical Negro graduate earns fully as much as the white.

Unemployment rates are persistently higher for Census Negroes than for whites. About half the differential in rates is to be accounted for by differences between the two groups in their distribution by occupation, education, age, and region, however. These differences are largely the result of historical discrimination, of course, but the fact is that *present* discrimination by employers on the basis of color accounts for much less unemployment than the gross figures would suggest. One important factor behind unemployment differentials is place of residence: boys and girls who live in districts where there is a relative surplus of unskilled workers are at a manifest disadvantage whatever their color. Occupation and income of parents is another: boys and girls whose parents own businesses or "know people" have an advantage in finding jobs. Class culture is still another factor: lower-class youths are less likely than others to look for jobs, and the lower their class culture the less acceptable they are to employers. Even after correcting for everything possible, something is left that must be explained on racial grounds, especially job discrimination. Still, considering all these other factors, white prejudice and any specifically Negro characteristics account for much less of the difference in employment rates than would otherwise appear.

The income of the Census Negro is low as compared to that of the white. However, when one controls for region of origin, rural or urban origin, and education, the difference is greatly reduced. Much of what looks like "racial" poverty is really "rural Southern" poverty.

The Census Negro spends as much as a third more for housing than do whites at a given income level but "it is far from clear that the residential segregation does in fact lead to higher housing prices for equivalent quality for Negroes." Studies made in Chicago show that when differences in income, occupation, location, and some other variables are taken into account, the Negro's housing costs are not very different from the white's. In Chicago, at least, the Statistical Negro pays about the same rent and lives at about the same density as the white.

The proportion of Negro children in households without a father present is very high. Whether it is higher than among whites of the same income, education, rural-urban origin, and class culture is not clear, however. An investigation conducted just before the First World War in the then predominantly Irish Middle West Side of New York found that about half the families there were fatherless.

Sexual promiscuity in the Negro slum is notorious. This is largely if not wholly a class characteristic, however. In another report on the predominantly Irish Middle West Side of half a century ago, mention is made of "the hopelessly unmoral attitude of the neighborhood," where "boys as young as seven and eight actually practice sodomy."

Negro youths in the slums are prone to violence, but here again it is unlikely that any racial factor is at work. *All* lower-class youths are prone to violence. Charles Loring Brace, a social worker of the 1880's, remarked that the youth gangs then plaguing New York consisted mainly of the American-born children of Irish and German immigrants. He went on to say:

> *The intensity of the American temperament is felt in every fibre of these children of poverty and vice. Their crimes have the unrestrained and sanguinary character of a race accustomed to overcome all obstacles. . . . The murder of an unoffending old man . . . is nothing to them. They are ready for any offense or crime, however degraded or bloody.*

The arrest rate of the Census Negro is undoubtedly higher than that of the Statistical Negro. According to economist Belton Fleisher, it is being of low income, not being black, that is most important in disposing one toward the kinds of crimes that juveniles commit. Probably the same is true for most other kinds of crimes as well. Most crimes are committed by lower-income and lower-class people, and many Negroes fall into these categories. Also, Southerners as such are more given to violence than are other Americans, and the proportion of Negroes who are of Southern origin is of course high.

The argument here is not that purely racial factors are of little or no importance. It is all too obvious that racial prejudice enters into every sphere of life. Cultural differences (apart from *class*-cultural differences)—and conceivably even biological ones as well—also account in some degree for the special position of the Negro, as they do for that of every ethnic group. If there is something about Jewish culture that makes the Jew tend to be upwardly mobile, there may be something about Negro culture that makes the Negro tend not to be. Strangely (considering the great number of sociologists and social anthropologists produced by American universities in the last two or three decades and considering the importance of the problem), very little is known about the personality and culture of the Negro or of other racial and ethnic groups in the city. Eventually, systematic study may reveal deep cultural differences among ethnic groups. It is very unlikely, however, that any differences in racial (or ethnic) culture will have as much explanatory importance for the matters under discussion here as do differences in income, education, place of origin, and—above all—class culture.

One way to estimate the importance of racial prejudice in the city is to ask how matters would change if overnight all Negroes turned white (or, if it be preferred, all whites black), thus making job and housing discrimination on color grounds impossible. If this were to happen, the Negro would in some ways be better off. But it is easy to overestimate the speed with which improvements in his situation would occur as well as the number of people who would be benefited in the short run.

If, overnight, Negroes turned white, most of them would go on living under much the same handicaps for a long time to come. The great majority of New Whites would continue working at the same jobs, living in the same neighborhoods, and sending their children to the same schools.

There would be no sudden mass exodus from the blighted and slum neighborhoods where most Negroes now live. By and large, New Whites would go on living in the same neighborhoods for the simple reason that they could not afford to move to better ones. Most of them would still be near the bottom of the income scale and would therefore buy or rent the cheapest housing on the market, which is to say the oldest, most run-down housing in the highest-density districts of the inner city. After a few years many would be living on the same blocks with Old Whites of the same (low) income level as themselves, but this change would be of slight importance, since the neighborhoods would be about as poor as before. In the very worst sections, New Whites would be an overwhelming majority for a long time to come, the reason being that Negroes constitute most of the poorest of the poor. Stores, schools, churches, and other community institutions and facilities there would still be segregated. For example, New White children would go to school only with New White children, and the slum school would remain a slum school. Negro incomes are growing as fast as white, but while Negroes are increasingly well-off *absolutely*, the gap remains nearly constant in *relative* terms.

With the end of racial discrimination, some New Whites would quickly climb the job and income ladder and then leave the slums and the blighted areas. Unfortunately, however, these would be few in number; the end of racial discrimination would not improve the job situation of most New Whites in the first generation at least. They would earn as little as before because they would still be unskilled. As for the well-trained, many would gain by the end of prejudice, but many would lose by it too. At present, most Negro professionals and politicians (the latter meaning all who act in representative capacities qua Negroes) have an advantage in not having to compete with whites; of the middle-class Negroes who do compete with whites, some receive a premium for being black. By putting them into competition with Old Whites, the end of racial discrimination would, in the short run at least, hurt perhaps as many New Whites as it would help.

It may be objected that in the absence of racial discrimination the Negro would soon become as well educated as the white and would then move into what are now "white" occupations. Although this would happen to some extent, there would not, unfortunately, be enough such movement to change the situation fundamentally. The reason is that while the New Whites were raising their educational level, the Old Whites would also be raising *theirs*; since the Old Whites would have a big head start, the gap between them and the New Whites would only widen if both groups made the same percentage increases in their rates of progress. The disparity between white and nonwhite levels of educational attainment, Otis Dudley Duncan calculates, "can hardly disappear in less than three-quarters of a century."

How painfully slow any improvement in the occupational position of the Negro relative to that of the white is likely to be may be judged from the experience of the past few decades. In the 1940's the relative occupational position of Negro males improved by 5 percent on an index representing the main occupational categories, and in the next decade there was a further improvement of 1 percent. The total improvement, however, erased only about one-fifth of the gross difference that existed to begin with. Of course, racial discrimination was widespread in the 1940's and 1950's, but there was less of it than there had been before. After twenty years the relative (but not the absolute) disadvantage of the Negro was almost unchanged. Special programs that will greatly change this prospect may perhaps be devised, although no very promising ones have appeared as yet.

One circumstance that would tend to hold the New White back is the size of his family. There were 60 percent more youths dependent on their parents among poor Negroes than among poor whites living in central cities in 1966; this situation was a consequence of the age distribution and birthrate of the Negro population and would not be affected by the end of prejudice and discrimination. Having more dependents and a lower income, the New White's disadvantage would still be compounded: that is, the amount of capital per child that he could invest in education and training would be much less than that available to the Old White.

Finally, it must be said that many New Whites would suffer indignities and humiliations not so different from those to which the Negro now is subject. The treatment that the lower-class white receives is in many ways like that of the victim of racial prejudice—and a larger proportion of New Whites would be lower class. In one respect their new (class) status might be harder to bear than their former (racial) one; for the victim of race prejudice can take some comfort, however small, in the knowledge that he is being treated unjustly.

Much of what appears (especially to Negroes) as race prejudice is really class prejudice or, at any rate, class antipathy. Similarly, much of what appears (especially to whites) as "Negro" behavior is really lower-class behavior. The lower class is relatively large among Negroes; it appears even larger than it is to those whites who fail to distinguish a Negro who exhibits outward signs— lack of skill, low income, slum housing, and so on—which in a white would mark him as lower class, from one whose culture is working, middle, or even upper class but whose opportunities have been limited by discrimination and whose income is low.

How much outward resemblance there is between class antipathy and racial prejudice may be seen from sociologists' accounts of the treatment often accorded to the white lower class. A. B. Hollingshead, for example, describes in *Elmtown's Youth* the social structure of a "typical" Midwestern county seat, the population of which in 1940 was white (there was only one Negro family) and consisted mostly of native-born Protestants, many descended from "old American stock." In this all-American community, nearly a quarter of the population had the status of pariahs. Class V (lower-class) families

are excluded from the two leading residential areas. . . . Employers do not like to hire them unless labor is scarce or they can be induced to work for low wages. . . . Class V persons are almost totally isolated from organized community activities. . . . They knew that their children were discriminated against in the school system by both the teachers and the pupils. . . . The Class V's get the bad jobs, such as helping in the junk yards and hauling garbage and ashes. . . . Class V persons give the impression of being resigned to a life of frustration and defeat in a community that despises them for their disregard of morals, lack of "success" goals, and dire poverty.

Hollingshead summarizes the community's view of the lower class— "the scum of the city"—as follows:

They have no respect for the law, or themselves.

They enjoy their shacks and huts along the river or across the tracks and love their dirty, smoky, low-class dives and taverns.

Whole families—children, in-laws, mistresses, and all—live in one shack.

This is the crime class that produces the delinquency and sexual promiscuity that fills the paper.

Their interests lie in sex and its perversion. The girls are always pregnant; the families are huge; incestual relations occur frequently.

They are not inspired by education, and only a few are able to make any attainments along this line.

They are loud in their speech, vulgar in their actions, sloppy in their dress, and indifferent toward their plight. Their vocabulary develops as profanity is learned.

If they work, they work at very menial jobs.

Their life experiences are purely physical, and even these are on a low plane.

They have no interest in health and medical care.

The men are too lazy to work or do odd jobs around town.

They support the Democratic party because of the relief obtained during the depression.

This group lives for a Saturday of drinking or fighting. . . .

The community's view of the lower class is not, apparently, based entirely on prejudice. Class V parents, Hollingshead says, are "indifferent to the future":

They will leave a job casually, often without notice . . . . 8 percent of the mothers and 46 percent of the fathers had been convicted once or more in the local courts. . . . Serial monogamy is the rule. . . . one-fifth to one-fourth of all births are illegitimate. . . . The mean [number of children] is 5.6 per mother. . . . Disagreements leading to quarrels and vicious fights, followed by desertion by either the man or the woman, possibly divorce, is not unusual. . . . The burden of child care, as well as support, falls on the mother more often than on the

*father when the family is broken. . . . Before the sixteenth birthday is reached . . .
75 percent of the class V's have left school. . . .*

If something like one-quarter of the population of a typical Midwestern town is (more or less correctly) perceived in this way, it should not be surprising that a sizable part of the population of a large city is perceived (also more or less correctly) in the same way. Racial and ethnic prejudice obviously do not account for the low status of so many Elmtown people. Why, then, should the same attitudes be attributed to racial prejudice when the Class V's are Negroes (or Puerto Ricans or Mexicans or whatever) rather than white, Protestant, native-born Americans?

Obviously, racial prejudice is manifested when, as often happens, the Negro is automatically regarded as lower-class simply on the basis of his skin color or when he is treated as if he were lower-class even though it is clear that he is not. But to treat the lower-class Negro exactly like the lower-class white is not, on the face of it, to show racial prejudice.

Although, in principle, it is easy to distinguish racial prejudice from class prejudice as well as prejudice ("an irrational attitude of hostility on the basis of supposed characteristics," according to the dictionary) from justifiable antipathy (a rational attitude of hostility on the basis of objective characteristics), doing so in practice would usually require a wisdom greater than Solomon's. Concretely, racial and class prejudice are usually inextricably mixed, and so are prejudice and justifiable antipathy. Consider the following:

A Negro drifter not long ago was arrested for breaking into a liquor store and swiping a bottle. He smashed the neck, took a swig and was caught with the goods, so to speak inside him. Two policemen carted him off to the station house for booking. He was a moderately difficult prisoner, swaying around as they tried to fingerprint him. But he had joshed them into a good mood and all three were making something of a joke about the fingerprinting. The Negro then shoved a bit, saying "C'mon you m____r f____ers." The cops immediately turned upon him and beat him up. The word he had used is not a word to which lower-middle-class Irishmen or Italians take kindly—even in jest, and especially from a Negro (although that particular epithet is a commonplace of lower-class Negro speech).

In a case like this, it is impossible to say what part was played by "racial prejudice." Negroes may be convinced that the drifter would not have been beaten if he had been white. On the other hand, readers of *Elmtown's Youth* may well conclude that a white, Protestant, "old-stock American" of Class V would have gotten exactly the same treatment.

Obstacles of many kinds, some insuperable, are placed in the way of Negroes who want to move into white neighborhoods. This fact, however, does not adequately explain the existence of neighborhoods that are wholly or almost wholly black. In many inner-city areas Negroes now constitute the main body of low-skilled, low-paid labor; this in itself would account for their being the main body of residents in the poorer parts of the city. No doubt, also, many Negroes *prefer* black neighborhoods and would live in them even if their opportunities to live in white ones were excellent (which, to repeat, they generally are not). A careful poll of Negro opinion in a sample of non-Southern metropolitan areas and in New York, Chicago, Atlanta, and Birmingham revealed in late 1964 that hardly any Negroes wanted to live in neighborhoods that were mostly white. The detailed findings are presented in the table.

TYPE OF NEIGHBORHOOD NEGROES PREFER*
(in percent)

Neighborhood	Metro	N.Y.	Chic.	Atl.	Birm.	Total
Mostly Negro	55	52	68	74	69	62
Mixed or no difference	38	35	25	18	27	31
Mostly white	4	9	5	5	1	4
Don't know	3	3	4	2	3	3
Total	100	100	100	100	100	100

SOURCE: Gary T. Marx, *Protest and Prejudice*, p. 176.
* If all equally well kept up.

The practice of calling all Negro neighborhoods "segregated" and "ghettoes" misrepresents the situation seriously and perhaps dangerously. In the technical language of many sociologists, a Negro neighborhood would be called segregated even if every family in it had recently turned down an excellent opportunity to live among whites; it is "unevenness in the distribution of white and Negro households" within a neighborhood, whatever the motive or cause of the unevenness, that constitutes segregation for the sociologist. The lay reader, unaware that the word is used in a Pickwickian sense, supposes that the "ghetto" studied by such sociologists and described in the newspapers must be the result of white prejudice. That it may be, partly or wholly, the result of circumstances (namely, that large numbers of unskilled Negro workers came all at once to the inner city and occupied all the low-cost housing then available) or of the Negroes' own preference is not likely to occur to him. Negroes, hearing incessantly that they are "segregated" and that they live in "ghettoes," are given additional grounds for supposing that they are in all cases "forced" to do what they would sometimes—perhaps often—do of their own accord as a matter of course. One can only conjecture, but it seems plausible that the universal practice of using "ghetto" and "segregated" in reference to any all-Negro neighborhood tends to condition Negroes to the idea—which is usually a half-truth at most—that white prejudice "forces" them to live in poor housing and among other Negroes. If this is so, the semantic confusion goes a long way toward making bad matters worse.

One of the few studies to shed light on why Negroes live apart from whites was published in 1964 by a team of researchers from Brandeis University. They made the study for the Boston Urban Renewal Administration, which wanted to know how many of the families in the Washington Park neighborhood—a middle-income "ghetto"—were likely to remain there if the neighborhood was rehabilitated. When interviewers first talked to the families, they assumed that most of them would want to move to predominantly white neighborhoods. There was nothing to stop them from doing so. The renewal agency had given them lists of housing that they might rent or purchase in white neighborhoods at prices they could afford. Moreover, most of them were very dissatisfied where they were; they strongly criticized the neighborhood schools and they complained also of inadequate shopping facilities, insufficient police protection, and noise and disorder in the streets. Since they could easily leave the "ghetto," it was reasonable to expect them to do so.

In fact, only thirty-three of the families (13 percent) did leave, and of these only nine left the Negro community. A large majority of the families did not even look at the housing listed as available. Some did not look at it because they were sure that they would be turned down on one pretext or another if they decided that they wanted it, but most were just not interested. (Incidentally, the few who inspected the listed housing encountered no prejudice.)

The main reason why the Washington Park people did not move, the researchers finally concluded, was that they had good housing at bargain prices where they were. They were paying a median rent of $85 per month, which was only 12 percent of their income. The carrying charges on a house in the suburbs would be between $125 and $150. Most of the families could afford this much—two-thirds of them had incomes of over $7,800—but they preferred to use their money for other things. As the researchers put it, "One might describe them as having been 'spoiled' by their current low costs of housing." In this respect the Negroes were just like the Italians in the West End of Boston whom Gans had studied a few years before. "People were so used to paying low rents," Gans found, "that their whole mode of life was adjusted to them. Any apartment that rented for more than $50 for five or six rooms was thought to be outrageously expensive."

Another reason why most of the Washington Park people chose not to move was that they wanted to be near friends and relatives. This motive, too, may have had little or nothing to do with race: Gans's Italians also liked being near friends and neighbors—that was why he called them "urban villagers." In every large city ethnic groups of the second, third, fourth, and even later generations—Irish, German, Scandinavian, Polish, Jewish, and Italian, among others—lived in self-imposed isolation and sent their children to schools that were to a high degree ethnically homogeneous.

In the case of the Negro, as in that of other ethnic groups, prejudice is not the *only* force creating spatial separation. To some extent separation is also imposed by the group upon itself in order to maintain its identity and its distinctive conception of life. As Ralph Ellison has written:

. . . it is a misunderstanding to assume that Negroes want to break out of Harlem. They want to transform the Harlems of their country. These places are precious to them. These places are where they have dreamed, where they have lived, where they have loved, where they have worked out life as they could. . . . it isn't the desire to run to the suburbs or to invade "white" neighborhoods that is the main concern with my people in Harlem. They would just like to have a more human life there. A slum like Harlem isn't just a place of decay. It is also a form of historical and social memory.

Even if more "segregation" is voluntary than most people realize, the fact remains that a great deal is *not* voluntary. There are many neighborhoods into which it is all but impossible for a black family to move and many more in which blacks are, to put it mildly, unwelcome. By no means all of this hostility represents *racial* prejudice, however. Some of it is simply snobbery (it is safe to say that, if the Washington Park Negroes had been blue-collar rather than white-collar, the white neighborhoods would have been less open to them), and some of it is the more or less justifiable distaste and fear that working- and middle-class people feel toward lower-class ones. (If a Negro is assumed to be lower-class simply because he is black and not because of anything he does, that, of course, is prejudice pure and simple.) This distaste and fear is probably as common among Negroes as among whites: the lower-class Negro is usually as unwelcome in or near a middle-class Negro neighborhood as in or near a middle-class white one. Still, even when these motives are added to voluntary "segregation," there is no doubt that much segregation based on race prejudice remains.

As the Washington Park case shows, it is not the absence of white faces that makes the "ghetto" objectionable to the Negro. Rather, it is the feeling that he is not perfectly free to live wherever he pleases and, also, the inadequacy of the stores, schools, playgrounds, and other facilities of his neighborhood. Once it is established, as in Washington Park, that he can live in a white neighborhood if he wishes, and once the facilities of the neighborhood are brought up to a standard of adequacy, the Negro very often prefers to live among other Negroes.

Like everyone else, too, he prefers to live among people whose class culture is not very different from his own. The main trouble with the "ghetto" (when it is without walls) is that so many of its residents are lower- or lower-working-class. This is perhaps the principal reason why its stores carry low-quality goods at high prices, why its alleys are strewn with garbage, why there are rats in the cellars, why the school is a blackboard jungle, why the streets are noisy and disorderly, why police protection is poor, and all the rest.

The middle- and upper-working-class Negro, then, if he is to be anywhere near his friends and relatives and in a community to which he feels he "belongs," must live among people whose style of life he finds repugnant. His situation differs fundamentally from that of, say, the Italian described by Gans in that the Italian belongs to a group that is predominantly working- and lower-middle-class. The middle-class Italian can live in comfort and without annoyance or embarrassment in the midst of an all-Italian neighborhood because the lower class is now too small to be noticeable. By contrast, the middle-class Negro who lives in an all-Negro district can rarely avoid contact with the slum. The choice open to him is painful: he may move to a white neighborhood, paying more for housing than he is used to, cutting himself off from relatives and friends, and risking insult and even injury from prejudiced neighbors; or he may suffer the inconveniences, annoyances, and hazards of living in or near a slum.

This problem does not exist for the lower-class Negro, who usually feels very much at home in the slum, or for the upper-class one, who can insulate himself from it by living in an expensive apartment house, working and shopping downtown, and sending his children to private schools. The problem is acute, however, for middle- and upper-working-class people whose incomes and work routines do not permit much insulation, and who are often distressed at the possibility of slipping—psychologically if not physically—into a state from which they have only recently managed to emerge. This thought, one suspects, is what lies behind Kenneth B. Clark's call for a struggle "to prevent decadence from winning over the remaining islands of middle class society." His rhetoric has to do entirely with the hatefulness, callousness, and brutality of whites, but what he seems to mean by "decadence" is lower-class culture. The "dark ghetto" is, in the last analysis, really the lower-class one.

The movement of the Negro up the class scale appears as inexorable as that of all other groups. The number of middle- and upper-class Negroes is in many areas already large enough to allow the formation of predominantly middle- and upper-class neighborhoods and suburbs—places large enough to support stores, churches, restaurants, and local public services of the sort that middle- and upper-class people desire. Between 1959 and 1967, the number of Negro families in metropolitan areas with incomes of $10,000 or more per year increased from 187,000 to 601,000. This suggests that the time is at hand when the Negro to whom the slum is intolerable will be able to leave it *without at the same time having to leave the society of other Negroes.*

Urban renewal, if extensive, will hasten the formation of Negro upper- and middle-class neighborhoods in two ways: first, by forcibly dislodging the lower class from neighborhoods that are chosen for rehabilitation or conservation, and second, by subsidizing the middle- and upper-working-class people who remain and by assuring them that the powers of government will be used to bring their neighborhood up to a middle-class standard and to keep it there. Both of these things happened in the Washington Park neighborhood. One resident told a member of the Brandeis research team:

> For the first two years . . . we were dissatisfied and looked forward to moving. We were particularly concerned because of the behavior of our Negro neighbors. Liquor bottles were thrown in the yard, there were fights every night in the apartments across the street and girls were raped in the neighborhood. It was not safe. But the last two years we have thought less about moving. . . . There has been an improvement in the neighborhood. Most of the low-class Negroes have moved to Dorchester; those remaining seem to have more pride in the neighborhood. We don't find liquor bottles in our yard anymore. A housing project for the elderly has been built nearby. As a result the neighborhood has been up-graded.

The "upgrading" of some neighborhoods will often mean the "downgrading" of others. As more and more Negroes withdraw into middle- and upper-class communities, the concentration of the lower class in the slum will necessarily increase. Very probably the "worsening" of the slum will be seen not as a consequence of the improved position of Negroes generally, but rather as further evidence of callousness and neglect by the "white power structure." "We have absentee leadership, absentee ministers, absentee merchants," a resident of Watts complained after the riot there. Apparently, he thought that this was a problem that someone—presumably the government—should do something to solve. The increasing isolation of the lower class is a problem, to be sure, but it is hard to see what can be done about it. The upper classes will continue to want to separate themselves physically from the lower, and in a free country they probably cannot be prevented from doing so.

"Whatever their origin," writes sociologist Urie Bronfenbrenner, "the most immediate, overwhelming, and stubborn obstacles to achieving quality and equality in education now lie as much in the character and way of life of the American Negro as in the indifference and hostility of the white community." This observation also is true of areas other than education. Prejudice against the Negro has declined sharply since the Second World War, while his other handicaps have grown. It is not likely, however, that the Negro man-on-the-street will fully recognize the changes that have occurred; he still has the lowest-paid and most menial jobs, he still lives in the worst neighborhoods, and he still sends his children to inadequate and all-black schools. Naturally, he concludes that the same old cause—"Whitey"—is still producing the same old effects. That these effects are now being produced largely (not entirely, of course) by other causes, especially differences of education, income, and—in the case of those who are lower class—class culture is something that he cannot be expected to see for himself or to believe if it is pointed out to him, especially when the pointing out is done by a white.

Negro leaders cannot be expected to explain that prejudice is no longer *the* obstacle. Even those of them who understand that it is not are bound to pretend otherwise. Like every specialist, the Negro leader is prone to magnify to himself as well as to others the importance of his specialty, seeing every problem in terms of it. Even when he recognizes that the situation of most Negroes would not be fundamentally different even if there were no racial prejudice at all, the logic of his position as a leader prevents him from saying so. To acknowledge that nonracial factors are more important than racial ones would cool the zeal of his supporters, give aid and comfort to the enemy, and destroy his very reason for being. So long as there is *any* racial prejudice at work, the leader cannot risk seeming to tolerate it, as he would if he emphasized those other (nonracial) aspects of the situation which from a practical (but not a moral) standpoint are vastly more important. For the race leader, there is everything to gain and nothing to lose by treating all problems as if they derived solely from the racial one.

Whites, too, will find prejudice a peculiarly satisfying explanation for the troubles of the Negro. . . . It is characteristic of upper- and middle-class culture not only to try to improve oneself and one's society but also to blame oneself for not doing more and succeeding better. Members of these classes are prone to see all social problems in terms of their own moral shortcomings —to say, for example, that the Negro is "forced to live in a ghetto" even when it is clear that he *chooses* to live among other Negroes. The Brandeis researchers, for example, refer to Washington Park as a "ghetto" even though their main finding is that most families live there by choice. Another study reports that the question "Do you think Puerto Ricans can live anywhere they want to if they can afford the rent?" was answered "yes" by 87 percent of a sample of New York Puerto Ricans, but calls the *barrio* a "ghetto" nevertheless.

The motives that produce this overemphasis on prejudice are understandable. It is graceless of the white, to say the very least, to run any risk of underemphasizing it. There is the feeling, too, that it can do no harm—and may do some good—to err on the side of seeing more prejudice than is really there. Besides, even if prejudice is not important causally, it is very important morally.

There are, however, at least two serious dangers in widespread overemphasis on prejudice as a cause of the Negro's troubles. The first is that it may lead to the adoption of futile and even destructive policies and to the nonadoption of others that might do great good. It is clear, for example, that if improving the housing of Washington Park Negroes is the goal, programs built on the assumption that the main problem is prejudice will lead nowhere.

The other, perhaps more serious danger in the overemphasis of prejudice is that it raises still higher the psychic cost of being Negro, a cost cruelly high under the best of circumstances. It is bad enough to suffer real prejudice, as every Negro does, without having to suffer imaginary prejudice as well. To refer once more to Washington Park, it is worth noting that some of the people there who did not look at the housing listed as available in white neighborhoods "knew" that Negroes could not buy it and that they would only be humiliated if they tried. In short, the overemphasis on prejudice encourages the Negro to define all his troubles in racial terms. Driving it into him that he is forced to live in a ghetto, the victim of the white man's hate and greed, and so on, makes it all the more difficult for him to feel that he is a man first and a Negro second.

Violence in the Cities

Richard C. Wade

Violence is no stranger to American cities. Almost from the very beginning, cities have been the scenes of sporadic violence, of rioting and disorders, and occasionally virtual rebellion against established authority. Many of these events resulted in only modest property damage and a handful of arrests. Others were larger in scale with deaths running into the scores and damages into the millions. This paper attempts to survey briefly some of these outbreaks and to analyze their origins and consequences. We confine ourselves, however, to the larger ones, and omit any discussion of individual acts of violence or the general level of crime. In addition, to keep these remarks relevant to the present crisis, we have confined our analysis to disorders in urban areas.

There has been, in fact, a good deal more violence and disorder in the American tradition than even historians have been willing to recognize. The violence on the frontier is, of course, well known, and in writing, movies, and television it has been a persistent theme in our culture. Indeed, one of America's favorite novelists, James Fenimore Cooper, transformed the slaughter and mayhem of Indians into heroic, almost patriotic, action. As the literary historian David Brion Davis has observed: "Critics who interpret violence in contemporary literature as a symptom of a sick society may be reassured to know that American writers have always been preoccupied with murder, rape, and deadly combat." To be sure, violence is not "as American as cherry pie," but it is no newcomer to the national scene.

Though serious scholarship on this dimension of the American past is shamefully thin, it is already quite clear that disorder and violence in our

From Richard C. Wade, "Violence in the Cities: A Historical View," in Urban Violence ed. by Charles U. Daly, pp. 7–26. Copyright © 1969. Reprinted by permission of the University of Chicago Center for Policy Study and the author.

cities were not simply occasional aberrations, but rather a significant part of urban development and growth. From the Stamp Act riots of the pre-revolutionary age, to the assaults on immigrants and Catholics in the decades before the Civil War, to the grim confrontation of labor and management at the end of the nineteenth century and its sporadic reappearance after World War I and during the depression, through the long series of racial conflicts for two centuries, American cities have known the physical clash of groups, widescale breakdown of established authority, and bloody disorder.

Nor is it hard to see why this early history had more than its share of chaos. American cities in the eighteenth and nineteenth centuries were very young. They had not yet the time to develop a system of orderly government; there was no tradition of habitual consent to local authority; there was no established police system. In addition, these cities grew at a spectacular rate. In the twentieth century, we have used the term "exploding metropolis" to convey the rapid pace of urbanization. It is not often remembered that the first "urban explosion" took place more than a century ago. Indeed, between 1820 and 1860 cities grew proportionately faster than they had before or ever would again. The very speed of this urban development was unsettling and made the maintenance of internal tranquillity more difficult.

The problem was further compounded by the fact that nearly every American city was born of commerce. This meant that there was always a large transient population—seamen engaged in overseas trade, rivermen plying the inland waters, teamsters and wagonmen using the overland routes, and a constant stream of merchants and salesmen seeking customers. At any moment the number of newcomers was large and their attachments to the community slight. Hence when they hit town, there was always some liveliness. After exhausting the cities' museums and libraries, sailors and teamsters would find other things to do. In the eighteenth and nineteenth century, transients comprised a significant portion of those who engaged in rioting and civil disorders.

In addition to being young, rapidly growing, and basically commercial, American cities also had very loose social structures. Unlike the Old World, they had no traditional ruling group, class lines were constantly shifting, and new blood was persistently pumped into these urban societies. One could say that up until the last part of the nineteenth century, mercantile leaders dominated municipal government; but even that commercial leadership changed continually. Later, immigrant groups shared high offices in municipal affairs, thus underlining the shifting nature of the social structure of most cities. Within this looseness there was always a great deal of mobility, with people rising and falling in status not only from generation to generation but within a single lifetime.

This fluid social system contrasted sharply with other, older societies, yet it contained a high incidence of disorder. For it depended on the constant acceptance of new people and new groups to places of influence and importance, and their incorporation into the system on a basis of equality with others. This acceptance was only grudgingly conceded, and often only after some abrasive episodes. The American social structure thus had a large capacity to absorb revolutionary tensions and avoid convulsive upheavals. But it also bred minor social skirmishes which were not always orderly. It is significant that in the pre-Civil War South, where slavery created a more traditional social structure, there was less rioting and civil disorder than in the North (though one ought not underestimate the individual violence against the slave built into institutional bondage).

The American social structure was also unique because it was composed not only of conventional classes, but also of different ethnic, religious, and racial groups. They had at once an internal cohesion that came from a common background and a shared American experience and also a sense of sharp differences with other groups, especially with the country's older stock. These groups, the Negro excepted, were initially both part of the system and yet outside of it. The resultant friction, with the newcomers pressing for acceptance and older groups striving for continued supremacy, was a fruitful source of disorder and often violence. Since it was in the city that these groups were thrown together, became aware of their differences, and struggled for survival and advancement, it would be on the streets rather than on the countryside that the social guerrilla warfare would take place.

If the internal controls in the American social structure were loose, the external controls were weak. The cities inherited no system of police control adequate to the numbers or to the rapid increase of the urban centers. The modern police force is the creation of the twentieth century; the establishment of a genuinely professional system is historically a very recent thing. Throughout the eighteenth and nineteenth century, the force was small, untrained, poorly paid, and part of the political system. In case of any sizable disorder, it was hopelessly inadequate; and rioters sometimes routed the constabulary in the first confrontation. Josiah Quincy, for example, in Boston in the 1820's had to organize and arm the teamsters to re-establish the authority of the city in the streets. Many prudent officials simply kept out of the way until the worst was over. In New York's draft riots, to use another instance, the mayor wandered down to see what the disturbance was all about and nearly got trampled in the melee.

Moreover, since some of the rioting was political, the partisanship of the police led official force to be applied against one group, or protection to be withheld from another. And with every turnover in the mayor's office, a substantial and often a complete change occurred in the police. In Atlanta, for instance, even where there was only one party, each faction had its own men in blue ready to take over with the changes in political fortunes. In some places where the state played a role in local police appointments, the mayor might even be deprived of any control at all for the peace of the city. In New York in the 1850's there was an awkward moment when there were two police forces—the Municipals and the Metropolitans—each the instrument of opposing parties. At the point of the most massive confusion, one group tried to arrest the mayor and an armed struggle took place between the two competing forces.

The evolution toward more effective and professional forces was painfully slow. Separating the police from patronage proved difficult, the introduction of civil service qualifications and protection came only in this century, and the development of modern professional departments came even later. To be sure, after a crisis—rioting, widescale looting, or a crime wave—there would be a demand for reform, but the enthusiasm was seldom sustained and conditions returned quickly to normal. The ultimate safety of the city thus resided with outside forces that could be brought in when local police could not handle the mob.

These general considerations account in large part for the high level of disorder and violence in American cities over the past three centuries. The larger disorders, however, often stemmed from particular problems and specific conditions and resulted in widescale bloodshed and destruction. Though these situations varied from place to place and time to time, it is perhaps useful to divide them into a few categories. Some rioting was clearly political, surrounding party struggles and often occasioned by legislation or an election. Some sprang from group conflict, especially the resistance to the rising influence of immigrant groups. Still others stemmed from labor disputes. And the largest, then as now, came out of race conflict. A few examples of each will convey some of their intensity and scale.

Politics has always been a fruitful source of disorders. Indeed, one of the most significant groups of riots surrounded the colonial break with Great Britain. In Boston, Samuel Adams and other radical leaders led the otherwise directionless brawling and gang warfare around the docks and wharfs into a political roughhouse against British policy. The Stamp Tax Riots, the Townshend Duty Riots and, of course, the Boston Massacre were all part of an organized and concerted campaign by colonial leaders. The urban middle classes initially tolerated the disorders because they too opposed certain aspects of British policy; they later pulled back when they felt that radical leadership was carrying resistance beyond their own limited objectives. Yet for nearly a decade, rioting and organized physical force was a part of the politics of the colonies.

*   *   *

Attacks against immigrants comprise another theme in the story. Often the assault by older, more established groups was against individuals or small groups. But in other cases it would be more general. The string of riots against Catholic churches and convents in the nineteenth century, for example, represented an attack on the symbols of the rise of the new groups. In the summer of 1834, for instance, a Charlestown (Mass.) convent was sacked and burned to the ground; scuffles against the Irish occurred in various parts of nearby Boston; some Irish houses were set afire. At the outset, the episode was carefully managed; then it got out of hand as teenage toughs got into action. Nor was this an isolated incident.

Characteristic of this period too was the resistance to the incorporation of immigrants into the public life of the city. "Bloody Monday" in Louisville in 1855 will perhaps serve as an illustration. Local politicians had become worried about the increase of the immigrant (German and Irish) vote. The Know-Nothings (a party built in part on anti-immigrant attitudes) determined to keep foreign-born residents away from the polls on election day. There was only a single voting place for every ward, thus numbering only eight in the entire city. Know-Nothing followers rose at dawn and occupied the booths early in the morning. They admitted their own reliables, but physically barred their opponents. The pre-election campaign had been tense and bitter with threats of force flying across party lines. By this time some on each side had armed themselves. Someone fired a shot, and the rioting commenced. When it was all through, "Quinn's Row," an Irish section, had been gutted, stores looted, and Catholic churches damaged. A newspaper which was accused of stirring up feeling only barely escaped destruction. The atrocities against the Irish were especially brutal, with many being beaten and shot. Indeed, some of the wounded were thrown back into the flames of ignited buildings. Estimates of the dead range from 14 to 100, though historians have generally accepted (albeit with slim evidence) 22 as the number killed.

Labor disputes have also often spawned widescale disorder. Indeed, at the turn of the century, Winston Churchill, already a keen student of American affairs, observed that the United States had the most violent industrial relations of any western country. Most of this rioting started with a confrontation of labor and management over the right to organize, or wages and hours, or working conditions. A large portion of these strikes found the workers in a vulnerable if not helpless position, a fact which has led most historians to come down on the side of labor in these early disputes. Moreover, unlike the disorders we have previously discussed, these were nationwide in scope—occurring at widely scattered points. There was no question of their being directed since a union was usually involved and it had some control over local action throughout the country. Yet the violence was seldom uniform or confined to strikers. It might flare up in Chicago and Pittsburgh, while St. Louis, where the issues would be the same, might remain quiescent. Often, as in the case of the railroad strike of 1877, the damage to life and property was large. In the Homestead lockout alone, 35 were killed and the damage (in 1892 dollars) ran to $2,500.00. In the 1930's the organizing steel, auto, and rubber unions brought a recrudescence of this earlier grisly process.

*   *   *

Of all the sources of civil disorder, however, none has been more persistent than race. Whether in the North or South, whether before or after the Civil War, whether nineteenth or twentieth century, this question has been at the root of more physical violence than any other. There had been some sporadic slave uprisings before emancipation, the largest being the Nat Turner rebellion in 1831. But most which moved from plot to action occurred on the countryside rather than in the cities. Yet even the fear of a slave insurrection took its toll; in 1822, for instance, Charleston, South Carolina, officials, acting on tips and rumors, hanged 37 Negroes and deported many more for an alleged plot to capture and burn the city. Seven years later, in a free state, whites invaded Cincinnati's "Little Africa" and burned and killed and ultimately drove half the colored residents from town. In the same period mobs also assaulted abolitionists, sometimes killing, otherwise sacking buildings and destroying printing presses.

Even the New York City riot against the draft in 1863 took an ugly racial twist before it had run its course. The events themselves arose out of the unpopularity of the draft and the federal government's call for more men as Lee headed into Pennsylvania. The situation was further complicated by a crisis in the police department as a result of the conflicting claims of command by a Republican mayor and a Democratic governor. The rioting broke out July 13 and the first target was the provost marshal's office. Within a short time 700 people ransacked the building and then set it afire. The crowd would not let the firemen into the area and soon the whole block lay gutted. Later the mob began to spill over into the Negro area where many blacks were attacked and some killed.

The police were helpless as the riot spread. The few clashes with the mob saw the police retreat; the crowd wandered about almost at will. Political leaders did not want to take the consequences for action against the mob, and soon it started to head toward the business district. Slowly the police reorganized, by Tuesday they began to win engagements with the rioters, and in a little while they were able to confine the action to the original area. The mobs were, however, better armed and organized and gave a good account of themselves in pitched battle. On the third day federal troops arrived and the control swung over to the authorities and quiet was restored. But in three days the casualties ran to at least 74 dead and many times that number wounded. The property damage was never accurately added up, but claims against the county exceeded $1,500,000 by 1865.

Emancipation freed the Negro from bondage, but it did not grant him either equality or immunity from white aggression. From the New Orleans riot of 1866, through the long list of racial disorders to the end of World War II with datelines running through Atlanta, Springfield, East St. Louis, Washington, Mobile, Beaumont, Chicago, Detroit, and Harlem, [all these riots] reveal something of the depth of the crisis and the vulnerability of American cities to racial disorders. These riots were on a large scale, involved many deaths, millions of dollars of property damage, and left behind deep scars which have never been fully erased. Most of these riots involved the resort to outside military help for containment; all exposed the thinness of the internal and external controls within our urban society.

In fact, the war had scarcely ended before racial violence erupted in New Orleans. The occasion of the outbreak was a Negro procession to an assembly hall where a debate over enfranchising the blacks was to take place. There was some jostling during the march and a shot fired; but it was only after the arrival at the convention that police and special troops charged the black crowd. In the ensuing struggle [the] Negroes were finally routed, but guns, bricks, and stones were generously used. Many Negroes fell on the spot; others were pursued and killed on the streets trying to escape. Later General Sheridan reported that "at least nine-tenths of the casualties were perpetrated by the police and citizens by stabbing and smashing in the heads of many who had already been wounded or killed by policemen." Moreover, he added that it was not just a riot but "an absolute massacre by the police . . . a murder which the mayor and police . . . perpetrated without the shadow of necessity." Federal troops arrived in the afternoon, took possession of the city, and restored order. But 34 Negroes and 4 whites were already dead and over 200 injured.

Smaller places, even in the North, were also affected with racial disorder. In August 1908, for instance, a three-day riot took its toll in Springfield, Illinois. The Negro population in the capital had grown significantly in the years after the turn of the century, and some whites sensed a political and economic threat. On August 13th a white woman claimed she had been violated by a Negro. An arrest was made and the newspapers carried an inflammatory account of the episode. Crowds gathered around the jail demanding the imprisoned black, but the sheriff quickly transferred the accused and another Negro to a prison in a nearby town without letting the public know. "The crowd outside was in an ugly mood," writes an historian of the riot, "the sun had raised tempers; many of the crowd had missed their dinners, which added to their irritation; and the authorities seemed to be taking no heed of their presence. By sundown the crowd had become an ugly mob."

The first target of the rioters was a restaurant whose proprietor presumably had driven the prisoners from jail. Within a few minutes his place was a shambles. They then headed for the Negro section. Here they hit homes and businesses either owned by or catering to Negroes. White owners quickly put white handkerchiefs in their windows to show their race; their stores were left untouched. A Negro was found in his shop and was summarily lynched. Others were dragged from streetcars and beaten. On the 15th the first of 5,000 national guardsmen reached Springfield; very quickly the mob broke up and the town returned to normal. The death toll reached six (four whites and two blacks); the property damage was significant. As a result of the attack,

Springfield's Negro population left the city in large numbers hoping to find better conditions elsewhere, especially in Chicago.

A decade later the depredations in East St. Louis were much larger, with the riot claiming the lives of 39 Negroes and 9 whites. The best student of this episode points out that the 1917 riot was not a sudden explosion but resulted from "threats to the security of whites brought on by the Negroes' gains in economic, political and social status; Negro resentment of the attempts to 'kick him back in his place'; and the weakness of the external forces of constraint—the city government, especially the police department." Tensions were raised when the Aluminum Ore Company replaced white strikers with Negro workers. In addition to these factors, race had become a political issue in the previous year when the Democrats accused Republicans of "colonizing" Negroes to swing the election in East St. Louis. The kindling seemed only to lack the match.

On May 28 came the fire. A Central Trades and Labor Union delegation formally requested the Mayor to stop the immigration of Negroes to East St. Louis. As the men were leaving City Hall they heard a story that a Negro robber had accidentally shot a white man during a holdup. In a few minutes the word spread; rumor replaced fact. Now it was said the shooting was intentional; that a white woman was insulted; that two white girls were shot. By this time 3,000 people had congregated and the cry for vengeance went up. Mobs ran downtown beating every Negro in sight. Some were dragged off the streetcars, others chased down. The police refused to act except to take the injured to hospitals and to disarm Negroes. The next day the National Guard arrived to restore order.

Two days later the governor withdrew troops although tension remained high. Scattered episodes broke the peace, but no sustained violence developed. The press, however, continued to emphasize Negro crimes and a skirmish broke out between white pickets and black workers at the Aluminum Company. Then on July 1 some whites drove through the main Negro neighborhood firing into homes. The colored residents armed themselves, and when a similar car, this time carrying a plainclothesman and reporter, went down the street the blacks riddled the passing auto with gunshot.

The next day was the worst. At about 10:00 A.M. a Negro was shot on the main street and a new riot was underway. An historian of the event asserted that the area along Collinsville Avenue between Broadway and Illinois Avenue became a "bloody half mile" for three or four hours. "Streetcars were stopped: Negroes, without regard to age or sex, were pulled off and stoned, clubbed and kicked. . . . By the early afternoon, when several Negroes were beaten and lay bloodied in the street, mob leaders calmly shot and killed them. After victims were placed in an ambulance, there was cheering and handclapping." Others headed for the Negro section and set fire to homes on the edge of the neighborhood. By midnight the South End was in flames and black residents began to flee the city. In addition to the dead, the injured were counted in the hundreds and over 300 buildings were destroyed.

Two summers later the racial virus felled Chicago. Once again, mounting tension had accompanied the migration of blacks to the city. The numbers jumped from 44,000 in 1910 to 109,000 ten years later. Though the job market remained good, housing was tight. Black neighborhoods could expand only at the expense of white ones, and everywhere the transition areas were filled with trouble. Between July 1, 1917, and March 1921, there had been 58 bombings of Negro houses. Recreational areas also witnessed continual racial conflict.

The riot itself began on Sunday, July 27, on the 29th Street Beach. There had been some stone-throwing and sporadic fighting. Then a Negro boy, who had been swimming in the Negro section, drifted into the white area and drowned. What happened is not certain, but the young blacks charged he had been hit by stones and demanded the arrest of a white. The police refused, but then arrested a Negro at a white request. When the Negroes attacked the police, the riot was on. News of the events on the beach spread to the rest of the city. Sunday's casualties were 2 dead and 50 wounded. On Monday, attacks were made on Negroes coming from work; in the evening cars drove through black neighborhoods with whites shooting from the windows. Negroes retaliated by sniping at any white who entered the Black Belt. Monday's accounting found 20 killed and hundreds wounded. Tuesday's list was shorter, a handful dead, 139 injured. Wednesday saw a further waning and a reduction in losses in life and property. Rain began to fall; the Mayor finally called in the state militia. After nearly a week a city which [had] witnessed lawlessness and warfare quieted down and began to assess the implications of the grisly week.

The Detroit riot of 1943 perhaps illustrates the range of racial disorders that broke out sporadically during World War II. There had been earlier conflicts in Mobile, Los Angeles, and Beaumont, Texas, and there would be some others later in the year. No doubt the war with its built-in anxieties and accelerated residential mobility accounted for the timing of these outbreaks. In Detroit, the wider problem was compounded by serious local questions. The Negro population in the city had risen sharply, with over 50,000 arriving in the 15 months before the riot; this followed a historical increase of substantial proportions which saw black residents increase from 40,000 to 120,000 in the single decade between 1920 and 1930. These newcomers put immense pressures on the housing market, and neighborhood turnover at the edge of the ghetto bred bitterness and sometimes violence; importantly, too, recreational areas became centers of racial abrasiveness.

On June 20 the riot broke out on Belle Isle, a recreational spot used by both races, but predominantly by Negroes. Fistfighting on a modest basis soon escalated, and quickly a rising level of violence spread across the city. The Negro ghetto—ironically called Paradise Valley—saw the first wave of looting and bloodshed. The area was, as its historians have described it, "spattered with blood and littered with broken glass and ruined merchandise. The black mob had spared a few shops owned by Negroes who had chalked COLORED on their windows. But almost every store in the ghetto owned by a white had been smashed open and ransacked." Other observers noted that "crudely organized gangs of Negro hoodlums began to operate more openly. Some looters destroyed property as if they had gone berserk."

The next morning saw the violence widen. The police declared the situation out of control and the mayor asked for state troops. Even this force was ineffective, and finally the Governor asked for federal help. Peace returned under the protection of 6,000 men; and the troops remained for more than a week. The dead numbered 34, 25 Negroes and 9 whites; property damage exceeded $2,000,000. And almost as costly was the bitterness, fear, and hate that became part of the city's legacy.

*   *   *

This survey, which is only suggestive and not exhaustive, indicates that widescale violence and disorder have been man's companion in the American city from the outset. Some generalizations out of this experience might be useful in the light of the present crisis.

First, most of the rioting has usually been either limited in objective or essentially sporadic. This, of course, is not true of racial conflict, but it is characteristic of a large number of the others. In those, the event was discrete; there was no immediate violent sequel. After a labor dispute, especially if it involved union recognition, bitterness and hate persisted, but there was no annual recurrence of the violence. Attacks on immigrants seldom produced an encore, though they might have an analogue in some other city in the same month or year. In short, though there was enough disorder and mob action to create a persistent anxiety, the incidence of overt conflict was irregular enough to preclude predictions of the next "long hot summer."

Second, this sporadic quality meant that the postmortems were usually short and shallow. It was characteristic to note the large number of teenagers who got involved; to attribute the disruption to outsiders (especially anarchists and communists); to place a large responsibility on the newspapers for carrying inflammatory information and spreading unfounded rumors; to blame the local police for incompetence, for prejudice, for intervening too soon or too late, or at all. After any episode, the urge to fix blame led to all kinds of analyses. The historian of the 1877 railroad violence, for example, observes that "the riots were variously ascribed to avarice, the expulsion of the Bible from the schools, the protective tariff, the demonetization of silver, the absence of General Grant, the circulation of the *Chicago Times* and original sin." Others saw in it a labor conspiracy or a communist plot. And the *New York Times* could assert after the Chicago riot in 1919 that: "The outbreak of race riots in Chicago, following so closely on those reported from Washington, shows clearly enough that the thing is not sporadic (but has) . . . intelligent direction and management . . . (It seems probable) that the Bolshevist agitation has been extended among the Negroes."

There were a few exceptions. After the Chicago race riot, for example, an Illinois commission studied the event in some detail and also examined the deteriorating relations between the races which lay at the bottom. Others occasionally probed beneath the surface [to get] at the deeper causes of unrest. But most cities preferred to forget as soon as possible and hoped for an end to any further disorder. Indeed, even the trials that followed most riots show how rapidly popular interest faded. The number of people brought to trial was small and the number of convictions extremely small; and, most significantly, there was little clamor for sterner measures.

Third, if the analyses of the riots were shallow, the response of cities and legislatures was not very effective. After quiet was restored, there would almost certainly be a discussion of police reform. Customarily little came of it, though in Louisville the utter ineptness and obvious partisanship of the police in 1855 prompted a change from an elective to an appointive force. Legislation usually emphasized control. As early as 1721, Massachusetts responded to growing disorders with an anti-riot act. And Chicago's Commercial Club made land available for Fort Sheridan after the events of 1877 in order to have troops nearby for the protection of the city. But most cities rocked back to normal as soon as the tremors died down.

Fourth, there was a general tendency to rely increasingly on outside forces for containing riots. Partly, this resulted from the fact that in labor disorders local police and even state militia fraternized with strikers and could not be counted on to discipline the workers. Partly, it was due to inadequate numbers in the face of the magnitude of the problem. Partly, too, it stemmed from the fact that sometimes the police were involved in the fighting at the outset and seemed a part of the riot. The first resort was usually to state troops; but they were often unsatisfactory, and the call for federal assistance became more frequent.

Fifth, while it is hard to assess, it seems that the bitterness engendered by riots and disorders was not necessarily irreparable. Though the immigrants suffered a good deal at the hands of nativists, it did not slow down for long the process of their incorporation into American life. Ten years after Louisville's "Bloody Monday" the city had a German mayor. The trade unions survived the assaults of the nineteenth century and a reduction of tension characterized the period between 1900 and the depression (with the notable exception of the post-war flare-ups). And after the violence of the 1930's, labor and management learned to conduct their differences, indeed their strikes, with reduced bloodshed and violence. It is not susceptible of proof, but it seems that the fury of the defeated in these battles exacted a price on the victors that ultimately not only protected the group but won respect, however grudgingly, from the public.

At any rate, the old sources of major disorders, race excepted, no longer physically agitate American society. It has been many years since violence has been a significant factor in city elections and no widespread disorders have even accompanied campaigning. Immigrant groups have now become so incorporated in American life that they are not easily visible and their election to high offices, indeed the highest, signals a muting of old hostilities. Even when people organized on a large scale against minority groups—such as the Americans' Protective Association in the 1890's or the Ku Klux Klan in the 1920's—they have seldom been able to create major riots or disorders. And though sporadic violence occasionally breaks out in a labor dispute, what is most remarkable is the continuance of the strike as a weapon of industrial relations with so little resort to force. Even the destruction of property during a conflict has ceased to be an expectation.

Sixth, race riots were almost always different from other kinds of disorders. Their roots went deeper; they broke out with increasing frequency; and their intensity mounted rather than declined. And between major disorders the incidence of small-scale violence was always high. Until recently, the Negro has largely been the object of the riot. This was true not only in northern cities where changing residential patterns bred violence, but also in the South where this question was less pervasive. In these riots the lines were sharply drawn against the Negroes, the force was applied heavily against them, and the casualties were always highest among blacks.

Finally, in historical perspective, if racial discord be removed, the level of large-scale disorder and violence is less ominous today than it has been during much of the past. As we have seen, those problems which have produced serious eruptions in the past no longer do so. In fact, if one were to plot a graph, omitting the racial dimension, violence and disorder over a long period have been reduced. Indeed, what makes the recent rioting so alarming is that it breaks so much with this historical trend and upsets common expectations.

Yet to leave out race is to omit the most important dimension of the present crisis. For it is race that is at the heart of the present discord. Some analysts, of course, have argued that the problem is class and they emphasize the numbers caught in widening poverty, and the frustration and envy of poor people in a society of growing affluence. Yet it is important to observe that though 68 percent of the poor people in this country are white, the disorders stem almost wholly from black ghettoes. The marginal participation of a few whites in Detroit and elsewhere scarcely dilutes the racial foundations of these disorders.

In fact, a historical survey of disorders only highlights the unique character of the present problem. For the experience of the Negro in American cities has been quite different from any other group. And it is in just this difference that the crisis lies. Because the black ghetto is unlike any ghettoes that our cities have known before. Of course, other groups knew the ghetto experience too. As newcomers to the city they huddled in the downtown areas where they met unspeakably congested conditions, occupied the worst housing, got the poorest education, toiled, if fortunate enough to have a job, at the most menial tasks, endured high crime rates, and knew every facet of deprivation.

The urban slum had never been a very pleasant place, and it was tolerable only if the residents, or most of them, thought there was a way out. To American immigrants generally the ghetto was a temporary stage in their incorporation into American society. Even some of the first generation escaped, and the second and third generation moved out of the slums in very large numbers. Soon they were dispersed around the metropolitan area, in the suburbs as well as the pleasant residential city wards. Those who remained behind in the old neighborhoods did so because they chose to, not because they had to. By this process, millions of people from numberless countries, of different national and religious backgrounds, made their way into the main current of American life.

It was expected that Negroes would undergo the same process when they came to the city. Thus, there was little surprise in the first generation when black newcomers did indeed find their way into the central city, the historic staging ground for the last and poorest arrivals. But the ghetto proved to be not temporary. Instead of colored residents dispersing in the second generation, the ghetto simply expanded. Block by block it oozed out into the nearby white neighborhoods. Far from breaking up, the ghetto grew. In fact, housing became more segregated every year; and the walls around it appeared higher all the time. What had been temporary for other groups seemed permanent to Negroes.

The growth of the Negro ghetto created conditions which had not existed before and which generated the explosiveness of our present situation. In the first place, the middle-class Negroes became embittered at their exclusion from the decent white neighborhoods of the city and suburbs. These people, after all, had done what society expected of them; they got their education, training, jobs, and income. Yet even so they were deprived of that essential symbol of American success—the home in a neighborhood of their own choosing where conditions would be more pleasant and schools better for their children. For this group, now about a third of all urban Negroes, the exclusion seemed especially cruel and harsh.

As a result they comprise now a growingly alienated and embittered group. The middle-class blacks are now beginning to turn their attention to organizing among the poor in the worst parts of the ghetto. Their children make up the cadres of black militants in the colleges. And when the riots come, they tolerate the activity even though they usually do not themselves participate. In short, the fact of the ghetto forces them to identify with race, not class. When the riots break, they feel a bond with the rioters, not white society. This had not been true of the emerging middle class of any immigrant group before.

If the ghetto has new consequences for the middle class, it also creates a new situation among the poorer residents of the ghetto, especially for the young people. They feel increasingly that there is no hope for the future. For other groups growing up in the ghetto there had always been visible evidence that it was possible to escape. Many before had done it; and everyone knew it. This produced the expectation that hard work, proper behavior, some schooling, and a touch of luck would make it possible to get ahead. But the young Negro grows up in increasing despair. He asks himself—"What if I do all they say I should—stay in school, get my training, find a job, accumulate some money—I'll still be living here, still excluded from the outside world and its rewards." He asks himself, "What's the use?" Thus, the hopelessness, despair, and frustration mounts, and the temperature of the ghetto rises. Nearly all of our poverty programs are stumbling on the problem of motivation. To climb out of the slum has always required more than average incentive. Yet this is precisely what is lacking in the ghetto youth.

The present riots stem from the peculiar problems of the ghetto. By confining Negroes to the ghetto we have deprived them of the chance to enter American society on the same terms as other groups before them. And they know increasingly that this exclusion is not a function of education, training, or income. Rather, it springs from the color of their skin. This is what makes race the explosive question of our time; this is what endangers the tranquillity of our cities. In the historian's perspective, until the ghetto begins to break, until the Negro middle class can move over this demeaning barrier, until the young people can see Negroes living where their resources will carry them and hence get credible evidence of equality, the summers will remain long and hot.

SUGGESTIONS FOR FURTHER READING

The literature on urban history and the urban crisis has expanded rapidly in the past decade. The best general introduction is Charles N. Glaab and A. Theodore Brown, *A History of Urban America (New York, 1967). A valuable analysis of recent trends in the writing of urban history, along with valuable bibliographic information, is Richard C. Wade, "An Agenda for Urban History," in George Athan Billias and Gerald N. Grob, eds., *American History: Retrospect and Prospect (New York, 1971), pp. 367–398. (The same essay also appears in Herbert J. Bass, ed., The State of American History [New York, 1971].) Arthur M. Schlesinger, The Rise of the City (New York, 1933) is an early effort to direct historians' attention to urban history; Schlesinger finds a developing urban consensus in the late nineteenth century. The anti-urban tradition in America can be approached through Morton and Lucia White, *The Intellectual versus the City (Cambridge, Mass., 1962). On the contemporary urban crisis, Jeanne

Lowe, *Cities in a Race with Time (New York, 1967) and Mitchell Gordon, *Sick Cities: Psychology and Pathology of American Urban Life (New York, 1965) are pessimistic, while Jane Jacobs, *The Death and Life of Great American Cities (New York, 1961) and Robert Weaver, *The Urban Complex: Human Values in Urban Life (New York, 1964) find more hope.

The best place to begin a study of immigration is Oscar Handlin, *The Uprooted (Boston, 1951), a portion of which is reprinted here. See also Handlin's *Boston's Immigrants (Cambridge, Mass., 1941). John Higham, *Strangers in the Land: Patterns of American Nativism, 1860–1925 (New Brunswick, 1955) describes some of the sharp conflicts between the immigrants and native Americans.

On the problems of assimilation, see Nathan Glazer and Daniel Patrick Moynihan, *Beyond the Melting Pot: The Negroes, Puerto Ricans, Jews, Italians and Irish of New York City (Cambridge, Mass., 1963). An important study of New York City blacks is Gilbert Osofsky, *Harlem: The Making of a Ghetto (New York, 1965).

* Available in paperback edition.

5
THE PROGRESSIVE MOVEMENT

Progressivism was a broad and diverse reform movement that had its roots in the 1890's, but came to a climax on the national level during the administrations of Theodore Roosevelt and Woodrow Wilson. It affected all areas of American life, including art, literature, religion, and education, but it was also a political movement founded on the idea that the problems arising in an industrialized America could be solved only by expanding democracy and social justice. Reformers in the cities sought to promote clean, honest, efficient government, and often to throw the bosses out. Reformers in the states paraded under the banner of "give the government back to the people," seeking the initiative, the referendum, the recall, the direct election of senators and many other reforms which had been supported by the Populists. Muckrakers sought to expose corruption in the world of business and politics. Social workers and other reformers fought to regulate child labor, clean up the slums, and promote better working conditions for both men and women. On the national level, leaders of both political parties sought ways to deal with the giant industrial combinations and turned to regulation, control, and "trust busting." Everywhere progressives were concerned with solving the many problems created by industrialism.

Not all progressives agreed on the objectives of the movement or even the best methods for reform; similarly historians have also disagreed about the essential nature of progressivism. To some historians the progressive era was a time of fundamental conflict between reformers on one side and businessmen and political bosses on the other. Their emphasis is usually on the Populist origins of progressivism. These scholars agree with William Allen White, a leading mid-western progressive, who remarked that the progressives "caught the Populists in swimming and stole all their clothing except the frayed underdrawers of free silver." They see the movement as drawing its chief support from the mid-western farmer and small businessman who were engaged in a bitter struggle for survival with the eastern bankers and corporation presidents.

Another group of historians interpret the progressive movement as much more than an extension of Populism; indeed, its dominant spirit becomes not "rural and provincial" but "urban, middle-class and nationwide." These historians often explain the movement in terms of what Richard Hofstadter has called "the status revolution." This thesis attempts to show that a group of middle-class, well-educated citizens including lawyers, doctors, preachers, educators, and small businessmen who had usually held positions of leadership were being displaced in the late nineteenth century by the rising power of labor union leaders, corporation executives, and political bosses. Frustrated by their loss of status and power, driven by a sense of responsibility or guilt when confronted by the problems of urbanism and industrialism, they became reformers not so much to improve society as to give themselves a feeling of importance.

Regardless of how the historian explains the motivation of the reformers, he usually sees the progressive era as a time of great exuberance and optimism when a lot of people thought they could make the world a better place in which to live. But would progress come because there was nothing fundamentally wrong in the world, or would it come through bitter conflict with the forces of evil? The progressives themselves were not sure, and historians have not been able to agree on an answer.

In the selections that follow Russell Nye sees the progressives building on the Populist anti-business heritage. Indeed, he defines the progressive period as the time when business control and dominance was drawing to a close. George Mowry, on the other hand, finds the secret to understanding the progressives in the failure of most of them to adjust to an industrial age, rather than in a real conflict between reformers and businessmen. Mowry, unlike Nye, sees very little continuity between Populism and progressivism. He emphasizes the anti-urban, and anti-labor and nostalgic aspects of the movement but at the same time notes the urban and middle-class origins of the reformers. Eric Goldman, however, sees progressivism as a part of a long and sincere attempt to promote social justice in America. He pictures the progressives as having a real concern for labor and the immigrant. Goldman inevitably finds some conflict; to him the progressive era was a time when there was a "condition of excitement" because there were real problems to be solved and many people stood ready with the solutions. Gabriel Kolko, on the other hand, sees progressivism as a movement dominated by businessmen who believed that "the general welfare of a community could be best served by satisfying the concrete needs of business." He describes a conservative consensus and directly attacks those liberal historians who, in the words of Arthur M. Schlesinger, Jr., agree that "liberalism in America has been ordinarily the movement on the part of the other sections of society to restrain the power of the business community." Using as a case study the regulation of the meat packing industry, a reform movement usually considered one of the triumphs of progressive regulation, he argues that the regulation was engineered by the packing industry for its own benefit.

How important were the differences which divided reformers from their opponents during the progressive period? Was there a widespread agreement on fundamentals which led progressives merely to seek minor adjustments in a basically sound society? Or did progressive reformers recognize deep-seated problems and seek major changes? Was progressivism essentially anti-business, or did liberal reformers and the businessmen share the same basic goals?

Progressivism:
Anti-Business Reform

Russell Nye

The wave of agrarian protest washed itself away in Bryan's defeat. The crusade of 1896, and the "dull and colorless reign of privilege" (Altgeld's phrase) that followed it, settled nothing. The issues of the eighties and nineties were driven underground by the Spanish war and militarism, the upsurge of prosperity, the to-be-or-not-to-be of imperialism. But the old difficulties were still unsolved—the trust, the "plutocrat," the twin problems of good government and representative government. What were the economic and political functions of wealth? What were the social and economic functions of government? What of Big Business? What of the farmer and the worker? They all boiled down to a single question, what is democracy?

The plain fact was (and many saw it clearly) that the American dream was simply not coming true. America, "the hope of the human race" as Turgot had called it, was not realizing its promise. The difference between what was and what might be was very great. The nineteenth-century Midwestern radicals tried to change the system and, with Bryan, lost "the first battle." The twentieth-century leaders reformed the army and mapped new offensives. They were a new kind of captain, trained in the West Point of state politics, with the same objectives as the tattered militia who preceded them.

The initial blow of the twentieth century was struck by the "muckrakers," who provided a sort of cutting edge to a three-pronged reform movement in politics, society, and economics at the turn of the century. Henry D.

From Midwestern Progressive Politics by Russell Nye (East Lansing, 1951), pp. 169–73, 180–81, 184–87, 190, 208–9, 224–25, 233–35, 242. Reprinted by permission of The Michigan State University Press.

Lloyd, and before him Bellamy and George, warned of the dangers of wealth and corporate power. B. O. Flower, an Illinois-born editor who imbibed Midwest radicalism at its source, ran energetic attacks on business and privilege in his magazine, the Arena, and shared with Lloyd the credit for pioneering in the journalism of exposure. Flower (who edited the Arena from 1889 to 1896, then the Chicago New Time, and then rejoined the Arena) was undoubtedly one of the most influential of the early reform editors before 1900. His magazines published articles by such well-known dissenters as Henry George, Hamlin Garland, Eugene Debs, George Herron, Frances Willard, and Frank Parsons and were filled with discussions of railroads and trusts, the Australian ballot, municipal ownership, and co-operatives.

The real upswing of muckraking journalism came, however, with the appearance of the cheap popular magazine. The four old standards (Scribner's, Harper's, the Century, and the Atlantic—all sedate, literate, and Eastern controlled)—were hardly the proper outlets for exposure of corruption and graft. The newer inexpensive ones (Munsey's, Cosmopolitan, Colliers, the American, Everybody's, McClure's) and the more radical intellectual ones (the Arena, Review of Reviews, the Outlook) suited the purpose admirably. The ten-cent magazine quadrupled the magazine-reading public after 1893.

"Muckraking" (as Theodore Roosevelt later named it) came into being after 1900. Lloyd, Flower, and the editors of Everybody's and the Independent started it, but when S. S. McClure in 1901 put Lincoln Steffens on the trail of the grafting politicians and later sent Ida M. Tarbell after Standard Oil, the lid was off. Every politician, every corporation, every executive was under suspicion, every public and private citizen open to investigation. Most of the writers were newspapermen rather than political scientists or economists, sentimental rather than doctrinaire liberals, but they all hated social and political injustice and pursued it relentlessly in print.

Steffens found political corruption of the grimiest sort in St. Louis, Minneapolis, Pittsburgh, New York, Philadelphia, and Chicago, and wrote it up in The Shame of the Cities. Next he inspected Ohio, Rhode Island, New Jersey, California, and Wisconsin; except for Wisconsin, he did not like what he saw and said so in The Struggle for Self-Government. As the time came to draw some generalizations from his observations of democracy in action, Steffens turned into less of a muckraker and more of a political philosopher. The trail of boodle, he discovered, led from city hall to state capitol to Washington itself—corruption was simply characteristic of the American political system on all levels. Reluctantly he was forced to the conclusion that the people themselves preferred "bad" to "good" government, that machines and corruption existed because the voter wished them to. America was so involved in business, and business so in need of special privileges, that it was more satisfactory to wink at someone else's "pull" while getting your own than to live under rigidly honest government. The remedy lay, Steffens decided, not in reforming politics but in reforming the voter (a point already noted by

Jane Addams in *Democracy and Social Ethics*), by entirely removing privilege from politics, and by reverting to a co-operative economic system—a path that eventually led Steffens straight to Russia.

Steffens' articles set the journals afire. McClure himself took to the road; C. E. Russell, Ben Lindsey, C. P. Connolly, George Kernan, Burton Hendrick, and others found Pennsylvania, Montana, Colorado, and Delaware as "corrupt and contented" as the states on Steffens' beat. When Steffens trained his sights on Washington, as did David Graham Phillips, Ernest Crosby, Alfred Lewis, and Benjamin Hampton, he found corruption rife in the Congress itself.

Meanwhile, others put big business under the microscope. Ida Tarbell's scholarly and damning study of Standard Oil set the pattern for Russell's study of the beef trust, Ray Stannard Baker's of the railroads, Welliver's of General Electric, Lewis' of International Harvester, Hendricks' of life insurance, Lawson's of Wall Street, and a dozen more. Muckraking moved on to other fields, too. Gentle Jake Riis wrote on the slums; Samuel Hopkins Adams investigated pure food; Will Irwin, Upton Sinclair, and others probed journalism. Churches were scrutinized for commercialism and connections with wealth, and the journals went to work on Belgian rule in the Congo, prison reform, loan sharks, prostitution, literary immorality, various sects—the thing was getting out of hand by 1910 when the public began to tire of it. It became harder to find new muck to rake, and big business discovered that withholding advertising from unco-operative magazines robbed them of a great deal of reforming zeal. Business also launched a counter-offensive of its own, beginning when the anthracite coal industry hired Ivy Lee in 1906 as publicity agent (he later was hired by the Pennsylvania Railroad and Standard Oil), a practice followed by other corporations until the "public relations counselor" became standard business equipment.

Muckraking, both good and bad, was part of a wider political, social, and intellectual reaction to industrial expansion and political corruption, a result of the same forces that produced Bryan, Theodore Roosevelt, Wilson, and La Follette. It was an exposure of fraudulent, misrepresentative government, of monopoly, of industrial immorality, of the trust—essentially the same tendencies in political, social, and economic life criticized by the agrarian radicals of the 1870's. The Grangers, and their descendants the Populists, had said the same things in a general way. The muckrakers offered proof and gave dates, names, places. The Grangers and Populists turned to government for help with little success. Now it was clear why. Government itself was under the thumb of the very forces they were fighting, as the Midwestern farmer and small businessman suspected all along. Like Populism and later progressivism, muckraking was an attack on privilege, on the exploitation of the many by the few, on social and economic malpractice. Steffens' conclusions were not so far removed from those of Jerry Simpson, nor Ida Tarbell's from General Weaver's.

The investigations of the muckrakers into city governments accelerated a trend toward municipal reform that reached back to the nineties and the Populist tradition. The Populists, and their agrarian predecessors, demanded clean, efficient, and representative government on a state and national scale; their urban counterparts demanded the same thing in the city. . . .

The movement for civic reform knew no regional boundaries (though perhaps it was strongest in the West), for municipal corruption was not specifically a regional problem. But certainly the Grangers and the Populists paved the way for it. Like them, the civic reformers had one aim—to make government more representative and more efficient—and they encountered (as the agrarians did) the monopoly, the corporation, and the machine. All intended to abolish privilege in government, whether it be the corporation working against the farmer or the traction tycoon against the city dweller. The personnel of the two movements showed some similarities and later greater differences. The early reform mayors—Pingree, Jones, and Johnson— came from Populist trust busting, Georgism, and Christian socialism, whereas the later reformers of the muckraker era were academic, well-schooled, urbane young attorneys, not crusaders but efficiency experts. The city reformers would no doubt have arrived had no Grangers or Populists existed, but the Grange, Farmers' Alliance, and People's party awakened the public conscience, drew the lines of conflict, and started the argument. Civic reform tied in with the Midwest agrarian radical tradition, doing locally what the Populists wished to do nationally. The cities, said Brand Whitlock, were really "working models of the larger democracy" that earlier Populists and later progressives visioned.

The twentieth-century progressive movement was, like its predecessors, deeply rooted in the social and economic soil of the times. American politics has been usually a direct reflection of current patterns of thought—embracing attitudes in business, science, education, economics, the church, and the home —and a manifestation of contemporary ideas that expresses itself among other ways in platforms and candidates. Thus the Grangers, the Farmers' Alliance, and the Populists were compounds of many elements, expressions of what the people (or a considerable segment of it) believed at a particular time. The elements themselves were concentrated for the most part in the agrarian Midwest, where the conflict between the old and new economics was most apparent, where the traditions of frontier discontent were strongest. . . .

Despite the dozens of young leaders it developed after 1900, the Midwest never really produced a politician of major stature (with the exception of La Follette) who might have tied Midwest progressivism into one neat bundle and delivered it bound and sealed on the White House doorstep. Neither did the Granger or Populist movements, whose leaders were colorful, astute, and sincere, but none of whom possessed the qualities needed to organize a political movement on a national rather than a regional scale. Bryan, the best of them, had neither the gifts to begin with nor the ability to develop them.

Excepting La Follette, the later progressives—honest and skillful men all—were no more than good noncommissioned officers, while La Follette himself was too inflexible, too rigid, too much the lone wolf to become the prairie Jackson that the Midwest progressive tradition demanded. The reason for the Midwest's failure to produce a national leader lay in the fact that the movement itself was a distinctively Midwestern thing that developed regional politicians who were chiefly concerned with regional problems. Progressivism in its Eastern phase—as represented by Theodore Roosevelt and Woodrow Wilson—attained national power and dealt with national issues, but it was not the same thing.

The drift of Midwestern progressive thought in the early 1900's was away from its Jeffersonian-Jacksonian-frontier sources. The ends remained the same, but the methods changed. As the frontier faded, the old eighteenth-century idea of untrammeled individualism and decentralized political power disappeared with it, for in the industrial nineteenth century individualism by itself was hardly enough to secure democracy. Jefferson thought he had secured it when he established the principle that there should be no political or legal check upon the individual's life, liberty, and pursuit of happiness. But the feudalism and royal tyranny he feared might threaten his democracy were replaced in the industrial age by the lords of the trusts, the knights of transportation, the corporate kings, the ministerial bosses. The Jacksonian period believed that in spoils, in the ability of the ordinary man, in the complex safeguards of intricate governmental machinery—there lay safety for the common people; but the boss and the corporation took over the machinery and bought the office. The Granger and the Populist dimly realized that the goals of the old democratic tradition could be attained only by modifications of the old methods and principles. Paradoxically, he found that the preservation of individualism required the introduction of certain restraints upon it. He could restrain it through the only agency—the government—that lay more or less under his direct control.

The most distinctive tendency in twentieth-century Midwestern progressivism, therefore, was its shift away from pure individualism toward social control, a trend already noticeable in the agrarian radicalism of the nineteenth century. Here was an effort to fit the individualism of the old frontier (and of Darwinism) to the new circumstances of an industrial society, an adjustment designed to give the citizen the same advantages under new social and economic conditions that he had enjoyed under the old. . . . "[We must stop] trying to apply a logic, true and proper for an individualistic era, to a new socialistic era," C. L. Deyo wrote in the *Public*. "All our fundamental conceptions will have to be exchanged for new ones in which the *social* side shall have due emphasis." If the individual's welfare—his pursuit of happiness—was the object of democracy, how might one, in trying to evolve a democratic capitalistic society, avoid the perils of a dog-eat-dog individualism on the one hand or the regimentation of socialism or communism on the other? The progressives chose a middle path between the two extremes. Their aim was not simply to restrict individualism, but to restrict in order to conserve the values of democracy.

This course was called by Charles McCarthy of Wisconsin "The New Individualism." It was not socialism, nor was it close to it. True, the Midwest progressive was occasionally willing to accept a so-called "socialistic" method to gain his desired objective. But the progressive, McCarthy explained, believed he could fulfill the promises of socialism without losing the essentials of private ownership and private enterprise. As Jane Addams remarked, since no political party or economic school possessed exclusive right to any device for eradicating poverty or obtaining political and social justice, the progressive had a right to borrow from socialism if he wished. Restrictions on laissez faire were, to the progressive, merely effective ways of preserving laissez faire itself.

Another major principle, a bequest of Populism, was the progressive's faith in and trust of the popular majority. The assumption was that every normal citizen who was mentally and morally qualified had both the right and the duty to participate directly in his government. "The composite judgment is always safer and wiser and stronger and more unselfish than the judgment of any one individual mind," wrote La Follette. "The people have never failed in any great crisis in history." The real cure for the ills of democracy, the Midwest progressive believed, was more democracy. His aim in politics therefore was simply to make government responsible and representative. Or as La Follette put it, "The very backbone of true representative government is the direct participation in the affairs of government by the people."

To insure a government that was both responsible and representative, Midwestern progressives believed it vitally necessary that the people control their government, both before and after elections. Machines and bosses controlled it only when they were allowed to steal the political machinery—something that pre-election measures such as the short ballot, the direct primary, the corrupt-practices act, and revised registration and voting systems were intended to prevent. As post-election controls they suggested the initiative, referendum, recall, and city home rule. Special influence must be removed, the structure of government so modified as to allow a greater direct participation by the citizen in the conduct of public business. The whole purpose of progressivism, said La Follette, was "to uphold the fundamental principles of representative government." It was an attempt to adapt the old democratic system to the needs of a new society, "a movement of a new generation toward more democracy in human relationships."

A third major principle of progressivism was its belief that the functions of government should be extended to meet the growing needs of the people. The state was not to be simply a negative factor in society, its influence happiest when least, but a positive factor, doing some things that no other agency could do, and others that no other agency could do so well. "He is really a Progressive," wrote Walter Owen in La Follette's Magazine, "who first discovers any wrongs and suggests the appropriate governmental action to prevent further abuse." Progressivism represented the culmination of an old frontal attack (the Grangers were its vanguard) on the laissez-faire concept of governmental do-nothingism, an assault seconded by economists like Ely and sociologists like Ward. It was the last phase of a movement away from the agrarian-Jeffersonian idea that government was merely a way to keep the individual's pursuit of life, liberty, and happiness within bounds, that government was "anarchy plus the street constable." The earlier agrarians never foresaw that the new industrial capitalism would find that "hands-off" concept of government exactly to its liking. The Populists realized, and the post-1900 progressives knew it more surely, that the tradition of government noninterference defeated the ends of democratic government itself. It had to be modified and adapted to secure democracy and extend it—hence the name "progressive." . . .

The real leader of Midwestern progressivism, and its greatest, was Robert Marion La Follette. The Midwest had been laboring to produce a leader for thirty years when he appeared on the scene in 1900. Under him progressivism captured a state and in turn furnished the pattern for the capture of the region; he carried it himself into the Senate and up to the doors of the White House. He had what the others lacked, expressed the tradition best, gave it its wisest and clearest direction, and when he died, it died with him. . . .

La Follette was closer to the people and closer to the Midwest than any politician after Bryan. Unlike Bryan's, his appeal to the public was rational, rather than emotional. He had none of Bryan's crowd-swaying hypnosis, speaking instead in a rapid, intense fashion, flooding his audience with statistics, figures, and examples. The fact that he could keep a crowd of farmers on the edge of their seats for three hours by reciting tariff schedules and tax rates (as he once did on Chautauqua) is a tribute to a skill less flamboyant than Bryan's but one certainly equally effective. He once spoke for fifty-three consecutive nights, without the slightest flagging of his own energy or the audience's interest, a political feat only Bryan himself could equal.

La Follette was a small, wiry man, with a shock of black (later iron-gray) hair and a tendency toward swift and sharp gesture. He was honest, serious, almost inhumanly intense, and thoroughly uncompromising. He was perfectly willing to jeopardize his career, as he did a dozen times, to keep his principles, and the hate and vituperation that often came his way affected him not one iota. "I can no more compromise, or seem to compromise . . . ," he said, "than I could by wishing it add twenty years to my life." His principles were always clear, his course equally so. Cold, severe, almost austere in manner, La Follette did not invite easy friendship. He never had fun in politics (as Theodore Roosevelt did), nor did he inspire the devotion that Bryan did. It would be difficult to choose, from the group of men who knew him best and followed him, one who was a really close friend, for his complete and selfless dedication to his cause wrapped him about like armor. In truth, with his solid, lined face, his tremendous idealism, his rigid indifference to any blandishments of friendship, party, place, profit, or power, La Follette was a trifle frightening. No one ever took Bob La Follette lightly or disinterestedly. "The politician cannot exist without absolute, unyielding, uncompromising honesty," he said, and he lived it out to the letter.

La Follette's Wisconsin cut the pattern, and the whole Midwest copied it. Progressivism after 1900 at one time or another had complete control of every state but Illinois, Michigan, Ohio, and Indiana. For that matter, it spread elsewhere under the leadership of men like Hiram Johnson in California, Charles Evans Hughes in New York, Woodrow Wilson in New Jersey, Bass in New Hampshire, and so on. But in the Middle West, where it started, progressivism was considerably more than simply a swing toward honest government. It was a definite and coherent political philosophy, a concept of democracy that grew naturally out of Grangerism and Populism. Behind it were Weaver and Bryan, Donnelly and Lloyd, Altgeld and Simpson, and a distinctively Midwestern, agrarian, Jeffersonian, frontier tradition. . . .

The assassin's bullet that cut down McKinley put a man already committed to progressivism into the White House. Both the political leaders of the Midwest and the city and state reformers of the East had begun their work, and T.R. seemed to be the national leader they all prayed for. No man ever stepped into the Presidency with a greater following or more personal power than Theodore Roosevelt. Not quite forty-three, vigorous, and energetic, with a sharp intellect, a quick mind, and a thirst for information, Roosevelt certainly possessed superb equipment for a politician. He was an experienced administrator, with a genius for personal contracts and a good sense of public relations, his appeal wide and his personal charm devastating. He could, as John Hay once said, "organize the unorganizable" by sheer personality.

Roosevelt was also a wizard at group diplomacy. He had an ambidextrous ability to please everybody, to have something for everyone, to catch the prevailing tone of any time or the temper of any group—cowboy, war hero, stern prosecutor of graft and crime, brilliant (though superficial) scholar, and so on. When the country went to war, T.R. was there with the Rough Riders and in the headlines. How many knew or cared that he was second in command, and who heard of Colonel Wood, his superior? If the public criticized college football, there was T.R. with a carefully balanced statement on the matter. If the public liked cowboys, T.R. owned a ranch, had cowboys to lunch, and wore a cowboy hat and a red bandanna to the 1900 Republican convention. He knew Bat Nelson, Bob Fitzsimmons, John L. Sullivan, President Eliot of Harvard, Booker T. Washington, Confederate soldiers (his uncle fought for the South), college professors, stockbrokers— name a prominent man in any walk of life and Roosevelt probably knew him. With his gift for phrases—the "big stick," the "square deal," the "malefactors of great wealth"—he said dramatically and concisely what people thought and wanted to hear. "Teddy" was a familiar face peering out of the newspaper and a familiar name in the headlines before he even went to Washington to serve as Vice-President under McKinley. He seemed in 1901 to be the heaven-sent answer to the progressive prayer for a national leader. . . .

Whether or not Roosevelt was really a progressive during his two terms as President is an open question. It is doubtful that he possessed, during the years 1900 to 1908, a coherent and organized theory of politics beyond his general desire to institute honest and efficient government. It was not until after he had retired from the Presidency that he developed, under the influence of Eastern intellectuals such as Herbert Croly, a more distinctively progressive political philosophy. From 1900 to 1908 Roosevelt's three chief interests, as shown in his speeches and actions, were regulation of corporations, conservation, and the extension of governmental power in social and economic areas, all of them in agreement with Midwestern progressive aims. Yet his policy toward corporations was certainly not that of Bryan and the Populists, nor that of La Follette and the post-1900 Midwesterners. "As a matter of fact," he confided to a friend in 1908, "I have let up in every case where I have had any possible excuse for so doing." He took a middle road between the Populist-Granger principle of destroying trusts and the La Follette policy of regulating them to insure competition. Roosevelt chose to take his stand on the principle of establishing the right to regulate, a wholly different emphasis. He considered the "rural Tories" of the Midwest, who wished to curb the trust or smash it, as no progressives at all, but simply wreckers. Conservation and social legislation, as La Follette pointed out, were progressive issues indeed, but significantly they were not controversial party issues either. Roosevelt's progressivism, it was suspected, stopped where party politics began. The Midwestern states, said La Follette, had done much more on all counts than T.R. had done in seven and one-half years.

In other words, certain Midwestern progressives felt in 1908 that Roosevelt was either not a progressive at all or (more charitably) a progressive of decidedly limited aims and enthusiasms. He talked a great deal, but failed to produce. "This cannonading," wrote La Follette of T.R.'s crusades, "first in one direction and then the other, filled the air with noise and smoke, which confused and obscured the line of action, but when the battle cloud drifted by and quiet was restored, it was always a matter of surprise that so little had really been accomplished." Louis Post, somewhat to the left of La Follette, thought Roosevelt "incapable of cooperation . . . and generally irresponsible," concluding that "progressivism would be stronger without him." Eugene Debs, on the socialist left and one of the gentlest of men, could barely speak or write of him with restraint. But a good many progressives held their tongues, content to accept what minor progress T.R. had undoubtedly made and to hope for more under Taft.

Roosevelt's real contribution to Midwestern progressivism did not come from the fact that he was part of it (for he was not) nor from what he accomplished for it, for he accomplished little. It lay instead in the leadership he assumed in the progressive movement at large—a leadership that the Midwest accepted with reservations, but nevertheless accepted. There was in the nation in 1900 a vague but powerful drift toward honest, efficient, and representative government. Roosevelt became its spearhead. Whether he led the way or whether he stepped in at the head of a procession that had already formed (Roosevelt believed the latter) is beside the question. He was important to progressivism because he was the first President after the Civil War who understood what had happened to the nation socially, politically, and economically since 1865. He dramatized the conflict between progressivism and conservatism, made it alive and important, and caught the imagination of the people with it, even though he did not resolve it. For reasons of temperament he was unable to resolve it, since his principles dissolved too often into glittering generalities. "We are neither for the rich man nor the poor man as such, but for the upright man, rich or poor," is a cheeringly liberal statement, but one difficult to put into law books. Yet his contributions to the rising wave of progressivism were not inconsiderable. The teeth, the eyeglasses, the bouncing vitality, the "big stick" and the "strenuous life," the St. George-like sallies against the trusts—all of these were trademarks of a muscular, youthful, aggressive, optimistic democracy that captured the nation's fancy. . . .

Though there was a tendency to establish tighter governmental regulation of industry during the period 1900 to 1908, the trend toward consolidation and combination in business slowed down, but it did not stop. "It really seems hard . . . ," said Jim Hill, thinking of the old freebooting days, "that we should now be compelled to fight for our lives against political adventurers who have never done anything but pose and draw a salary." But the plain fact was that the public, which had long watched business running politics, could see no reason why politics should not run business. For decades the railroads and other business combinations had bought the people's legislators and packed the people's conventions. It was not much use for businessmen to cry after 1900 that business was private business, removed from politics, for it never had been removed from politics.

The truth was that the era of the businessman was drawing to a close. The temper of national life had changed since 1870, the philosophy of democracy was no longer so popularly nor so solidly based on Darwin and Adam Smith. The issues of 1870 were by no means fully settled—indeed, the real settlement had hardly begun—but the alliance between government and business was not so strong as before, the trust under closer rein, the financier not quite so firmly certain of his ground.

Progressivism: Middle-Class Disillusionment

George Mowry

As a group, the reform mayors and governors, their prominent supporters, and the muckrakers were an interesting lot. Considering the positions they held, they were very young. Joseph W. Folk was only thirty-five when elected governor, Theodore Roosevelt forty, Charles Evans Hughes and Hiram Johnson forty-four, and Robert La Follette forty-five. The average age of the important progressive leaders who upset the Southern Pacific Railroad machine in California was a little over thirty-eight. The tale of a rather typical young reformer was that of Joseph Medill Patterson of the Chicago *Tribune* family. Patterson's grandfather founded the *Tribune*, his father was general manager of the paper, and his cousin was Robert McCormick, who controlled the paper for over thirty years. Patterson sharply reacted against the reigning conservatism by winning a seat in the Illinois legislature at the age of twenty-four on a platform advocating the municipal ownership of all city utilities in the state. Two years later he resigned from the Chicago Commission of Public Works to become a Socialist because, he announced, it was impossible to reform the city and the country under capitalism. In 1906 he published a diatribe against wealth in the *Independent* entitled "The Confessions of a Drone," and followed it two years later with a book of similar tone.[1] Obviously, this was a period, like the ones after the War of 1812 and in the 1850's,

[1] George E. Mowry, *The California Progressives* (Berkeley and Los Angeles, 1952), p. 87; *The Public*, April 8, 1905; *Independent*, LXI (1906), pp. 493–495; Joseph Medill Patterson, *Little Brother of the Rich* (Chicago, 1908).

when energetic and incautious youth took command. And in each instance the departure of the elder statesmen portended great changes.

Some of these reformers, like Golden Rule Jones, Charles Evans Hughes, and Tom Johnson, were self-made men, although Hughes's father was a minister, and Johnson's, a Confederate colonel, had come from the upper stratum of Kentucky society. A surprising number of them came from very wealthy families, with names like du Pont, Crane, Spreckels, Dodge, Morgenthau, Pinchot, Perkins, McCormick, and Patterson. The quip was made that this was a "millionaire's reform movement." But the great majority of the reformers came from the "solid middle class," as it then was called with some pride. That their families had been of the economically secure is indicated by the fact that most of them had had a college education in a day when a degree stamped a person as coming from a special economic group. It is interesting to note that most of the women reformers and social workers had gone to college. Occupationally also the reformers came from a very narrow base in society. Of a sample of over four hundred a majority was lawyers, as might be expected of politicians, and nearly 20 percent of them newspaper editors or publishers. The next largest group was from the independent manufacturers or merchants, with the rest scattered among varied occupations, including medicine, banking, and real estate. A statistical study of sixty of the wealthier reformers reveals that the largest single group of twenty-one was manufacturers or merchants, ten lawyers, six newspaper publishers, while nineteen more had inherited their wealth. Quite a few among the latter group had no definite occupation save that of preserving their family fortune and indulging in reform. Of the sixty only about half attended college, a figure much lower than that for the entire group of reformers. Of this number just 50 percent came from three institutions, Harvard, Princeton, and Yale.[2]

If names mean anything, an overwhelming proportion of this reform group came from old American stock with British origins consistently indicated. Except for the women, who were predominantly Midwestern, the reformers' places of origin were scattered over the country roughly in proportion to population densities. Practically all of them by 1900, however, lived in northern cities, most of the Southerners having left their section during early manhood. Religious affiliations were surprisingly difficult to get, and no really trustworthy national sample was obtained. The figures collected were not at all consonant with national church membership statistics. Representatives of the Quaker faith bulked large among the women reformers, as did members of the Jewish religion among the very wealthy. But for the group as a whole the religious descendants of Calvin and Knox predominated, with the Congregationalists, Unitarians, and Presbyterians in the vast majority. Thus it seems likely that the intellectual and religious influence of New England was again dominating the land.

---

[2] These statistics and the ones following came from a series of studies in the writer's seminar. The figures were rechecked and are in the author's possession.

Whether Democrats or Republicans, the overwhelming number of this group of twentieth-century reformers had been conservatives in the nineties. If Republican, they had almost to a man followed the way of Theodore Roosevelt, Robert La Follette, Lincoln Steffens, and William Allen White to support William McKinley. Most of the progressive Democrats had not been supporters of Bryan, but, like Woodrow Wilson, John Johnson, and Hoke Smith of Georgia, had either followed the Gold Democratic ticket or had remained silent during the election of 1896. Yet from four to six years later most of these men were ardent advocates of municipal gas and water socialism, and were opposed to their regular party machines to the extent of leading either nonpartisan movements in the municipalities or rebellious splinter groups in the states. Moreover, the new century found most of them, except on the currency issue, supporting many of the 1896 Populist and Bryanite demands. Before the Progressive years were finished they and their kind had not only secured the inception of a host of the Populists' reforms, but had contributed a few of their own.

Obviously, a good many questions arise about the motivation of this economically secure, well-educated, middle-class group. On the surface it looked as if the progressive movement was simply a continuation under different leadership of the Populist cause. According to William Allen White, Populism had "shaved its whiskers, washed its shirt, put on a derby, and moved up into the middle class. . . ." But White's remark scarcely probed beneath the surface. Populism arose from farmer distress in a period of acute depression. Its reforms were belly reforms. The movement was led by angry men and women not too far removed from the Grange hall. Except for the western silver men, they were incensed at the mounting figures of farm foreclosures and a withering countryside. To the contrary, progressivism arose in a period of relative prosperity. Its reforms were more the results of the heart and the head than of the stomach. Its leaders were largely recruited from the professional and business classes of the city. A good many were wealthy men; more were college graduates. As a group they were indignant at times, but scarcely ever angry. What caused them to act in the peculiar way they did? A part of the answer lies in the peculiar economic and social position in which this middle-class group found itself at about the turn of the century, a part in the intellectual and ethical climate of the age, a part in the significant cluster of prejudices and biases that marked the progressive mind.

"The world wants men, great, strong, harsh, brutal men—men with purpose who let nothing, nothing, nothing stand in their way," Frank Norris wrote in one of his novels. This worship of the strong man, so characteristic of the age, produced a cult of political leadership with ominous overtones for later years. Tempered at this time with the ethics of the social gospel, the cult produced an image far less frightening: an image of men dedicated to the social good, an image approximating the hope of Plato for his guardians. These strong good men, "the change-makers," Harold Frederic wrote, were the protectors of morality, the originators of progress. They were ambitious men and ruthless, but only ruthless in their zeal for human advancement. They were supremely alone, the causative individuals. Far from being disturbed when isolated, David Graham Phillips's hero Scarborough was only concerned when he was "propped up" by something other than his own will and intelligence. "I propose," he commented, "never to 'belong' to anything or anybody."[3]

In 1872 a future progressive, Henry Demarest Lloyd, confessed that he wanted power above all things, but "power unpoisoned by the presence of obligation." That worship of the unfettered individual, the strong pride of self, the strain of ambition, and the almost compulsive desire for power ran through progressive rhetoric like a theme in a symphony. From Frank Norris's strong-minded heroes to Richard Harding Davis's men of almost pure muscle these feelings were a badge of a restless, sensitive, and troubled class. They were never far below the surface in the character of Theodore Roosevelt. Robert La Follette knew them, and Woodrow Wilson had more than his share of them. While still a scholar and teacher, Wilson poured out his frustration with the contemplative life: "I have no patience with the tedious world of what is known as 'research,' " he wrote to a friend. "I should be complete if I could inspire a great movement of opinion. . . ."[4]

A few progressive leaders like William Jennings Bryan and Golden Rule Jones really thought of themselves as servants of the people,[5] and almost completely identified themselves with their constituents. But most progressives set themselves apart from the crowd. Mankind was basically good and capable of progress, but benign change scarcely issued from the masses. Rather it was only accomplished through the instrumentality of a few great and good men. Woodrow Wilson believed that efficient government could come only from "an educated elite," William Kent thought that progress never came from the bottom, and Roosevelt often spoke of government as the process of "giving justice from above." Occasionally, when the electorate disagreed with them, the progressives contented themselves with the thought that truth "was always in the minority" and a possession alone of the "few who see." In 1912 Walter Lippmann wrote that since men could do anything but govern themselves, they were constantly looking for some "benevolent guardian." To the progressive politician that guardian, of course, was patterned after his image of himself.[6] . . .

A small reform-minded minority in 1900 was outspoken in defense of

[3] Frank Norris, A Man's Woman (New York, 1900), p. 71; David Graham Phillips The Cost (Indianapolis, 1904), p. 17.

[4] Quoted in Daniel Aaron, Men of Good Hope (New York, 1951), p. 139; Richard Hofstadter, The American Political Tradition and the Men Who Made It (New York, 1948), p. 243.

[5] Frances G. Newland, Public Papers (New York, 1932), p. 311.

[6] Theodore Roosevelt, "Who Is a Progressive?" The Outlook, C (1912), 2; The Public, April 18, 1903; Walter Lippmann, Drift and Mastery (New York, 1914), p. 189.

the large industrial and commercial city as the creator of the good life. Some of them saw the city as a place of refuge from an ugly countryside and from a hostile natural environment. Remembering his own bleak and lonely boyhood on an upstate New York farm, the novelist Harold Frederic condemned a daily communion with nature that starved the mind and dwarfed the soul. Theodore Dreiser bluntly described the natural processes as inimical to man as a species. Others felt the fascination of the city, a place of excitement and of opportunity. Lincoln Steffens recalled that he felt about the concrete canyons of New York as other youths felt about the wild West. For people like Jane Addams, Jacob Riis, and Hutchins Hapgood the city offered a place to work and an avenue to opportunity.

For the great majority of the new century's reformers, however, the city contained almost the sum of their dislikes. It was a "devilsburg of crime" sucking into its corrupt vortex the "young, genuine, strong and simple men from the farm." There, if successful, they became "financial wreckers" who made their money strangling legitimate enterprises and other human beings. If they were failures—that is, if they remained factory workers—they gradually became like the machine they tended, "huge, hard, brutal, strung with a crude blind strength, stupid, unreasoning." At the worst such unfortunates became the flotsam of the slums, making the saloon their church and the dive their home. The native American lost not only his morals in the city but also his talent for creative work and his sense of beauty. "Sometimes, I think, they'se poison in th' life in a big city," Mr. Dooley remarked, "the flowers won't grow there. . . ." If a man stayed in the city long enough, one of David Graham Phillips' characters remarked, he would almost inevitably lose those qualities that made him an American: one had to go West to see a "real American, a man or a woman who looks as if he or she would do something honest or valuable. . . ."[7]

With such intense antiurban feelings, it is small wonder that the United States began to romanticize its pioneer past and its agrarian background. Following the Spanish War historical novels fairly poured from the publishers. The public appetite for western stories had one of its periodic increases, and the virtues of the countryside were extolled in even the best literature. In one of Ellen Glasgow's first novels the country, "with its ecstatic insight into the sacred plan of things," is contrasted with the city's "tainted atmosphere." Almost repeating William Jennings Bryan in 1896, Miss Glasgow wrote that the country was the world as God had planned it, the city as man had made it. The cult of the frontier, first introduced into historical scholarship by Frederick Jackson Turner in 1890, and the new emphasis upon agrarian virtues

[7] For varied expressions of this antiurbanism, see Irving Bacheller, *Eben Holden* (Boston, 1900), p. 336; Alice H. Rice, *Mrs. Wiggs of the Cabbage Patch* (New York, 1901), p. 29; Winston Churchill, *The Dwelling-Place of Light* (New York, 1917), p. 79; Finley Peter Dunne, *Mr. Dooley in Peace and War* (Boston, 1898), p. 125; D. G. Phillips, *Golden Fleece* (New York, 1903), pp. 57–58.

were zealously reflected by the more sensitive politicians. William Jennings Bryan, Theodore Roosevelt, Robert La Follette, and Woodrow Wilson all showed to varying degrees this national nostalgia, this reactionary impulse. Roosevelt in particular saw the great city as the creator of national weakness and possible disintegration, and the countryside as the nation's savior. It was the man on the farm, he wrote, who had consistently done the nation the "best service in governing himself in time of peace and also in fighting in time of war." Dangerous elements to the commonwealth lurked in every large city, but among the western farmers of the West "there was not room for an anarchist or a communist in the whole lot." What Professor Richard Hofstadter has called the agrarian myth, but which might better be called the agrarian bias, was one of the more important elements that went into the making of the progressive mind.[8]

A part of the progressive's romantic attraction to the countryside at this particular time can be explained by the alien character of the urban population. In 1903 the Commissioner of Immigration reported that the past year had witnessed the greatest influx of immigrants in the nation's history. But far from being pleased, the Commissioner was plainly worried. An increasing percentage of these newcomers, he pointed out, belonged to an "undesirable foreign element," the "indigestible" aliens from south Europe. The public was neither surprised at the figures of the report nor shocked by its adjectives. It had been made increasingly sensitive to the changing patterns of immigration by numerous periodical articles and newspaper items calling attention to the alien nature of the eastern seaboard cities. As the immigrant tide welled stronger each year, the nativist spirit that had been so obviously a part of the mental complex leading to the Spanish War increased in intensity. Throughout the decade editors, novelists, and politicians competed with each other in singing the praises of the "big-boned, blond, long-haired" Anglo-Saxon with the blood of the berserkers in his veins, and in denigrating Jack London's "dark pigmented things, the half castes, the mongrel bloods, and the dregs of long conquered races. . . ." In Frank Norris's novels the really despicable characters run all to a type. Braun, the diamond expert in Vandover; Zerkow, the junk dealer in McTeague; the flannel-shirted Grossman in The Pit; and Behrman in The Octopus were all of the same religion and approximately from the same regions in Europe. One of the themes in Homer Lea's The Vermillion Pencil was the extra-national loyalty of the Catholic bishop who intrigued endlessly for the Church and against the State. Although Chester Rowell frankly admitted that California needed "a class of servile labor," he was adamantly opposed to

---

[8] Ellen Glasgow, The Descendant (New York, 1897), p. 254; Roosevelt to George Otto Trevelyan, March 9, 1905, and to Kermit Roosevelt, January 1, 1907, Roosevelt MSS.; The Public, November 14, 1903.

the admission of Orientals, who were dangerous to the state and to "the blood of the next generation."[9]

The progressives, of course, had no monopoly of this racism. Such conservatives as Elihu Root, Henry Cabot Lodge, and Chauncey Depew, and even radicals like Debs, shared their views to a degree. But for one reason or another neither conservative nor radical was as vocal or as specific in his racism as was the reformer. No more eloquent testimony to the power of racism over the progressive mind is evident than in the writings of the kindly, tolerant Middle Westerner William Allen White. In a book published in 1910 White explained nearly all of America's past greatness, including its will to reform, in terms of the nation's "race life" and its racial institutions, "the home and the folk moot." Nor would this genius, this "clean Aryan blood," White promised, be subjected to a debilitating admixture in the future despite the incoming hordes. "We are separated by two oceans from the inferior races and by an instinctive race revulsion to cross breeding that marks the American wherever he is found."[10] Such diverse reformers as Theodore Roosevelt, Albert J. Beveridge, Chester Rowell, Frank Parsons, Hoke Smith, Richard W. Gilder, and Ray Stannard Baker, with more or less emphasis, echoed White's sentiments. . . .

Since the progressive usually came from a comfortable part of society and a general attack upon property was usually furthest from his mind, this assault upon great wealth put him in a rather ambiguous position. The one way out of the paradox was to draw a line between good and bad wealth. For some the limit of private fortunes was the total that man could "justly acquire." For others the measurement was made in terms of service to society. Tom Johnson, for example, believed that the law could be so drawn that men would be able "to get" only the amount "they earned." Still others argued that there must be a point where additional money ceased to be salubrious for a man's character and became instead a positive evil force. Wayne MacVeagh, Garfield's Attorney General, suggested that all people could be divided into three classes: those who had more money than was good for them, those who had just enough, and those who had much less than was morally desirable. Just where the exact lines should be drawn, most progressives would not say. But the imputation that the state ought to redivide wealth on a morally desirable basis found a receptive audience. To George F. Baer's claim that coal prices should be the sum of "all the traffic will bear," the editors of The Outlook replied that property was private not by any natural right but by an "artificial arrangement made by the community." "If under those artificial arrangements," the editorial continued, "the community

9 *Literary Digest, XXVII* (1903), p. 158; Jack London, *The Mutiny of the Elsinore* (New York, 1914), pp. 197–198. See also John Higham, *Strangers in the Land, Patterns of American Nativism, 1860–1925* (New Brunswick, N.J., 1955), pp. 131 ff.
10 William Allen White, *The Old Order Changeth* (New York, 1910), pp. 128, 197, 253.

is made to suffer, the same power that made them will find a way to unmake them." Thus in the progressive mind the classical economic laws repeatedly described in the past as natural had become artificial arrangements to be re-arranged at any time the community found it morally or socially desirable. Admittedly the formulations of new ethical standards for a division of national wealth were to be extremely difficult. But once the progressive had destroyed the popular sanction behind the "laws" of rent, prices, and wages, there was to be no complete turning back. A revolution in human thought had occurred. Man, it was hoped, would now become the master and not the creature of his economy. And the phrases punctuating the next fifty years of history—the "square deal," the New Deal, the Fair Deal, the just wage, the fair price—attested to his efforts to make the reality square with his ambitions.[11]

After revisiting the United States in 1905, James Bryce, the one-time ambassador from Great Britain, noted that of all the questions before the public the ones bearing on capital and labor were the most insistent and the most discussed. Certainly for many a progressive the rise of the labor union was as frightening as the rise of trusts. True, he talked about them less because nationally they were obviously not as powerful as were the combines of capital. But emotionally he was, if anything, more opposed to this collectivism from below than he was to the collectivism above him in the economic ladder.[12]

"There is nothing ethical about the labor movement. It is coercion from start to finish. In every aspect it is a driver and not a leader. It is simply a war movement, and must be judged by the analogues of belligerence and not by industrial principles." This statement by a Democratic progressive illustrates the ire of the small and uncertain employer who was being challenged daily by a power he often could not match. In their lawlessness and in their violence, remarked another, unions were "a menace not only to the employer but to the entire community."[13] To the small employer and to many middle-class professionals unions were just another kind of monopoly created for the same reasons and having the same results as industrial monopoly. Unions, they charged, restricted production, narrowed the available labor market, and raised wages artificially in the same manner that trusts were restricting production, narrowing competition, and raising their own profits. "Every step in trade unionism has followed the steps that organized capital has laid down before it," Clarence Darrow observed in a speech before the Chicago Henry George Association. The ultimate direction of the two monopolies was as clear to the individual entrepreneur as it was to Darrow.

---

[11] *The Public*, September 23, 1905, and February 3, 1906; Wayne MacVeagh, "An Appeal to Our Millionaires," *North American Review*, June, 1906; *The Outlook*, LXXVI (1904), 240.

[12] James Bryce, "America Revisited," *The Outlook*, LXXIX (1905), p. 848.

[13] *The Public*, June 13, 1903; *The Outlook*, LXVIII (1901), p. 683.

Either trade unionism would break down, a Midwestern editor argued, or it would culminate in "a dangerously oppressive partnership" with the stronger industrial trusts. The end result was equally obvious to such men: a steady decrease in opportunity for the individual operating as an individual, an economy of statics, an end to the open society. The burden of the industrial evolution, Darrow said in concluding his speech, "falls upon the middle class."[14] And Howells' traveler from Altruria put the case even more graphically: "the struggle for life has changed from a free fight to an encounter of disciplined forces, and the free fighters that are left get ground to pieces between organized labor and organized capital." . . .

" 'I am for labor,' or 'I am for capital,' substitutes something else for the immutable laws of righteousness," Theodore Roosevelt was quoted as saying in 1904. "The one and the other would let the class man in, and letting him in is the one thing that will most quickly eat out the heart of the Republic." Roosevelt, of course, was referring to class parties in politics. Most progressives agreed with Herbert Croly that a "profound antagonism" existed between the political system and a government controlled by a labor party.[15] In San Francisco in 1901, in Chicago in 1905, and in Los Angeles in 1911, when labor used or threatened direct political action, the progressive reacted as if touched by fire. Chicago was a "class-ridden" city, remarked one progressive journal, which would not redeem itself until the evil pretensions of both organized capital and labor had been suppressed. In Los Angeles, where a Socialist labor group came within a hair's breadth of controlling the city, the progressives combined with their old enemies, the corporation-dominated machine, to fight off the challenge, and as a result never again exerted the power they once had in the city. Apropos of that struggle punctuated by a near general strike, dynamite, and death, the leading California progressive theorist, Chester Rowell, expostulated that no class as a class was fit to rule a democracy; that progress came only from the activities of good citizens acting as individuals. Class prejudice and class pride excused bribery, mass selfishness, lawlessness, and disorder. This class spirit emanating from both business and labor was "destroying American liberty." When it became predominant, Rowell concluded, American institutions would be dead, for peaceful reform would no longer be possible, and "nothing but revolution" would remain.[16]

At various times and places the progressive politician invited the support of organized labor, but such co-operation was almost invariably a one-way

[14] Chicago Record Herald, June 26, 1903; The Public, June 11, 1903.
[15] Charles H. Cooley, Human Nature and the Social Order (New York, 1902), p. 72; Ray Stannard Baker, "The Rise of the Tailors," McClure's, XXIV (1904), p. 14. For other expressions of the same spirit, see Simon Patten, The New Basis of Civilization (New York, 1907), p. 84; John N. McCormick, The Litany and the Life (Milwaukee, 1904), p. 93; H. B. Brown, "Twentieth Century," Forum, XIX (1895), p. 641; The Public, November 26, 1914; Jacob A. Riis, "Theodore Roosevelt, The Citizen," The Outlook, LXXVI (1904), p. 649; Croly, Promise, p. 129.
[16] The Public, May 13, 1905, and June 17, 1905; Fresno Republican, November 20, 1911.

street. Somewhat reminiscent of the early relations between the British Liberal and Labor parties, it worked only if the progressive rather than the labor politician was in the driver's seat. In Maine, for example, when labor attempted to lead a campaign for the initiative and referendum, it was defeated in part by progressives, who two years later led a successful campaign on the same issues.[17] In the progressive literature the terms "captain of industry" and "labor boss" were standard, while "labor statesman" was practically unknown. Roosevelt's inclination to try labor lawbreakers in a criminal court is well known; his administration's failure to indict criminally one corporation executive is eloquent of the limits of his prejudice. Progressive literature contained many proposals for permitting corporations to develop until they had achieved quasi-monopoly status, at which time federal regulation would be imposed. No such development was forecast for labor. Unions were grudgingly recognized as a necessary evil, but the monopolistic closed shop was an abomination not to be tolerated with or without government regulation. In the Chicago teamsters' strike of 1905 Mayor Dunne ordered the city police to be "absolutely impartial" toward both capital and labor. But he also insisted that the strikers not be allowed to block the teams of nonunion men or the delivery of nonunion-marked goods.[18]

A few progressives, of course, hailed the rise of labor unions as an advance in democracy. But the majority, while sincerely desirous of improving the plight of the individual workingman, was perhaps basically more hostile to the union than to corporate monopoly. If the progressive attention was mostly centered on the corporation during the decade, it was largely because the sheer social power of the corporation vastly overshadowed that of the rising but still relatively weak unions. When confronted with a bleak either-or situation, progressive loyalties significantly shifted up and not down the economic ladder.

Emotionally attached to the individual as a causative force and to an older America where he saw his group supreme, assaulted economically and socially from above and below, and yet eager for the wealth and the power that flowed from the new collectivism, the progressive was at once nostalgic, envious, fearful, and yet confident about the future. Fear and confidence together for a time inspired this middle-class group of supremely independent individuals with a class consciousness that perhaps exceeded that of any other group in the nation. This synthesis had been a long time developing. Back in the early 1890's Henry George had remarked that the two dangerous classes to the state were "the very rich" and "the very poor." Some years afterward a Populist paper referred to the "upper and lower scum" of society. At about the same time the acknowledged dean of American letters had inquired just where the great inventions, the good books, the beautiful pictures, and the

---

[17] J. William Black, "Maine's Experience with the Initiative and Referendum," *Annals of the American Academy of Political Science,* XLII, pp. 164–165.
[18] *The Public,* April 15, 1905.

just laws had come from in American society. Not from the "uppermost" or "lowermost" classes, Howells replied. They had come mostly from the middle-class man. In the first decade of the twentieth century the progressive never questioned where ability and righteousness resided. Nor was he uncertain of the sources of the nation's evils. "From above," one wrote, "come the problems of predatory wealth. . . . From below come the problems of poverty and pigheaded and brutish criminality."[19]

As the progressive looked at the sharply differentiated America of 1900, he saw "pyramids of money in a desert of want." For William Allen White the world was full of "big crooks" and the "underprivileged." The polar conditions of society assaulted the progressive conscience and threatened progressive security. Supremely individualistic, the progressive could not impute class consciousness, or, as he would have phrased it, class selfishness, to himself. His talk was therefore full of moral self-judgments, of phrases like "the good men," "the better element," "the moral crowd." From the Old Source, he paraphrased, "Thou shalt not respect the person of the poor, nor honor the person of the great; in righteousness shalt thou judge thy neighbor." His self-image was that of a "kind-hearted man" dealing in justice. William Kent publicly stated that he could not believe in the class struggle because every great reform of the past had been wrought by men who were not "selfishly interested." "I believe," he concluded, "altruism is a bigger force in the world than selfishness."[20]

Since the progressive was not organized economically as was the capitalist and the laborer, he chose to fight his battles where he had the most power —in the political arena. And in large terms his political program was first that of the most basic urge of all nature, to preserve himself, and secondly to refashion the world after his own image. What the nation needed most, wrote a Midwestern clergyman, was an increase in the number of "large-hearted men" to counteract the class organization of both capital and labor. "Solidarity," Herbert Croly stated, "must be restored." The point of reconcentration around which the hoped-for solidarity was to take place, of course, was the middle class. It was to "absorb" all other classes, thought Henry Demarest Lloyd. It was to be both the sum and substance of the classless state of the future.[21]

The progressive mentality was a compound of many curious elements. It contained a reactionary as well as a reform impulse. It was imbued with a burning ethical strain which at times approached a missionary desire to create a heaven on earth. It had in it intense feelings of moral superiority over both

[19] Aaron, Men of Good Hope, pp. 84, 193; Jackson (Michigan) Industrial News, March 8, 1894; California Weekly, December 18, 1908.

[20] William Allen White to Henry J. Allen, July 28, 1934, in Walter Johnson (ed.), Selected Letters of William Allen White, 1899–1943 (New York, 1947), p. 348; San Francisco Bulletin, September 8, 1911.

[21] William J. McCaughan, Love, Faith and Joy (Chicago, 1904), p. 206; Croly, Promise of American Life, p. 139; Aaron, Men of Good Hope, p. 160.

elements of society above and below it economically. It emphasized individual dynamism and leadership. One part of it looked backward to an intensely democratic small America; another looked forward to a highly centralized nationalistic state. And both elements contained a rather ugly strain of racism.

The progressive mentality was generated in part from both a fear of the loss of group status and a confidence in man's ability to order the future. Had progressive militancy come in a more despondent intellectual and ethical climate and in a bleaker economic day, group fear might have won over group hope. Its more benign social ends might then have been transmuted into something more malignant. But in the warm and sunny atmosphere of 1900 the optimistic mood prevailed. . . .

A Condition of Excitement

Eric Goldman

At first the new reformers had no special name for themselves. "Liberal" was too closely associated with Clevelandism. "Populist" called up the dour radicalism of the Nineties. Gradually the term "progressivism" took its place after "liberalism" and "Populism" as the label for another, quite different attempt to reform post-Civil War America.

In many fundamentals progressivism continued Populism. For both movements, the central problem was opportunity and they aimed to "restore" opportunity by quite similar programs. Government was to be democratized in order to make it more amenable to reform. Reform meant primarily the ending of governmental interventions that benefited large-scale capital and a rapid increase in the interventions that favored men of little or no capital. Many of progressivism's specific proposals came straight from Populism, including the direct election of United States senators, the initiative and the referendum, anti-trust action, a federal income tax, the encouragement of trade-unions, and an eight-hour day. In the spirit of Populism, progressives took up new proposals for direct democracy or the advancement of lower-income groups, most notably popular primaries, the recall of elected officials, workmen's compensation legislation, and minimum-wage and maximum-hour laws. The new reform also continued Populism's political recognition of women. The cities were producing their own female activists, and these women, for the most part talented and well educated, made effective advocates of feminism in the eyes of progressives.

Yet progressivism was not simply the Populist buggy rolled out for a new century. More urban in its base, progressivism was much more genuinely concerned with the problems of labor and was far more inclined to include small businessmen and white-collar workers in the groups it wanted to help. Equally important, progressivism was developing its own special attitude toward the immigrant.

The progressives did not entirely drop Populism's anti-immigrant feeling. One of the country's best-known progressive spokesmen, the sociologist Edward Ross, provided the era's most effective formula for fear of immigration by arguing that the "squalid" newcomers bred rapidly while the old stock, "struggling to uphold a decent standard of living," stopped at two or three children. Many progressives also carried over the Populist fear that unlimited immigration kept wage scales down and consequently they continued the Populist demand for restriction of the influx. But progressivism as a movement was far more friendly than Populism to the immigrants who had already arrived. It was tending toward a genuine acceptance of the newcomer, even toward espousal of an important role for him.

Progressives made up the dominant element in the settlement houses that were undertaking the first systematic "Americanization" work, and the Americanization they advocated was no one-way street. The immigrant was not only to learn, settlement workers emphasized; he was to teach. While assimilating, he was to preserve the parts of his heritage which did not conflict with adjustment to the United States and he was to enrich American culture by bringing to it desirable ideas or customs from his old-country background. This type of Americanization was enthusiastically approved by Israel Zangwill, a British Jew who had become familiar with American settlement work by serving as head of an organization that helped Russian Jews flee the pogroms to the United States. In 1908 Zangwill wrote his enthusiasm into *The Melting Pot*, one of those occasional literary works that both express and further a social movement.

The chief characters of Zangwill's play were all immigrants in New York City—an Irish Catholic, a Jew-hating nobleman who had personally conducted pogroms in Russia, his daughter, and a young Russian Jew whose parents had been murdered at the order of the nobleman. The theme was the general benefit to be derived from what Zangwill called an "all-around give-and-take," between the various groups of immigrants and between all the newcomers and the old stock. At the end of the play, as the Jew and the Jew-killer's daughter prepared to marry, the young man looked out to a sunset and proclaimed it "the fires of God round His crucible."

DAVID: *There she lies, the great Melting Pot—listen! Can't you hear the roaring and the bubbling?* (he points east). *There gapes her mouth—the harbour where a thousand mammoth feeders come from the ends of the world to pour in their human freight. . . . Celt and Latin, Slav and Teuton, Greek and Syrian,—black and yellow—*

VERA: *Jew and Gentile—*
DAVID: *Yes, East and West, and North and South, the palm and the pine, the pole and the equator, the crescent and the cross—how the great alchemist melts and fuses them with his purging flame! . . . Ah, Vera, what is the glory of Rome and Jerusalem where all nations and races come to worship and look back, compared with the glory of America, where all races and nations come to labour and look forward!*

"Romantic claptrap," the New York Times critic snorted, and Zangwill's gushing prose is certainly hard to read today without wincing. But in a more sentimental era, the play provided for thousands of progressives an exciting expression of their desire for an attitude toward the immigrant that was more generous and hopeful than Populist snarling.

In the political field, progressivism was altering Populism by the greater degree to which it sought centralization. The Populists may not have been afraid of pyramided power, and the progressives certainly did not ignore reform possibilities on the municipal and state levels. But the increasing urge to centralize was showing itself in a number of ways, of which the two most important were greater dependence on federal rather than state action and on executives rather than legislatures.

The progressives were men in a hurry, and even at their best legislatures must always seem slow and cumbersome. The legislatures of the turn of the century, reformers constantly learned in additional ways, were hardly legislatures at their best. At the same time, able individuals were showing the prodigies that could be performed by one skillful reformer in an executive position. Under the circumstances, progressives relied increasingly on the "good man" who would bring to reform the decisiveness of a Carnegie and would maneuver, drive, or skirt around a legislature. The desire to provide efficient by-passes heightened progressive enthusiasm for the administrative commission, the device which gave long-time, quasi-legislative powers to a few men appointed by the executive.

Simultaneously progressives were becoming discouraged about the potentialities of action by the states. The problem with which the reformers were most concerned, the large corporation, did not yield readily to state action. No one of the huge businesses operated in only one state, and state regulations usually ended up in creating a maze of conflicting statutes that hindered the efficiency of corporations without exacting from them any real social responsibility. Worse yet, state social legislation was being thrown out by state courts almost as fast as it was passed. Quite obviously, Washington was no perfect base for reform. But the federal Constitution did explicitly empower Congress to regulate interstate commerce and national action did seem the logical way to regulate corporations operating on a national scale. In the early 1900's, much more than in the Populist era, reform eyes were focusing on Washington.

If progressivism was going beyond Populism in its attitude toward centralization, it was pulling back in another important respect. Progressivism virtually gave up the Populist attempt to make the Southern Negro an equal citizen. It paid little attention to the Negro problem as a whole and, to the extent that it worried over the black man at all, gave its support to the program of a Negro whose whole life had been a preparation for compromise.

Born to slavery and to poverty so great that his bed was a bundle of rags, Booker T. Washington had been helped to his education by a series of kindly whites. The Negro school he was invited to run, Tuskegee Institute, was founded on the initiative of Southern whites, and continued white aid permitted Washington to build Tuskegee from a dilapidated shanty for thirty students to forty-six substantial buildings offering thirty trades to fourteen hundred pupils. It is possible to exaggerate the amount of faith in the white man which this background gave Booker Washington. His was a practical, canny mind, operating in a situation that suggested bargaining Negro equality for some Negro advances. ("Actually," W. E. B. Du Bois once remarked, "Washington had no more faith in the white man than I do," which was saying that he had little faith indeed.) But whatever was going on behind that calm, pleasant face of Booker Washington, he spoke no belligerence toward the white man and no call for immediate equality.

When he was asked to address the Atlantic Cotton Exposition in 1895, Washington put his philosophy into sentences that immediately became famous as the "Atlanta Compromise." The Negro should accept political inequality, Washington said, provided he was given the opportunity to advance economically and educationally; in time, having prepared himself for the wise use of the vote, he would be granted the privilege. Washington bluntly repudiated any drive for social equality. "In all things that are purely social," he declared in his most widely quoted sentence, "we can be as separate as the fingers, yet one as the hand in all things essential to mutual progress."

In the early 1900's Washington's argument had the force of apparent success. His program was the first to promise any substantial advance for the Negro which the nation as a whole seemed willing to accept. Tuskegee Institute and similar schools were rapidly turning out trained Negroes who could train others and, by supporting themselves in decency, win respect for the whole race. In the decade between 1900 and 1910, Negro illiteracy throughout the country declined from forty-four to thirty percent, while the number of farms owned by Southern Negroes increased at a rate four times more swiftly than the growth of the Negro population. Progressives interested in the Negro observed all this and remembered the violence and quick failure that had come with Populist attempts at equality. They were inclined to become enthusiastic, to help make Booker T. Washington the first Negro national hero—and to let well enough alone.

In other, less important details, progressivism also moved away from Populism, but the core of the differences between the movements lay in a consideration that no discussion of specific variations would adequately reveal.

Agrarian-dominated Populism, with its desperate sense of being left behind, its doubts whether anyone could be both a businessman and a decent citizen, its inclination to suspect the man with well-fitted clothes or polished grammar, was not the only base of progressivism. The new reform was a product of the cities as much as of the farms, an amalgam of the Best People's liberalism and of the nobody's Populism, a middle doctrine for a nation rapidly committing itself to middle-class ways of thinking.

Progressivism accepted business America, even was enthusiastic about it, and aimed merely to correct abuses. It prized cultivation, manner, and efficiency; quite characteristically, progressivism restored liberalism's emphasis on civil-service reform. Above all, progressivism replaced Populist grimness with a gusty, dawn-world confidence, worrying about America but not worrying about it enough to turn to extremes. The ominous Populist distinction between "producing" and "nonproducing" classes fast disappeared from reform terminology. To the progressive, America was never farmers or industrial workers locked in a class struggle with big capital. America was always "the people," some of whom were richer and more powerful than others, but all of whom could be given back their birthright of opportunity by moderate, practical moves.

The restoration of opportunity by giving stronger powers to more democratized governments, a businesslike restoration with no disreputable caterwauling—such was the least common denominator of the thinking that was rising out of the union of liberalism and Populism. It was a denominator to which each progressive added his own integers; it had its confusions, its vagaries, and its dodges. But it was a sweepingly appealing program, the most national one since the Republican platform that rode Lincoln into the White House, and for most progressives it carried the kind of emotional intensity that whirls political movements ahead.

"In fact," the progressive journalist Ray Stannard Baker has remembered his mood in the early 1900's, "I used to be sure reform would sweep the country, that is, I always used to be sure until I talked to the man next to me on the street car." Throughout progressive America a growing confidence in the program was accompanied by a growing awareness that the program alone was not enough. Progressivism was face to face with a potent set of hostile ideas, ideas that had been tangled up with the middle-class rejection of Populism and that did not quickly wither as the middle-class attitude moved toward dissent. Somehow the progressives had to dissolve away the argument that their whole program was unscientific, contrary to human nature, antidemocratic, unconstitutional, and immoral. . . .

Blurrings, tendencies, trends—but in the first decade of the twentieth century the main current of progressivism was the one on which Teddy Roosevelt bobbed along so gaily. He might scourge minority nationalists, but Du Bois and Brandeis were both admirers as his Administrations drew to a close. He might suddenly turn on the muckrakers, even, on occasion, thwack the unions or help the United States Steel trust, but for the overwhelming number of American reformers Roosevelt was progressivism incarnate, and that progressivism was bringing an all-excusing sense of achievement. The new reform not only ruled the White House and hundreds of state and local governments. Progressives could take deeper satisfaction in the way that economic and social change was becoming the central subject of the day, the exciting, even the glamour subject, replacing the older generation's awed discussions of captains of industry with ebullient talk about the goodness, the inevitability, the sheer fun of re-doing America.

Late in 1904 Mrs. Sarah P. Decker took her ample self to the rostrum of the General Federation of Women's Clubs, turned a carefully coiffured head to the delegates, and said: "Ladies, you have chosen me your leader. Well, I have an important piece of news to give you. Dante is dead. He has been dead for several centuries, and I think it is time that we dropped the study of his *Inferno* and turned our attention to our own." It was that way everywhere in the country, on all social levels. In Chicago an immigrant worker walked up to her boss and demanded better toilet facilities with the statement: "Old America is gone. There is new times." In middle-class New York, pretty young Frances Perkins was reading the reform books the President was always recommending, and vowing that "the pursuit of social justice would be my vocation." In Baltimore a socialite horseman turned the city upside down with full-page advertisements preaching Rauschenbusch's dictum that "the greatest thing a millionaire can do is to make the rise of future millionaires impossible." Thirty-three Protestant denominations joined in a Federal Council dedicated to Reform Darwinian Christianity, Walter Lippmann proudly took over the presidency of the Harvard Socialist Club, a muckraking novelist, Winston Churchill, led both Rex Beach and *The Trail of the Lonesome Pine* on the best-seller lists, and Clarence Darrow was invited to address the Ulysses S. Grant Chapter of the Daughters of the American Revolution in Ashtabula, Ohio.

There was, said Theodore Roosevelt in the only understatement of his entire career, "a condition of excitement and irritation in the public mind. . . ."

The Triumph of Conservatism

Gabriel Kolko

Assuming that the burden of proof is ultimately on the writer, I contend that the period from approximately 1900 until the United States' intervention in the war, labeled the "progressive" era by virtually all historians, was really an era of conservatism. Moreover, the triumph of conservatism that I will describe in detail throughout this book was the result not of any impersonal, mechanistic necessity but of the conscious needs and decisions of specific men and institutions.

There were any number of options involving government and economics abstractly available to national political leaders during the period 1900–1916, and in virtually every case they chose those solutions to problems advocated by the representatives of concerned business and financial interests. Such proposals were usually motivated by the needs of the interested businesses, and political intervention into the economy was frequently merely a response to the demands of particular businessmen. In brief, conservative solutions to the emerging problems of an industrial society were almost uniformly applied. The result was a conservative triumph in the sense that there was an effort to preserve the basic social and economic relations essential to a capitalist society, an effort that was frequently consciously as well as functionally conservative.

I use the attempt to preserve existing power and social relationships as the criterion for conservatism because none other has any practical meaning. Only if we mechanistically assume that government intervention in the economy, and a departure from orthodox laissez faire, automatically benefits the

Reprinted with permission of The Macmillan Company from The Triumph of Conservatism: A Reinterpretation of American History, 1900–1916 *by Gabriel Kolko.* © *by The Free Press, a Division of The Macmillan Company, 1963.*

general welfare can we say that government economic regulation by its very nature is also progressive in the common meaning of that term. Each measure must be investigated for its intentions and consequences in altering the existing power arrangements, a task historians have largely neglected.

I shall state my basic proposition as baldly as possible so that my essential theme can be kept in mind, and reservations and intricacies will be developed in the course of the book. For the sake of communication I will use the term *progressive* and *progressivism*, but not, as have most historians, in their commonsense meanings.

Progressivism was initially a movement for the political rationalization of business and industrial conditions, a movement that operated on the assumption that the general welfare of the community could be best served by satisfying the concrete needs of business. But the regulation itself was invariably controlled by leaders of the regulated industry, and directed toward ends they deemed acceptable or desirable. In part this came about because the regulatory movements were usually initiated by the dominant businesses to be regulated, but it also resulted from the nearly universal belief among political leaders in the basic justice of private property relations as they essentially existed, a belief that set the ultimate limits on the leaders' possible actions.

It is business control over politics (and by "business" I mean the major economic interests) rather than political regulation of the economy that is the significant phenomenon of the Progressive Era. Such domination was direct and indirect, but significant only insofar as it provided means for achieving a greater end—political capitalism. *Political capitalism* is the utilization of political outlets to attain conditions of stability, predictability, and security—to attain rationalization—in the economy. *Stability* is the elimination of internecine competition and erratic fluctuations in the economy. *Predictability* is the ability, on the basis of politically stabilized and secured means, to plan future economic action on the basis of fairly calculable expectations. By *security* I mean protection from the political attacks latent in any formally democratic political structure. I do not give to *rationalization* its frequent definition as the improvement of efficiency, output, or internal organization of a company; I mean by the term, rather, the organization of the economy and the larger political and social spheres in a manner that will allow corporations to function in a predictable and secure environment permitting reasonable profits over the long run. My contention in this volume is not that all of these objectives were attained by World War I, but that important and significant legislative steps in these directions were taken, and that these steps include most of the distinctive legislative measures of what has commonly been called the Progressive Period.

Political capitalism, as I have defined it, was a term unheard of in the Progressive Period. Big business did not always have a coherent theory of economic goals and their relationship to immediate actions, although certain individuals did think through explicit ideas in this connection. The advocacy of specific measures was frequently opportunistic, but many individuals with similar interests tended to prescribe roughly the same solution to each concrete problem, and to operationally construct an economic program. It was never a question of regulation or no regulation, of state control or laissez faire; there were, rather, the questions of what kind of regulation and by whom. The fundamental proposition that political solutions were to be applied freely, if not for some other industry's problems then at least for one's own, was never seriously questioned in practice. My focus is on the dominant trends, and on the assumptions behind these trends as to the desirable distribution of power and the type of social relations one wished to create or preserve. And I am concerned with the implementation and administration of a political capitalism, and with the political and economic context in which it flourished.

Why did economic interests require and demand political intervention by the *federal* government and a reincarnation of the Hamiltonian unity of politics and economics?

In part the answer is that the federal government was *always* involved in the economy in various crucial ways, and that laissez faire never existed in an economy where local and federal governments financed the construction of a significant part of the railroad system, and provided lucrative means of obtaining fortunes. This has been known to historians for decades, and need not be belabored. But the significant reason for many businessmen welcoming and working to increase federal intervention into their affairs has been virtually ignored by historians and economists. This oversight was due to the illusion that American industry was centralized and monopolized to such an extent that it could rationalize the activity in its various branches voluntarily. Quite the opposite was true.

Despite the large number of mergers, and the growth in the absolute size of many corporations, the dominant tendency in the American economy at the beginning of this century was toward growing competition. Competition was unacceptable to many key business and financial interests, and the merger movement was to a large extent a reflection of voluntary, unsuccessful business efforts to bring irresistible competitive trends under control. Although profit was always a consideration, rationalization of the market was frequently a necessary prerequisite for maintaining long-term profits. As new competitors sprang up, and as economic power was diffused throughout an expanding nation, it became apparent to many important businessmen that only the national government could rationalize the economy. Although specific conditions varied from industry to industry, internal problems that could be solved only by political means were the common denominator in those industries whose leaders advocated greater federal regulation. Ironically, contrary to the consensus of historians, it was not the existence of monopoly that caused the federal government to intervene in the economy, but the lack of it.

*   *   *

Meat Inspection: Theory and Reality

In October, 1904, a young man named Upton Sinclair arrived in Chicago with a $500 stake from Fred S. Warren, editor of *The Appeal to Reason*. After seven weeks of interviews and observation in the stock yard area, Sinclair sent back stories to Warren on the working conditions, filth, and gore of the packing industry, and his novel *The Jungle* electrified the nation, spreading Sinclair's name far and wide and, finally, bringing the Beef Trust to its knees. The nation responded, Roosevelt and Congress acted by passing a meat inspection law, and the Beef Trust was vanquished. Or so reads the standard interpretation of the meat inspection scandal of 1906.

Unfortunately, the actual story is much more involved. But the meat inspection law of 1906 was perhaps the crowning example of the reform spirit and movement during the Roosevelt presidency, and the full story reveals much of the true nature of progressivism.

Alas, the movement for federal meat inspection did not begin with the visit of Sinclair to Chicago in 1904, but at least twenty years earlier, and it was initiated as much by the large meat packers themselves as by anyone. The most important catalyst in creating a demand for reform or innovation of meat inspection laws was the European export market and not, as has usually been supposed, the moralistic urgings of reformers. And since the European export market was more vital to the major American meat packers than anyone else, it was the large meat packers who were at the forefront of reform efforts.

Government meat inspection was, along with banking regulation and the crude state railroad regulatory apparatus, the oldest of the regulatory systems. In principle, at least, it was widely accepted. The major stimulus, as always, was the desire to satisfy the European export market. As early as December, 1865, Congress passed an act to prevent the importation of diseased cattle and pigs, and from 1877 on, agents of the Commissioner of Agriculture were stationed in various states to report on diseases.

In 1879 Italy restricted the importation of American pigs because of diseases, and in 1881 France followed suit. Throughout the 1880's the major European nations banned American meat, and the cost to the large American packers was enormous. These packers learned very early in the history of the industry that it was not to their profit to poison their customers, especially in a competitive market in which the consumer could go elsewhere. For the European nation this meant turning to Argentine meat, to the American consumer to another brand or company. The American meat industry . . . was competitive throughout this period, mainly because the level of investment required to enter packing was very small and because there were no decisive economies in large size. In 1879 there were 872 slaughtering and meat packing establishments, but there were 1,367 in 1889. Chicago in the late 1870's had established a municipal system of inspection, but it left much to be desired and was weakened over time. In 1880, after England banned the importation of cattle with pleuropneumonia, the livestock growers initiated a campaign for legislation designed to prevent the spread of the disease. The Grange and many state legislatures joined the movement, and in 1880 Rep. Andrew R. Kiefer of Minnesota introduced a bill to prohibit the transportation of diseased livestock from infected to clean areas. Similar bills designed to halt the spread of pleuropneumonia followed, but failed to gather sufficient support. In late 1882, however, exposés in the Chicago papers of diseased meat led to reforms in municipal inspection, and the major packers cooperated with the city health department to set up more examining stations to root out disease. Other cities also created inspection systems at this time, although they varied in quality.

Despite the failure of Congress to legislate on the matter, in 1881 the Secretary of the Treasury created an inspection organization to certify that cattle for export were free of pleuropneumonia. Such limited efforts and haphazard municipal inspection, despite packer support, were inadequate to meet exacting European standards. In March, 1883, Germany banned the importation of American pork, cutting off another major export market. Congress was forced to meet the threat to the American packers, and in May, 1884, established the Bureau of Animal Industry within the Department of Agriculture "to prevent the exportation of diseased cattle and to provide means for the suppression and extirpation of pleuropneumonia and other contagious diseases among domestic animals." Despite the research and regulatory activities of the bureau, which by 1888 cost one-half million dollars per year, the Department of Agriculture from 1885 on began appealing for additional federal regulation to help improve exports to Europe. Its major impetus was to fight European restrictions, not to aid the American consumer, and in doing so it effectively represented the interests of the major American packers who had the most to gain from the Department's success.

Rather than improving, the situation further deteriorated with a hog cholera epidemic in 1889 worsening the American export position. Congress acted to meet the challenge, and in August, 1890, responding to the pressure of the major packers, passed a law providing for the inspection of all meat intended for export. But since provision was not made for inspection of the live animal at the time of slaughter, the foreign bans remained in effect. Desperate, in March, 1891, Congress passed the first major meat inspection law in American history. Indeed, the 1891 Act was the most significant in this field, and the conclusion of the long series of efforts to protect the export interests of the major American packers. The Act provided that all live animals be inspected, and covered the larger part of the animals passing through interstate trade. Every establishment in any way involved in export was compelled to have a Department of Agriculture inspector, and violations of the law could be penalized by fines of $1,000, one year in prison, or both. Hogs were required to have microscopic examinations as well as the usual pre- and post-mortem inspections. The law, in brief, was a rigid one, and had the desired effect. During 1891 and 1892, prohibitions on importing American pork were removed by Germany, Denmark, France, Spain, Italy, and Austria.

The Act of 1891 satisfied the health standards of European doctors, but greatly distressed the European packing industry. Slowly but surely the European nations began imposing new medical standards in order to protect their own meat industries. Major American packers failed to appreciate the retaliatory tactics of their foreign competitors, and protested to the Department of Agriculture, which pressured the Department of State into helping it defend the vital interests of the American meat industry. The government's meat inspection organization, in the meantime, gradually extended control over the greater part of the interstate meat commerce, and in 1895 was aided by another act providing for even stronger enforcement. In 1892 the Bureau of Animal Industry gave 3.8 million animals ante- and post-mortem examinations; it examined 26.5 million animals in 1897. It maintained 28 abattoirs in 12 cities in 1892, 102 abattoirs in 26 cities in 1896. The inspection extended to packaged goods as well, despite the rumors that American soldiers during the Spanish-American War were being served "embalmed meat" that damaged their digestive systems—rumors strongly denied by Harvey W. Wiley, the leading American advocate of pure food legislation. By 1904, 84 percent of the beef slaughtered by the Big Four packers in Chicago, and 100 percent of the beef slaughtered in Ft. Worth, was being inspected by the government; 73 percent of the packers' entire U.S. kill was inspected. It was the smaller packers that the government inspection system failed to reach, and the major packers resented this competitive disadvantage. The way to solve this liability, most of them reasoned, was to enforce and extend the law, and to exploit it for their own advantage. They were particularly concerned about the shipment of condemned live stock to smaller, noninspected houses, and applied pressure on the bureau to stop the traffic. When the Association of Official Agricultural Chemists created a committee in 1902 to determine food standards for meat products, the major meat companies cooperated with the effort and agreed with the final standards that were created.

When Sinclair arrived in Chicago in late 1904 to do a story for *The Appeal to Reason* he was primarily interested in writing a series on the life of Chicago's working class. His contact with the local socialists led him to Adolph Smith, a medically qualified writer for the English medical journal, *The Lancet*, and one of the founders of the Marxist Social Democratic Federation of England. Smith proved to be of great aid to Sinclair, supplying him with much information. In January, 1904, Smith published a series of articles in *The Lancet* attacking sanitary and especially working conditions in the American packing houses. Smith's series was hardly noticed in the United States—certainly it provoked no public outcry. In April, 1905, *Success Magazine* published an attack on diseased meat and packer use of condemned animals. This article also failed to arouse the public, which was much more concerned with alleged monopoly within the meat industry than with sanitary conditions.

The inability of these exposés to capture the attention of the public was especially ironic in light of the unpopularity of the packers. Charles Edward Russell had just completed his series in *Everybody's Magazine* on "The Greatest Trust in the World," an exaggerated account that nevertheless did not raise the question of health conditions. The Bureau of Corporations' report on beef displeased the public, and made the Roosevelt Administration especially defensive about the packers. The Bureau of Animal Industry, at the same time, feared that attacks on the quality of inspection would reflect on the integrity of the bureau and damage the American export market—and advised against the publication of the *Success Magazine* article.

Roosevelt had been sent a copy of *The Jungle* before its publication, but took no action after it was released. The controversy over it was carried on for several months by J. Ogden Armour, Sinclair, and the press, and Roosevelt was dragged into the matter only after Senator Albert J. Beveridge presented a new inspection bill in May, 1906. In February, shortly before *The Jungle* received wide attention, the Department of Agriculture ordered the packers to clean up their toilet and sanitary conditions for workers, even though it had no legal power to do so. J. Ogden Armour, in early March, took to the *Saturday Evening Post* to defend government meat inspection. He pointed out that the Chicago packing houses had always been open to the public, and that the stockyards, for the past six years, had been in the process of total reconstruction. The large packers, Armour insisted, strongly favored inspection.

Attempt to evade it would be, from the purely commercial viewpoint, suicidal. No packer can do an interstate or export business without Government inspection. Self-interest forces him to make use of it. Self-interest likewise demands that he shall not receive meats or by-products from any small packer, either for export or other use, unless that small packer's plant is also "official"—that is, under United States Government inspection.

This government inspection thus becomes an important adjunct of the packer's business from two viewpoints. It puts the stamp of legitimacy and honesty upon the packer's product and so is to him a necessity. To the public it is insurance against the sale of diseased meats.

Armour's reference to the small packers reflected his genuine concern with the increasing growth of competitors, the number of companies in the field increasing by 52 percent from 1899 to 1909. And since the six largest packers slaughtered and sold less than 50 percent of the cattle, and could not regulate the health conditions of the industry, government inspection was their only means of breaking down European barriers to the growth of American exports.

In March, at least, Roosevelt was not thinking of legislative reform in beef. Although he favored "radical" action, he told Sinclair in a discussion over socialism, "I am more than ever convinced that the real factor in the elevation of any man or any mass of men must be the development within his or their hearts and heads of the qualities which alone can make either the individual, the class or the nation permanently useful to themselves and to others." Roosevelt was ready to allow the triumph of personal conversion rather than legislation in March, but in April his alienation with the packers went somewhat further. In March, 1906, a District Court dismissed the Justice Department's case against the Big Four packers on the grounds that their voluntary production of evidence to the Bureau of Corporations in 1904, on which evidence the suit was heavily based, gave them immunity under the Fifth Amendment. On April 18, Roosevelt sent Congress a message denying the packers' contention that Garfield had promised them immunity—which he had—and calling for legislation denying immunity to voluntary witnesses or evidence. By May, when Beveridge brought in his proposed meat legislation, the unpopular and grossly misunderstood major packers were ready to welcome the retaliatory legislation against them.

Historians, unfortunately, have ignored Upton Sinclair's important contemporary appraisal of the entire crisis. Sinclair was primarily moved by the plight of the workers, not the condition of the meat. "I aimed at the public's heart," he wrote, "and by accident I hit it in the stomach." Although he favored a more rigid law, Sinclair pointed out that

the Federal inspection of meat was, historically, established at the packers' request; . . . it is maintained and paid for by the people of the United States for the benefit of the packers; . . . men wearing the blue uniforms and brass buttons of the United States service are employed for the purpose of certifying to the nations of the civilized world that all the diseased and tainted meat which happens to come into existence in the United States of America is carefully sifted out and consumed by the American people.

Sinclair was correct in appreciating the role of the big packers in the origins of regulation, and the place of the export trade. What he ignored was the extent to which the big packers were already being regulated, and their desire to extend regulation to their smaller competitors.

In March, 1906, sensing the possibility of a major public attack on its efficiency, the Department of Agriculture authorized an investigation of the Chicago office of the Bureau of Animal Industry. Although the report of the inquiry admitted that the inspection laws were not being fully applied because of a lack of funds, it largely absolved its bureau. Soon after, realizing that the Department of Agriculture report was too defensive, Roosevelt sent Charles P. Neill, the Commissioner of Labor, and James B. Reynolds to Chicago to make a special report. Neill, an economist with no technical knowledge of the packing industry, and Reynolds, a civil service lawyer, had never been exposed to the mass slaughtering of a packing house, and like Sinclair were sensitive, middle-class individuals. Roosevelt regarded the Department of Agriculture report as critical, but he hoped the Neill-Reynolds report would vindicate the worst.

Senator Albert J. Beveridge, in the meantime, began drafting a meat inspection bill at the beginning of May. Drafts passed back and forth between Beveridge and Secretary of Agriculture James Wilson, and Reynolds was frequently consulted as well. Wilson wished to have poultry excluded from the law, and diseased but edible animals passed. By the end of May, when a final bill had been agreed upon, Wilson strongly defended the Beveridge proposal. The measure was submitted as an amendment to the Agriculture Appropriation Bill, and the big packers indicated at once that they favored the bill save in two particulars. They wanted the government to pay for the entire cost of inspection, as in the past, and they did not want canning dates placed on meat products for fear of discouraging the sales of perfectly edible but dated products. Save for these contingencies, the Beveridge Amendment received the support of the American Meat Packers' Association and many major firms. The packers' objections were embodied in the amendments to the Beveridge proposal made in the House by James W. Wadsworth, chairman of the Committee on Agriculture.

Roosevelt immediately opposed the Wadsworth amendments, and threatened to release the Neill-Reynolds report if the House failed to support his position. The House supported Wadsworth, and Roosevelt sent the report along with a special message to Congress on June 4. He must have had qualms as to what it would prove, for he hedged its findings by asserting that "this report is preliminary," and that it did not discuss the entire issue of the chemical treatment of meats. The report, the packers immediately claimed, reluctantly but definitely absolved them, but also "put weapons into the hands of foreign competitors."

The Beveridge Amendment passed the Senate on May 25 without opposition. To strengthen his position, Wadsworth called hearings of the Committee of Agriculture for June 6 through June 11. Two significant facts emerge from the testimony, both of which Wadsworth intended making. Charles P. Neill's testimony revealed that the sight of blood and offal, and the odors of systematic death, had deeply shocked the two investigators, and that they had often confused the inevitable horrors of slaughtering with sanitary conditions. Roosevelt had erred in sending to the slaughterhouses two inexperienced Washington bureaucrats who freely admitted they knew nothing of canning. The major result of the hearings was to reveal that the big

Chicago packers wanted more meat inspection, both to bring the small packers under control and to aid their position in the export trade. Formally representing the large Chicago packers, Thomas E. Wilson publicly announced "We are now and have always been in favor of the extension of the inspection, also to the adoption of the sanitary regulations that will insure the very best possible conditions," including nearly all the recommendations of the Neill-Reynolds report. "We have always felt that Government inspection, under proper regulations, was an advantage to the live stock and agricultural interests and to the consumer," but the packers strongly opposed paying for the costs of their advantage. The packers opposed dating canned food because of its effects on sales, but had no objection to reinspection of older cans or the banning of any chemical preservatives save saltpeter.

Although segments of the press immediately assumed that the packing industry opposed regulation that presumably damaged their interests—and historians have accepted their version—most contemporaries, including Beveridge, knew better. Upton Sinclair was critical of the bill from the start, and called for municipal slaughter houses. On June 29, as the packers and live-stock growers were urging passage of the Beveridge amendment with the government footing the expenses, Beveridge announced that "an industry which is infinitely benefited by the Government inspection ought to pay for that inspection instead of the people paying for it." The value of meat inspection for the export trade, Senator Henry C. Hansbrough of North Dakota declared, is obvious. What was wrong with the entire measure, Senator Knute Nelson pointed out, was that "the American consumers and the ordinary American farmer have been left out of the question. Three objects have been sought to be accomplished—first, to placate the packers; next, to placate the men who raise the range cattle, and, third, to get a good market for the packers abroad."

The battle that followed was not on the basic principle of a meat inspection law, but on the issue of who should pay for the cost of administering it and on the problem of placing dates on processed meat. During the committee hearings, Wadsworth asked Samuel H. Cowan, the lawyer of the National Live Stock Association, to prepare a bill with the modifications acceptable to the big packers. This he did, and it was rumored in the press that Roosevelt had given Cowan's efforts his tacit approval. If an agreement between Roosevelt and Wadsworth was, in fact, reached, it was surely secret, although the two men had at least two private discussions between June 1 and 15. On June 15 the President dashed off an attack on Wadsworth's bill that was intended for the press. Wadsworth, Roosevelt claimed, was working for the packers. "I told you on Wednesday night," Wadsworth answered, referring to their private conversation, "when I submitted the bill to you, that the packers insisted before our committee on having a rigid inspection law passed. Their life depends on it, and the committee will bear me out in the statement that they placed no obstacle whatever in our way. . . ."

The House stood firm on its bill, and there was a stalemate for a week. Since an efficient inspection bill was to the interests of the packers, the New York *Journal of Commerce* announced on June 18, they should be willing to pay its costs. But the House conferees could not be made to budge on the issues of the government assuming the cost of inspection and the dating of cans and processed meats. Beveridge abdicated, and on June 30 the bill was signed by the President. The bill, George Perkins wrote J. P. Morgan, "will certainly be of very great advantage when the thing once gets into operation and they are able to use it all over the world, as it will practically give them a government certificate for their goods. . . ."

The most significant aspect of the new law was the size of the appropriation—$3 million as compared to the previous peak of $800,000—for implementing it. The law provided for the post-mortem inspection of all meat passing through interstate commerce. In this respect, the law was a systematic and uniform application of the basic 1891 Act, but it still excluded intrastate meat. Indeed, even in 1944 only 68 percent of the meat output was covered by federal laws. The new law was unique insofar as it extended inspection to meat products and preservatives, and determined standards for sanitation within the plants. The basic purpose of Sinclair's exposé, to improve the conditions of the working class in the packing houses, could have been achieved either through better wages or socialism. Although they now had cleaner uniforms at work, their homes and living conditions were no better than before, and if they became diseased they were now thrown out of the packing houses to fend for themselves. "I am supposed to have helped clean up the yards and improve the country's meat supply—though this is mostly delusion," Sinclair later wrote. "But nobody even pretends to believe that I improved the condition of the stockyard workers."

Yet historians have always suggested that Sinclair brought the packers to their knees, or that The Greatest Trust in the World collapsed before the publication of the Neill-Reynolds report. Given the near unanimity with which the measure passed Congress, and the common agreement on basic principles shared by all at the time, there is an inconsistency in the writing of historians on this problem. If the packers were really all-powerful, or actually opposed the bill, it is difficult to explain the magnitude of the vote for it. The reality of the matter, of course, is that the big packers were warm friends of regulation, especially when it primarily affected their innumerable small competitors.

In late August the packers met with officials of the Department of Agriculture to discuss the problem of complying with the law. ". . . the great asset that you gentlemen are going to have," Secretary Wilson told them, "when we get this thing to going will be the most rigid and severe inspection on the face of the earth." According to the minutes of the meeting, the packers responded to this proposition with "loud applause" and not with a shudder. The purpose of the law "is to assure the public that only sound and wholesome meat and meat food products may be offered for sale," Swift & Co. and other giant packers told the public in large ads. "It is a wise law. Its enforcement must be universal and uniform."

Meat inspection ceased to be a significant issue during the remainder of the Progressive Era. Beveridge, for several years after the passage of the 1906 Act, tried to restore his defeated amendments, but he had no support from either Roosevelt or other important politicians. Secretary of Agriculture Wilson, among others, opposed Beveridge's efforts to have the packers pay for the expenses of inspection. The packers naturally resisted all attempts to saddle them with the costs, but strongly defended the institution of meat inspection and "the integrity and efficiency of the Bureau's meat inspection service." Despite the urging of the American Meat Packers' Association, which wanted action to eradicate tuberculosis and other diseases in livestock, the issue of meat inspection died.

*   *   *

The Lost Democracy

The American political experience during the Progressive Era was conservative, and this conservatism profoundly influenced American society's response to the problems of industrialism. The nature of the economic process in the United States, and the peculiar cast within which industrialism was molded, can only be understood by examining the political structure. Progressive politics is complex when studied in all of its aspects, but its dominant tendency on the federal level was to functionally create, in a piecemeal and haphazard way that was later made more comprehensive, the synthesis of politics and economics I have labeled "political capitalism."

The varieties of rhetoric associated with progressivism were as diverse as its followers, and one form of this rhetoric involved attacks on businessmen—attacks that were often framed in a fashion that has been misunderstood by historians as being radical. But at no point did any major political tendency dealing with the problem of big business in modern society ever try to go beyond the level of high generalization and translate theory into concrete economic programs that would conflict in a fundamental way with business supremacy over the control of wealth. It was not a coincidence that the results of progressivism were precisely what many major business interests desired.

Ultimately businessmen defined the limits of political intervention, and specified its major form and thrust. They were able to do so not merely because they were among the major initiators of federal intervention in the economy, but primarily because no politically significant group during the Progressive Era really challenged their conception of political intervention. The basic fact of the Progressive Era was the large area of consensus and unity among key business leaders and most political factions on the role of the federal government in the economy. There were disagreements, of course, but not on fundamentals. The overwhelming majorities on votes for basic progressive legislation is testimony to the near unanimity in Congress on basic issues.

Indeed, an evaluation of the Progressive Era must concede a much larger importance to the role of Congress than has hitherto been granted by historians who have focused primarily on the more dramatic Presidents. Congress was the pivot of agitation for banking reform while Roosevelt tried to evade the issue, and it was considering trade commissions well before Wilson was elected. Meat and pure food agitation concentrated on Congress, and most of the various reform proposals originated there. More often than not, the various Presidents evaded a serious consideration of issues until Congressional initiatives forced them to articulate a position. And businessmen seeking reforms often found a sympathetic response among the members of the House and Senate long before Presidents would listen to them. This was particularly true of Roosevelt, who would have done much less than he did were it not for the prodding of Congress. Presidents are preoccupied with patronage to an extent unappreciated by anyone who has not read their letters.

The Presidents, considered—as they must be—as actors rather than ideologists, hardly threatened to undermine the existing controllers of economic power. With the possible exception of Taft's Wickersham, none of the major appointees to key executive posts dealing with economic affairs were men likely to frustrate business in its desire to use the federal government to strengthen its economic position. Garfield, Root, Knox, Straus—these men were important and sympathetic pipelines to the President, and gave additional security to businessmen who did not misread what Roosevelt was trying to say in his public utterances. Taft, of course, broke the continuity between the Roosevelt and Wilson Administrations because of political decisions that had nothing to do with his acceptance of the same economic theory that Roosevelt believed in. The elaborate relationship between business and the Executive created under Roosevelt was unintentionally destroyed because of Taft's desire to control the Republican Party. Wilson's appointees were quite as satisfactory as Roosevelt's, so far as big business was concerned, and in his concrete implementation of the fruits of their political agitation—the Federal Reserve Act and the Federal Trade Commission Act—Wilson proved himself to be perhaps the most responsive and desirable to business of the three Presidents. Certainly it must be concluded that historians have overemphasized the basic differences between the Presidents of the Progressive Era, and ignored their much more important similarities. In 1912 the specific utterances and programs of all three were identical on fundamentals, and party platforms reflected this common agreement.

This essential unanimity extended to the area of ideologies and values, where differences between the Presidents were largely of the sort contrived by politicians in search of votes, or seeking to create useful images. None of the

Presidents had a distinct consciousness of any fundamental conflict between their political goals and those of business. Roosevelt and Wilson especially appreciated the significant support business gave to their reforms, but it was left to Wilson to culminate the decade or more of agitation by providing precise direction to the administration of political capitalism's most important consequences in the Progressive Era. Wilson had a small but articulate band of followers who seriously desired to reverse the process of industrial central-ization—Bryan and the Midwestern agrarians reflected this tradition more than any other group. Yet ultimately he relegated such dissidents to a secondary position—indeed, Wilson himself represented the triumph of Eastern Democ-racy over Bryanism—and they were able to influence only a clause or amend-ment, here and there, in the basic legislative structure of political capitalism.

But even had they been more powerful, it is debatable how different Bryanism would have been. Bryan saw the incompatibility between giant cor-porate capitalism and political democracy, but he sought to save democracy by saving, or restoring, a sort of idealized competitive capitalist economy which was by this time incapable of realization or restoration, and was in any event not advocated by capitalists or political leaders with more power than the agrarians could marshal. Brandeis, for his part, was bound by enigmas in this period. Big business, to him, was something to be ultimately rejected or justified on the basis of efficiency rather than power accumulation. He tried to apply such technical criteria where none was really relevant, and he overlooked the fact that even where efficient or competitive, business could still pose irreconcilable challenges to the political and social fabric of a democratic community. Indeed, he failed to appreciate the extent to which it was com-petition that was leading to business agitation for federal regulation, and finally he was unable to do much more than sanction Wilson's actions as they were defined and directed by others.

There was no conspiracy during the Progressive Era. It is, of course, a fact that people and agencies acted out of public sight, and that official state-ments frequently had little to do with operational realities. But the imputation of a conspiracy would sidetrack a serious consideration of progressivism. There was a basic consensus among political and business leaders as to what was the public good, and no one had to be cajoled in a sinister manner. If détentes, private understandings, and the like were not publicly proclaimed it was merely because such agreements were exceptional and, generally known, could not have been denied to other business interests also desiring the security they provided. Such activities required a delicate sense of public relations, since there was always a public ready to oppose preferential treatment for special businesses, if not the basic assumptions behind such arrangements.

Certainly there was nothing surreptitious about the desire of certain businessmen for reforms, a desire that was frequently and publicly proclaimed, although the motives behind it were not appreciated by historians and al-though most contemporaries were unaware of how reforms were implemented after they were enacted. The fact that federal regulation of the economy was conservative in its effect in preserving existing power and economic relations in society should not obscure the fact that federal intervention in the economy was conservative in purpose as well. This ambition was publicly proclaimed by the interested business forces, and was hardly conspiratorial.

It is the intent of crucial business groups, and the structural circumstances within the economy that motivated them, that were the truly significant and unique aspects of the Progressive Era. The effects of the legislation were only the logical conclusion of the intentions behind it. The ideological consensus among key business and political leaders fed into a stream of common action, action that was sometimes stimulated by different specific goals but which nevertheless achieved the same results. Political leaders, such as Roosevelt, Wilson, and their key appointees, held that it was proper for an industry to have a decisive voice or veto over the regulatory process within its sphere of interest, and such assumptions filled many key businessmen with confidence in the essential reliability of the federal political mechanism, especially when it was contrasted to the unpredictability of state legislatures.

Business opposition to various federal legislative proposals and measures did exist, of course, especially if one focuses on opposition to particular clauses in specific bills. Such opposition, as in the case of the Federal Reserve Bill, was frequently designed to obtain special concessions. It should not be allowed to obscure the more important fact that the essential purpose and goal of any measure of importance in the Progressive Era was not merely endorsed by key representatives of businesses involved; rather such bills were first proposed by them.

One can always find some businessman, of course, who opposed federal regulation at any point, including within his own industry. Historians have relished in detailing such opposition, and, indeed, their larger analysis of the period has encouraged such revelations. But the finding of division in the ranks of business can be significant only if one makes the false assumption of a monolithic common interest among all capitalists, but, worse yet, assumes that there is no power center among capitalists, and that small-town bankers or hardware dealers can be equated with the leaders of the top industrial, financial, and railroad corporations. They can be equated, of course, if all one studies is the bulk of printed words. But in the political as well as in the economic competition between small and big business, the larger interests always managed to prevail in any specific contest. The rise of the National Association of Manufacturers in the Progressive Era is due to its antilabor position, and not to its opposition to federal regulation, which it voiced only after the First World War. In fact, crucial big business support could be found for every major federal regulatory movement, and frequent small business support could be found for any variety of proposals to their benefit, such as price-fixing and legalized trade associations. Progressivism was not the triumph of small business over the trusts, as has often been suggested, but the victory of big businesses in achieving the rationalization of the economy that only the federal government could provide.

Still, the rise of the N.A.M. among businessmen in both pro- and anti-regulation camps only reinforces the fact that the relationship of capitalists to the remainder of society was essentially unaltered by their divisions on federal intervention in the economy. In terms of the basic class structure, and the conditions of interclass relationships, big and small business alike were hostile to a labor movement interested in something more than paternalism and inequality. In this respect, and in their opposition or indifference to the very minimal social welfare reforms of the Progressive Era (nearly all of which were enacted in the states), American capitalism in the Progressive Era acted in the conservative fashion traditionally ascribed to it. The result was federal regulation in the context of a class society. Indeed, because the national political leadership of the Progressive Period shared this *noblesse oblige* and conservatism toward workers and farmers, it can be really said that there was federal regulation because there was a class society, and political leaders identified with the values and supremacy of business.

This identification of political and key business leaders with the same set of social values—ultimately class values—was hardly accidental, for had such a consensus not existed the creation of political capitalism would have been most unlikely. Political capitalism was based on the functional unity of major political and business leaders. The business and political elites knew each other, went to the same schools, belonged to the same clubs, married into the same families, shared the same values—in reality, formed that phenomenon which has lately been dubbed The Establishment. Garfield and Stetson met at Williams alumni functions, Rockefeller, Jr. married Aldrich's daughter, the Harvard clubmen always found the White House door open to them when Roosevelt was there, and so on. Indeed, no one who reads Jonathan Daniels' remarkable autobiography, *The End of Innocence*, can fail to realize the significance of an interlocking social, economic, and political elite in American history in this century.

The existence of an Establishment during the Progressive Era was convenient, even essential, to the functional attainment of political capitalism, but it certainly was not altogether new in American history, and certainly had antecedents in the 1890's. The basic causal factor behind national progressivism was the needs of business and financial elements. To some extent, however, the more benign character of many leading business leaders, especially those with safe fortunes, was due to the more secure, mellowed characteristics and paternalism frequently associated with the social elite. Any number of successful capitalists had long family traditions of social graces and refinement which they privately doubted were fully compatible with their role as capitalists. The desire for a stabilized, rationalized political capitalism was fed by this current in big business ideology, and gave many businessmen that air of responsibility and conservatism so admired by Roosevelt and Wilson. And, from a practical viewpoint, the cruder economic conditions could also lead to substantial losses. Men who were making fortunes with existing shares of the market preferred holding on to what they had rather than establishing control over an industry, or risking much of what they already possessed. Political stabilization seemed proper for this reason as well. It allowed men to relax, to hope that crises might be avoided, to enjoy the bountiful fortunes they had already made.

Not only were economic losses possible in an unregulated capitalism, but political destruction also appeared quite possible. There were disturbing gropings ever since the end of the Civil War: agrarian discontent, violence and strikes, a Populist movement, the rise of a Socialist Party that seemed, for a time, to have an unlimited growth potential. Above all, there was a labor movement seriously divided as to its proper course, and threatening to follow in the seemingly radical footsteps of European labor. The political capitalism of the Progressive Era was designed to meet these potential threats, as well as the immediate expressions of democratic discontent in the states. National progressivism was able to short-circuit state progressivism, to hold nascent radicalism in check by feeding the illusions of its leaders—leaders who could not tell the difference between federal regulation of business and federal regulation for business.

Political capitalism in America redirected the radical potential of mass grievances and aspirations—of genuine progressivism—and to a limited extent colored much of the intellectual ferment of the period, even though the amorphous nature of mass aspirations frequently made the goals of business and the rest of the public nearly synonymous. Many well-intentioned writers and academicians worked for the same legislative goals as businessmen, but their innocence did not alter the fact that such measures were frequently designed by businessmen to serve business ends, and that business ultimately reaped the harvest of positive results. Such innocence was possible because of a naive, axiomatic view that government economic regulation, per se, was desirable, and also because many ignored crucial business support for such measures by focusing on the less important business opposition that existed. The fetish of government regulation of the economy as a positive social good was one that sidetracked a substantial portion of European socialism as well, and was not unique to the American experience. Such axiomatic and simplistic assumptions of what federal regulation would bring did not take into account problems of democratic control and participation, and in effect assumed that the power of government was neutral and socially beneficent. Yet many of the leading muckrakers and academics of the period were more than naive but ultimately conservative in their intentions as well. They sought the paternalism and stability which they expected political capitalism to bring, since only in this way could the basic virtues of capitalism be maintained. The betrayal of liberalism that has preoccupied some intellectual historians did not result from irrelevant utopianism or philosophical pragmatism, but from the lack of a truly radical, articulated alternative economic and political program capable of synthesizing political democracy with industrial reality. Such a program was never formulated in this period either in America or Europe.

*   *   *

The question remains: Could the American political experience, and the nature of our economic institutions, have been radically different than they are today? It is possible to answer affirmatively, although only in a hypothetical, unreal manner, for there was nothing inevitable or predetermined in the peculiar character given to industrialism in America. And, abstractly regarding all of the extraneous and artificial measures that provided shape and direction to American political and economic life, and their ultimate class function, it would be possible to make a case for a positive reply to the question. Yet ultimately the answer must be a reluctant "No."

There can be no alternatives so long as none are seriously proposed, and to propose a relevant measure of fundamental opposition one must understand what is going on in society, and the relationship of present actions to desired goals. To have been successful, a movement of fundamental change would have had to develop a specific diagnosis of existing social dynamics and, in particular, the variable nature and consequences of political intervention in the economy. It would have, in short, required a set of operating premises radically different than any that were formulated in the Progressive Era or later. Populism rejected, on the whole, the values of business even as it was unable to articulate a viable alternative. Intellectually it left a vacuum, and, more important, the movement was dead by 1900. The Socialist Party suffered from the fetishistic belief in the necessity of centralization that has characterized all socialist groups that interpreted Marx too literally, and it had a totally inaccurate estimate of the nature of progressivism, eventually losing most of its followers to the Democrats. The two major political parties, as always, differed on politically unimportant and frequently contrived details, but both were firmly wedded to the status quo, and the workers were generally their captives or accomplices. No socially or politically significant group tried to articulate an alternative means of organizing industrial technology in a fashion that permitted democratic control over centralized power, or participation in routine, much less crucial, decisions in the industrial process. No party tried to develop a program that suggested democracy could be created only by continuous mass involvement in the decisions that affected their lives, if the concentration of actual power in the hands of an elite was to be avoided. In brief, the Progressive Era was characterized by a paucity of alternatives to the status quo, a vacuum that permitted political capitalism to direct the growth of industrialism in America, to shape its politics, to determine the ground rules for American civilization in the twentieth century, and to set the stage for what was to follow.

SUGGESTIONS FOR FURTHER READING

Much of the writing on American history in the twentieth century has been influenced by the progressive movement. Beard and Parrington, of course, felt the impact directly, but later writers like Eric Goldman in *Rendezvous with Destiny* (New York, 1952) are also sympathetic to the progressive point of view. George E. Mowry, *The Era of Theodore Roosevelt, 1900–1912* (New York, 1958) and Arthur S. Link, *Woodrow Wilson and the Progressive Era, 1910–1917* (New York, 1954) are balanced studies that fit the two major progressive politicians into the larger progressive movement and in the process reduce some of the conflict that earlier writers emphasized. Samuel P. Hays, *The Response to Industrialism* (Chicago, 1957), and Robert Wiebe, *The Search for Order, 1877–1920* (New York, 1967) see adjustment, consolidation, order, and efficiency, rather than conflict, as the keys to the period. But Wiebe in *Businessmen and Reform: A Study of the Progressive Movement* (Cambridge, Mass., 1962), unlike Kolko, describes the business community as divided during the period. James Weinstein, *The Corporate Ideal in the Liberal State, 1900–1918* (Boston, 1968) finds a conservative business consensus, but Allen F. Davis, *Spearheads for Reform* (New York, 1967) still finds the quest for social justice a part of the movement. For a convenient selection of writings and a good bibliography see David M. Kennedy, ed. *Progressivism: The Critical Issues* (Boston, 1971).

* Available in paperback edition.

6
THE NEW DEAL

The depression following the stock market crash in the fall of 1929 revealed important weaknesses in the American economic system, weaknesses that had not been corrected by earlier reforms of the Populists and progressives, weaknesses only suspected by a few during the 1920's. Hungry men and women fought over garbage dumped in the street. Farmers, forced to burn their corn for fuel, watched sullenly as their creditors came to evict them from their farms, and some of them talked of revolution. A group of unemployed Army veterans marched on Washington in the summer of 1932 to demand immediate payment of their bonus, only to be driven out of town by troops and tanks and tear gas.

"Only a foolish optimist can deny the dark realities of the moment," declared the newly elected President of the United States, Franklin Delano Roosevelt, in his inaugural address. Roosevelt went on to announce that he interpreted his victory in the elections of the previous November as a "mandate" for "direct, vigorous action" under active leadership. This leadership he promised to give.

The result was the New Deal, a period of intensive legislative activity lasting roughly from 1933 to 1938. Virtually no part of the economy failed to feel the effects of the New Deal legislation. The unemployed received aid and work; farmers were helped with measures to cut production and support prices; working people organized unions under the protection of federal law. The banks and the stock exchange came under strict government supervision and the government used its money to institute flood control, rural electrification, and other forms of natural resource conservation.

New Deal legislation won Franklin D. Roosevelt and the Democratic Party a great deal of support among the American people. But at the same time, the New Deal program elicited some of the sharpest opposition in American political history. When New Dealers noted that their goals were the Three R's—Relief, Recovery, and Reform—many opponents bitterly insisted that a fourth "R," Revolution, be added, arguing that the New Deal had turned the country toward socialism.

Few historians accept the view that the New Deal was socialistic either in its goals or its results, but some do argue that it was revolutionary in that it marked a radical break with the traditions and methods of the past. They maintain that the reforms so altered the nature of the relationship between government and society that they marked a fundamental change to which the term revolutionary may be aptly applied. Others, however, argue that the New Deal was in reality conservative, that the legislation passed in the early thirties was really designed to conserve the American system, which was facing a dangerous crisis. As such, the New Deal was radical neither in intent nor in method, having borrowed its techniques, its personnel, and its goals from a long tradition of American reform. Examples of these views may be seen in the following selections.

In the first selection, Frank Freidel, the biographer of Franklin Roose-

269

velt, views the New Deal in historical perspective, and decides that it borrowed much from the progressive era. In total, Freidel concludes, the New Deal represents a conservative solution to the problems of the thirties. Some businessmen, of course, thought that Roosevelt was endangering the American way of life and leading the country toward socialism, but, Freidel argues, most of the businessman's problems were of his own making; Roosevelt certainly preferred to be, and usually was, conciliatory rather than hostile toward the business community. To Freidel the fact that in recent years the opposition party as well as the business community have accepted most of the New Deal measures proves that the Roosevelt reforms were in the tradition of the American consensus.

Carl Degler, like Freidel, views the New Deal sympathetically, but he finds Roosevelt's reforms revolutionary. In fact he sees a fundamental political reorientation because of the depression and the New Deal. While Freidel finds continuity and a conservative consensus, Degler sees a sharp break with the past and a radical consensus. In the last selection Howard Zinn, a New Left historian, is harshly critical of the New Deal. "What the New Deal did," he argues, "was to refurbish middle class America," and to adopt just enough reform "to get the traditional social mechanisms moving again." Roosevelt, according to Zinn, missed the opportunity to reconstruct society, alter the American business system, and promote justice for the Negro. Zinn would agree with Freidel that the New Deal was conservative and promoted a middle-class consensus, but while Freidel seems to approve of the conservatism of the New Deal, Zinn is bitterly opposed.

Without question, the legislation of the New Deal years had a great impact on American life, an impact that continues today. But what was the exact nature of that impact? Did the New Deal legislation mark a radical change in American society? Did the problems of the depression bring about a revolutionary break with the past? Or was the New Deal a conservative reform movement which sought to make only those innovations which would prevent revolutionary change? Is it fair to judge the New Deal from the perspective of the present, or should we view its accomplishments and limitations within the context of the 1930's?

Conservative Reform
Movement

Frank Freidel

In less than a generation, the New Deal has passed into both popular legend and serious history. The exigencies of American politics long demanded that its partisans and opponents paint a picture of it either in the most glamorous whites or sinister blacks. Long after the New Deal was over, politicians of both major parties tried at each election to reap a harvest of votes from its issues.

Gradually a new generation of voters has risen which does not remember the New Deal and takes for granted the changes that it wrought. Gradually too, politicians have had to recognize that the nation faces new, quite different problems since the second World War, and that campaigning on the New Deal has become as outmoded as did the "bloody shirt" issue as decades passed after the Civil War. At the same time, most of the important manuscript collections relating to the New Deal have been opened to scholars so rapidly that careful historical research has been possible decades sooner than was true for earlier periods of United States history. (The Franklin D. Roosevelt papers and the Abraham Lincoln papers became available for research at about the same time, just after the second World War.)

It has been the task of the historians not only to analyze heretofore hidden aspects of the New Deal on the basis of the manuscripts, but also to remind readers of what was once commonplace and is now widely forgotten. A new generation has no firsthand experience of the depths of despair into which the depression had thrust the nation, and the excitement and eagerness

From The New Deal in Historical Perspective, Service Center #25, by Frank Freidel, 2nd ed. (Washington, D.C., 1965), pp. 1–20. Reprinted by permission of the American Historical Association.

271

with which people greeted the new program. Critics not only have denied that anything constructive could have come from the New Deal but they have even succeeded in creating the impression in the prosperous years since 1945 that the depression really did not amount to much. How bad it was is worth remembering, since this is a means of gauging the enormous pressure for change.

Estimates of the number of unemployed ranged up to thirteen million out of a labor force of fifty-two million, which would mean that one wage-earner out of four was without means of support for himself or his family. Yet of these thirteen million unemployed, only about a quarter were receiving any kind of assistance. States and municipalities were running out of relief funds; private agencies were long since at the end of their resources. And those who were receiving aid often obtained only a pittance. The Toledo commissary could allow for relief only 2.14 cents per person per meal, and the Red Cross in southern Illinois in 1931 was able to provide families with only seventy-five cents a week for food. It was in this crisis that one of the most flamboyant members of the Hoover administration suggested a means of providing sustenance for the unemployed: restaurants should dump left-overs and plate scrapings into special sanitary cans to be given to worthy unemployed people willing to work for the food. It was a superfluous suggestion, for in 1932 an observer in Chicago reported:

> Around the truck which was unloading garbage and other refuse were about thirty-five men, women, and children. As soon as the truck pulled away from the pile, all of them started digging with sticks, some with their hands, grabbing bits of food and vegetables.

The employed in some instances were not a great deal better off. In December 1932 wages in a wide range of industries from textiles to iron and steel, averaged from a low of 20 cents to a high of only 30 cents an hour. A quarter of the women working in Chicago were receiving less than 10 cents an hour. In farming areas, conditions were equally grim. In bitter weather on the Great Plains, travelers occasionally encountered a light blue haze that smelled like roasting coffee. The "old corn" held over from the crop of a year earlier would sell for only $1.40 per ton, while coal cost $4 per ton, so many farmers burned corn to keep warm. When Aubrey Williams went into farm cellars in the Dakotas in the early spring of 1933 farm wives showed him shelves and shelves of jars for fruits and vegetables—but they were all empty. Even farmers who could avoid hunger had trouble meeting payments on their mortgages. As a result a fourth of all farmers in the United States lost their farms during these years.

Despairing people in these pre-New Deal years feared President Herbert Hoover had forgotten them or did not recognize the seriousness of their plight. As a matter of fact he had, more than any other depression president in American history, taken steps to try to bring recovery. But he had functioned largely through giving aid at the top to prevent the further collapse of banks and industries, and the concentric rings of further collapses and unemployment which would then ensue. Also he had continued to pin his faith upon voluntary action. He felt that too great federal intervention would undermine the self-reliance, destroy the "rugged individualism" of the American people, and that it would create federal centralization, thus paving the way for socialism.

President Hoover was consistent in his thinking, and he was humane. But it would have been hard to explain to people like those grubbing on the Chicago garbage heap, why, when the Reconstruction Finance Corporation was loaning $90,000,000 to a single Chicago bank, the President would veto a bill to provide federal relief for the unemployed, asserting, "never before has so dangerous a suggestion been seriously made in this country." It was not until June 1932 that he approved a measure permitting the RFC to loan $300,000,000 for relief purposes.

It seems shocking in retrospect that such conditions should have existed in this country, and that any President of either major party should so long have refused to approve federal funds to alleviate them. It adds to the shock when one notes that many public figures of the period were well to the right of the President—for instance, Secretary of the Treasury Andrew Mellon —and that almost no one who was likely to be in a position to act, including Governor Roosevelt of New York, was ready at that time to go very far to the left of Hoover.

Roosevelt, who was perhaps the most advanced of the forty-eight governors in developing a program to meet the depression, had shown little faith in public works spending. When he had established the first state relief agency in the United States in the fall of 1931, he had tried to finance it through higher taxes, and only later, reluctantly, abandoned the pay-as-you-go basis. He was, and he always remained, a staunch believer in a balanced budget. He was never more sincere than when, during the campaign of 1932, he accused the Hoover administration of having run up a deficit of three and three-quarters billions of dollars in the previous two years. This, he charged, was "the most reckless and extravagant past that I have been able to discover in the statistical record of any peacetime Government anywhere, any time."

Governor Roosevelt's own cautious record did not exempt him from attack. In April 1932, seeking the presidential nomination, he proclaimed himself the champion of the "forgotten man," and talked vaguely about raising the purchasing power of the masses, in part through directing Reconstruction Finance Corporation loans their way. This little was sufficient to lead many political leaders and publicists, including his Democratic rival, Al Smith, to accuse Roosevelt of being a demagogue, ready to set class against class.

Smith and most other public figures, including Roosevelt, favored public works programs. A few men like Senators Robert F. Wagner of New York and Robert M. La Follette of Wisconsin visualized really large-scale spending on public construction, but most leaders also wanted to accompany the spending with very high taxes which would have been deflationary and thus have defeated the program. None of the important political leaders, and none of the economists who had access to them, seemed as yet to visualize the decisive intervention of the government into the economy of the sort that is considered commonplace today. The term "built-in stabilizers" had yet to be coined.

The fact was that Roosevelt and most of his contemporaries, who like him were products of the Progressive Era, were basically conservative men who unquestioningly believed in the American free enterprise system. On the whole, they were suspicious of strong government, and would indulge in it only as a last resort to try to save the system. This was their limitation in trying to bring about economic recovery. On the other hand, part of their Progressive legacy was also a humanitarian belief in social justice. This belief would lead them to espouse reforms to improve the lot of the common man, even though those reforms might also take them in the direction of additional government regulation. Roosevelt as governor had repeatedly demonstrated this inconsistency in his public statements and recommendations. He had ardently endorsed states rights and small government in a truly Jeffersonian way. Then in quite contrary fashion (but still in keeping with Jeffersonian spirit applied to twentieth-century society) he had pointed out one or another area, such as old age security, in which he believed the government must intervene to protect the individual.

At this time, what distinguished Governor Roosevelt from his fellows were two remarkable characteristics. The first was his brilliant political skill, which won to him an overwhelming proportion of the Democratic politicians and the general public. The second was his willingness to experiment, to try one or another improvisation to stop the slow economic drift downward toward ruin. During the campaign of 1932, many a man who had observed Roosevelt felt as did Harry Hopkins that he would make a better president than Hoover, "chiefly because he is not afraid of a new idea."

Roosevelt's sublime self-confidence and his willingness to try new expedients stood him in good stead when he took over the presidency. On that grim March day in 1933 when he took his oath of office, the American economic system was half-paralyzed. Many of the banks were closed; the remainder he quickly shut down through presidential proclamation. Industrial production was down to 56 percent of the 1923–25 level. Yet somehow, Roosevelt's self-confidence was infectious. People were ready to believe, to follow, when he said in words that were not particularly new, "The only thing we have to fear is fear itself." He offered "leadership of frankness and vigor," and almost the whole of the American public and press—even papers like the

Chicago *Tribune* which soon became bitter critics—for the moment accepted that leadership with enthusiasm.

For a short period of time, about one hundred days, Roosevelt had behind him such overwhelming public support that he was able to push through Congress a wide array of legislation which in total established the New Deal. It came in helter-skelter fashion and seemed to go in all directions, even at times directions that conflicted with each other. There was mildly corrective legislation to get the banks open again, a slashing of government costs to balance the budget, legalization of 3.2 beer, establishment of the Civilian Conservation Corps, of the Tennessee Valley Authority, and of a wide variety of other agencies in the areas of relief, reform, and, above all in those first months, of recovery.

What pattern emerged in all of this legislation? How sharply did it break with earlier American political traditions? The answer was that it represented Roosevelt's efforts to be President to all the American people, to present something to every group in need. And it was based squarely on American objectives and experience in the Progressive Era and during the first World War. It went beyond the Hoover program in that while the word "voluntary" remained in many of the laws, they now had behind them the force of the government or at least strong economic incentives.

It has been forgotten how basically conservative Roosevelt's attitudes remained during the early period of the New Deal. He had closed the banks, but reopened them with relatively little change. Indeed, the emergency banking measure had been drafted by Hoover's Treasury officials. What banking reform there was came later. His slashing of the regular government costs was something he had promised during his campaign, and in which he sincerely believed and continued to believe. He kept the regular budget of the government low until the late thirties. While he spent billions through the parallel emergency budget, he did that reluctantly, and only because he felt it was necessary to keep people from starving. He was proud that he was keeping the credit of the government good, and never ceased to look forward to the day when he could balance the budget. For the first several years of the New Deal he consulted frequently with Wall Streeters and other economic conservatives. His first Director of the Budget, Lewis Douglas, parted ways with him, but late in 1934 was exhorting: "I hope, and hope most fervently, that you will evidence a real determination to bring the budget into actual balance, for upon this, I think, hangs not only your place in history but conceivably the immediate fate of western civilization." (Douglas to FDR, November 28, 1934).

Remarks like this struck home with Roosevelt. Douglas's successors as Director of the Budget held much the same views, and Henry Morgenthau, Jr., who became Secretary of the Treasury at the beginning of 1934, never failed to prod Roosevelt to slash governmental expenditures.

We should add parenthetically that Roosevelt always keenly resented the untrue newspaper stories that his parents had been unwilling to entrust him with money. As a matter of fact he was personally so thrifty when he was in the White House that he used to send away for bargain mail-order shirts, and when he wished summer suits, switched from an expensive New York tailor to a cheaper one in Washington. This he did despite the warning of the New York tailor that he might thus lose his standing as one of the nation's best-dressed men.

Financial caution in governmental affairs rather typifies Roosevelt's economic thinking throughout the entire New Deal. He was ready to go much further than Hoover in construction of public works, but he preferred the kind which would pay for themselves, and did not think there were many possibilities for them in the country. His estimate before he became president was only one billion dollars worth. In 1934, he once proposed that the government buy the buildings of foundered banks throughout the nation and use them for post-offices rather than to construct new buildings. This is how far he was from visualizing huge public works expenditures as a means of boosting the country out of the depression. His course in this area was the middle road. He wished to bring about recovery without upsetting the budget any further than absolutely necessary. He did not launch the nation on a program of deliberate deficit financing.

When Roosevelt explained his program in a fireside chat at the end of July 1933, he declared:

> It may seem inconsistent for a government to cut down its regular expenses and at the same time to borrow and to spend billions for an emergency. But it is not inconsistent because a large portion of the emergency money has been paid out in the form of sound loans . . . ; and to cover the rest . . . we have imposed taxes. . . .
>
> So you will see that we have kept our credit good. We have built a granite foundation in a period of confusion.

It followed from this that aside from limited public works expenditures, Roosevelt wanted a recovery program which would not be a drain on governmental finances. Neither the Agricultural Adjustment Administration nor the National Recovery Administration were. He had promised in the major farm speech of his 1932 campaign that his plan for agricultural relief would be self-financing; this was achieved through the processing tax on certain farm products. The NRA involved no governmental expenditures except for administration.

Both of these programs reflected not the progressivism of the first years of the century, but the means through which Progressives had regulated production during the first World War. This had meant regulation which would as far as possible protect both producers and consumers, both employers and employees. Here the parallel was direct. The rest of Roosevelt's program did not parallel the Progressives' wartime experience, for during the war, in terms of production regulation had meant channeling both factories and farms into the maximum output of what was needed to win the war. Now the problem in the thirties was one of reducing output in most areas rather than raising it, and of getting prices back up rather than trying to hold them down.

Certainly the nation badly needed this sort of a program in 1933. The products of the fields and mines and of highly competitive consumers' goods industries like textiles were being sold so cheaply that producers and their employees alike were close to starvation. The overproduction was also wasteful of natural resources. In an oilfield near Houston, one grocer advertised when 3.2 beer first became legal that he would exchange one bottle of beer for one barrel of oil. They were worth about the same. In other heavy industries like automobiles or farm machinery, production had been cut drastically while prices remained high. One need was to bring prices throughout industry and agriculture into a more equitable relationship with each other, and with the debt structure.

The NRA scheme in theory would help do this. Its antecedents were in the regulatory War Industries Board of the first World War, and indeed it was run by some of the same men. The War Industries Board had functioned through industrial committees; in the twenties these committees had evolved into self-regulatory trade associations. Unfortunately, as Roosevelt had found when he headed the association created to discipline one of the largest and most chaotic of industries, the American Construction Council, self-regulation without the force of law behind it, had a tendency to break down. When the depression had hit, some businessmen themselves had advocated the NRA scheme, but Hoover would have none of it. Roosevelt was receptive.

The theory was that committees in a few major fields like steel, textiles, bituminous coal and the like, would draw up codes of fair practice for the industry. These would not only stabilize the price structure, but also protect the wages and working conditions of labor. Even consumers would benefit, presumably through receiving more wages or profits, and thus enjoying larger purchasing power with which to buy goods at somewhat higher prices.

In practice, the NRA program went awry. Too many committees drew up too many codes embodying many sorts of unenforceable provisions. There was a code even for the mopstick industry. What was more important, some manufacturers rushed to turn out quantities of goods at the old wage and raw material level before the code went into effect, hoping then to sell these goods at new higher prices. Consequently during the summer of 1933 there was a short NRA boom when industrial production jumped to 101 percent of the 1923–25 level, and wholesale prices rose from an index figure of 60.2 in March to 71.2 by October. The crop reduction program of the AAA led to a corresponding rise in agricultural prices.

Had consumers at the same time enjoyed a correspondingly higher purchasing power, the recovery scheme might well have worked. Some of its designers had visualized pouring the additional dollars into consumers' pockets through a heavy public works spending program. Indeed the bill which created the NRA also set up a Public Works Administration with $3,300,000,000 to spend. This money could have been poured here and there into the economy where it was most needed to "prime the pump." But Roosevelt and his most influential advisers did not want to give such an enormous spending power to the administrator of the NRA, nor had they really accepted the deficit spending school of thought. Hence while some of the money being spent by the New Deal went for immediate relief of one form or another, it went to people so close to starvation that they were forced to spend what they received on bare necessities. This was of little aid in priming the pump. The public works fund, which could have served that purpose, went to that sturdy old Progressive, "Honest Harold" Ickes. He slowly went about the process of allocating it in such a way that the government and the public would get a return of one hundred cents (or preferably more) on every dollar spent. Raymond Moley has suggested that if only the cautious Ickes had headed the NRA and the impetuous Johnson the Public Works Administration the scheme might have worked.

Without a huge transfusion of dollars into the economy, the industrial and agricultural recovery programs sagged in the fall of 1933. Roosevelt turned to currency manipulation to try to get prices up. He explained to a critical Congressman, "I have always favored sound money, and do now, but it is 'too darned sound' when it takes so much of farm products to buy a dollar." Roosevelt also accepted a makeshift work relief program, the Civil Works Administration, to carry the destitute through the winter.

Already the New Deal honeymoon was over, and in 1934 and 1935 a sharp political struggle between Roosevelt and the right began to take form. To conservatives, Roosevelt was shattering the constitution with his economic legislation. Al Smith was attacking the devaluated currency as "baloney dollars," and was writing articles with such titles as "Is the Constitution Still There?" and "Does the Star-Spangled Banner Still Wave?" Former President Hoover published his powerful jeremiad, *The Challenge to Liberty*.

Many businessmen complained against the NRA restrictions, the favoritism allegedly being shown to organized labor, and the higher taxes. Although some of them had advocated the NRA, the significant fact was that the thinking of most businessmen seems to have remained about what it had been in the 1920's. They were eager for aid from the government, as long as it involved no obligations on their part or restrictions against them. They wanted a government which could protect their domestic markets with a high tariff wall, and at the same time seek out foreign markets for them, a court system which could discipline organized labor with injunctions, and a tax structure which (as under Secretary of the Treasury Mellon) would take no enormous bite of large profits, and yet retain disciplinary levies on the lower-middle income groups. All these policies they could understand and condone. The New Deal, which would confer other benefits upon them, but require corresponding obligations, they could not.

This hostile thinking which began to develop among the business community was sincere. Businessmen genuinely believed that under the New Deal program too large a share of their income had to go to organized labor, and too much to the government. They freely predicted federal bankruptcy as the deficit began to mount. If they had capital to commit, they refused to expend it on new plants and facilities (except for some introduction of labor-saving machinery). They were too unsure of the future, they complained, because they could not tell what that man in the White House might propose next. Business needed a "breathing spell," Roy Howard wrote Roosevelt, and the President promised one. Nevertheless, the legislative requests continued unabated.

All this, important though it is in delineating the ideology of business-men, is not the whole story. The fact is that during the long bleak years after October 1929 they had slipped into a depression way of thinking. They regarded American industry as being over-built; they looked upon the American market as being permanently contracted. By 1937 when industrial production and stock dividends were up to within ten percent of the 1929 peak, capital expenditures continued to drag along the depression floor. Industrialists did not engage in the large-scale spending for expansion which has been a significant factor in the boom since 1945. As late as 1940 to 1941, many of them were loathe to take the large defense orders which required construction of new plants. Unquestionably the pessimism of businessmen during the thirties, whether or not linked to their hatred of Roosevelt and fear of the New Deal, was as significant a factor in perpetuating the depression, as their optimism since the war has been in perpetuating the boom.

The paradox is that some of the New Deal measures against which the businessmen fought helped introduce into the economy some of the stabilizers which today help give businessmen confidence in the continuation of prosperity. These came despite, not because of, the businessmen. Roosevelt long continued to try to co-operate with the leaders of industry and banking. Their anger toward him, and frequently-expressed statements that he had betrayed his class, at times bewildered and even upset him. For the most part he laughed them off. He hung in his bedroom a favorite cartoon. It showed a little girl at the door of a fine suburban home, apparently tattling to her mother, "Johnny wrote a dirty word on the sidewalk." And the word, of course, was "Roosevelt."

To some of his old friends who complained to him, he would reply with patience and humor. Forever he was trying to point out to them the human side of the problem of the depression. Perhaps the best illustration is a witty interchange with a famous doctor for whom he had deep affection. The doctor wired him in March 1935:

"Pediatricians have long been perplexed by difficulty of weaning infant from breast or bottle to teaspoon or cup. The shift often establishes permanent neurosis in subsequent adult. According to report in evening paper twenty-two million citizen infants now hang on federal breasts. Can you wean them, doctor, and prevent national neurosis?"

Roosevelt promptly replied:

As a young interne you doubtless realize that the interesting transitional process, which you describe in your telegram, presupposes that the bottle, teaspoon, or cup is not empty. Such vehicles of feeding, if empty, produce flatulence and the patient dies from a lack of nutrition.

The next question on your examination paper is, therefore, the following:

Assuming that the transitional period has arrived, where is the Doctor to get the food from to put in the new container?

As time went on, and the attacks became virulent from some quarters, at times even passing the bounds of decency, Roosevelt struck back vigorously. During his campaign in 1936 he excoriated the "economic royalists." When he wound up the campaign in Madison Square Garden, he declared:

We had to struggle with the old enemies of peace—business and financial monopoly, speculation, reckless banking, class antagonism, sectionalism, war profiteering. They had begun to consider the Government of the United States as a mere appendage to their own affairs. And we know now that Government by organized money is just as dangerous as Government by organized mob.

Never before in all our history have these forces been so united against one candidate as they stand today. They are unanimous in their hate for me—and I welcome their hatred.

To these sharp words Roosevelt had come from his position early in the New Deal as the impartial arbiter of American economic forces. He had come to them less because of what he considered as betrayal from the right than through pressure from the left. How had this pressure applied between 1934 and the campaign of 1936?

Back in 1934, while the economic temperature chart of the near frozen depression victim had fluctuated up and down, still dangerously below normal, the dispossessed millions began to look at the New Deal with despair or even disillusion. Those workers going on strike to obtain the twenty-five or thirty-five cents an hour minimum wage or the collective bargaining privileges promised by the NRA began to wisecrack that NRA stood for the National Run-Around. Some of them and of the unemployed millions in northern cities still dependent upon meager relief handouts, began to listen to the stirring radio addresses of Father Charles Coughlin. Old people began to pay five cents a week dues to Dr. Francis Townsend's clubs, which promised them fantastically large benefits. Throughout the South (and even in parts of the North) the dispossessed small farmers listened with enthusiasm to the exhortations of the Louisiana Kingfish, Huey Long, that he would share the wealth to make every man a king.

Many Democratic politicians were surprisingly oblivious to these rumblings and mutterings. Much of the private conversation of men like Vice President John Nance Garner sounded like the public demands of the Liberty Leaguers: cut relief and balance the budget. Garner, who spent the 1934 campaign hunting and fishing in Texas, predicted the usual mid-term loss of a few congressional seats back to the Republicans. Instead the Democrats picked up a startling number of new seats in both houses of Congress. The dispossessed had continued to vote with the Democratic party—but perhaps because there was no alternative but the Republicans who offered only retrenchment. Charles Beard commented that the 1934 election was "thunder on the left."

President Roosevelt, who was brilliantly sensitive to political forces, sensed fully the threat from the left. At the beginning of that crisis year 1935 he proposed in his annual message to Congress the enactment of a program to reinforce "the security of the men, women, and children of the nation" in their livelihood, to protect them against the major hazards and vicissitudes of life, and to enable them to obtain decent homes. In this increased emphasis upon security and reform, Professor Basil Rauch sees the beginnings of a second New Deal.

Certainly the pattern as it emerged in the next year was a brilliant one. Roosevelt neutralized Huey Long with the "soak the rich" tax, the "holding company death sentence," and with various measures directly of benefit to the poorer farmers of the South. Before an assassin's bullet felled Long, his political strength was already undercut. Similarly Roosevelt undermined the Townsend movement by pressing passage of the Social Security Act, which provided at least small benefits for the aged, at the same time that a congressional investigation disclosed how men around Townsend were fattening themselves on the nickels of millions of the aged. As for Father Coughlin, the Treasury announced that money from his coffers had gone into silver speculation at a time he had been loudly advocating that the government buy more silver at higher prices. More important, Coughlin had less appeal to employed workers after the new National Labor Relations Act raised a benign federal umbrella over collective bargaining. For the unemployed, a huge and substantial work relief program, the Works Progress Administration, came into existence.

Partly all this involved incisive political counterthrusts; partly it was a program Roosevelt had favored anyway. In any event, combined with Roosevelt's direct and effective appeal in radio fireside chats, it caused the dispossessed to look to him rather than to demagogues as their champion.

Millions of them or their relations received some direct aid from the New Deal, whether a small crop payment or a WPA check. Millions more received wage boosts for which they were more grateful to Roosevelt than to their employers. Others through New Deal mortgage legislation had held onto their farms or homes. All these people, benefitting directly or indirectly, looked to Roosevelt as the source of their improved economic condition, and they were ready to vote accordingly. Roosevelt, who had been nominated in 1932 as the candidate of the South and the West, the champion of the farmer and the middle-class "forgotten man," after 1936 became increasingly the leader of the urban masses and the beneficiary of the growing power of organized labor.

What happened seems sharper and clearer in retrospect than it did at the time. Secretary Ickes, recording repeatedly in his diary during the early months of 1935 that the President was losing his grip, was echoing what many New Dealers and part of the public felt. They did not see a sharp shift into a second New Deal, and that is understandable. Roosevelt ever since he had become president had been talking about reform and from time to time recommending reform measures to Congress. He seems to have thought at the outset in two categories, about immediate or short-range emergency recovery measures to bring about a quick economic upswing, and also in terms of long-range reform legislation to make a recurrence of the depression less likely. Some of these reform measures like TVA had been ready for immediate enactment; others, like a revision of banking legislation and the social security legislation, he had planned from the beginning but were several years in the making. Frances Perkins has vividly described in her memoirs the lengthy task she and her associates undertook of drafting and selling to Congress and the public what became the Social Security Act of 1935.

Then Roosevelt had to face the additional factor that the emergency legislation had not succeeded in bringing rapid recovery. He had to think in terms of more permanent legislation with which to aim toward the same objectives. That meant he ceased trying to save money with a temporary program of cheaper direct relief, and switched instead to work relief (in which he had always believed) to try to stop some of the moral and physical erosion of the unfortunates who had been without employment for years.

In part the Supreme Court forced the recasting of some of his legislation. It gave a mercy killing in effect to the rickety, unwieldy NRA code structure when it handed down the Schechter or "sick chicken" decision of May 1935. On the whole the NRA had been unworkable, but it had achieved some outstanding results—in abolishing child labor, in bringing some order in the chaotic bituminous coal industry, and the like. Roosevelt was furious with the court, since the decision threatened to undermine all New Deal economic regulation. He charged that the justices were taking a horse and buggy view of the economic powers of the government. There followed six months later the court invalidation of the Triple-A processing tax, which for the moment threw out of gear the agricultural program.

The answer to these and similar Supreme Court decisions was Roosevelt's bold onslaught against the court after he had been re-elected in the great landslide of 1936. He had carried every state but Maine and Vermont; he considered himself as having a great mandate from the people to continue his program. Nor had he any reason to doubt his ability to push a court reform program through Congress, since the already bulging New Deal majorities had become still bigger. He was wrong; he failed. His failure came as much as anything through a great tactical error. He disguised his program as one to bring about a speedier handling of cases, when he should have presented it frankly as a means of ending the court obstruction of the New Deal. This obstruction was real. Many corporations openly flaunted the National Labor Relations Act, for example, they were so confident that the Supreme Court would invalidate it.

However laudable the end, to many a well-educated member of the middle class who had supported Roosevelt even through the campaign of 1936, Roosevelt's resort to subterfuge smacked of the devious ways of dictators. In 1937, Americans were all too aware of the way in which Hitler and Mussolini had gained power. It was not that any thinking man expected Roosevelt to follow their example, but rather that many objected to any threat, real or potential, to the constitutional system including the separation of powers. After Roosevelt, they argued, the potential dictator might appear. It may be too that times had improved sufficiently since March 1933 so that constitutional considerations could again overweigh economic exigencies. In any event, Roosevelt lost his battle—and won his war.

While the struggle was rocking the nation, the justices began exercising the judicial self-restraint which one of their number, Harlan F. Stone, had urged upon them the previous year. They surprised the nation by upholding the constitutionality of the National Labor Relations Act and the Social Security Act. In large part this eliminated the necessity for the New Dealers to make any change in the personnel of the court, and thus helped contribute to Roosevelt's defeat in Congress. Further, the fight had helped bring into existence a conservative coalition in Congress which from this time on gave Roosevelt a rough ride. Many old-line Democratic congressmen now dared proclaim in public what they had previously whispered in private. All this added up to a spectacular setback for Roosevelt—so spectacular that it is easy to overlook the enormous and permanent changes that had come about.

In the next few years the Supreme Court in effect rewrote a large part of constitutional law. The federal and state governments were now able to engage in extensive economic regulation with little or no court restraint upon them. The limits upon regulation must be set for the most part by the legislative branch of the government, not the judiciary. Not only were the National

Labor Relations Act and Social Security constitutional, but a bulging portfolio of other legislation.

These laws were not as spectacular as the measures of the Hundred Days, but in the bulk they were far more significant, for they brought about lasting changes in the economic role of the federal government. There was the continued subsidy to agriculture in order to maintain crop control—based upon soil conservation rather than a processing tax. There were all the agricultural relief measures which came to be centralized in the Farm Security Administration. Although that agency has disappeared, most of its functions have continued in one way or another. There was a beginning of slum clearance and public housing, and a continuation of TVA, held constitutional even before the court fight. There was a stiffening of securities regulation. There was a continuation of much that Roosevelt had considered beneficial in the NRA through a group of new laws usually referred to as the "little NRA." These perpetuated the coal and liquor codes, helped regulate oil production, tried to prevent wholesale price discriminations and legalized the establishment of "fair trade" prices by manufacturers. Most important of all, the Fair Labor Standards Act of 1937 set a national minimum of wages and maximum of hours of work, and prohibited the shipping in interstate commerce of goods made by child labor. These are lasting contributions of the New Deal, either substantial laws in themselves or the seeds for later legislation.

What then, is to be said of the recession and the anti-monopoly program? A Keynesian point of view is that public works spending, the other New Deal spending programs, and the payment of the bonus to veterans of the first World War (over Roosevelt's veto, incidentally), all these together had poured so such money into the economy that they brought about a substantial degree of recovery, except in employment, by the spring of 1937. At this point Roosevelt tried to balance the budget, especially by cutting public works and work relief expenditures. The result was a sharp recession. Roosevelt was forced to resort to renewed pump-priming, and in a few months the recession was over.

Even this recession experience did not convert Roosevelt to Keynesianism. Keynes once called upon Roosevelt at the White House and apparently tried to dazzle him with complex mathematical talk. Each was disappointed in the other. In 1939, after the recession when a protégé of Mrs. Roosevelt's proposed additional welfare spending, Roosevelt replied by listing worthwhile projects in which the government could usefully spend an additional five billions a year. Then he pointed out that the deficit was already three billions, which could not go on forever. How, he inquired, could an eight billion dollar deficit be financed.

As for economists, many of them saw the answer in the enormous spending power which would be unleashed if the government poured out billions in time of depression. To most of them the lesson from the recession was that the only way to right the economy in time of upset was through spending.

As for businessmen, they could see in the recession only the logical outcome of Roosevelt's iniquitous tinkering with the economy. They had been especially angered by the protection the Wagner Act had given to protective bargaining with the resulting militant expansion of organized labor. Roosevelt reciprocated the businessmen's feelings and blamed the recession upon their failure to co-operate. To a considerable degree he went along with a powerful handful of Progressive Republicans and Western Democrats in the Senate, like William E. Borah of Idaho and Joseph O'Mahoney of Wyoming, in attacking corporate monopoly as the villain. There are some indications, however, that the anti-monopoly program that he launched in the Department of Justice through the urbane Thurman Arnold was intended less to bust the trusts than to forestall too drastic legislation in the Congress. Roosevelt gave his strong backing to Arnold's anti-trust division only for the first year or two, and Arnold functioned for the most part through consent decrees. These in many instances allowed industries to function much as they had in the NRA days. The new program was in some respects more like a negative NRA than the antithesis of the NRA.

Thus from the beginning of the New Deal to the end, Roosevelt functioned with a fair degree of consistency. He heartily favored humanitarian welfare legislation and government policing of the economy, so long as these did not dangerously unbalance the budget. He preferred government co-operation with business to warfare with it.

Many of the New Dealers went far beyond Roosevelt in their views, and sometimes saw in his reluctance to support them, betrayal rather than a greater degree of conservatism. They had valid grievances some of the time when Roosevelt stuck to a middle course and seemed to them to be compromising away everything for which they thought he stood, in order to hold his motley political coalitions together. It is a serious moral question whether he compromised more than necessary, and whether at times he compromised his principles. It has been charged that his second four years in the White House represented a failure in political leadership.

In terms of gaining immediate political objectives, like the fiasco of the court fight, and the abortive "purge" in the 1938 primaries, this is undoubtedly true. In terms of the long-range New Deal program, I think the reverse is the case. These were years of piecemeal unspectacular consolidation of the earlier spectacular changes. It was many years before historians could say with certainty that these changes were permanent. By 1948 various public opinion samplings indicated that an overwhelming majority of those queried, even though Republican in voting habits, favored such things as social security and the TVA. The election of a Republican President in 1952 did not signify a popular repudiation of these programs. In the years after 1952 they were accepted, and in some instances even expanded, by the Republican administration. The only serious debate over them concerned degree, in which the Republicans were more cautious than the Democrats. The New Deal changes have even come for the most part to be accepted by the business community, although the United States Chamber of Commerce now issues manifestoes against federal aid to education with all the fervor it once directed against Roosevelt's proposals. The fact is that the business community in part bases its plans for the future upon some things that began as New Deal reforms. It takes for granted such factors as the "built-in stabilizers" in the social security system—something, incidentally, that Roosevelt pointed out at the time the legislation went into effect.

In January 1939 Roosevelt, concerned about the threat of world war, called a halt to his domestic reform program. What he said then, concerning the world crisis of 1939, is remarkably applicable to the United States more than two decades later:

We have now passed the period of internal conflict in the launching of our program of social reform. Our full energies may now be released to invigorate the processes of recovery in order to preserve our reforms, and to give every man and woman who wants to work a real job at a living wage.

But time is of paramount importance. The deadline of danger from within and from without is not within our control. The hour-glass may be in the hands of other nations. Our own hour-glass tells us that we are off on a race to make democracy work, so that we may be efficient in peace and therefore secure in national defense.

The Third American Revolution

Carl N. Degler

Twice since the founding of the Republic, cataclysmic events have sliced through the fabric of American life, snapping many of the threads which ordinarily bind the past to the future. The War for the Union was one such event, the Great Depression of the 1930's the other. And, as the Civil War was precipitated from the political and moral tensions of the preceding era, so the Great Depression was a culmination of the social and economic forces of industrialization and urbanization which had been transforming America since 1865. A depression of such pervasiveness as that of the thirties could happen only to a people already tightly interlaced by the multitudinous cords of a machine civilization and embedded in the matrix of an urban society.

In all our history no other economic collapse brought so many Americans to near starvation, endured so long, or came so close to overturning the basic institutions of American life. It is understandable, therefore, that from that experience should issue a new conception of the good society.

"Hunger Is Not Debatable"

The economic dimensions of the Great Depression are quickly sketched— too quickly perhaps to permit a full appreciation of the abyss into which the economy slid between 1929 and 1933. The value of stocks on the New York Exchange, for example, slumped from a high of $87 billion in 1929 to a mere $19 billion in 1933. Wholesale prices dropped 38 percent by 1933 and farm prices seemed almost to have ceased to exist: they were 60 percent

From *Out of Our Past* by Carl N. Degler, pp. 379–93, 410–16. Copyright © 1959 by Carl N. Degler. Reprinted with the permission of Harper & Row, Publishers.

below the low level of 1929. Within less than three years, realized national income plummeted to almost half of what it had been in the last boom year; and the same was true of industrial production. The human cost of this catastrophic breakdown in the complicated industrial machine, *Fortune* magazine estimated in September, 1932, was 10 million totally unemployed or 25 million people without any source of income.

To worsen matters, the industrial stagnation was accompanied by a spreading fever of bank failures. First here and there, then all over the country, the banks began to close their doors in the faces of their depositors. By the beginning of 1933, the financial self-confidence of the nation reached a dangerously low level, requiring the new administration of Franklin Roosevelt, as its first official act, to order the closing of all banks. In all, more than 10,000 deposit banks failed in the five years after 1929. If the banks, the custodians of the measure of value, proved to be unsound, men might well wonder what was left to cling to as the winds of disaster gained in fury.

Unnerving as the failure of the banks undoubtedly was, for most people the Great Depression became starkly real only when unemployment struck. No one knew whom it would hit next; the jobless were everywhere—in the cities, in the towns, on the farms. Their helplessness, their bewilderment, were often written in their faces, reflected in their discouraged gaits, and mirrored in their run-down dwellings. John Dos Passos reported seeing the unemployed of Detroit in 1932 living in caves scooped out of giant abandoned sand piles. Though it was said that no one would be allowed to starve, *Fortune*, in September, 1932, suggested that some had already. The magazine counted the millions of the unemployed and told of families subsisting on a single loaf of bread for over a week or of going without food for two or three days on end. Discarded and spoiled vegetables or wild dandelions were the substance of meals for some families. Other reports in 1933 told of at least twenty-nine persons who died of starvation in New York City. Moreover, thousands must have died from diseases which gained an easy foothold in weakened and underfed bodies; but these unfortunates were never counted. Food, casually consumed in good times, suddenly became the focus of existence for thousands. In their desperation some urban folk actually tried to wring their food from the barren soil of the city. In Gary, Indiana, for example, 20,000 families were raising food on lots lent by the city; Robert and Helen Lynd reported that in Middletown in 1933, 2,500 of the town's 48,000 people eked out their food budgets with relief gardens.

The spreading unemployment generated new and deep-seated fears. When the unkempt veterans of the First World War camped in Washington in 1932, demanding a bonus to tide them over their joblessness, a fearful and unsure President had them dispersed by troops armed with tear gas. And when Congress in that same year voted a 10 percent cut in government salaries, President Hoover sent a secret message urging that the enlisted men of the Army and the Navy be excluded from such decreases so that in case of domestic troubles the federal government would not be compelled to rely upon disgruntled troops.

Nor was it only the federal government that felt uneasy in the presence of the specter which was stalking the land. Malcolm Cowley, in an eyewitness account, described how the trucks bearing the disillusioned veterans out of Washington were quickly sped through town after town, the local authorities fearing that some of the unemployed veterans would jump off and become burdens on already overtaxed communities. Cowley tells of one citizen in Washington, not a marcher at all, who was hurriedly bundled into a truck by mistake and could not get off until he reached Indianapolis!

Driven by their desperation, some Americans began to talk of violence. Mutterings of revolution and threats to return with rifles were heard among the bonus marchers as they left Washington. Out on the farms, the dissatisfaction of the veterans was matched by sullen farmers who closed the courts and disrupted mortgage auctions to save their homes. The ugly turn which the discontent could take was revealed by the arrest of a man in Wisconsin in 1932 on suspicion of having removed a spike from the railroad track over which President Hoover's train was to pass. In that bleak year it was not uncommon for the President of the United States to be booed and hooted as he doggedly pursued his ill-starred campaign for re-election. To Theodore Dreiser, as the cold night of the depression settled over the land, it seemed that Karl Marx's prediction "that Capitalism would eventually evolve into failure . . . has come true."

Even for the Lords of Creation, as Frederick Lewis Allen was to call them, the Great Depression was an unsettling and confusing experience. "I'm afraid, every man is afraid," confessed Charles M. Schwab of United States Steel. "I don't know, we don't know, whether the values we have are going to be real next month or not." And in the very early months of the Roosevelt administration, Harold Ickes, attending a dinner of the Chamber of Commerce of the United States, could sense the pitiable impotence to which the nation's industrial leaders had sunk. "The great and the mighty in the business world were there in force," he rather gleefully noted in his diary, "and I couldn't help thinking how so many of these great and mighty were crawling to Washington on their hands and knees these days to beg the Government to run their businesses for them."

But it was the unspectacular, the everyday dreariness of unemployment that must have cut the deepest and endured the longest as far as the ordinary American was concerned. The simplest things of life, once taken for granted, now became points of irritation. "I forget how to cook good since I have nothing to cook with," remarked one housewife. Children lost their appetites upon seeing the milk and mush "that they have seen so often." Even the rare treat of fresh meat could not awaken an appetite long accustomed to disappointment and pallid food.

The routine entertainments of the poor were casualties to unemployment. "Suppose you go to a friend's house and she gives you a cup of tea and something," the wife of an unemployed worker told a social worker. "You feel ashamed. You think, now I got to do the same when she comes to my house. You know you can't so you stay home." Shifts in entertainment patterns among the unemployed were revealed in a study made of some 200 families in New Haven. Before the breadwinner lost his job, some 55 percent went to the movies; once unemployment hit, however, only 16 percent did. In the days when work was to be had, only 13 percent found recreation in "sitting around the house," but now 25 percent did so. With the loss of their jobs, 12 percent of the men admitted they "chatted and gossiped" for recreation, although none of them did when they had work.

Unemployment's effect upon the family was often more profound and far-reaching. In recounting the case history of the Raparka family, one sociologist wrote that when Mr. Raparka "lost his job in the fall of 1933, he dominated the family. Two years later it was Mrs. Raparka who was the center of authority." Again and again social workers chronicled the alteration in the father's position in the family during a period of unemployment. Humiliation settled over many a father no longer able to fulfill his accustomed role in the family. "I would rather turn on the gas and put an end to the whole family than let my wife support me," was the way one unemployed father put it. One investigator found that one-fifth of her sample of fifty-nine families exhibited a breakdown in the father's authority, particularly in the eyes of the wife. For example, one wife said, "When your husband cannot provide for the family and makes you worry so, you lose your love for him."

Fathers discovered that without the usual financial power to buy bikes or bestow nickels, their control and authority over children were seriously weakened and sometimes completely undermined. In one family where the father was unemployed for a long time, his role was almost completely taken over by the eldest son. The father himself admitted: "The son of twenty-two is just like a father around the house. He tries to settle any little brother-and-sister fights and even encourages me and my wife." In the same family, a younger son who was working summed up his relationship to his parents in a few words. "I remind them," he said, "who makes the money. They don't say much. They just take it, that's all. I'm not the one on relief." In such circumstances, it is no exaggeration to say that the massive weight of the depression was grinding away at the bedrock of American institutions.

The ties of a home struck by unemployment were weak and the opportunities for fruitful and satisfying work were almost totally absent in 1932–33. *Fortune* reported in February, 1933, that something like 200,000 young men and boys were traveling around the country on railroad trains for lack of anything better to do. Tolerated by the railroads because of their obvious poverty and lack of jobs, the boys were often suffering from disease and malnutrition. The authorities in Los Angeles asserted, for example, that 25 percent of those coming into the city needed clinical attention and 5 percent required hospitalization. During a single season, one railroad announced, fifty such footloose boys were killed and one hundred injured. From Kansas City it was reported that girl wanderers, dressed in boy's clothing, were on the increase. To many such young people, now grown, the Great Depression must still seem the most purposeless, the most enervating period of their lives.

What Robert and Helen Lynd concluded for their study of Middletown in 1935 can be applied to America as a whole: ". . . the great knife of the depression had cut down impartially through the entire population cleaving open lives and hopes of rich as well as poor. The experience has been more nearly universal than any prolonged recent emotional experience in the city's history; it has approached in its elemental shock the primary experiences of birth and death."

The End of Laissez Faire

Perhaps the most striking alteration in American thought which the depression fostered concerned the role of the government in the economy. Buffeted and bewildered by the economic debacle, the American people in the course of the 1930's abandoned, once and for all, the doctrine of laissez faire. This beau ideal of the nineteenth-century economists had become, ever since the days of Jackson, an increasingly cherished shibboleth of Americans. But now it was almost casually discarded. It is true, of course, that the rejection of laissez faire had a long history; certainly the Populists worked to undermine it. But with the depression the nation at large accepted the government as a permanent influence in the economy.[1]

Almost every one of the best-known measures of the federal government during the depression era made inroads into the hitherto private preserves of business and the individual. Furthermore, most of these new measures survived the period, taking their places as fundamental elements in the structure of American life. For modern Americans living under a federal government of transcendent influence and control in the economy, this is the historic meaning of the great depression.

Much of what is taken for granted today as the legitimate function of government and the social responsibility of business began only with the legislation of these turbulent years. Out of the investigation of banking and bankers in 1933, for example, issued legislation which separated commercial

---

[1] A complementary and highly suggestive way of viewing this trend away from laissez faire, of which the events of the 1930's are a culmination, is that taken in K. William Kapp, *The Social Costs of Private Enterprise* (Cambridge, Mass., 1950). Kapp observes that for a long time private enterprise had shifted the social costs of production—like industrially polluted water, industrial injuries, smoke nuisances and hazards, unemployment, and the like—onto society. The decline of laissez faire has, in this view, actually been a movement to compel industry to pay for those social costs of production which it has hitherto shirked.

banking from the stock and bond markets, and insured the bank deposits of ordinary citizens. The stock market, like the banks, was placed under new controls and a higher sense of responsibility to the public imposed upon it by the new Securities and Exchange Commission. The lesson of Black Tuesday in 1929 had not been forgotten; the classic free market itself—the Exchange—was hereafter to be under continuous governmental scrutiny.

The three Agricultural Adjustment Acts of 1933, 1936, and 1938, while somewhat diverse in detail, laid down the basic lines of what is still today the American approach to the agricultural problem. Ever since the collapse of the boom after the First World War, American agriculture had suffered from the low prices born of the tremendous surpluses. Unable to devise a method for expanding markets to absorb the excess, the government turned to restriction of output as the only feasible alternative. But because restriction of output meant curtailment of income for the farmer, it became necessary, if farm income was to be sustained, that farmers be compensated for their cut in production. Thus was inaugurated the singular phenomenon, which is still a part of the American answer to the agricultural surplus, of paying farmers for *not* growing crops. The other device introduced for raising farm prices, and still the mainstay of our farm policy, came with the 1938 act, which provided that the government would purchase and store excess farm goods, thus supporting the price level by withdrawing the surplus from the competitive market. Both methods constitute a subsidy for the farmer from society at large.[2]

Though the Eisenhower administration in the 1950's called for a return to a free market in farm products—that is, the removal of government supports from prices—very few steps have been taken in that direction, and probably very few ever will.[3] A free market was actually in operation during the twenties, but it succeeded only in making farmers the stepchildren of the golden prosperity of that decade. Today the farm bloc is too powerful politically to be treated so cavalierly. Moreover, the depression has taught most Americans that a free market is not only a rarity in the modern world but sometimes inimical to a stable and lasting prosperity.

Perhaps the most imaginative and fruitful of these innovations was the Tennessee Valley Authority, which transformed the heart of the South. "It was and is literally a down to earth experiment," native Tennesseean Broadus

---

[2] On the day that the first AAA was declared unconstitutional, a Gallup poll revealed that, although the nation as a whole did not like the AAA, the farmers of the South and Midwest did. As a result, invalidation of the act by the Court did not mean the end of such a policy, but only the beginning of a search to find a new way of accomplishing the same end. Hence there were successive AAA's, whereas, when NRA was declared unconstitutional in 1935, it was dropped, primarily because neither business nor labor, for whose interests it had been organized, found much merit in its approach to their problems.

[3] As reported in the *New York Times*, July 2, 1958, forecasts for the fiscal year 1958–59 see government subsidies to agriculture reaching $6 billion—an all-time high.

Mitchell has written, "with all that we know from test tube and logarithm tables called on to help. It was a union of heart and mind to restore what had been wasted. It was a social resurrection." For the TVA was much more than flood and erosion control or even hydroelectric power—though its gleaming white dams are perhaps its most striking and best-known monuments. It was social planning of the most humane sort, where even the dead were carefully removed from cemeteries before the waters backed up behind the dams. It brought new ideas, new wealth, new skills, new hope into a wasted, tired, and discouraged region.

At the time of the inception of the TVA, it was scarcely believable that the "backward" South would ever utilize all the power the great dams would create. But in its report of 1956, the Authority declared that the Valley's consumption of electricity far exceeded that produced from water sites: almost three-quarters of TVA's power is now generated from steam power, not from waterfall. In large part it was the TVA which taught the Valley how to use more power to expand its industries and to lighten the people's burdens. Back in 1935, Drew and Leon Pearson saw this creation of consumer demand in action. "Uncle Sam is a drummer with a commercial line to sell," they wrote in *Harper's Magazine*. "He sold liberty bonds before, but never refrigerators."

Measured against textbook definitions, the TVA is unquestionably socialism. The government owns the means of production and, moreover, it competes with private producers of electricity.[4] But pragmatic Americans—and particularly those living in the Valley—have had few sleepless nights as a consequence of this fact. The TVA does its appointed job and, as the recent fight over the Dixon and Yates contract seemed to show, it is here to stay. It, too, with all the talk of "creeping socialism," has been absorbed into that new American Way fashioned by the experimentalism of the American people from the wreckage of the Great Depression.

Undoubtedly social security deserves the appellation "revolutionary" quite as much as the TVA; it brought government into the lives of people as nothing had since the draft and the income tax. Social security legislation actually comprises two systems: insurance against old age and insurance in the event of loss of work. The first system was completely organized and operated by the federal government; the second was shared with the states—

---

[4] The extent of the intellectual changes which the depression measures introduced can be appreciated by a quotation from President Hoover's veto in 1931 of a bill to develop a public power project in what was later to be the TVA area. "I am firmly opposed to the Government entering into any business the major purpose of which is competition with our citizens." Emergency measures of such a character might be tolerated, he said. "But for the Federal government deliberately to go out and build up and expand such an occasion to the major purpose of a power and manufacturing business is to break down the initiative and enterprise of the American people; it is destruction of equality of opportunity amongst our people; it is the negation of the ideals upon which our civilization has been based."

but the national government set the standards; both were clear acknowledgment of the changes which had taken place in the family and in the business
of making a living in America. No longer in urban America could the old
folks, whose proportion in the society was steadily increasing, count on being
taken in by their offspring as had been customary in a more agrarian world.
Besides, such a makeshift arrangement was scarcely satisfying to the self-
respect of the oldsters. With the transformation of the economy by industrialization, most Americans had become helpless before the vagaries of the
business cycle. As a consequence of the social forces which were steadily
augmenting social insecurity, only collective action by the government could
arrest the drift.

To have the government concerned about the security of the individual
was a new thing. Keenly aware of the novelty of this aim in individualistic
America,[5] Roosevelt was careful to deny any serious departure from traditional
paths. "These three great objectives—the security of the home, the security
of livelihood, and the security of social insurance," he said in 1934, constitute
"a minimum of the promise that we can offer to the American people." But
this, he quickly added, "does not indicate a change in values."

Whether the American people thought their values had changed is not
nearly as important as the fact that they accepted social security. And the
proof that they did is shown in the steady increase in the proportion of the
population covered by the old-age benefit program since 1935; today about
80 percent of nonfarm workers are included in the system. Apart from being
a minimum protection for the individual and society against the dry rot of
industrial idleness, unemployment insurance is now recognized as one of the
major devices for warding off another depression.

It is true, as proponents of the agrarian life have been quick to point out,
that an industrialized people, stripped as they are of their economic self-
reliance, have felt the need for social insurance more than people in other
types of society. But it is perhaps just as important to recognize that it is
only in such a highly productive society that people can even dare to dream
of social security. Men in other ages have felt the biting pains of economic
crisis, but few pre-industrial people have ever enjoyed that surfeit of goods
which permits the fat years to fill out the lean ones. But like so much else
concerning industrialism, it is not always easy to calculate whether the boons
it offers exceed in value the burdens which it imposes.

For the average man, the scourge of unemployment was the essence of
the depression. Widespread unemployment, permeating all ranks and stations
in society, drove the American people and their government into some of

[5] Characteristically enough, as his memoirs show, President Hoover had long been interested in both old-age and unemployment insurance, but always such schemes were to be
worked out through private insurance companies, or at best with the states—never under
the auspices of the federal government. "It required a great depression," he has written
somewhat ruefully, "to awaken interest in the idea" of unemployment insurance.

their most determined and deliberate departures from the hallowed policy of "hands off." But despite the determination, as late as 1938 the workless still numbered almost ten million—two thirds as great as in 1932 under President Hoover. The governmental policies of the 1930's never appreciably diminished the horde of unemployed—only the war prosperity of 1940 and after did that—but the providing of jobs by the federal government was a reflection of the people's new conviction that the government had a responsibility to alleviate economic disaster. Such bold action on the part of government, after the inconclusive, bewildered approach of the Hoover administration, was a tonic for the dragging spirits of the people.[6]

A whole range of agencies, from the Civil Works Administration (CWA) to the Works Progress Administration (WPA), were created to carry the attack against unemployment. It is true that the vast program of relief which was organized was not "permanent" in the sense that it is still in being, but for two reasons it deserves to be discussed here. First, since these agencies constituted America's principal weapon against unemployment, some form of them will surely be utilized if a depression should occur again. Second, the various relief agencies of the period afford the best examples of the new welfare outlook, which was then in the process of formation.

Though in the beginning relief programs were premised on little more than Harry Hopkins' celebrated dictum, "Hunger is not debatable," much more complex solutions to unemployment were soon worked out. The relief program of the WPA, which after 1935 was the major relief agency, was a case in point. In 1937, *Fortune* magazine commented on "the evolution of unemployment relief from tool to institution"—a recognition of the importance and duration of relief in America. "In 1936, the federal government was so deeply involved in the relief of the unemployed," *Fortune* contended, "that it was not only keeping them alive, but it was also giving them an opportunity to work; and not only giving them an opportunity to work but giving them an opportunity to work at jobs for which they were peculiarly fitted; and not only giving them an opportunity to work at jobs for which they

---

[6] It was the misfortune of Herbert Hoover to have been President at a time when his considerable administrative and intellectual gifts were hamstrung by his basic political philosophy, which, instead of being a guide to action, served as an obstacle. Much more of an old-fashioned liberal than a reactionary, and deeply attached to the Jeffersonian dogma of the limited powers of the federal government, Hoover was psychologically and philosophically unable to use the immense powers and resources of his office in attacking the urgent threat of unemployment. Back in 1860–61, another President—James Buchanan —had been paralyzed in the midst of a national crisis by his limited conception of the federal power, but in that instance his inaction was palliated by the fact that his successor was to take office within less than three months. Hoover, however, wrestled with the depression for three years, and all during that trying period he stoutly held to his rigid intellectual position that federally supplied and administered relief would destroy the foundations of the nation. Never has an American President, including the two Adamses, defied overwhelming popular opinion for so long for the sake of his own ideals as Herbert Hoover did then; and never has a President since Buchanan fallen so quickly into obscurity as Hoover did after March 4, 1933.

were peculiarly fitted, but creating for them jobs of an interest and usefulness which they could not have expected to find in private employment." The statement somewhat distorts the work of the WPA, but it sums up the main outlines of the evolution of the relief program.

The various artistic and cultural employment programs of the WPA are excellent examples of how relief provided more than employment, though any of the youth agencies like the Civilian Conservation Corps or the National Youth Administration (it subsidized student work) would serve equally well. At its peak, the Federal Writers' Project employed some 6,000 journalists, poets, novelists, and Ph.D.'s of one sort or another; unknowns worked on the same payroll, if not side by side, with John Steinbeck, Vardis Fisher, and Conrad Aiken. The $46 million expended on art—that is, painting and sculpture—by the WPA in 1936–37 exceeded the artistic budget of any country outside the totalitarian orbit—and there art was frankly propagandistic. *Fortune*, in May, 1937, found the American government's sponsorship of art singularly free of censorship or propaganda. The magazine concluded that "by and large the Arts Projects have been given a freedom no one would have thought possible in a government run undertaking. And by and large that freedom has not been abused." During the first fifteen months of the Federal Music Project, some fifty million people heard live concerts; in the first year of the WPA Theater, sixty million people in thirty states saw performances, with weekly attendance running to half a million. T. S. Eliot's *Murder in the Cathedral*, too risky for a commercial producer, was presented in New York by the Federal Theater to 40,000 people at a top price of 55 cents.

"What the government's experiments in music, painting, and the theater actually did," concluded *Fortune* in May, 1937, "even in their first year, was to work a sort of cultural revolution in America." For the first time the American audience and the American artist were brought face to face for their mutual benefit. "Art in America is being given its chance," said the British writer Ford Madox Ford, "and there has been nothing like it since before the Reformation. . . ."

Instead of being ignored on the superficially plausible grounds of the exigencies of the depression, the precious skills of thousands of painters, writers, and musicians were utilized. By this timely rescue of skills, tastes, and talents from the deadening hand of unemployment, the American people, through their government, showed their humanity and social imagination. Important for the future was the foresight displayed in the conserving of artistic talents and creations for the enrichment of generations to come.

The entrance of the federal government into a vast program of relief work was an abrupt departure from all previous practice, but it proved enduring. "When President Roosevelt laid it down that government had a social responsibility to care for the victims of the business cycle," *Fortune* remarked prophetically in 1937, "he set in motion an irreversible process." The burden of unemployment relief was too heavy to be carried by local government or private charities in an industrialized society; from now on, the national government would be expected to shoulder the responsibility. "Those who are on relief and in close contact otherwise with public matters realize that what has happened to the country is a bloodless revolution," wrote an anonymous relief recipient in *Harper's* in 1936. The government, he said, has assumed a new role in depressions, and only the rich might still be oblivious to it. But they too "will know it by 1940. And in time," they will "come to approve the idea of everyone having enough to eat."[7] Few people escaped the wide net of the depression: "Anybody sinks after a while," the anonymous reliefer pointed out. "Even you would have if God hadn't preserved, without apparent rhyme or reason, your job and your income." That the depression was a threat to all was perhaps the first lesson gained from the 1930's.

The second was that only through collective defense could such a threat be met. By virtue of the vigorous attack made upon the economic problems of the thirties by the government, the age-old conviction that dips in the business cycle were either the will of God or the consequence of unalterable economic laws was effectively demolished. As recently as 1931, President Hoover had told an audience that some people "have indomitable confidence that by some legerdemain we can legislate ourselves out of a world-wide depression. Such views are as accurate as the belief that we can exorcise a Caribbean hurricane." From the experience of the depression era, the American people learned that something could and ought to be done when economic disaster strikes. No party and no politician with a future will ever again dare to take the fatalistic and defeatist course of Herbert Hoover in 1929–33.

As the enactment of the Employment Act of 1946 showed, the prevention of depression now occupies top listing among the social anxieties of the American people. The act created a permanent Council of Economic Advisers to the President, to keep him continuously informed on the state of the economy and to advise him on the measures necessary to avoid an economic decline. And the Joint Committee on the Economic Report does the same for Congress.

Today political figures who indignantly repudiate any "left-wing" philosophy of any sort readily accept this inheritance from the depression. "Never again shall we allow a depression in the United States," vowed Republican candidate Eisenhower in 1952. As soon as we "foresee the signs of any recession and depression," he promised, ". . . the full power of private industry, of municipal government, of state government, of the Federal Government will be mobilized to see that that does not happen." Ignoring the fact that as a

[7] The providing of work relief instead of the dole did more than fill hungry stomachs; it re-established faith in America and in one's fellow man. "I'm proud of our United States," said one relief recipient. "There ain't no other nation in the world that would have sense enough to think of WPA and all the other A's." The wife of one WPA worker was quoted as saying, "We aren't on relief any more—my man is working for the government."

prospective federal official he had promised more than he could deliver, he innocently and accurately added, "I cannot pledge you more than that." Sensing the tremendous importance of the matter to the American people, Eisenhower made substantially the same statement three other times—at Yonkers, Peoria, and Pittsburgh. At Yonkers he said that he had "repeated this particular pledge over and over again in the United States" and that he and his associates were "dedicated to this proposition. . . ."

In the White House, Eisenhower continued to reflect this underlying and persistent fear that a depression would once again stride through the land. According to the account in Robert Donovan's semiofficial *Eisenhower: The Inside Story*, at session after session of the Cabinet during the recession of 1953–54, it was the President who stressed the urgency of the economic situation. It was he who constantly prodded Arthur F. Burns of the Council of Economic Advisers to prepare plans with which to forestall a serious drop in the economic indicators. Indeed as late as June, 1954, just after Burns had delivered an optimistic report on the condition and future of the economy, as Donovan tells it, "The President . . . was still concerned about whether the administration was doing enough. Even though it jarred the logic of some members of the Cabinet, he insisted, everything possible must be done to restore vigor to the economy. It was important, the President said, to produce results and to err on the side of doing too much rather than too little."

In the midst of the recession of 1957–58, Vice-President Nixon, speaking on April 24, 1958, specifically repudiated the Hoover approach of permitting the economy to right itself without government intervention. "Let us recognize once and for all," he told his audience, "that the time is past in the United States when the Federal Government can stand by and allow a recession to be prolonged or to deepen into depression without decisive Government action." Though Eisenhower was obviously worried that hasty measures might bring on further inflation, on May 20, in a public address, he agreed with the Vice-President that the government had "a continuing responsibility . . . to help counteract recession." In the same speech the President enumerated concrete measures already taken, such as extension of unemployment benefits, speeding up of defense and civilian procurement, acceleration of government construction projects, and the easing of credit by the Federal Reserve.

The Republican administration's evident acceptance of the new obligations of government in the economy is strikingly suggestive of the shock which the depression dealt conventional economic thought in America. . . .

Was It a New or Old Deal?

One of the most enduring monuments to the Great Depression was that congeries of contradictions, naïveté, humanitarianism, realistic politics, and economic horse sense called the New Deal of Franklin D. Roosevelt. As the governmental agent which recast American thinking on the responsibilities of government, the New Deal was clearly the offspring of the depression. As we have seen, it was also more than that: it was a revitalization of the Democratic party; it was the political manifestation of that new spirit of reform which was stirring among the ranks of labor and the Negro people.

In their own time and since, the New Deal and Franklin Roosevelt have had a polarizing effect upon Americans. Probably at no time before Roosevelt has the leader of a great democratic nation come to symbolize as he did the hopes and the fears of so many people.[8] Not even Jackson, in whom Roosevelt himself recognized a President of his own popularity- and hatred-producing caliber, could rival him. Over a decade after Roosevelt's death, the mention of his name still evokes emotions, betrayed by the wistful look in the eye or in the hard set of the jaw. The election of 1956, moreover, demonstrated once again that the Old Guard of the Republican party still fights the dead Roosevelt while the Democratic party wanders leaderless in his absence. This too is a measure of the political revolution he led.

For the Democratic party, Roosevelt was like a lightning rod, drawing to himself all the venom and hatred of the opposition, only to discharge it harmlessly; nothing, it seemed, could weaken his personal hold on the affections of the majority of Americans. That something more was involved than sheer popularity is shown by the example of Dwight Eisenhower. Though held in even greater popular esteem, Eisenhower has been unable to invest his party with his own vote-getting power; Republicans lose though Eisenhower wins. The difference between F.D.R. and Ike is that one stood for a program, a hope, and a future, while the other stands for himself as a good, well-intentioned man whom all instinctively trust and perhaps even admire. The one is a leader of a nation, the other a popular hero. Roosevelt is already a member of that tiny pantheon of great leaders of Americans in which Washington, Jackson, Lincoln, and Wilson are included; it is difficult to believe that Eisenhower will be included. His monument is more likely to be inscribed: "The best-liked man ever to be President."

In the thirties, as now, the place of the New Deal in the broad stream of American development has been a matter of controversy. Historians and commentators on the American scene have not yet reached a firm agreement —if they ever will—as to whether the New Deal was conservative or radical in character, though it does appear that the consensus now seems to lean

---

[8] According to Harold Ickes, Roosevelt was profoundly struck by the adoration which was bestowed upon him by his admirers. During the 1936 campaign, the President told Ickes "that there was something terrible about the crowds that lined the streets along which he passed. He went on to explain what he meant, which was exclamations from individuals in the crowd, such as 'He saved my home,' 'He gave me a job,' 'God bless you, Mr. President,' etc." In May, 1936, Marquis Childs published an article in *Harper's*, entitled "They Hate Roosevelt," in which he described and tried to account for the unreasoning hatred for the President on the part of what Childs called the upper 2 percent of the population.

toward calling it conservative and traditional.[9] Certainly if one searches the writings and utterances of Franklin Roosevelt, his own consciousness of conservative aims is quickly apparent. "The New Deal is an old deal—as old as the earliest aspirations of humanity for liberty and justice and the good life," he declared in 1934. "It was this administration," he told a Chicago audience in 1936, "which saved the system of private profit and free enterprise after it had been dragged to the brink of ruin. . . ."

But men making a revolution among a profoundly conservative people do not advertise their activity, and above all Franklin Roosevelt understood the temper of his people.[10] Nor should such a statement be interpreted as an insinuation of high conspiracy—far from it. Roosevelt was at heart a conservative, as his lifelong interest in history, among other things, suggests. But he was without dogma in his conservatism, which was heavily interlaced with genuine concern for people.[11] He did not shy away from new means and new approaches to problems when circumstances demanded it. His willingness to experiment, to listen to his university-bred Brains Trust, to accept a measure like the TVA, reveal the flexibility in his thought. Both his lack of theoretical presuppositions and his flexibility are to be seen in the way he came to support novel measures like social security and the Wagner Act. Response to popular demand was the major reason. "The Congress can't stand the pressure of the Townsend Plan unless we have a real old-age insurance system," he complained to Frances Perkins, "nor can I face the country without having . . . a solid plan which will give some assurance to old people of systematic assistance upon retirement." In like manner, the revolutionary NLRA was adopted as a part of his otherwise sketchy and rule-of-thumb philosophy of society. Though ultimately Roosevelt championed the Wagner bill in the House, it was a belated conversion dictated by the foreshadowed success of the measure and the recent invalidation of the NRA. In his pragmatic and common-sense reactions to the exigencies of the depression, Roosevelt, the easygoing conservative, ironically enough became the embodiment of a new era and a new social philosophy for the American people.

"This election," Herbert Hoover presciently said in 1932, "is not a mere

[9] For example, one of the most recent short evaluations of the New Deal, by a most knowledgeable historian, Arthur Link, concludes as follows: "The chief significance of the reform legislation of the 1930's was its essentially conservative character and the fact that it stemmed from a half century or more of discussion and practical experience and from ideas proposed as well by Republicans as by Democrats." *American Epoch* (New York, 1955), p. 425.

[10] It is significant that only once during the 1932 campaign, according to Ernest K. Lindley, did Roosevelt call for "a revolution"; and then he promptly qualified it to "the right kind, the only kind of revolution this nation can stand for—a revolution at the ballot box."

[11] When an economist suggested to F.D.R. that the depression be permitted to run its course and that then the economic system would soon right itself—as Frances Perkins tells the story—the President's face took on a "gray look of horror" as he told the economist: "People aren't cattle you know!"

shift from the ins to the outs. It means deciding the direction our nation will take over a century to come." The election of Franklin Roosevelt, he predicted, would result in "a radical departure from the foundations of 150 years which have made this the greatest nation in the world." Though Hoover may be charged with nothing more than campaign flourishing, it is nevertheless a fact that his speech was made just after Roosevelt's revealing Commonwealth Club address of September. Only in this single utterance, it should be remembered, did Roosevelt disclose in clear outline the philosophy and program which was later to be the New Deal. "Every man has a right to life," he had said, "and this means that he has also a right to make a comfortable living. . . . Our government, formal and informal, political and economic," he went on, "owes to everyone an avenue to possess himself of a portion of that plenty [from our industrial society] sufficient for his needs, through his own work." Here were the intimations of those new goals which the New Deal set for America.

Accent as heavily as one wishes the continuity between the reforms of the Progressive era and the New Deal, yet the wide difference between the goals of the two periods still remains. The Progressive impulse was narrowly reformist: it limited business, it assisted agriculture, it freed labor from some of the shackles imposed by the courts, but it continued to conceive of the state as policeman or judge and nothing more. The New Deal, on the other hand, was more than a regulator—though it was that too, as shown by the SEC and the reinvigoration of the antitrust division of the Justice Department. To the old goals for America set forth and fought for by the Jeffersonians and the Progressives the New Deal appended new ones. Its primary and general innovation was the guaranteeing of a minimum standard of welfare for the people of the nation. WPA and the whole series of relief agencies which were a part of it, wages and hours legislation, AAA, bank deposit insurance, and social security,[12] each illustrates this new conception of the federal government. A resolution offered by New Deal Senator Walsh in 1935 clearly enunciated the new obligations of government. The resolution took notice of the disastrous effects of the depression "upon the lives of young men and women . . ." and then went on to say that "it is the duty of the Federal Government to use every possible means of opening up opportunities" for the youth of the nation "so that they may be rehabilitated and restored to a *decent standard of living* and ensured proper development of their talents. . . ."

But the guarantor state as it developed under the New Deal was more active and positive than this. It was a vigorous and dynamic force in the so-

---

[12] Social security is an excellent example of how, under the New Deal, reform measures, when they conflicted with recovery, were given priority. In siphoning millions of dollars of social security taxes from the purchasing power of the workers, social security was a deflationary measure, which must have seriously threatened the precariously based new economic recovery. For this reason and others, Abraham Epstein, the foremost authority in America on social security, denounced the act as a "sharing of poverty."

ciety, energizing and, if necessary, supplanting private enterprise when the general welfare required it. With the Wagner Act, for example, the government served notice that it would actively participate in securing the unionization of the American worker; the state was no longer to be an impartial policeman merely keeping order; it now declared for the side of labor. When social and economic problems like the rehabilitation of the Valley of the Tennessee were ignored or shirked by private enterprise, then the federal government undertook to do the job. Did private enterprise fail to provide adequate and sufficient housing for a minimum standard of welfare for the people, then the government would build houses. As a result, boasted Nathan Straus, head of the U.S. Housing Authority, "for the first time in a hundred years the slums of America ceased growing and began to shrink."

Few areas of American life were beyond the touch of the experimenting fingers of the New Deal; even the once sacrosanct domain of prices and the valuation of money felt the tinkering. The devaluation of the dollar, the gold-purchase program, the departure from the gold standard—in short, the whole monetary policy undertaken by F.D.R. as a means to stimulate recovery through a price rise—constituted an unprecedented repudiation of orthodox public finance. To achieve that minimum standard of well-being which the depression had taught the American people to expect of their government, nothing was out of bounds.

But it is not the variety of change which stamps the New Deal as the creator of a new America; its significance lies in the permanence of its program. For, novel as the New Deal program was, it has, significantly, not been repudiated by the Eisenhower administration, the first Republican government since the reforms were instituted. Verbally, it is true, the Republican administration has had to minimize its actual commitments to the New Deal philosophy, and it tends to trust private business more than the New Dealers did— witness, for example, its elimination of the minor governmental manufacturing enterprises which competed with private firms. But despite this, the administration's firm commitment to the guaranteeing of prosperity and averting depression at all costs is an accurate reflection of the American people's agreement with the New Deal's diagnosis of the depression. Nor has the Republican party dared to repeal or even emasculate the legislation which made up the vitals of the New Deal: TVA, banking and currency, SEC, social security, the Wagner Act, and fair treatment of the Negro. The New Deal Revolution has become so much a part of the American Way that no political party which aspires to high office dares now to repudiate it.

It may or may not be significant in this regard (for apothegms are more slippery than precise) but it is nonetheless interesting that Roosevelt and Eisenhower have both been impressed with the same single sentence from Lincoln regarding the role of government. "The legitimate object of Government," wrote Lincoln, "is to do for a community of people whatever they need to have done but cannot do at all or cannot do so well for themselves in their separate or individual capacities." Twice, in 1934 and again in 1936, F.D.R. in public addresses used this expression to epitomize his own New Deal, and Robert Donovan in his officially inspired book on the Eisenhower administration writes that this same "fragment of Lincoln's writing . . . Eisenhower uses time and again in describing his own philosophy of government." Between Lincoln and Eisenhower there was no Republican President, except perhaps Theodore Roosevelt, who would have been willing to subscribe to such a free-wheeling description of the federal power; in this can be measured the impact of the New Deal and the depression.

The conclusion seems inescapable that, traditional as the words may have been in which the New Deal expressed itself, in actuality it was a revolutionary response to a revolutionary situation. In its long history America has passed through two revolutions since the first one in 1776, but only the last two, the Civil War and the depression, were of such force as to change the direction of the relatively smooth flow of its progress. The Civil War rendered a final and irrevocable decision in the long debate over the nature of the Union and the position of the Negro in American society. From that revolutionary experience, America emerged a strong national state and dedicated by the words of its most hallowed document to the inclusion of the black man in a democratic culture. The searing ordeal of the Great Depression purged the American people of their belief in the limited powers of the federal government and convinced them of the necessity of the guarantor state. And as the Civil War constituted a watershed in American thought, so the depression and its New Deal marked the crossing of a divide from which, it would seem, there could be no turning back.

Middle-Class America Refurbished

Howard Zinn

When we compel the past to speak, we want neither the gibberish of total recall nor the nostalgia of fond memories; we would like the past to speak wisely to our present needs. And so we have a good reason for trying to recapture some of the lost dialogue of the New Deal years—that which was carried on, with varying degrees of tension, inside and outside the Roosevelt circle.

The New Dealers themselves were articulate, humane, and on occasion profound. Among them were the "brains trust" (Adolf A. Berle, Raymond Moley, Rexford Guy Tugwell), the cabinet members (Henry Wallace, Frances Perkins, Harold Ickes, and others), the administrators of the alphabetic agencies (Harry Hopkins, David Lilienthal, and others), the Congressional spokesmen (Robert F. Wagner, Hugo Black, and others). And above them all was Franklin D. Roosevelt himself. They had no clearly defined set of goals, beyond that of extricating the nation from the depression of 1929–1932. In the course of easing the crisis, however, they found themselves—pushed partly by the cries of alarm on all sides, partly by inner humanitarian impulses—creating new laws and institutions like the Tennessee Valley Authority, the social security system, farm subsidies, minimum wage standards, the National Labor Relations Board, and public housing.

These accomplishments were considerable enough to give many Americans the feeling they were going through a revolution, while they successfully evaded any one of a number of totalitarian abysses into which they might have fallen. So it is not surprising that the New Deal left a glow of enthusiasm, even adoration, in the nation at large.

Yet, when it was over, the fundamental problem remained—and still remains—unsolved: how to bring the blessings of immense natural wealth and staggering productive potential to every person in the land. Also unsolved was the political corollary of that problem; how to organize ordinary people to convey to national leadership something more subtle than the wail of crisis (which speaks for itself); how to communicate the day-to-day pains felt, between emergencies, in garbage-strewn slums, crowded schools, grimy bus stations, inadequate hospital wards, Negro ghettos, and rural shacks—the environment of millions of Americans clawing for subsistence in the richest country in the world.

When the reform energies of the New Deal began to wane around 1939 and the depression was over, the nation was back to its normal state: a permanent army of unemployed; twenty or thirty million poverty-ridden people effectively blocked from public view by a huge, prosperous, and fervently consuming middle class; a tremendously efficient yet wasteful productive apparatus that was efficient because it could produce limitless supplies of what it decided to produce, and wasteful because what it decided to produce was not based on what was most needed by society but on what was most profitable to business.

What the New Deal did was to refurbish middle-class America, which had taken a dizzying fall in the depression, to restore jobs to half the jobless, and to give just enough to the lowest classes (a layer of public housing, a minimum of social security) to create an aura of good will. Through it all, the New Dealers moved in an atmosphere thick with suggestions, but they accepted only enough of these to get the traditional social mechanism moving again, plus just enough more to give a taste of what a truly far-reaching reconstruction might be.

This harsh estimate of New Deal achievements derives from the belief that the historian discussing the past is always commenting—whether he realizes it or not—on the present; and that because he is part of a morally responsible public, his commentary should consider present needs at the expense, if necessary, of old attachments. It is fruitless today to debate "interpretations" of the New Deal. We can no longer vote for or against Roosevelt. We can only affect the world around us. And although this is the 1960's, not the 1930's, some among us live very high, and some live very low, and a chronic malaise of lost opportunities and wasted wealth pervades the economic aid.

It is for today, then, that we turn to the thinking of the New Deal period. Although the New Deal gave us only fragments of solutions, it did leave us—perhaps because those were desperate years, and desperation stimulates innovation—with a public discussion more intense and more sweeping than any we have had before or since. People outside the New Deal entourage, invited or not, joined that discussion and extended the boundaries of political and economic imagination beyond those of the New Dealers—sometimes to the left, sometimes to the right, sometimes in directions hard to plot.

Among these were philosophers, writers, critics, lawyers, poets, college professors, journalists, dissident politicians, or commentators without special portfolio. Their names are still known today: John Dewey, Charles Beard, Reinhold Niebuhr, Paul Douglas, Stuart Chase, John Maynard Keynes, Norman Thomas, Oswald Garrison Villard, Heywood Broun, Max Lerner, Morris Cohen, Walter White, Edmund Wilson, Felix Frankfurter, John Steinbeck, John L. Lewis, Upton Sinclair.

Their thinking does not give us facile solutions, but if history has uses beyond that of reminiscence, one of them is to nourish lean ideological times with the nectars of other years. And although the present shape of the world was hardly discernible in 1939, certain crucial social issues persist in both eras. Somehow, in the interaction between the ideas of the New Dealers themselves and those of social critics who gathered in various stances and at various distances around the Roosevelt fire, we may find suggestions or approaches that are relevant today.

I

The word "pragmatic" has been used, more often perhaps than any other, to describe the thinking of the New Dealers. It refers to the experimental method of the Roosevelt administration, the improvisation from one step to the next, the lack of system or long-range program or theoretical commitment. Richard Hofstadter, in fact, says that the only important contribution to political theory to come out of the Roosevelt administration was made by Thurman Arnold, particularly in his two books, *The Symbols of Government* and *The Folklore of Capitalism*. Hofstadter describes Arnold's writing as "the theoretical equivalent of FDR's opportunistic virtuosity in practical politics—a theory that attacks theories." As the chief expression of Roosevelt's "ideology," Arnold's work deserves some attention.

All through both his books, in a style of cool irony, Arnold cuts away at "preconceived faiths," "preconceived principles," "theories and symbols of government," "high-sounding prejudices," "traditional ideals," "moral ideals," "permanent cures." In the last paragraphs of *The Symbols of Government*, he writes:

So long as the public hold preconceived faiths about the fundamental principles of government, they will persecute and denounce new ideas in that science, and orators will prevail over technicians. So long as preconceived principles are considered more important than practical results, the practical alleviation of human distress and the distribution of available comforts will be paralyzed. . . . The writer has faith that a new public attitude toward the ideals of law and economics is slowly appearing to create an atmosphere where the fanatical alignments between opposing political principles may disappear and a competent, practical, opportunistic governing class may rise to power. . . .

Because the Roosevelt administration did, in fact, experiment and improvise without a total plan, FDR's "pragmatism" has come, for many, to be the most important statement about the thinking of the New Dealers. This emphasis on the method rather than on the substance of that thinking tends to obscure what may be its greatest significance.

Most statesmen experiment: Tsar Nicholas instituted a Duma, Lenin encouraged private enterprise for several years, Bismarck sponsored social welfare measures, Mao Tse-tung introduced back-yard steel furnaces, and George Washington supported a national bank. These examples show that experimentation can be linked to a variety of social ideals. Some statesmen engage in more experiments than others, and in a time of crisis one who is willing to undertake a vast number of them deserves commendation, as Roosevelt does. The truly important question that can be asked about the thinking of any government is: in what direction, and how far, is it willing to experiment? What goals, what ideals, what expectations direct that experimentation?

Thurman Arnold himself contributed to this misplaced emphasis on method rather than substance. He was so anxious to demolish old myths that stood in the way of the welfare measures of the New Deal that mythology itself became his chief concern. He was so intent on sweeping away old debris, that he became obsessed, ironically, with a folklore of his own, in which the idea of debris-clearing crowded out the concept of what he wanted to plant in the cleared area.

Examining Arnold's *The Symbols of Government*, one sees that what started him on a crusade against myths was that he sought to expose the symbolism that stood in the way of bringing cheap electric power to people and of instituting relief, public works, social security. His strongest expression on social justice was his statement that: "Those who rule our great industrial feudalism still believe inalterably the old axioms that man works efficiently only for personal profit; that humanitarian ideals are unworkable as the principal aim of government or business organization; that control of national resources, elimination of waste, and a planned distribution of goods would destroy both freedom and efficiency."

As was true of his associate, Thurman Arnold, FDR's experimentalism and iconoclasm were not devoid of standards and ideals. They had a certain direction, which was toward governmental intervention in the economy to prevent depression, to help the poor, and to curb ruthless practices in big business. Roosevelt's speeches had the flavor of a moral crusade. Accepting the nomination at the Democratic Convention of 1932, he said that "the Federal Government has always had and still has a continuing responsibility for the broader public welfare," and pledged "a new deal for the American people." In a campaign speech that year at the Commonwealth Club in San Francisco, he said: "Our government . . . owes to every one an avenue to possess himself of a portion of that plenty sufficient for his needs, through his own work." In his 1936 speech accepting the nomination, he spoke of the power of the "economic royalists" and said: "Our allegiance to American institutions requires the overthrow of this kind of power."

But FDR's ideas did not have enough clarity to avoid stumbling from one approach to another: from constant promises to balance the budget, to large-scale spending in emergencies; from an attempt to reconcile big business interests and labor interests (as in the National Recovery Act), to belated support for a pro-labor National Labor Relations Act; from special concern for the tenant farmer (in the Resettlement Administration), to a stress on generous price supports for the large commercial farmer (in the Agricultural Adjustment Act of 1938).

His ideas on political leadership showed the same indecision, the same constriction of boundaries, as did his ideas about economic reform. Roosevelt was cautious about supporting the kind of candidates in 1934 (Socialist Upton Sinclair in California, Progressive Gifford Pinchot in Pennsylvania) who represented bold approaches to economic and social change; and when he did decide to take vigorous action against conservative Congressional candidates in 1938, he did so too late and too timorously. He often attempted to lead Congress in a forceful way to support his economic program; yet his leadership was confined to working with the existing Congressional leadership, including many Southern conservatives who ruled important committees. Roosevelt's political daring did not extend to building new political forces among the poor, the unemployed, the tenant farmers, and other disadvantaged groups, with whose support he might have given the country a bolder economic program.

The circle of men around Roosevelt, the cabinet members and administrators, was an odd mixture of liberals and conservatives who often worked at cross-purposes. Rexford Guy Tugwell, a bold advocate of national planning to help the lower-income groups, was close to Roosevelt for several years; but so was Raymond Moley, who believed in a kind of planning more beneficial to business interests. Even the liberal New Dealers, with rare exceptions, hesitated to carry their general concern for the underprivileged too far. Frances Perkins, the Secretary of Labor, had the humanitarian instincts of a first-rate social worker, but she seemed often to be trailing behind the labor movement, rather than helping to give it direction. (The most advanced piece of New Deal labor legislation was the Wagner Act, but Secretary Perkins wrote later: "I myself, had very little sympathy with the bill.") Progressive Secretary of the Interior Harold Ickes was offset by conservative Secretary of Commerce Daniel Roper. And although Roper was succeeded in 1939 by Harry Hopkins, there remained in the cabinet a powerful force for fiscal conservatism and budget-balancing—Secretary of the Treasury Henry Morgenthau.

The experimentalism of the New Deal, in short, had its limits: up to these limits, Roosevelt's social concern was genuinely warm, his political courage huge, his humanitarian spirit unfailing; beyond them, his driving force weakened. Thus, by 1938, with the nation out of the worst of the depression, with a skeletal structure of social reform in the statute books, and with that year's Congressional elections showing a sudden waning of political approbation, the Roosevelt program began to bog down. As it slid to its close, it left behind a mountain of accomplishment, and ahead, mountains still unclimbed. Many millions—businessmen, professionals, unionized workingmen, commercial farmers—had been given substantial help. Many millions more—sharecroppers, slum-dwellers, Negroes of North and South, the unemployed—still awaited a genuine "new deal."

II

Why did the New Deal sputter out around 1938–1939? One important factor seems to be that the urgency of 1933–1935 was gone. By 1939, although there were still nine million unemployed, the sense of panic was over. After all, unemployment was normal in America. Harry Hopkins had said in 1937 that even in prosperity it was "reasonable to expect a probable minimum of 4,000,000 to 5,000,000 unemployed." The American nation had developed over the years a set of expectations as to what constituted "normal" times and by 1938 it was approaching these.

Hopkins' statement and the administration's inaction indicate that the ideals of the New Dealers did not extend very far beyond the traditional structure of the American economy. They had wanted to get out of the terrible economic despair of 1932 and 1933 and to establish certain moderate reforms. These aims had been accomplished. True, some of the New Dealers, including FDR himself, did speak of what still remained to be done. But once the nation was restored to close to the old balance—even if income was still distributed with gross inequality, even if rural and urban slums crisscrossed the land, even if most workingmen were still unorganized and underpaid, and a third of the nation still, in FDR's words, "ill-nourished, ill-clad, ill-housed"—the driving force of the New Deal was gone.

Why were the expectations and ideals of the New Deal (its folklore, its symbols, according to Thurman Arnold) so limited? Why did the New Dealers not declare that the government would continue spending, experimenting, and expanding governmental enterprises—until no one was unemployed, and all slums were gone from the cities, until no family received below-subsistence incomes and adequate medical care was available to everyone, until anyone who wanted a college education could get one? True, there were political obstacles to realizing such objectives, but to state them as goals would itself have constituted the first step toward overcoming those obstacles. For this might have enabled FDR to do what political scientist James MacGregor Burns asserts was not done: to build "a solid, organized mass base" among labor and other underprivileged groups.

Humanitarianism pure and simple can go only so far, and self-interest must carry it further. Beyond the solicitude felt by the New Dealers for the distressed, beyond the occasionally bold rhetoric, there was not enough motive power to create a radically new economic equilibrium; this would have to be supplied by the groups concerned themselves; by the tenant farmers, the aged, the unemployed, the lowest-paid workers in the economy. Those who *did* organize—the larger farm operators, the several million industrial workers who joined the CIO—improved their position significantly. But as Paul Douglas, then an economics professor at the University of Chicago and now a United States Senator, wrote in 1933:

> *Along with the Rooseveltian program must go . . . the organization of those who are at present weak and who need to acquire that which the world respects, namely, power. . . . Unless these things are done, we are likely to find the permanent benefits of Rooseveltian liberalism to be as illusory as were those of the Wilsonian era.*

Many organized movements sprang up in the 1930's, spurred by need and encouraged by the new atmosphere of innovation. The Townsend Movement sought $200 a month pensions for the aged. Father Charles Coughlin's panacea of "Social Justice" was heard by millions of radio listeners. Huey Long, the Louisiana Senator, excited many others with his "Share the Wealth" plan. The National Negro Congress, the Farmers Union, and the American Youth Congress all represented special needs and all hurled their energies into the boiling political pot in Washington.

But there was no political program around which these disparate groups could effectively unite. And many of them began to lose their thrust when their demands were partially met. Even the Congress of Industrial Organizations, the largest and most successful of those mass movements born in the depression and stimulated by New Deal legislation, came eventually to represent a special interest of its own.

The Madisonian argument that political stability would be assured in a federal republic of many states, because an uprising in one would die for lack of support, applied also in the economic sphere, where no single economic interest, fierce as it might be in its own domain, ever developed a concern wide enough to embrace society at large. Perhaps one reason is that in the United States every little rebellion, every crisis, has been met with enough concessions to keep general resentment below the combustible level, while isolated aggrieved groups fought their way up to the point of complacency.

But if—as Paul Douglas forecasts—the underprivileged are the only ones who can supply the driving force for a sharp change in their condition, then it is probably the intellectuals of society who will furnish the theories, state the ideals, define the expectations. And so it is from those thinkers who clustered, half-friendly, half-reproachful, around the New Deal, their ideological reach less restrained, perhaps, by the holding of power, that our generation may find suggestions.

III

Almost immediately, with John Dewey, we are brought face to face with the proof that it is not the fact of experimentalism, but the definition of its boundaries, that is of supreme significance. He was one of the fathers of American pragmatism, the theoretician par excellence of the experimental method. In an article of 1918, he expressed the view of pragmatic experimentation that he held to the end of his life in 1952.

The question is whether society . . . will learn to utilize the intelligence, the insight and foresight which are available, in order to take hold of the problem and to go at it, step by step, on the basis of an intelligent program—a program which is not too rigid, which is not a program in the sense of having every item definitely scheduled in advance, but which represents an outlook on the future of the things which most immediately require doing, trusting to the experience which is got in doing them to reveal the next things needed and the next steps to be taken.

Roosevelt and Dewey were both experimentalists and they both operated within a range of ideals; but that range, for John Dewey, involved goals that went well beyond Roosevelt's farthest bounds. Roosevelt wrote to newspaper publisher Roy Howard on September 2, 1935, that his legislation was "remedial," described the New Deal program as involving "modifications in the conditions and rules of economic enterprise" and said that: "This basic program, however, has now reached substantial completion." Undoubtedly he was bending over backward to satisfy an anxious and influential citizen. And his program did go on to embrace a minimum wage law, public housing, and other measures. But that was largely because of the momentum already created for reform and because of pressures among the public. The Roosevelt vision had been stretched almost to its limits.

In Dewey's 1935 lectures at the University of Virginia, he said:

The only form of enduring social organization that is now possible is one in which the new forces of productivity are cooperatively controlled and used in the interest of the effective liberty and the cultural development of the individuals that constitute society. Such a social order cannot be established by an unplanned and external convergence of the actions of separate individuals, each of whom is bent on personal private advantage. . . . Organized social planning, put into effect for the creation of an order in which industry and finance are socially directed . . . is now the sole method of social action by which liberalism can realize its professed aims.

Both Roosevelt and Dewey believed in moving step by step. But FDR wanted to preserve the profit system; Dewey was willing to reshape it drastically. Because Dewey's aim was larger, his steps were longer ones, taken two or three at a time, and were less haphazard. "In short," he said, "liberalism must now become radical. . . . For the gulf between what the actual situation makes possible and the actual state itself is so great that it cannot be bridged by piecemeal policies undertaken ad hoc." Dewey was very conscious of the dangers of totalitarianism, but he believed that the spirit of free expression could remain alive, even while liberalism went on to "socialize the forces of production." Among pragmatists, apparently, crucial distinctions exist.

Part of Roosevelt's "pragmatism" was his rejection of doctrinaire ideas of the left. Marxism was in the air all around him. Many intellectuals were enthusiastic about the Five Year Plans of Soviet Russia. British Marxists were influential: Harold J. Laski lectured and wrote extensively in the United States; John Strachey popularized the concepts of socialism in The Nature of Capitalist Crisis (1935) and other works. Some in depression-ridden America were attracted to Marxism's claims that society could be analyzed "scientifically": that economic crisis was inevitable where production was complex and gigantic, yet unplanned; that exploitation of working people was built into a system where private profit was the chief motive; that the state was not neutral but an instrument of those who held economic power; that only the working class could be depended on to take over society and move it towards a classless, strifeless commonwealth. A true pragmatist might at least have explored some of the suggestions of Marxist thought. Roosevelt's thinking, however, remained in a kind of airtight chamber that allowed him to regulate what currents he would permit inside—and Marxism was not one of them.

Nevertheless, to steer clear of the theories of the Marxists, as of the Hooverian folklore of "free enterprise," "thrift," and "laissez-faire," left a vast middle ground of which Roosevelt explored only one sector. Edmund Wilson, for instance, a social critic and essayist, also rejected Marxian dialectics; yet he tried to extract from it some truths. He wrote with apparent warmth of the idea that (as he put it, in an imaginary restatement of a more acceptable Marxism): ". . . if society is to survive at all, it must be reorganized on new principles of equality." Others, not Marxists, but more demanding in their notion of reform than was the New Deal, reconnoitered beyond its ideological fences.

Reinhold Niebuhr, a theologian and social philosopher who carried the Social Gospel to new borders in the 1930's, urged that "private ownership of the productive processes" be abandoned, yet he hoped that through an alliance among farmers, industrial workers, and the lower income classes, the transition to a new order could be accomplished without violence. Stuart Chase, an economist who wrote a series of widely selling books in the 1930's, suggested that old alternatives had been swept aside by the onrush of technology, that the choice was no longer between capitalism and socialism; there was a need, he said, for some uncategorizable collectivist society whose "general objective will be the distribution of the surplus, rather than a wrangling over the ownership of a productive plant which has lost its scarcity position."

William Ernest Hocking, a Harvard philosopher, asked for "collectivism of a sort," but neither the collectivism of a "headless Liberalism" or of a "heady" Communism or Fascism. He wrote: "What the State has to do with production is to drive into economic practice the truth that there is little or no capital whose use is not 'affected by a public interest.'" Hocking said: "Economic processes constitute a single and healthy organism only when the totality of persons in a community who have a right to consume *determine what is produced*. . . ." Hocking was setting goals quite beyond the Rooseveltian ones.

Upton Sinclair, a muckraker since the early part of the century, preached a non-Marxist, home-grown socialism that attracted enough adherents to bring him very close to winning the gubernatorial election in California in 1934. Sinclair prophesied that "in a cooperative society every man, woman, and child would have the equivalent of $5000 a year income from labor of the able-bodied young men for three or four hours per day." This prophecy was certainly utopian in 1933, but such vision, even if it were going to be bent and modified in practice, might carry a program of social reform much further —and perhaps win more powerful blocs of electoral support—than did the more moderate goals of the New Deal.

A program may be pragmatic in its willingness to explore various means, yet be certain of its goals; it may be limited in how far it is willing to go, and yet be clear about the direction of its thrust. There is a difference between experimentation and vacillation. Robert MacIver, a distinguished social scientist, was impressed in 1934 by the variety of new institutions created under Roosevelt, but wondered if they meant "the inauguration of a period of social and cultural reformation." He asked: "The new institutions are here, but the essential point is—Who shall control them?" There was uncertainty about the New Deal, particularly in its first two years, when the National Recovery Act set out to create large planning organizations for industry in which big business seemed to be making the important decisions. It led some liberals and radicals to see in it possible Fascist aims, led some important businessmen to support it, and kept political loyalties crisscrossed in a happy chaos.

After 1935 (although ambiguity remained in specific areas like trust-busting), the over-all direction of the New Deal became clear: it was sympathetic to the underprivileged, and to organized labor, and it was pervaded by a general spirit of liberal, humanitarian reform. But also the scope of the New Deal became clear. This limitation is shown in a number of issues that the New Deal faced, or sometimes tried to avoid facing, between 1933 and 1939: the problem of planning; the question of how to deal with monopolistic business; the controversy over deficit financing and the extension of public enterprise; the creation of an adequate system of social security.

IV

When Roosevelt told students at Oglethorpe University during his 1932 campaign that he was in favor of "a larger measure of social planning," it was not clear how large this measure was. Was he willing to go as far as his own advisor, Columbia professor Rexford Guy Tugwell? Tugwell attacked the profit motive, said that "planning for production means planning for consumption too," declared that "profits must be limited and their uses controlled," and said he meant by planning "something not unlike an integrated group of enterprises run for its consumers rather than for its owners." The statement, he said, that "business will logically be required to disappear" is "literally meant" because: "Planning implies guidance of capital uses. . . . Planning also implies adjustment of production to consumption; and there is no way of accomplishing this except through a control of prices and of profit margins." To limit business in all these ways, he said, meant in effect "to destroy it as business and to make of it something else."

Raymond Moley, who played a direct role in shaping Roosevelt's early legislation, also deplored the lack of planning in the New Deal. But Moley was interested in planning for quite different groups. Tugwell was concerned with the lower classes' lack of purchasing power. Moley, although he too was moved by a measure of genuine concern for deprived people, was most worried about "the narrow margin of profit" and "business confidence." In the end, Roosevelt rejected both ideas. Whatever planning he would do would try to help the lower classes, for example, the Tennessee Valley Authority. On the other hand, the planning would not be national; nor would it interfere with the fundamental character of the American economy, based as it was on corporate profit; nor would it attempt any fundamental redistribution of wealth in the nation. And the TVA embodied these too because it represented *piecemeal* planning.

David Lilienthal's defense of this method, in his book on the TVA, comes closest to the New Deal approach. "We move step by step—from where we are," wrote Lilienthal. Not only was any notion of national economic planning never seriously considered, but after the TVA, the moving "step by step" did not carry very far. Housing developments and several planned communities were inspiring, but came nowhere near matching the enormity of the national need.

Ambiguity persisted longest in the policy towards monopoly and oligopoly. The NRA was a frank recognition of the usefulness—or at least, the inevitability—of large enterprise, when ordered by codes. The Securities Exchange Commission and the Public Utilities Holding Company Act moved back (but weakly, as William O. Douglas recognized at the time) to the Brandeis idea of trying to curb the size and strength of large enterprises. Roosevelt's basic policy towards giantism in business, although he vigorously attacked "economic royalists" in 1936, remained undetermined until 1938, when he asked Congress for a sweeping investigation of monopoly. And although he was clearly returning to the idea of restraining the power of big business, one sentence in his message to Congress reveals his continuing uncertainty: "The power of the few to manage the economic life of the Nation must be diffused among the many or be transferred to the public and its democratically responsible government."

The first alternative was an obviously romantic notion; the second was really much farther than either Congress or FDR was prepared to go. Hence, the Temporary National Economic Committee, after hearing enough testimony to fill thirty-one volumes and forty-three monographs, was unwilling, as William Leuchtenburg writes, "to tackle the more difficult problems or to make recommendations which might disturb vested interests." Roosevelt had come close to expressing, but he still did not possess, nor did he communicate to the nation, a clear, resolute goal of transferring giant and irresponsible economic power "to the public and its democratically responsible government." The restraints on the New Dealers' thinking is shown best perhaps by Adolf A. Berle, who said that prosperity depended on either a gigantic expansion of private activity or nationalization of key industries. Yet, knowing private industry was not going to fill the need, he did not advocate nationalization —nor did any other New Dealer.

Roosevelt was experimental, shifting, and opportunistic in his espousal of public enterprise and the spending that had to accompany such governmental activity. As James MacGregor Burns says: "Roosevelt had tried rigid economy, then heavy spending, then restriction of spending again. He had shifted back and forth from spending on direct relief to spending on public works." The significant measure, however, was not the swings of the pendulum, but the width of the arcs. When FDR went all-out for spending, it was still only a fraction of what the British economist John Maynard Keynes was urging as a way of bringing recovery. An American Keynesian, Professor Alvin Hansen, was arguing that the economy was "mature" and therefore required much more continuous and powerful injections of governmental spending than was being given.

Roosevelt himself had introduced into public discussion the idea of a "yardstick," which the Tennessee Valley Authority represented—a public enterprise that would, by competing with private producers, force them to bend more towards the needs of the consumer. (Later FDR tried, unsuccessfully, to get Congress to introduce "seven little TVA's" in other river valleys.) But the vast implications of the concept were left unexplored. When political scientist Max Lerner called for government-owned radio stations and government-subsidized newspapers to break into the growing monopolization of public opinion by giant chains, there was no response. TVA, a brief golden period of federal theater, a thin spread of public housing, and a public works program called into play only at times of desperation, represented the New Deal's ideological and emotional limits in the creation of public enterprise.

It is one thing to experiment to discover the best means of achieving a certain objective; it is quite another thing to fail to recognize that objective. The Social Security System, as set up, was not an experiment to find the best type of system. Roosevelt knew from the beginning that it was not the most effective way to handle the problems of poverty for the aged, the unemployed, and the helpless. Behind the basic political problem of getting the bill passed lay fundamental narrowness of vision. Social security expert Abraham Epstein pointed this out at the time, and it was noted on the floor of Congress. Henry E. Sigerist, a physician and student of welfare medicine in other countries, wrote patiently and clearly about the need for socialized medicine, answered the arguments against it, and explained how it might operate.

Thus, if the concept of New Deal thought is widened to include a large circle of thinkers—some close to the administration itself, others at varying distances from it—we get not panaceas or infallible schemes but larger commitments, bolder goals, and greater expectations of what "equality" and "justice" and "security" meant.

V

For our view of the New Deal as a particularly energetic gyroscopic motion putting the traditional structure aright again, we have what the natural scientists might call a set of "controls"—a way of checking up on the hypothesis —one in the area of race relations, another in the experience of war.

In the field of racial equality, where there was no crisis as in economics, where the gyroscope did not confront a sharply tilted mechanism, there was no "new deal." The special encumbrances of the depression were lifted for Negroes as for many other Americans, but the *permanent* caste structure remained unaltered by the kind of innovations that at least threatened the traditional edifice in economics. The white South was left, as it had been since the Compromise of 1877, to deal with Negroes as it chose—by murder, by beatings, by ruthless exclusion from political and economic life; the Fourteenth Amendment waited as fruitlessly for executive enforcement as it had in all earlier administrations since Grant. Washington, D.C., itself remained a tightly segregated city. And the Harlems of the North continued as great symbols of national failure.

The warm belief in equal rights held by Eleanor Roosevelt, as well as by FDR himself, the appointments of Mary McLeod Bethune, Robert Weaver, and others to important secondary posts in the government, even the wide distribution of relief and WPA jobs, were not enough to alter the fundamental injustice attached to being a Negro in the United States. The disposition of the New Deal to experiment could have led to important accomplishments, but the clear goal of ending segregation, as with comparable objectives in economics, was never established.

With the coming of World War II, economic and social experimentation blossomed under Roosevelt's leadership and involved a good measure of national planning, jobs for everyone, and a vast system of postwar educational benefits to eighteen million veterans. There was little inhibition; new, radically different national goals were not required for the traditional objective of winning at war. With such an aim, policy could be fearless and far-reaching.

Some coming generation perhaps, while paying proper respects to the spirit of the New Deal, may find, as William James put it, "the moral equivalent of war"—in new social goals, new expectations, with imaginative, undoctrinaire experimentation to attain them. If, in such an adventure, the thought of the past can help, it should be put to work.

SUGGESTIONS FOR FURTHER READING

The New Deal has already inspired more writing than many periods in American history, and most of it has been favorable. A balanced, general account, tightly packed and entertainingly written, is William E. Leuchtenburg, *Franklin Roosevelt and the New Deal (New York, 1963). Leuchtenburg emphasizes the change in American life brought about by the New Deal, but not to the extent that Mario Einaudi does in The Roosevelt Revolution (New York, 1959). Arthur Schlesinger, Jr. has completed three volumes of his major study of The Age of Roosevelt (*The Crisis of the Old Order, *The Coming of the New Deal, and *The Politics of Upheaval [Boston, 1957, 1959, 1960]). Schlesinger writes exciting history and shows Roosevelt, the pragmatic-idealist, moving from cooperation with the business community early in his first term to a more critical attitude after 1935.

The best one-volume biography of Roosevelt is James MacGregor Burns, *Roosevelt: The Lion and the Fox (New York, 1956). Burns, like most historians, views Roosevelt as essentially conservative on political and economic issues. Edgar Robinson, The Roosevelt Leadership, 1933–45 (Philadelphia, 1955) is the best evaluation of the New Deal from the right. Much recent writing looks at the New Deal from the left and is critical, arguing that the reforms of the 1930's did not go far enough. See Paul K. Conkin, *The New Deal (New York, 1967) and Barton Bernstein, "The New Deal: The Conservative Achievement of Liberal Reform," in Bernstein, ed., *Towards a New Past: Dissenting Essays in American History (New York, 1968).

Alonzo L. Hamby, *The New Deal: Analysis and Interpretation (New York, 1969) is a convenient collection of essays; Howard Zinn, ed., *New Deal Thought (Indianapolis, 1966) is a good collection of contemporary documents; Richard S. Kirkendall, "The New Deal as Watershed," Journal of American History, XIV (March 1968), is a guide to the recent literature.

* Available in paperback edition.

7

THE UNITED STATES AS A WORLD POWER

Americans have always been deeply involved with the rest of the world. As colonials they often found themselves participants in England's wars. By taking advantage of the antagonism against England, they were able to secure military and financial aid from the Continent during the Revolution. In the early years of national independence, American merchants attempted to wend their way through the clashing interests of France and England, a profitable yet dangerous venture which ultimately led the new nation into a second war with England. After 1815, Americans turned their attention inward, opening and settling new lands and building a national market. Nevertheless, relations with foreign countries remained important. Foreign investment as well as income from lucrative foreign trade helped to finance the westward movement and canal and railway building.

Although America was never isolated from the rest of the world it was not until the end of the nineteenth century that the nation emerged as a major world power. A short but successful war with Spain in 1898 symbolized America's new position in the world. Spain ceded Guam and Puerto Rico to the United States; the Philippines although promised independence, remained under U.S. control; and Cuba received only nominal independence, remaining virtually a protectorate of the United States. The United States had embarked upon an imperialist venture.

More important than the actual acquisition of new territories was the growing influence and power of the United States in world affairs. In 1904, the so-called "Roosevelt Corollary to the Monroe Doctrine" announced to the world that the United States reserved to itself the right to intervene in Latin America: ". . . in the Western Hemisphere the adherence of the United States to the Monroe Doctrine may force the United States, however reluctantly, in flagrant cases of . . . wrongdoing or impotence, to the exercise of an international police power." Nor was this simply a paper declaration. In the years which followed the United States intervened in the internal affairs of a number of Latin American countries including the Dominican Republic, Nicaragua, and Haiti.

While the United States was building a canal at the Isthmus of Panama and establishing and protecting its influence in Latin America, there were growing signs of tension among the great European powers. Yet few Americans envisioned full scale world war; after all, all of Europe had not been locked in conflict since the defeat of Napoleon in 1815. Thus when war did come in 1914, most Americans were shocked. If they tended to favor Britain and its allies, they were adamant in their opinion that the United States should not become involved. But the United States was again unable to stay out of Europe's wars. On April 2, 1917 President Wilson read a war message to Congress. The issue at stake, the president argued, was democracy: "The world must be made safe for democracy."

Making the world safe for democracy proved more elusive than military defeat of the central powers. A League of Nations, designed to solve international differences peaceably, was established as part of the peace treaties, but the United States Senate refused to ratify the treaties and the United States never became a member of the League. The result, however, was not complete isolation of the United States from the rest of the world. The government aided in working out a solution to the reparations question, participated in conferences designed to limit naval armaments, cooperated with a number of League of Nations agencies, and jointly sponsored the Kellogg-Briand pact in which some 63 nations renounced "recourse to war for the solution of international controversies." In Latin America the dominance of the United States continued under the Republican administrations of the 1920's.

The Great Depression revealed grave domestic problems which occupied the energies of Americans during the 1930's. News from abroad, however, was disquieting: the rise of Hitler and Mussolini and the obvious expansionist aims of Japan aroused alarm. Nevertheless, Americans were determined not to repeat the mistake of becoming involved in the wars of the great powers. The Neutrality Acts passed by Congress beginning in 1935 legislated non-involvement. Arms shipments to either side in a war were prohibited and Americans were warned that they traveled on belligerent ships at their own risk.

Isolation, however, could not be maintained. By mid-1940 Hitler had overrun western Europe and Britain was threatened by invasion; in September an aggressive Japan signed a military and economic alliance with Germany and Italy. Rearmament in the United States was stepped up and strict neutrality gave way to support for England and opposition to Japan as Americans began to realize the growing menace to their security. Then on Sunday, December 7, 1941 Japan attacked Pearl Harbor. On the following day Congress declared war on Japan. Three days later Italy and Germany declared war on the U.S. and Congress responded with a declaration of war against these powers.

The attitude of the United States after the Second World War was very different from that following World War I. Isolationism was all but dead. Although most Americans envisioned a post-war world of peace and friendship among the war-time allies—Britain, the USSR, and the United States— they also seemed to realize that the nation's participation in the post-war world was essential. The onset of the cold war led not to disillusionment, disgust, and a withdrawal into isolation, but to a fuller participation of the United States in world affairs.

Thus it is clear that in the last three-quarters of a century the United States has emerged as a major economic and military power, a power, moreover, which has played an increasingly large role in world affairs. Less obvious are the reasons for this change. Some historians have emphasized the connection between economic development and foreign relations. They have seen the nation's foreign policy basically as an accommodation to the needs of the business community and particularly of big business. Business engaged in foreign trade and foreign investment needed support and protection and received it from the politicians. Other historians find little relationship between economics and foreign policy. They emphasize instead moral fervor born of nationalism or the desire to extend democracy, or they point to strategic requirements, the need to protect our borders from real or potential enemies.

American diplomatic relations have always been the subject of debate, but never has this debate assumed the proportions and intensity that it has since the start of the cold war. The reasons are obvious enough. Military technology has reached the point where total destruction of the world is possible; diplomacy therefore deals with matters of life or death not only for Americans but for a large portion of the world's population. Examples of this debate may be followed in the selections below.

In the first selection, John Spanier argues that American security after World War II required the establishment of a balance of power in Europe and Asia that would serve to block Communist expansion. This required, Spanier continues, a realistic foreign policy, one that recognized and was willing to use the weapons of power politics and one that accepted the necessity of "a happy marriage between diplomacy and force." But the American experience worked against such a realistic view; Americans tended to think of foreign relations in moral terms and to ignore the realities of power politics. New conditions, he concludes, demanded a change in American attitudes. In the next selection, William G. Carleton discusses some of the changes that came as a result of cold war experiences. He discovers a growing realism after 1945. Although he notes differences of opinion, he finds that these differences were for the most part within the context of a more realistic view of power politics. Americans, he concludes, "were learning." Clearly, both Spanier and Carleton deny that foreign policy is determined by the needs of an economic elite. Indeed, both stress national interests rather than class interests and both argue that a basic American consensus at home often continues to create difficulties in the formulation of an effective and realistic foreign policy.

In the next selection, Ronald Steel deals with the war in Vietnam. He sees the war as a result, in part, of the realism which Spanier and Carleton seem to advocate. Although he strongly opposes the war, he does not view it as an accident: "Vietnam is precisely the kind of war the American military machine, as perfected in the mid-1960's, was designed to fight." But, according to Steel, if the war is not simply a tactical error, it is also not the result of the machinations of a military elite. Rather, it arose from mistaken American attitudes. Americans, he concludes, must learn to distinguish between "interventions necessary to defend the United States and its most intimate allies, and those which spring from a euphoria of power." In short, what America needs is a new consensus to replace the one that led us into a tragic war.

Paul A. Baran and Paul M. Sweezy view American post-World War II diplomacy in a much different light. They are persuaded that American policies derived from the need to protect the economic interests of the giant American corporations. They note, however, that although business interests dictate an imperialist foreign policy, there is very little opposition to this policy because of the general feeling that it promotes economic well-being for the entire nation. In the final selection, Gabriel Kolko analyzes the formation of American foreign policy. He denies that this policy arises from "capriciousness, accident, and chance," maintaining instead that it is the result of the "predominance of the economic ruling class which is the final arbiter and beneficiary" of both domestic and foreign policies. Opposition is tolerated only when it is neither serious nor effective; if necessary, a consensus is maintained by repression exercised by the ruling elite.

According to a popular cliché in American politics, partisan debate stops at our borders. While there is ample justification for debate on domestic issues, our foreign relations, where the security of the nation is at stake, must be bi-partisan if the best interests of the country are to be served. Although often expressed, this attitude has seldom been followed in practice. Few major foreign policy decisions have been made without intense debate. Yet how significant is this debate? What are the issues which have divided Americans? More important, are there basic divisions of interest determining foreign policy even when these divisions are not publicly expressed? Has American diplomacy derived from a basic consensus of American opinion? Or has it arisen from the interests of particular classes in American society? If foreign policy is in the interests of the few, how do policy makers gain acceptance of their policies from the masses of the American people and their representatives? What means—if any—are available to those who oppose particular policies and who wish to bring about changes?

The American Approach to Foreign Policy

John Spanier

Following World War I, the English geopolitician Halford MacKinder wrote: "Who rules East Europe commands the Heartland [largely Russia and China, plus Iran and Afghanistan]: Who rules the Heartland commands the World-Island [Eurasia and Africa]: Who rules the World-Island commands the World." Some years later, an American geopolitician, Nicolas Spykman, paraphrased MacKinder in a reply to his thesis: "Who controls the Rimland [the peripheral areas of the Eurasian continent] rules Eurasia; who rules Eurasia controls the destinies of the world."

No two maxims could have summed up the history of the post-World War II era more aptly. The Soviet Union and Communist China now occupy most of the Heartland; surrounding them along a 20,000-mile periphery lie the exposed and weaker Rimland nations—the Scandinavian and West European countries, Italy, Greece, Turkey, the Arab countries, Iran, Afghanistan, India, Burma, Thailand, Malaya, Indochina, and Korea (with Britain, Indonesia, and Japan lying just off the Eurasian continent). It is the Communists' aim to extend their control to these nations. This would leave the United States and the Americas—the Western Hemisphere—a lone island in a totalitarian sea. American security would then be, at best, very precarious and could be maintained only by the organization of our society as a "garrison state," a condition incompatible with any interpretation of the "American way of life." At worst, the United States would be at the mercy of the Soviet bloc controlling the Eurasian continent. The ability of the United States to ensure its own security—indeed, its survival—under these circumstances depends upon its

From John Spanier, American Foreign Policy Since World War II, 4th rev. ed., 1971, pp. 1–17. Reprinted by permission of Frederick A. Praeger, Inc.

capacity to establish a balance of power in Eurasia in order to prevent the Communists from expanding into the Rimland or neutralizing those nations.

As far back as the 1830's, a prophetic Frenchman, Alexis de Tocqueville, had foreseen this struggle which dominates our age:

> There are, at the present time, two great nations in the world which seem to tend toward the same end, although they started from different points: I allude to the Russians and the Americans. . . . The Anglo-American relies upon personal interest to accomplish his ends and gives free scope to the unguided exertions and common sense of the citizens; the Russians center all the authority of society in a single arm: the principal instrument of the former is freedom; of the latter is servitude. Their starting point is different, and their courses are not the same; yet each of them seems to be marked out by the will of Heaven to sway the destinies of half the globe.

Yet, the United States in 1945 could not have been less equipped to conduct the struggle and to assume the global responsibilities involved. American experience in foreign affairs, in comparison with that of the other great powers of the world, had been limited. Consequently, the United States was essentially a novice in the art she now had to practice—the art of "power politics." For over a century the nation had cut itself off from Europe and pursued a policy of isolationism, or what today would be called neutralism or nonalignment. Like the new nations of the post-World War II era, the United States, as the world's first new nation to emerge from colonial subjection, refused to involve herself in the quarrels of Britain, France, and the other European powers. "Europe has a set of primary interests, which to us have none, or a very remote relation. Hence she must be engaged in frequent controversies, the causes of which are essentially foreign to our concerns," said George Washington in his Farewell Address. Therefore, he continued, it would be unwise

> to implicate ourselves, by artificial ties, in the ordinary vicissitudes of her politics, or the ordinary combinations and collisions of her friendships, or enmities: Our detached and distant situation invites and enables us to pursue a different course. . . . Why forego the advantages of so peculiar a situation? Why quit our own to stand upon foreign ground? Why, by interweaving our destiny with that of any part of Europe, entangle our peace and prosperity in the toils of European ambition, Rivalship, Interest, Humour or Caprice?

Why, indeed?

The republic was young, hardly yet conscious of its national identity. American nationalism had been aroused during the War of Independence. But once the British had been defeated and ejected, each of the thirteen colonies had become more interested in its own affairs than in those of the Confederation. The Confederation was a "league of states" in which loyalty to the states took precedence; it was a "firm league of friendship," not a united nation. For example, when Jefferson talked of "my country," he was referring to Virginia, not to the United States. The resulting interstate rivalries and conflicts, the absence of any effective central government, and the lack of an international status for the Confederation led to the formation of the "more perfect union." But once the colonial master who had formerly united the people in common opposition had been removed, how could this new union gain its sense of identity as a new nation? The answer given by the leaders of the young republic—and this answer is still given by the leaders of most of today's new nations—was to continue pursuing an anticolonial policy. This is essential for a new nation's national cohesion. It was colonial subjugation that first kindled the spirit of revolt and awakened the people's sense of national consciousness. It is by continuing to "fight colonialism"—both the specific former colonial ruler and colonialism in general—that this feeling of nationalism is strengthened. Since it was Europe that colonized the world, the rejection of Europe is essential to the formation of the new nation's sense of identity. Therefore, it cannot realign itself with the old colonial master, even when its security is threatened. Whether this threat comes from the Holy Alliance or Communism, the newborn state cannot in most circumstances "stand up and be counted." It must remain independent, for only its assertion against Europe—or, as we say today, "the West"—will foster its growth of national consciousness.

Avoiding "foreign entanglements," as Jefferson called it, is also necessary for the young nation's "economic development." How will it become strong enough to defend the country against possible foreign attacks or assert its prestige against disrespectful, "neocolonial" treatment by the older nations of the world? How can it tie the various parts of the nation together into an effective union and subordinate local and regional loyalties to a primary national loyalty? And finally, how can it provide a better life and standard of living for its new citizens? These are the three vital questions that confront the leaders of all new states, for the government must prove to its people that the recently formed nation is worthy of their support and allegiance because it can furnish them with a secure and decent life. Hamilton, the father of American industrialism, was keenly aware of these needs, particularly the security of the nation. Industrialization thus became a necessity if the United States was to defend her national security, safeguard her independence, and gain the respect of those states who still considered her a colonial weakling and inferior. The continuing friction with Britain during the first years after independence made this clear. The British treated the young republic in an arrogant and high-handed fashion as if it were still a colony; they refused to vacate the Northwest frontier and impressed American sailors by stopping American ships on the high seas and taking the sailors off. Not surprisingly, the lesson of the War of 1812 (also known as the Second War of Independence) was the need for industrialization and strength. But the purpose of industrialization is to do more than augment national power; it is also to strengthen the still fragile political bonds of union with economic bonds. Industrialization, with its high degree of specialization and division of labor, welds together the many areas of a country and binds the people living therein into a closer union; once strangers to each other—hardly thinking of one another as countrymen and fellow nationals—they will be compelled to travel and communicate as the imperative of economic interdependence envelops the entire nation in one large market. The people thereby become "nationalized" as industrialization molds the consciousness of the new citizens and impresses upon them an awareness that they are members of one nation who will all have to work together if their common aspirations are to be fulfilled. Finally, it enables the new nation to raise its people's standard of living. This is the ultimate test of the new political order—its ability to confer economic benefits, or, more succinctly, its ability to "pay off." This is not to deny the importance of such other values as national independence and self-government. However, if man does not live by bread alone, he cannot survive without bread either; and the crucial issue therefore becomes the new order's capacity to furnish its citizens with at least the basic necessities of life, if not a degree of affluence and leisure. It was precisely the opportunities the American political and economic system afforded to its people to improve their material condition that drew the millions of immigrants to these shores. Freedom alone would not have proved such a powerful magnet. Indeed, it is doubtful that freedom can be established, let alone survive, in conditions of poverty. A degree of affluence and a reasonably equitable distribution of income seem to be prerequisites for the blossoming of a democracy, although they are not the sole prerequisites. In any case, the conclusion is clear: Economic development is vital if the new nation is to grow strong, united, and prosperous. In fact, the term "economic development" is a misnomer. It is the *political* results of this development that are essential to the future of the new state. Economic development might more appropriately be called "nation-building."

Granted that, in the American instance—as for new nations after 1945—the avoidance of foreign entanglements was thus a realistic policy, the subsequent American understanding of international relations proved to be unrealistic. For the priority of internal political and economic tasks, all of which were reinforced by the opening of the West and the subsequent transcontinental drive to the Pacific, led to the depreciation of the importance of foreign policy and the role that power plays in protecting the nation's interests. The ability of the United States to live in isolationism during the nineteenth century and a good part of the twentieth century was attributed, not to the nation's geographic distance from Europe or to the Royal Navy as the protector of the *Pax Britannica*, but to the nature of democracy. The United States was more than just the world's first "new nation"; it was also the world's first democracy and, as such, the first country in history that would devote itself to improving the lot of the common man, granting each individual the opportunity to enrich and ennoble his life. ("Give me your tired, your poor, your huddled masses yearning to be free," reads the inscription on the Statue of Liberty.) The more perfect union was to be an egalitarian society. European concepts of social hierarchy, nobility and titles, and bitter class struggles were not to be planted in its democratic soil. "Here the free spirit of mankind, at length, throws its last fetters off," exclaimed one writer. America was to be a "beacon lighting for all the world the paths of human destiny," wrote Emerson. From the very beginning of their national life Americans believed strongly in their destiny—to spread, by example, the light of freedom to all men and to lead mankind out of the wicked ways of the Old World. The massive immigration of the nineteenth century—particularly after 1865—was to reinforce this sense of destiny. "Repudiation of Europe," as John Dos Passos once said, "is, after all, America's main excuse for being." Europe stood for war, poverty, and exploitation; America for peace, opportunity, and democracy. But the United States was not merely to be a beacon of a superior democratic domestic way of life. It was also to be an example of a morally superior democratic pattern of international behavior. The United States would voluntarily reject power politics as unfit for the conduct of its foreign policy. Democratic theory posits that man is a rational and moral creature, and that differences among men can be settled by rational persuasion and moral exhortation. Indeed, granted this assumption about man, the only differences that could arise would simply be misunderstandings; and since man is endowed with reason and a moral sense, what quarrels could not be settled, given the necessary good will? Peace—the result of harmony among men—was thus the natural or normal state.

Conversely, conflict was considered a deviation from this norm, caused primarily by wicked statesmen whose morality and reason had been corrupted by the exercise of uncontrolled authority. Power politics was an instrument of selfish and autocratic rulers—that is, men unrestrained by democratic public opinion—who loved to wield it for their own personal advantage. To them, war was a grand game. They could remain in their palatial homes, continuing to eat well and to enjoy the luxuries of life. They suffered none of the hardships of war. These hardships fell upon the ordinary people; it was they who had to leave their families to fight, to endure the higher taxes made necessary by the costs of war, possibly to see their homes destroyed and their loved ones maimed or killed. It was only the despot who thought of war as a sport, as a sort of "bully" fox hunt; the common man, who had to endure all the cruelties of war, was therefore by his very nature peaceful. The conclusion was clear: Undemocratic states were inherently warlike and evil; democratic nations, in which the people controlled and regularly changed their leaders, were peaceful and moral.

American experience seemed to support this conclusion. The United States was a democracy and she was at peace. Furthermore, peace seemed to be the normal state of affairs. It was therefore logical that democracy and peaceful behavior and intentions should be thought of as synonymous. Americans never asked themselves whether democracy was really responsible for the peace they enjoyed, or whether this peace they assumed to be a natural condition was the product of other forces. The constant wars of Europe appeared to provide the answer: European politics were power politics, and this was because of the undemocratic nature of European regimes. Americans were therefore relieved that they had long ago, at the time of the Revolutionary War, cut themselves off from Europe and its constant class conflicts and power politics. America had to guard her democratic purity and abstain from any involvement in the affairs of Europe lest she be soiled and corrupted. Nonalignment was therefore the morally correct policy which allowed the United States to quarantine herself from contact with Europe's hierarchical social structures and immoral international habits. At the same time, by confusing the results of geography and international politics with the supposed consequence of democracy, Americans could smugly enjoy a self-conferred moral superiority. It was the Monroe Doctrine, proclaimed in 1823, which first stressed, officially and explicitly, this ideological difference between the New and Old Worlds. It declared specifically that the American political system was "essentially different" from that of Europe, whose nations were constantly engaged in warfare. The implication was very clear: Democratic government equals peace, and aristocratic government—which was identified with despotism—means war.

But this association of peace with democracy was not the only reason for the American depreciation of power politics. Another was that the United States was an overwhelmingly one-class society in which almost all men shared the same set of middle-class, capitalistic, and democratic values or beliefs. America was unique among nations in this respect. The European countries were, by contrast, three-class societies. In addition to the middle-class, they contained in their bodies politic an aristocratic class whose energies were devoted either to maintaining itself in power or to recapturing power in order to return to the glorious days of a feudal past. Moreover, European urbanization and industrialism during the nineteenth century gave birth to a proletariat which, because it felt that it did not receive a fair share of the national income, became a revolutionary class. The nations of the Old World were, in short, a composite of three elements: a reactionary aristocracy, a democratic middle class, and a revolutionary proletariat. Or, to put it another way, these nations had, in an intellectual as well as a political sense, a right, a center, and a left. The United States had only a center, both intellectually and politically. This country had never experienced a feudal past and therefore possessed no large and powerful aristocratic class on the right; and because it was, by and large, an egalitarian society, it also lacked a genuine left-wing movement of protest, such as socialism or Communism. America was, as De Tocqueville had said, "born free" as a middle-class, individualistic, capitalistic, and democratic society. We were not divided by the kind of deep ideological conflicts which in France, for instance, set one class of Frenchmen against another. No one class was ever so afraid of another that it preferred national defeat to domestic revolution—as in France in the late 1930's, when the bourgeoisie was so apprehensive of a proletarian upheaval that its slogan became "Better Hitler than Blum [the French Socialist leader]."

Americans are, in fact, in such accord on their basic values that whenever the nation is threatened from the outside, the public becomes fearful of internal disloyalty. It is one of the great ironies of American society that although Americans possess this unity of shared beliefs to a greater degree than any other people, their apprehension of external danger leads them, first, to insist upon a general and somewhat dogmatic reaffirmation of loyalty to the "American way of life," and then to a hunt for internal groups or forces that might betray this way of life. Disagreement tends to become suspect as disloyalty; men are accused of "un-American" thinking and behavior, and labeled "loyalty or security risks." Perhaps only a society so overwhelmingly committed to one set of values could be so sensitive to internal subversion and so fearful of internal betrayal; perhaps only a society in which two or more ideologies have long since learned to live together could genuinely tolerate diverse opinions. Who has ever heard of "un-British" or "un-French" activities? The United States has often been called a "melting pot" because of the many different nationality groups it comprises; but before each generation of immigrants has been fully accepted into American society, it has had to be "Americanized." Few Americans have ever accepted diversity as a value. American society has, in fact, taken great pride in destroying diversity through assimilation.

It was precisely this overwhelming agreement on the fundamental values of American society and Europe's intense class struggles that reinforced the American misunderstanding of the nature and functions of power on the international scene. Dissatisfied groups never developed a revolutionary ideology because the growing prosperity spread to them before they could translate their grievances against the capitalistic system into political action. America —politically secure and economically prosperous—therefore remained unaware of two important principles: that conflict is the natural offspring of clashing interests and groups, and that power plays a vital role in protecting, promoting, and compromising interests. By contrast, the European states, with their internal class struggles and external conflicts among themselves, never failed to appreciate the nature and role of power.

Politics did not, in any event, seem very important to Americans. The United States matured during the nineteenth century, the era of *laissez-faire* capitalism, whose basic assumption was that man was economically motivated. It was self-interest that governed the behavior of man; it might be referred to as "enlightened self-interest," but it was nevertheless self-interest. Each individual, seeking to maximize his wealth, responded to the demand of the free market. In an effort to increase his profit, he supplied the product the consumers wanted. The laws of demand and supply therefore transformed each person's economic selfishness into socially beneficial results. The entire society would prosper. The free market was thus considered the central institution that provided "the greatest good of the greatest number." Politics mattered little in this self-adjusting economic system based upon individuals' actions whose combined efforts resulted in the general welfare. The best government was the government that governed least. Arbitrary political interference with the economic laws of the market would only upset the results these laws were intended to produce. Private property, profit, the free market were thus the keys to assuring the happiness of mankind by providing him with abundance. Capitalism, in short, reflected the materialism of the age of industrialization.

To state the issue even more bluntly: Economics was good, politics was bad. This simple dichotomy came naturally to the capitalist middle class. Were the benefits of economic freedom not as "self-evident" as the truths stated in the Declaration of Independence? And had this economic freedom not been gained only by a long and bitter struggle of the European middle class to cut down the authority of the powerful monarchical state, and finally to overthrow it by revolution in France? The middle class, as it had grown more prosperous and numerous, had become increasingly resentful of paying taxes from which the aristocracy was usually exempt, of the restrictions placed upon trade and industry, of the absence of institutions in which middle-class economic and political interests were represented, of the class barriers to the social status that came with careers in the army and in the bureaucracy, and of the general lack of freedom of thought and expression. Since the middle class identified the power of the state with its own lack of freedom, its aim was to restrict this power. Only by placing restraints upon the authority of the state could it gain the individual liberty and, above all, the right to private enterprise it sought. Democratic philosophy stated these claims in terms of the individual's "natural rights" against the state. The exercise of political authority was thus equated with the abuse of that authority and the suppression of personal freedoms. The power of the state had therefore to be restricted to the minimum to ensure the individual's maximum political and economic liberties. It was with this purpose in mind that the American Constitution divided authority between the states and the Federal Government, and, within the latter, among the executive, legislative, and judicial branches. Federalism and the separation of powers were deliberately designed to keep all governments—and especially the national government—weak. Man's secular problems would be resolved not by the state's political actions but by the individual's own economic actions in society.

Again, both man's economic motivation and the benefits of a government that acts least were considered to be reflected in the American experience. Millions came to the United States from other lands to seek a better way of life. America was the earthly paradise where all men, no matter how poor or humble they had been in the old country, could earn a respectable living. A virgin and underdeveloped land, America presented magnificent opportunities for individual enterprise. First, there was the Western frontier with its rich soil; later, during the Industrial Revolution, the country's bountiful natural resources were exploited. The environment, technology, individual enterprise, and helpful governmental policies enabled the American people to become the "people of plenty." But to earn money was not only economically necessary in order to attain a comfortable standard of living; it was also psychologically necessary in order to gain social status and to earn the respect of one's fellow citizens.

Individual self-esteem is determined by the community in every society, for the individual can only judge his own worth by the standards of that society. In a class society, status can be easily recognized by certain upper-class traits, such as the clothes a man wears, the manners with which he conducts himself, and the way he pronounces his words. His education is, in fact, the key to his status. But in an egalitarian society, the successful man can be recognized only by his affluence; only the fact that he is richer than his peers, that he has more possessions, that he can afford to indulge in "conspicuous consumption" distinguishes him from other men. It follows logically that if material gain is the exclusive or at least principal sign of differentiation among men and if it confers upon them social respect and position, everyone will preoccupy himself with the pursuit and accumulation of the "almighty dollar." If men are judged primarily by their economic achievements, they will concentrate on "getting ahead." It is not surprising, therefore, that money comes closer to being the common standard of value in the United States than in any other country. For money is the symbol of power and prestige; it is the sign of success, just as failure to earn enough money is a token of personal failure. It has been said, not without some justice, that the American prefers two cars to two mistresses.

It was hardly surprising that in these circumstances the solution to international problems should be thought of in economic terms. Economics was identified with social harmony and the welfare of all men; politics was equated with conflict and war and death. Just as the "good society" was to be the product of free competition, so the peaceful international society would be created by free trade. An international *laissez-faire* policy would benefit all states just as a national *laissez-faire* policy benefited each individual within these states. Consequently, people all over the world had a vested interest in peace in order to carry on their economic relations. Trade and war were incompatible. Trade depended upon mutual prosperity (the poor do not buy much from one another). War impoverishes and destroys and creates ill-will among nations. Commerce benefits all the participating states; the more trade, the greater the number of individual interests involved. Commerce was consequently nationally and individually profitable and created a vested interest in peace. War, by contrast, was economically unprofitable and therefore obsolete. Free trade and peace, in short, were one and the same cause.

Thus the United States entered the twentieth century with a relative unawareness of the role that power plays in the relations among nations, even though as a highly industrialized and powerful nation she was at the turn of the century increasingly exerting a dominating influence in the Western Hemisphere. At no time was this attitude more vividly demonstrated than at the point of our entry into World War I and during the interwar period. It was Germany's unrestricted submarine warfare in early 1917 that brought us into that conflict; it was thus the German High Command's fatal decision that propelled the United States into the war. Yet, our security demanded this entry. The balance of power in the European battlefield was about to collapse: Britain and France were nearing financial exhaustion; Britain's food supply had reached near-starvation level because of the effectiveness of the German submarine campaign; the French Army had suffered such enormous casualties during a series of offensives that it had mutinied; and above all, the Czarist Empire was about to collapse, and this would allow the Germans to transfer some 2 million troops to the Western Front for their 1918 spring offensives. If the Western Allies had then been defeated, as seemed quite likely, the United States would have had to confront a Germany astride the whole continent, dominating European Russia, and in alliance with Austria-Hungary and the Ottoman Empire, extending her influence over the Balkans and the Middle East as far as the Persian Gulf. This would have posed a grave threat to American security, since Germany would have been in substantial control of the Heartland and the European Rimland. The United States, therefore, had good reason to ally herself with Britain and France to safeguard her own security before this menacing situation matured. But she did not— and would not have, if Germany had not launched its unrestricted submarine warfare in the spring of 1917.

The United States thus entered the war in a political vacuum. The American people were never aware of the power realities and security interests which made American participation in the war absolutely necessary. Rather, they believed they were fighting a war for freedom and democracy, conducting a crusade to destroy German despotism and militarism and to banish power politics forever. It is hardly surprising, therefore, that once the war had burned out this crusading spirit, the American public, still blissfully unaware of the relationship between American independence and the balance of power, should again wish to retire into its prewar isolationist state. The United States thus refused to help protect herself, although Britain and France had been exhausted by the four years of fighting and Germany remained second only to the United States as potentially the most powerful country in the world. We refused to face the responsibility that attended the possession of great power. Instead of playing our proper role in world affairs and attempting to preserve the international balance, thereby heading off the next war, we buried our head in the sand for more than twenty years. The result was that a renascent Germany—allied this time with Italy and Japan (plus the Soviet Union from 1939 to 1941)—once again sought to dominate the world. In December, 1941, Japan's attack on Pearl Harbor precipitated the American entry into World War II. Our ostrich policy had not prevented the waves of world politics from once more lapping our shores.

This American depreciation of power, so evident in these events, has meant that the United States draws a clear-cut distinction between war and peace in its approach to foreign policy. Peace is characterized by a state of harmony among nations; power politics, or war, is considered abnormal. In peacetime, one need pay little or no attention to foreign problems; indeed, to do so would divert men from their individual materialistic concerns and upset the whole scale of social values. The effect of this attitude is clear: Americans turn their attention toward the outside world only with the greatest reluctance and only when provoked—that is, when the foreign menace has become so clear that it can no longer be ignored. Or, to state it somewhat differently, the United States rarely initiates policy; the stimuli which are responsible for the formulation of American foreign policy come from beyond America's frontiers.

Once Americans are provoked, however, and the United States has to resort to force, the employment of this force can be justified only in terms of the universal moral principles with which the United States, as a democratic country, identifies itself. Resort to this evil instrument, war, can be justified only by presuming noble purposes and completely destroying the immoral enemy who threatens the integrity, if not the existence, of these principles. American power must be "righteous" power; only its full exercise can ensure salvation or the absolution of sin. The national aversion to violence thus becomes transformed into a national glorification of violence, and our wars become ideological crusades to make the world safe for democracy—by democratizing it or by converting the authoritarian or totalitarian states into peaceful, democratic states and thereby banishing power politics for all time. Once that aim has been achieved, the United States can again withdraw into itself, secure in the knowledge that American works have again proved to be "good works." In this context, foreign affairs are an annoying diversion from more important domestic matters. But such diversions are only temporary, since maximum force is applied to the aggressor or warmonger to punish him for his provocation and to teach him that aggression is immoral and will not be rewarded. As a result, American wars are total wars—that is, wars aimed at the total destruction of the enemy.

Not only does the American approach to international politics consider peace and war as two mutually exclusive states of affairs; it also divorces force from diplomacy. In peacetime, diplomacy unsupported by force is supposed to preserve the harmony among states. But in wartime, political considerations are subordinated to force. Once the diplomats have failed to keep the peace with appeals to morality and reason, military considerations become primary. During war, the soldier is placed in charge. Just as the professional medical man has the responsibility for curing his patients of their several maladies, so the military "doctor" must control the curative treatment of the international society when it is infected with the disease of power politics. General Douglas MacArthur has aptly summed up this attitude: when diplomacy has failed to preserve the peace, he said, "you then go to force; and when you do that, the balance of control . . . is the control of the military. A theater commander, in any campaign, is not merely limited to the handling of his troops; he commands the whole area politically, economically, and militarily. . . . when politics fail, and the military take over, you must trust the military."

The United States, then, has traditionally rejected the concept of war as a political instrument and the Clausewitzian definition of war as the continuation of politics by other means. Instead, it has regarded war as a politically neutral operation which should be guided by its own professional rules and imperatives. The military officer is a nonpolitical man who conducts his campaign in a strictly military, technically efficient manner. And war is a purely military instrument whose sole aim is the destruction of the enemy's forces and of his despotic regime so that his people can be democratized.

War is thus a means employed to abolish power politics; war is conducted to end all wars. This same moralistic attitude which is responsible for our all-or-nothing approach to war—either to abstain from the dirty game of power politics or to crusade for its complete elimination—also militates against the use of diplomacy in its classical sense: to compromise interests, to conciliate differences, and to moderate and isolate conflicts. While, on the one hand, Americans regard diplomacy as a rational process for straightening out misunderstandings between nations, they are, on the other hand, extremely suspicious of diplomacy. If the United States is by definition moral, it obviously cannot compromise; for a nation endowed with a moral mission can hardly violate its own principles. That would constitute appeasement and national humiliation. The nation's principles would be transgressed, the nation's interests improperly defended, the national honor stained. For to compromise with the immoral enemy is to be contaminated with evil. Moreover, to reach a settlement with him, rather than wiping him out in order to safeguard our principles, would be a recognition of our weakness. This attitude toward diplomacy which, in effect, prevents its use as an instrument of compromise thus reinforces our predilection for war as a means of settling our international problems. For war allows us to destroy our evil opponent, while permitting us to keep our moral mission intact and unsullied by any compromises which could infect our purity.

The result of this depreciation of power and moralistic approach to foreign policy is the inability of the United States to relate military power to political objectives. Yet, only if the two are combined can a nation conduct an effective foreign policy. Diplomacy, as an instrument by which the nation's interests are guarded without resort to force, cannot achieve its aims unless it is supported by military strength. It is precisely this strength which safeguards a nation's interests and enables it to head off crises, instead of having to pay the terrible costs of war involved in actually applying this force once the threat has become clear. Power can be employed in administering pressure upon an opponent, forcing him to be conciliatory if he wishes to avoid a clash. Military strength, in short, can act as an incentive for an adversary to compromise; for if he is unwilling to be conciliatory, he is faced with the prospect of defeat in battle. A diplomacy unsupported by a proper military power and strategy thus spells impotence. Good intentions by themselves are insufficient and must be supplemented by power. It may be true, as some like to say, that right is might; but superior moral ideals, unsupported by a political and military strategy, inevitably lead to their self-defeat. Faith without works, as Christianity has taught us, is not enough.

In the past, American foreign policy has not been characterized by such a happy marriage between diplomacy and force. Even when the United States has been involved in foreign affairs, its policy has featured the divorce of political aims from military strategy. In peacetime, the United States has, at best, possessed a skeleton military establishment; and during hostilities, it has simply maximized its strength to achieve total defeat of the enemy. American diplomacy in peacetime has been paralyzed by a lack of strength; during war, purely military objectives have become paramount. The American approach to foreign policy has been an all-or-nothing affair, characterized by either complete abstention and impotence or total commitment and strength.

The situation which faced the United States in 1945, however, no longer allowed her to abstain from this struggle. The Soviet threat required a long-range policy which would effectively combine the political, military, and economic factors of power; above all, it demanded a permanent commitment. There could be no disengagement from this conflict if the United States wished to survive as a free nation. Engagement was the only course.

An Appraisal of American Foreign Policy

William G. Carleton

American achievements in foreign policy since 1945 had been great, greater than most Americans realized. In 1946 the Russians were threatening Trieste, Greece, Turkey, and Iran; they had vast economic claims in West Germany; France looked to the East as much as to the West; the Germans were sullen and disliked the West almost as much as the East; the European economy was shattered; all Europe lay defenseless (except for fear of the atomic bomb) before any Russian attack. Since that time barriers had been thrown up before Trieste, Greece, Turkey, and Iran; Yugoslavia had become a partial ally; the Russians had been shut out of West Germany; France had become an ally of the West; West Germany had come into the Western community; Europe had survived economically; and the Russians no longer had an open and easy path to aggression. NATO had performed a noteworthy job. Even by 1954, the Allies could mass over 500,000 men on the critical German front against the Soviet 300,000. NATO was greatly strengthened by Germany's admission in 1954 and by Germany's subsequent rearmament, still behind schedule, however, in 1957. By 1956, Allied countries from Norway to Turkey could provide a common command of well over a hundred divisions—armed, equipped, based, and in position. More and more NATO bases and fields were being erected. The number of minesweepers, jet planes, and tactical atomic weapons available to NATO continued to mount.

One of the most constructive measures had been the Marshall Plan, which did so much to restore the war-exhausted European economies, weaken Communist parties and the forces of subversion, and lay the basis for much greater economic cooperation among the nations of western Europe. However, the promise of the Marshall Plan to regenerate the European economy and revolutionize its technological and managerial methods was left unfulfilled by the virtual cutting off of economic aid.

In Asia, the American record was less impressive, but not as unsatisfactory as many supposed. Red China, in spite of fears of Chinese aggression in southern Asia, was involved in herculean tasks of internal development. Besides, technological backwardness in Asia allowed more time there than in Europe for the development of a constructive program.

It may reasonably be argued that by concentrating on the sheer power phase of the world situation, by insisting on rearmament and by building military alliances, the United States contributed decisively to preventing Soviet aggressions and subversions and even an overt Soviet attempt to upset the balance of power, and to so restraining the Soviet Union in general as to rescue many of the new nations of Asia and many of the new social revolutions from inclusion in a possible Eurasian-tight monolithism, thus helping to keep the developing civilization of the future flexible, diverse, pluralistic, and free. The shift in Soviet tactics after 1953 may in part have been the result of Western rearmament and the West's military alliances.

By standing squarely against overt aggressions in Korea and in Egypt and by working through the United Nations to check such aggressions, the United States helped establish successful precedents for effective security by localized international actions, by actions which did not ripen into general wars.

Most notable, the United States exercised its vast power in such a manner as to earn the respect of many proud and suspicious nations, which had first feared an American "imperialism." American encouragement of a West European federation, which in the future might be a rival and competitor of the United States, was an action immediately expedient but certainly generous. The fact that the nations of western Europe wanted American troops stationed on the European continent and American air bases located there, that they regarded such troops and bases not as threats to their liberties but as guarantees of their liberties, is a tribute to the restrained uses of American power.

However, American foreign policy has also had its failures. In China, the absorption of the anti-imperialist revolution into the Communist Revolution was certainly a colossal American reverse. Yet it is difficult to see how the triumph of the Communist Revolution in China could have been averted without the large-scale intervention of the United States in behalf of Chiang Kai-shek, not only with supplies and arms but also with impressive American military forces, something which even the most rabid critics of America's China policy were never willing to advocate. After Chiang Kai-shek's Kuomintang deserted the principles of Sun Yat-sen and became increasingly corrupt and inefficient, no middle way, no nationalist, anti-imperialist, and social-democratic force appeared in China with sufficient strength to stand as a real alternative to Mao's communism, which itself claimed to be the heir of Sun's principles. In China, there was no middle ground between reaction and Red Revolution, no promising social-democratic center which the United States could support.

A partitioned Germany still stood as a supreme challenge to American foreign policy. Partition could be no final answer. As long as Germany remained truncated, every settlement in Europe—NATO, Western European Union, ECSC, and Euratom—remained provisional. Between Western integration and the reunification of Germany, Germans would overwhelmingly choose the unity of their country. Could both be accomplished peacefully? What, if any, bargain could be struck with the Russians which would allow this? Winston Churchill's suggestion of an Eastern Locarno, a mutual non-aggression and assistance pact in which the West, a reunited Germany, the Soviet, and Poland would all guarantee the German-Polish boundaries and promise to fight, if need be, to protect them from any violation, offered a tangible solution possibly acceptable to the Russians. Churchill had insisted that the justifiable fears of the Russians, the Poles, and the Czechs of a reunited Germany would have to be met by the West. This proposed Locarno, however, would have to overcome many obstacles. Could the German-Polish borders be drawn in a way satisfactory to both the Germans and the Poles? What of East Prussia, Silesia, and Polish occupation of eastern Germany to the Oder and the western Neisse? Would America guarantee the borders of a Poland under Soviet domination, and just how Titoist or independent would Poland have to be to justify such an American guarantee? Would Russia insist on a complete neutralization of Germany or only on a military neutralization, allowing Germany a free hand in integrating itself with the West on nonmilitary matters? Unattractive as Churchill's proposal seemed to most Americans, the further growth of truly independent Titoism in Poland and a relaxation of tensions, enough for the West to acquiesce in a military neutralization of Germany (West German withdrawal from NATO) which at the same time allowed Germany in all other matters to integrate with the West, might within the decade make some such plan feasible. But if a reunited and strong Germany were free to integrate itself in a nonmilitary way with western Europe, how could such integration be safely made? What would balance German power? Would not Germany soon dominate the various economic and functional combinations which gradually were coming to constitute the West European community? Merely to pose these questions shows how far we still are from a solution of the German question, which is the key to the future of Europe.

The Americans had failed to win the confidence of the anti-imperialist revolutions, those which had not merged with communism, to the degree that should have been "natural." The Americans had a long anti-colonial tradition and were committed to self-determination of peoples. Yet Americans had not made the most of this, and they seemed to forget that Jefferson, Franklin, Lincoln, Whitman, Twain, Wilson, and the second Roosevelt were inspiring names among many of the leaders of the anti-colonial revolutions. And the Americans were still having trouble understanding the collectivist movements abroad and the social aspects and the indigenous collectivism inherent in the anti-imperialist revolutions, and hence they were still having difficulty playing constructive social politics. It should have been obvious by 1957 that to stand for constructive social politics (for a limited and nontotalitarian collectivism) abroad was no betrayal of free enterprise at home, because conditions abroad were so different from conditions in North America. And it was no excuse to say that the United States had to take into consideration the sensitivity of the old colonial powers, particularly Britain and France, which were its chief allies, because the nature of the anti-imperialist revolutions was well understood in those countries. Britain had voluntarily withdrawn from most of its Asian empire, and large elements in Britain, not only the Bevanites but also the Attlee and Gaitskell Labourites, most of the Liberals, and even many of the Conservatives, would have welcomed a bold American program of constructive social politics in the underdeveloped countries. Indeed, there were repeated complaints by prominent Britons that American policy emphasized the military too much and the social too little.

The most surprising failure, because of America's vaunted boast that it stood for the market economy and for international capitalism, was America's continued economic nationalism. Indeed, it seemed that while America had abandoned political isolation it had clung to economic isolation. The ugly dollar-gap appeared year after year. Eventually this might contribute to an economic depression in the West, or to greater economic federation in West Europe, or to both.

Nevertheless, by mid-century it was fairly clear that the twentieth century probably would prove to be the most constructive century in the world's history. The new nationalism at work in the world had within itself an international cooperativeness, even a federative tendency, which the old nationalism had never had. And the great scientific, technological, anti-imperialist, and social revolutions of the time gave promise of a vastly better life for the mass of mankind. Dynamic American capitalism, Keynesianism, social democracy, and even communism were making gigantic inroads into mass poverty, disease, and ignorance. However, the world's rising population, as neo-Malthusians pointed out, and the armaments race, with attendant terrors of atomic war, posed threats to the world's economy. A mitigating circumstance was the fact that the world was becoming more aware of these threats.

By mid-century, too, it was also fairly clear that in several senses the twentieth century was to be an American century. The Americans had assumed the leadership of the non-Soviet world. The Americans had taken theoretical nuclear physics, mostly developed in western Europe, and developed atomic energy, which, if it did not lead to total disaster, would likely contribute enormously to the world's growing abundance. It might also, because of mutual terrors, do what all the world's great ethical teachers had thus far failed to do, lead to peace, to a *pax atomica*. And paradoxically, even the great social revolutions among the backward peoples, even the Communist revolutions, were being inspired by American example, because a dynamic drive behind the social revolutions was to get *American* technology and mass production in a hurry. Even in the Soviet Union, Henry Ford was a hero along with Karl Marx, in actual practice probably more of a hero. But this would be robbed of some of its paradox should the Communist societies, because of social and class pluralization produced by this very industrialism, be forced eventually to liberalize or burst their rigid Marxist bonds.

American Opinion and American Foreign Policy

Nearly two decades after Pearl Harbor, American opinion still reflected traditional American sentiments with respect to foreign policy, but in altered proportions. It also reflected some new attitudes born of recent experience.

First, there were the idealistic or doctrinaire internationalists who still conceived of international organization in terms of completed or near-perfect systems. The World Federalists represented this view, and so also did those who would abolish the big-five veto in the United Nations and in other drastic ways so revolutionize the organization as to imperil its very existence. This group was a declining one.

Second, there were the unilateralists, who inclined to think that America could still go it alone, could follow the policy Senator Taft had described as that of the free hand. The unilateralists fell roughly into two groups: the isolationists and the imperialists.

The isolationists in turn were composed of two wings: the pacifists and the nationalists. The pacifists came largely from the evangelical and pietistic Protestant sects, and many of them hovered between isolationism and doctrinaire internationalism. The career of W. J. Bryan had reflected this hesitation between isolationist pacifism and platonic internationalism. The nationalists believed that America's peculiar geographical position still gave it a relative immunity from the world's troubles and that the power and ideological conflicts among the European and Asian countries would so embroil them as to lead to Eurasian balances and counterbalances, leaving the United States in a relatively safe position. These views were exemplified in the writings of Charles A. Beard, which still carried weight with a diminishing number of Americans. Sometimes the nationalist and the pacifist merged, as in Herbert Hoover. Hoover's concept of "a defense perimeter" and "a Western Hemisphere bastion" may have had in it a measure of lingering Quakerism. Paradoxically, if Hoover's policy were to prevail it would be largely because a majority came to believe that the new cataclysmic weapons had altered old basic concepts of war in such a way as to make America's defense less dependent on vast ground forces abroad.

The other branch of the unilateralists, the imperialists, were the spiritual heirs of Albert J. Beveridge and William Randolph Hearst. The imperialists were represented by General MacArthur and by Senators McCarthy and Knowland, and they believed that America's allies did not give sufficient support to American ideas and American foreign policy and that the United States, because of its wealth, power, and responsibility, ought to go ahead with bold pro-Chiang, pro-Rhee policies of its own in Asia, even at the cost of separation from its allies and alienation of neutralist opinion in Asia. This group was not reconciled to the permanency of the Red Revolution in China, and it believed that China could still be redeemed from the Communists.

Nationalists and imperialists found much in common besides their unilateralism: both were suspicious of Britain, both found much popular support among Americans of German and Irish descent, both tended to a doctrinaire view of free enterprise yet clung to mercantilist trade policies, both disliked the collective elements in the anti-imperialist revolutions, both looked upon social politics abroad as "globaloney" and "Afghanistanism," both increasingly played upon American fears of inflation as an additional argument for paring foreign aid.

Third, there were the cooperationists, those who believed in formulating American foreign policy in close consultation and concert with other governments. Their approach was pragmatic: they would cooperate both within the United Nations and within a series of power-politics alliances. The cooperationists refused to compartmentalize the world; they tended to view all aspects of foreign policy as an integrated whole. For instance, the cooperationists had seen clearly that the heavy sacrifices of the French in Indo-China had made France timid in Europe, had made her more fearful of a revived and rearmed Germany. They also saw that if southeast Asia fell to the Communists, Japan —a deficit area needing Asian trade—would be cut off from the continent and face permanent economic dislocation. What would happen then to the defense-perimeter strategy based on Japan and other Pacific islands? The cooperationists clearly predominated in the Democratic Party, and they were represented in the Republican Party by the majority Willkie-Vandenberg-Dulles-Dewey-Eisenhower wing. The cooperationists had largely formulated postwar American policy, although there were times when they had had to yield to other views. There had been much yielding in economic policy to the nationalists, and in China policy to the imperialists. In most international political matters the cooperationists were clearly the stronger, but in economic matters, conceptions of American self-interest were still more on the side of the nationalists.

By 1957, the cooperationists tended to divide into two wings. One wing emphasized the sheer power phase of the world situation. Members of this wing insisted that America should make use of allies, whatever their ideology, who had effective power now and the will to use it. In this view, an alliance with Chiang, Rhee, and Franco should always take precedence over winning the friendship of weak and wavering countries like Burma and India and Indonesia, the alliance with Britain and France should always take precedence over winning the friendship of the weak and "erratic" Arab states. The other wing insisted that while effective power was important, so also were ideology, the good will of the mass populations of the new and rising nations, and the integrity of collective security. This wing tended to move in its thinking toward the Asian-African bloc and to resist even Britain and France when these powers violated collective-security principles.

What was the attitude of America's powerful business community toward international affairs? The cooperationists were strong among those businessmen who represented international banking and gigantic industries like steel, automobiles, electrical equipment—those more and more interested in foreign markets. These wanted to revive, with some modifications, the mid-nineteenth-century world of international capitalism. They looked with increasing favor on a real revolution in America's tariff policies. The center of this group was New York. The nationalists were strong among those whose markets were almost exclusively in the United States. Their center was Chicago. If events should push the nationalists toward imperialism, that imperialism likely would be neomercantilistic.

It was remarkable the way the Eisenhower policies managed more or less to satisfy almost all elements in American opinion. The Administration's new look and its cutbacks in the armed forces pleased the unilateralists, while its essential policies still pleased the cooperationists. The Administration had maintained the alliances with Chiang, Rhee, and Franco, yet it was friendly with Tito, moved considerably in the direction of the Asian-African bloc, and did not hesitate to invoke collective-security measures against Britain and France in the Suez crisis. In making specific decisions on tariff rates under the reciprocal trade program, Eisenhower alternated between pleasing the nationalists and pleasing the free-traders.

That some nationalistic attitudes persisted in American opinion and American policy should not be surprising, because national interest is still the pivot of a nation's foreign policy. It would be a long time before Americans or any other nationals agreed that what was good for the world was also always and necessarily good for their particular country. Nor is it unusual for a country taking the lead in international politics to intersperse parochial and seemingly archaic and inconsistent policies among its international policies. Many a Roman of Augustan times carried into his world imperialism Catoesque misgivings and throw-backs, and in many ways the British carried their "insularity" and their "little England" attitudes and policies into their nineteenth-century world policies. It was naïve to think that American isolationist and unilateralist attitudes and policies would disappear. They would, of course, continue to affect Americans and American policies for a long time to come. Even many of America's political cooperationists were nationalists in trade policies. And all Americans, cooperationists as well as unilateralists, were at times beset by hesitation, doubt, and even gloom about American leadership in world affairs. Now power politics would get in the way of collective security, and then collective security would get in the way of power politics. Americans were still having trouble understanding the collectivist movements abroad, and the social aspects of the anti-colonial revolutions, and hence they were still having difficulty playing constructive social politics.

In spite of their leadership and their achievements, the dominant mood of Americans with respect to the world was a profound pessimism. So deep was the gloom in certain quarters that there was some danger that a national neurosis, a self-guilt complex, was developing. Americans were soul-searching: Were they responsible for the fall of China? Why had they dismantled German industry? Why had they demobilized in 1945? Why had Truman pulled back American troops in Germany? Why had not Roosevelt let Truman in on the secrets of foreign policy? What was there in the American form of government which produced a deadly hiatus after Roosevelt's death? Why had Roosevelt acted as he did at Yalta? Why had Americans got into World War II? Why had they not joined the League of Nations? Why had they got into World War I? Was it really true that Americans no longer had any real freedom to choose the degree of their world participation? Why had those Democratic Presidents got them into those "foreign wars"? Few Americans saw clearly that the world troubles of their time went back to deep-seated historic forces with roots in the pre-1914 era, fewer still discerned that they were probably threading their way to a new world, a better and more stable world than the pre-1914 world had been.

The pessimism notwithstanding, there was no possibility of a return to the old isolation or the old policy of the free hand. Americans were in world politics, mostly as cooperationists, to stay; and they were learning. They were learning that foreign policy is never-ending and that it cannot be turned on and off; that tensions and crisis situations are more or less normal; that there are many aspects and many values involved in any given international situation; that problems are rarely solved, and never completely and one-sidedly; that there are few short cuts and summary grand actions that do not backfire; that the "solutions" to given problems are likely in turn to lead to new problems and challenges.

Americans were learning, too, that there is no single approach to international relations. At first the American approach had been legalistic and moralistic. Then after 1945 Americans discovered the importance of power, of power-politics, and they tended to put too much reliance on armaments and military alliances. Now they were learning that power, vastly important as it is, is not the only or even always the decisive factor in international relations. Americans were learning that foreign policy, if it is to touch reality at all points, must avoid the single-track approach and be positively and avow-edly pluralistic, as diverse and varied as history, as inclusive as life itself.

However, the kind of pluralism existing in the world would not always square with the kind of pluralism existing in America. Moreover, while America was the most multi-group society in the world, it also had more consensus on its basic social values—the essential goodness of a liberal-capitalist, middle-class, democratic society—than any other country in the free world. It was inevitable that America's "monolithic liberalism" in ide-ology would sometimes conflict with social values elsewhere, even with the varied social values of its allies in the free world. And to add to the complex-ity, America's multi-group society resulted, in practical and specific situations, in the application of more pressure on the American government than on any other government in the world. Then too, American leaders were not drawn from an inbred aristocratic elite as were those of Britain when Britain was the leading power in the world; nor were they drawn from a monolithic party elite as were the Soviet leaders. The American consensus on basic social values would make the American foreign policy, in the long run, ideologically con-sistent, if not always realistic. But America's multi-group pressures would frequently make the application of American foreign policy in practical and specific situations inconsistent and even ambivalent. These were basic ele-ments in the American society which time and international experience were unlikely to alter. This consensus on American social values vis-à-vis the rest of the world and this process of diverse group conflict and compromise at home with respect to specific measures abroad would continue to make the formu-lation of American foreign policy extraordinarily difficult.

No More Vietnams?

Ronald Steel

Yesterday's heresy becomes today's cliché. What a few years ago would have been labeled as isolationist, if not vaguely traitorous, is now the new orthodoxy. "We cannot impose ideals on others and still call ourselves men of peace," President Nixon declared, in outlining a new low posture for the United States and a scaling down of foreign commitments. This is a far cry from John Kennedy's summons to "pay any price, bear any burden, meet any hardship, support any friend, oppose any foe to assure the survival and the success of liberty" anywhere in the world. And it is welcome deflation from Lyndon Johnson's proclamation in the Inaugural Address of January 1965 that "the American covenant called on us to help show the way for the liberation of man."

After Vietnam, the Dominican Republic, and the Greek junta, it is not so easy for an American President to speak with a straight face of the nation's foreign policy being based on the "liberation of man" or the "survival of liberty." The self-glorifying rhetoric of the 1960s has given way to a more studied pragmatism based on the old concepts of self-interest and balance of power. "Our interests," President Nixon has told us, "must shape our commitments, rather than the other way around." Being a good politician, he recognizes that the nation is fed up with self-assumed obligations to set the world right and with undeclared wars conducted under the tattered banners of a discredited globalism.

No more Vietnams is what the public wants. Yet it is not enough to say that we made a mistake and won't do it again. Most people still believe that the war in Vietnam is some kind of aberration, an event totally without precedent in our national history, and one that will never happen again. But this is to ignore Korea, Lebanon, and Cuba. What is unique about Vietnam is not the fact of our intervention, but its scale. It has already cost some $100 billion, tied down three-quarters of a million men around Southeast Asia, and taken more casualties than the Korean War. Did we stumble into it by accident? Hardly. The war was a result of a succession of conscious political decisions made by three successive American presidents. Rather than a new departure in our way of looking at the world, it was quite consistent with the unexpressed principles of our foreign policy. Vietnam happened because it was time for it to happen, because we had the military power to make it happen.

Vietnam is precisely the kind of war the American military machine, as perfected in the mid-1960s, was designed to fight. When he came to power, John F. Kennedy inherited a military strategy based on "massive retaliation" with nuclear weapons. Clearly such a strategy was ineffective in dealing with the revolutionary disturbances shaking the Third World and imperiling American influence in such areas as the Caribbean and Southeast Asia. The ability to fight "limited war," Kennedy told Congress in a special defense message in March 1961, should be the "primary mission" of our overseas forces. An avid reader of the manuals of Mao and Che, Kennedy believed that guerrillas had to be met on their own terrain if forces of "national liberation" were to be defeated. Robert McNamara was brought in to reorganize the Pentagon and set up amphibious strike forces. In such cold-war intellectuals as Walt Rostow, Maxwell Taylor, Roger Hilsman, and Richard Bissell, Kennedy found zealous advocates for the new counter-guerrilla warfare. Kennedy ordered the expansion of the Special Forces training center at Fort Bragg, and, over the Army's objections, reinstated the green beret as the symbol of the new counter-guerrilla elite force. In the fall of 1961 General Taylor, head of the Counter-Insurgency Committee, went to Vietnam with Walt Rostow and returned urging increased American intervention, including a military task force. In December Kennedy ordered the military build-up to begin.

The arms race took a dramatic jump during the next few years. Billions of dollars flowed into the Pentagon to increase American nuclear superiority and to provide weapons to fight insurrectionary movements in the Third World. The liberals around Kennedy believed they had a mission to bring about an American-style peace based upon political stability and economic development. They saw the underdeveloped nations achieving "take-off" points to economic growth through infusions of foreign aid and technical expertise. And they were convinced that world peace and American security demanded an ideological balance of power. They were ready to intervene wherever necessary to maintain that balance. American military power—both nuclear missiles and conventional forces—had been increased precisely for that purpose. After the Cuban missile crisis of October 1962, when they took the world to the brink of nuclear war and successfully faced down the Russians, they were ready to intervene wherever it seemed necessary.

Vietnam provided the opportunity in the guise of an obligation. Although American intervention in Vietnamese affairs extended back to the early 1950s, Eisenhower had clearly set the limits of American assistance to Saigon. The liberal interventionists, however, were eager to show that wars of national liberation would not pay. Vietnam was their showcase. When Diem failed to live up to their expectations, and when his brother showed signs of political independence verging on talks with the North Vietnamese, the right-wing generals were allowed to get rid of him. With the murder of Diem the legitimacy of the Saigon regime was undermined. This was followed shortly by Kennedy's assassination and the intensified American commitment to an anti-communist government in Saigon.

Under President Johnson, who eagerly embraced their theories of "nation-building" and communist containment, the liberals lost control of the war. Yet they dug in more deeply to vindicate themselves and the views they held. Vietnam was their war. "It took a visionary liberal administration," William Pfaff has written, "fully to translate the globalism of American rhetoric into a program of national action. Vietnam was deliberately made into a test of liberal international reform by the Kennedy and Johnson administrations—of liberal 'nation building,' carried on behind a shield of green beret counter-insurgent warfare—against the Asian communist 'model' of radical national transformation."

By the time of Lyndon Johnson's electoral triumph, on a platform of peace and social reform, the Pentagon was ready for the full-scale military intervention that had been engineered in the White House. "McNamara's prodigious labors to strengthen and broaden the US military posture were about completed," according to Townsend Hoopes, a Pentagon official who turned against the war, ". . . US 'general purpose' forces were now organized to intervene swiftly and with modern equipment in conflicts of limited scope, well below the nuclear threshold." In February 1965 Johnson began the bombing of North Vietnam, in June American troops were officially authorized to enter combat, and in July the President ordered an increase in American forces from 75,000 to 125,000. Within four years Kennedy's 16,000 "advisers" had swollen to an American expeditionary force of half a million men, and the Vietnamese civil war became an American war. As the economist Joseph Schumpeter wrote of ancient Egypt's military forces, "created by wars that required it, the machine now created the wars it required."

We intervened from a euphoria of power, generated in part by our success in the Cuban missile crisis and our military superiority over the Russians. The liberals wanted to prove that guerrilla wars were not the wave of the future, and were determined to keep South Vietnam as an anti-communist outpost in Southeast Asia. But they grossly underestimated the price.

As the cost of intervention mounted, so the rhetoric rose to meet the occasion. What began as a military-aid program to a harassed neo-colonial outpost that had been abandoned by the French and picked up by Dulles was transformed into a full-scale war. The very scale of our intervention transformed the Vietnamese civil war into a test of American resolve. By our intervention we created the problem that was used to justify our involvement.

As the scale of war increased, so Washington sought various theories to explain why it was worth the cost. First it was to help our friends in the South deal with communist-led insurgents. Then it was to push back an "aggression" from the North, although Hanoi's troops did not enter the war until after the American intervention. We were there, it was said, to honor our treaty commitments, although the SEATO treaty provided only for consultation in case of attack, or to stop that amorphous but virulent force known simply as "Asian communism," or even to prevent the miraculously amphibious Chinese from invading southern California and speeding east along the interstate highway system. Vietnam, we were told, was a test case for wars of national liberation, and if the Vietcong were defeated, guerrillas from the Andes to the Sahara would turn in their rifles and slink home. In a moment of desperation, Lyndon Johnson even evoked the principle of envy, declaring that "they want what we've got," thereby suggesting that we are in Vietnam to defend electric carving knives and remote control TV from the greedy hands of the Vietcong. Later President Nixon, pursuing Johnson's policies while changing his tactics, again trotted out the balance-of-power theory, saying that to abandon the Saigon generals "would threaten our long-term hopes for peace in the world."

Nearly a year after assuming office with a promise to end the war, President Nixon presented a plan which called for the gradual withdrawal of American combat troops and their replacement by South Vietnamese soldiers. The plan was tendered as a supplement to the peace talks in Paris between the United States and North Vietnam. Yet it was clearly meant as an alternative to negotiations, since no nation would reduce its military power in the field while conducting negotiations on its own withdrawal. The purpose of "Vietnamization," as Walter Lippmann pointed out, was "not to buy concessions from Hanoi with our military withdrawal, but to buy patience and endurance from the American people for an indefinitely long American occupation in South Vietnam."

Vietnamization cleverly defused popular opposition to the war by withdrawing some of the troops while retaining the bases and the commitment to an anti-communist South Vietnam. Its drawback, as Hoopes observed, was that it committed the American people "to the endless support of a group of men in Saigon who represented nobody but themselves, preferred war to the risks of a political settlement, and could not remain in power more than a few months without our large-scale assistance." Yet what could the American people do about it? In the elections of 1964 and 1968 they twice voted for peace, first in rejecting Barry Goldwater and electing a man who said he would not send American boys to die in Vietnam, and then in repudiating the Humphrey-Johnson administration. Both times their wishes were ignored by presidents who circumvented Constitutional restrictions and pursued the war on their own authority for reasons they declared to be vital to the national interest.

If elections cannot change foreign policy, what is the validity of the political process? If Americans can be sent to die in battle as a result of decisions made by the executive branch, what is the meaning of the Constitutional obligation of Congress to declare acts of war? Traditional politics no longer provides a solution for political ills or implements the popular will. This has led to an increasing emphasis on direct action, on popular participation, on decentralization, and, when all else seems to fail, on violence. Unable to affect the decisions that control their lives—whether they be on the wars they die in, the polluted air they breathe, or the schools where their children fail to receive an education—the American people are driven to strike out against bureaucracy and many of the very principles of government that they have been trained to take for granted.

There has been a crisis of faith in the political process, just as there has been in the realm of science and technology. We have learned that technology destroys even as it creates, and that its gifts, such as DDT and the internal-combustion engine, are bought with our own lives. Our faith in man's future has been shaken as we realize that in the name of progress the very forces that make possible human life on the earth are being tampered with and perhaps inadvertently destroyed. In our political life, as in our personal lives, we are repelled by the cult of bigness, and are turning, more in desperation than in hope, to various forms of decentralization. Those who once believed that only big government could solve the problems of a complex society now put an equally abiding faith in the virtues of the local community.

Both radicals and reactionaries profess to find salvation in local control, the former in flight from the technology and the war machine that are oppressing their lives, the latter in an effort to hold on to the old ways. To both the Right and the Left, government itself has become a kind of enemy, and faith in political solutions has broken down. The whole society is pervaded by a deep and destructive sense of powerlessness. Among conservatives this feeling seeks its outlet against those who threaten the established order—hippies, dropouts, militants. These are the people who chant that they love Mayor Daley and applaud police violence against young demonstrators. Among radicals this alienation and powerlessness results in desperate attempts to change unresponsive institutions. The universities, of course, are the obvious targets because there the ideals of community seem most betrayed by arbitrary and unresponsive administrators. This feeling was well expressed by the student newspaper at the Santa Barbara campus of the University of California, following rioting, mass arrests, and destruction: "If we have any community at all, it is a community based on common frustrations—born of powerlessness, alienation from one's pre-programmed life, and contempt for authoritarian institutions." It is a complaint that even conservatives could share, for it is a common American condition.

Vietnam intensified, although it did not create, this sense of powerlessness, of being unable to affect the decisions that can, literally, mean the difference between life and death. The war took perfectly decent young Americans, taught them to use napalm and machine guns, sent them across the world to a totally alien society with instructions to kill "communists," and justified this in the name of freedom. It is not surprising that some of our most sensitive young people, rather than fight a war they consider morally wrong, have preferred to go to jail or seek a saner life in another country. Nor is it even surprising that atrocities like those at Songmy have occurred, for the kind of war we are fighting in Vietnam is a brutalizing experience. It infects everything we do, and comes back to haunt us at home. We were all at Songmy, in one way or another.

There is a great revulsion in this country against the rhetorical globalism of the past two decades. A Harris poll taken early in 1970 showed six out of ten people saying Vietnam was a terrible mistake, with a full one-third volunteering that "we should mind our own business and stop policing the world." In these results the pollsters found "overtones of a new isolationism." No doubt Americans are tired of the violence that has been committed in the name of peace, of the two wars fought since 1950 for objectives that seem increasingly specious and hypocritical, of the unending interventions that are conducted in the tired vocabulary of anti-communism, of the sacrifice of their own social needs to an insatiable war machine that declares itself to be the repository of patriotism. No doubt they see no reason why more money should be spent on MIRVs and ABMs when America and Russia have already stockpiled nuclear weapons with the explosive power of fifteen tons of TNT for every man, woman, and child on earth. But the people have always wanted peace, and they rarely get it—particularly when their leaders believe they have the power to obtain what they want by force of arms.

America is not aggressive by nature. As great powers go, it has been relatively restrained in its use of force. But it has undeniably used its power aggressively, not only in Vietnam, but in the Spanish-American war, and in seizing half of Mexico in the war of 1848. So long as that power is untempered, it will be used whenever military and political leaders think it should be used. So long as we have a military machine anywhere near its present size, it will always find work for itself to do. It will have bases to defend in one or another of the various unstable and revolution-prone countries of the Third World. It will issue solemn assurances, as Air Force generals did in Vietnam early in 1965, that a few well-placed bombs will take care of revolutionaries and communists. And there will be government officials, on loan from corporations and universities, who will tell us that American military intervention is necessary for something noble-sounding like stability or self-determination.

After Korea everyone said there would be no more Koreas. And there weren't. But there was Vietnam. Now it is a cliché to say there will be no more Vietnams. And there probably won't be—in Vietnam. But unless our military power to fight counterrevolutionary wars is reduced, and unless our attitudes change, there might very well be further American military interventions in Asia and the Caribbean. Even while President Nixon asserted that our allies should be able to defend themselves, he declared regarding Asia that "we shall provide a shield if a nuclear power threatens the freedom of a nation allied with us, or of a nation whose security we consider vital to our security and the security of the region as a whole." We are allied with forty-two nations and, judging from past behavior, consider virtually every non-communist country in the world as being vital to our security. Does that mean we are supposed to go to war whenever the President considers it "vital"? Who gave him the authority to provide nuclear shields for whatever Asian nations he desires? Even while saying there must be no more Vietnams, the administration conducted a covert war in Laos and invaded Cambodia without bothering to inform its government or the American Congress.

The legacy of globalism still weighs heavily on American foreign policy. Having intervened actively for thirty years, it has become almost a reflex action. Whenever there is talk of retrenching commitments, the global interventionists raise the specter of isolationism. They say that the experience of Vietnam may induce us to turn inward and ignore our responsibilities to the rest of the world. The danger is exaggerated. With the world's most powerful economy and mightiest military force, the United States could never again be isolationist. Regardless of how many Americans might desire it, the nation's economic and political interests make it impossible.

Yet it might not be a bad thing if we did ignore some of our self-assumed "responsibilities" for building democratic, capitalistic nations out of feudal societies. The results of isolationism could, in most cases, hardly be much worse than the results of our interventionism, which, except for Europe, have ranged from the stupid, as in Lebanon, Cuba, and the Dominican Republic, to the tragic, as in Vietnam. They have brought no credit on us, nor have they appreciably advanced the causes of freedom and self-determination we are ostensibly promoting. It long ago became obvious, even before Tet and Songmy, that the best thing we could have done for the Vietnamese was to have left them alone. "We had to destroy the village in order to save it," an American officer said as his troops moved into a lifeless wasteland of devastated homes and mutilated bodies. It could be the epitaph for our whole adventure in Vietnam.

By now it is a truism to say that we ought to set our own house in order before we declare ourselves responsible for the welfare of the entire world. It might even be said that we don't have any idea of what the welfare of other societies might be, and not very much understanding of how to improve our own. The emphasis is now on national priorities and on saving this country from drowning in its own pollution, or turning into a police state, or descending into the savagery of a race war. But powerful voices like President Nixon's still cling to the old rhetoric and warn us of the disasters that would occur "if America were to become a dropout in assuming the responsibility for defending peace and freedom in the world."

It is questionable that such disasters would occur, since outside of Western Europe (and in such countries as Greece and Portugal, not even there) the United States has not been occupied in defending peace and freedom. It has simply sought to maintain the status quo and prevent revolutionary groups, particularly those led or thought to be led by communists, from coming to power. The moral imperatives of our foreign policy, our interventions in support of self-serving oligarchies and military strongmen, have never fooled anyone but ourselves. America is not going to be a dropout in defending her own interests. No nation is, if it has the strength to do otherwise. But America would do well to cease the hypocrisy which seeks to justify its interventions in the name of a higher morality. Then it might be easier for our officials, not to mention the public they are supposed to be serving, to distinguish between interventions necessary to defend the United States and its most intimate allies, and those which spring from a euphoria of power.

No more Vietnams? It would be unwise to take any bets on it. The heady rhetoric of the 1960s has been deflated, but great power still provides an irresistible temptation. There will be a danger of more Vietnams until there is a world power balance that will make such unilateral interventions far more hazardous. Only then are we likely truly to have "our interests . . . shape our commitments, rather than the other way around." Undeniably we have learned something from Vietnam. But it may be simply that we should never again intervene in Vietnam.

If we are to avoid more Vietnams, we have to shake loose from our global fantasies and begin our perfection of the human race within our own frontiers. There is certainly a great deal to do within a society which a century after the liberation of the slaves still has not been able to grant the Negro full equality, a society which is plagued by violence in the streets and guilt in the heart, a society which has achieved unprecedented material riches and yet is sick from a debilitating alienation, and where the ideals of American democracy are mocked by the reality of radical prejudice, where individual decency is in constant conflict with social irresponsibility, where prosperity has assured neither justice nor tolerance, where private affluence dramatizes the shame of public squalor, where wealth has brought psychoanalysis, and where power has bred anxiety and fear.

Vietnam has not caused our troubles, but it has clearly intensified them and made Americans aware of their severity. It is not only the ideals of the nation that are being tested, but its very survival as a free society. Our power has not brought us security, any more than our wealth has brought us tranquillity. Nor have the noble ideals on which this nation was founded insured social justice for the millions of Americans who, because of race, or poverty, or misfortune, have been excluded from the system and the benefits it is supposed to provide. The dispossessed are now finding a voice, and their cause is being taken up by young idealists on campuses and elsewhere who, despite the hostility of their elders and mounting repression by the authorities, maintain a persistent belief that the promise of American life can be made real to all Americans.

For more than three decades this country has been absorbed in foreign affairs, foreign aid, and foreign wars. In the remaining years of this decade, and of this century, it might be better for America, and for the world, if we turn to the needs of our own divided, unhappy, insecure society. When he visited this country a century ago, Thomas Huxley wrote:

I cannot say that I am in the slightest degree impressed by your bigness, or your material resources, as such. Size is not grandeur, and territory does not make a nation. The great issue, about which hangs the terror overwhelming fate, is what are you going to do with all these things?

What are we going to do with them? The task of diplomacy in the years ahead is not to remake the world in the American image through wars of intervention and a self-deceiving imperialism. Rather, it is to help create, in cooperation with others, a tolerable international order from which the fear of instantaneous obliteration has been lifted. Having failed to bring the world democracy, we can at least try to make it safe for diversity. America's worth to the world will not be measured by the solutions she seeks to impose on others, but by the degree to which she achieves her own ideals at home. That will be a fitting challenge to our ideals and a test of whether "any nation so conceived, and so dedicated, can long endure."

Militarism and Imperialism

Paul A. Baran
and Paul M. Sweezy

The American oligarchy's need for a huge military machine must be sought elsewhere than in a non-existent threat of Soviet aggression. Once we recognize this and free our minds of the cant and confusion generated by the oligarchy's ideological and propagandistic distortions, we shall soon discover what we are looking for: the same implacable hatred of socialism, the same determination to destroy it, that has dominated the leading nations of the capitalist world from the time the Bolsheviks seized power in November 1917. The central purpose has always been the same: to prevent the expansion of socialism, to compress it into as small an area as possible, and ultimately to wipe it off the face of the earth. What has changed with changing conditions are the methods and strategies used to achieve these unchanging goals. . . .

The implementation of this global policy of anti-Communism required, among other things, the following:

(1) The speediest rehabilitation and strengthening of the traditional centers of capitalist power and their integration into a military alliance dominated by the United States. These objectives were accomplished through the Marshall Plan, announced in June 1947, just three months after the Truman Doctrine; and through the North Atlantic Treaty Organization, negotiated during the next year and signed in April 1949. A similar turn in policy soon occurred in Japan, culminating in the signing of a separate peace treaty in 1951. The underlying conditions for the revival of capitalism in Western Europe and Japan were much more favorable than they appeared.

From Paul A. Baran and Paul M. Sweezy, *Monopoly Capital*, pp. 186–187, 190–207, 210–213. Reprinted by permission of the Monthly Review Press. Copyright © 1966 by Paul M. Sweezy.

Fixed capital and trained manpower were amply available; needed were large infusions of working capital, and these the United States was able to supply. In solving this problem, Washington may be said to have scored its one really large-scale, solid foreign policy success of the postwar period.

(2) The weaving of a network of military pacts and bases around the entire perimeter of the socialist bloc. This operation began with NATO and has been going on ever since. The network now includes, in addition to NATO, the Southeast Asia Treaty Organization, the Central Treaty Organization (originally known as the Baghdad Pact), and bilateral treaties or "mutual assistance" agreements with dozens of countries everywhere: Spain, Turkey, Pakistan, the Philippines, Formosa, Japan, and many others. By 1959, the United States had, according to Fleming, a total of 275 major base complexes in 31 countries and more than 1,400 foreign bases, counting all sites where Americans were then stationed and sites designed for emergency occupation. These bases cost nearly $4 billion and were manned by approximately a million American troops.

(3) Above all, United States policy required arms of all kinds and descriptions and the men to use them, to lend muscle and sinew to this world-wide skeleton of alliances, thus establishing the "positions of strength" from which the expansion of socialism could be stemmed and enough counter-pressure could in due course be brought to bear to force its retreat. Failing these objectives, the military establishment would be designed to be powerful enough to wage and win a war against the Soviet Union, thus clearing the way for the final liquidation of socialism by purely military means.

To sum up: the need of the American oligarchy for a large and growing military machine is a logical corollary of its purpose to contain, compress, and eventually destroy the rival world socialist system.

We cannot leave this subject of the need for military strength without inquiring into the causes of capitalist hostility to the existence of a rival world socialist system. If, as some people seem to think, this hostility is based largely on irrational prejudices and fears, like the sedulously cultivated belief in Soviet aggressiveness, then there would seem to be at least a chance that in time more rational views might come to prevail. In that case, peaceful coexistence and disarmament could be looked upon not as propaganda slogans in the struggle between the two systems but as realizable goals. On the other hand, if the prejudices and fears are, as so often happens, simply masks for deep-rooted interests, then we would have to assess the outlook differently.

First, we must dispose of one very common argument purporting to prove that the spread of socialism is a mortal threat to the existence of the capitalist system. It is often said that capitalism cannot exist without foreign trade and that every advance of socialism means a constriction of capitalism's trading area. Hence, the argument continues, for the leading capitalist countries, even if they are not threatened by powerful internal socialist movements, the struggle against socialism is quite literally a struggle for survival. Put in this form, the reasoning from capitalist interests involves a *non sequitur*. It is true that capitalism is inconceivable without foreign trade, but it is not true that socialist countries are unwilling or unable to trade with capitalist countries. Hence the spread of socialism taken by itself, does not imply any reduction of the trading area open to the capitalist countries. One can even go further. Bourgeois economists never tire of repeating that the more industrially developed a country is, the greater its potential as a trading partner. Since underdeveloped countries industrialize more rapidly under socialism than under capitalism, the leading capitalistic countries, on this argument, should welcome the spread of socialism in the underdeveloped parts of the capitalist world. That they do not but instead resist it tooth and nail must be explained on other grounds.

The problem is in reality much more complex and can only be fruitfully posed in quite different terms. Capitalist governments do not, in general, trade with each other. Most trade in the capitalist world is carried on by private enterprises, mainly by large corporations. What these corporations are interested in is not trade as such but profits: the reason they and the governments they control are opposed to the spread of socialism is not that it necessarily reduces their chances of importing or exporting (though of course it may), but that it does necessarily reduce their opportunities to profit from doing business with and in the newly socialized area. And when account is taken of the fact that for corporations in the leading capitalist countries, profit rates from doing business with and in the less developed and underdeveloped countries are generally higher than domestic profit rates, the reason for the vehemence of opposition to the spread of socialism in precisely those areas will be appreciated.

We advisedly use the general term "doing business with and in" rather than the more limited "buying from and selling to." The international relationships and interests of the typical giant corporation today are likely to be diverse and extremely complex, much more so than mere exporting or importing. There is perhaps no better way to make this clear than by summarizing the world-wide scope and character of what is unquestionably the leading United States "multinational corporation"—Standard Oil of New Jersey. The facts and figures which follow are taken from official publications of the company.

In terms of dollar assets, Jersey Standard is the largest industrial corporation in the United States, the total at the end of 1962 amounting to $11,488 million. Aggregate revenues for the same year were $10,567 million and net income (profit) $841 million. It is only when these figures are broken down geographically, however, that the crucial importance of foreign operations becomes clear. As of the end of 1958, the percentage distribution of assets and profits by regions was as follows:

	Assets	Profits
United States and Canada	67	34
Latin America	20	39
Eastern Hemisphere	13	27
Total	100	100

While two thirds of Jersey's assets were located in North America, only one third of its profits came from that region. Or to put the point differently, Jersey's foreign investments were half as large as its domestic investments but its foreign profits were twice as large as its domestic profits. The indicated profit rate abroad is thus four times the domestic rate.

That Jersey's operations are truly world-wide can be gathered from the facts that in 1962 the company sold its products in more than a hundred countries and owned 50 percent or more of the stock in 275 subsidiaries in 52 countries. Table I enumerates such subsidiaries by country of organization. Summarizing by regions, we find that Jersey had 114 subsidiaries in the United States and Canada, 77 in Europe, 43 in Latin America, 14 in Asia, 9 in Africa, and 18 elsewhere.

TABLE I   SUBSIDIARIES OF STANDARD OIL

United States	77	Switzerland	2
Canada	37	Uruguay	2
Great Britain	24	Venezuela	2
Panama	17	Algeria	1
France	12	Danzig	1
Bahamas	8	Dominican Republic	1
Italy	6	Egypt	1
Sweden	6	El Salvador	1
Colombia	5	Finland	1
Netherlands	5	Hungary	1
Australia	4	India	1
Brazil	4	Indonesia	1
Chile	4	Kenya	1
Germany	4	Luxembourg	1
Philippines	4	Madagascar	1
Argentina	3	Mexico	1
Denmark	3	New Zealand	1
Ireland	3	Paraguay	1
Japan	3	Peru	1
Netherlands Antilles	3	Republic of Congo	1
Norway	3	Singapore	1
Austria	2	South Africa	1
Belgium	2	Spain	1
Bermuda	2	Surinam	1
Iraq	2	Tunisia	1
Malaya	2		
Morocco	2	Total	275

The tremendous variety and scope of Jersey's foreign operations might lead one to suppose that over the years the company has been a large and consistent exporter of capital. Nothing could be further from the truth. Apart from a small initial export of capital many years ago, the expansion of Jersey's foreign assets has been financed from the profits of its foreign operations. Moreover, so great have been these foreign profits that after all foreign expansion needs have been taken care of, there have still been huge sums left over for remittance to the parent company in the United States. Separate figures on the amount of these remittances from foreign profits are not published, but an idea of the order of magnitude is conveyed by the following figures for 1962. In that year, as already noted, total profits were $841 million. Of this sum, $538 million were paid out as dividends to stockholders, the vast majority of whom are residents of the United States. The remaining $303 million were added to the company's investments, at home and abroad. Elsewhere in the same Annual Report that records these figures we learn that profits from operations in the United States in 1962 were $309 million. This figure, it will be seen, is $229 million less than the amount of dividends paid. In other words, approximately 40 percent of dividends paid to stockholders plus whatever net investment was made in the United States during the year were financed from the profits of foreign operations. In a word: Standard Oil of New Jersey is a very large and consistent *importer* of capital.

At this point, however, we must pause and ask whether Standard Oil of New Jersey is really an ideal type which helps us to distill the essence of capitalist reality, or whether on the contrary it may not be an exceptional case which we should ignore rather than focus attention on.

Up to the Second World War, it would have been correct to treat Standard Oil as a sort of exception—a very important one, to be sure, exercising tremendous, and at times even decisive, influence on United States world policy. Nevertheless in the multinational scope and magnitude of its operations not only was it far ahead of all the others; there were only a handful which could be said to be developing along the same lines. Many United States corporations of course had large interests in import and export trade, and quite a few had foreign branches or subsidiaries. In neither respect, however, was the situation much different in 1946 from what it had been in 1929. Indeed, direct foreign investments of United States corporations actually declined from $7.5 billion to $7.2 billion, or by 4 percent, between these two dates. Most of the giant corporations which dominated the American economy in those years were, in the words of *Business Week*, "domestically oriented enterprises with international operations" and not, like Standard Oil, "truly world oriented corporations."

A big change took place during the next decade and a half. To quote *Business Week* again, "In industry after industry, U.S. companies found that their overseas earnings were soaring, and that their return on investment abroad was frequently much higher than in the U.S. As earnings abroad began to rise, profit margins from domestic operations started to shrink . . . This is the combination that forced development of the multinational company." As a result, of course, foreign direct investments of American corporations shot up—from $7.2 billion in 1946 to $40.6 billion in 1963, a more than fivefold increase in the years since the Second World War. Parallel to this growth in foreign investments has gone an increase in the sales and profits of foreign branches and subsidiaries. In manufacturing (excluding petroleum and mining), sales of such affiliates amounted to $18.3 billion in 1957 (the first year for which figures are available) and to $28.1 billion in 1962, an increase of 54 percent in six years.

Some idea of the growing relative importance of these foreign operations of American corporations may be gathered from Table II, which presents data on the sales of foreign manufacturing affiliates, total domestic manufacturing sales, and nonagricultural merchandise exports. (See Table II)

TABLE II   GROWTH OF FOREIGN AND DOMESTIC MANUFACTURING SALES AND MERCHANDISE EXPORTS, 1957–1962
(Billions of dollars)

	Sales of Foreign Manufacturing Affiliates	Total Domestic Manufacturing Sales	Merchandise Exports (Excluding foodstuffs)
1957	18.3	341	16.8
1958	n.a.	314	13.8
1959	21.1	356	13.7
1960	23.6	365	16.6
1961	25.6	368	16.9
1962	28.1	400	17.3

n.a. = not available
SOURCES: Foreign sales, Fred Cutler and Samuel Pizer, "Foreign Operations of U.S. Industry," *Survey of Current Business*, October 1963; domestic sales and exports, *Economic Indicators*, current issues.

It would of course be preferable to compare the foreign and domestic sales and exports of those corporations which have foreign branches or subsidiaries; and it would be still better if we could include the profits of these corporations from foreign and domestic operations respectively. If such data were available, we could form a very clear picture of the degree of involvement of the United States giant corporations in foreign activities. But even the figures presented in Table II bear eloquent testimony to the rapid growth of that involvement. In the six years beginning with 1957, the sales of foreign affiliates grew by 54 percent, while total domestic manufacturing sales expanded only 17 percent and nonagricultural exports hardly changed at all.

So much for the record of recent years. If we look ahead, we find that

American corporate business, far from regarding its expansion abroad as having come to an end, is relying heavily for its future prosperity on the continued penetration of other countries' economies. "America as the 'land of opportunity' is beginning to lose that title in the eyes of many U.S. businessmen," says a Special Report in *U.S. News & World Report*. And the Report goes on to tell why:

> These businessmen increasingly are deciding that markets abroad—not those in this country—offer the biggest potential for future growth. The feeling grows that the U.S. market, while huge, is relatively "saturated."
>
> It is overseas that businessmen see the big, untapped market with hundreds of millions of customers wanting—and increasingly able to buy—all kinds of products and services.
>
> To go after this market, U.S. firms are building and expanding factories all around the world. Since 1958, more than 2,100 American companies have started new operations in Western Europe alone. . . .
>
> All types of businesses—from autos to baby foods—predict a glowing future for markets outside the U.S.
>
> Says L. E. Spencer, president of Goodyear Tire & Rubber Company of Canada: "Foreign markets will expand several times as fast as North American markets over the next 10 years."
>
> From C. C. Smith, vice president of International Business Machines' World Trade Corporation: "The rate of increase in our foreign business is greater than in the U.S. in every major product category. In time, we expect volume to overtake that in the U.S."
>
> Listen to the comment by an official of Colgate-Palmolive Company: "You're in a saturated market here in the U.S., where new products are the only answer to growth. Abroad there are millions of people each year who reach the stage in their cultural, social and economic development where they buy soap, toothpaste, other things we sell."
>
> This flat prediction is made by Fred J. Borch, president of General Electric Corporation: "Regardless of economic or political ups and downs, the most rapidly expanding markets will be abroad in the next 25 years."
>
> Against that background, the survey of U.S. firms abroad turned up these major findings—
>
> 1. Foreign sales of U.S. companies are growing much faster than sales of the same companies in this country. Often, the percentage gains are three or four times as great.
>
> 2. Profit rates abroad generally are higher than those in similar activities in the U.S. Many firms report a percentage return "twice as high abroad as in America." Most cite lower wage costs overseas—and less competition.
>
> 3. Foreign markets usually can best be tapped by an on-the-scene operation, rather than by exporting from the U.S. A plant abroad can avoid tariff and other trade barriers erected against exports from this country. . . .

It thus appears both from the record of the past and from the plans and hopes for the future that American corporate business has irrevocably embarked on the road long since pioneered by Standard Oil. Standard is still the model of a multinational corporation, but it is no longer an exception. It simply shows us in the most developed form what the other giants either already are or are in the process of becoming.

As it happens, the recent history of Standard Oil of New Jersey also supplies us with a textbook example of why multinational corporations are profoundly hostile to the spread of socialism. Before the Cuban Revolution, Jersey was heavily involved in Cuba in several ways. It owned refining facilities on the island and operated an extensive distribution system, involving altogether properties valued at $62,269,000. In addition, Jersey's Cuban subsidiary bought its crude from Creole Petroleum, Jersey's Venezuelan subsidiary, at the high prices maintained by the international oil cartel. The company therefore reaped profits in two countries and on three separate operations—sale of crude, refining of crude, and sale of finished products. As a result of the Revolution, the company's properties in Cuba were nationalized without compensation, and Creole lost its Cuban market. More than $60 million in assets and all three sources of current profit were lost in one blow—and without in any way involving exports from or imports to the United States.

It might be argued that if Jersey and the United States government had pursued different policies toward Cuba, the revolutionary regime would have been glad to continue buying oil from Venezuela, which after all is the nearest and most rational source of supply. This is no doubt true—but with a big proviso. The revolutionary regime would have been glad to continue buying oil from Venezuela, but it would not have been glad to continue paying prices and meeting terms of payment dictated by Standard Oil. And since it could turn to the Soviet Union as an alternative source of supply, it was no longer obliged to go on submitting to the cartel's terms. Hence to remain in the Cuban market, Jersey would at the least have had to cut its prices and offer better credit terms. This not only would have meant less profits on sales to Cuba but would have threatened the whole structure of cartel prices. Jersey and Washington decided instead to make war on the Cuban Revolution.

That what is at stake in the conflict between the United States and Cuba is not trade between the two countries is confirmed by Cuba's relations with other capitalist countries. Long after the socialization of the Cuban economy, the Havana government was vigorously promoting its trade with Britain, France, Spain, Canada, Japan—in short, with any country willing and able to do business with Cuba. It is true, of course, that Cuba's capacity to export and import has been seriously curtailed by the disorganization and other difficulties of the early years of the change-over to socialism, but there seems to be no reason to doubt the Cubans' own contention that in a few years the island will be a much better trading partner than it was under the old neo-colonial regime. Nor is there any reason to doubt that the United States could capture a major share of the Cuban trade if the blockade were called off and normal relations re-established between the two countries.

But this is not what really interests the giant multinational corporations which dominate American policy. What they want is *monopolistic control* over foreign sources of supply and foreign markets, enabling them to buy and sell on specially privileged terms, to shift orders from one subsidiary to another, to favor this country or that depending on which has the most advantageous tax, labor, and other policies—in a word, they want to do business on their own terms and wherever they choose. And for this what they need is not trading partners but "allies" and clients willing to adjust their laws and policies to the requirements of American Big Business.

Against this background, one can see that Cuba's crime was to assert, in deeds as well as in words, her sovereign right to dispose over her own resources in the interests of her own people. This involved curtailing and, in the struggle which ensued, eventually abrogating the rights and privileges which the giant multinational corporations had previously enjoyed in Cuba. It was because of this and not because of a loss of trade, still less because of any irrational fears or prejudices, that the corporations and their government in Washington reacted so violently to the Cuban Revolution.

It might perhaps be thought that since Cuba is a small country, the violence of the reaction was out of all proportion to the damage suffered. But this would be to miss the main point: What makes Cuba so important is precisely that she is so small, plus the fact that she is located so close to the United States. If Cuba can defect from the "free world" and join the socialist camp with impunity, then any country can do so. And if Cuba prospers under the new setup, all the other underdeveloped and exploited countries of the world will be tempted to follow her example. The stake in Cuba is thus not simply the exploitability of one small country but the very existence of the "free world" itself, that is to say, of the whole system of exploitation.

It is this fact that has dictated the Cuban policy of the United States. The strategy has been to damage and cripple the Cuban economy in every possible way, with a threefold objective. First, it is hoped that the Cuban people will sooner or later become disillusioned with their revolutionary leadership, thus setting the stage for a successful counterrevolution. Second, the people of the underdeveloped countries are to be taught that revolution does not pay. And third, the burden of supporting the Cuban economy thrown on the rest of the socialist camp, and especially on the Soviet Union as its economically most developed member, is to be maximized so that these other socialist countries may be induced to use their influence to restrain any new revolutions which might place further burdens on their already overstrained economies.

This is of course not the only way the "free world" is being defended. The United States failed to understand the nature of the revolution which overthrew the Batista regime in Cuba until it was too late to keep the revolutionaries from consolidating their power. Every precaution is being taken to see that the same mistake is not made again. All revolutionaries are automatically suspect; no regime is too reactionary to merit all-out United States backing.

Partly, this backing takes the form of so-called economic aid—in reality handouts to corrupt oligarchies designed to insure their loyalty to Washington rather than to the interests of their own countries. And partly it takes the form of military aid, which is predominantly of two types.

First, there is direct participation by United States armed forces on the territory of the client state: stationing of troops in bases controlled by the United States (as we saw above, there are some 275 major base complexes and 1,400 bases either occupied by or prepared for American forces); "emergency" deployment of troops anywhere on the host country's national territory that the two governments may decide (Lebanon in the summer of 1958, Thailand in the spring of 1962, the Dominican Republic in the spring of 1965); and various kinds of advisory and training missions accredited to the armed forces of the clients (in 1957, a total of forty Army, Navy, and Air Force missions were in Latin America alone, in every country except Mexico). As South Vietnam shows, training missions can be quickly and almost imperceptibly transformed into counterrevolutionary combat forces.

The second form of military aid is the provision of material and financial support for the armed forces of the client states. While the dozens of military assistance pacts which the United States has signed with underdeveloped countries around the world are ostensibly designed to meet the "threat" of aggression from the Soviet Union or China, no serious military planner imagines that this is the real purpose. Such a threat, if it really existed, could be countered only by the United States itself, and an attempt to coordinate military strategy with a large number of feeble allies would be a source of weakness rather than strength. The real purpose of this military aid is clearly spelled out by Lieuwen in his pioneer study of the role of the military in Latin America:

> Those [military] policies . . . are not designed to meet the military threat of communism, but rather to gain Latin America's friendship, to win its cooperation and support in the United Nations and the Organization of American States. The Rio military alliance, the M[utual] D[efense] A[ssistance] Pacts, the arms grants, the reimbursable aid, the work of the I[nter] A[merican] D[efense] B[oard] and of the military missions—all of these have no great military significance. They are designed, above all, to draw the Latin American officer corps, which exercise great influence over the political scene in most of the republics, closer to the United States, in the hope that they will exclude Soviet influence, give the United States their support, maintain political stability, ensure continued access to strategic raw materials, and provide rights to the use of bases.

To put the matter more bluntly, the purpose of United States military aid to underdeveloped countries is to keep them in the American empire if they are already there and to bring them in if they are not—and in any case to insure that there are no further defections from the "free world." The consequences for the recipient countries are tragic. "What we are doing," said the Colombian statesman Eduardo Santos, "is building up armies which weigh nothing in the international scale but which are juggernauts for the internal life of each country. Each country is being occupied by its own army." And the same point is made and heavily underlined in a remarkable study of relations between the United States and Pakistan published by a group of Pakistani students in London:

> In the long run, the worst aspect of military aid lies in the complete change it produces in the balance of social and political forces in favor of conservatism and established vested interests. The dragon seeds sown by military aid have produced a fearful crop of military officers, with their social roots in the most conservative sections of our society, who have learnt to sit in judgment on our people. It is an overwhelming force without any countervailing force to hold it in check.

This world-wide spawning of little military machines loyal to Washington does not in any way reduce the need for a big military machine in the United States itself. As the tide of revolutionary protest rises in the exploited countries of the "free world," it is only by increasingly direct and massive intervention by American armed forces that the old order can be held together a while longer. As the shift to nuclear weapons and intercontinental missiles proceeds, even the pretense that the global system of bases is for protection against Russian aggression is given up. "Little by little," writes Cyrus L. Sulzberger, foreign affairs columnist of the New York Times, "the requirement for bases on the periphery of the NATO area is dwindling. Medium-range and long-range plus seaborne missiles are changing the emphasis of our counter-strike force. But the time has not yet come when one can envision the disappearance of all need for U.S. overseas bases; on the contrary." There follows a revealing analogy with British policy after the Napoleonic Wars, though the naked term "empire" is used only in referring to that bygone era:

> Today Washington stresses preparations to fight limited wars if necessary. These need mobility, the ability to transfer men and supplies from one quarter to the other, using staging points abroad. They also necessitate what is called "forward stockpiling" at strategically important havens.
>
> A study of this particular problem is now under way in the Pentagon. After the Napoleonic Wars, the British Navy made such a study to ascertain London's requisites in defending its vast overseas empire. Later the U.S. Navy made a similar analysis of how to operate globally.
>
> The focus of present Washington research is more on aspects of limited war than total war. . . .
>
> Likewise, the administration sees the possibility we might be engaged in limited wars on other fronts, conflicts similar to that in South Vietnam where we

are not belligerents but are increasingly committed. For example, were Iran to be subjected to Russian pressure, initial efforts to aid it might be "limited" rather than "total." To be ready for such actions, the United States must maintain sufficient bases overseas to permit accumulation of stocks for swift reaction by other means than holocaust.

Is not Sulzberger really saying that the United States, like Great Britain in the nineteenth century, needs a global military machine to police a global empire? But, as we know, the United States needs a global military machine also for carrying on its unremitting struggle against the advance of socialism. And the truth is that policing the empire and fighting socialism are rapidly becoming, if they are not already, one and the same. For the threat to the empire comes from revolutionary movements which, like the American Revolution two hundred years ago, are sparked by a deep-seated yearning for national independence and are fueled by an increasingly urgent need for economic development, which experience is proving cannot be achieved by underdeveloped countries today except on the basis of public enterprise and comprehensive planning—in short, only if their nationalist revolutions are also socialist revolutions.

As these two great socio-political transformations merge into a single process, so likewise does the struggle against them. For the United States to defend its empire today means to fight socialism, not only in the empire but wherever it exists; for socialism is by its very nature an international movement which gains strength everywhere from a success anywhere. Hence all revolutions must be opposed, every source which gives them material or moral aid must be weakened and if possible destroyed. It is this two-sided, worldwide commitment to the political and social status quo which defines and determines the military needs of the United States oligarchy. . . .

It would be misleading to leave the impression that only the oligarchy has favored the steady increase in military spending during these years. If one assumes the permanence of monopoly capitalism, with its proved incapacity to make rational use for peaceful and humane ends of its enormous productive potential, one must decide whether one prefers the mass unemployment and hopelessness characteristic of the Great Depression or the relative job security and material well-being provided by the huge military budgets of the 1940's and 1950's. Since most Americans, workers included, still do assume without question the permanence of the system, it is only natural that they should prefer the situation which is personally and privately more advantageous. And in order to rationalize this preference, they have accepted the official ideology of anti-Communism which appears to justify an unlimited expansion of the military establishment as essential to national survival.

Against this background it is easy to understand why there has been so little political opposition in recent years to expanding military budgets. In a Congress normally characterized by fierce fighting among lobbies and pressure groups, a majestic unanimity emerges as soon as a request is made for additional billions for the armed services, with Congressmen vying with one another for the honor of proposing the largest increases.

The people's representatives in their enthusiasm even pay little attention to the strictly military rationality of how the money is spent. "My own experience in the Senate," says William Proxmire, Democratic Senator from Wisconsin, "has shown me the painful inability of our democracy to resist the momentum of excessive spending and waste that accompanies our vast military establishment." And he gives a graphic illustration, the Senate's reaction to strong urging by Secretary of Defense McNamara against spending more on B-52 and B-58 bombers than the President had already requested:

> Only three Senators joined me in voting for my amendment, which would have eliminated this appropriation. In the Senate debate, we had made an overwhelming case against spending more than half a billion dollars in this way. Yet some 95 percent of the Senators voting that day rejected the logic of the case, rejected the advice of the President, the Secretary of Defense and his aides, and voted to appropriate the funds. This was more money than was spent in that year by the federal government for medical research; more than was spent for all federal housing programs; more than the budgets allocated to the U.S. Forest Service, the National Park Service, and the Fish and Wildlife Service combined.

No wonder Senator Proxmire concludes that "as a rationalization for federal expenditure, national defense has few peers. Programs that wouldn't get a second look from Congress flit through if they are attached to an armed forces appropriation." The views of Proxmire, reputed to be one of the more liberal members of the Senate, might be discounted as likely to be exaggerated. This would hardly apply to Senator Richard B. Russell of Georgia, a conservative Southerner, Chairman of the Senate Armed Services Committee, and often described as the most powerful individual in the Congress. Here is Senator Russell in a colloquy on the Senate floor with Senator Proxmire:

> There is something about preparing for destruction that causes men to be more careless in spending money than they would be if they were building for constructive purposes. Why that is so I do not know; but I have observed, over a period of almost thirty years in the Senate, that there is something about buying arms with which to kill, to destroy, to wipe out cities, and to obliterate great transportation systems which causes men not to reckon the dollar cost as closely as they do when they think about proper housing and the care of the health of human beings.

A more devastating condemnation of a whole social order would be hard to imagine. Nor, as we have seen, are the reasons so mysterious as Senator Russell seems to think. The Cold War, the well-known Harvard economist Sumner Slichter explained in 1949, "increases the demand for goods, helps sustain a high level of employment, accelerates technical progress and thus helps the country to raise its standard of living. . . . So we may thank the Russians for helping make capitalism in the United States work better than ever." And a few months later *U.S. News & World Report*, published by the ultra-conservative David Lawrence, spelled out the same idea with brutal candor:

> *Government planners figure they have found the magic formula for almost endless good times. . . . Cold War is the catalyst. Cold War is an automatic pump primer. Turn a spigot, the public clamors for more arms spending. Turn another, the clamor ceases. Truman confidence, cockiness, is based on this "Truman formula."* Truman era of good times, President is told, can run much beyond 1952. *Cold War demands, if fully exploited, are almost limitless.*

U.S. News & World Report was still saying the same thing in 1954. Following news that the United States had exploded the world's first hydrogen bomb, it commented: "What H-bomb means to business. A long period . . . of big orders. In the years ahead, the effects of the new bomb will keep on increasing. As one appraiser put it: 'The H-bomb has blown depression-thinking out the window.'"

Here at last monopoly capitalism had seemingly found the answer to the "on what" question: On what could the government spend enough to keep the system from sinking into the mire of stagnation? On arms, more arms, and ever more arms.

The Limits of Consensus

Gabriel Kolko

For a growing number of Americans the war in Vietnam has become the turning point in their perception of the nature of American foreign policy, the traumatizing event that requires them to look again at the very roots, assumptions, and structure of a policy that is profoundly destructive and dangerous. Vietnam is the logical outcome of a consistent reality we should have understood long before the United States applied much of its energies to ravaging one small nation.

We can only comprehend Vietnam in the larger context of the relations of the United States to the Third World, removing from our analytic framework superfluous notions of capriciousness, accident, and chance as the causal elements in American foreign and military policy. For the events in Vietnam expose in a sustained and systematic manner those American qualities that have led to one of the most frightful examples of barbarism of mechanized man against man known to modern history. The logical, deliberative aspects of American power at home and its interest abroad show how fully irrelevant are notions of accident and innocence in explaining the diverse applications of American power today, not only in Vietnam but throughout the Third World. If America's task of repressing the irrepressible is doomed to failure because it is impossible for six percent of the world's population to police and control the globe, critics of American policy should not attribute the undertaking to omission or ignorance. For if the United States can impose its will on the recalcitrant revolutionaries everywhere it will gain immensely thereby, and its losses will be proportionately great if it fails.

*   *   *

From The Roots of American Foreign Policy, pp. xi–xii, 3–26, 83–87. Copyright © 1969 by Gabriel Kolko. Reprinted by permission of Beacon Press.

The Men of Power

To comprehend the nature and function of power in America is to uncover a critical analytic tool for assessing the character of the American historical experience and the role of the United States in the modern world. The failure of most of an entire generation of American intellectuals and scholars to make the phonemenon of power a central concern has permitted a fog of obscurantism and irrelevance to descend upon the study of American life in the twentieth century.

Stated simply, the question is: What are the political and economic dimensions of power in American society, how does power function, and who benefits from it? The correlations of these structural aspects of power are either curious or critical, incidental, and perhaps colorful, or of decisive importance. The structure of power may be described empirically, but power may also reflect a more elusive configuration of social attitudes and forces that makes it possible for one class to prevail in American history—or it may involve aspects of both the tangible and the intangible.

For the most part, the handful of students of American power have concentrated on the investigation of the social status and origins of men of power, an exercise that has meaning only if one can show distinctive political behavior on the part of men of power with lower social status. Indeed, one must assess the psychology of decision-makers, the genesis of their power, and the source of their conduct in the context of the structure and function of American power at home and in the world, a critical evaluation that permits one to determine whether a "military-industrial complex," a unique bureaucratic mentality, or something more substantial is the root of American policy nationally and internationally. It forces us to determine whether, for example, the presence of a Harriman-family lawyer in one key post is, in itself, crucial to understanding the goals and motives of his behavior and American policies, or whether powerful men freely use one decision-making mechanism or another in a situation in which the results are largely the same because more fundamental interests and goals define the range of action and objectives of all decision-makers. The permanence and continuity in American national and international policy for the better part of this century, scaled to the existence and possibilities of growing national strength, suggests that the study of power in America must also define the nature and function of American interests at the same time.

If, in the last analysis, the structure of power can only be understood in the context in which it functions and the goals American power seeks to attain, the fact that the magnitude of such a vast description requires a full history of twentieth century America should not deter social analysts from highlighting the larger contours of the growth of modern American bureaucracies, if only to make the crucial point that these bureaucratic structures are less the source of power than the means by which others direct power in

America for predetermined purposes. That society is one in which bureaucrats do not represent their own tangible interests, save if they wear other and more important hats, but those of what one must tentatively call that of the "power system," and when their own aspirations become dysfunctional, leaders remove them on behalf of more pliable men. For behind the bureaucrats exist levels of economic and political power, whether latent or exercised, the objectives and maintenance of which no one can abandon without far-reaching, indeed revolutionary, alterations in policy and the very nature of American society itself. It is this ultimate power that defines the limits of bureaucratic conduct and the functions of the state.

Politicians create bureaucracies for specific purposes, and that these structures develop their own administrative codes and techniques, or complex mystifying rationales, is less consequential than their objective and functions. Congress created such bureaucratic power in the United States first during the era 1887–1917 as a result of class-oriented elements seeking to rationalize via political systems the unpredictable elements of economic life in a modern technology. To study how rather than why political power operates in a class society, a formalism that Max Weber contributed to conservative descriptive social analysis, is to avoid the central issue of the class nature and function of the modern state. After the turn of the century the political parties cultivated bureaucracy purely as an instrumentality serving and reflecting class interests—bureaucracy with no independent power base and nowhere to find one within the American power structure. Given the decisive role of the businessmen in the creation of modern American bureaucracy and the "positive state," it should be neither surprising nor impractical that they staff the higher levels of the bureaucratic mechanisms of American power with men from business.

Policy, in brief, preceded bureaucratic rationalism, with Congress serving as a lobby for, and objective of, various business interests. Given the consensual nature of social and political priorities in America, and the essentially repressive manner in which the authorities handle nonconformity to consensus when it becomes a potential threat, political power in American society is an aspect of economic power—economic power often sharply in conflict by region or size or interest, but always operative within certain larger assumptions about the purposes of victory for one side or the other. Often this disunity among competing economic interests is so great as to mean mutual neutralization and ineffectuality, and frequently the divergent factions couch their goals in rhetorical terms—"anti-monopoly" being the most overworked—which has made "liberal" phraseology the useful ideology of corporate capitalism.

This diversity and conflict within the ranks of business and politicians, usually described as a pluralist manifestation, has attracted more attention than it deserves and leads to amoebic descriptions of the phenomenon of interbusiness rivalry in a manner that obscures the much more significant dimensions of common functions and objectives. The critical question for the study of what passes as conflict in American society must be: What are the major positions, and who wins and why? The motives of the losers in the game of politics, or of those who created pressures others redirected for their own ends, is less critical than the actual distribution of power in society. It is in this context of the nature of power and its function that the scholar should study bureaucracies, with less concern for social mobility than the concept of purpose and goals the bureaucracy serves. Only in this manner can we understand the interests and actions that are functional and irrevocable as part of the logic of American power and not the result of mishap, personalities, or chance. If powerful economic groups are geographically diffuse and often in competition for particular favors from the state, superficially appearing as interest groups rather than as a unified class, what is critical is not who wins or loses but what kind of socioeconomic framework they *all* wish to compete within, and the relationship between themselves and the rest of society in a manner that defines their vital function as a class. It is this class that controls the major policy options and the manner in which the state applies its power. That they disagree on the options is less consequential than that they circumscribe the political universe.

Despite the increasingly technical character of modern political and economic policy, and the need to draw on individuals with appropriate backgrounds for the administration of policy—especially businessmen—it is the structural limits and basic economic objectives of policy that define the thrust of American power nationally and internationally. The source of leadership is important, and has been since the turn of the century, but it may not be decisive. What is ultimately of greatest significance is that whether leadership comes from Exeter-Harvard or Kansas, the results have been the same, and an outcome of the nature of power in America and the role of the United States in the world.

The Limits of Consensus. American politics in the twentieth century has been a process of change and shifting rewards within predictable boundaries and commitments that are ultimately conservative and controlled as to the limited social and economic consequences it may achieve. No decisive or shattering social and economic goals have cracked the basic structure and distribution of power in all its forms, and if some have used democratic and liberal rhetoric to explain motion within these boundaries it is less consequential than the functional material contours of the system itself. Indeed, it is the illusion of the possibility of significant change—of true freedom in society—that helps make possible its practical suppression via liberal politics and gradualism which, as historical fact, never exceed predetermined orbits and assumptions.

One must never infer that such illusions are the sole source of conservative order—as witnessed by the response of those with power during rare periods when genuine opposition shatters the mythologies. For though freedom is a posture decision-makers tolerate among the politically impotent, those in power act to make certain that all others remain ineffectual. When their own policies are subject to severe trials, or appear to be failing, they cannot afford the luxury of organized opposition and functional freedoms which can shatter their hegemony over the normal, usually passive social apathy. The history of civil liberties in the United States is testimony to the fact that when freedom moves from rhetoric to social challenge it is suppressed insofar as is necessary. Functional freedom is the ability to relate to power or forces with the potential for achieving authority, that is, the decision-making establishment or those who seek to transform or replace it. So long as intellectuals or the people exercise this right "responsibly," which is to say to endorse and serve the consensus their rulers define, abstract freedoms flourish in public pronouncements and slogans because they lead nowhere. Hence the dissenter has the freedom to become a victim in the social process and history, and a battery of sedition, espionage, criminal anarchy, or labor laws exist in readiness for the appropriate moment of social tension and the breakdown in the social and ideological consensus which exists during periods of peace and stability. The celebrants of American freedom rarely confront the concepts of order that underlie the large body of law for suppression that always exists in reserve.

A theory of consensus is indispensable for comprehending the nature of decision-making and power in American society, but a social analyst must always consider that theory from the viewpoint of its role when some socially critical and potentially dynamic groups and classes cease to endorse or sanction the consensus, because then consensus is based on discipline and becomes, for practical purposes, authoritarian on matters of measurable power. For only challenges to a political and social system and crises reveal its true character—when established power threatens to break down and formal democracy is nearly transformed into functional, true freedom.

The essential, primary fact of the American social system is that it is a capitalist society based on a grossly inequitable distribution of wealth and income that has not been altered in any essential manner in this century. Even if there has not been *decisive* class conflict within that structure, but merely conflict limited to smaller issues that were not crucial to the existing order, one can accurately describe American society as a static class structure serving class ends. A sufficiently monolithic consensus might voluntarily exist on the fundamental questions indispensable to the continuation of the existing political and economic elites, and the masses might respect or tolerate the primary interest of a ruling class in the last analysis. The prevailing conception of interests, the critical values of the society, did not have to be essentially classless, as Louis Hartz and recent theorists of consensus have argued, but merely accepted by those segments of society without an objective stake in the constituted order. This dominant class, above all else, determines the nature and objectives of power in America. And for this reason no one can regard business as just another interest group in American life, but as the keystone of power which defines the essential preconditions and functions of the larger American social order, with its security and continuity as an institution being the political order's central goal in the post-Civil War historical experience.

On the national level, reform and legislation have led to class ends and the satisfaction of class needs, and that the purposes of decision-makers in 1968 should be any different than in 1888 makes sense only if one can posit and prove a drastic alteration in the distribution of economic power.

One may base such an analysis on a functional view of American reform, on the consequences of legislation rather than the motives of all reformers, motives that are ultimately paramount among those who are to be regulated and who have power. Social theory, muckrakers, and intellectuals did not and do not influence important businessmen, who have never aspired to have reforming crusaders regulate and direct their affairs. Businessmen have always preferred that their own lawyers and direct representatives play that role in matters of the most intimate relevance to their economic fortunes, though not necessarily in lesser affairs, and it is a fact that the government has ultimately drawn most critical political decision-makers from, or into, the higher reaches of economic life. In this setting, we should see American reform primarily as a question of technical and efficiency engineering—of social rationalization— to advance the welfare and interests of specific business interests first and society generally, but always within critical ideological boundaries and assumptions. With only occasional differences on tangential points, political authorities have shared, or conformed to, the practical applications of this conservative consolidation usually called "progressivism" or "liberalism."

Yet the critical question arises as to why, in such an economic context of inequality, poverty, and many years of unemployment, there has never been a class opposition to constituted politics and power. In brief, quite apart from the efficacy of the alternatives, why has no anti-capitalist mass movement emerged, as in Western Europe, to create that essential political option which is the indispensable precondition for true pluralism and freedom in America? For the United States is a class society, with measurable oppression, but also without decisive class conflict as of this time. It is also a society serving class ends with the consensual support or apathetic toleration of the dispossessed classes. This consensus, which serves the interest of a single class rather than all of society, exists in an altogether different situation than what theorists of consensus have described, but the social and historic outcome is the same.

The phenomenon of consensus and its causes are simply too complex to describe in light of existing evidence. But it is necessary to pose certain critical questions in order to comprehend whether consent alone is important in explaining the nature and durability of American power and the decision-making structure. What happens when the consensus is shattered and ceases to receive traditional adherence or toleration? Does the fact that all of society may at times share an ideology legitimate it? Or is it more consequential that the economically critical and powerful class endorses the ideology that serves it best—a fact that makes the ideology operate during those rare periods when consensus breaks down? And can core commitments of the public be evaluated by any measurable techniques that permit valid social generalization?

If the history of Left politics in the United States is co-option for some, it is also repression for many others: grandfather clauses, poll taxes, and other means for applying the stick when the carrot was insufficient or deemed inappropriate. The history of the militant labor movement, black struggles, southern populism, socialism, and even the current anti-war and civil rights movements all bear testimony to the fact that when politics and social movements do not legitimize the existing order consensus becomes mandatory conformity and suppression. Authority and power exist quite beyond general social sanctions and rest on specific interests and the ability to impose restraints, and the ruling class has never permitted decision-makers in the governmental apparatus who do not advance and conform to the interests of the state—for psychological reasons or whatever—to introduce dysfunctional elements or policies into governmental affairs. This enforced consensus from above and social cohesion due to the relatively rare exercise of ever latent authority and repression has been the truly revealing aspect of the nature and purpose of American power and capitalist interests. Yet whether voluntaristic or otherwise, these shared values make the origins of decision-makers, or the identity of their special governmental agencies, less consequential than the binding and permanent commitments of ruling groups and their social and economic system.

For this reason, mass consent in a society based on a relatively small elite predominance is less significant, and the operative causal agents in society are the interests and goals of men of power—and their will and ability to retain their mastery—rather than [the] masses who also endorse those objectives. It is the commitments of those able to implement their beliefs and goals, rather than of the powerless, that creates racism in the employment practices of corporations; and it is elite authoritarianism, which remains constant in the historical process, rather than working class biases—which vary with circumstances and interest and often disappear functionally—that leads to authoritarian institutions.

Yet even if the social and power weight of specific opinion and class interests, as opposed to its existence among all sectors of society, is primary, it is still vital to comprehend the elusive character of what is now called "public opinion" or "consensus." What is more significant than opinion is the ultimate implications of apathy and ignorance of elite-sanctioned policies, a condition that reveals the limits of the integrative possibilities of elite-controlled "mass culture" from above. For the most part, in matters of foreign affairs, workers are no more or less belligerent or pacifistic than executives and professionals—when they are forced to register an opinion. The theory of public attitudes as the fount of the decision-making process reinforces a democratic theory of legitimacy, which, for reasons of sentimental tradition at home and ideological warfare abroad, is a useful social myth. But the close and serious student of modern American foreign relations will rarely, if ever, find an instance of an important decision made with any reference to the alleged general public desires or opinions. What is more significant is the fact of ignorance and lack of interest among the vast majority of the population during a period of crisis as to the nature of essential issues and facts, a condition that neutralizes their role in the decision-making process even more and cultivates an elitist contempt for the inchoate role of "the people" as nothing more than the instrument or objective, rather than the source, of policy. The persistent fluctuations in such mass attitudes alone assure that for practical guidance the decision-makers must refer to their own tangible and constant values and priorities. Yet what no one has ever shown is the extent to which this mass apathy reflects the manipulative and moronizing impact of modern communications, or a superior intelligence based on the individual's awareness that he has no power or influence after all, and that he has a very different identity and interest in the social process than the managers and rulers of society.

The Versatile Rulers. If the manipulated values and consensual ideology coincide with the objective and material interests of the decision-makers, the fact is important but not necessarily the sole causal factor of their conduct, for even where personal interests do not exist the policies are the same. The function of bureaucracy is to serve constituted power, not itself. While it often can be relevant that an individual in government is directly connected with a business interest, even one in a field deeply concerned with the topic over which he has jurisdiction, we can determine the ultimate significance of this connection only if more disinterested men adopt different policies. Historically, by and large, they have not. In our own era the reasons for this continuity in policy and action are critical, and they reveal the institutional and interest basis of American power in the world, a power that transcends factions and men.

American diplomacy has traditionally been the prerogative of the rich and well placed. Even if they had a lifetime career in government, the intrinsic nature of the structure until 1924 required professional diplomats to be men of independent means, and that tradition persisted until today in various forms. In 1924 the Diplomatic Corps, which paid salaries so low that only the sons of the well-to-do and rich could advance very far in it, was merged with the Consular Corps into the Foreign Service to establish a merit system. In 1924, 63 percent of the diplomatic officers were Harvard-Princeton-Yale graduates, as opposed to 27 percent of the ambassadors for the years 1948, 1958, and 1963. Of the 1,032 key federal executive appointees between March 4,

1933, and April 30, 1965, 19 percent had attended these three elite schools, ranging from 16 percent under Roosevelt to 25 percent during the Johnson Administration. Somewhat lower on the scale of rank, in 1959 the three universities produced 14 percent of all Foreign Service executives, while nearly two-thirds of those in the Service were the sons of business executives and owners or professionals. At the level of all civilian federal executives above GS-18 ranking, or the very highest group, 58 percent were the sons of this upper income and status occupational category.

Sociologists such as C. Wright Mills, and often journalists as well, have made too much of these social origins, for while interesting and important there is no proof such connections are decisive. Twenty-six percent of the highest federal executives come from working class and farmer origins, and an increasingly larger percentage from the non-Ivy League schools, and there is no evidence whatsoever to prove that social and educational origins determine policies of state. That elite origins and connections accelerated personal advancement is now sufficiently self-evident not to warrant excessive attention, much less to make these standards the key criterion for explaining the sources and purposes of American power. In brief, the basic objectives, function, and exercise of American power, and not simply its formal structure and identity, are paramount in defining its final social role and significance. Without denigrating the important contribution of Mills, which was brilliant but inconsistent, such an approach fails to come to grips with the dynamics of American power in its historical setting.

A class structure, and predatory rule, can exist within the context of high social mobility and democratic criteria for rulership, perhaps all the better so because it co-opts the elites and experts of the potential opposition and totally integrates talent into the existing society. The major value in essentially static structural studies of key decision-makers is to illustrate the larger power context in which administrators made decisions, but not to root the nature of those decisions in the backgrounds or individual personalities of an elite. In brief, correlation may not be causation in the power structure, and should high status, rich men ever seek to make decisions dysfunctional to the more permanent interests of dominant power interests, even more powerful leaders would immediately purge them from decision-making roles. The point is that while such men are unlikely to make socially dysfunctional decisions, so is anyone else who rises to the top of a structure with predetermined rules and functions. To measure power that is latent as well as active, it is often easier to study the decision-makers themselves. The other approach, and by far the more difficult, is to define objective and impersonal interests and roles for the larger classes and sectors of American society, their relationship to each other and to the world, and the manner in which they have exercised their relative power.

The analyst must utilize both approaches, and should consider everything useful, including the investigation of status, celebrities, core elites, military elites—the important and trivial, as Mills discovered—and he should discount the trivial and establish the correlations in the hope of revealing causes. If Mills made it clear that there were levels of power among those who shared it, and an inner power core that transcended local society and celebrities, he slighted the economic basis of American politics and exaggerated the causal and independent importance of the military. To him, the social and educational origins of the elite were too critical, thereby excluding the possibility of a power elite "democratized" within its own ranks or selection process but still in the traditional dominant relationship to the remainder of society. Offhand, I assume that in this process it is worth striking a final balance and integration and rejecting certain factors. Social origins and education, and the possibility of the existence of an Establishment based on common heritage and interests, are of lesser concern than the currently operative ties of decision-makers, for the father's words or the impressions of old school days wear off, and the responsibilities of men are measurable in the present rather than in the past.

A more select group reveals far more than a collection as large as W. Lloyd Warner's 12,929 federal executives, and on this assumption I investigated the career cycles and origins of the key American foreign policy decision-makers from 1944 through 1960, excluding the Presidents. My major premise was that even if I could show that such men neither began nor ended in business, there were still many other and more valid ways of gauging the nature of foreign policy. We examined the State, Defense or War, Treasury and Commerce Departments, plus certain relevant executive level agencies . . . and considered only those with the highest ranks. The study included 234 individuals with all their positions in government during 1944–60, comprising the lesser posts if an individual attained the highest executive level. As a total, these key leaders held 678 posts and nearly all of them were high level and policy-making in nature.

The net result of this study, however imperfect, revealed that foreign policy decision-makers are in reality a highly mobile sector of the American corporate structure, a group of men who frequently assume and define high level policy tasks in government, rather than routinely administer it, and then return to business. Their firms and connections are large enough to afford them the time to straighten out or formulate government policy while maintaining their vital ties with giant corporate law, banking, or industry. The conclusion is that a small number of men fill the large majority of key foreign policy posts. Their many diverse posts make this group a kind of committee government entrusted to handle numerous and varied national security and international functions at the policy level. Even if not initially connected with the corporate sector, career government officials relate in some tangible manner with the private worlds predominantly of big law, big finance, and big business.

Of the 234 officials examined, 35.8 percent, or eighty-four individuals, held 63.4 percent of the posts. Thirty men from law, banking, and investment firms accounted for 22 percent of all the posts which we studied, and another fifty-seven from this background held an additional 14.1 percent—or a total of 36.1 percent of the key posts. Certain key firms predominated among this group: members of Sullivan & Cromwell, or Carter, Ledyard & Milburn, and Coudert Brothers, in that order among law firms, held twenty-nine posts, with other giant corporate-oriented law firms accounting for most of the remainder. Dillon, Read & Co., with four men, and the Detroit Bank, with only Joseph M. Dodge, accounted for eighteen and ten posts, respectively, and two men from Brown Brothers, Harriman held twelve posts—or forty posts for three firms. It was in the nature of their diverse functions as lawyers and financiers for many corporate industrial and investment firms, as Mills correctly perceived, that these men preeminently represented the less parochial interests of all giant corporations, and were best able to wear many hats and play numerous roles, frequently and interchangeably as each corporate or government problem—or both—required. Nothing reveals this dual function more convincingly than their career cycles. Despite the fact that Sullivan & Cromwell and Dillon, Read men tended to go into the State Department, or lawyers from Cahill, Gordon, Zachry & Riendel to the Navy Department, general patterns of distribution by economic interests—save for bankers in the governmental banking structure—are not discernible. And with one possible exception, all the men from banking, investment, and law who held four or more posts were connected with the very largest and most powerful firms in these fields.

In the aggregate, men who came from big business, investment, and law held 59.6 percent of the posts, with only forty-five of them filling 32.4 percent of all posts. The very top foreign policy decision-makers were therefore intimately connected with dominant business circles and their law firms. And whether exercised or not, scarcely concealed levels of economic power exist beneath or behind the government, and indeed high mobility in various key posts reinforces such interlockings. This continuous reality has not altered with successive administrations, as the state has called upon Fair Dealers and modern Republicans alike to serve as experts in running a going operation which they are asked to administer efficiently within certain common definitions of its objectives. Whether Democrats, such as James Forrestal of Dillon, Read, or Republicans, such as John Foster Dulles of Sullivan & Cromwell, the continuous contact and advice they have received from their colleagues in the world of finance, law, and business have always colored their focus. The operative assumption of such men, as Forrestal once put it, is that "What I have been trying to preach down here is that in this whole world picture the Government alone can't do the job; it's got to work through business. . . . That means that we'll need to, for specific jobs, be able to tap certain people. . . ." It is this process of "tapping" for high level policy tasks that has accounted for high mobility and the concentration of posts in few hands.

Perhaps of even greater interest is the special nature of the government career officials and their relationship to business during their extended professional lives. These sixty men, 25.6 percent of the total, held 31.7 percent of the posts considered, in part because, being full-timers, they were available for a greater number of tasks. But for many of these men government became a stepping stone toward business careers, and we can only speculate on how this possible aspiration influenced their functional policies on economic and other questions while they were in government. "The lure of industry was such that I couldn't pass it up," a former career officer and head of the C.I.A. for fourteen months, Admiral William F. Raborn, Jr., confessed in discussing why he had taken his government post in the first place. "I went there with the thought I could go when I wanted to." Over half these men, perhaps enticed in the same manner, later took up nongovernmental posts, though a significant fraction returned to government for special tasks. Conversely, however, any government employee thwarting the interests of American businesses, as expressed in foreign and national security affairs, risks losing possible future posts, even if he goes to foundations or university administrations. Most of these new private positions were in law firms and industry. But certain of these key career officials who never left for business or new careers the State Department had selected under its pre-1924 or conventional rules, where independent wealth and social connections were always helpful. The fact that John M. Cabot, Assistant Secretary of State and a Boston Cabot, also held the largest number of posts among the twenty-six full-time career officials we examined is not inconsequential. It is within this career group that the conventional elite social background predominates.

For the most part, the technical and policy nature of foreign policy and military security issues has necessitated the selection of men with requisite business backgrounds. The choice of William L. Clayton, rags-to-riches head of the largest world cotton export firm, to deal with United States foreign economic policy between 1944–47 was rational and both a cause and reflection of policy. What is most instructive was that Woodrow Wilson and Cordell Hull, President and Secretary of State (1933–44), a professor and small town politician, formulated the essential foreign economic policy, and it is here that we must see the larger ideological and consensual definition of foreign policy as ultimately transcending the decision-maker recruitment process.

Business as the Fount. The organizational rungs of governmental power take many other businessmen into the lower hierarchies of administration in much the same manner as their seniors function at the very highest levels. These lower tiers of operation are too extensive to measure in their entirety here, but it is sufficient to point to several readily documented expressions. Such lines of contact are perfectly logical, given the objectives of American policy abroad, and given the fact that Washington generally assigns the management of the government's relationship to various problems to the businessmen or their representatives with business connections or backgrounds in the various areas. And it is both convenient and more than logical that key federal executives recruit former associates for critical problem-solving posts for which they have responsibility. There is no conflict of interest because the welfare of government and business is, in the largest sense, identical.

This will mean that key law firm executives with major corporate connections will draw on former clients, whom they may again soon represent at the termination of their governmental service; it will simplify the task of the business representatives in Washington—about two-thirds of the top two hundred manufacturing firms maintain them on a full-time basis—who may wish assistance with marketing, legislative, or legal matters. The Government will invariably choose advisers to international raw materials and commodity meetings from the consuming industries, and will select key government executives concerned with specific issues—such as oil—from the interested industry. The existence of businessmen and their lawyers in government, in short, gives the lobbyists and those not in government something to do—successfully—insofar as it is to their interest. These men interact in different roles and at various times, for today's assistant secretary may be tomorrow's senior partner or corporate president. However much such men may have competing specific economic objectives, conflicts that may indeed at times neutralize their mutual goals, what is essentially common among such elites, whether or not they are cooperative, makes them a class with joint functions and assumptions and larger economic objectives that carry with it the power to rule. This is not to say such well placed officials with industry backgrounds are the only source of government policy, but that they exist and, more important, given the larger aims of government it is entirely rational to select personnel in this fashion. From this viewpoint the nature of the bureaucracy is essentially an outcome rather than a cause of policy.

Examples of interlocking government-business leadership are numerous even below the highest decision-making echelons. In the Department of the Interior, to cite one instance, the large majority of key personnel in the Office of Oil and Gas or the Petroleum Administration for Defense in the decade after 1946 came from the industry, often just on loan for fixed periods of time. These bodies, which are largely a continuation of wartime boards, have permitted the regulation of the petroleum industry via governmental agencies, free from the threat of antitrust prosecution and for the welfare of the industry. Pleased with the arrangement, the industry has supplied many of the key administrators and consultants the government needs on a no-compensation basis.

No less typical is the Business and Defense Services Administration of the Department of Commerce (BDSA), created in the fall of 1953. Composed of 184 industry groups during the period 1953–55, the BDSA committees dealt with a vast number of goods and the problems of their industry, recommending action to the government that was the basis of profitable action and regulation of various economic sectors. These ranged from the division of government purchases among industry members to the review of proposed Export-Import Bank and World Bank loans for the construction of competing industries abroad. In effect, BDSA committees have served themselves via the government in a classic fashion, the precedents for which range back to the early nineteenth century. In this regard they are no different in genesis and function from the federal regulatory movement initiated in 1887.

At every level of the administration of the American state, domestically and internationally, business serves as the fount of critical assumptions or goals and strategically placed personnel. But that this leadership in foreign and military affairs, as integrated in the unified hands of men who are both political and economic leaders, comes from the most powerful class interests is a reflection as well as the cause of the nature and objectives of American power at home and abroad. It is the expression of the universality of the ideology and the interests and material power of the physical resources of the ruling class of American capitalism, the latter being sufficient should consensus break down. The pervasiveness of this ideological power in American society and its measurable influence on mass culture, public values, and political opinions is the most visible reality of modern American life to the contemporary social analyst. It means that one can only assess the other institutional structures, the military in particular, in relation to the predominance of the economic ruling class which is the final arbiter and beneficiary of the existing structure of American society and politics at home and of United States power in the world.

*   *   *

A Theory of United States Global Role

In their brilliant essay on the political economy of nineteenth-century British imperialism, John Gallagher and Ronald Robinson have described a process that parallels the nature of the United States expansion after 1945:

> Imperialism, perhaps, may be defined as a sufficient political function of this process of integrating new regions into the expanding economy; its character is largely decided by the various and changing relationships between the political and economic elements of expansion in any particular region and time. Two qualifications must be made. First, imperialism may be only indirectly connected with economic integration in that it sometimes extends beyond areas of economic development, but acts for their strategic protection. Secondly, although imperialism is a function of economic expansion, it is not a necessary function. Whether imperialist phenomena show themselves or not, is determined not only by the factors

of economic expansion, but equally by the political and social organization of the regions brought into the orbit of the expansive society, and also by the world situation in general.

It is only when the politics of these new regions fail to provide satisfactory conditions for commercial or strategic integration and when their relative weakness allows, that power is used imperialistically to adjust those conditions. Economic expansion, it is true, will tend to flow into the regions of maximum opportunity, but maximum opportunity depends as much upon political considerations of security as upon questions of profit. Consequently, in any particular region, if economic opportunity seems large but political security small, then full absorption into the extending economy tends to be frustrated until power is exerted upon the state in question. Conversely, in proportion as satisfactory political frameworks are brought into being in this way, the frequency of imperialist intervention lessens and imperialist control is correspondingly relaxed. It may be suggested that this willingness to limit the use of paramount power to establishing security for trade is the distinctive feature of the British imperialism of free trade in the nineteenth century, in contrast to the mercantilist use of power to obtain commercial supremacy and monopoly through political possession.

In today's context, we should regard United States political and strategic intervention as a rational overhead charge for its present and future freedom to act and expand. One must also point out that however high that cost may appear today, in the history of United States diplomacy specific American economic interests in a country or region have often defined the national interest on the assumption that the nation can identify its welfare with the profits of some of its citizens—whether in oil, cotton, or bananas. The costs to the state as a whole are less consequential than the desires and profits of specific class strata and their need to operate everywhere in a manner that, collectively, brings vast prosperity to the United States and its rulers.

Today it is a fact that capitalism in one country is a long-term physical and economic impossibility without a drastic shift in the distribution of the world's income. Isolated, the United States would face those domestic backlogged economic and social problems and weaknesses it has deferred confronting for over two decades, and its disappearing strength in a global context would soon open the door to the internal dynamics which might jeopardize the very existence of liberal corporate capitalism at home. It is logical to regard Vietnam, therefore, as the inevitable cost of maintaining United States imperial power, a step toward saving the future in something akin to its present form by revealing to others in the Third World what they too may encounter should they also seek to control their own development. That Vietnam itself has relatively little of value to the United States is all the more significant as an example of America's determination to hold the line as a matter of principle against revolutionary movements. What is at stake, according to the "domino" theory with which Washington accurately perceives the world, is the control of Vietnam's neighbors, Southeast Asia and, ultimately, Latin America.

The contemporary world crisis, in brief, is a by-product of United States response to Third World change and its own definitions of what it must do to preserve and expand its vital national interests. At the present moment, the larger relationships in the Third World economy benefit the United States, and it is this type of structure America is struggling to preserve. Moreover, the United States requires the option to expand to regions it has not yet penetrated, a fact which not only brings it into conflict with Third World revolutions but also with an increasingly powerful European capitalism. Where neocolonial economic penetration via loans, aid, or attacks on balanced economic development or diversification in the Third World are not sufficient to maintain stability, direct interventions to save local *compradors* and oligarchies often follow. Frequently such encroachments succeed, as in Greece and the Dominican Republic, but at times, such as Vietnam, it is the very process of intervention itself that creates its own defeat by deranging an already moribund society, polarizing options, and compelling men to choose— and to resist. Even the returns to the United States on partial successes have warranted the entire undertaking in the form not just of high profit ratios and exports, but in the existence of a vast world economic sector which supplies the disproportionately important materials without which American prosperity within its present social framework would eventually dry up.

The existing global political and economic structure, with all its stagnation and misery, has not only brought the United States billions but has made possible, above all, a vast power that requires total world economic integration not on the basis of equality but of domination. And to preserve this form of world is vital to the men who run the American economy and politics at the highest levels. If some of them now reluctantly believe that Vietnam was not the place to make the final defense against tides of unpredictable revolutionary change, they all concede that they must do it somewhere, and the logic of their larger view makes their shift on Vietnam a matter of expediency or tactics rather than of principle. All the various American leaders believe in global stability which they are committed to defend against revolution that may threaten the existing distribution of economic power in the world.

When the day arrives that the United States cannot create or threaten further Vietnams, the issue at stake will be no less than the power of the United States in the world. At that point, both the United States and the rest of the world will undergo a period of profound crises and trauma, at home as well as abroad, as the allocation of the earth's economic power is increasingly removed from American control. *If*, in the process of defending their prerogatives, the leaders of the United States during those trying years do not destroy the globe, piecemeal as in Vietnam or in a war with China or Russia, we shall be on the verge of a fundamentally new era for the United States and mankind. The elimination of that American hegemony is the essential precondition for the emergence of a nation and a world in which mass hunger, suppression, and war are no longer the inevitable and continuous characteristics of modern civilization.

SUGGESTIONS FOR FURTHER READING

A short and readable interpretive survey which attacks Americans' moralistic approach to foreign policy is George F. Kennan, *American Diplomacy, 1900–1950* (Chicago, 1953). A scholar and career diplomat, Kennan played an instrumental role in American policy formation after World War II. Kennan's influence is clearly reflected in the works of Spanier and Carleton, parts of which are reprinted above. For a related view emphasizing post-World War II foreign policy, see Hans J. Morgenthau, *In Defense of the National Interest* (New York, 1951). The notions of idealism and realism in American diplomacy are surveyed perceptively by Robert E. Osgood, *Ideals and Self-Interest in America's Foreign Relations* (Chicago, 1953).

In two influential books, William Appleman Williams stresses the connection between domestic economic development and diplomacy: *The Tragedy of American Diplomacy* (Cleveland, 1959; revised edition, New York, 1962) and *The Roots of the Modern American Empire* (New York, 1969). Important also is C. Wright Mills, *The Power Elite* (New York, 1956).

The conflict of opinion discussed here may be followed in detailed studies of other periods. For the period leading up to the Spanish-American War see Walter LaFeber, *The New Empire* (Ithaca, 1963) who considers economic developments and Julius W. Pratt, *Expansionists of 1898* (Baltimore, 1936) who denies the influence of the business community. Charles C. Tansill, *America Goes to War* (New York, 1938) emphasizes economic factors which brought the United States into World War I while Ernest R. May, *World War and American Isolation, 1914–1917* (Cambridge, Mass. 1959) minimizes economics.

Ernest R. May has written a perceptive bibliographical essay, "Emergence to World Power," in John Higham, *The Reconstruction of American History* (New York, 1962). A short, but useful annotated bibliography dealing with the post-World War II period is included in John Spanier's *American Foreign Policy Since World War II* (4th revised edition; New York, 1971). See also Alexander De Conde, *New Interpretations in American Foreign Policy* (1957), a pamphlet published by the American Historical Association's Service Center for Teachers of History.

* Available in paperback edition.

8
THE AGE OF ANXIETY
AND PROTEST

It is always difficult for the historian to interpret the events of the recent past, but the years since World War II, with their bewildering technical advances, unprecedented international crises, and rapid changes at home, present special problems. One thing is clear: World War II marked the beginning of a new era of responsibility for the United States. But responsibility abroad often led to frustration and stalemate on the domestic scene. The threat of Communism was exaggerated in the minds of many Americans. Disturbed by a cold war which seemed endless and by a war in Korea that could not be won, some Americans imagined that subversive agents were everywhere undermining American democracy. Rightist organizations confused liberals and progressives with Communists, and any criticism or dissent with subversion. In the mid-fifties Senator Joseph McCarthy led a witch hunt designed to ferret out the Communists in government, but succeeded only in threatening the basic American right of free speech.

Although the worst of the anti-Communist hysteria touched only a few, the post-war years were marked by a general reaction against reform. Harry Truman pulled the upset of the century in 1948 by defeating the Republican candidate, Thomas Dewey, but Truman had little success in extending the social legislation of the New Deal. The conservative temper was further strengthened by the election of General Dwight D. Eisenhower in 1952. Eisenhower called himself a "progressive conservative" and a "modern Republican" and his presidency was a time of equilibrium and holding the line.

Complacency and conformity characterized the 1950's. The American left collapsed and there was a noticeable absence of any meaningful ideological or political conflict in America. Both major parties were coalitions of diverse elements with conservatives and liberals in both camps. Labor leaders acted like businessmen, and the skilled workmen joined the middle class, moved to the suburbs with millions of other Americans and enjoyed the general prosperity of the post-war years. David Riesman and William Whyte described the conformity of "organization men" and the decline of the puritan ethic. American students became part of a "silent generation."

In some ways the 1960's witnessed a turn away from the conformity and complacency of the 1950's. John F. Kennedy's margin of victory over Richard Nixon in 1960 was razor thin, but the young president brought a spirit of idealism to the office that captured the imagination of the young. They joined the Peace Corps to try to do something concrete about the world's problems, and enlisted in the war on poverty—suddenly rediscovered among the affluence. They also cooperated with the civil rights movement initiated by America's Negro citizens. A Supreme Court decision in 1954 had made school desegregation unconstitutional, but it was a group of dedicated young leaders, both black and white, who implemented the decision by organizing bus boycotts, protest marches, and sit-ins. Some of the young, impatient with the slow progress being made by politicians, formed leftist organizations and sought more direct action. At the same time the radical right, which saw a great Communist conspiracy at work in the country, also gained strength.

President Kennedy had greater success in changing the spirit of the times than he had in getting social legislation through Congress. Tragically, in November of 1963, he was murdered in Dallas, so one can only guess at what he might have accomplished in a second term. In 1964 Barry Goldwater of Arizona mobilized the conservative and rightist discontent and to the surprise of many won the Republican nomination for the Presidency. He promised to provide "a choice not an echo" but his candidacy helped Lyndon B. Johnson win the most overwhelming presidential victory in modern American history. Provided with a cooperative Congress and a consensus which included not only labor, the farmers, the Negroes, and the intellectuals, but a large portion of the business community as well, Johnson in 1965 pushed through Congress a program of social legislation which in many ways completed the New Deal.

But the Johnson consensus faded rapidly after 1965. His program did not silence the critics from either the left or the right, and his attempt to build a "Great Society" through mobilizing the important interest groups into a great consensus failed to satisfy those who suggested that real social advance is forged only through social conflict. The expansion of the war in Vietnam evoked widespread discontent and protest; the increasing militancy of blacks and students heightened the tension and enlarged the conflict. A riot in the black ghetto of Watts in Los Angeles in 1965 was but the prelude to a series of "long hot summers" in the cities. In 1967, forty-one cities were shaken by riots. The National Advisory Commission on Civil Disorders reported the next year that "our nation is moving toward two societies, one black, one white—separate and unequal."

Bitterness and violence increased during the election year of 1968. The country seemed hopelessly divided, and when civil rights leader Martin Luther King and presidential hopeful Robert F. Kennedy were gunned down by assassins, many concluded that the country was sick with hate and violence. The war in Vietnam became a focal point for critics and a major campaign issue in the primary campaign. The primary victories of Senator Eugene McCarthy of Wisconsin, who campaigned on a peace platform, along with the rising tide of discontent, helped produce President Johnson's announcement in March that he would not seek reelection. But when the Democratic convention, meeting in Chicago, chose Vice-President Hubert H. Humphrey, who supported the Johnson war policy, to head its ticket, thousands of protesting young people continued to clash with police as millions of horrified Americans watched the conflict on television. American coalition politics seemed to have broken down in 1968.

Richard M. Nixon was elected by a narrow margin in 1968, but with George Wallace running on an independent ticket and taking thirteen percent of the vote, Nixon was a minority president. He promised to work to bring the country back together, but the war went on and the country remained sharply divided. When in the spring of 1970, American forces invaded Cambodia, thousands of students protested. Violence broke out on hundreds of campuses; on two of them—Kent State in Ohio and Jackson State in Mississippi—several students were killed in clashes with the National Guard. Urban strife also continued as a portion of the black militants and New Left resorted to planned violence. The police responded in kind; indeed, many charged that the police sometimes initiated the violence against militant students and blacks. "There is in the American psyche today an alienation from the central government that is new in our experience," Richard Rovere announced. And George Reedy, a former aide to President Johnson and clearly a member of the Establishment, wrote, "The question is raised: Can our political system cope with the strains? The answer is probably not."

It appeared to some that these statements were too pessimistic. By the end of 1971 tensions had abated some. President Nixon's promise to withdraw from Vietnam blunted some of the protest; the cities were relatively quiet during the summer of 1971. Some observers were convinced that most Americans still wanted to work within the system; others argued that the relative calm was the result of an apathy born of discouragement, frustration, and fear of repression. At the same time, the entire country watched apprehensively as inflation continued in the midst of an economic recession marked by increasing unemployment.

The following selections approach some of the bewildering problems of contemporary America from several different angles. Kevin Phillips argues on the basis of population statistics and election returns that 1968 marked the end of the New Deal-Democratic coalition and the beginning of a new Republican consensus. This emerging Republican majority is based, he argues, on a moderately conservative "silent majority" of suburbanites and those moving into the "Sun Belt States," plus traditionally Democratic voters from the working class and the South who are switching to the Republican party. Phillips assumes that the American system of coalition politics will continue to work in the future, with the minority Democratic party playing an important and creative opposition role. In the next selection, Theodore J. Lowi questions the concept of coalition politics, arguing that American party politics, by their very nature, force an artificial consensus by denying voters a real choice. Surface consensus hides important differences, thus making the system "impervious to social change." He concludes that the nation needs some "productive disorder" and that unless the political parties provide real options, people will act outside of the two-party system. Some of the selections that follow deal with efforts to bring about change by means of action outside the traditional party system.

One such group is the "Radical Right," which is discussed by Daniel Bell. He is not sympathetic with their views and suggests that the far right represents the only group in America with an ideology. He finds them to be a dispossessed class which projects an imagined, but dangerous conflict onto society. The radical right's commitment and methods, he argues, threaten to disrupt the "fragile consensus that underlies the American political system."

The next two selections, by William Whyte and by Paul Jacobs and Saul Landau, compare two college generations, one from the mid-fifties and the other from the mid-sixties. Perhaps neither is typical, but the organization men of the fifties, content with security, conformity, and the political center, contrast sharply with the new radicals of the sixties, who are militantly determined to reconstruct American society. Jacobs and Landau, writing in 1966, have an optimistic faith that the new radicals can transform the country, but in the next selection, written five years later, Larry Nachman, basing his analysis on books written by some prominent radicals, sees conflict, disagreement, and error within the New Left. Like Jacobs and Landau, Nachman is sympathetic—if critical—but he is no longer as optimistic as the earlier writers. He argues that a radical movement, if it is to be effective, cannot stand completely outside the system, a point he illustrates by considering the tactics of the Women's Liberation Movement.

The last two selections represent a fundamental disagreement within the movement for black equality. Bayard Rustin argues that the future of the black's struggle for equal rights depends not on blacks alone but on a "coalition of progressive forces," which would create a sympathetic political majority in the United States—in other words, a consensus for black equality. Vincent Harding, on the other hand, traces the development of black radicalism in America, viewing it as arising largely from the failure of the civil rights movement to achieve real and lasting results. Working within the system, he suggests, has brought only law and order and death to black leaders while black visions of justice and hope based on rebellion and conflict have led to the same result. Young blacks today "see blood, but they are determined it shall not be theirs alone." Harding concludes on a note of doubt. He is certainly not optimistic about the future.

Obviously the debate over consensus and conflict raises fundamental questions about the recent American past and about contemporary society. The debate is not just of historical significance, for its outcome will affect the lives of all who pick up this book. Is it possible to build a better America through consensus politics and by working within the system, or does worthwhile reform and change in domestic and foreign policy come only after sharp and fundamental conflict? Is it possible to include the business community in the same political coalition with labor and the black community, or does social progress inevitably collide with business interests? Is there a new coalition emerging in the country based upon a silent majority upset by the political and social developments of recent years? Or has the whole concept of coalition politics reached a point of bankruptcy in the United States? What is the role of the radicals on both the right and the left? Is the conflict and the conspiracy they describe real or imagined? Is either group powerful enough to disrupt the traditional political pattern?

As a college student yourself, do you more nearly fit William Whyte's description of the "organization man," or are you a new radical? Perhaps you want to be classified somewhere in between, but is it possible or desirable to be in the middle? What, after all, should be the role of the educated person in America? Should he try to conform to the values of his society or should he try to change them? Indeed, does he, as some have argued, have an obligation to promote change? If change is your goal, what is the best means of bringing it about? Is it best to work within the context of American coalition politics or is it more effective to work outside of traditional institutions?

The Emerging Republican Majority

Kevin Phillips

Far from being the tenuous and unmeaningful victory suggested by critical observers, the election of Richard M. Nixon as President of the United States in November, 1968, bespoke the end of the New Deal Democratic hegemony and the beginning of a new era in American politics. To begin with, Nixon was elected by a Republican Party much changed from that deposed in 1932; and such party metamorphosis has historically brought a fresh political cycle in its wake. Secondly, the vastness of the tide (57 percent) which overwhelmed Democratic liberalism—George Wallace's support was clearly an even more vehement protest against the Democrats than was Nixon's vote—represented an epochal shifting of national gears from the 61 percent of the country's ballots garnered in 1964 by Lyndon Johnson. This repudiation visited upon the Democratic Party for its ambitious social programming, and inability to handle the urban and Negro revolutions, was comparable in scope to that given conservative Republicanism in 1932 for its failure to cope with the economic crisis of the Depression. And ironically, the Democratic debacle of 1968 followed the Party's most smashing victory—that of 1964—just as the 1932 toppling of the Grand Old Party succeeded the great landslide of 1928.

* * *

Considerable historical and theoretical evidence supports the thesis that a liberal Democratic era has ended and that a new era of consolidationist Republicanism has begun. To begin with, the 1932–68 Democratic reign spanned thirty-six years and a social revolution. History indicates that this is the usual longevity of an American political cycle. For example, the modern American political system dates from the election of Andrew Jackson in 1828, which precipitated a Democratic predominance lasting until Lincoln's triumph in 1860. Contrary to general legend, the Civil War did not seat the Republicans firmly in the national saddle, however effectively it unseated the hitherto predominant Democrats. As a matter of fact, once the Southern states had returned to the Union, things settled into something of a stalemate. No president elected between 1876 and 1892 won a majority of the popular vote. Finally, in 1896, the Bryan-McKinley contest tarred the Democrats with the brush of agrarianism and revivalism, thus cementing Republican rule based on the populous, industrial Northeast and Great Lakes. Thereafter, except for the eight-year Wilson Administration, the GOP held national sway until the advent of the Great Depression and the election of Franklin D. Roosevelt in 1932. Actually, the coming of age of urban America had begun to swing the pendulum towards the Democrats even before the Depression, as witness Al Smith's 1928 breakthroughs in the Northeast; however, many Republicans blamed Franklin Roosevelt's personal popularity and refused to face the socioeconomic fact that a new Democratic majority had come into being. Thirty-six years later, it too gave way to change.

To structure a mathematical perspective reaching back to 1828, political history divides into four cycles: 1828–60, 1860–96, 1896–1932 and 1932–68. All four cycles lasted thirty-two or thirty-six years, and all four included steady rule by one party, with an interregnum of just eight years when the lesser party held power. The interregnums were: (1) the tenures of Whig generals Harrison and Taylor amidst the otherwise Democratic span of 1828–60; (2) the two Grover Cleveland administrations in the 1860–96 post-Civil War era; (3) the two Woodrow Wilson administrations amidst the 1896–1932 rule of industrial Republicanism; and (4) the Eisenhower years in the middle of the 1932–68 New Deal Democratic cycle. The Nixon administration seems destined by precedent to be the beginning of a new Republican era.

Another bulwark of cyclical change is the obsolescence of the prevailing ideology or impetus of the dominant party. The principal force which broke up the Democratic (New Deal) coalition is the Negro socioeconomic revolution and liberal Democratic ideological inability to cope with it. Democratic "Great Society" programs aligned that party with many Negro demands, but the party was unable to defuse the racial tension sundering the nation. The South, the West and the Catholic sidewalks of New York were the focal points of conservative opposition to the welfare liberalism of the federal government; however, the general opposition which deposed the Democratic Party came in large part from prospering Democrats who objected to Washington dissipating their tax dollars on programs which did them no good. The Democratic Party fell victim to the ideological impetus of a liberalism which had carried it beyond programs taxing the few for the benefit of the many (the New Deal) to programs taxing the many on behalf of the few (the Great Society).

Back in 1932, the Democratic Party took office with a popular mandate to develop a new governmental approach to the problems of economic and social welfare which the Depression had brought into painful focus. Basically, Roosevelt's New Deal liberalism invoked government action to deal with situations from which the government had hitherto remained aloof; i.e., the malpractice of corporations, unemployment, malnutrition, lack of rural electricity, collapsed farm prices and managerial intolerance of organized labor. But in the years since 1932, federal interventionism has slowly changed from an innovative policy into an institutionalized reflex. Great Society liberalism propounded federally controlled categorical grant-in-aid programs and bureaucratic social engineering as the answer to crises big and little just as inevitably as Calvin ("The business of America is business") Coolidge sermonized laissez-faire economics during the formative period of the Depression. And just as the political inability of laissez-faire Republicanism to handle the post-1929 economic crisis signaled the end of one cycle and the beginning of another, so did the breakdown of New Deal liberalism in the face of a social and urban crisis which clearly demands its own ideological innovation. In all likelihood, 1968 marks the beginning of an era of decentralizing government, whereby Washington can regain the public confidence necessary to mobilize the inchoate American commitment to housing, education and employment opportunity.

Gone are the days when a conservative Establishment—Wall Street, the Episcopal Church, the great metropolitan newspapers, the U.S. Supreme Court and Manhattan's East Side—harassed Franklin D. Roosevelt and his fledgling New Deal. Today, these same institutions, now liberal, vent their spleen on populist conservatism. The contemporary Establishment reflects the institutionalization of the innovative political impetus of thirty years ago: the middle-aged influence and affluence of the New Deal. This is a good sign of change. By the time a once-popular political upheaval has become institutionalized in the partners' rooms of Wall Street and the salons of Fifth Avenue, a counter-movement has invariably taken hold in the ordinary (now middle-class) hinterlands of the nation.

A fourth and last theory on which a new political cycle can be predicated rests on the post-1945 migration of many white Americans (including many of the traditionally Democratic white ethnic groups) to suburbia and the Sun Belt states of Florida, Texas, Arizona and California. This trend parallels, and is partially a result of, concurrent Southern Negro migration to the principal cities of the North. The Negro problem, having become a national rather than a local one, is the principal cause of the breakup of the New Deal coalition.

Previous American population shifts have generally triggered major political changes: (1) The rise of the trans-Appalachian "New West" in the early Nineteenth Century overpowered the conservatism of the Eastern Seaboard and provided the base of Jacksonian democracy. (2) The admission of California, Oregon and the Yankee-settled Farm states to the Union tipped the balance against the South and subsequently buoyed the Republicans throughout the post-Civil War era. (3) The expansion of the United States across the plains and Rocky Mountains added new Republican states to the Union, while the vast influx of European immigrants whose sweat ran the mills and factories of the Northeast laid down a vital foundation for the 1896–1932 era of industrial Republicanism. And (4) the coming of age of urban and immigrant America, rendered more painful by the Depression, established a national Democratic hegemony rooted in the cities which lasted from 1932 to 1968. Today, the interrelated Negro, suburban and Sun Belt migrations have all but destroyed the old New Deal coalition. Chart 1 [p. 403] vividly illustrates the declining population and power of the big cities. Some Northern cities are nearly half Negro, and new suburbia is turning into a bastion of white conservatism; moreover, growing Northern-based Negro political influence has prompted not only civil rights measures obnoxious to the South but social legislation and programs anathema to the sons and daughters of Northern immigrants. As in the past, changing population patterns have set the scene for a new political alignment.

American voting patterns are a kaleidoscope of sociology, history, geography and economics. Of course, the threads are very tangled and complex, but they can be pulled apart. The "science" in political science is not entirely a misnomer; voting patterns can be structured and analyzed in such a way as to show an extraordinary amount of social and economic behaviorism at work. Once the correct framework has been erected, national voting patterns can be structured, explained, correlated and predicted to a surprising degree. The trick is to build the framework.

For a century, the prevailing cleavages in American voting behavior have been ethnic and cultural. Politically, at least, the United States has not been a very effective melting pot. In practically every state and region, ethnic and cultural animosities and divisions exceed all other factors in explaining party choice and identification. From New York City, where income level has only minimally influenced the mutual hostility of Jews and Irish Catholics; to Wisconsin, where voting analysis requires an ethnic map of the state's Welsh, Belgian, French, Swiss, Finnish, Polish, Dutch, German, Danish, Swedish, Norwegian and Yankee populations; to Missouri, where partisanship has long pivoted on Virginian, New England, hillbilly and German settlement patterns and ensuing Civil War sympathies—everywhere ethnic, regional and cultural loyalties constitute the principal dynamics of American voting. Inasmuch as most of the Catholic ethnic groups live in Northern states where the rural Protestant population—their obvious political opposition—has been Republican, they have generally voted Democratic. Today these loyalties are ebbing along with the Republicanism of the Yankee countryside.

Beneath the checkerboard of ethnic settlement which extends from Maine's French Catholic Aroostook Valley to the Norwegian fishing villages of Alaska's Inland Passage—the South, except for its Negroes and Latin fringe, is largely Anglo-Saxon—the basic roots of American voting patterns have long rested in the regionalism of Civil War loyalties. And these in turn have reflected patterns of Yankee, Middle Atlantic and Southern settlement. During the hundred years after the founding of the Republican Party in 1854, GOP strength was principally rooted in Yankee New England and its outliers from upstate New York to Oregon. Democratic voting, based on Southern antecedents and Civil War sentiment, prevailed from Delaware west through Kentucky, Missouri, Oklahoma and the Southwest, as well as the eleven states of the old Confederacy. The two cultures met in the Missouri, Mississippi and Ohio valleys, though the "border" was irregular and outposts of one group sometimes pushed into the general territory of the other. For example, Virginian settlements were made in north-central Ohio and New England-planted towns can be found in northern Missouri.

Given the extent to which Civil War loyalties underlay the Republican-Democratic party alignment until the end of the New Deal era, the contemporary ebb of Republicanism in its bailiwicks of Yankee tradition and the more striking disintegration of the Democratic Party in its former Southern and Border fiefs suggests that a full-scale delineation of the scope and spread of both behavioral streams can shed real light on the forces and prospects of the emerging conservative and Republican majority. To a degree little appreciated by most Americans, the cultural patterns of the Northeast and the coastal South traveled due west across the pre-Civil War Mississippi Valley so that the county-by-county partisanship of, say, Indiana, can be largely explained in terms of Yankee, Middle Atlantic or Southern settlement. A number of pre-Civil War travelers and observers discussed this phenomenon, and one of the best descriptions is that written in 1834 by a contemporary emigration counselor named Baird:

The emigration to the Valley of the Mississippi seems to have gone in columns, moving from the East almost due west, from the respective states . . . From New England, the emigrant column advanced through New York, peopling the middle and western parts of that state in its progress; but still continuing, it reached the northern part of Ohio, then Indiana and finally Illinois. A part of the same column . . . is diverging into Michigan . . . The Pennsylvania and New Jersey column advanced within the parallels of latitude of those states in west Pennsylvania, and still continuing, advanced into the middle and southern parts of Ohio, and extended even into the middle parts of Indiana and Illinois. The Virginia column advanced first into the western part of the state and Kentucky— which was long a constituent part of it—thence into the southern parts of Indiana and Illinois, until it had spread over almost the whole of Missouri. The North Carolina column advanced into East Tennessee, thence into West Tennessee, and also into Missouri. And the South Carolina and Georgia column has moved upon the extensive and fertile lands of Alabama (and Mississippi) . . . In Arkansas, the emigrating columns of Kentucky and Tennessee predominate.

The above mentioned fact furnishes a better key than any other that I know of, to furnish a correct knowledge of the diversity of customs and manners which prevail in the Valley of the Mississippi. For if one knows what are the peculiarities of the several states east of the Allegheny mountains, he may expect them, with some shades of difference occasioned by local circumstances, in the corresponding parallels of the West. Slavery keeps nearly within the same parallels and so does nearly every other peculiarity.

Thus, what seems like uselessly remote historical data—the details of the peopling of the United States—is actually quite vital to understanding the dynamics of the upcoming political cycle. On the one hand, the Democrats are scoring gains in Yankee and Scandinavian areas of Civil War-era Republican tradition; yet on the other hand, they are suffering a much greater loss in Southern-oriented territory reaching beyond Dixie to Delaware Bay, the Ohio and Missouri valleys and the far Southwest. . . . Not only is the Democratic Party's loss more extensive than its gain, but the loss is occurring in those sections of the nation—Florida, the Gulf Coast, Texas, Arizona and Southern California—where population growth is centered. The Yankee countryside and the old Northeastern cities are losing both people and political power. A century ago, for example, Maine had more congressmen than Texas; Rhode Island more than Florida. The 1970 Census is expected to award Texas and Florida thirty-nine to Maine and Rhode Island's collective four.

*   *   *

The long-range meaning of the political upheaval of 1968 rests on the Republican opportunity to fashion a majority among the 57 percent of the American electorate which voted to eject the Democratic Party from national power. To begin with, more than half of this protesting 57 percent were firm Republicans from areas—Southern California to Long Island's Suffolk County—or sociocultural backgrounds with a growing GOP bias. Some voted for George Wallace, but most backed Richard Nixon, providing the bulk of his Election Day support. Only a small minority of 1968 Nixon backers— perhaps several million liberal Republicans and independents from Maine and Oregon to Fifth Avenue—cast what may be their last Republican presidential ballots because of the partisan re-alignment taking place. The third major anti-Democratic voting stream of 1968—and the most decisive—was that of the fifteen million or so conservative Democrats who shunned Hubert Humphrey to divide about evenly between Richard Nixon and George Wallace. Such elements stretched from the "Okie" Great Central Valley of California to the mountain towns of Idaho, Florida's space centers, rural South Carolina, Bavarian Minnesota, the Irish sidewalks of New York and the Levittowns of Megalopolis. . . .

Although most of George Wallace's votes came from Democrats rather than Republicans, they were conservatives—Southerners, Borderers, German and Irish Catholics—who had been trending Republican prior to 1968. . . . The Wallace vote followed the cultural geography of obsolescent conservative (often Southern) Democratic tradition. There was no reliable Wallace backing among blue-collar workers and poor whites as a class; industrial centers in the Yankee sphere of influence from Duluth to Scranton, Fall River and Biddeford shunned the Alabama ex-governor with a mere 2 percent to 3 percent of the vote. Areas of eroding Democratic tradition were the great breeding grounds of Wallace voters.

In the South, Wallace drew principally on conservative Democrats quitting the party they had long succored and controlled. Generally speaking, Wallace's Southern strength was greatest in the Democratic Party's historic (pre-1964) lowland strongholds, while the Alabaman's worst Southern percentages came in the Republican highlands. White voters throughout most sections of the Deep South went two-to-one for Wallace. In the more Republican Outer South, only one white voter out of three supported the third-party candidate. In the South as a whole, 85 to 90 percent of the white electorate cast Nixon or Wallace votes against the re-aligning national Democratic Party in 1968, an unprecedented magnitude of disaffection which indicates the availability of the Wallace vote to the future GOP.

Four of the five Wallace states had gone Republican in 1964, and although the Alabaman greatly enlarged the scope of Southern revolt by attracting most of the (poor white or Outer South Black Belt) Southerners who had hitherto resisted Republican or States Rights candidacies, much of his tide had already been flowing for Goldwater. Nor does the Nixon Administration have to bid much ideologically for this electorate. Despite his success in enlarging the scope of white Southern revolt, George Wallace failed to reach far enough or strongly enough beyond the Deep South to give his American Independent Party the national base required for a viable future. Republican Nixon won most of the Outer South, establishing the GOP as the ascending party of the local white majority. Having achieved statewide success only in the Deep South, and facing competition from a Southern Republicanism mindful of its opportunity, the Wallace movement cannot maintain an adequate political base and is bound to serve, like past American third parties, as a way station for groups abandoning one party for another. Some Wallace voters were longtime Republicans, but the great majority were conservative Democrats who have been moving—and should continue to do so—towards the GOP.

The linkage of Wallace voting to the obsolescent Democratic loyalties of certain areas and groups can also be proved far beyond the old Confederacy. . . . The pattern of Wallace support in the Ohio Valley, instead of standing out in backlash-prone industrial areas, followed rural contours of traditional Democratic strength, moving farthest north along the Scioto

River, central Ohio's roadway of Virginia and Kentucky migration. And in New York and Pennsylvania, . . . certain levels of Wallace support probed farthest north along the Susquehanna, Delaware and Hudson valleys, outliers of traditionally Democratic non-Yankee rural strength. Out West, Wallace percentages were greatest in the Oklahoma- and Texas-settled towns of California's Central Valley, the populist mining and logging counties of the Rocky Mountains, the traditionally Democratic Mormon reaches of Idaho, and in Alaska's long-Democratic sluice and sawmill districts.

In addition to Western or Southern Democrats of conservative or populist bent, Wallace also scored well among Catholics, but only in certain areas. From Maine to Michigan, across most of the belt of Yankee-settled territory where local cleavage, though changing, still pits Protestant Republicans against urban Catholic Democrats, the Catholic trend away from the Democrats was slight. However, in the greater New York area, as well as Gary and Cleveland, where minority group (Negro and/or Jewish) power has taken control of local Democratic machinery, Catholic backing of Wallace was considerable. Here . . . Catholics are leaving the Democratic Party.

The common denominator of Wallace support, Catholic or Protestant, is alienation from the Democratic Party and a strong trend—shown in other years and other contests—towards the GOP. Although most of Wallace's votes came from Democrats, he principally won those in motion between a Democratic past and a Republican future. In the last few weeks of the campaign, labor union activity, economic issues and the escalating two-party context of October, 1968, drew many Wallace-leaning Northern blue-collar workers back into the Democratic fold. Only those fully alienated by the national Democratic Party stuck with Wallace in the voting booth. Offered a three-party context, these sociopolitical streams preferred populist Wallace; a two-party context would have drawn them into the GOP. Three quarters or more of the Wallace electorate represented lost Nixon votes.

A few states—Mississippi or Alabama—may indulge in future third-party or states rights efforts. The Wallace party itself, however, has dubious prospects, being not a broad-based national grouping but a transient 1968 aggregation of conservative Democrats otherwise trending into the Republican Party. Generally speaking, the South is more realistic than its critics believe, and nothing more than an effective and responsibly conservative Nixon Administration is necessary to bring most of the Southern Wallace electorate into the fold against a Northeastern liberal Democratic presidential nominee. Abandonment of civil rights enforcement would be self-defeating. Maintenance of Negro voting rights in Dixie, far from being contrary to GOP interests, is essential if southern conservatives are to be pressured into switching to the Republican Party—for Negroes are beginning to seize control of the national Democratic Party in some Black Belt areas.

Successful moderate conservatism is also likely to attract to the Republican side some of the Northern blue-collar workers who flirted with George

Wallace but ultimately backed Hubert Humphrey. Fears that a Republican administration would undermine Social Security, Medicare, collective bargaining and aid to education played a major part in keeping socially conservative blue-collar workers and senior citizens loyal to the 1968 Democratic candidate. Assuming that a Nixon Administration can dispel these apprehensions, it ought to be able to repeat—with much more permanence—Eisenhower's great blue-collar success of 1956. Sociologically, the Republican Party is becoming much more lower-middle class and much less establishmentarian than it was during the Nineteen-Fifties, and pursuit of an increasing portion of the Northern blue-collar electorate—an expansion of its 1968 Catholic triumph in greater New York City—would be a logical extension of this trend.

Although the appeal of a successful Nixon Administration and the lack of a Wallace candidacy would greatly swell the 1972 Republican vote in the South, West, Border and the Catholic North, the 1972 GOP may well simultaneously lose a lesser number of 1968 supporters among groups reacting against the party's emerging Southern, Western and New York Irish majority. . . . Yankees, Megalopolitan silk-stocking voters and Scandinavians from Maine across the Great Lakes to the Pacific all showed a distinct Democratic trend in the years between 1960 and 1968. Such disaffection will doubtlessly continue, but its principal impact has already been felt. Richard Nixon won only 38 percent of the total 1968 presidential vote on Manhattan's rich East Side; he took only 44 percent of the ballots in Scarsdale, the city's richest suburb; New England's Yankee counties and towns produced Nixon majorities down 10 percent to 15 percent from 1960 levels; fashionable San Francisco shifted toward the Democrats; and Scandinavian Minnesota and Washington state backed Humphrey, as did the Scandinavian northwest of Wisconsin.

. . . All of these locales shifted *towards* the Democrats during the 1960–68 period. Because the local re-alignment pivoted on liberal Republicans rather than conservative Democrats, these areas evidenced little or no support for George Wallace. Beyond the bounds of states that went Democratic in 1968, the Yankee, silk-stocking establishmentarian and Scandinavian trends predominate only in Vermont, New Hampshire and Oregon. Although Northern California, Wisconsin, Ohio's old Western Reserve, central Iowa and parts of the Dakotas are likewise influenced, other conservative trends—those of Southern California suburbanites, German Catholics of the upper Farm Belt and the quasi-Southern Democrats of the Ohio Valley—should keep those states Republican. Yankee, Northeastern silk-stocking and Scandinavian disaffection with the GOP is concentrated in states which the party has already lost, and it menaces only a few states which the GOP won in 1968.

The upcoming cycle of American politics is likely to match a dominant Republican Party based in the Heartland, South and California against a minority Democratic Party based in the Northeast and the Pacific Northwest (and encompassing Southern as well as Northern Negroes). With such support behind it, the GOP can easily afford to lose the states of Massachusetts,

New York and Michigan—and is likely to do so except in landslide years. Together with the District of Columbia, the top ten Humphrey states— Hawaii, Washington, Minnesota, Michigan, West Virginia, New York, Connecticut, Rhode Island, Massachusetts and Maine—should prove to be the core of national Democratic strength. . . . The new battlegrounds of quadrennial presidential politics are likely to be California, Ohio and Pennsylvania.

Unluckily for the Democrats, their major impetus is centered in stagnant Northern industrial states—and within those states, in old decaying cities, in a Yankee countryside that has fewer people than in 1900, and in the most expensive suburbs. Beyond this, in the South and West, the Democrats dominate only two expanding voting blocs—Latins and Negroes. From space-center Florida across the booming Texas plains to the Los Angeles–San Diego suburban corridor, the nation's fastest-growing areas are strongly Republican and conservative. Even in the Northeast, the few rapidly growing suburbs are conservative-trending areas. . . . Because of this demographic pattern, the South and West are gaining electoral votes and national political power at the expense of the Northeast. . . . The conservative Sun Belt cities are undergoing a population boom—and getting more conservative—while the old liberal cities of the Northeast decline. . . . The Northeast is steadily losing relative political importance to the Sun Belt.

CHART 1   THE DECLINE IN THE BIG CITY PRESIDENTIAL VOTE, 1960–68

City*	Total Major Party Vote for President (In Thousands)		
	1960	1964	1968
New York City	3,081	2,811	2,591
Chicago	1,674	1,607	1,433
Los Angeles	1,053	1,079	1,012
Philadelphia	914	910	826
Detroit	743	681	598
Baltimore	317	317	290
Cleveland	338	302	263
St. Louis	304	268	221
Milwaukee	309	298	256
San Francisco	341	324	272
Boston	292	255	225

* The eleven largest cities of 1960 (excluding Sun Belt Houston); several will no longer be on the list when the 1970 Census is completed.

One of the greatest political myths of the decade—a product of liberal self-interest—is that the Republican Party cannot attain national dominance without mobilizing liberal support in the big cities, appealing to "liberal" youth, empathizing with "liberal" urbanization, gaining substantial Negro support and courting the affluent young professional classes of "suburbia." The actual demographic and political facts convey a very different message.

. . . The big city political era is over in the United States. Chart 1 lists the considerable 1960–68 slippage in the presidential vote cast by the leading big cities. With Negroes moving into the cities, whites have moved out. Moreover, white urban populations are getting increasingly conservative. Richard Nixon and George Wallace together won 40 percent of the vote in liberal New York City. Perhaps more to the point, leading big city states like New York, Michigan and Massachusetts are no longer necessary for national Republican victory.

Youth is important, but voters under 25 cast only 7.4 percent of the nation's ballots in 1968. And while many Northeastern young people are more liberal and Democratic than their parents—especially the affluent and anarchic progeny of the Establishment—the reverse seems to be true in Southern, Border, Rocky Mountain, Catholic, lower-middle-class and working-class areas. In these locales, the young electorate's trend against local political tradition helps the GOP, as does resentment of the blithe nihilism of the children of the affluent society.

While urbanization is changing the face of America, and the GOP must take political note of this fact, it presents the opposite of a problem. A generation ago, the coming of age of the working-class central cities condemned the Republican Party to minority status, but the new "urbanization"—suburbanization is often a better description—is a middle-class impetus shaping the same ignominy for the Democrats. All across the nation, the fastest-growing urban areas are steadily increasing their Republican pluralities, while the old central cities—seat of the New Deal era—are casting steadily fewer votes for Democratic liberalism. No major American city is losing population so rapidly as arch-Democratic and establishmentarian Boston, while the fastest-growing urban area in the nation is Southern California's staunchly conservative Orange County, and the fastest growing cities are conservative strongholds like Phoenix, Dallas, Houston, Anaheim, San Diego and Fort Lauderdale.

Substantial Negro support is not necessary to national Republican victory in light of the 1968 election returns. Obviously, the GOP can build a winning coalition without Negro votes. Indeed, Negro-Democratic mutual identification was a major source of Democratic loss—and Republican or American Independent Party profit—in many sections of the nation.

. . . The liberal and Democratic 1960–68 shifts of a few (now atypical) silk-stocking counties were dwarfed by the conservative trends of the vast new tracts of middle-class suburbia. Actually, the Democratic upswing in a number of rich suburban areas around New York, Boston and Philadelphia is nothing more than an extension of the liberal establishmentarian behavior of Manhattan's East Side, Boston's Beacon Hill and Philadelphia's Rittenhouse Square. Typical suburban behavior is something else again.

Centered in the Sun Belt, the nation's heaviest suburban growth is solidly middle-class and conservative. Contemporary suburban expansion in the Northeast pales next to the spread of the Florida, Texas, Arizona and Southern California suburbs. Rapid, although less spectacular, suburban growth is occurring in the areas around Camden (New Jersey), Washington, D.C., Richmond, Atlanta, Memphis, St. Louis, Chicago, Oklahoma City, Tulsa and Denver. These suburbs are also conservative, often highly so. And even the few fast-growing Northeastern suburban counties—Suffolk, New York; Burlington, New Jersey; Prince Georges, Maryland—are conservative-trending, middle-class sections. The principal exception is Maryland's rich but fast-expanding Montgomery County, liberal seat of the upper echelons of Washington's federal bureaucracy.

From a national perspective, the silk-stocking liberal suburbs of Boston, New York, Philadelphia, San Francisco and (to a lesser extent) Chicago and Washington cast only a minute fraction of the ballots wielded by the preponderance of unfashionable lower-middle- and middle-income suburbs. And because more and more new suburbanites come from lower-middle-income backgrounds, this gap should widen.

The National Commission on Urban Problems, chaired by former Illinois Senator Paul Douglas, has drawn attention to the increasingly powerful shift of blue-collar and lower-middle-class population to suburbia, but surprisingly few establishment liberals understand or admit these demographic facts of life. Instead, they typically portray the large conservative majority of Americans as a mere obsolescent and shrinking periphery of society, meanwhile painting their own peer group as the expanding segment of the nation committed to cosmopolitan thinking, technological sophistication and cultural change.

This myopia has considerable precedent. Since the days of Alexander Hamilton and the Federalists, the United States—and the Northeast in particular—has periodically supported a privileged elite, blind to the needs and interests of the large national majority. The corporate welfarists, planners and academicians of the Liberal Establishment are the newest of these elites, and their interests—for one thing, a high and not necessarily too productive rate of government social, educational, scientific and research spending—are as vested as those of Coolidge-Hoover era financiers and industrialists. The great political upheaval of the Nineteen-Sixties is not that of Senator Eugene McCarthy's relatively small group of upper-middle-class and intellectual supporters, but a populist revolt of the American masses who have been elevated by prosperity to middle-class status and conservatism. Their revolt is against the caste, policies and taxation of the mandarins of Establishment liberalism.

Granted that the new populist coalition includes very few Negroes—

they have become almost entirely Democratic and exert very little influence on the GOP—black solidarity within the Democratic Party is rapidly enlarging Negro influence and job opportunities in many old Northern central cities. In New York, few Negroes have deserted the Democratic Party even to support Republican liberals Rockefeller, Javits, and Lindsay. . . . These intensely Democratic Negro loyalties are not rooted in fear of the GOP or its promise of a return to law and order, but in a realization that the Democratic Party can serve as a vehicle for Negro advancement—just as other groups have used politics to climb the social and economic ladder of urban America.

Ethnic polarization is a longstanding hallmark of American politics, not an unprecedented and menacing development of 1968. As illustrated throughout this book, ethnic and cultural division has so often shaped American politics that, given the immense midcentury impact of Negro enfranchisement and integration, reaction to this change almost inevitably had to result in political realignment. Moreover, American history has another example of a persecuted minority—the Nineteenth-Century Irish—who, in the face of considerable discrimination and old-stock animosity, likewise poured their ethnic numbers into the Democratic Party alone, winning power, jobs and socioeconomic opportunity through local political skill rather than the benevolence of usually-Republican national administrations.

For a half-century after the Civil War, the regular Democratic fidelity of the unpopular Irish city machines helped keep much of the nation Republican, and it seems possible that rising Negro participation in (national) Democratic politics from Manhattan to Mississippi may play a similar role in the post-1968 cycle. Growing Negro influence in—and conservative Southern, Western and Catholic departure from—the Democratic Party also suggests that Northeastern liberals ought to be able to dominate the party, which in turn must accelerate the sectional and ideological re-alignment already underway.

To the extent that the ethnic and racial overtones of American political behavior and alignment are appreciated, they are often confused or mis-stated. For example, far from being opposed by all non-whites, Richard Nixon was strongly supported by one non-white group—the Chinese. San Francisco's Chinese electorate was more Republican in 1968 than the city's white population. Nor is today's Republican Party Protestant rather than Catholic. In New York City, the party is becoming the vehicle of the Italians and Irish, and in the Upper Farm Belt—Wisconsin, Minnesota and North Dakota—German Catholics are moving to the fore. From the first days of the Republic, American politics have been a maze of ethnic, cultural and sectional oppositions and loyalties, and this has not deterred progress or growth. The new popular conservative majority has many ethnic strains, and portraits showing it as a white Anglo-Saxon Protestant monolith are highly misleading.

The emerging Republican majority spoke clearly in 1968 for a shift away from the sociological jurisprudence, moral permissiveness, experimental residential, welfare and educational programing and massive federal spending by which the Liberal (mostly Democratic) Establishment sought to propagate liberal institutions and ideology—and all the while reap growing economic benefits. The dominion of this impetus is inherent in the list of Republican-trending groups and potentially Republican Wallace electorates of 1968: Southerners, Borderers, Germans, Scotch-Irish, Pennsylvania Dutch, Irish, Italians, Eastern Europeans and other urban Catholics, middle-class suburbanites, Sun Belt residents, Rocky Mountain and Pacific Interior populists. Democrats among these groups were principally alienated from their party by its social programs and increasing identification with the Northeastern Establishment and ghetto alike. Except among isolationist Germans, resentment of the Vietnamese war, far from helping to forge the GOP majority, actually produced *Democratic* gains among the groups most affected: silk-stocking Megalopolitans, the San Francisco-Berkeley-Madison-Ann Arbor electorate, Scandinavian progressives and Jews. As for the Republican trend groups, nothing characterizes their outlook so much as a desire to dispel the Liberal Establishment's philosophy of taxation and redistribution (partly to itself) and reverse the encroachment of government in the social life of the nation.

Shorn of power, stripped of vested interests in misleading and unsuccessful programs, the Liberal Establishment may narrow its gap between words and deeds which helped to drive racial and youthful minorities into open revolt. So changed, Democratic liberalism will once again become a vital and creative force in national politics, usually too innovative to win a presidential race, but injecting a needed leavening of humanism into the middle-class *realpolitik* of the new Republican coalition.

Because the Republicans are little dependent on the Liberal Establishment or urban Negroes—the two groups most intimately, though dissimilarly, concerned with present urban and welfare policies—they have the political freedom to disregard the multitude of vested interests which have throttled national urban policy. The GOP is particularly lucky not to be weighted down with commitment to the political blocs, power brokers and poverty concessionaires of the decaying central cities of the North, now that national growth is shifting to suburbia, the South and the West. The American future lies in a revitalized countryside, a demographically ascendant Sun Belt and suburbia, and new towns—perhaps mountainside linear cities astride monorails 200 miles from Phoenix, Memphis or Atlanta. National policy will have to direct itself towards this future and its constituencies; and perhaps an administration so oriented can also deal realistically with the central cities where Great Society political largesse has so demonstrably failed.

When new eras and alignments have evolved in American politics, the ascending party has ridden the economic and demographic wave of the future: with Jefferson, a nation pushing inland from the Federalist seaboard and Tidewater; with Jackson, the trans-Appalachian New West; with Lincoln, the free-soil West and industrial North; with McKinley, a full-blown industrial North feeding from a full dinner pail; and with Roosevelt, the emergence of the big cities and the coming of age of the immigrant masses. Now it is Richard Nixon's turn to build a new era on the immense middle-class impetus of Sun Belt and suburbia. Thus, it is appropriate that much of the emerging Republican majority lies in the top growth states (California, Arizona, Texas and Florida) or new suburbia, while Democratic trends correlate with stability and decay (New England, New York City, Michigan, West Virginia and San Francisco-Berkeley).

. . . The GOP core areas are the Mountain, Farm and Outer South states. The Deep South will become a GOP core area once it abandons third-party schemes. The Democratic stronghold is obvious: New York and New England. Most of the upcoming cycle's serious presidential campaign strategy will relate to three battleground areas: (1) the Pacific; (2) the Ohio-Mississippi Valley (Ohio, Indiana, Illinois, Kentucky and Missouri); and (3) the non-Yankee Northeast (New Jersey, Pennsylvania, Delaware and Maryland). Overall trends favor the Republicans in each of these battlegrounds. . . .

The Artificial Majority

Theodore J. Lowi

The election of 1970 was an overwhelming bore. James Reston observed in *The New York Times* that "None have come forward," and he, like many others, had in mind such leaders as Humphrey, Muskie, Stevenson, Bayh, McGovern, Tunney, Kennedy, Mondale, Hart, and House members and gubernatorial candidates too numerous to mention. On the Republican side, many candidates stuck like barnacles to their Democratic opponents, and couldn't be pried loose to give voters a clear view of the difference. Humphrey ran a virtual law-and-order campaign; Stevenson absolutely avoided distinction until late in the campaign; Tunney seemed just younger, not better.

The only excitement was the uncertainty of outcome in a few states. But if politics is to be more than a winter replacement for night baseball, mere excitement is not enough.

There was only one surprise, and it was not the stridency of Spiro Agnew. What he did was absolutely typical of Republicans, especially at the end of periods of war, when there is usually a Republican majority and a bit of panic in the air as to whether all the killing accomplished anything toward ridding the world of America's enemies. If it had not been Agnew, some other figure would have taken the lead that Nixon took during the 1950s. The surprise was the frailty of the liberals, liberal Democrats mainly, but Republican liberals as well. It was the unwillingness of these people to bring to the electorate the message that the country is in trouble; the reluctance of these usually thoughtful public men to define our problems in terms that might lead to meaningful public policies. The surprise lay in their willingness to let Agnew define the agenda and the terms of discourse. In politics, as in the courtroom, he who does that has gone a long way toward winning the debate.

From Theodore J. Lowi, "The Artificial Majority," The Nation, CCXI (December 2, 1970), pp. 591–94. Reprinted by permission of The Nation.

Of course, it was not a matter of personal frailty. These men have all demonstrated courage upon occasion. There is something about the political system itself that explains their espousal of politics-as-usual at a time when everything else is unusual. So the question really is: what kind of electoral and party system do we have that it can be impervious to social change and disorder?

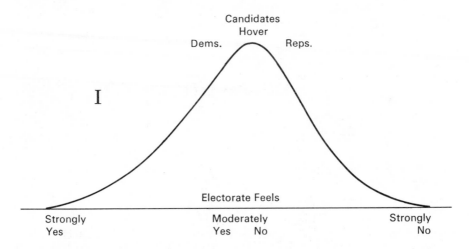

How the Electorate Looks to the Candidates

Part of the answer lies in the assumption of centrality, which goes back to Locke and passes to us through a host of American historians and political scientists. It supposes that the American spirit is, as the statistician would say, "normally distributed." Americans, it is argued, think very much alike about many fundamental things. And when they disagree, they do not clash with much passion. Only a very small percentage of the population feels intensely about issues, and they are best treated as exceptions, as intellectual outsiders. Extreme disagreement means unwillingness to compromise, and that violates one of the unwritten but sacred rules of American politics. The attitudes of Americans are assumed to distribute themselves like the model given in Diagram I.

That is not necessarily a true description of Americans. It is only a model, but it is the model that political personalities carry around in their heads. . . . They might have been surprised to learn from *The Real Majority* that the electorate had moved a bit to the right; but no one could tell the candidates, and no one tried to tell them, that the mass of voters had ceased to hover around dead center.

This assumption is reinforced by the opinion polls, but in a peculiar way. It is doubtful that the polls influence people by reporting results with which the previously uncommitted align themselves. The more likely explanation is a "McLuhan effect"—the medium is indeed the message. Polling agencies, first of all, ask only certain questions; there is simply no room for everything on the questionnaire. Often the only issues touched upon are those that have been on the agenda for some time, and it is probable that for many of these, opinion hovers around the center.

A second important factor in polling is the way in which questions are asked and responses are structured. For example, the respondent may be asked how he feels about "the law-and-order issue," and he will have to pick a single response (either For or Against; or Strongly For, For, Against, Strongly Against—"Please check only one"). Or the question could be more specific: "Do you favor appropriating more money for the local police department?" In either case, the respondent on the usual opinion poll cannot expand on his response. Instead, he undertakes an inner dialogue, trying to balance all his plusses and minuses in order to give the interviewer his best accounting, which is really a complex response expressed in terribly simple terms. It is a "net response," a "Well, yes and no," or a "Well, I don't know," or, to be safe, a "moderate Yes" or "Maybe not."

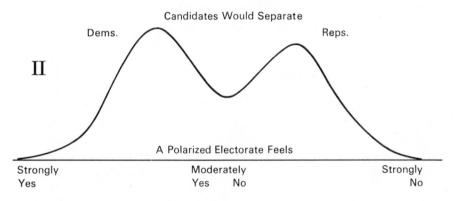

How the Electorate Actually Looks on Some Issues

The polling agency must then code these responses for entry on computer cards. These "net responses" have to be treated centrally, as moderate yesses and noes. At one level that is accurate; yet many of these middle-ground respondents may actually feel very intensely about certain aspects of the questions, but were given no opportunity on the questionnaire to express these intensities. The result is reaffirmation of the assumption of centrality. Reaffirmation is putting it too mildly. The polls lend Scientific Validation to the assumption of centrality.

Two most important results flow from this assumption of centrality. First, if candidates or parties believe that voters are overwhelmingly in the middle, it would be irrational of them to develop appeals and campaign strategies that were not center-oriented. Exactly the same problem arises in merchandising. Competing service stations occupy all four corners of a single intersection, where the traffic patterns are concentrated. To move slightly away from that center would be to move from the site of best exposure. Similarly, the candidates feel that, if they moved "away from center," they would be moving down the slope of the curve, where obviously there are fewer voters—if it is true that they are so distributed.

Over the years, a few major party candidates—Taft and Goldwater are the most important examples—have made a different assumption. They thought it more probable that voters were distinctly partisan and tended to distribute themselves "bi-modally," like a camel's hump, rather than in a single, central mode. In that case it would be rational to move to one or the other side of center, as suggested in Diagram II. Only Goldwater got a Presidential nomination and the opportunity to test this theory. His defeat does not necessarily prove that there are no clearly divisive issues in the country, but it obviously convinced most candidates for all public offices that the centricity assumption was the safest.

The second result of assuming centricity is the self-fulfilling prophecy. If candidates assume that voters are moderate and centrally distributed, and if they conduct their appeals accordingly, they help bring about that very situation.

This second consequence is not as simple as it sounds, because it does not happen merely because the politicians influence thousands of voters to be moderate by making moderate appeals. That may be the effect in a few cases, but more often something else happens, as we can see all too clearly in the 1970 campaigns.

Centricity prevails, first of all, because the candidates give the voters no choice but centricity. Even if the polls did not tilt the responses in favor of moderation, the candidates would. They hang together so closely around a mean that voters must vote for a middle-of-the-road position or stay home.

And even that is not the most important part of the process. How do candidates hang close together? They do it by "strategic obfuscation." In other words, they define the issues in terms so general that each candidate can virtually subsume the other. That is why the Democrats let the Agnew Republicans define the terms of discourse in 1970, why they so readily accepted "Law and Order" as the issue.

Law and Order is a generalized concept, a basket phrase that includes six, eight, even ten specific issues. Supporting this generalized form of law and order, the Democratic candidate could say, "I'm for Law and Order— with justice," as the Republicans were saying, "I'm for Law and Order— with safety." Thus they create the impression of debate, while in fact they agree to define as irrelevant to the campaign the specific issues that are part of the law-and-order basket.

At least two things follow from this. First, each voter goes through the same internal dialogue as does the respondent to an opinion poll. He has only one vote and must use it according to his own balancing of the various issues in the law-and-order package. This pulls him toward the center because, if he is to vote at all, he must vote "on net" as a Democrat or a Republican.

But a second, fascinating thing happens: the extremes are eliminated statistically! Let us say that six hard-core issues are hidden underneath the candidate's definition of law and order. Let us even propose that the electorate is polarized on all six of these, so that voter distributions on attitudes toward racial integration, student radicals, police powers and restraints, preventive detention, the Black Panthers and unilateral withdrawal are all bi-modal, like the camel's hump, with most voters intensely for or intensely against. See then what happens when the six are treated simultaneously under the law-and-order concept, rather than one issue at a time, as in a real debate.

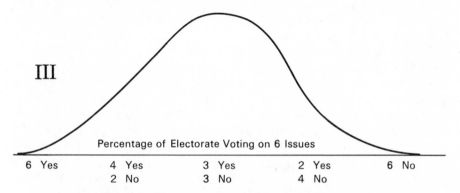

How the Electorate Actually Looks When Six (or more) Polarized Issues Are Presented Simultaneously

Diagram III is the almost inevitable result of grouping issues in one basket, because the same people are not intensely for or against all the issues. Racial questions are salient to certain voters, who will feel intensely "yes" or "no" about questions in that field. But many of these people care little one way or another about preventive detention or students. Thus only a very few highly militant types will be consistent *and* intense on all six (or eight or ten) issues.

You can be almost certain that when politicians advance conglomerate rather than specific definitions of issues they will produce, quite artificially, the impression of centrality. In effect, the Real Majority is an Artificial Majority, created by artifice, and in fact combining very unlike positions. As the great political scientist E. E. Schattschneider put it thirty years ago, "Persuasion is unnecessary or secondary. Politicians take people as they find them. The politician has a technical specialty based on a profitable discovery about the behavior of numbers."

This explains the paradox of political quiescence in the midst of social disorder. When they can, politicians avoid polarized issues; when avoidance becomes impossible, they lump controversies together and thus cancel out the extremes. This is probably the controlling reason why American electoral and party politics are so stable, and so isolated from the big issues of the day. It also suggests that, as the social turmoil increases, the separation between party politics and society becomes ever greater.

This pattern also suggests why there is rarely much to be gained from looking to party and electoral politics as agents of great changes. American party politics is designed to maintain the system. It maintains good things about the system, and it militates against removing bad things. And once change comes, usually through other channels, party politics adjusts and maintains the change as well. For example, a party politics all by itself would never have spread suffrage to Southern blacks; but once the suffrage was expanded, a party politics emerged to help realize a more effective participation.

Once in a great while political parties and elections do become channels of change. Students of these critical elections, particularly V. O. Key, Dean Burnham and Duncan MacRae, have located perhaps five national elections in 180 years that directly produced significant changes in the system. The last such "critical election" was probably 1928 (when Herbert Hoover defeated Alfred Smith), following which parties were for a brief while organized in ways relevant to making significant public policies. Students of these matters have probably been expecting another critical election for several years now, since the conditions again seem ripe. But one has not come because the polls have made politicians far more rational than they used to be, and rationality hath made cowards of them all.

It now strikes them as being safer and surer to follow the opinion pattern than to try occasionally to shape it. They fail to realize that in trying to follow opinion they are in fact shaping it—through the mechanism of the self-fulfilling prophecy.

Consequently, change will come, if it does, from forces and organizations outside the party-political system. The election just held was good proof of this, for there has never been a better opportunity for candidates to embrace change. Changes come through social movements, through cumulative shifts of emphasis in education, through scientific breakthroughs, through an occasional muckraking book. Changes often come through more aristocratic channels, such as Supreme Court decisions or capitalistic advancement of important new technologies.

We need to revise our outlook toward campaigns and elections. Party and electoral politics can be understood only if accepted as the way to buy stability—Law and Order in the broadest sense. When we want a little productive disorder, we must look elsewhere. And if in large numbers we were to turn away from party politics, treating elections as the great bore they have become, perhaps that would bring on a critical election, because politicians would try a little harder to get our attention.

The Radical Right: The Dispossessed

Daniel Bell

The American has never yet had to face the trials of Job. . . . Hitherto America has been the land of universal good will, confidence in life, inexperience of poisons. Until yesterday, it believed itself immune from the hereditary plagues of mankind. It could not credit the danger of being suffocated or infected by any sinister principle. . . .

George Santayana,
*Character and Opinion
in the United States*

In the winter of 1961–62, the "radical right" emerged into quick prominence on the American political scene. The immediate reasons for its appearance are not hard to understand. The simple fact was that the Republican Party, now out of power, inevitably began to polarize (much as the Democrats, if they were out of power, might have split over the civil rights and integration issue), and the right wing came to the fore. The right-wing Republicans have an ideology—perhaps the only group in American life that possesses one today—but during the Eisenhower administration they had been trapped because "their" party was in power, and the American political system, with its commitment to deals and penalties, does not easily invite ideological—or even principled—political splits. An administration in office, possessing patronage and prestige, can "paper over" the inherent divisions within a party. But out of office, such conflicts are bound to arise, and so they did within the G.O.P.

From Daniel Bell, "The Dispossessed," Daniel Bell, ed., The Radical Right (Garden City, N.Y.: Doubleday & Company, 1962), pp. 1–5, 8–21, 41–45. Reprinted by permission of the author.

Clearly there is more to all this than merely a contest for power within a party. Something new has been happening in American life. It is not the rancor of the radical right, for rancor has been a recurrent aspect of the American political temper. Nor is it just the casting of suspicions or the conspiracy theory of politics, elements of which have streaked American life in the past. What is new, and this is why the problem assumes importance far beyond the question of the fight for control of a party, is the ideology of this movement—its readiness to jettison constitutional processes and to suspend liberties, to condone Communist methods in the fighting of Communism.

Few countries in the world have been able to maintain a social system that allows political power to pass peacefully from one social group to another without the threat of hostilities or even civil war. In the mid-twentieth century, we see such historical centers of civilization as France, let alone states just beginning to work out viable democratic frameworks, torn apart by ideological groups that will not accept a consensual system of politics. The politics of civility, to use Edward Shils' phrase, has been the achievement of only a small group of countries—those largely within an Anglo-Saxon or Scandinavian political tradition. Today, the ideology of the right wing in America threatens the politics of American civility. Its commitment and its methods threaten to disrupt the "fragile consensus" that underlies the American political system.

I believe that the radical right is only a small minority, but it gains force from the confusions within the world of conservatism regarding the changing character of American life. What the right as a whole fears is the erosion of its own social position, the collapse of its power, the increasing incomprehensibility of a world—now overwhelmingly technical and complex—that has changed so drastically within a lifetime.

The right, thus, fights a rear-guard action. But its very anxieties illustrate the deep fissures that have opened in American society as a whole, as a result of the complex structural changes that have been taking place in the past thirty years or so. And more, they show that the historic American response to social crisis, the characteristic American style, is no longer adequate to the tasks.

The Emergence of the Radical Right

Social groups that are dispossessed invariably seek targets on whom they can vent their resentments, targets whose power can serve to explain their dispossession. In this respect, the radical right of the early 1960s is in no way different from the Populists of the 1890s, who for years traded successfully on such simple formulas as "Wall Street," "international bankers," and "the Trusts," in order to have not only targets but "explanations" for politics. What lends especial rancor to the radical right of the 1960s is its sense of betrayal not by its "enemies" but by its "friends."

After twenty years of Democratic power, the right-wing Republicans hoped that the election of Dwight Eisenhower would produce its own utopia: the dismantling of the welfare state, the taming of labor unions, and the "magical" rollback of Communism in Europe. None of this happened. Eisenhower's Labor Secretary courted the unions, social security benefits increased, and, during the recession, unemployment benefits were extended, while the government, in good Keynesian style, ran a twelve-billion-dollar budgetary deficit. In foreign policy, Secretary of State Dulles first trumpeted a "liberation policy," and then retreated, talked brinkmanship but moved cautiously, announced a policy of "massive retaliation," and, toward the end of his tenure, abandoned even that, so that the subsequent Eisenhower moves toward summitry were no different from, or from a "hard" right line were "softer" than, the Truman–Acheson containment policy. Thus eight years of moderation proved more frustrating than twenty years of opposition.

Once the Democrats were back in office, the charge of softness in dealing with Communism could again become a political, as well as an ideological, issue. And the radical right was quick to act. The abject failure in Cuba—the name of the landing place for the abortive invasion, the Bay of Pigs, itself became a cruel historical joke—seemed to reinforce the picture of the United States that emerged out of the stalemate in Korea a decade ago—of a lurching, lumbering power, lacking will, unsure of its strength, indecisive in its course, defensive in its posture. The theme of the radical right was voiced by Rear Admiral Chester Ward (ret.), the Washington director of the American Security Council, who declared, "Americans are tired of defeats. They are tired of surrenders covered up as 'negotiated settlements.' They are, indeed, tired of so much talk and little action by our leaders. For the first time in sixteen years of the cold war, a demand for victory is beginning to roll into Washington."

Thus the stage was set.

The factors that precipitated the radical right into quick notoriety in early 1961 were the rancor of their attacks and the flash spread of the movement in so many different places. McCarthyism in the mid-1950s was never an organized movement; it was primarily an atmosphere of fear, generated by a one-man swashbuckler cutting a wide swath through the headlines. In some localities—in Hollywood, on Broadway, in some universities—individual vigilante groups did begin a drumbeat drive against Communists or former fellow-travelers, but by and large the main agitation was conducted in government by Congressional or state legislators, using agencies of legislative investigation to assert their power. In contrast, the radical right of the 1960s has been characterized by a multitude of organizations that seemingly have been able to evoke an intense emotional response from a devoted following.

Three elements conjoined to attract public attention to the radical right. One was the disclosure of the existence of the John Birch Society, a secretive, conspiratorial group obedient to a single leader, Robert Welch, who argued that one could combat the methods of Communism only with Communist methods. Thus, membership lists were never disclosed, fronts were organized to conduct campaigns (such as the one to impeach Chief Justice Warren, which turned, with heavy-handed jocularity, into calls to "hang" him), and a symbol of patriotism was put forth in the name of an Army captain who had been shot in China by the Communists.

The second was the fashionable spread of week-long seminars of anti-Communist "schools," conducted by evangelist preachers who adapted old revivalist techniques to a modern idiom, which swept sections of the country, particularly the Southwest and California. These schools promised to initiate the student into the "mysteries" of Communism by unfolding its secret aims, or unmasking the philosophy of "dialectical materialism." And, third, there was the disclosure of the existence of extreme fanatic groups, such as the Minutemen, who organized "guerrilla-warfare seminars," complete with rifles and mortars, in preparation for the day when patriots would have to take to the hills to organize resistance against a Communist-run America. Such fringe movements, ludicrous as they were, illustrated the hysteria that had seized some sections of the radical right. . . .

The Psychological Posture

The psychological stock-in-trade of the radical right rests on a threefold appeal: the breakdown of moral fiber in the United States; a conspiracy theory of a "control apparatus" in the government which is selling out the country; and a detailed forecast regarding the Communist "takeover" of the United States.

Central to the appeal of the radical right is the argument that old-fashioned patriotism has been subverted by the cosmopolitan intellectual. An editorial in the *National Review* on the space flight of astronaut John Glenn sums up this theme in striking fashion. Glenn, said the editorial, is an authentic American hero because he is unashamed to say that he gets a thrill when the American flag goes by and because he will openly acknowledge the guidance of God.

It is "American" as in older storybooks, as in legends, and myths and dreams— brought up to technological date, of course—as, let's say it plainly, in the pre-1930 Fourth of July celebrations; and the Saturday Evening Post covers before they, too, not long ago, went modern; and a touch of soap opera. Yes, a bit corny —for that is the traditional American style. Too corny by far for the Norman Cousinses, Arthur Schlesingers, Adlai Stevensons, Henry Steele Commagers, Max Lerners, John Kenneth Galbraiths, and those others of our enlightened age—so many of them now fluttering around the Kennedy throne—who have long left behind the old provincial corn for a headier global brew.

Here one finds the praise of the "simple virtues"—they are always simple—the evocation of small-town life, the uncluttered Arcadia, against the modern, the sophisticated, the cosmopolitan. But the Glenn flight, according to the editorial, proved more: it proved the victory of "man" against the "mechanical" and, implicitly, against the intellectual. "This and that went wrong, we all learned, with the unbelievably complex mechanism of Glenn's ship, as it whirled through the emptiness of Space," continued the *National Review*.

The altitude control thingamajigs didn't work right. There were troubles in some of the communication instruments. A signal indicated that the latching of the heat shield was precarious. This and that went wrong with the mechanism, and man took over and brought Friendship 7 to its strange harbor. . . . And that is fine news, though it should hardly be news. It is good technically, because we Americans, with our gadgetry obsession and our wish for too much convenience, safety and comfort, tend to crowd all our machines and vehicles with too immensely many tricky devices. Every additional transistor in these automatic mechanisms means that many more connections to loosen; every valve can fail to open; every fuse can blow. Many sober engineers believe that this over-complication habit accounts for not a few of our missile and space troubles. . . . It is better news still, philosophically, we might say, because it reminds us that there is no such thing, and never will be, as a "thinking" machine. Only man thinks, wills, decides, dares. No machine, on land, in sea, air or space, can do man's job for him: can choose, for good or ill.

The fact that "man" is also the one who designs the machines is, of course, beside the point of the editorial. Its implication is fairly clear: don't let anyone tell us that space (or politics, economics, or life) is complicated; machines can never be perfect ("every valve can fail to open; every fuse can blow"); only "man" (not the scientist, the intellectual, or the unsober engineer) can think. In short, America will be back on an even keel when the simple virtues prevail.

The theme of conspiracy haunts the mind of the radical rightist. It permits him to build up the image of the children of darkness and the children of light. It exempts him from having to specify empirical proofs. General Edwin Walker told a Congressional committee that a "control apparatus" was "selling out the Constitution, national sovereignty and national independence," but when asked to specify the members of the control apparatus, he replied that he could not name the individuals, but that the apparatus could be identified "by its effects—what it did in Cuba—what it did in the Congo—what it did in Korea."

The irony of this reply is that it is cut from the same cloth as vulgar Bolshevik explanation: accident and contingency are ruled out of history, subjective intentions are the prattlings of "bourgeois morality," history is plot and objective consequence. Just as in a concentration camp—or any extreme situation—a victim adopts unconsciously the mode, manner, and even swagger of the aggressor, so men like General Walker seem to have become mesmerized by the enemies they have studied so assiduously and with such horrified fascination.

And to round out their picture of horror, the radical right has given us an exact forecast of things to come. Just as the "enthusiastic" preachers of Baptist fundamentalism would predict with Biblical certainty the date of the end of the world, so the fundamentalists of the radical right make their own predictions of the end of liberty in the United States. Fred Schwarz has named 1973 as the date set by the Communists for the take-over of America. In his lectures, Schwarz builds up the picture of the ultimate fate in store for his audience once the Communists win. "When they come for you, as they have for many others, and on a dark night, in a dank cellar, they take a wide-bore revolver with a soft-nose bullet, and they place it at the nape of your neck. . . ."

A more elaborate fantasy is provided in *The John Franklin Letters*, a Birchite novel that was circulated in 1959, and then withdrawn. The novel pictures an America Sovietized by the Communists in 1970. The beginning of the end comes in 1963, when the World Health Organization sends in a Yugoslav inspector, under powers granted by the President of the United States, to search any house he chooses. The Yugoslav discovers in the house of a good American a file of anti-Communist magazines, seizes them as dele-terious to the mental health of the community, and is shot by the American, who escapes to the woods. But the infiltration continues. By 1970, the United States, thanks to the global do-gooders, has become part of a World Author-ity dominated by the Soviet-Asian-African bloc, and this Authority suspends the country's right to govern itself because of the "historic psychological genocide" against the Negro race. United Nations administrators, mostly Red Chinese, are sent in to rule. Harlem, triumphant, arises and loots the liquor stores. The city proletariat, its sense of decency destroyed by public housing, begins to raid the suburbs. In short order, twenty million Americans are "done away with," while the people are subjected to torture by blow-torch and rock-'n'-roll—the latter on television.

Meanwhile, the good American begins to fight back. As far back as 1967, John Franklin and his friends had been stockpiling rifles. And now they act. Franklin describes in gory detail a total of fourteen patriotic mur-ders: two by fire, one by hammer, one by strangling, two by bow and arrow, one by defenestration, one by drowning, and the rest by shooting. These brave actions are sufficient to turn the tide—despite the atom bomb, a huge invasion army, and absolute terror. By 1976, the people all over the world go into the streets, and everywhere Communism falls. The assumption is that Communism is so inefficient, it cannot build heavy tanks or heavy weapons. All that is necessary is the courage of a few determined men, practicing the "simple virtues," to overthrow this clumsy Moloch.

"This, of course," as Murray Kempton remarks,

is the Bircher's dream. America slides unresistingly into Communism; a few Mike Hammers find their rifles; and in five years the world is free. The Birch mind is only the Mickey Spillane mind. There is that lingering over and savoring of pure physical violence, the daydream of the disarmed. Reading The John Franklin Letters we can recognize Robert Welch's voice. He is Charles Atlas saying to us again that we need only mail the letter and back will come the muscles which we will use to throw the bully off the beach and have the girl turn to us with eyes shining with the sudden knowledge of how special we are.

The distinctive theme of the radical right is that not only is Communism a more threatening force today than at any other time in the past forty years, but that the threat is as great domestically as it is externally. If one points out, in astonishment, that the American Communist Party is splintered badly, its membership at the lowest point since the mid-1920s, its influence in the trade-union movement nil, and that not one intellectual figure of any consequence today is a Communist, the rightist replies do not confront these assertions at all. They range from the question that, if this is so, how did it happen that the United States "lost" China, Czechoslovakia, and Cuba to the Communists, to the outright charges, like General Walker's, that the highest officials of the Democratic Party are members of the "Communist conspiracy," or to Robert Welch's claim that former President Eisenhower was a "tool" of the Communists and that his brother Milton is an avowed one. Defeat can be possible only if sinister men were at the helm.

In fact, so great is the preoccupation with the alleged domestic threat that only rarely in the press of the radical right is there any mention of Russia's military prowess, its scientific equipment, or its ability to propel intercontinental ballistic missiles. When such facts are raised, it is often asserted either that such strength is a sham or that whatever knowledge Russia has was "stolen" from the United States (the claim made, for example, by Medford Evans, now an adviser to General Walker, in his book The Secret War for the A-Bomb, Chicago, Regnery Press, 1953). For a considerable period of time, in fact, the magazines of the radical right refused to acknowledge that the Russians had sent a sputnik to the moon, or that they had sent a man into space, and, like the Daily Worker unmasking a capitalist conspiracy, they gleefully pounced on inconsistencies in news stories to assert that we were all being hoodwinked by a hoax (as were, presumably, the American tracking stations).

The existence of an extreme internal threat is crucial to the ideological, if not the psychological, posture of the radical right, for if it admitted that such a threat is dubious, then the debate would have to shift to ground about which it has little comprehension, or rightists would have to admit— as Eisenhower did—that the area of maneuverability in foreign policy is highly limited. If the threat was conceded to be largely external, one would have to support an expanded federal budget, large military expenditures, foreign aid to allies, and also confront the intractable fact that American might alone is insufficient to defeat the Russians—or that victory for anyone would not be possible once war began!—and that the United States has to take into account the forces working for independence in the former colonial world.

The unwillingness of the radical right to recognize Russian military strength as a prime factor in the balance of terror, and the compulsive pre-occupation with a presumed internal threat, can perhaps be clarified by a little-understood psychological mechanism—the need to create "fear-justify-ing" threats in order to explain fright that is provoked by other reasons. For example, a child who is afraid of the dark may tell his parents that the creaking noises he hears in the house indicate that there are burglars down-stairs. It does not reassure the child if he is told that there is no burglar, or that the noises are harmless, for he needs the story to justify the fear he feels. In fact, it upsets the child to be "reassured." (The simplest answer is to tell the child that if there are burglars downstairs, his father is strong enough to handle them or the police are close by.) Similarly, a study by Prasad of rumors in India following an earthquake revealed that people in the areas adjacent to the earthquake, who had heard about the quake but had had no direct experience of it, persisted in believing and spreading ru-mors that a new earthquake was coming. The function of such stories was to justify, psychologically, the *initial* apprehensions, which had little basis in experience. In short, the radical right, having a diffused sense of fear, needs to find some story or explanation to explain, or justify, that fear. One can deny the external reality, and build up the internal threat, through such psychological mechanisms.

One sees among the radical right, particularly among individuals in its upper-middle-class following who have never seen a Communist, the most extraordinary apprehensions about the extent of current Communist infil-tration in government. If one asks them to explain these attitudes, one is constantly reminded of Alger Hiss and Harry Dexter White. Yet whatever the actuality of past Communist infiltration in the government—and its ex-tent has been highly distorted as to the actual influence exerted—none of this offers any proof about the current status of Dean Rusk or W. W. Rostow, or any of the present foreign-policy advisers of the Kennedy admin-istration. Yet the *internal* threat is the one that is primarily harped upon, along with suspicions of the "soft" attitudes of the current administration.

It is largely among the extremist fringes of the radical right that such paranoid views are peddled. But most of the radical right, uneasily aware of the difficulty of maintaining the position that the Communist Party alone constitutes the internal threat, has shifted the argument to a different and more nebulous ground—the identification of Communism with liberal-ism. "I equate the growth of the welfare state," says Dan Smoot, a former F.B.I. agent whose program, *The Dan Smoot Report*, is heard on thirty-two television and fifty-two radio stations, "with Socialism and Socialism with Communism." Thus it is argued that the administration is unwilling (for ideological reasons) or incapable (for intellectual reasons) of "getting tough" with Communism. And in this fashion, the foreign-policy issue is tied in with a vast array of right-wing domestic issues, centering around the income tax and the welfare state.

But with this shift in the argument, the nature of the debate becomes clearer. What the right wing is fighting, in the shadow of Communism, is essentially "modernity"—that complex of attitudes that might be defined most simply as the belief in rational assessment, rather than established custom, for the evaluation of social change—and what it seeks to defend is its fading dominance, exercised once through the institutions of small-town America, over the control of social change. But it is precisely these established ways that a modernist America has been forced to call into question.

The Crisis in National Style

Every country has a "national style," a distinctive way of meeting the problems of order and adaptation, of conflict and consensus, of individual ends and communal welfare, that confront any society. The "national style," or the characteristic way of response, is a compound of the values and the national character of a country. As anyone who has read travelers' accounts knows, there has long been agreement on the characteristics of the American style.

The American has been marked by his sense of achievement, his activism, his being on the move, his eagerness for experience. America has always been "future-oriented." Europe represented the past, with its hierarchies, its fixed statuses, its ties to antiquity. The American "makes" himself, and in so doing transforms himself, society, and nature. In Jefferson's deism, God was not a transcendental being but a "Workman" whose intricate design was being unfolded on the American continent. The achievement pattern envisaged an "endless future," a life of constant improvement. Education meant preparation for a career rather than cultivation. When Samuel Gompers, the immigrant labor leader, was asked what labor's goal was, he gauged the American spirit shrewdly in answering, simply, "More."

Hand in hand with achievement went a sense of optimism, the feeling that life was tractable, the environment manipulable, that anything was possible. The American, the once-born man, was the "sky-blue, healthy-minded moralist" to whom sin and evil were, in Emerson's phrase, merely the "soul's mumps and measles and whooping cough." In this sense the American has been Graham Greene's "quiet American" or, to Santayana, "inexperienced of poisons." And for this reason Europeans have always found America lacking in a sense of the esthetic, the tragic, or the decadent.

American achievement and masculine optimism created a buoyant sense of progress, almost of omnipotence. America had never been defeated. America was getting bigger and better. America was always first. It had the tallest buildings, the biggest dams, the largest cities. "The most striking expression of [the American's] materialism," remarked Santayana, "is his singular preoccupation with quantity."

And all of this was reflected in distinctive aspects of character. The emphasis on achievement was an emphasis on the individual. The idea that society was a system of social arrangements that acts to limit the range of individual behavior was an abstraction essentially alien to American thought; reality was concrete and empirical, and the individual was the moral unit of action. That peculiar American inversion of Protestantism, the moralizing style, found its focus in the idea of reform, but it was the reform of the individual, not of social institutions. To reform meant to remedy the defects of character, and the American reform movement of the nineteenth century concentrated on sin, drink, gambling, prostitution, and other aspects of individual behavior. In politics, the moralistic residue led to black-and-white judgments; if anything was wrong, the individual was to blame. Since there were good men and bad men, the problem was to choose the good and eschew the bad. Any defect in policy flowed from a defect in the individual, and a change in policy could begin only by finding the culprit.

All of this—the pattern of achievement, of optimism and progress, and the emphasis on the individual as the unit of concern—found expression in what W. W. Rostow has called the "classic" American style. It was one of *ad-hoc* compromise derived from an implicit consensus. In the American political debates, there were rarely, except for the Civil War, an appeal to "first principles," as, say, in France, where every political division was rooted in the alignments of the French Revolution, or in the relationship of the Catholic Church to the secular state. In the United States, there were three unspoken assumptions: that the values of the individual were to be maximized, that the rising material wealth would dissolve all strains resulting from inequality, and that the continuity of experience would provide solutions for all future problems.

In the last fifteen years, the national self-consciousness has received a profound shock. At the end of World War II, American productivity and American prodigality were going to inspire an archaic Europe and a backward colonial system. But the American century quickly vanished. The fall of China, the stalemate in Korea, the eruption of anti-colonialism (with the United States cast bewilderingly among the archvillains), the higher growth rates in the western European economies at a time when growth in this country has slowed considerably, and the continued claims of Khrushchev that Communism is the wave of the future have by now shattered the earlier simple-minded belief Americans had in their own omnipotence, and have left almost a free-floating anxiety about the future. In a crudely symbolic way, the Russian sputniks trumped this country on its own ground—the boastful claim of always being first. Getting to the moon first may be, as many scientists assert, of little scientific value, and the huge sums required for such a venture might be spent more wisely for medical work, housing, or scientific research, but having set the "rules of the game," the United States cannot now afford to withdraw just because, in its newly acquired sophistication, it has perhaps begun to realize that such competitions are rather childish.

But these immediate crises of nerve only reflect deeper challenges to the adequacy of America's classic national style. That style, with its *ad-hoc* compromise and day-to-day patching, rather than consistent policy formation, no longer gives us guides to action. The classic notion was that rights inhered in individuals. But the chief realization of the past thirty years is that not the *individual* but *collectivities*—corporations, labor unions, farm organizations, pressure groups—have become the units of social action, and that individual rights in many instances derive from group rights, and in others have become fused with them. Other than the thin veil of the "public consensus," we have few guide lines, let alone a principle of distributive justice, to regulate or check the arbitrary power of many of these collectivities.

A second sign that the classic style has broken down appears in the lack of any institutional means for creating and maintaining necessary public services. On the municipal level, the complicated political swapping among hundreds of dispersed polities within a unified economic region, each seeking its own bargains in water supply, sewage disposal, roads, parks, recreation areas, crime regulation, transit, and so on, makes a mockery of the *ad-hoc* process. Without some planning along viable regional lines, local community life is bound to falter under the burdens of mounting taxes and social disarray.

And, third, foreign policy has foundered because every administration has had difficulty in defining a national interest, morally rooted, whose policies can be realistically tailored to the capacities and the constraints imposed by the actualities of world power. The easy temptation—and it is the theme of the radical right—is the tough-talking call for "action." This emphasis on action—on getting things done, on results—is a dominant aspect of the traditional American character. The moralizing style, with its focus on sin and on the culpability of the individual, finds it hard to accept social forces as a convincing explanation of failure, and prefers "action" instead. Americans have rarely known how to sweat it out, to wait, to calculate in historical terms, to learn that "action" cannot easily reverse social drifts whose courses were charted long ago. The "liberation" policy of the first Eisenhower administration was but a hollow moralism, deriving from the lack of any consistent policy other than the need to seem "activist"—again part of the classic style—rather than from a realistic assessment of the possibility of undermining Soviet power in eastern Europe. Until recently, there has been little evidence that American foreign policy is guided by a sense of historical time and an accurate assessment of social forces.

Styles of action reflect the character of a society. The classic style was worked out during a period when America was an agrarian, relatively homogeneous society, isolated from the world at large, so that ad-hoc measures were a realistic way of dealing with new strains. As an adaptive mechanism, it served to bring new groups into the society. But styles of action, like rhetoric, have a habit of outliving institutions. And the classic style in no way reflects the deep structural changes that have been taking place in American life in the past quarter of a century. . . .

The Polarities of American Politics and the Prospects of the Radical Right

A meaningful polarity within the American consensus has always been part of the American search for self-definition and self-identity. Jefferson versus Hamilton, Republicanism versus Federalism, Agrarianism versus Capitalism, the frontier West versus the industrial East. However significant such polarities may have been in the past, there seems to be little meaningful polarity today. There is no coherent conservative force—and someone like Walter Lippmann, whose The Public Philosophy represents a genuine conservative voice, rejects the right, as it rejects him—and the radical right is outside the political pale, insofar as it refuses to accept the American consensus. Nor does a viable left exist in the United States today. The pacifist and Socialist elements have been unable to make the peace issue salient. The radicals have been unable to develop a comprehensive critique of the social disparities in American life—the urban mess, the patchwork educational system, the lack of amenities in our culture. Among the liberals, only the exhaustion of the "received ideas," such as they were, of the New Deal remains. It is a token of the emptiness of contemporary intellectual debate that from the viewpoint of the radical right, the Americans for Democratic Action constitutes the "extreme left" of the American political spectrum, and that Life, in order to set up a fictitious balance, counterposes the tiny Councils of Correspondence, a loosely organized peace group led by Erich Fromm and David Riesman, as the "extreme left," to the "extreme right" of the John Birch Society.

The politics of conflict in any country inevitably has some emotional dimension, but in the United States, lacking a historically defined doctrinal basis—as against the ideological divisions of Europe—it takes on, when economic-interest-group issues are lacking, a psychological or status dimension. In this psychological polarity, the right has often been splenetic, while the mood of the left has traditionally been one of ressentiment. Today the politics of the radical right is the politics of frustration—the sour impotence of those who find themselves unable to understand, let alone command, the complex mass society that is the polity today. In our time, only the Negro community is fired by the politics of resentment—and this resentment, based on a justified demand for equity, represents no psychological polarity to the radical right. Insofar as there is no real left to counterpoise to the right, the liberal has become the psychological target of that frustration.

One of the reasons why psychological politics can flare up so much more easily here than, say, in Great Britain is the essentially "populist" character of American institutions and the volatile role of public opinion. In the ill-defined, loosely articulated structure of American life, public opinion rather than law has been the more operative sanction against nonconformists and dissenters. Though Americans often respond to a problem with the phrase "there ought to be a law," their respect for law has been minimal, and during periods of extreme excitement, whether it be the vigilante action of a mob or the removal of a book from a school library, the punitive sanctions of opinion quickly supersede law. The very openness or egalitarianism of the American political system is predicated on the right of the people to know, and the Congressional committees, whether searching into the pricing policies of corporations or the political beliefs of individuals, have historically based their investigative claims on this populist premise.

It has always been easier to "mobilize" public opinion on legislation here than it is in England, and in the United States the masses of people have a more direct access to politics. The Presidential-election system (as against a ministerial system), with the candidates appealing to every voter and, if possible, shaking every hand, involves a direct relation to the electorate. And in the Congressional system, individual constituents, through letters, telephone calls, or personal visits, can get through immediately to their representatives to affect his vote. The Congressional system itself, with its elaborate scaffolding of Senatorial prerogative, often allows a maverick like Borah, Norris, or Robert La Follette to dominate the floor, or a rogue elephant like Huey Long or Joseph McCarthy to rampage against the operations of the government.

But while the populist character of the political institutions and the sweeping influence of public opinion allow social movements to flare with brush-fire suddenness across the political timberland, the unwieldy party system, as well as the checks and balances of the Presidential and judicial structures, also act to constrain such movements. In a few instances, notably the temperance crusade, a social movement operating outside the party system was able to enforce a unitary conception of social behavior on the country; and even then prohibition was repealed in two decades. Until recently, the party and Presidential system have exerted a "discipline of compromise" that has put the maverick and the rogue elephant outside the main arena of the political game.

Within this perspective, therefore, what are the prospects of the radical right? To what extent does it constitute a threat to democratic politics in the United States? Some highly competent political observers write off the radical right as a meaningful political movement. As Richard Rovere has written,

The press treats the extreme Right as though it were a major tendency in American politics, and certain politicians are as much obsessed with it as certain others are with the extreme Left. If a day arrives when the extreme Right does become a major movement, the press and the obsessed politicians may have a lot to answer for. For the time being, there seems no reason to suppose that its future holds anything more than its present. There is no evidence at all that the recent proliferation of radical, and in some cases downright subversive, organizations of a Rightist tendency reflects or has been accompanied by a spread of ultra-conservative views. On the contrary, what evidence there is suggests that the organizations are frantic efforts to prevent ultra-conservatism from dying out.

In his immediate assessment, Rovere is undoubtedly right. In the spring of 1962, both former Vice-President Nixon and Senator Goldwater had moved to dissociate themselves from the extremist right. Nixon quite sharply repudiated the Birchites, on the premise that they are already a political liability, and Goldwater did so more cautiously in expressing his concern that, if not the Birchites, then its leader, Robert Welch, may have gone too far. Yet the future is more open than Rovere suggests. It is in the very nature of an extremist movement, given its tensed posture and its need to maintain a fever pitch, to mobilize, to be on the move, to act. It constantly has to agitate. Lacking any sustained dramatic issue, it can quickly wear itself out, as McCarthyism did. But to this extent the prospects of the radical right depend considerably on the international situation. If the international situation becomes stable, it is likely that the radical right may run quickly out of steam. If it were to take a turn for the worse—if Laos and all of Vietnam were to fall to the Communists; if, within the Western Hemisphere, the moderate regimes of Bolivia and Venezuela were to topple and the Communists take over—then the radical right could begin to rally support around a drive for "immediate action," for a declaration of war in these areas, for a pre-emptive strike, or similar axioms of a "hard line." And since such conservatives as Nixon and Goldwater are committed, at least rhetorically, to a tough anti-Communist position, they would either be forced to go along with such an extreme policy or go under.

Yet, given the severe strains in American life, the radical right does present a threat to American liberties, in a very different and less immediate sense. Democracy, as the sorry history of Europe has shown, is a fragile system, and if there is a lesson to be learned from the downfall of democratic government in Italy, Spain, Austria, and Germany, and from the deep divisions in France, it is that the crucial turning point comes, as Juan Linz has pointed out, when political parties or social movements can successfully establish "private armies" whose resort to violence—street fightings, bombings, the break-up of their opponents' meetings, or simply intimidation—cannot by controlled by the elected authorities, and whose use of violence is justified or made legitimate by the respectable elements in society.

In America, the extreme-right groups of the late 1930s—the Coughlinites, the German-American Bund, the native fascist groups—all sought to promote violence, but they never obtained legitimate or respectable support. The McCarthyite movement of the early 1950s, despite the rampaging antics of its eponymous leader, never dared go, at least rhetorically, outside the traditional framework in trying to establish loyalty and security tests. The Birchers, and the small but insidious group of Minutemen, as the epitome of the radical right, are willing to tear apart the fabric of American society in order to instate their goals, and they did receive a temporary aura of legitimacy from the conservative right.

Barbarous acts are rarely committed out of the blue. (As Freud says, first one commits oneself in words, and then in deeds.) Step by step, a society becomes accustomed to accept, with less and less moral outrage and with greater and greater indifference to legitimacy, the successive blows. What is uniquely disturbing about the emergence of the radical right of the 1960s is the support it has been able to find among traditional community leaders who have themselves become conditioned, through an indiscriminate anti-Communism that equates any form of liberalism with Communism, to judge as respectable a movement which, if successful, can only end the liberties they profess to cherish.

Young Men of the 1950's:
A Generation of Bureaucrats

William H. Whyte, Jr.

When I was a college senior in 1939, we used to sing a plaintive song about going out into the "cold, cold world." It wasn't really so very cold then, but we did enjoy meditating on the fraughtness of it all. It was a big break we were facing, we told ourselves, and those of us who were going to try our luck in the commercial world could be patronizing toward those who were going on to graduate work or academic life. We were taking the leap.

Seniors still sing the song, but somehow the old note of portent is gone. There is no leap left to take. The union between the world of organization and the college has been so cemented that today's seniors can see a continuity between the college and the life thereafter that we never did. Come graduation, they do not go outside to a hostile world; they transfer.

For the senior who is headed for the corporation it is almost as if it were part of one master scheme. The locale shifts; the training continues, for at the same time that the colleges have been changing their curriculum to suit the corporation, the corporation has responded by setting up its own campuses and classrooms. By now the two have been so well molded that it's difficult to tell where one leaves off and the other begins.

The descent, every spring, of the corporations' recruiters has now become a built-in feature of campus life. If the college is large and its placement director efficient, the processing operation is visibly impressive. I have never been able to erase from my mind the memory of an ordinary day at Purdue's placement center. It is probably the largest and most effective placement operation in the country, yet, much as in a well-run group clinic, there seemed hardly any activity. In the main room some students were quietly studying company literature arranged on the tables for them; others were checking the interview timetables to find what recruiter they would see and to which cubicle he was assigned; at the central filing desk college employees were sorting the hundreds of names of men who had registered for placement. Except for a murmur from the row of cubicles there was little to indicate that scores of young men were, every hour on the half hour, making the decisions that would determine their whole future life.

Someone from a less organized era might conclude that the standardization of this machinery—and the standardized future it portends—would repel students. It does not. For the median senior this is the optimum future; it meshes so closely with his own aspirations that it is almost as if the corporation was planned in response to an attitude poll.

Because they are the largest single group, the corporation-bound seniors are the most visible manifestation of their generation's values. But in essentials their contemporaries headed for other occupations respond to the same urges. The lawyers, the doctors, the scientists—their occupations are also subject to the same centralization, the same trend to group work and to bureaucratization. And so are the young men who will enter them. Whatever their many differences, in one great respect they are all of a piece: more than any generation in memory, theirs will be a generation of bureaucrats.

They are, above all, conservative. Their inclination to accept the status quo does not necessarily mean that in the historic sweep of ideas they are conservative—in the more classical sense of conservatism, it could be argued that the seniors will be, in effect if not by design, agents of revolution. But this is a matter we must leave to later historians. For the immediate present, at any rate, what ideological ferment college men exhibit is not in the direction of basic change.

This shows most clearly in their attitude toward politics. It used to be axiomatic that young men moved to the left end of the spectrum in revolt against their fathers and then, as the years went on, moved slowly to the right. A lot of people still believe this is true, and many businessmen fear that twenty years of the New Deal hopelessly corrupted our youth into radicalism. After the election of 1952 businessmen became somewhat more cheerful, but many are still apprehensive, and whenever a poll indicates that students don't realize that business makes only about 6 percent profit, there is a flurry of demands for some new crusade to rescue our youth from socialistic tendencies.

If the seniors do any moving, however, it will be from dead center. Liberal groups have almost disappeared from the campus, and what few remain are anemic. There has been no noticeable activity at the other end of the spectrum either. When William Buckley, Jr., produced God and Man at Yale, some people thought this signaled the emergence of a strong right-wing movement among the young men. The militancy, however, has not proved particularly contagious; when the McCarthy issue roused and divided their elders, undergraduates seemed somewhat bored with it all.

Their conservatism is passive. No cause seizes them, and nothing so exuberant or willfully iconoclastic as the Veterans of Future Wars has re-appeared. There are Democrats and Republicans, and at election time there is the usual flurry of rallies, but in comparison with the agitation of the thirties no one seems to care too much one way or the other. There has been personal unrest—the suspense over the prospect of military service assures this—but it rarely gets resolved into a thought-out protest. Come spring and students may start whacking each other over the head or roughing up the townies and thereby cause a rush of concern over the wild younger generation. But there is no real revolution in them, and the next day they likely as not will be found with their feet firmly on the ground in the recruiters' cubicles.

Some observers attribute the disinterest to fear. I heard one instructor tell his colleagues that in his politics classes he warned students to keep their noses clean. "I tell them," he said, "that they'd better realize that what they say might be held against them, especially when we get to the part about Marx and Engels. Someday in the future they might find their comments bounced back at them in an investigation."

The advice, as his colleagues retorted, was outrageously unnecessary. The last thing students can be accused of now is dangerous discussion; they are not interested in the kind of big questions that stimulate heresy and whatever the subject—the corporation, government, religion—students grow restive if the talk tarries on the philosophical. Most are interested in the philosophical only to the extent of finding out what the accepted view is in order that they may accept it and get on to the practical matters. This spares the bystander from the lofty bulling and the elaborate pose of unorthodoxy that my con-temporaries often used to effect, but it does make for a rather stringent utilitarianism.

Even in theological seminaries, this impatience to be on with the job has been evident. Writes Norman Pittenger, professor at General Theological Seminary:

It is a kind of authoritarianism in reverse. Theological students today, in contrast to their fellows of twenty years ago, want "to be told." I have gone out of my way to ask friends who teach in seminaries of other denominations whether they have recognized the new tendency. Without exception they have told me that they find the present generation of students less inquiring of mind, more ready to accept an authority, and indeed most anxious to have it "laid on the line."

In the seminary this means that the lecturer or teacher must be unusually careful lest his opinion, or what "the Bible says" or "the church teaches," shall be taken as the last word. . . . What troubles many of us is that students today are not willing enough to think things through for themselves. If this is what the Bible says, then how does it say it and why, and how do we know that this is indeed the teaching of Scripture? If this is what the church teaches, why does it teach it, what evidence can be given for the teaching and what right has the church to teach at all? Or if a professor says that such-and-such a view is correct, why does he say it and what real evidence can he produce that his statement is true? It would be better and healthier if the new respect for authority were more frequently found in combination with a spirit of inquiry, a ready willingness to think through what is authoritatively declared, and a refusal ever to accept anything simply because some reputable expert makes the statement.

In judging a college generation, one usually bases his judgment on how much it varies from one's own, and presumably superior, class, and I must confess that I find myself tempted to do so. Yet I do not think my generation has any license to damn the acquiescence of seniors as a weakening of intellectual fiber. It is easy for us to forget that if earlier generations were less content with society, there was a great deal less to be contented about. In the intervening years the economy has changed enormously, and even in retrospect the senior can hardly be expected to share former discontents. Society is not out of joint for him, and if he acquiesces it is not out of fear that he does so. He does not want to rebel against the status quo because he really likes it—and his elders, it might be added, are not suggesting anything bold and new to rebel for.

Perhaps contemporaryism would be a better word than conservatism to describe their posture. The present, more than the past, is their model; while they share the characteristic American faith in the future also, they see it as more of same. As they paraphrase what they are now reading about America, they argue that at last we have got it. The big questions are all settled; we know the direction, and while many minor details remain to be cleared up, we can be pretty sure of enjoying a wonderful upward rise.

While the degree of their optimism is peculiarly American, the spirit of acquiescence, it should be noted, is by no means confined to the youth of this country. In an Oxford magazine, called, aptly enough, *Couth*, one student writes this of his generation:

It is true that over the last thirty years it has been elementary good manners to be depressed. . . . But . . . we are not, really, in the least worried by our impending, and other people's present, disasters. This is not the Age of Anxiety. What distinguishes the comfortable young men of today from the uncomfortable young men of the last hundred years . . . is that for once the younger generation is not in revolt against anything. . . . We don't want to rebel against our elders. They are much too nice to be rebellable-against. Old revolutionaries as they are, they get rather cross with us and tell us we are stuffy and prudish, but even this can't provoke us into hostility. . . . Our fathers . . . brought us up to see them not as the representatives of ancient authority and unalterable law but as rebels against our grandfathers. So naturally we have grown up to be on their side, even if we feel on occasion that they were a wee bit hard on their fathers, or even a little naïve.

More than before, there is a tremendous interest in techniques. Having no quarrel with society, they prefer to table the subject of ends and concentrate instead on means. Not what or why but *how* interests them, and any evangelical strain they have they can sublimate; once they have equated the common weal with organization—a task the curriculum makes easy—they will let the organization worry about goals. "These men do not question the system," an economics professor says of them, approvingly. "They want to get in there and lubricate and make them run better. They will be technicians of the society, not innovators."

The attitude of men majoring in social science is particularly revealing on this score. Not so very long ago, the younger social scientist was apt to see his discipline as a vehicle for protest about society as well as the study of it. The seniors that set the fashion for him were frequently angry men, and many of the big studies of the twenties and thirties—Robert and Helen Lynd's *Middletown*, for example—did not conceal strong opinions about the inequities in the social structure. But this is now old hat: it is the "bleeding-heart" school to the younger men (and to some not so young, too), for they do not wish to protest; they wish to collaborate. Reflecting the growing reconciliation with middle-class values that has affected all types of intellectuals, they are turning more and more to an interest in methodology, particularly the techniques of measurement. Older social scientists who have done studies on broad social problems find that the younger men are comparatively uninterested in the problems themselves. When the discussion period comes, the questions the younger men ask are on the technical points; not the what, or why, but the how.

The urge to be a technician, a collaborator, shows most markedly in the kind of jobs seniors prefer. They want to work for somebody else. Paradoxically, the old dream of independence through a business of one's own is held almost exclusively by factory workers—the one group, as a number of sociologists have reported, least able to fulfill it. Even at the bull-session level college seniors do not affect it, and when recruiting time comes around they make the preference clear. Consistently, placement officers find that of the men who intend to go into business—roughly one half of the class—less than 5 percent express any desire to be an entrepreneur. About 15 to 20 percent plan to go into their fathers' business. Of the rest, most have one simple goal: the big corporation.

And not just as a stopgap either. When I was a senior many of us liked to rationalize that we were simply playing it smart; we were going with big companies merely to learn the ropes the better to strike out on our own later. Today, seniors do not bother with this sort of talk; once the tie has been established with the big company, they believe, they will not switch to a small one, or, for that matter, to another big one. The relationship is to be for keeps.

It is not simply for security that they take the vows. Far more than their predecessors they understand bigness. My contemporaries, fearful of anonymity, used to talk of "being lost" in a big corporation. This did not prevent us from joining corporations, to be sure, but verbally, at least, it was fashionable to view the organization way with misgivings. Today this would show a want of sophistication. With many of the liberals who fifteen years ago helped stimulate the undergraduate distrust of bigness now busy writing tracts in praise of bigness, the ideological underpinnings for the debate have crumbled.

The fact that a majority of seniors headed for business shy from the idea of being entrepreneurs is only in part due to fear of economic risk. Seniors can put the choice in moral terms also, and the portrait of the entrepreneur as a young man detailed in postwar fiction preaches a sermon that seniors are predisposed to accept. What price bitch goddess Success? The entrepreneur, as many see him, is a selfish type motivated by greed, and he is furthermore, unhappy. The big-time operator as sketched in fiction eventually so loses stomach for enterprise that he finds happiness only when he stops being an entrepreneur, forsakes "21," El Morocco, and the boss's wife and heads for the country. Citing such fiction, the student can moralize on his aversion to entrepreneurship. His heel quotient, he explains, is simply not big enough.

Not that he is afraid of risk, the senior can argue. Far from being afraid of taking chances, he is simply looking for the *best* place to take them in. Small business is small because of nepotism and the roll-top desk outlook, the argument goes; big business, by contrast, has borrowed the tools of science and made them pay off. It has its great laboratories, its market-research departments, and the time and patience to use them. The odds, then, favor the man who joins big business. "We wouldn't hesitate to risk adopting new industrial techniques and products," explains a proponent of this calculated-risk theory, "but we would do it only after we had subjected it to tests of engineers, pre-testing in the market and that kind of thing." With big business, in short, risk-taking would be a cinch.

In turning their back on the Protestant Ethic they are consistent; if they do not cherish venture, neither do they cherish what in our lore was its historic reward. They are without avarice. Reflecting on the difference between the postwar classes and his own class of 1928, an erstwhile Yale history professor confessed that the former were so unmercenary he was almost a little homesick for his own. "We were a terrible class. It was the days of the roasted lark, Hell's entries, of the white-shoe boys. Everyone was playing the stock market—they even had a ticker down at the Hotel Taft—and I wound up for a while in a bucket shop down in Wall Street. But today you don't hear that kind of talk. They don't want a million. They are much more serious, much more worth while." He shook his head nostalgically.

Others have been similarly impressed. One recruiter went through three hundred interviews without one senior's mentioning salary, and the experience is not unusual. Indeed, sometimes seniors react as if a large income and security were antithetical. As some small companies have found to their amazement, the offer of a sales job netting $15,000 at the end of two years is often turned down in favor of an equivalent one with a large company netting $8,000. Along with the $8,000 job, the senior says in justification, goes a pension plan and other benefits. He could, of course, buy himself some rather handsome annuities with the extra $7,000 the small company offers, but this alternative does not suggest itself readily.

When seniors are put to speculating how much money they would like to make twenty or thirty years hence, they cite what they feel are modest figures. Back in forty-nine it was $10,000. Since then the rising cost of living has taken it up higher, but the median doesn't usually surpass $15,000. For the most part seniors do not like to talk of the future in terms of the dollar —on several occasions I have been politely lectured by someone for so much as bringing the point up.

In popular fiction, as I will take up later, heroes aren't any less materialistic than they used to be, but they are decidedly more sanctimonious about it. So with seniors. While they talk little about money, they talk a great deal about the good life. This life is, first of all, calm and ordered. Many a senior confesses that he's thought of a career in teaching, but as he talks it appears that it is not so much that he likes teaching itself as the sort of life he associates with it—there is a touch of elms and quiet streets in the picture. For the good life is equable; it is a nice place out in the suburbs, a wife and three children, one, maybe two cars (you know, a little knock-about for the wife to run down to the station in), and a summer place up at the lake or out on the Cape, and, later, a good college education for the children. It is not, seniors explain, the money that counts.

They have been getting more and more relaxed on the matter each year. In the immediate postwar years they were somewhat nervous about the chances for the good life. They seemed almost psychotic on the subject of a depression, and when they explained a preference for the big corporation, they did so largely on the grounds of security. When I talked to students in 1949, on almost every campus I heard one recurring theme: adventure was all very well, but it was smarter to make a compromise in order to get a depression-proof sanctuary. "I don't think A T & T is very exciting," one senior put it, "but that's the company I'd like to join. If a depression comes there will always be an A T & T." (Another favorite was the food industry: people always have to eat.) Corporation recruiters were unsettled to find that seniors seemed primarily interested in such things as pension benefits and retirement programs.

Seven years of continuing prosperity have made a great difference. Students are still interested in security but they no longer see it as a matter of security *versus* opportunity. Now, when they explain their choice, it is that the corporation is security *and* opportunity both. If the questionnaires that

I have been giving groups of college seniors over the past six years are any indication, students aiming for the big corporation expect to make just as much money as those who say they want to start their own business or join a small one.

Who is to blame them for being contented? If you were a senior glancing at these ad headlines in the *Journal of College Placement*, how much foreboding would you feel?

A World of Expanding Opportunity
Opportunity Unlimited
Careers Unlimited
The Horizons Are Unlimited for College Graduates at Union Carbide
A Gateway to Lifetime Security
A Wise Choice Today Puts You Ahead of Your Future
Why They're Sure They're in the Right Job at Harnschfeger
To the Young Man Bent on Conquering the Unknown
A Second Education
Growth Company in a Growth Industry
"Brain Box" Needs Brains
So You Want to Go Into Business
Why College Graduates Should Consider Union Carbide
A Man Can Grow and Keep On Growing With Owens-Illinois Glass Co.
A Bright Future With RCA
Dow Offers the Graduate a Bright Future
More and Better Jobs
Exceptional Opportunities for College Man in Textile Sales
An Equitable Life Insurance Man is "A Man on His Way Up"
Ground-Floor Opportunities in Transistors
Vitro Offers Your Graduates the Engineers of Tomorrow!
Your Opportunity for a Lifetime Career
Opportunity for Your College Graduates
Opportunities for Math Majors
An Unusual Opportunity for Outstanding Math Majors
The Sky is Our World
The Sky is the Limit!

It would be enough to make a man cynical. But the students are not a cynical lot. When they talk about security they like to make the point that it is the psychic kind of security that interests them most. They want to be of service. Occasionally, their description of service borders on the mawkish, as though the goal was simply to defend the little people, but underneath there is real concern. Seniors want to do something *worth while.*

This worth-whileness needs some qualification. To listen to seniors talk, one would assume that there has been an upsurge of seniors heading toward such service careers as the ministry. There is no evidence of such a rush. The public variety of service doesn't attract either. Seniors scarcely mention politics as a career and even for the more aseptic forms of public service they show little enthusiasm; the number aiming for the foreign services or the civil services has been declining, and this decline was well under way before the Washington investigations.

If they are going to be worth while, seniors want to be worth while with other people. Their ideal of service is a gregarious one—the kind of service you do others right in the midst of them and not once removed. A student at a round-table discussion on the pursuit of happiness put it this way: "People who are just selfish and wrapped up in themselves have the most trouble. And people who are interested in other people . . . are the type of person that is not too much concerned with security. Somehow the security is provided in the things they do, and they are able to reach out beyond themselves."

The kind of work that students want to do within the corporation illumines the character of this concept of worthwhileness. What the preferences show is a strong inclination toward the staff rather than the line. In a check I made of two hundred corporation-bound students of the classes of '55 and '56, only 12 percent said they were aiming for production work, while roughly a third indicated a staff job.

Of these, the personnel slot is the glamour one. When seniors first expressed this yen for personnel work right after the war, many people thought it was simply a temporary phenomenon. The veterans of the postwar classes labored under the idea that because they had "handled people" in the services they were ideally suited for personnel work, and the advice given them by Veterans Administration counselors further confirmed them in the belief. But the years have gone by, and the quest has persisted. Wearily, placement directors explain that the work is semiprofessional, that there are few openings in it, and that in any event they are rarely open to recruits. It still doesn't seem to make much difference. With a phrase that has become a standing joke in placement circles, the senior explains that it is the job for him just the same—he likes people.

His vision of the job is a mirage. The actual work is connected more with time study, aptitude testing, and stop watches than adjusting people, but to the senior it seems to promise the agreeable role of a combination YMCA worker, office Solomon, and father confessor to the men at the lathes. It promises also to be somewhat out of the main stream. Much like life in the services, it seems to offer a certain freedom from competition; it is a technician's job, the job of one who services others. For a class intent on the happy mean, it is the all-around package: not only does it promise economic security, it promises spiritual security as well.

Because the quest has been so long unrequited, seniors have been turning to public relations. In some colleges it has already outdistanced personnel work as a choice. But it is really the same job they are thinking about. The senior does not see himself worrying about seating lists for banquets, ghost-writing speeches, or the like; in his vision he sees the universal man of the future, testing the pulse of the workers to see that they are happy, counseling with educators and clergymen for better inter-group communication, spell-binding the mossbacks with advocacy of the common man. As in personnel work, he will be nice to everybody on company time.

When seniors check such ostensibly line occupations as sales, they still exhibit the staff bias. For they don't actually want to sell. What they mean by sales is the kind of work in which they will be technical specialists helping the customer, or, better yet, master-minding the work of those who do the helping. They want to be sales engineers, distribution specialists, merchandising experts—the men who back up the men in the field.

If they must sell in the old, vulgar sense of the word, they want to do it as a member of a group and not as a lone individual. And most definitely they do not want to sell on commission. This has been made quite clear in the reception given life insurance recruiters. Except when they have home office jobs to offer, insurance recruiters have always had fairly rough going in the colleges, but it's now so difficult that sometimes they sit in the interview room a whole day without a senior once coming near them. Mainly out of commiseration for the recruiters, one placement director uses a stratagem to force students into signing up for insurance interviews. "I tell them it's good for the practice," he explains. "I also tell them that if they don't turn up for these interviews I won't let them have a crack later at those nice big corporations."

Those who mark down finance as a choice are also staff-minded. Few ever mention speculating or investing in stocks and bonds. Their interest in finance is administrative rather than accumulative; they are primarily interested in credit, mortgage loan work, trust and estate work, and financial analysis.

A distinction is in order. While the fundamental bias is for staff work, it is not necessarily for a staff job. If the choice is offered them, a considerable number of students will vote for "general managerial" work, and many who choose personnel or public relations do so with the idea that it is the best pathway to the top line jobs. Seniors see no antithesis; in their view the line and staff have become so synonymous that the comfortable pigeonhole and the ladder, to mix some favorite metaphors, are one and the same. Their concept of the manager subsumes the two. As older executives are so fond of telling them, the "professionalization" of the executive is making a new kind of man, and more literally than the older men know, the younger ones believe every word of it. In fact, of course, as well as in the senior's fancy, the manager's work has been shifted more to the administrative. But not half so much as seniors would like to see it. In this respect, as so many business-school people hopefully say, seniors are way ahead of everybody else.

But not so very much. The bureaucrat as hero is new to America, and older, conventional dreams of glory do linger on—the lawyer brilliantly turning the tables in cross-examination, the young scientist discovering the secret in the microscope late at night. Even in corporations' institutional advertising there is some cultural lag—many an ad still shows us the young man dreaming by himself of new frontiers as he looks up at a star or a rainbow or a beautiful hunk of alto-cumulus clouds. But slowly the young man at the microscope is being joined by other young men at microscopes; instead of one lone man dreaming, there are three or four young men. Year by year, our folklore is catching up with the needs of organization man.

In *Executive Suite* we catch a glimpse of the hero in mid-passage. In clean-cut Don Walling, the hitherto junior executive, what senior could not feel that there, with the grace of God, would go he? In Walling have been resolved all the conflicts of organization life; he puts everything he has into his work and plays baseball with his boy; he cares little about money and his ranch house is beautiful; he is a loyal subordinate and gets to be president. He is not fully the new model—he is too pushy, he plays too rough in the clinches for that—but he could almost be the class valedictorian as he electrifies his elders with his ringing, if somewhat hazy, statement of belief. Management man does not work to make money for himself and the company. Business is *people*, and when you help people to rise to their fullest you make them fulfill themselves, you create more and better goods for more people, you make happiness.

While the trust in organization is very strong among the majority group of college seniors headed for a business career, it is less so with a smaller group who say, at least, that they prefer a small firm. In the course of sessions during the past few years I have had with different undergraduate groups, to get the discussion rolling I have asked the students to answer several hypothetical questions on the "ideal" relationship between an individual and the demands of organization. I attach no great statistical significance to the actual figures, but I have kept the terms the same with each group, and I have noticed that consistently there is a difference between the answers of those headed for big organization and those not. As is brought out more forcefully by the kind of questions that the students themselves later asked, the big-corporation men are more inclined to the group way than the others.

Here is how a total of 127 men answered the two chief questions: on the question of whether research scientists should be predominantly the team player type, 56 percent of the men headed for a big corporation said yes, versus 46 percent of the small-business men. On the question of whether the key executive should be basically an "administrator" or a "bold leader," 54 percent of the big-corporation men voted for the administrator, versus only 45 percent of the small-business men. Needless to say, the weightings varied from college to college, and often the influence of a particular teacher was manifest—in one class the students complained that they probably seemed so chary of big business because they had been "brain-washed" by a liberal instructor. Whatever the absolute figures, however, there was generally the same relative difference between the big-business and the small-business men.

These differences raise an interesting question. It is possible that the majority group might be less significant than the minority—that is to say, the more venturesome may become the dominant members of our society by virtue of their very disinclination to the group way. As a frankly rapacious young salesman put it to me, the more contented his run-of-the-mill contemporaries, the freer the field for the likes of him.

While this can only be a matter of opinion at this date, I doubt that our society, as it is now evolving, will suffer such a double standard. The corporation-bound man may be an exaggeration of his generation's tendencies but only in degree, not in character. Other occupations call for different emphases, but on the central problem of collective versus individual work, young men going into other fields, such as teaching or law or journalism, show the same basic outlook.

Seniors do not deny that the lone researcher or the entrepreneur can also serve others. But neither do they think much about it. Their impulses, their training, the whole climate of the times, incline them to work that is tangibly social. Whether as a member of a corporation, a group medicine clinic, or a law factory, they see the collective as the best vehicle for service.

To a degree, of course, this is a self-ennobling apologia for seeking the comfortable life—and were they thoroughly consistent they would more actively recognize that public service is social too. But it is not mere rationalization; the senior is quite genuine in believing that while all collective effort may be worth while, some kinds are more so. The organization-bound senior can argue that he is going to the main tent, the place where each foot pound of his energy will go the farthest in helping people. Like the young man of the Middle Ages who went off to join holy orders, he is off for the center of society.

The New Radicals
of the 1960's

Paul Jacobs
and Saul Landau

I. The Movement's Themes

The Movement is a mélange of people, mostly young; organizations, mostly new; and ideals, mostly American. In 1960 and 1961 the Freedom Riders and Negro college students who sat-in in the South were acting in the spirit of The Movement. Most of those who protested against President Kennedy's Cuban policy in 1962 were responding to the impulse of The Movement. That same impulse took them south for the Student Nonviolent Coordinating Committee (SNCC) in 1963, got them arrested in Sproul Hall at the University of California in 1964, and marched them to Washington in 1965 to demonstrate their opposition to the war. Movement youth can be found today in the San Joaquin Valley of California, helping striking farm workers; some will become organizers in the slum communities of Northern cities; others will try to change the university system in America.

These young people believe that they must make something happen, that they are part of a movement stirring just below the surface of life hitherto accepted all over the world. So they identify with the Zengakuren students whose snake-dance demonstrations prevented President Eisenhower from visiting Japan, and wince at the photos of the young rebel shot by a policeman in Santo Domingo. They empathize with the young Soviet poets who read their poetry at the statue of Mayakovsky in Moscow until the police break up the meeting.

From The New Radicals, by Paul Jacobs and Saul Landau. Copyright © 1966 by Paul Jacobs and Saul Landau. Reprinted by permission of Random House, Inc.

How many people are in the American Movement? Certainly, it is possible to count those who are members of the organizations within The Movement, but that would be to misunderstand one of the basic facts of its nature: The Movement is organizations plus unaffiliated supporters, who outnumber by the thousands, and perhaps even hundreds of thousands, those committed to specific groups. The Movement's basic strength rests on those unaffiliated reserves, who are just as much a part of it as the organization youth.

The leitmotifs that dominate The Movement extend far beyond politics. The Movement is much more than anti-Vietnam marches, civil rights demonstrations, and student sit-ins. To be in The Movement is to search for a psychic community, in which one's own identity can be defined, social and personal relationships based on love can be established and can grow, unfettered by the cramping pressure of the careers and life styles so characteristic of America today.

The Movement rejects the careers and life styles of the American liberal, too, for to The Movement it is the liberal way of life and frame of mind that represent the evil of America. Those in The Movement feel that modern American liberals have substituted empty rhetoric for significant content, obscured the principles of justice by administrative bureaucracy, sacrificed human values for efficiency, and hypocritically justified a brutal attempt to establish American hegemony over the world with sterile anti-Communism. The Movement sees the liberals righteously proclaiming faith in American democracy from their comfortable suburban homes or offices, while the United States Air Force drops napalm on villages and poisons the rice paddies.

So, those in The Movement see not only the openly authoritarian or totalitarian society as an enemy but the administered, bureaucratic, dehumanized, rhetorical-liberal one as well. They reject liberal authority. They were stirred, momentarily, by President Kennedy's call for a commitment to freedom, but were so disappointed by his actions in Cuba and Vietnam that they turned on him with bitterness. And the Johnson Administration's foreign policy reinforces their view that America flouts, in action, the traditions of freedom and justifies the use of military instruments associated with the Nazis.

The new movement is also a revolt against the postwar "over-developed society," with its large bureaucracies in government, corporations, trade unions, and universities. To those in The Movement the new technologies of automation and cybernation, with their computers and memory-bank machines, are instruments of alienation, depersonalizing human relations to a frightening degree. The brain machines and the translation of human qualities into holes punched into a card are viewed as devices that break down communication and destroy community in the interests of efficiency. Technology's emphasis on routine efficiency has created a set of values, rationalized by its supporters as representing "the facts of modern life." But The Movement sees these values as false, imposed on the whole society without "the consent of the governed." Even worse, the decision-making over which the governed no longer have control extends far beyond politics: in the technological order every aspect of the people's lives is under the control of administrators far removed from responsibility to the governed. And the elders of those in The Movement have exchanged their decision-making right for the comforts of American affluence. All that remains is nineteenth-century rhetoric about democracy and freedom, and technology has drained the words of their content.

In their personal life style, their aesthetic sense, many in The Movement reject affluence and its associated symbols. The ambition to escape from poverty is no spur to action in their lives, for many are children of America's post-Depression *nouveau* middle class. Their parents are the once-poor scholars who head rich academic institutes; the ex-union organizers who run their own large businesses; the former slum dwellers who develop segregated real-estate tracts; the families once on the WPA who live in suburbia—all those who have made it. But their parents' desire to own, to accumulate, to achieve the status and prestige which go with material wealth, are meaningless goals to the children. To them television is not a wonder but a commonplace, and they see the $5,000 a year their parents spend on the analyst as too high a price to pay for the loss of human values.

The marvels of the space age are commonplace to them, too, and the voices to which they listen are not those of the orbiting astronauts exchanging banalities. They respond instead to the sense and sound of friendship and community, to the exultation they feel when thousands of people link hands and sing "We Shall Overcome." And to achieve that feeling of community, of life, they have been willing to sacrifice most middle-class comforts.

They are willing to do this, for until they enter The Movement their inability to affect the quality of their own lives disturbs them profoundly. Those of the upper middle class were trapped, protected to the point of coddling through their childhood and early teens, sated with *nouveau* affluence by the time they were twenty. They knew they could achieve a place in the society of their parents, but it was not a society in which they wanted a place; it offered little beyond physical comfort. They believed the ideals they were taught, and felt miserable when the ideals were exposed as empty words. Their awareness that Negroes and millions of poor have been left out of the society moved them to act rather than depend on the persuasion techniques advocated by their elders.

Many of them were born in the year of The Bomb, and so their history begins with the history of nuclear destruction. The twenties and even the thirties are almost prehistory to them, and the burning issues which agitated the older generation's radicals and liberals are devoid of meaning. Some know of the mid-fifties' McCarthyism and the House Un-American Activities Committee (HUAC), but the internecine wars of the thirties have little personal significance for them.

In some measure, too, the modes of extreme personal behavior adopted by this group—their permissive view of marijuana or hallucinogenics like LSD, their matter-of-fact acceptance of sexual freedom and their habitual profanity—are part of their search for identity. That search assumes a rejection of everything connected with their old identity and of the technological, bureaucratic values they see as dominant in American life. It is also possible that their difficulties in finding personal meaning in the routine politics of the civil rights struggle and their anguish in seeing the country carry out a foreign policy they believe to be totally bad force these young people into seeking meaning in experiences. They think the ivory-towered men of ideas have cheated them, lied to them, and that action and spontaneous experience will show them truth.

Above all, those in The Movement now restlessly seek to find a new politics and a new ideology that will permit them to link existential humanism with morally acceptable modes of achieving radical social change.

II. The Movement's Origins

The Movement's origins are elusive and have many strands. In the 1930s and 1940s the radical movement encompassed a broad spectrum of organizations and political beliefs: the Communists and their front groups; the socialists, Trotskyists, and other anti-Stalinist organizations; sections of the CIO and a few other unions. The Communist groups, drawing worldwide support, dominated American radicalism, since their size and prestige were greater than any of the other political tendencies. And although the American Communist Party was shaken in 1939 by the Stalin-Hitler nonaggression pact, the Nazi attack on the Soviet Union returned them to political acceptability.

But by the mid-fifties the old movement was nearly dead. The Communist Party had declined badly in the postwar period, because of government persecution and its own internal weaknesses. The trade unions were no longer crusading, many once radical anti-Communists had become supporters of the Establishment, and the socialists were barely distinguishable from the liberal Democrats.

Then, when today's young radicals were still in junior high school, the entire Communist world was shaken by the revelations about Stalin made at the 20th Party Congress. The Communist movement soon suffered further blows from the uprisings in Hungary and Poland. The Labor Youth League (LYL), the Communist Party youth group, was disbanded shortly after the shock of 1956, but it would have declined from internal stress anyway. At the very time the American Marxists were being disillusioned by the actions of Soviet socialism, England, France, and Israel joined in an invasion of Egypt. A few intellectuals, faced with Western imperialism and brutal Soviet Marxism, began seeking a fresh way out of the crisis, developing what C. Wright Mills described as The New Left.

It started in England, where in 1957 a group of university intellectuals published two new journals, *Universities and Left Review* and *The New Reasoner*. In 1959 they merged into the *New Left Review*. Many of the editors had been members of or had been close to the Communist Party at Oxford. For them the failure of Marxism was more a failure of the vulgar Communist Marxists than of the theory. In the new journals the ideals of socialism were rediscovered, and the kind of humanist analysis that had been forgotten through purges, war, and Cold War was revived. Often, too, *New Left Review* debated ideas that could not comfortably be talked about within the framework of Soviet Marxism: alienation and humanism.

New Left political clubs of college and working-class youth followed the magazine's formation, and through 1959 this small group lit a new spark under dormant English radicalism—Aldermaston marches in support of peace and against nuclear testing grew larger each year, and the Labour Party swung to the New Left position on nuclear weapons, for one year.

By the end of the fifties concern for racial justice was developing among American students. A strong reaction to the indignities of fear and anxiety heaped on the country by McCarthy and a general rejection of the symbols of American affluence were growing. Some youth responded with the "beat" mood; others developed an interest in the new British intellectual radicalism; still others rejected the style of life practiced by J. D. Salinger's characters.

Simultaneously, a group in the American pacifist movement, strongly influenced by pacifist leader A. J. Muste, was developing a "third camp" position, which rejected both the American and Soviet Cold War positions, concentrating instead on attempting to create a third force to resist all militarism. Many "third camp" pacifists had been involved in the civil rights struggle, to which they had brought the nonviolent techniques that they had been studying and practicing since the outbreak of World War II. And although their original interest and commitment had an informal religious base, they moved over easily to politics.

As McCarthyism waned in the late fifties a group of university intellectuals, much like the British New Left although less vigorous and certain, began to develop around the universities of Wisconsin, California at Berkeley, and Chicago. At Wisconsin the Socialist Club was formed by ex-LYLers and younger undergraduates who had never experienced Communist Party schooling; at Berkeley a similar group called SLATE formed a student political party; at Chicago a student political party founded in the early fifties was revived.

At Wisconsin the success of the Socialist Club and the inspiration of the British New Left were combined with the teaching of William Appleman Williams, the historian, who attempted to use Marxism creatively to understand American history. The result was the publication of *Studies on the Left*, "a journal of research, social theory and review." Several months later at the University of Chicago a group of graduate students began to publish *New University Thought*.

The difference between the magazines was essentially over the use of the word "left." At a meeting held in Madison, Wisconsin, in 1960 to discuss merging the two magazines, the Chicago group, most of whom had had some experience with Communist youth groups as had the Wisconsin editors, argued that the word "left" and certainly the word "socialism" was so discredited as to be useless. The *Studies* editors argued that since they were socialists and Marxists, they should say so. One of their regrets was that during the McCarthy period they had been forced to mask their true political beliefs.

The advent of *Studies* and *New University Thought* marked the transition from old left Marxist dogma to a new period, even though most of the editors were Marxists who retained some loyalty to the Soviet Union, at least as a force for peace and reason. But the editors were also deeply concerned with scholarship, and saw themselves not so much as professional Movement people but as a new breed of university professor.

Meanwhile new journals appeared at Columbia, at Harvard, at campuses all over the country, reflecting the increased activity among intellectual radicals. These publications and the discussions over their contents were not limited to politics but covered every aspect of life from sexual freedom and pornography to civil rights and peace issues.

Another generation graduated from high school, and the colleges and universities became breeding grounds for campus political activity and the civil rights drive. Some of the young people in The Movement began to exhibit an inclination for activism and a spirit of anti-intellectualism, in part a rejection of the very university system in which they were involved. "The University" came to be regarded as part of the Establishment, and as the point of immediate contact, the most oppressive part.

Unlike their immediate predecessors, who had published magazines like *Studies* and *New University Thought*, this new group of youth activists knew little about the debates of the thirties. They learned about Stalinism, Trotskyism, and Social Democracy only in an academic context. Outside the classroom they referred with a sneer to the "old days"—the thirties, forties, and now the fifties. Like the rest of American society, the old left, they believed, had in some way "betrayed" them: they had "sold out" or else were "hung up" on old and dead battles. To most of these young people Marx, Lenin, and Trotsky had little relevance for what they understood to be America's problems. They simultaneously refused to identify with the Soviet Union or to be greatly concerned about injustice in any of the Communist societies. Their enemy was the American society and its Establishment.

Many of the young people in this activist generation were the children of parents who had been the radicals and left liberals of the thirties and the forties. At home they had heard the discussions about civil rights, and they knew of the political pall that hung over the country during the McCarthy era. They had learned a set of ideals from their parents and now, much to their parents' discomfiture, they were trying to put those ideals into practice.

And so by 1960 this new generation was throwing itself against American society, literally and figuratively. They found a new hero in Castro, the man of action, the man without an ideology, whose only interest seemed to be bettering the life of the Cuban people. They responded to the youthful Castro with enthusiasm and demanded "fair play" for the Cuban Revolution.

In May 1960 they were ready for an action of their own, and the opportunity was provided by the House Un-American Activities Committee. Hundreds of students from the campuses of the University of California at Berkeley and San Francisco State College, joined by some of the people who were moving away from the inactivity of the "beat" coffee houses, demonstrated physically against the Committee's San Francisco hearing. And after the demonstration, which received enormous publicity, they scorned the allegation that they had been led or inspired by the Communists. That charge, which they knew to be untrue, only reinforced their feelings of distrust for the celebrants of American society.

They identified, too, with the Freedom Riders who went South in 1960 and 1961; for this again meant taking direct action with their own bodies against segregation. They were not interested in theory, and so the long historical articles even in such left journals as *Studies* were not seen by them as being relevant.

This new activist Movement influenced even those who thought of themselves as being outside of society. As the apolitical "beats"—almost alone as symbols of protest in the fifties—turned their concern to concrete issues of racial equality and peace, their style, dress, and decor affected the activists. Arguments about politics began to include discussions of sexual freedom and marijuana. The language of the Negro poet-hipster permeated analyses of the Cuban Revolution. Protests over the execution of Caryl Chessman ultimately brought together students and some Bohemians—the loose and overlapping segments of what was to become known as The Movement.

President Kennedy gauged accurately the need of many youth to participate in programs for justice, and a few of the new activists were attracted to the Peace Corps. The Peace Corps stressed, at least in its appeal, a non-paternalistic, activist program in which people would be helped to help themselves, but most activists rejected the Peace Corps or any other government program. They felt American society supported racism, oppressive institutions, capital punishment, and wars against popular movements in underdeveloped countries. "Alienation" was used to describe the society's effects on its citizens, and American society was seen as the source of injustice and suffering everywhere. While opposed to injustice and suppression of liberty in general, the activists did not feel the same outrage against Castro or Mao or Khrushchev that they could against their own rulers. It was "our" fault. Brought up and nurtured on the United Nations and liberal political values, hearing them articulated so well by President Kennedy and Adlai

Stevenson, they demanded purity at home first, and when it was not forth-coming, quickly became convinced that it was impossible, that there was something rotten at the core of American society.

This dashing of hopes, the feeling that they had succumbed to what turned out to be only rhetoric on the part of Kennedy and Stevenson, was an important part of their turning so bitterly against the Establishment.

And while the older ones among them had been able to articulate their views in a speech or a pamphlet, some of the younger ones, those who came into The Movement later and rejected politics—a small but growing number of middle-class youth—made a virtue of their inability to articulate and analyze coherently. They talked "from the gut," stumblingly, haltingly, using the language of the new folksingers, deliberately adopting a style that was the antithesis of what they had heard from their professors.

In their revulsion against the liberal intellectuals who were celebrating America and the end of ideology, the young activists rejected all ideology and traditional party politics, turning instead to where the action was, to SNCC, formed in 1960 by Negroes and whites, Southern and Northern. SNCC wasn't political; it was concerned with right and wrong, with people. The SNCC ideal of morality in action also provided the spur for the Students for a Democratic Society (SDS) and its community and campus programs: the decision to act was reinforced by the role of the liberal intellectuals in the 1961 Bay of Pigs episode and the 1962 missile crisis.

What began perhaps as a rebellion against affluence and liberal hypocrisy grew in a few years into a radical activism that protested injustice at the very core of the society. But when even this was tolerated by the structures that were under attack, some of the young radicals began to think about some-thing beyond rebellion or radical protest. The Movement now is struggling to develop an ideology that will guide them toward building an organization that can compete for political power.

Crisis in the New Left

Larry David Nachman

Four of the defendants in the Chicago conspiracy trial, Abbie Hoffman, Jerry Rubin, Tom Hayden and Dave Dellinger, published books in the last year that portray and reflect the strains and divisions that beset the American Left as it begins a new decade.

Woodstock Nation (Random House) is a story, a memoir—perhaps it would be best to match extravagance for extravagance and say that *Woodstock Nation* is Abbie Hoffman's first novel. The story turns on a simple episode: during the great Woodstock festival, Hoffman stepped up to the microphone to make a statement and was thrown off the platform by Peter Townshend of the rock group, The Who. The performers felt that Hoffman was interfering with their show and that he was intruding politics into a celebration. The incident was insignificant but it was related to a larger event whose significance is harder to assess—the impasse of the American Left.

Three events of 1969 had special meaning for the American Left. The first was the breakup of SDS, that loose coalition of old Left, New Left and hippies, which had helped energize the university campus. In its stead, on the one hand, were the well-organized youth branches of the old, rigid and authoritarian Marxist organizations, and, on the other hand, the Weatherman faction in which Americans saw the gradual emergence of an underground, terroristic organization. The second event was Woodstock.

The special spirit of the New Left had been the unusual combination of deep concern its members displayed for both politics and the problems of self and alternative social and cultural forms. But just at the time

From Larry David Nachman, "The Movement Seeks a Mass," The Nation, CCXII, January 11, 1971, pp. 39–45. Reprinted by permission of the Nation.

when politics seemed increasingly desiccated, futile and frustrating, Wood-stock provided an instant legend of immediate personal liberation through those good and joyous modes of self-exploration which the Left had learned so well to appreciate: sex, rock and drugs. That the event did not bring one into contact with the social and political reality of the nation was an added attraction to those who could not forget that the great radical social event of the previous August had been the "siege of Chicago."

The third important occurrence of 1969 was the Chicago conspiracy trial. It promised a chance to re-create the political energy and direction of the Left, but that is not what happened. The trial's significance came to lie in its other side, in the emergence of political repression as a national policy of high priority. However much radicals might find strength in their courage, the new repression put a constant additional strain on them and made them feel more intensely the political isolation that had been gnaw-ing at the Left for several years.

When black nationalism emerged in 1965, it cut the nascent white Left off from the masses of black Americans, and since then the Left has had to get along without the political and psychological support of direct connection with a mass base. In the first stages of the anti-war movement, it did not seem to matter. Moral outrage over the war and the excitement of touching the conscience of the nation seemed sufficient to sustain peo-ple in their political opposition. But the capacity of established institutions, particularly the Presidency and the political parties, to weather this oppo-sition and continue the war made radicals uneasy about the future of a political movement that was building only on itself.

Much of what has happened to the Left in the last three years can be described in terms of the blows it suffered as it moved away from its natural constituency of educated, white middle-class youth, and attempted to forge links with other groups. Indeed, the various divisions on the Left can, in part, be understood in terms of the particular mass base with which a given radical group would like to identify: the workers (orthodox Marxist-Leninists), Third World revolutionaries (Weatherman, et al.), or the Black Panther Party as the "vanguard" of American blacks (Peace and Freedom Party, etc.). On the other hand, the cultural radicals, who continued to suspect the reality of these proposed alliances, no longer seemed concerned about politics.

Abbie Hoffman had been a key figure in the fusing of culture and politics. In *Woodstock Nation*, surveying the split between them, he re-sembles a child whose parents have separated. He is sympathetic to both, angry at both for failing to remain together, and conscious that he alone now represents the union disunited. His own preference is for a politics built on cultural radicalism.

Political revolution leads people into support for other revolutions rather than having them get involved in their own. Cultural revolution requires people to change the way they live and act in the revolution rather than passing judgments on how the other folks are proceeding.

He is saying that people's politics must have a vital connection with the social and political reality they experience in their daily lives. His mistake is to restrict that connection to those who have established "outlaw" communities or life styles. To oppose war making or racism of one's own country is completely different from envisioning oneself as part of the resistance offered by the victims of those policies. However, Hoffman shares with Mark Rudd a suspicion of any politics that is built around moral reaction to others' suffering. He differs from Rudd in his convictions that people can organize effectively only around their own suffering, and that those in the process of liberating themselves from the white middle class do suffer from real oppression. At the New Haven Panther rally the following May he was to say, "the most oppressed people in America are white middle-class youth." He therefore attacks Rudd for lacking self-consciousness and self-awareness. "Mark Rudd is facing fifteen years on a drug bust and I talk about it more than he does." Hoffman knows that white radicals can never constitute an American branch of the Vietcong or of the Cuban revolution. Those who think they can are deluding themselves and failing to recognize that "deep down they're hippies just like us."

But though a hippie, Hoffman is a political hippie and he could not at all be happy with a situation in which "the Left was moving to Stalinism and the hippies were moving to the country (as usual)." As a political activist, he was concerned about the dangers of political isolation. He notes that liberal financial support for radical political causes was diminishing, whereas cultural radicalism was proving very profitable indeed. Besides enjoying the proceeds from sales of rock albums, festival tickets and other paraphernalia, the capitalists were learning to incorporate in advertisements the forms, language and artifacts of the hippies in order to appeal to young people and to those who would like to have as much fun as their dreams told them young people were having. In *Woodstock Nation*, Hoffman describes how he tried to persuade the promoters of the festival to contribute part of the profits to movement causes. It is typical of so many of his enterprises—the Free Store, the Movement Speakers' Bureau, the guides on how to get free goods and services. All these activities are directed to the important and impossible goal of creating a self-sufficient radical community.

That community is a fantasy, a portent of a better but distant future. But much too often Hoffman forgets that and confuses his fantasy with present social reality. Cultural radicalism not only has its origins in the American middle class but persists in being a middle-class phenomenon. Who else can afford it? Large numbers of young people are giving their

lives new directions, exploring new life styles, and abandoning the career-
ism and professionalism of the fifties, but few of them are severing completely their ties to the actual institutions of our society. Very few indeed
will live in communes. When Abbie Hoffman tells college audiences that
they should "drop out," they cheer him; but next day they return to their
classes.

Failure to distinguish the real potential for change from his unreal
exaggerations produces the major ambiguity that lies at the heart of Hoffman's book. On one side, he argues that cultural radicals are "outlaws";
their life style brings them automatically into conflict with either the legal
system or social mores. That being so, their estrangement from society will
intensify as the cultural radicals are harassed and jailed; and at the same
time they will become more closely knit as they share a common oppression. On the other hand, Hoffman sees that the ambiance of hippie life
can be easily assimilated into the consumerism of affluent society. Woodstock, on that level, becomes a weekend with entertainment in the country
for some nice kids from the suburbs.

There was real poignancy in his aborted attempt to speak to the multitude gathered on the slopes of Bethel. He was flying on acid and brood-
ing about John Sinclair who was, and is, serving a ten-year sentence in
Michigan for possession of two marijuana cigarettes. Soft drugs flowed
freely at Woodstock and no attempt was made to enforce the law. By
speaking to the crowd of Sinclair, Hoffman would bring them back to the
political reality they had forgotten. They would be reminded of a man
whose youth was being consumed by the rigid enforcement of a stupid
and repressive law. Sinclair was for Hoffman the symbol of what those at
the festival had left behind—not only the problems of poverty, war and
racism but a consciousness of their own struggle with the Establishment.
In the end, Hoffman was not permitted to speak: the order of the day was
"No politics here."

But at bottom how different is Abbie Hoffman from those he felt
were ignoring their political commitments? Has he not, in his own way,
also gone off to the country? He has repeatedly argued that he has been
arrested and prosecuted for his life style, for what he was rather than what
he did.

> When I appear in the Chicago courtroom, I want to be tried not because
> I support the National Liberation Front—which I do—but because I have long
> hair.

That position was echoed by several of his co-defendants, but did it
happen? The prosecutors, to be sure, made hay over the defendants' personal habits, but that is the custom of prosecutors. Whatever the defendants came to think, they were prosecuted, not for their long hair and not

even because they supported the Vietcong (a support which could not have any effective meaning in terms of political action) but because they actively opposed the war in Vietnam.

Opposition to the war—or to any other governmental policy—is not mere dissent. The latter is verbal or written criticism of acts and policies of state. And in a society in which the means of reaching large numbers of people are controlled by relatively few, dissent does not constitute a threat to power. Opposition, on the contrary, involves a real challenge to institutions. It consists of political actions which have the twofold purpose of exposing wrongs done by government and withdrawing the consent upon which the moral authority of the government rests. And, though the anti-war activists had become frustrated and impatient, they were putting a strain on the government and limiting somewhat its options at home and abroad.

Hoffman understands as well as any one the basis of radical politics. At his trial, he stated strongly the justification for civil disobedience:

> But when the decorum is oppression, the only dignity that free men have is the right to speak out. . . . We cannot respect a law, a law that is tyranny and a law that is trying us, and the courts are in a conspiracy of tyranny, and when the law is tyranny the only order is insurrection and disrespect, and that's what we showed, and that's what all honorable men of free will will show.

When he speaks that way he reveals his own decency and moral insight. He also states the feelings of a new generation that can no longer venerate or give unconditional loyalty to their institutions, because they have seen what crimes those institutions can commit. But when Abbie Hoffman says in *Woodstock Nation*, "I think kids should kill their parents," he not only violates that basic decency which consists in retaining some human bonds even with those you oppose but reveals a deep contempt for those he courts, most of whom share his opposition to the structure and policies of the government but who have neither the will nor the desire to kill their parents, ritually or literally.

I am not condemning Abbie Hoffman for some chance remark, grue-some as it is. Such phrases are characteristic of his theatrical flourishes and are based on his commitment to use the medium of art ("theatre of the streets") to engage people emotionally in politics, even if it means pro-voking hostility. There is a larger issue here. A constellation of experiences has produced a major error of the Left. In the first place, the experience of the intractability and unresponsiveness of political institutions has not only brought the salutary rejection of the authority of those institutions but has meant for many radicals that on principle they should not have any con-cern for any of the processes of government. This principle has cut radicals off from those around them. To replace the political reality they have lost, they have turned elsewhere—to the revolutionary societies in the Third World. But for American radicals these societies cannot be a field of political activity. They must act here or nowhere. Too many have, in effect and unknown to themselves, chosen the latter course.

This flight from political reality reinforces another tendency. Radicals have discovered deep layers of oppression in their institutions and repression in the accepted morality. They have become distrustful of the existing world and have sought in their imagination to discover new possibilities. Like radicals before them, they have learned that what is is not necessarily what has to be. But from questioning everything and seeing that anything is possible, many came to feel that everything is permitted. Street theatre as comedy is a magnificent political weapon. It holds institutions up to derision and makes the powerful seem ridiculous and contemptible. But when the hostility, aggression and violence ever present in our society become the substance of street theatre, a real danger arises. Such theatre does not represent the conversion of art into reality but of reality into art. Radicals, then, reproduce what they have always railed against: the turning of pain and horror into a mere spectacle—Vietnam as television entertainment. Violence as theatre or as play must be distinguished from real violence which hurts, injures and kills. Finally, imagination and speculation must halt before one reality—the living human being in his mortal flesh. The vision that does not take account of him is already dehumanized and can produce a world no better than the one we have always known.

But Abbie Hoffman is a gentle, restrained lamb in comparison to Jerry Rubin. In Jerry Rubin,

> The blood-dimmed tide is loosed, everywhere
> The ceremony of innocence is drowned.

Hoffman himself once described with considerable accuracy the distinction between the two of them. He wrote: "Jerry wants to show the clenched fist. I want to show the clenched fist and the smile. He wants the gun. I want the gun and the flower."

By all accounts, Jerry Rubin is a brilliant political organizer. In his book, *Do It* (Simon & Schuster), he shows intelligence, occasional tenderness and, of course, his famous manic wit. But these are secondary considerations if one is to take Jerry Rubin seriously—and I believe he must be taken seriously if America is to know its radicals and if radicals are to know themselves. This is not to say that Jerry Rubin is a typical radical, but he carries with him, unalloyed, the anger and rage of a decade of struggle. *Do It* reveals the smoldering rage that is present to some degree in every American radical.

Every radical knows that anger and rage as a background feeling that boils to the surface at moments like the Kent State killings. But in Jerry Rubin the emotions are always on the surface; they are his driving force and the basis of his politics. Their explanation lies in the structure of contemporary America and in its recent history. The problems which have engaged radicals—racism, poverty and war—are obsolete problems; they should and could have been dealt with long ago. It is grotesque that in 1971 one still must assert against a recalcitrant political reality that it is wrong for blacks to be treated worse than whites, and that it is wrong for the most powerful nation in history to be concentrating its resources on slaughtering hundreds of thousands of Southeast Asians.

The buoyancy and elation of the first stages of the civil rights and anti-war movements came from the sense that they presented a moral issue but not a moral debate. The issue need only be revealed to the public and there would be change. In both cases, bitterness arose when the Left discovered how tenaciously older, outmoded policies were clung to. Moreover, one should never forget how terrible a strain it has been for people to oppose actively the might of the state. There have been deaths in this struggle. Young men and women have spent time in jail or in living with fear. Careers have been risked, people have emigrated or cut their ties with their families and their social roots. And yet the infamy continues.

Radicals lack a tragic sense and Americans lack one even more so. Actions are supposed to bring results; failure is not to be accepted. Is an American capable of acting with the foreknowledge that his act will not succeed? I return here to the theme of political frustration. Frustration could, of course, have provided a useful lesson. It could have brought about a deeper understanding of political power and social institutions and it could have purged people of their dreams of instant success. It could have led to a commitment to long-run effort, both within and outside the political system. Such a commitment to the long run is, of course, painfully hard in the presence of actual human suffering. What alone can justify it is that there is no real political alternative.

In Jerry Rubin one sees the triumph of the anti-politics of apocalyptic fantasy:

When in doubt, burn. Fire is the revolutionary's god. Fire is instant theater. No words can match fire. Politicians only notice poverty when the ghettos burn. The burning of the first draft card caused earth tremors under the Pentagon.
Burn the flag. Burn churches.
Burn, burn, burn.

That is the cry of one who yearns with all his heart to act, to do something in the world. Violence is embraced as an equivalent of action. But for Jerry Rubin, violence is still fantasy—he burns nothing. As fantasy, violence becomes a mode of dealing with the anger and rage within. It is psychic satisfaction, but it is politically empty. Jerry Rubin, too, has gone to the country.

And because of the pervasiveness of this rhetoric, young people have been saying lately, "I don't believe in violence and I don't believe in electoral politics, so I cannot really be political." It is ironic that Jerry Rubin and many like him have re-established the traditional American definition of politics as either violence or elections. At the same time, this rhetoric supports those liberals and conservatives who over the years have, loosely and wrongly, used the word "violence" to describe demonstrations, protest marches and sit-ins.

So even more than Hoffman, Rubin has cut himself off from his own political world. He connects with his own dreams of destruction, with the Panthers, the Vietcong and with the Cuban revolution, but how is all that related to concrete political acts? And how does it affect those very many Americans who are seriously troubled by the policies and structure of their government, and yet either do not identify with revolutionary movements abroad or do not even have a radical political consciousness? These issues can best be discussed by turning to a more deliberate and systematic thinker, Tom Hayden.

Tom Hayden's *Trial* (Holt, Rinehart & Winston) is an extensive and penetrating analysis of the New Left. It is, perhaps, the most brilliant book yet written on contemporary American radicalism. Hayden exemplifies some of the most important elements of that radicalism: he has been a civil rights activist, student organizer, and local community worker. *Trial* displays the workings of an analytic and considerate mind, grappling with some of the most complex issues of the age. He picks up, examines, and tries to do justice to all the various positions on the Left.

His basic thesis is that the United States Government has entered a new hard-line period at home and abroad. The government has dug in to fight revolution in the Third World and opposition at home. But the fury of the war in Southeast Asia and the domestic political repression, Hayden believes, are signs of weakness and symptoms of the collapse of the power of the American empire. Hayden's analysis, thus, should spur radicals on to greater militancy as they face new and grave threats. At the same time, he shares the traditional optimism of radicals, telling them that victory is assured, time is on their side. The authorities "can kill but never win." A small radical movement, having few resources save its courage and its intellectual and moral energy, which is in the midst of active opposition to the United States Government, the military, finance capital, heavy industry and the mass media, can ill afford delusions of grandeur. Hayden's argument must be looked at more closely.

Part of his optimism lies in the importance he attaches to the generational conflict.

The rise of an American student movement in the last decade is a revolutionary, not routine, event. . . . For the time being . . . "youth" is more important than "economic class" in analyzing the American struggle.

Hayden has here seized upon one of the most important facts about American radicalism: that a significant section of the middle class has defected from the very institutions to which they were heir. If the new and coming generation is inherently radical, then one can confidently await the future in which the present holders of power are quite simply outlived. But the weakness in Hayden's analysis is his confidence that college students will continue to be radicalized. When dealing with the young, it is important to remember that new people are coming on the scene all the time.

The student generation of the last decade was exceptionally political, but their being political depended on the development of places in which it was possible to be political. Demonstrations, from marches to sit-ins, were a means of involving people from the highly committed to the marginally committed. The flexibility inherent in such a range of tactics permitted the opposition to grow. But gradually over the last few years, the highly committed radicals have avoided any action which was not adequate to their level of commitment. Those who have a concern for issues but are without militancy no longer have a place to act, since the initiation or organization of action usually depends upon the most committed. The result is that political radicals have become more and more isolated and tend to talk only to one another. On the other hand, fewer college students seem to become politically engaged. Last fall was an exceptionally quiet one on the American campus. There is a good chance that the near future will see a college student typified by a cynicism that extends equally to the established political system and to any political action whatsoever.

But optimism can produce a peculiar kind of blindness, even in a careful and serious political analyst. Hayden talks of creating "free territories" (e.g., Haight-Ashbury, the East Village, etc.) of resistance. Whatever weakness the United States Government has been showing, one would think it will be a long time before it will lack the power to take on the East Village.

Yet the real core of moral and political weakness in Hayden's position is to be seen in his conviction that the white Left must attach itself solidly to the cause of the Black Panther Party. The very last words of Hayden's book are:

All those who value their own liberation must go with the Panthers and Bobby [Seale] as they become symbols of humanity making a time-honored stand: Freedom or Death.

The white Left has adulated the Panthers from the start. Norman Mailer once perceptively observed that the black Left has had more influence on the white Left than on the black masses. The reason for the Panthers' hold on the white Left is apparent: the Panthers are the only militant black group that is willing to enter into alliances with whites, and white radicals, intensely conscious of the bitter heritage of American racism, wish desperately to unite with black people in the struggle against that racism.

Hayden, along with many radicals, does in thought what the Panthers have certainly not been able to do in fact. He sees the Panthers as representative of all black people. To support the Panthers is to support the black people. To oppose them is to oppose the blacks. It was a striking characteristic of the Chicago trial that as it went on the defendants tended more and more to subordinate the issues of the trial to the Panther issue. Now it is true that the Panthers have been brutally attacked by police across the nation. But to defend the Panthers against these attacks it is not necessary to approve of whatever they may do.

The debacle that this identification with the Panthers brought about was seen in the Chicago defendants' taking up the cause of the New Haven Panthers. The "facts are irrelevant," Tom Hayden announced in a speech on behalf of the accused Panthers. But if the facts are irrelevant then we no longer live in a common moral and political universe. Those who are "objectively" our friends are always good and right; our "objective" enemies are bad and wrong. In such a world, violence is indeed the only possible political relationship.

Hayden's statement, moreover, reveals that he had a shrewd notion as to what the facts might have been. In any event, they became clear in the trial that followed. A Panther, wrongly suspected of being a police spy, was tortured for several days and then murdered. Lonnie McLucas, a convicted and self-confessed participant in the act, seems to have been deeply disturbed by the crime, and one gets the sense that he was trapped by Panther rhetoric and the Panther mystique into a position where he was no longer capable of saying no. One dead, several convicted, others awaiting trial; all Panthers—these facts are supremely relevant, and one is permitted to ask what a group that does this to its own people can possibly offer to anyone else. Tom Hayden has the wisdom to know that in politics and morality means are ends.

A radical movement always begins to create within itself the structures that will eventually form the basis of the new society.

Would Tom Hayden have the murder of Alex Rackley be part of the basis of the new society? If so, how many will want to join him in building it?

But yet, on another level, what does white radical support for the Panthers mean? One detects that for most white supporters it involves a psychic identification with the Panthers' guns. Once again, sustained political action is hard and, in terms of immediate results, unrewarding. Dreams of violence and destruction are comforting and satisfying for those whose deepest and coldest fear is that things will, after all, not change significantly in the foreseeable future. Has even Tom Hayden gone to the country?

Recent American radicalism came into being through contact with American political life. Political consciousness developed as even larger numbers of people, particularly college students, came to grips with some of the basic elements of American life and began to confront the institutions that sustained the policies which they rejected. The Vietcong did not teach Americans new lessons; Johnson, McNamara, Nixon, the March on the Pentagon, the 1968 Democratic National Convention and the demonstrations surrounding it, Berkeley—these were what created a new political consciousness. Any program for the revitalization of a radical opposition must concentrate on American institutions and a strategy that is relevant to the American experience. The time has again come to remember that fundamental political question, "What is to be done?" What am I to do tomorrow and all the rest of my tomorrows?

Too much of the recent debate on the Left has sounded like the argument, "Mine is bigger than yours." Each group tries to demonstrate its greater militancy and thus prove its superior radicalism. It is fortunate in this state of affairs that one can still turn to that most anomalous of radicals, Dave Dellinger.

Dellinger's *Revolutionary Non-Violence* (Bobbs-Merrill) is a compilation of articles dating back to 1943. That, in itself, is remarkable. Dellinger is able to draw on an unusually long experience of being a radical. Always somewhat aloof from the old Left, he must have known depths of political isolation which younger radicals can hardly imagine. But most important, he has had the experience of acting when his acts could bring no immediate political result. Most notably, he served two prison terms as a draft resister in World War II.

Dellinger is unfortunately no theorist. His political analysis is uneven; sometimes sharp, sometimes flaccid. What he is, what he knows himself to be, is a political activist. He is, like all men, fallible in his political judgments. But he has a deep sense of what action involves and his radicalism is built around his profound understanding of the quality of the political act. "A potentially revolutionary movement becomes what it does."

The radical is a prophet and educator. By his actions, he is bearing "moral witness" to the wrongs of the society. At the same time, what *he* does bears witness to what could be. A radical movement must be an exemplary model of what an alternative society would be like. At their best, the civil rights and anti-war movements had such moral strength. And it was when they were at their best that they were attracting large numbers of people. The moral view which leads the radical into action must be present in the actions themselves. Again, there are no means, only ends:

Now it is our responsibility to see that righteousness continues to be on our side, both in the objectives for which we struggle and in the spirit and activities by which we carry on that struggle.

Radicalism exists in the realm of spirit; it always has the quality of fantasy and of the ideal. Other political positions are rooted in the existing social and political reality; they correspond to actual interests. Radicalism belongs to the imagination and involves the vision of new possibilities in the world. Radicalism, thus, always carries with it the twofold danger that it will never connect with the world in which men live and that the unreachable goals it sets for itself will lead to paralyzing or self-destructive frustration.

Dellinger gently criticizes Martin Luther King for having fallen "into the trap of White House politics." He is right insofar as radicals ought not to accept the legitimacy and authority of institutions and should not believe them to be self-correcting. But I believe that Dellinger detaches himself too completely from the institutions in which not only most Americans but most radicals live out their lives. He realizes the need for democratization of both social and political institutions, but he does not fully appreciate the importance of some work within institutions.

The way in which a radical can connect his vision with the actual world around him is to take that world seriously. The politically conscious college generation of the sixties has now graduated. There are radicals in teaching, journalism, social work, city planning, medicine, law, etc. Full-time activists, such as Hoffman, Rubin, Hayden and Dellinger, cannot be models for these people. They must learn to create their own models. A movement whose only ideal is the person who stands completely outside the system will be hopelessly elitist and hopelessly small. In their working lives, radicals are now in a position to begin to make some real but limited changes in society. The directions in which they should move are toward greater internal democracy in their institutions and more direct institutional commitment to serve the needs of the community. Already hospitals and universities are feeling the pressures from a new politically and socially conscious staff. It is to be hoped that this trend will continue and be extended. Furthermore, this kind of action provides a diversity of models for younger people who want neither to drop out nor to end their political lives at graduation.

On the great national political issues, people like Dave Dellinger will continue to be invaluable. There is a charming irony in the new radical judgment that demonstrations don't work. Did the Left really believe the political system was so responsive that three to five years of demonstrations ought to have changed the government from its course? It will take persistent pressure and confrontation over decades to make any real change in the basic structure of American political life. The political tactics used in the sixties must be revived and made a permanent part of the political scene. Demonstrations should be understood for what they are, simultaneously acts of political pressure and of political education. Nor should more conventional political tactics be avoided on principle. The presence of a radical opposition should be brought to bear wherever it can be felt.

It is no accident that one of the few vital radical groups remaining is the Women's Liberation movement. Women's Lib uses a wide variety of tactics: sit-ins, marches, lobbying, electoral politics. It thus enables a broad spectrum of women to participate in a common politics: each woman able to choose the political mode she is most comfortable with. Women's Lib encourages people to work within their own institutions to break down patterns of sex discrimination. And the group is careful not to alienate its own potential constituency. This approach, which was once typical of the antiwar movement, is a good model to follow. Radicalism can return to the specific structures and institutions of American life or we can all go to the country.

The Future of the Civil Rights Movement

Bayard Rustin

I

The decade spanned by the 1954 Supreme Court decision on school de-segregation and the Civil Rights Act of 1964 will undoubtedly be recorded as the period in which the legal foundations of racism in America were destroyed. To be sure, pockets of resistance remain; but it would be hard to quarrel with the assertion that the elaborate legal structure of segregation and discrimination, particularly in relation to public accommodations, has virtually collapsed. On the other hand, without making light of the human sacrifices involved in the direct-action tactics (sit-ins, freedom rides, and the rest) that were so instrumental to this achievement, we must recognize that in desegregating public accommodations, we affected institutions which are relatively peripheral both to the American socio-economic order and to the fundamental conditions of life of the Negro people. In a highly industrialized, 20th-century civilization, we hit Jim Crow precisely where it was most anachronistic, dispensable, and vulnerable—in hotels, lunch counters, terminals, libraries, swimming pools, and the like. For in these forms, Jim Crow does impede the flow of commerce in the broadest sense: it is a nuisance in a society on the move (and on the make). Not surprisingly, therefore, it was the most mobility-conscious and relatively liberated groups in the Negro community—lower-middle-class college students—who launched the attack that brought down this imposing but hollow structure.

The term "classical" appears especially apt for this phase of the civil

From Bayard Rustin, "From Protest to Politics," Commentary (February 1965), pp. 25–31. Reprinted from Commentary, by permission; copyright © 1965 by the American Jewish Committee.

rights movement. But in the few years that have passed since the first flush of sit-ins, several developments have taken place that have complicated matters enormously. One is the shifting focus of the movement in the South, symbolized by Birmingham; another is the spread of the revolution to the North; and the third, common to the other two, is the expansion of the movement's base in the Negro community. . . . Birmingham remains the unmatched symbol of grass-roots protest involving all strata of the black community. It was also in this most industrialized of Southern cities that the single-issue demands of the movement's classical stage gave way to the "package deal." No longer were Negroes satisfied with integrating lunch counters. They now sought advances in employment, housing, school integration, police protection, and so forth.

Thus, the movement in the South began to attack areas of discrimination which were not so remote from the Northern experience as were Jim Crow lunch counters. At the same time, the interrelationship of these apparently distinct areas became increasingly evident. What is the value of winning access to public accommodations for those who lack money to use them? The minute the movement faced this question, it was compelled to expand its vision beyond race relations to economic relations, including the role of education in modern society. And what also became clear is that all these interrelated problems, by their very nature, are not soluble by private, voluntary efforts but require government action—or politics. Already Southern demonstrators had recognized that the most effective way to strike at the police brutality they suffered from was by getting rid of the local sheriff— and that meant political action, which in turn meant, and still means, political action within the Democratic party where the only meaningful primary contests in the South are fought.

And so, in Mississippi, thanks largely to the leadership of Bob Moses, a turn toward political action has been taken. More than voter registration is involved here. A conscious bid for *political power* is being made, and in the course of that effort a tactical shift is being effected: direct-action techniques are being subordinated to a strategy calling for the building of community institutions or power bases. Clearly, the implications of this shift reach far beyond Mississippi. What began as a protest movement is being challenged to translate itself into a political movement. Is this the right course? And if it is, can the transformation be accomplished?

II

The very decade which has witnessed the decline of legal Jim Crow has also seen the rise of *de facto* segregation in our most fundamental socio-economic institutions. More Negroes are unemployed today than in 1954, and the unemployment gap between the races is wider. The median income of Negroes has dropped from 57 percent to 54 percent of that of whites. A higher percentage of Negro workers is now concentrated in jobs vulnerable to automation than was the case ten years ago. More Negroes attend de facto segregated schools today than when the Supreme Court handed down its famous decision; while school integration proceeds at a snail's pace in the South, the number of Northern schools with an excessive proportion of minority youth proliferates. And behind this is the continuing growth of racial slums, spreading over our central cities and trapping Negro youth in a milieu which, whatever its legal definition, sows an unimaginable demoralization. Again, legal niceties aside, a resident of a racial ghetto lives in segregated housing, and more Negroes fall into this category than ever before.

These are the facts of life which generate frustration in the Negro community and challenge the civil rights movement. At issue, after all, is not *civil rights*, strictly speaking, but social and economic conditions. Last summer's riots were not race riots; they were outbursts of class aggression in a society where class and color definitions are converging disastrously. How can the (perhaps misnamed) civil rights movement deal with this problem?

Before trying to answer, let me first insist that the task of the movement is vastly complicated by the failure of many whites of good will to understand the nature of our problem. There is a widespread assumption that the removal of artificial racial barriers should result in the automatic integration of the Negro into all aspects of American life. This myth is fostered by facile analogies with the experience of various ethnic immigrant groups, particularly the Jews. But the analogies with the Jews do not hold for three simple but profound reasons. First, Jews have a long history as a literate people, a resource which has afforded them opportunities to advance in the academic and professional worlds, to achieve intellectual status even in the midst of economic hardship, and to evolve sustaining value systems in the context of ghetto life. Negroes, for the greater part of their presence in this country, were forbidden by law to read or write. Second, Jews have a long history of family stability, the importance of which in terms of aspiration and self-image is obvious. The Negro family structure was totally destroyed by slavery and with it the possibility of cultural transmission (the right of Negroes to marry and rear children is barely a century old). Third, Jews are white and have the *option* of relinquishing their cultural-religious identity, intermarrying, passing, etc. Negroes, or at least the overwhelming majority of them, do not have this option. There is also a fourth, vulgar reason. If the Jewish and Negro communities are not comparable in terms of education, family structure, and color, it is also true that their respective economic roles bear little resemblance.

This matter of economic role brings us to the greater problem—the fact that we are moving into an era in which the natural functioning of the market does not by itself ensure every man with will and ambition a place in the productive process. The immigrant who came to this country during the late 19th and early 20th centuries entered a society which was expanding territorially and/or economically. It was then possible to start at the bottom, as an unskilled or semi-skilled worker, and move up the ladder, acquiring new skills along the way. Especially was this true when industrial unionism was burgeoning, giving new dignity and higher wages to organized workers. Today the situation has changed. We are not expanding territorially, the western frontier is settled, labor organizing has leveled off, our rate of economic growth has been stagnant for a decade. And we are in the midst of a technological revolution which is altering the fundamental structure of the labor force, destroying unskilled and semi-skilled jobs—jobs in which Negroes are disproportionately concentrated.

Whatever the pace of this technological revolution may be, the *direction* is clear: the lower rungs of the economic ladder are being lopped off. This means that an individual will no longer be able to start at the bottom and work his way up; he will have to start in the middle or on top, and hold on tight. It will not even be enough to have certain specific skills, for many skilled jobs are also vulnerable to automation. A broad educational background, permitting vocational adaptability and flexibility, seems more imperative than ever. We live in a society where, as Secretary of Labor Willàrd Wirtz puts it, machines have the equivalent of a high school diploma. Yet the average educational attainment of American Negroes is 8.2 years.

Negroes, of course, are not the only people being affected by these developments. It is reported that there are now 50 percent fewer unskilled and semi-skilled jobs than there are high school dropouts. Almost one-third of the 26 million young people entering the labor market in the 1960's will be dropouts. But the percentage of Negro dropouts nationally is 57 percent, and in New York City, among Negroes 25 years of age or over, it is 68 percent. They are without a future. . . .

I would advise those who think that self-help is the answer to familiarize themselves with the long history of such efforts in the Negro community, and to consider why so many foundered on the shoals of ghetto life. It goes without saying that any effort to combat demoralization and apathy is desirable, but we must understand that demoralization in the Negro community is largely a common-sense response to an objective reality. Negro youths have no need of statistics to perceive, fairly accurately, what their odds are in American society. Indeed, from the point of view of motivation, some of the healthiest Negro youngsters I know are juvenile delinquents: vigorously pursuing the American Dream of material acquisition and status, yet finding the conventional means of attaining it blocked off, they do not yield to defeatism but resort to illegal (and often ingenious) methods. They are not alien to American culture. They are, in Gunnar Myrdal's phrase, "exaggerated Americans." To want a Cadillac is not un-American; to push a cart in the garment center is. If Negroes are to be persuaded that the conventional path (school, work, etc.) is superior, we had better provide evidence which is now sorely lacking. It is a double cruelty to harangue Negro youth about education and training when we do not know what jobs will be available for them. When a Negro youth can reasonably foresee a future free of slums, when the prospect of gainful employment is realistic, we will see motivation and self-help in abundant enough quantities.

Meanwhile, there is an ironic similarity between the self-help advocated by many liberals and the doctrines of the Black Muslims. Professional sociologists, psychiatrists, and social workers have expressed amazement at the Muslims' success in transforming prostitutes and dope addicts into respectable citizens. But every prostitute the Muslims convert to a model of Calvinist virtue is replaced by the ghetto with two more. Dedicated as they are to maintenance of the ghetto, the Muslims are powerless to affect substantial moral reform. So too with every other group or program which is not aimed at the destruction of slums, their causes and effects. Self-help efforts, directly or indirectly, must be geared to mobilizing people into power units capable of effecting social change. That is, their goal must be genuine self-help, not merely self-improvement. Obviously, where self-improvement activities succeed in imparting to their participants a feeling of some control over their environment, those involved may find their appetites for change whetted; they may move into the political arena.

III

Let me sum up what I have thus far been trying to say: the civil rights movement is evolving from a protest movement into a full-fledged *social movement*—an evolution calling its very name into question. It is now concerned not merely with removing the barriers to full *opportunity* but with achieving the fact of *equality*. From sit-ins and freedom rides we have gone into rent strikes, boycotts, community organization, and political action. As a consequence of this natural evolution, the Negro today finds himself stymied by obstacles of far greater magnitude than the legal barriers he was attacking before: automation, urban decay, *de facto* school segregation. These are problems which, while conditioned by Jim Crow, do not vanish upon its demise. They are more deeply rooted in our socio-economic order; they are the result of the total society's failure to meet not only the Negro's needs, but human needs generally.

These propositions have won increasing recognition and acceptance, but with a curious twist. They have formed the common premise of two apparently contradictory lines of thought which simultaneously nourish and antagonize each other. On the one hand, there is the reasoning of the New York *Times* moderate who says that the problems are so enormous and complicated that Negro militancy is a futile irritation, and that the need is for "intelligent moderation." Thus, during the first New York school boycott, the *Times* editorialized that Negro demands, while abstractly just, would necessitate massive reforms, the funds for which could not realistically be anticipated; therefore the just demands were also foolish demands and would only antagonize white people. Moderates of this stripe are often correct in perceiving the difficulty or impossibility of racial progress in the context of present social and economic policies. But they accept the context as fixed. They ignore (or perhaps see all too well) the potentialities inherent in linking Negro demands to broader pressures for radical revision of existing policies. They apparently see nothing strange in the fact that in the last twenty-five years we have spent nearly a trillion dollars fighting or preparing for wars, yet throw up our hands before the need for overhauling our schools, clearing the slums, and really abolishing poverty. My quarrel with these moderates is that they do not even envision radical changes; their admonitions of moderation are, for all practical purposes, admonitions to the Negro to adjust to the status quo, and are therefore immoral.

The more effectively the moderates argue their case, the more they convince Negroes that American society will not or cannot be reorganized for full racial equality. Michael Harrington has said that a successful war on poverty might well require the expenditure of $100 billion. Where, the Negro wonders, are the forces now in motion to compel such a commitment? If the voices of the moderates were raised in an insistence upon a reallocation of national resources at levels that could not be confused with tokenism (that is, if the moderates stopped being moderates), Negroes would have greater grounds for hope. Meanwhile, the Negro movement cannot escape a sense of isolation.

It is precisely this sense of isolation that gives rise to the second line of thought I want to examine—the tendency within the civil rights movement which, despite its militancy, pursues what I call a "no-win" policy. Sharing with many moderates a recognition of the magnitude of the obstacles to freedom, spokesmen for this tendency survey the American scene and find no forces prepared to move toward radical solutions. From this they conclude that the only viable strategy is shock; above all, the hypocrisy of white liberals must be exposed. These spokesmen are often described as the radicals of the movement, but they are really its moralists. They seek to change white hearts—by traumatizing them. Frequently abetted by white self-flagellants, they may gleefully applaud (though not really agreeing with) Malcolm X because, while they admit he has no program, they think he can frighten white people into doing the right thing. To believe this, of course, you must be convinced, even if unconsciously, that at the core of the white man's heart lies a buried affection for Negroes—a proposition one may be permitted to doubt. But in any case, hearts are not relevant to the issue; neither racial affinities nor racial hostilities are rooted there. It is institutions—social, political, and economic institutions—which are the ultimate molders of collective sentiments. Let these institutions be reconstructed *today*, and let the ineluctable gradualism of history govern the formation of a new psychology.

My quarrel with the "no-win" tendency in the civil rights movement (and the reason I have so designated it) parallels my quarrel with the moderates outside the movement. As the latter lack the vision or will for fundamental change, the former lack a realistic strategy for achieving it. For such a strategy they substitute militancy. But militancy is a matter of posture and volume and not of effect.

I believe that the Negro's struggle for equality in America is essentially revolutionary. While most Negroes—in their hearts—unquestionably seek only to enjoy the fruits of American society as it now exists, their quest cannot *objectively* be satisfied within the framework of existing political and economic relations. The young Negro who would demonstrate his way into the labor market may be motivated by a thoroughly bourgeois ambition and thoroughly "capitalist" considerations, but he will end up having to favor a great expansion of the public sector of the economy. At any rate, that is the position the movement will be forced to take as it looks at the number of jobs being generated by the private economy, and if it is to remain true to the masses of Negroes.

The revolutionary character of the Negro's struggle is manifest in the fact that this struggle may have done more to democratize life for whites than for Negroes. Clearly, it was the sit-in movement of young Southern Negroes which, as it galvanized white students, banished the ugliest features of McCarthyism from the American campus and resurrected political debate. It was not until Negroes assaulted *de facto* school segregation in the urban centers that the issue of quality education for *all* children stirred into motion. Finally, it seems reasonably clear that the civil rights movement, directly and through the resurgence of social conscience it kindled, did more to initiate the war on poverty than any other single force.

It will be—it has been—argued that these by-products of the Negro struggle are not revolutionary. But the term revolutionary, as I am using it, does not connote violence; it refers to the qualitative transformation of fundamental institutions, more or less rapidly, to the point where the social and economic structure which they comprised can no longer be said to be the same. The Negro struggle has hardly run its course; and it will not stop moving until it has been utterly defeated or won substantial equality. But I fail to see how the movement can be victorious in the absence of radical programs for full employment, abolition of slums, the reconstruction of our educational system, new definitions of work and leisure. Adding up the cost of such programs, we can only conclude that we are talking about a refashioning of our political economy. It has been estimated, for example, that the price of replacing New York City's slums with public housing would be $17 billion. Again, a multi-billion dollar federal public-works program, dwarfing the currently proposed $2 billion program, is required to reabsorb unskilled and semi-skilled workers into the labor market—and this must be done if

Negro workers in these categories are to be employed. "Preferential treatment" cannot help them.

I am not trying here to delineate a total program, only to suggest the scope of economic reforms which are most immediately related to the plight of the Negro community. One could speculate on their political implications —whether, for example, they do not indicate the obsolescence of state government and the superiority of regional structures as viable units of planning. Such speculations aside, it is clear that Negro needs cannot be satisfied unless we go beyond what has so far been placed on the agenda. How are these radical objectives to be achieved? The answer is simple, deceptively so: *through political power.*

There is a strong moralistic strain in the civil rights movement which would remind us that power corrupts, forgetting that the absence of power also corrupts. But this is not the view I want to debate here, for it is waning. Our problem is posed by those who accept the need for political power but do not understand the nature of the object and therefore lack sound strategies for achieving it; they tend to confuse political institutions with lunch counters.

A handful of Negroes, acting alone, could integrate a lunch counter by strategically locating their bodies so as *directly* to interrupt the operation of the proprietor's will; their numbers were relatively unimportant. In politics, however, such a confrontation is difficult because the interests involved are merely *represented.* In the execution of a political decision a direct confrontation may ensue (as when federal marshals escorted James Meredith into the University of Mississippi—to turn from an example of non-violent coercion to one of force backed up with the threat of violence). But in arriving at a political decision, numbers and organizations are crucial, especially for the economically disenfranchised. (Needless to say, I am assuming that the forms of political democracy exist in America, however imperfectly, that they are valued, and that elitist or putschist conceptions of exercising power are beyond the pale of discussion for the civil rights movement.)

Neither that movement nor the country's twenty million black people can win political power alone. We need allies. The future of the Negro struggle depends on whether the contradictions of this society can be resolved by a coalition of progressive forces which becomes the *effective* political majority in the United States. I speak of the coalition which staged the March on Washington, passed the Civil Rights Act, and laid the basis for the Johnson landslide—Negroes, trade unionists, liberals, and religious groups.

There are those who argue that a coalition strategy would force the Negro to surrender his political independence to white liberals, that he would be neutralized, deprived of his cutting edge, absorbed into the Establishment. Some who take this position urged last year that votes be withheld from the Johnson-Humphrey ticket as a demonstration of the Negro's political power. Curiously enough, these people who sought to demonstrate power through the non-exercise of it, also point to the Negro "swing vote" in crucial urban areas as the source of the Negro's independent political power. But here they are closer to being right: the urban Negro vote will grow in importance in the coming years. If there is anything positive in the spread of the ghetto, it is the potential political power base thus created, and to realize this potential is one of the most challenging and urgent tasks before the civil rights movement. If the movement can wrest leadership of the ghetto vote from the machines, it will have acquired an organized constituency such as other major groups in our society now have.

But we must also remember that the effectiveness of a swing vote depends solely on "other" votes. It derives its power from them. In that sense, it can never be "independent," but must opt for one candidate or the other, even if by default. Thus coalitions are inescapable, however tentative they may be. And this is the case in all but those few situations in which Negroes running on an independent ticket might conceivably win. "Independence," in other words, is not a value in itself. The issue is which coalition to join and how to make it responsive to your program. Necessarily there will be compromise. But the difference between expediency and morality in politics is the difference between selling out a principle and making smaller concessions to win larger ones. The leader who shrinks from this task reveals not his purity but his lack of political sense.

The task of molding a political movement out of the March on Washington coalition is not simple, but no alternatives have been advanced. We need to choose our allies on the basis of common political objectives. It has become fashionable in some no-win Negro circles to decry the white liberal as the main enemy (his hypocrisy is what sustains racism); by virtue of this reverse recitation of the reactionary's litany (liberalism leads to socialism, which leads to Communism) the Negro is left in majestic isolation, except for a tiny band of fervent white initiates. But the objective fact is that *Eastland* and *Goldwater* are the main enemies—they and the opponents of civil rights, of the war on poverty, of medicare, of social security, of federal aid to education, of unions, and so forth. The labor movement, despite its obvious faults, has been the largest single organized force in this country pushing for progressive social legislation. And where the Negro-labor-axis is weak, as in the farm belt, it was the religious groups that were most influential in rallying support for the Civil Rights Bill.

The durability of the coalition was interestingly tested during the election. I do not believe that the Johnson landslide proved the "white backlash" to be a myth. It proved, rather, that economic interests are more fundamental than prejudice: the backlashers decided that loss of social security was, after all, too high a price to pay for a slap at the Negro. This lesson was a valuable first step in re-educating such people, and it must be kept alive, for the civil rights movement will be advanced only to the degree that social and economic welfare gets to be inextricably entangled with civil rights.

The 1964 elections marked a turning point in American politics. The Democratic landslide was not merely the result of a negative reaction to Goldwaterism; it was also the expression of a majority liberal consensus. The near unanimity with which Negro voters joined in that expression was, I am convinced, a vindication of the July 25th statement by Negro leaders calling for a strategic turn toward political action and a temporary curtailment of mass demonstrations. Despite the controversy surrounding the statement, the instinctive response it met with in the community is suggested by the fact that demonstrations were down 75 percent as compared with the same period in 1963. But should so high a percentage of Negro voters have gone to Johnson, or should they have held back to narrow his margin of victory and thus give greater visibility to our swing vote? How has our loyalty changed things? Certainly the Negro vote had higher visibility in 1960, when a switch of only 7 percent from the Republican column of 1956 elected President Kennedy. But the slimness of Kennedy's victory—of his "mandate"—dictated a go-slow approach on civil rights, at least until the Birmingham upheaval.

Although Johnson's popular majority was so large that he could have won without such overwhelming Negro support, that support was important from several angles. Beyond adding to Johnson's total national margin, it was specifically responsible for his victories in Virginia, Florida, Tennessee, and Arkansas. Goldwater took only those states where fewer than 45 percent of eligible Negroes were registered. That Johnson would have won those states had Negro voting rights been enforced is a lesson not likely to be lost on a man who would have been happy with a unanimous electoral college. In any case, the 1.6 million Southern Negroes who voted have had a shattering impact on the Southern political party structure, as illustrated in the changed composition of the Southern congressional delegation. The "backlash" gave the Republicans five House seats in Alabama, one in Georgia, and one in Mississippi. But on the Democratic side, seven segregationists were defeated while all nine Southerners who voted for the Civil Rights Act were re-elected. It may be premature to predict a Southern Democratic party of Negroes and white moderates and a Republican Party of refugee racists and economic conservatives, but there certainly is a strong tendency toward such a realignment; and an additional 3.6 million Negroes of voting age in the eleven Southern states are still to be heard from. Even the *tendency* toward disintegration of the Democratic party's racist wing defines a new context for Presidential and liberal strategy in the congressional battles ahead. Thus the Negro vote (North as well as South), while not *decisive* in the

Presidential race, was enormously effective. It was a dramatic element of a historic mandate which contains vast possibilities and dangers that will fundamentally affect the future course of the civil rights movement.

The liberal congressional sweep raises hope for an assault on the seniority system, Rule Twenty-two, and other citadels of Dixiecrat-Republican power. The overwhelming of this conservative coalition should also mean progress on much bottlenecked legislation of profound interest to the movement (e.g., bills by Senators Clark and Nelson on planning, manpower, and employment). Moreover, the irrelevance of the South to Johnson's victory gives the President more freedom to act than his predecessor had and more leverage to the movement to pressure for executive action in Mississippi and other racist strongholds.

None of this *guarantees* vigorous executive or legislative action, for the other side of the Johnson landslide is that it has a Gaullist quality. Goldwater's capture of the Republican party forced into the Democratic camp many disparate elements which do not belong there, Big Business being the major example. Johnson, who wants to be President "of all people," may try to keep his new coalition together by sticking close to the political center. But if he decides to do this, it is unlikely that even his political genius will be able to hold together a coalition so inherently unstable and rife with contradictions. It must come apart. Should it do so while Johnson is pursuing a centrist course, then the mandate will have been wastefully dissipated. However, if the mandate is seized upon to set fundamental changes in motion, then the basis can be laid for a new mandate, a new coalition including hitherto inert and dispossessed strata of the population.

Here is where the cutting edge of the civil rights movement can be applied. We must see to it that the reorganization of the "consensus party" proceeds along lines which will make it an effective vehicle for social reconstruction, a role it cannot play so long as it furnishes Southern racism with its national political power. (One of Barry Goldwater's few attractive ideas was that the Dixiecrats belong with him in the same party.) And nowhere has the civil rights movement's political cutting edge been more magnificently demonstrated than at Atlantic City, where the Mississippi Freedom Democratic Party not only secured recognition as a bona fide component of the national party, but in the process routed the representatives of the most rabid racists—the white Mississippi and Alabama delegations. While I still believe that the FDP made a tactical error in spurning the compromise, there is no question that they launched a political revolution whose logic is the displacement of Dixiecrat power. They launched that revolution within a major political institution and as part of a coalition effort.

The role of the civil rights movement in the reorganization of American political life is programmatic as well as strategic. We are challenged now to broaden our social vision, to develop functional programs with concrete objectives. We need to propose alternatives to technological unemployment, urban decay, and the rest. We need to be calling for public works and training, for national economic planning, for federal aid to education, for attractive public housing—all this on a sufficiently massive scale to make a difference. We need to protest the notion that our integration into American life, so long delayed, must now proceed in an atmosphere of competitive scarcity instead of in the security of abundance which technology makes possible. We cannot claim to have answers to all the complex problems of modern society. That is too much to ask of a movement still battling barbarism in Mississippi. But we can agitate the right questions by probing at the contradictions which still stand in the way of the "Great Society." The questions having been asked, motion must begin in the larger society, for there is a limit to what Negroes can do alone.

Black Radicalism

Vincent Harding

The living annals of oppressed and troubled peoples abound in wry, unanswerable comments; it is said among black people here that when Lenin was told there were black conservatives in America, he raised his eyebrows and exclaimed: "Oh! And what precisely do they have to conserve?" In an age when instantaneous global communications were only beginning to be exploited, this was a natural question for an outsider to ask, and especially for a stranger who dealt in revolution. At a time when lynchings and emasculations of Negroes were public celebrations, when urban riots meant that white mobs were raging for the lives of defenseless Negroes, who could fault such a question from afar? For anyone who was close to the black communities of the United States, however, there was an answer: They had their *lives* to conserve.

Throughout most of their strange black pilgrimage in this often threatening land, the struggle to stay alive—to conserve their lives and the lives of their children—has been the dominant concern of Afro-Americans. The bravado cry of "Liberty or Death!" has sprung from their lips no more readily than from the lips of other men. Their shaping of revolutionary institutions has not been a significant activity. Neither radical words nor deeds have surged easily from black people in America. They have, instead, survived within the realities of Claude McKay's poignant lines:

> . . . I was born, far from my native clime,
> Under the white man's menace, out of time.

The complete text of "Black Radicalism: The Road from Montgomery" by Vincent Harding was originally published in Dissent: Explorations in the History of American Radicalism, edited by Alfred F. Young, © 1968 by Northern Illinois University Press. Abridged version reprinted by permission of the publisher.

For most of those who live as an indelibly marked minority in the heart of such a menace, conservatism—at least in public—comes as naturally as breathing. (And, like breathing, it often seems a necessary condition for staying alive.) Indeed, even the special black breed that has courageously dared to raise voices of protest in the midst of such a hostile situation has had to come to terms with their distance from "home," and their darkly obvious status as the outnumbered ones. So for those who have been at once black, angry, and wise, protest has never moved easily over into radicalism. Even when protest has made this leap, most of its actions and energies have been defensive. Black radicalism, therefore, has been focused largely on the means for realizing "the American promise" rather than on shaping new, dissenting goals.

One facet of the dilemma was described a decade ago by one of the most famous black radicals, Paul Robeson. In his autobiographical statement, *Here I Stand*, Robeson delineated what he called "a certain protective tactic of Negro life in America." Speaking from bitter experience, this politically sensitive artist said:

Even while demonstrating that he is really an equal . . . the Negro must never appear to be challenging white superiority. Climb up if you can—but don't act "uppity." Always show that you are grateful. (Even if what you have gained has been wrested from unwilling powers, be sure to be grateful lest "they" take it all away.) Above all, do nothing to give them cause to fear you, for then the oppressing hand, which might at times ease up a little, will surely become a fist to knock you down again!

Robeson's conclusions are confirmed by Lerone Bennett, another perceptive recorder of the black experience, in *The Negro Mood*. "The history of the Negro in America . . . has been a quest for a revolt that was not a revolt . . . a revolt . . . that did not seem to the white power structure to be an open revolt."

If in one sense these analyses are being outstripped by the pace of current events in the nation's black communities, they nonetheless describe much that has happened up to now (and the death of Martin Luther King appeared to many persons as additional proof of their validity). Such insights, moreover, suggest a set of guidelines for understanding the nature of black radicalism in America.

At what point does black radicalism begin? Perhaps it begins when black men lose or repress their fear of the descending white fist and carry Negro protest to one of its logical conclusions, regardless of the consequences. Perhaps it begins when sensitive, restive souls lose faith in "the myth of Negro progress" within the American system. Perhaps we may speak of black radicalism when men are pressed by our society to seek alternatives (even though chimerical and "unrealistic") to the American way of life for

Afro-Americans. Even now, black radicalism is more a reaction than a calcu-lated strategy, more an agonized thrust than a body of thought; and this is one of its weaknesses.

Inchoate though they may be, as one sorts out the elements of the Afro-American experience with radicalism, several themes can be identified. First of all, it becomes clear that the classic, primarily European terms of "left" and "right" or "communist" and "capitalist" usually provide insuffi-cient contexts for a discussion of American black radicalism. Even the some-times helpful separation into social, political, economic, and racial radicalism at last becomes a tiresome burden in probing the subject. This radicalism, which grows out of a situation as emotionally weighted and psychologically distorted as the black-white encounter in America, cannot adequately be described in terms that are largely intellectual and theoretical. For such "irrational" reasons (among others), those classic "radicals," the Communists, found American black revolutionaries a very difficult brood to cultivate.

Another thematic reality is that in every generation there has been a group of black radicals (marked with the blood that always accompanies new births and violent deaths) that has moved far beyond the acceptable or customary lines of protest and revolt. Sometimes this has been simply a personal groping with the menace; sometimes it has been organized. At various times the emphasis of the radical approach has been on armed self-defense; and occasionally it has urged armed uprisings against the status quo. In each generation the "radical edge" has reached a different point in the overall experience, but it has always been present—marked by despair, alien-ation, fierce anger, and sometimes even by hope.

A third continuity is found in the constantly recurring, religiously ori-ented themes of apocalyptic messianism and atonement. Basically this has implied the conviction that there could be no ultimate deliverance for blacks (or whites) without a black-led rebellious movement, which would involve levels of anguish and blood-letting surpassing those of the Civil War. From the first attempts to capture their slave ships to the current talk of "taking over the ghettos," the black radical impulse has been informed by a vision of blood, a vision often understood as being of divine origin.

Usually, however, the goal of black radicalism has appeared to be the simplistic, "moderate" goal of assimilation into American society; but many radicals have realized there is nothing simple or moderate about such an aim. They knew that the American nation would have to be drastically trans-formed before it would fully open itself to the native-yet-alien presence in its midst. This was what a black leader of the Communist Party meant when she said, in the 1930's, "It is impossible to take one step in the direction of winning for the Negro people their elementary rights that is not revolution-ary." Nevertheless, other radicals eventually became convinced that such a transformation is impossible. Thus black nationalism and black zionism also have sought to chart a course in the endless search. Their path, of course, has not been towards assimilation.

Against such a background it becomes clear that the transformation of black radicals from the singing, integration-directed marchers of Montgomery, Alabama, in 1955 into the avowed guerrilla fighters and alienated rebels of the late 1960's was in keeping with historical precedents.

I

In 1955 Martin Luther King and the black community in Montgomery faced a situation that contained much that was new as well as much that was brutally old. Social, political, and economic injustices to Negro citizens were evident on every hand; the South was considered the major bastion of enforced second-class citizenship; and segregation in public facilities seemed the most blatant example of racial humiliation. But there was something new as well. The previous spring the Bandung Conference in Southeast Asia had reminded the world how much World War II had done to intensify the struggles of formerly colonized people in wrenching themselves free of Western domination. In New York City the United Nations was an expanding forum for the views of the formerly silent peoples of the earth. The United States was deeply engaged in ideological—and occasionally military—struggles with powers that were quick to exploit this nation's poor record as a protector of its own oppressed. Younger, better-educated black people and their families were moving from rural to urban areas and were determined to play a new role in American society.

In this context, and under the prodding of the National Association for the Advancement of Colored People, the Supreme Court in 1954 had declared that racial segregation in public schools was unconstitutional. Concern about school segregation focused on the South, for it was recognized that the decision, if firmly enforced, also could signal the end of many other institutionalized forms of segregation. Some blacks who saw this possibility now moved forward with a conviction that, for the first time, the nation's highest tribunal was on their side. At the same moment, the Court's decision was a call to fierce resistance for many white persons.

It was at this point that Martin Luther King entered the scene. The decision of a gentle black lady to retain her disputed seat on a segregated bus, then the decision of Montgomery's Negro community that her subsequent arrest be protested—these and other events helped press the twenty-six-year-old Baptist minister into the radical path. Neither his somewhat sheltered middle-class Atlanta background nor his rather conventional education had prepared him for such a mission, but he accepted it. Martin Luther King's brand of radicalism can be traced to a number of sources: the lives and the teachings of Christ and Gandhi, the thinking of Thoreau, the aborted hopes of James Farmer and A. Philip Randolph, the tough strategy talks of Bayard Rustin, and the exigencies of the situation. From these and other sources King shaped his old-new hope, catalyzed by his own creative impulses.

Love was the answer. Not sentimentality, but the tough and resolute love that refused bitterness and hatred but stood firmly against every shred of injustice. Few brands of black radicalism had ever required so much. Men were not only urged to stand and face the menace, they were called upon to be true to themselves and to reject the very weapons that had destroyed them for so long. They were called upon to transform American life by substituting moral and spiritual courage for its traditional dependence upon violence and coercion. This new (and untried) weapon could easily be distributed to—eventually—the overwhelming majority of ordinary black people. To the confused and often fearful white faces behind the menacing fists Dr. King addressed these words:

We will match your capacity to inflict suffering with our capacity to endure suffering. We will meet your physical force with soul force. We will not hate you, but we cannot . . . obey your unjust laws. Do to us what you will and we will still love you. Bomb our homes and threaten our children; send your hooded perpetrators of violence into our communities and drag us out on some wayside road, beating us and leaving us half dead, and we will still love you. But we will soon wear you down by our capacity to suffer. And in winning our freedom we will so appeal to your heart and conscience that we will win you in the process.

After the victory against segregation in public buses in Montgomery (which many persons explained away in legal terms), King sought to institutionalize his vision in the Southern Christian Leadership Conference. King and the SCLC still harbored David Walker's messianic hope that black people would lead the way to a redeemed America, but they would not use Walker's method. The new radical hope (is it not always radical to think of redemption for America?) was expressed in an SCLC document:

Creatively used, the philosophy of nonviolence can restore the broken community in America. SCLC is convinced that nonviolence is the most potent force available to an oppressed people in their struggle for freedom and dignity.

In uniting the broken community King and the SCLC sought to build what they called "the beloved community," in which black and white Americans of every social and economic level would recognize their bonds of human unity. . . .

II

As the sit-ins, freedom rides, and other demonstrations moved across the South, white resistance stiffened, and some black radicals were not convinced that nonviolence was their most effective weapon. They saw little evidence of the pliable "hearts and consciences" to which King had addressed his appeal; rather, they saw mobs, heard bombs, felt the impact of heavy clubs. Thereupon they chose Denmark Vesey, David Walker, and Nat Turner as the fathers of their black radicalism. Indeed, it was in North Carolina, the state in which the mass sit-in movement was born, that the newest call to armed Negro self-defense was sounded.

In 1959 Robert F. Williams, a Marine Corps veteran, drew attention to himself and to his branch of the NAACP in Monroe, North Carolina. Williams had changed the usual middle-class makeup of the association's branches by forming a group from laborers and other persons whose thoughts and inclinations were closer to his own. He had already begun to talk of Negroes' arming themselves when, in 1959, a white man was acquitted of charges of physical assault and attempted rape of a black woman, despite the testimony of a number of Negro witnesses.

This . . . shows [Williams said] that the Negro in the South cannot expect justice in the courts. He must convict his attackers on the spot. He must meet violence with violence, lynching with lynching.

The NAACP's national office immediately disassociated itself from Williams' statement and attempted to remove him from his position. Eventually, however, the local and state officials took care of this matter; they hounded the burly, outspoken black radical from the city and the state. But Williams was not silenced. In 1962, when nonviolence was still in its ascendancy, he maintained that

any struggle for liberation should be a flexible struggle. We must use non-violence as a means as long as this is feasible, but the day will come when conditions become so pronounced that non-violence will be suicidal. . . . The day is surely coming when we will see more violence on the same American scene. The day is surely coming when some of the same Negroes who have denounced our using weapons for self-defense will be arming themselves.

Events made Williams a prophet; but the question that continues to rise from such thinking is whether the call to armed self-defense is a conservative or a radical move? It can be argued that Williams—and others like him—simply become part of the violent pattern of American life and promise no more than its continuation. Can a nation that is built on violence be constructively transformed by violence? On the other hand one faces the perennial, inherent ambiguity in black radicalism: in the minds of some persons nothing could have been more radical, even in the 1960's, than the decision of Negroes to arm themselves. Williams' group, in arming itself, determined to defy both the southern mob and the southern police, who seemed ready to expose them to the mob's fury. On one such occasion a "very old . . . white man . . . started screaming and crying like a baby, [while saying:]

"God damn, God damn, what is this God damn country coming to that niggers have got guns, the niggers are armed and the police can't even arrest them."

Whatever the accuracy of definitions of black radicalism from the lips of very old southern white men, Williams soon would follow a familiar black radical path as he moved from Cuba to Moscow to Peking. Later, his call for armed self-defense would be accepted by a black revolutionary liberation struggle in America, and by 1968 he would be elected Provisional President of a separatist black nation in American exile.

Behind the most militant words and deepest commitments to black radicalism of all who have spoken of black revolution in America, whatever the variety, has been a battery of unresolved but realistic questions. How does an easily identifiable minority carry out such a revolution? Where does it find allies in a hostile and threatened nation? Against whom will the revolution be directed, and what are its goals? These were the questions of the early sixties, when nonviolence was counterposed against armed and militant self-defense.

After 1954 it was generally assumed that the enemy was the system of segregation in the South and that the major allies were the federal government, the liberals of the North, and the conscience of the nation. But step by step this assumption was transformed. More and more black persons began to ask whether segregation properly could be isolated in the South merely because it was supported by law only in that region. Others wondered how a "federal government" could be separate from the pervasive prejudice and discrimination black men had always found in the nation as a whole. Was the United States Congress really more liberal than the homeowners, real estate dealers, and corporations it represented? Was it not obvious that, when serious attempts were made to direct action into the North, there was a noticeable cooling of ardor among erstwhile allies, especially when issues of compensatory hiring, suburban housing, and integrated education were raised?

Moreover, as the nation became more deeply enmeshed in Vietnam, who was willing to approve the scores-of-billions-of-dollars price tag for the rehabilitation of the black communities? And what kind of radicalism was needed to force a complacent nation to confront the need to rehabilitate the black community? What kind of a "revolution" depended on federal troops to protect and advance it? These were some of the vexing questions of the post-Montgomery decade. In Birmingham, Alabama, in the spring of 1963, SCLC activists attempted tentative answers to some of those questions. More black people than ever before were called into the streets to face the prospect of jail. Larger numbers of children and young people were involved in SCLC-directed civil disobedience. At the same time, King's group raised its sights beyond the integration of public facilities: jobs for black people became part of the broader demands. But broader demands meant the willingness to launch in Birmingham a long siege of direct action, and SCLC did not seem prepared for such a trial. Besides, more and more young people of the city became involved in the protest, and their susceptibility to violent radicalism was not easy to control. Therefore the city's business leaders (forever concerned with images), the federal administration, and parts of the SCLC leadership seemed ready to bring the Birmingham campaign to a halt sooner than the results might have indicated. Thus the expanded agenda did not bring the predicted results, but some observers thought they saw the direction nonviolent action must take if it was to remain on the constantly moving forward edge of black radicalism.

One of the insights that emerged from the Birmingham demonstrations was the need for even larger attempts at civil disobedience, aimed at Washington, D.C., and utilizing the pent-up energies of thousands of black young people. A civil rights bill had finally been introduced in Congress, in response to Birmingham, but some SCLC staff members and others were determined to push the nation even beyond such legalities. It was proposed that A. Philip Randolph's old idea for a march on Washington be revived and that thousands of black people be brought to the capital for a massive act of nonviolent civil disobedience. The objective was to paralyze the life of the nation's capital until Congress and the country were willing to move much more meaningfully toward equality. But because of opposition within the civil rights establishment—from financial benefactors and from the highest level of the federal government—this massive nonviolent "attack" on the nation's capital became the "polite" March on Washington.

America had domesticated another radical movement. The militant speeches were censored, the taverns were closed for the day. Radicalism that sought to reach the heart of the black condition in America also sought to remain on good terms with the President and the Attorney General. It had been easily seduced, but the lesson was not lost on some of the younger militants. The words that had been censored from one of the speeches had questioned whether the federal government was truly an ally of the black movement, and some of these perceptive young people soon answered this question in the negative. Other radicals continued to urge that the nonviolent movement engage in massive civil disobedience or lose its relevance to the condition of black America.

At a SCLC convention soon after the Washington march, Wyatt Tee Walker, the conference's executive director, said:

The question is, whether we want to continue local guerrilla battles against discrimination and segregation or go to all-out war. . . . has the moment come in the development of the non-violent revolution that we are forced . . . on some appointed day . . . literally [to] immobilize the nation until she acts on our pleas for justice and morality? . . . Is the day far-off that major transportation centers would be deluged with mass acts of civil disobedience; airports, train stations, bus terminals, the traffic of large cities, interstate commerce, would be halted by the bodies of witnesses non-violently insisting on "Freedom Now"? I suppose a nationwide work stoppage might attract enough attention to persuade someone to do something to get this monkey of segregation and discrimination off our backs, once, now and forever. Will it take one or all of these?

Because Walker was known to be given to flights of rhetoric, it was difficult to ascertain how serious he was, but he seemed to sense the new mood. The nonviolent movement would die if it did not become more radical—to a degree that would shock most civil rights leaders and more radical than its chief financial backers would approve. Part of the familiar frustration was symbolized by Walker's vague reference to the need "to persuade someone to do something": *Who* should they try to persuade, with even the most radical action, and *what* should they be persuaded to do? Walker's organization did not support him, nor was there support for a proposed large cadre of nonviolent demonstrators who would commit themselves for at least a year of continuous action before they returned to their homes, jobs, or school. In the North, attempts at school boycotts, traffic disruption, and other forms of civil disobedience met with indifferent success. None of the major organizations was ready to move in the direction of large-scale civil disobedience. With court-enforced desegregation depriving the black movement of easily articulated goals for the struggle, momentum could not be built. Meanwhile, however, another kind of black momentum built fiercely.

III

In the summer of 1967 the transportation, commerce, commuting, and other schedules of more than one American city were totally disrupted by "witnessing" blacks, but not in the way that Walker had considered four years earlier. The young people who were to have been the core of the rejected nonviolent campaigns stormed angrily through the cities, witnessing with bricks, Molotov cocktails, and rifles. Much of their violence was a reaction to the callousness of American society at large, but it was certainly aggravated by the lack of meaningful alternatives, the result of the nonviolent movement's failure to move with the urgency the situation demanded.

What had happened between Walker's speech in 1963 and the immobilization of the cities by fear and fire in 1967? What turns black minds upon the path of alienation and armed violence? One of the crucial events was the bombing in Birmingham, less than a month after the March on Washington. The exhausted civil rights movement was mesmerized before the spectacle of the death of four black children in Birmingham, the result of a bomb that had been planted in the Sixteenth Street Baptist Church. Negro radicals saw this atrocity as a typical white American response to increasingly cautious, impotent, religiously oriented nonviolence. One of the younger black radicals wrote:

What was needed that Sunday [of the bombing] was ol' John Brown to come riding into Birmingham as he had ridden into Lawrence, Kansas, burning every building that stood and killing every man, woman and child that ran from his onslaught. Killing, killing, killing, turning men into fountains of blood, . . . until Heaven itself drew back before the frothing red ocean.

But the Liberal and his Negro sycophants would've cried, Vengeance accomplishes nothing. You are only acting like your oppressor and such an act makes you no better than him. John Brown, his hands and wrists slick with blood, would've said, oh so softly and so quietly, Mere Vengeance is folly. Purgation is necessary.

Atonement by blood is a persistent motif in the minds of black radicals.

Other youths were utterly embittered by the refusal of "liberal" northern political leaders even to admit that psychological violence and destruction was wreaked daily upon the lives of black ghetto-dwellers. Nothing was getting better for the submerged black people despite all the talk of "Negro progress" and "going too fast." Their schools were progressively miseducating more black children. Their houses were still decaying. Their incomes relative to whites' were decreasing. No one—radical or otherwise—seemed to be creating meaningful programs to deal with the immense problems, to challenge the widening alienation.

Equally significant, perhaps, was the growing perception that political leaders did not intend to take chances with their white constituencies by enforcing the civil rights legislation that had been enacted in 1964. When tough choices had to be made, they still seemed to favor the whites. In this "reconstruction," as in the first, the key to basic change for Negroes seemed to be in the hands of the white North, which in the mid-1960's appeared no more committed to full equality and restitution for black men than it had been a century before. Perhaps now, as then, politicians and people intuitively recognized that the social, economic, and political changes that were necessary for the rehabilitation of black America would constitute a revolution. What majority has ever presented a minority with a legislated revolution?

Therefore, as he had predicted, Robert Williams—in Cuba—spoke for more and more black persons when he said: "What is integration when the law says yes, but the police and howling mobs say no? Our only logical and successful answer is to meet organized and massive violence with massive and organized violence. Our people must prepare to wage an urban guerrilla war of self-defense." In Williams' opinion, racism had become so intrinsic a part of the nation's life that it could be exorcised only with "shock treatment." Only in this way, he said, could America be saved.

Other conclusions also were drawn from Williams' premise. By 1963 America's attention had been called to Elijah Muhammad's Nation of Islam, largely through the work of the group's outstanding spokesman, Malcolm X. The Nation, which claimed a tie to the Islamic peoples of the world, had its organizational roots in the broken black hopes of the 1930's. Focusing on the black lower classes and teaching a version of religious black nationalism, the group successfully attempted to rehabilitate some of society's most alienated black rejects, and Malcolm X was one of these. He had heard the teachings of the "messenger," Elijah Muhammad, while serving a term in prison for his activities as "Detroit Red," a pimp and a narcotics pusher.

Speaking for his group, Minister Malcolm said: "We don't think that it is possible for the American white man in sincerity to take the action necessary to correct the unjust conditions that 20 million black people here are made to suffer morning, noon, and night." From such a premise there followed a logical conclusion, one also derived from a long history of black radicalism. Malcolm continued,

Because we don't have any hope or confidence or faith in the American white man's ability to bring about a change in the injustices that exist, instead of asking or seeking to integrate into the American society we want to face the facts of the problem the way they are, and separate ourselves.

. . . This doesn't mean that we are anti-white or anti-American, or anti-anything. We feel, that if integration all these years hasn't solved the problem yet, then we want to try something new, something different and something that is in accord with the conditions as they actually exist.

Elijah Muhammad's people were moved by what was surely to come, by Malcolm's conviction that "we are living at the end of time," when "the earth will become all . . . Islam," and when those who reject the Prophet's teachings will be destroyed by Allah. They were separatists, therefore, because "we don't want to be wiped out with the American white man." What other conclusions were logical for those who had lost all faith in American whites but had gained a faith in a just and all-conquering God? Except for "Allah," of course, the script had been written in America many times over since 1800.

By 1964 this remarkable young radical had rejected Elijah Muhammad's version of the old script, apparently having decided against separatism, and therefore he was faced with the dilemma Frederick Douglass and others had faced before him. In a speech before an integrated group in New York that same year, Malcolm X demonstrated his ambivalence. First he predicted that

1964 will see the Negro revolt evolve and merge into the worldwide black revolution that has been taking place on this earth since 1945. The so-called revolt will become a real black revolution. . . . Revolutions are never . . . based upon . . . begging a corrupt society or a corrupt system to accept us into it. Revolutions overturn systems. And there is no system on this earth which has proved itself more corrupt, more criminal, than this system that in 1964 still colonizes 22 million . . . Afro-Americans.

But instead of describing the terrors of the coming revolution, he seemed to backtrack: "America is the only country in history in a position to bring about a revolution without violence and bloodshed by granting the suffrage to all black people." Like Douglass, however, he had to admit: "But America is not morally equipped to do so." Malcolm seemed to be caught in a painful ambivalence similar to that which had dogged the earlier radicals.

In an anguished display of mixed emotions and convictions, Malcolm nevertheless predicted that blacks' use of the franchise would "sweep all of the racists and the segregationists out of office." This, in his opinion, would "wipe out the Southern segregationism that now controls America's foreign policy, as well as America's domestic policy." More and more frequently Malcolm X proclaimed that, for the Negroes, it had to be "either ballots or bullets," either a revolution of votes or guerrilla warfare. How he expected to gain the franchise in a totally corrupt system was never made clear. (This, of course, is one of the basic dilemmas for all black leaders who have tried to help their people through a reformist ballot method. Who will vote with this minority, with those who are at once powerless and most in need of the help that can come only from a transformed society? Who will vote with them when giving that help may mean the loss of a significant share of power? In light of this conundrum, what shall black radicals do if they are determined to remain loyal to the way of life that has been blessed as most truly democratic by the rest of the society?)

Struggling with the problems of tactics and strategy, Malcolm X formed his own group, the Organization of Afro-American Unity. Avowedly black nationalist, he saw no other position for those who would work for, with, and in the black ghettos. As he traveled in various parts of the world his religious commitment deepened and was transformed. He also became more convinced of the classic black nationalist vision of the need for internationalizing the struggle of American Negroes, and with this in mind he began to seek aid from African leaders in bringing the plight of Afro-Americans before the United Nations. "Our African . . . Asian . . . [and] Latin-American brothers can throw their weight on our side, and . . . 800 million Chinamen are . . . waiting to throw their weight on our side." A troubled spirit, Malcolm moved through the ghettos and college campuses trying to construct a way where so many other brilliant black radicals before him had failed.

On self-defense he was positive and clear. Black men must exercise their right, he said, especially "in areas where the government has proven itself either unwilling or unable to defend the lives and the property of Negroes." On other issues he moved from guerrilla warfare to the ballot, but he never seemed to believe that the vote could be gained without the shedding of much blood, and perhaps not even then. On economic issues he took the predictable path of espousing socialism, partly because "almost every one of the countries that has gotten independence has devised some kind of socialistic system." Besides, he said, "you can't operate a capitalistic system unless you are vulturistic; you have to have someone else's blood to suck to be a capitalist. You show me a capitalist, I'll show you a bloodsucker."

Up to the time of his death, however, Malcolm had had no vision of the path to final liberation. Near the end of his life, and before a predominantly black audience, he succumbed to the natural temptation to oversimplify the problem and its solution. In late 1964 he said: "What we need in this country is the same type of Mau Mau here that they had over there in Kenya. . . . If they were over here, they'd get this problem straightened up just like that." But such loose words were testimony more to the desperation he felt before a host of enemies and an unfeeling nation than to the real level of his searching. His seeking was profound, burdened by all the agony that radical black integrity must carry, and it was complicated by his new vision of Islam and its commitment to an all-inclusive brotherhood of many-colored men. How could this be achieved in a country whose seeds of racism were embedded so deep? Perhaps all that one can, tentatively, say of him was compressed into the lines of Robert Hayden:

> He fell upon his face before
> Allah the raceless in whose blazing Oneness all . . .
>
> Were one. He rose renewed, renamed, became
> much more than there was time for him to be.

First among the black rebels to be cut down in the classic American style—by gunfire at a public meeting—Malcolm X had become a martyr and a saint even before his last breath escaped his body. He had helped bring modernity and a new respectability to black nationalism among the younger militants of his day. Even before he died the integrity of his life and his obvious identification with the masses among whom he had hustled and been reborn had deeply impressed the angry young men. Just before and just after his death a new flowering of militant black nationalist organizations testified to his impact on the ghettos. . . .

IV

With the new ideology fermenting, it was not long before the nation's news media sensationalized the situation through their vast image-creating (and image-destroying) techniques. At the same time, ironically, when the occasion came, one of the most articulate new voices had two of the most honored black prophets of the earlier radicalism as his foils. James Meredith, the black Mississippian who had caused a riot when he attempted to enter his state university in 1962, returned to Mississippi in June of 1966 to walk the length of the state on foot as a witness against black fear. After he was shot from ambush and hospitalized, the march was continued by leaders of what still was called the civil rights movement, among whom were Dr. King and

Stokely Carmichael, the self-possessed new chairman of SNCC. In the course of the rejuvenated march there were many open as well as private debates among the leaders about the need for a renewed emphasis on "blackness" in the movement. The debates were not really settled at that time but SNCC and Carmichael were the obvious victors in the jousting for publicity from the mass media, and King's international prestige served to bring public attention to the phrase that had been germinating for a long time.

"We shall overcome" already was tame enough for a Texas-born president to quote in a national address, but the young radicals had moved on. Thus the press corps and a people, both of them constantly in search of fearful sensations, found them in "Black Power" and Stokely Carmichael. Only the term, however, and the violent response of the public media and the nation, were new; its concepts were old. "Black Power" merely expressed the radicalism of Afro-Americans who had decided there was no physical escape from this land and who saw no future in an integration that demanded the giving up of blackness. "Black Power" therefore meant turning away from assimilation and emphasizing the existence and beauty of an authentic Afro-American culture. "Black Power" meant a movement of and for the masses that honored the memory of Marcus Garvey and Malcolm X and the early Adam Clayton Powell. It also meant a proud association with Africa and pan-Africanism and a connection with oppressed and colonized people all over the world. Who could not hear W. E. B. Du Bois' impeccable language paraphrased in Harlem slang?

Again it was the radicalism of those who had tried white allies and had found them wanting in the tasks of building the black community. Black power sent such allies away, some with less ceremony than others. It told them to work with the white menace and to transform it into something healthy and new. It sometimes indicated that one day there might be a meeting, after the work had been done on both sides of the wall, but only blacks could now move effectively among their teeming, disaffected masses. As in an earlier day, Black Power meant armed self-defense for many adherents, who later would advance the rhetoric and the reality of the positive benefits of violence. Its emphasis was on self-determination for black people in their communities, which included political, educational, and cultural self-determination. . . .

V

SNCC was only the clearest manifestation of a black radicalism that had many indigenous ghetto roots, as was shown when a National Conference on Black Power met in July, 1967, in Newark, New Jersey. Although various radicals seriously questioned the motivation of the conveners and would not attend, a thousand Afro-Americans came from scores of different communities (the Newark uprising earlier in the month was a spectacular spur to attendance).

The speeches, clothing, and variety of visions and commitments showed that every strain of black radicalism was represented at this meeting. Indeed, there was an awesome terror in the fact that—more than a century after the Civil War—these strains should still be so obvious in the North and often so strong: separatism, radical black nonviolence, armed struggle, the Harlem Mau Mau. And a telegram was received from Robert Williams, in Peking, urging a long guerrilla struggle. The entire scene was filled with a sense of angry, outraged determination, and sometimes one could sense an air of millennarian expectation.

White members of the press corps tasted black anger at some of the four-day sessions; indeed, their bodily eviction from one of the meeting places was symptomatic of the intensity and hostility of some of the younger radicals. Members of this group urged a march through the streets, in direct confrontation with the police riot forces that patrolled the area, to protest the fact that hundreds of blacks still were in jail as a result of the recent uprising. At the highly charged plenary session where this call was issued, more than at any other time, this group resembled conventional revolutionary elements. Rap Brown and others, however, reminded the activists that violent action alone did not make radicals or revolutionaries; Brown suggested that persons who would lead unarmed men to face the guns of the frightened Newark policemen were either irresponsible fools or agents provocateurs. "First go and get your guns," he counseled; "then lead the march."

There was no march, partly because there were few guns, but also because black radicalism had not yet found a leader who could challenge the romanticized memory of Malcolm X and rally the forces for such a desperate move. It is much more likely, however, that there was no march because black radicalism had not yet created a program sufficiently clear and compelling to demand the rational allegiance of those who must march and perhaps die. It was obvious to many participants at Newark that such an ideology and its accompanying program would not spring from so large and disparate a group of persons and organizations.

But it was equally evident that such a gathering, if only for purposes of initial contact, could be most important. The lack of a leader and a clearly articulated framework of thought did not negate the significance of the meeting. The African costumes of explosive color, the proudly "natural" hair styles, the many persons who had adopted African and Islamic names in exchange for their "slave names," the impassioned and sometimes dangerously fiery debate—all this testified to vitality in the radical edges of the black movement.

Although the dominant idiom of the conference was the language of the ghetto, how serious was the talk of beginning a national debate on possible partition? This is yet to be seen, especially when one reflects on the fact that the delegates were housed in two of Newark's most expensive, white-owned hotels and when one recalls the black action at the New Politics convention in Chicago one month later. (The luxurious housing reminded many persons of the continued dependence upon white benevolence, and the appearance in Chicago seems a strange prelude to black partition.) How significant was the constant discussion of black revolution? One of its foremost exponents, Ron Karenga, said: "We are the last revolutionaries in America. If we fail to leave a legacy of revolution for our children we have failed our mission and should be dismissed as unimportant." Although Karenga, like others, believes the cultural revolution of black consciousness is most important at the present time, he has vividly pictured the next stage:

When the word is given we'll see how tough your are. When it's "burn," let's see how much you burn. When it's "kill," let's see how much you kill. When it's "blow up," let's see how much you blow up. And when it's "take that white girl's head too," we'll really see how tough you are.

After the Newark Conference Rap Brown, SNCC's chairman, added his cry: "Straighten up America, or we'll burn you down.". . .

VI

In light of even so cursory an historical survey it is essential to question some of the interpretations of black radicalism in America. John P. Roche, in his introduction to Wilson Record's *Race and Radicalism*, agrees with that book's thesis that

the "radicalism" of the American Negro today is nothing more than a radical Americanism. Despite subjection to slavery and discrimination, the Negro has never massively responded to gospels of alienation but has persistently and with incredible patience fought for his rightful membership in the American community.

Because these lines were published in 1964, and probably were written at the apex of the nonviolent movement, Mr. Roche might be forgiven for some of his myopia. However, if we have established the fact that radicalism is never measured by "massive" responses, we must add an insistent question mark to such an evaluation of the black radical past. Alienation has often been at its heart, and alienation was its dominant hallmark in the past decade.

In many ways a much more sensitive appreciation of black radicalism is suggested by a European radical. Victor Serge's *Memoirs of a Revolutionary, 1901–1941* opens with lines that are strongly reminiscent of some of the men we have met in these pages.

Even before I emerged from childhood, I seem to have experienced, deeply at heart, that paradoxical feeling which was to dominate me all through the first part of my life: that of living in a world without any possible escape, in which there was nothing . . . but to fight for an impossible escape. I felt repugnance mingled with wrath and indignation, toward people whom I saw settled comfortably in this world. How could they not be conscious of their captivity, of their unrighteousness?

Irving Howe wrote, in response to this remarkably sensitive opening of the heart: "Few Americans could, in good faith, say as much: perhaps none but a handful of jail-hardened militants at the outer edge of the Negro movement who have chosen alienation from American society as a badge of honor."

Howe is only partly right. The number of alienated black militants greatly exceeds "a handful," and they are not on the "outer edge" of the Negro movement in America; indeed, the center of the movement draws closer to them each day. And they discovered their "badge of honor" buried deep within their breasts almost as soon as they came to know themselves.

What is the future of this black radicalism that claims no desire for membership in the American community? Will sensitive, justice-starved black aliens be condemned to an endless search for "an impossible escape"? Are they damned to move, like burning, cursing wraiths, in the midst of unending darkness? Or if they find, from some now unknown source, the strength to do the task, will their most noble vocation be to "tear this building down"? It may be that the growing number of radically engaged black intellectuals will avoid the pitfalls of despair, accommodation, and empty rhetoric and will, instead, propose acceptable alternatives to the society they increasingly scorn. Therefore,—if theory does indeed follow practice, if ideologies are most often worked out in the midst of fiery social transformation—the whole or partial tearing down may yet come, as a beginning rather than as an end.

Are there still grounds for radical hope? Perhaps some statements of the "shining black prince" of this generation's black radicals will help illuminate the enigmatic answers to this question. In one of his most thoughtful moments Malcolm X entered into the black radical religious tradition to speak of judgment and atonement:

I believe that God now is giving the world's so-called "Christian" white society its last opportunity to repent and atone for the crimes of exploiting and enslaving the world's non-white peoples, but is white America really sorry for her crimes against the black people? Does white America have the capacity to repent—and to atone? Does the capacity to repent, to atone, exist in a majority, in one-half, in even one-third of American white society? Indeed, how can white society atone for enslaving, for raping, for unmanning, for otherwise brutalizing millions of human beings, for centuries? What atonement would the God of Justice demand for the robbery of the black people's labor, their lives, their true identities, their culture, their history—and even their human dignity?

The former "Detroit Red" knew the ghettos well enough to be clear on what was *not* the answer: "A desegregated cup of coffee, a theater, public toilets—the whole range of hypocritical 'integration'—these are not atonement." Malcolm X was never given a clear answer nor did he provide one, but the man who saw life in America "like it is" also knew that it must get much better or much worse. "Only such real, meaningful actions as those which are sincerely motivated from a deep sense of humanism and moral responsibility can get at the basic causes that produce the racial explosions in America today." Without such actions, "the racial explosions are only going to grow worse."

This was written in 1964, a few months before the man who struggled to grow under the menace from Detroit Red to El-Hajj Malik El-Shabazz was given a personal reply to the questions he had so insistently raised. Nor was Martin King allowed to come any closer to the "Promised Land" of true freedom which he constantly spoke of. Would it really materialize in America as he desperately hoped to the end, or would there come instead some brutal fulfillment of the tragic nightmares both he and Malcolm had foreseen? Whether their deaths were an answer or only another question is not certain, but this much seems sure: Unless America becomes as different from the rest of the world as its most blind lovers already believe it is, the necessary radical social movement toward black liberation (and therefore toward the liberation of all) will not take place without the acute suffering and the shedding of blood that has long been predicted by black radicals. The hundreds of billions of dollars, the unfeigned national commitment, the transformation of priorities and energies will not be produced without stark agony, if they come at all.

There is still a minority among black radicals who view themselves not only as major architects of the new ways and seers of the new visions but also as suffering servants who must pay the price for the change. But there is a larger group, the young and rising black tide, which, despite its alienation, has been "too American" to accept (or understand) such a role. They see blood and they know it probably will be theirs. They hear the voices of police chiefs and other officials who promise to respond to their black rebellions and to riot commission reports with increased firepower. They realize that one police commissioner most likely speaks for many others when he says "We're in a war, and law enforcement is going to win." When they heard the President of the United States define "crime in the streets" as the major domestic problem, they knew he was speaking of them. These black young men see blood, but they are determined it shall not be theirs alone. Whatever they seek in life, they seek no separate death, and the words of Malcolm X are often on their lips: "It takes two to tango. If I go, you go"—a despairing invitation to the dance of death. Surely it is not an intellectual's radical program, but for black men (especially the young and cast-off) who consider themselves "under the white man's men-ace, out of time," it is understandable—in the absence of other programs.

Can the menace be lifted and the times set right? Or will the forces of law and order—and death—again prevail over radical black visions of justice and hope? Will every Martin Luther King have to be buried in his native land before he can really be "free at last"? Historians can deftly refer such questions to various prophets, and walk away, but it may be that the prophets of long ago who spoke of sowing and reaping will have the last, the final, word.

SUGGESTIONS FOR FURTHER READING

Any list of books on the recent past where history and current events merge is in danger of quickly becoming obsolete. Eric Goldman, *The Crucial Decade And After* (New York, 1960) is a lively account of consensus and complacency during the years 1945–1960. Daniel Bell, *The End of Ideology: On the Exhaustion of Political Ideas in the Fifties* (New York, 1959); David Riesman et al., *The Lonely Crowd* (New York, 1959); William H. Whyte, Jr., *The Organization Man* (New York, 1956), from which a chapter is reprinted here; Samuel Lubell, *Revolt of the Moderates* (New York, 1956) are important for understanding the conformity of the fifties. Edward Quinn and Paul J. Dolan, eds., *The Sense of the 60's* (New York, 1968) is a start at understanding a complex decade. William L. O'Neill, ed., *American Society Since 1945* (Chicago, 1969) is a collection of essays on the period.

There is a large and growing literature on the black revolution. A fine brief historical introduction is August Meier and Elliot Rudwick, *From Plantation to Ghetto* (New York, 1966). Works by participants themselves are invaluable in understanding the movement. See in particular Martin Luther King, Jr., *Stride Toward Freedom* (New York, 1958) and *Where Do We Go From Here: Chaos or Community?* (New York, 1967); Whitney M. Young, Jr., *To Be Equal* (New York, 1964); James Farmer, *Freedom—When?* (New York, 1965); Robert Williams, *Negroes with Guns* (New York, 1962); and *The Autobiography of Malcolm X* (New York, 1964). See also Charles E. Silberman, *Crisis in Black and White* (New York, 1964); C. Eric Lincoln, *The Black Muslims in America* (Boston, 1961); Howard Zinn, *SNCC: The New Abolitionists* (Boston, 1964). John H. Bracy, Jr., August Meier, and Elliot Rudwick, eds., *Black Nationalism in America* (Indianapolis, 1970) is a collection of documents with a good bibliography.

The essays in Daniel Bell, ed., *The Radical Right* (New York, 1963) are interesting attempts to make sense of a baffling movement; see also the essays in Richard Hofstadter, *The Paranoid Style in American Politics* (New York, 1965). A sympathetic account of the Kennedy years is Arthur M. Schlesinger, Jr., *A Thousand Days* (Boston, 1965).

Richard M. Scammon and Ben J. Wattenberg, *The Real Majority* (New York, 1970) argues that the majority of voters in the country have moved to the right. Two books important for understanding contemporary political and social thought are Theodore Roszak, *The Making of a Counter Culture (New York, 1970) and Charles A. Reich, *The Greening of America (New York, 1971). The latter argues that there is already a radical consensus in America based mostly on a life style which he calls Consciousness III. There are many books dealing with the young, the New Left, and the crisis on the campus. Lewis Feuer, *Conflict of Generations (New York, 1969) and Daniel J. Boorstin, *The Decline of Radicalism (New York, 1969) are generally critical of today's youth, while Kenneth Kenniston, *Young Radicals: Notes on Committed Youth (New York, 1968) and Paul Jacobs and Saul Landau, *The New Radicals: A Report with Documents (New York, 1966) are generally sympathetic.

* Available in paperback edition.

9
THE AMERICAN CHARACTER

No question has intrigued Americans more than that asked by Michel-Guillaume de Crèvecoeur during the Revolutionary War: "What then is the American, this new man?" Since that time literally thousands of Americans and foreign observers have asked that question anew. For, despite the efforts of perspicacious, sensitive commentators and highly trained specialists, the answer has been elusive.

The very fact that obvious and easily accepted American traits could not be found accounts, of course, for the fascination the question holds. Yet there is more to it than this. It might be just as difficult to describe and define the English character or the French character or the Italian character, but unlike Americans, Englishmen, Frenchmen, and Italians have given scant attention to the problem of trying to define what they were.

It is ironic that while Americans cannot agree on what an American is, they have devoted considerable attention to attempting to define what is un-American. Perhaps because we are so unsure of our identity, we constantly seek to set up certain rigid and mechanical standards to take the place of something we should all feel or take for granted. Or perhaps it is because we are so different and diverse, because we lack common characteristics which would arise from a long historical tradition, that we seek to set minimum standards. Maybe it is because we are so different that we must organize "Americanization" programs and search for "un-American activities" in our communities.

For whatever reason, Americans have been fascinated with the problem of discovering who they are. The reports and comments of thousands of visitors to our shores—Alexis de Tocqueville, Harriet Martineau, Charles Dickens, Frances Trollope, Lord Bryce, and Denis W. Brogan, to name but a few of the more insightful and better known—have been read eagerly in this country. Even those like Charles Dickens who heaped scorn upon us have been widely read. And the continued popularity of their works to the present day attests to the continued interest in the subject.

The search for an American character is a part of the consensus tradition in American history. Those who seek the American character have by the very definition of the problem accepted the notion of unity. Their premise (for which they feel no proof is required) is that there is an American character; their problem is to find it, describe it, and account for it. For such people there is something in the American environment and in the American experience which has molded a common American character. Thus there is not only a basic uniformity among Americans, but also a general continuity in American history: Certain relatively unchanging conditions have resulted in the creation of a relatively homogeneous population exhibiting basically common characteristics.

Not all of those who seek it find an American character; some find more than one. Accepting the argument that environment and experience create character, these people insist either that the American environment has changed so significantly over the years that there have been changes in the American character over time, or they argue that the environment at any given time is so diverse that different people experience different environments and hence have different characters.

Recently, the "rediscovery" of the poor, the blacks, the Indians, and the many immigrant groups in America—each with a different heritage—has caused some to question the concept of one American character shared by all. But at the same time, the increase in crime and violence during the last decade have caused some scholars looking into the past to suggest that a penchant for violence has been part of American society throughout its history. Not everyone agrees with the flat statement by black leader H. Rap Brown that "violence is necessary, and it's as American as cherry pie," but many historians and other commentators have emphasized the riots and labor upheavals and the vigilante and lynch-law traditions that certainly make our country one of the most violent in the Western world.

In the first selection which follows, David M. Potter finds an American character stemming from the experience of economic abundance. Michael Harrington is also concerned with the affluent society, but he argues that there is a large part of the American population which does not experience economic abundance and hence does not share a common character with those who do. For Harrington there are really two Americas.

Frederick Jackson Turner looks at the matter in a very different way. For him the most important factor creating an American character was the frontier experience. Yet implicit in his entire argument is the suggestion that there would probably be a change, for he finds (writing in 1893) that for the first time in American history there is no longer a frontier. David Riesman is much more explicit. He finds that changes in the American society in the last hundred years have resulted in distinct and significant changes in the American character over this period.

Thus to answer Crèvecoeur's question we must look back into American history and out into contemporary society. Were our experiences in the past similar enough to develop common characteristics which would set us apart from others? Was the American a "new man"? Or were our experiences so diverse that we must speak of several American characters? Have Americans changed over time? Has our society altered so fundamentally that we may speak of a changing American character? And what of today? Do businessmen and workers, Northerners and Southerners, Negroes and whites, urbanites and rural dwellers share a common character? Is the American tradition a violent one, and has that violent tradition become a part of the American character? Can the riots, the racial clashes, the lynchings, and the crime in America be explained by our frontier heritage? Or is violence a product of the very diversity of the American people?

Abundance and the Formation of Character

David M. Potter

Let us consider the situation of a six-month-old American infant, who is not yet aware that he is a citizen, a taxpayer, and a consumer.

This individual is, to all appearances, just a very young specimen of *Homo sapiens*, with certain needs for protection, care, shelter, and nourishment which may be regarded as the universal biological needs of human infancy rather than specific cultural needs. It would be difficult to prove that the culture has as yet differentiated him from other infants, and, though he is an American, few would argue that he has acquired an American character. Yet abundance and the circumstances arising from abundance have already dictated a whole range of basic conditions which, from his birth, are constantly at work upon this child and which will contribute in the most intimate and basic way to the formation of his character.

To begin with, abundance has already revolutionized the typical mode of his nourishment by providing for him to be fed upon cow's milk rather than upon his mother's milk, taken from the bottle rather than from the breast. Abundance contributes vitally to this transformation, because bottle feeding requires fairly elaborate facilities of refrigeration, heating, sterilization, and temperature control, which only an advanced technology can offer and only an economy of abundance can make widely available. I will not attempt here to resolve the debated question as to the psychological effects, for both mother and child, of bottle feeding as contrasted with breast feeding in infant nurture. But it is clear that the change-over to bottle feeding has encroached somewhat upon the intimacy of the bond between mother and child. The nature of this bond is, of course, one of the most crucial factors in the formation of character. Bottle feeding also must tend to emphasize the separateness of the infant as an individual, and thus it makes, for the first time, a point which the entire culture reiterates constantly throughout the life of the average American. In addition to the psychic influences which may be involved in the manner of taking the food, it is also a matter of capital importance that the bottle-fed baby is, on the whole, better nourished than the breast-fed infant and therefore likely to grow more rapidly, to be more vigorous, and to suffer fewer ailments, with whatever effects these physical conditions may have upon his personality.

It may be argued also that abundance has provided a characteristic mode of housing for the infant and that this mode further emphasizes his separateness as an individual. In societies of scarcity, dwelling units are few and hard to come by, with the result that high proportions of newly married young people make their homes in the parental ménage, thus forming part of an "extended" family, as it is called. Moreover, scarcity provides a low ratio of rooms to individuals, with the consequence that whole families may expect as a matter of course to have but one room for sleeping, where children will go to bed in intimate propinquity to their parents. But abundance prescribes a different regime. By making it economically possible for newly married couples to maintain separate households of their own, it has almost destroyed the extended family as an institution in America and has ordained that the child shall be reared in a "nuclear" family, so-called, where his only intimate associates are his parents and his siblings, with even the latter far fewer now than in families of the past. The housing arrangements of this new-style family are suggested by census data for 1950. In that year there were 45,983,000 dwelling units to accommodate the 38,310,000 families in the United States, and, though the median number of persons in the dwelling unit was 3.1, the median number of rooms in the dwelling unit was 4.6. Eighty-four percent of all dwelling units reported less than one person per room. By providing the ordinary family with more than one room for sleeping, the economy thus produces a situation in which the child will sleep either in a room alone or in a room shared with his brothers or sisters. Even without allowing for the cases in which children may have separate rooms, these conditions mean that a very substantial percentage of children now sleep in a room alone, for, with the declining birth rate, we have reached a point at which an increasing proportion of families have one child or two children rather than the larger number which was at one time typical. For instance, in the most recent group of mothers who had completed their childbearing phase, according to the census, 19.5 percent had had one child and 23.4 had had two. Thus almost half of all families with offspring did not have more than two children throughout their duration. In the case of the first group, all the children were "only" children throughout their childhood, and in the second group half of the children were "only" children until the second child was born. To state this in another, and perhaps a more forcible, way, it has been shown that among American women who arrived at age thirty-four during the year 1949 and who had borne children up to that time, 26.7 percent had borne only one child, and 34.5 percent had borne only two. If these tendencies persist, it would mean that, among families where there are children, hardly one in three will have more than two children.

The census has, of course, not got around to finding out how the new-style family, in its new-style dwelling unit, adjusts the life-practice to the space situation. But it is significant that America's most widely circulated book on the care of infants advises that "it is preferable that he [the infant] not sleep in his parents' room after he is about 12 months old," offers the opinion that "it's fine for each [child] to have a room of his own, if that's possible," and makes the sweeping assertion that "it's a sensible rule not to take a child into the parents' bed for any reason." It seems clear beyond dispute that the household space provided by the economy of abundance has been used to emphasize the separateness, the apartness, if not the isolation, of the American child.

Not only the nourishment and housing, but also the clothing of the American infant are controlled by American abundance. For one of the most sweeping consequences of our abundance is that, in contrast to other peoples who keep their bodies warm primarily by wearing clothes, Americans keep their bodies warm primarily by a far more expensive and even wasteful method: namely, by heating the buildings in which they are sheltered. Every American who has been abroad knows how much lighter is the clothing—especially the underclothing—of Americans than of people in countries like England and France, where the winters are far less severe than ours, and every American who can remember the conditions of a few decades ago knows how much lighter our clothing is than that of our grandparents. These changes have occurred because clothing is no longer the principal device for securing warmth. The oil furnace has not only displaced the open fireplace; it has also displaced the woolen undergarment and the vest.

This is a matter of considerable significance for adults but of far greater importance to infants, for adults discipline themselves to wear warm garments, submitting, for instance, to woolen underwear more or less voluntarily. But the infant knows no such discipline, and his garments or bedclothes must be kept upon him by forcible means. Hence primitive people, living in outdoor conditions, swaddle the child most rigorously, virtually binding him into his clothes, and breaking him to them almost as a horse is broken to the harness. Civilized peoples mitigate the rigor but still use huge pins or clips to frustrate the baby's efforts to kick off the blankets and free his limbs. In a state of nature, cold means confinement and warmth means freedom, so far as young humans are concerned. But abundance has given the American infant physical freedom by giving him physical warmth in cold weather.

In this connection it may be surmised that abundance has also given him a permissive system of toilet training. If our forebears imposed such training upon the child and we now wait for him to take the initiative in these matters himself, it is not wholly because the former held a grim Calvinistic doctrine of child-rearing that is philosophically contrary to ours. The fact was that the circumstances gave them little choice. A mother who was taking care of several babies, keeping them clean, making their clothes, washing their diapers in her own washtub, and doing this, as often as not, while another baby was on the way, had little choice but to hasten their fitness to toilet themselves. Today, on the contrary, the disposable diaper, the diaper service, and most of all the washing machine, not to mention the fact that one baby seldom presses upon the heels of another, make it far easier for the mother to indulge the child in a regime under which he will impose his own toilet controls in his own good time.

Thus the economy of plenty has influenced the feeding of the infant, his regime, and the physical setting within which he lives. These material conditions alone might be regarded as having some bearing upon the formation of his character, but the impact of abundance by no means ends at this point. In so far as it has an influence in determining what specific individuals shall initiate the infant into the ways of man and shall provide him with his formative impressions of the meaning of being a person, it must be regarded as even more vital. When it influences the nature of the relationships between these individuals and the infant, it must be recognized as reaching to the very essence of the process of character formation.

The central figures in the dramatis personae of the American infant's universe are still his parents, and in this respect, of course, there is nothing peculiar either to the American child or to the child of abundance. But abundance has at least provided him with parents who are in certain respects unlike the parents of children born in other countries or born fifty years ago. To begin with, it has given him young parents, for the median age of fathers at the birth of the first child in American marriages (as of 1940) was 25.3 years, and the median age of mothers was 22.6 years. This median age was substantially lower than it had been in the United States in 1890 for both fathers and mothers. Moreover, as the size of families has been reduced and the wife no longer continues to bear a succession of children throughout the period of her fertility, the median age of mothers at the birth of the last child was declined from 32 years (1890) to 27 years (1940). The age of the parents at the birth of both the first child and the last child is far lower than in the case of couples in most European countries. There can be little doubt that abundance has caused this differential, in the case of the first-born by making it economically possible for a high proportion of the population to meet the expenses of homemaking at a fairly early age. In the case of the last-born, it would also appear that one major reason for the earlier cessation of childbearing is a determination by parents to enjoy a high standard of living themselves and to limit their offspring to a number for whom they can maintain a similar standard.

By the very fact of their youth, these parents are more likely to remain alive until the child reaches maturity, thus giving him a better prospect of being reared by his own mother and father. This prospect is further reinforced by increases in the life-span, so that probably no child in history has ever enjoyed so strong a likelihood that his parents will survive to rear him. Abundance has produced this situation by providing optimum conditions for prolonging life. But, on the other hand, abundance has also contributed much to produce an economy in which the mother is no longer markedly dependent upon the father, and this change in the economic relation between the sexes has probably done much to remove obstacles to divorce. The results are all too familiar. During the decade 1940–49 there were 25.8 divorces for every 100 marriages in the United States, which ratio, if projected over a longer period, would mean that one marriage out of four would end in divorce. But our concern here is with a six-month-old child, and the problem is to know whether this factor of divorce involves childless couples predominantly or whether it is likely to touch him. The answer is indicated by the fact that, of all divorces granted in 1948, no less than 42 percent were to couples with children under eighteen, and a very large proportion of these children were of much younger ages. Hence one might say that the economy of abundance has provided the child with younger parents who chose their role of parenthood deliberately and who are more likely than parents in the past to live until he is grown, but who are substantially less likely to preserve the unbroken family as the environment within which he shall be reared.

In addition to altering the characteristics of the child's parents, it has also altered the quantitative relationship between him and his parents. It has done this, first of all, by offering the father such lucrative opportunities through work outside the home that the old agricultural economy in which children worked alongside their fathers is now obsolete. Yet, on the other hand, the father's new employment gives so much more leisure than his former work that the child may, in fact, receive considerably more of his father's attention. But the most vital transformation is in the case of the mother. In the economy of scarcity which controlled the modes of life that were traditional for many centuries, an upper-class child was reared by a nurse, and all others were normally reared by their mothers. The scarcity economy could not support many nonproductive members, and these mothers, though not "employed," were most decidedly hard workers, busily engaged in cooking, washing, sewing, weaving, preserving, caring for the henhouse, the garden, and perhaps the cow, and in general carrying on the domestic economy of a large family. Somehow they also attended to the needs of a numerous brood of children, but the mother was in no sense a full-time attendant upon any one child. Today, however, the economy of abundance very nearly exempts a very large number of mothers from the requirement of economic productivity in order that they may give an unprecedented share of their time to the care of the one or two young children who are now the usual number in an American family. Within the home, the wide range of labor-saving devices and the assignment of many functions, such as laundering, to service industries have produced this result. Outside the home, employment of women in the labor force has steadily increased, but the incidence of employment falls upon unmarried women, wives without children, and wives with grown children. In fact, married women without children are two and one-half times as likely to be employed as those with children. Thus what amounts to a new dispensation has been established for the child. If he belongs to the upper class, his mother has replaced his nurse as his full-time attendant. The differences in character formation that might result from this change alone could easily be immense. To mention but one possibility, the presence of the nurse must inevitably have made the child somewhat aware of his class status, whereas the presence of the mother would be less likely to have this effect. If the child does not belong to the upper class, mother and child now impinge upon each other in a relationship whose intensity is of an entirely different magnitude from that which prevailed in the past. The mother has fewer physical distractions in the care of the child, but she is more likely to be restive in her maternal role because it takes her away from attractive employment with which it cannot be reconciled.

If abundance has thus altered the relationship of the child with his parent, it has even more drastically altered the rest of his social milieu, for it has changed the identity of the rest of the personnel who induct him into human society. In the extended family of the past, a great array of kinspeople filled his cosmos and guided him to maturity. By nature, he particularly needed association with children of his own age (his "peers," as they are called), and he particularly responded to the values asserted by these peers. Such peers were very often his brothers and sisters, and, since they were all members of his own family, all came under parental control. This is to say that, in a sense, the parents controlled the peer group, and the peer group controlled the child. The point is worth making because we frequently encounter the assertion that parental control of the child has been replaced by peer-group control; but it is arguable that what is really the case is that children were always deeply influenced by the peer group and that parents have now lost their former measure of control over this group, since it is no longer a familial group. Today the nursery school replaces the large family as a peer group, and the social associations, even of young children, undergo the same shift from focused contact with family to diffused contact with a miscellany of people, which John Galsworthy depicted for grown people in the three novels of the *Forsyte Saga.* Again, the effects upon character may very well be extensive.

Abundance, then, has played a critical part in revolutionizing both the physical circumstances and the human associations which surround the American infant and child. These changes alone would warrant the hypothesis that abundance has profoundly affected the formation of character for such a child. But to extend this inquiry one step further, it may be worth while to consider how these altered conditions actually impinge upon the individual. Here, of course, is an almost unlimited field for investigation, and I shall only attempt to indicate certain crucial points at which abundance projects conditions that are basic in the life of the child.

One of these points concerns the cohesive force which holds the family together. The family is the one institution which touches all members of society most intimately, and it is perhaps the only social institution which touches young children directly. The sources from which the family draws its strength are, therefore, of basic importance. In the past, these sources were, it would seem, primarily economic. For agrarian society, marriage distinctively involved a division of labor. Where economic opportunity was narrowly restricted, the necessity for considering economic ways and means in connection with marriage led to the arrangement of matches by parents and to the institution of the dowry. The emotional bonds of affection, while always important, were not deemed paramount, and the ideal of romantic love played little or no part in the lives of ordinary people. Where it existed at all, it was as an upper-class luxury. (The very term "courtship" implies this upper-class orientation.) This must inevitably have meant that the partners in the majority of marriages demanded less from one another emotionally than do the partners of romantic love and that the emotional factor was less important to the stability of the marriage. Abundance, however, has played its part in changing this picture. On the American frontier, where capital for dowries was as rare as opportunity for prosperous marriage was plentiful, the dowry became obsolete. Later still, when abundance began to diminish the economic duties imposed upon the housewife, the function of marriage as a division of labor ceased to seem paramount, and the romantic or emotional factor assumed increasing importance. Abundance brought the luxury of romantic love within the reach of all, and, as it did so, emotional harmony became the principal criterion of success in a marriage, while lack of such harmony became a major threat to the existence of the marriage. The statistics of divorce give us a measure of the loss of durability in marriage, but they give us no measure of the factors of instability in the marriages which endure and no measure of the increased focus upon emotional satisfactions in such marriages. The children of enduring marriages, as well as the children of divorce, must inevitably feel the impact of this increased emphasis upon emotional factors, must inevitably sense the difference in the foundations of the institution which holds their universe in place.

In the rearing of a child, it would be difficult to imagine any factors more vital than the distinction between a permissive and an authoritarian regime or more vital than the age at which economic responsibility is imposed. In both these matters the modern American child lives under a very different dispensation from children in the past. We commonly think of these changes as results of our more enlightened or progressive or humanitarian ideas. We may even think of them as results of developments in the specific field of child psychology, as if the changes were simply a matter of our understanding these matters better than our grandparents. But the fact is that the authoritarian discipline of the child, within the authoritarian family, was but an aspect of the authoritarian social system that was linked with the economy of scarcity. Such a regime could never have been significantly relaxed within the family so long as it remained diagnostic in the society. Nor could it have remained unmodified within the family, once society began to abandon it in other spheres.

Inevitably, the qualities which the parents inculcate in a child will depend upon the roles which they occupy themselves. For the ordinary man the economy of scarcity has offered one role, as Simon N. Patten observed many years ago, and the economy of abundance has offered another. Abundance offers "work calling urgently for workmen"; scarcity found the "worker seeking humbly any kind of toil." As a suppliant to his superiors, the worker under scarcity accepted the principle of authority; he accepted his own subordination and the obligation to cultivate the qualities appropriate to his subordination, such as submissiveness, obedience, and deference. Such a man naturally transferred the principle of authority into his own family and, through this principle, instilled into his children the qualities appropriate to people of their kind—submissiveness, obedience, and deference. Many copybook maxims still exist to remind us of the firmness of childhood discipline, while the difference between European and American children—one of the most clearly recognizable of all national differences—serves to emphasize the extent to which Americans have now departed from this firmness.

This new and far more permissive attitude toward children has arisen, significantly, in an economy of abundance, where work has called urgently for the workman. In this situation, no longer a suppliant, the workman found submissiveness no longer a necessity and therefore no longer a virtue. The principle of authority lost some of its majesty, and he was less likely to regard it as the only true criterion of domestic order. In short, he ceased to impose it upon his children. Finding that the most valuable trait in himself was a capacity for independent decision and self-reliant conduct in dealing with the diverse opportunities which abundance offered him, he tended to encourage this quality in his children. The irresponsibility of childhood still called for a measure of authority on one side and obedience on the other, but this became a means to an end and not an end in itself. On the whole, permissive training, to develop independent ability, even though it involves a certain sacrifice of obedience and discipline, is the characteristic mode of child-rearing in the one country which most distinctively enjoys an economy of abundance. Here, in a concrete way, one finds something approaching proof for Gerth and Mills's suggestion that the relation of father and child may have its importance not as a primary factor but rather as a "replica of the power relations of society."

If scarcity required men to "seek humbly any kind of toil," it seldom permitted women to seek employment outside the home at all. Consequently, the woman was economically dependent upon, and, accordingly, subordinate to, her husband or her father. Her subordination reinforced the principle of authority within the home. But the same transition which altered the role of the male worker has altered her status as well, for abundance "calling urgently for workmen" makes no distinctions of gender, and, by extending economic independence to women, has enabled them to assume the role of partners rather than of subordinates within the family. Once the relation of voluntarism and equality is introduced between husband and wife, it is, of course, far more readily extended to the relation between parent and child.

If abundance has fostered a more permissive regime for the child, amid circumstances of democratic equality within the family, it has no less certainly altered the entire process of imposing economic responsibility upon the child, hence the process of preparing the child for such responsibility. In the economy of scarcity, as I have remarked above, society could not afford to support any substantial quota of nonproductive members. Consequently, the child went to work when he was as yet young. He attended primary school for a much shorter school year than the child of today; only a minority attended high school; and only the favored few attended college. Even during the brief years of schooling, the child worked, in the home, on the farm, or even in the factory. But today the economy of abundance can afford to maintain a substantial proportion of the population in nonproductive status, and it assigns this role, sometimes against their will, to its younger and its elder members. It protracts the years of schooling, and it defers responsibilities for an unusually long span. It even enforces laws setting minimal ages for leaving school, for going to work, for consenting to sexual intercourse, or for marrying. It extends the jurisdiction of juvenile courts to the eighteenth or the twentieth year of age.

Such exemption from economic responsibility might seem to imply a long and blissful youth free from strain for the child. But the delays in reaching economic maturity are not matched by comparable delays in other phases of growing up. On the contrary, there are many respects in which the child matures earlier. Physically, the child at the lower social level will actually arrive at adolescence a year or so younger than his counterpart a generation ago, because of improvement in standards of health and nutrition. Culturally, the child is made aware of the allurements of sex at an earlier age, partly by his familiarity with the movies, television, and popular magazines, and partly by the practice of "dating" in the early teens. By the standards of his peer group, he is encouraged to demand expensive and mature recreations, similar to those of adults, at a fairly early age. By reason of the desire of his parents that he should excel in the mobility race and give proof during his youth of the qualities which will make him a winner in later life, he is exposed to the stimuli of competition before he leaves the nursery. Thus there is a kind of imbalance between the postponement of responsibility and the quickening of social maturity which may have contributed to make American adolescence a more difficult age than human biology alone would cause it to be. Here, again, there are broad implications for the formation of character, and here, again, abundance is at work on both sides of the equation, for it contributes as much to the hastening of social maturity as it does to the prolongation of economic immaturity.

Some of these aspects of the rearing of children in the United States are as distinctively American, when compared with other countries, as any Yankee traits that have ever been attributed to the American people. In the multiplicity which always complicates social analysis, such aspects of child-rearing might be linked with a number of factors in American life. But one of the more evident and more significant links, it would seem certain, is with the factor of abundance. Such a tie is especially pertinent in this discussion, where the intention of the whole book has been to relate the study of character, as the historian would approach it, to the same subject as it is viewed by the behavioral scientist. In this chapter, especially, the attempt has been made to throw a bridge between the general historical force of economic abundance and the specific behavioral pattern of people's lives. Historical forces are too often considered only in their public and over-all effects, while private lives are interpreted without sufficient reference to the historical determinants which shape them. But no major force at work in society can possibly make itself felt at one of these levels without also having its impact at the other level. In view of this fact, the study of national character should not stand apart, as it has in the past, from the study of the process of character formation in the individual. In view of this fact, also, the effect of economic abundance is especially pertinent. For economic abundance is a factor whose presence and whose force may be clearly and precisely recognized in the most personal and intimate phases of the development of personality in the child. Yet, at the same time, the presence and the force of this factor are recognizable with equal certainty in the whole broad, general range of American experience, American ideals, and American institutions. At both levels, it has exercised a pervasive influence in the shaping of the American character.

The Other America

Michael Harrington

There is a familiar America. It is celebrated in speeches and advertised on television and in the magazines. It has the highest mass standard of living the world has ever known.

In the 1950's this America worried about itself, yet even its anxieties were products of abundance. The title of a brilliant book was widely misinterpreted, and the familiar America began to call itself "the affluent society." There was introspection about Madison Avenue and tail fins; there was discussion of the emotional suffering taking place in the suburbs. In all this, there was an implicit assumption that the basic grinding economic problems had been solved in the United States. In this theory the nation's problems were no longer a matter of basic human needs, of food, shelter, and clothing. Now they were seen as qualitative, a question of learning to live decently amid luxury.

While this discussion was carried on, there existed another America. In it dwelt somewhere between 40,000,000 and 50,000,000 citizens of this land. They were poor. They still are.

To be sure, the other America is not impoverished in the same sense as those poor nations where millions cling to hunger as a defense against starvation. This country has escaped such extremes. That does not change the fact that tens of millions of Americans are, at this very moment, maimed in body and spirit, existing at levels beneath those necessary for human decency. If these people are not starving, they are hungry, and sometimes fat with hunger, for that is what cheap foods do. They are without adequate housing and education and medical care.

The Government has documented what this means to the bodies of the poor, and the figures will be cited throughout this book. But even more basic, this poverty twists and deforms the spirit. The American poor are pessimistic and defeated, and they are victimized by mental suffering to a degree unknown in Suburbia.

This book is a description of the world in which these people live; it is about the other America. Here are the unskilled workers, the migrant farm workers, the aged, the minorities, and all the others who live in the economic underworld of American life. In all this, there will be statistics, and that offers the opportunity for disagreement among honest and sincere men. I would ask the reader to respond critically to every assertion, but not to allow statistical quibbling to obscure the huge, enormous, and intolerable fact of poverty in America. For, when all is said and done, that fact is unmistakable, whatever its exact dimensions, and the truly human reaction can only be outrage. As W. H. Auden wrote:

> Hunger allows no choice
> To the citizen or the police;
> We must love one another or die.

The millions who are poor in the United States tend to become increasingly invisible. Here is a great mass of people, yet it takes an effort of the intellect and will even to see them.

I discovered this personally in a curious way. After I wrote my first article on poverty in America, I had all the statistics down on paper. I had proved to my satisfaction that there were around 50,000,000 poor in this country. Yet, I realized I did not believe my own figures. The poor existed in the Government reports; they were percentages and numbers in long, close columns, but they were not part of my experience. I could prove that the other America existed, but I had never been there.

My response was not accidental. It was typical of what is happening to an entire society, and it reflects profound social changes in this nation. The other America, the America of poverty, is hidden today in a way that it never was before. Its millions are socially invisible to the rest of us. No wonder that so many misinterpreted Galbraith's title and assumed that "the affluent society" meant that everyone had a decent standard of life. The misinterpretation was true as far as the actual day-to-day lives of two-thirds of the nation were concerned. Thus, one must begin a description of the other America by understanding why we do not see it.

There are perennial reasons that make the other America an invisible land.

Poverty is often off the beaten track. It always has been. The ordinary tourist never left the main highway, and today he rides interstate turnpikes. He does not go into the valleys of Pennsylvania where the towns look like movie sets of Wales in the thirties. He does not see the company houses in rows, the rutted roads (the poor always have bad roads whether they live in the city, in towns, or on farms), and everything is black and dirty. And even if he were to pass through such a place by accident, the tourist would not meet the unemployed men in the bar or the women coming home from a runaway sweatshop.

Then, too, beauty and myths are perennial masks of poverty. The traveler comes to the Appalachians in the lovely season. He sees the hills, the streams, the foliage—but not the poor. Or perhaps he looks at a run-down mountain house and, remembering Rousseau rather than seeing with his eyes, decides that "those people" are truly fortunate to be living the way they are and that they are lucky to be exempt from the strains and tensions of the middle class. The only problem is that "those people," the quaint inhabitants of those hills, are undereducated, underprivileged, lack medical care, and are in the process of being forced from the land into a life in the cities, where they are misfits.

These are normal and obvious causes of the invisibility of the poor. They operated a generation ago; they will be functioning a generation hence. It is more important to understand that the very development of American society is creating a new kind of blindness about poverty. The poor are increasingly slipping out of the very experience and consciousness of the nation.

If the middle class never did like ugliness and poverty, it was at least aware of them. "Across the tracks" was not a very long way to go. There were forays into the slums at Christmas time; there were charitable organizations that brought contact with the poor. Occasionally, almost everyone passed through the Negro ghetto or the blocks of tenements, if only to get downtown to work or to entertainment.

Now the American city has been transformed. The poor still inhabit the miserable housing in the central area, but they are increasingly isolated from contact with, or sight of, anybody else. Middle-class women coming in from Suburbia on a rare trip may catch the merest glimpse of the other America on the way to an evening at the theater, but their children are segregated in suburban schools. The business or professional man may drive along the fringes of slums in a car or bus, but it is not an important experience to him. The failures, the unskilled, the disabled, the aged, and the minorities are right there, across the tracks, where they have always been. But hardly anyone else is.

In short, the very development of the American city has removed poverty from the living, emotional experience of millions upon millions of middle-class Americans. Living out in the suburbs, it is easy to assume that ours is, indeed, an affluent society.

This new segregation of poverty is compounded by a well-meaning ignorance. A good many concerned and sympathetic Americans are aware that there is much discussion of urban renewal. Suddenly, driving through the city, they notice that a familiar slum has been torn down and that there are towering, modern buildings where once there had been tenements or hovels. There is a warm feeling of satisfaction, of pride in the way things are working out: the poor, it is obvious, are being taken care of.

The irony in this . . . is that the truth is nearly the exact opposite to the impression. The total impact of the various housing programs in postwar America has been to squeeze more and more people into existing slums. More often than not, the modern apartment in a towering building rents at $40 a room or more. For, during the past decade and a half, there has been more subsidization of middle- and upper-income housing than there has been of housing for the poor.

Clothes make the poor invisible too: America has the best-dressed poverty the world has ever known. For a variety of reasons, the benefits of mass production have been spread much more evenly in this area than in many others. It is much easier in the United States to be decently dressed than it is to be decently housed, fed, or doctored. Even people with terribly depressed incomes can look prosperous.

This is an extremely important factor in defining our emotional and existential ignorance of poverty. In Detroit the existence of social classes became much more difficult to discern the day the companies put lockers in the plants. From that moment on, one did not see men in work clothes on the way to the factory, but citizens in slacks and white shirts. This process has been magnified with the poor throughout the country. There are tens of thousands of Americans in the big cities who are wearing shoes, perhaps even a stylishly cut suit or dress, and yet are hungry. It is not a matter of planning, though it almost seems as if the affluent society had given out costumes to the poor so that they would not offend the rest of society with the sight of rags.

Then, many of the poor are the wrong age to be seen. A good number of them (over 8,000,000) are sixty-five years of age or better; an even larger number are under eighteen. The aged members of the other America are often sick, and they cannot move. Another group of them live out their lives in loneliness and frustration: they sit in rented rooms, or else they stay close to a house in a neighborhood that has completely changed from the old days. Indeed, one of the worst aspects of poverty among the aged is that these people are out of sight and out of mind, and alone.

The young are somewhat more visible, yet they too stay close to their neighborhoods. Sometimes they advertise their poverty through a lurid tabloid story about a gang killing. But generally they do not disturb the quiet streets of the middle class.

And finally, the poor are politically invisible. It is one of the cruelest ironies of social life in advanced countries that the dispossessed at the bottom of society are unable to speak for themselves. The people of the other America do not, by far and large, belong to unions, to fraternal organizations, or to political parties. They are without lobbies of their own; they put forward no legislative program. As a group, they are atomized. They have no face; they have no voice.

Thus, there is not even a cynical political motive for caring about the poor, as in the old days. Because the slums are no longer centers of powerful political organizations, the politicians need not really care about their inhabitants. The slums are no longer visible to the middle class, so much of the idealistic urge to fight for those who need help is gone. Only the social agencies have a really direct involvement with the other America, and they are without any great political power.

To the extent that the poor have a spokesman in American life, that role is played by the labor movement. The unions have their own particular idealism, an ideology of concern. More than that, they realize that the existence of a reservoir of cheap, unorganized labor is a menace to wages and working conditions throughout the entire economy. Thus, many union legislative proposals—to extend the coverage of minimum wage and social security, to organize migrant farm laborers—articulate the needs of the poor.

That the poor are invisible is one of the most important things about them. They are not simply neglected and forgotten as in the old rhetoric of reform; what is much worse, they are not seen. . . .

Forty to 50,000,000 people are becoming increasingly invisible. That is a shocking fact. But there is a second basic irony of poverty that is equally important: if one is to make the mistake of being born poor, he should choose a time when the majority of the people are miserable too.

J. K. Galbraith develops this idea in *The Affluent Society*, and in doing so defines the "newness" of the kind of poverty in contemporary America. The old poverty, Galbraith notes, was general. It was the condition of life of an entire society, or at least of that huge majority who were without special skills or the luck of birth. When the entire economy advanced, a good many of these people gained higher standards of living. Unlike the poor today, the majority poor of a generation ago were an immediate (if cynical) concern of political leaders. The old slums of the immigrants had the votes; they provided the basis for labor organizations; their very numbers could be a powerful force in political conflict. At the same time the new technology required higher skills, more education, and stimulated an upward movement for millions.

Perhaps the most dramatic case of the power of the majority poor took place in the 1930's. The Congress of Industrial Organizations literally organized millions in a matter of years. A labor movement that had been declining and confined to a thin stratum of the highly skilled suddenly embraced masses of men and women in basic industry. At the same time this acted as a pressure upon the Government, and the New Deal codified some of the social gains in laws like the Wagner Act. The result was not a basic transformation of the American system, but it did transform the lives of an entire section of the population.

In the thirties one of the reasons for these advances was that misery was general. There was no need then to write books about unemployment and poverty. That was the decisive social experience of the entire society, and the apple sellers even invaded Wall Street. There was political sympathy from middle-class reformers; there were an élan and spirit that grew out of a deep crisis.

Some of those who advanced in the thirties did so because they had unique and individual personal talents. But for the great mass, it was a question of being at the right point in the economy at the right time in history, and utilizing that position for common struggle. Some of those who failed did so because they did not have the will to take advantage of new opportunities. But for the most part the poor who were left behind had been at the wrong place in the economy at the wrong moment in history.

These were the people in the unorganizable jobs, in the South, in the minority groups, in the fly-by-night factories that were low on capital and high on labor. When some of them did break into the economic mainstream —when, for instance, the CIO opened up the way for some Negroes to find good industrial jobs—they proved to be as resourceful as anyone else. As a group, the other Americans who stayed behind were not originally composed primarily of individual failures. Rather, they were victims of an impersonal process that selected some for progress and discriminated against others.

Out of the thirties came the welfare state. Its creation had been stimulated by mass impoverishment and misery, yet it helped the poor least of all. Laws like unemployment compensation, the Wagner Act, the various farm programs, all these were designed for the middle third in the cities, for the organized workers, and for the upper third in the country, for the big market farmers. If a man works in an extremely low-paying job, he may not even be covered by social security or other welfare programs. If he receives unemployment compensation, the payment is scaled down according to his low earnings.

One of the major laws that was designed to cover everyone, rich and poor, was social security. But even here the other Americans suffered discrimination. Over the years social security payments have not even provided a subsistence level of life. The middle third have been able to supplement the Federal pension through private plans negotiated by unions, through joining medical insurance schemes like Blue Cross, and so on. The poor have not been able to do so. They lead a bitter life, and then have to pay for that fact in old age.

Indeed, the paradox that the welfare state benefits those least who need help most is but a single instance of a persistent irony in the other America. Even when the money finally trickles down, even when a school is built in a poor neighborhood, for instance, the poor are still deprived. Their entire environment, their life, their values, do not prepare them to take advantage of the new opportunity. The parents are anxious for the children to go to work; the pupils are pent up, waiting for the moment when their education has complied with the law.

Today's poor, in short, missed the political and social gains of the thirties. They are, as Galbraith rightly points out, the first minority poor in history, the first poor not to be seen, the first poor whom the politicians could leave alone.

The first step toward the new poverty was taken when millions of people proved immune to progress. When that happened, the failure was not individual and personal, but a social product. But once the historic accident takes place, it begins to become a personal fate.

The new poor of the other America saw the rest of society move ahead. They went on living in depressed areas, and often they tended to become depressed human beings. In some of the West Virginia towns, for instance, an entire community will become shabby and defeated. The young and the adventurous go to the city, leaving behind those who cannot move and those who lack the will to do so. The entire area becomes permeated with failure, and that is one more reason the big corporations shy away.

Indeed, one of the most important things about the new poverty is that it cannot be defined in simple, statistical terms. Throughout this book a crucial term is used: aspiration. If a group has internal vitality, a will—if it has aspiration—it may live in dilapidated housing, it may eat an inadequate diet, and it may suffer poverty, but it is not impoverished. So it was in those ethnic slums of the immigrants that played such a dramatic role in the unfolding of the American dream. The people found themselves in slums, but they were not slum dwellers.

But the new poverty is constructed so as to destroy aspiration; it is a system designed to be impervious to hope. The other America does not contain the adventurous seeking a new life and land. It is populated by the failures, by those driven from the land and bewildered by the city, by old people suddenly confronted with the torments of loneliness and poverty, and by minorities facing a wall of prejudice.

In the past, when poverty was general in the unskilled and semiskilled work force, the poor were all mixed together. The bright and the dull, those who were going to escape into the great society and those who were to stay behind, all of them lived on the same street. When the middle third rose, this community was destroyed. And the entire invisible land of the other Americans became a ghetto, a modern poor farm for the rejects of society and of the economy.

It is a blow to reform and the political hopes of the poor that the middle class no longer understands that poverty exists. But, perhaps more important, the poor are losing their links with the great world. If statistics and sociology can measure a feeling as delicate as loneliness . . . the other America is becoming increasingly populated by those who do not belong to anybody or anything. They are no longer participants in an ethnic culture from the old country; they are less and less religious; they do not belong to unions or clubs. They are not seen, and because of that they themselves cannot see. Their horizon has become more and more restricted; they see one another, and that means they see little reason to hope.

. . . There is, in a sense, a personality of poverty, a type of human being produced by the grinding, wearing life of the slums. The other Americans feel differently than the rest of the nation. They tend to be hopeless and passive, yet prone to bursts of violence; they are lonely and isolated, often rigid and hostile. To be poor is not simply to be deprived of the material things of this world. It is to enter a fatal, futile universe, an America within America with a twisted spirit.

Perhaps the most classic (but still controversial) study of this subject is the book *Social Class and Mental Illness* by August B. Hollingshead and F. C. Redlich. Published in 1958, it summarizes a careful research project in New Haven, Connecticut. It is an academic, scholarly work, yet its statistics are the description of an abyss.

Hollingshead and Redlich divided New Haven into five social classes. At the top (Class I) were the rich, usually aristocrats of family as well as of money. Next came the executives and professionals more newly arrived to prestige and power. Then, the middle class, and beneath them, the workers with decent paying jobs. Class V, the bottom class, was made up of the poor. About half of its members were semiskilled, about half unskilled. The men had less than six years of education, the women less than eight.

As it turned out, this five-level breakdown was more revealing than the usual three-class image of American society (upper, middle, and lower). For it showed a sharp break between Class V at the bottom and Class IV just above it. In a dramatic psychological sense, the skilled unionized worker lived much, much closer to the middle class than he did to the world of the poor. Between Class IV and Class V, Hollingshead and Redlich found a chasm. This represents the gulf between working America, which may be up against it from time to time but which has a certain sense of security and dignity, and the other America of the poor.

Perhaps the most shocking and decisive statistic that Hollingshead and Redlich found was the one that tabulated the rate of treated psychiatric illness per 100,000 people in New Haven. These are their results:

Classes I and II	556 per 100,000
Class III	538
Class IV	642
Class V	1,659

From the top of society down to the organized workers, there are differences, but relatively small ones. But suddenly, when one crosses the line from Class IV to Class V, there is a huge leap, with the poor showing a rate of treated psychiatric illness of almost three times the magnitude of any other class.

But the mental suffering of the poor in these figures is not simply expressed in gross numbers. It is a matter of quality as well. In Classes I and II, 65 percent of the treated psychiatric illness is for neurotic problems, and only 35 percent for the much graver disturbances of psychoses. But at the bottom, in Class V, 90 percent of the treated illness is for psychosis, and only 10 percent for neurosis. In short, not only the rate but also the intensity of mental illness is much greater for the poor.

One of the standard professional criticisms of Hollingshead and Redlich is that their figures are for treated illness (those who actually got to a doctor or clinic) and do not indicate the "true prevalence" of mental illness in the population. Whatever merits this argument has in relation to other parts of the study, it points up that these particular figures are an understatement of the problem. The higher up the class scale one is, the more likely that there will be recognition of mental illness as a problem and that help will be sought. At the bottom of society, referral to psychiatric treatment usually comes from the courts. Thus, if anything, there is even more mental illness among the poor than the figures of Hollingshead and Redlich indicate.

The one place where this criticism might have some validity is with regard to the intensity of emotional disturbance. Only 10 percent of the poor who received treatment are neurotics, yet the poor neurotic is the least likely person in the society to show up for treatment. He can function, if only in an impaired and maimed way. If there were something done about this situation, it is quite possible that one would find more neurosis in the other America at the same time as one discovered more mental illness generally.

However, it is not necessary to juggle with statistics and explanations in order to corroborate the main drift of the New Haven figures. During the fifties the Cornell University Department of Psychiatry undertook an ambitious study of "Midtown," a residential area in New York City. The research dealt with a population of 170,000 from every social class, 99 percent of them white. (By leaving out the Negroes, there probably was a tendency to underestimate the problem of poverty generally, and the particular disabilities of a discriminated minority in particular.) The goal of the study was to discover "true prevalence," and there was interviewing in depth.

The Cornell scholars developed a measure of "mental health risk." They used a model of three classes, and consequently their figures are not so dramatic as those tabulated in New Haven. Yet they bear out the essential point: the lowest class had a mental health risk almost 40 percent greater than the highest class. Once again the world of poverty was given definition as a spiritual and emotional reality.

The huge brute fact of emotional illness in the other America is fairly well substantiated. The reasons behind the fact are the subject of considerable controversy. There is no neat and simple summary that can be given at the present time, yet some of the analyses are provocative for an understanding of the culture of poverty even if they must be taken tentatively.

One of the most interesting speculations came from the Cornell study of "Midtown" in New York City. The researchers developed a series of "stress factors" that might be related to an individual's mental health risk. In childhood, these were poor mental health on the part of the parents, poor physical health for the parents, economic deprivation, broken homes, a negative attitude on the part of the child toward his parents, a quarrelsome home, and sharp disagreements with parents during adolescence. In adult life, the stress factors were poor health, work worries, money worries, a lack of neighbors and friends, marital worries, and parental worries.

The Cornell team then tested to see if there was any relationship between these factors and mental health. They discovered a marked correlation. The person who had been subjected to thirteen of these stress factors was three times more likely to be mentally disturbed than the person who had felt none of them. Indeed, the researchers were led to conclude that the sheer number of stress factors was more important than the quality of stresses. Those who had experienced any three factors were of a higher mental risk than those who had experienced two.

If the Cornell conclusions are validated in further research, they will constitute an important revision of some widely held ideas about mental health. The Freudian theory has emphasized the earliest years and the decisive trauma in the development of mental illness (for example, the death of a parent). This new theory would suggest a more cumulative conception of mental illness: as stress piles upon stress over a period of time, there is a greater tendency toward disturbance. It would be an important supplement to the Freudian ideas.

But if this theory is right, there is a fairly obvious reason for the emotional torment of the other America. The stress factors listed by the Cornell study are the very stuff of the life of the poor: physical illness, broken homes, worries about work and money, and all the rest. The slum, with its vibrant, dense life hammers away at the individual. And because of the sheer, grinding, dirty experience of being poor, the personality, the spirit, is impaired. It is as if human beings dilapidate along with the tenements in which they live.

However, some scholars have attempted to soften the grimness of this picture with a theory about "drift." The poor, they argue, have a high percentage of disturbed people, not because of the conditions of life in the urban and rural slums, but because this is the group that gets all the outcasts of society from the rest of the classes. If this thesis were true, then one would expect to find failures from the higher classes as a significant group in the culture of the poor.

Hollingshead and Redlich tested this theory in New Haven and did not find any confirmation for it. The mentally impaired poor had been, for the most part, born poor. Their sickness was a product of poverty, instead of their poverty being a product of sickness. Similarly, in the Midtown study, no evidence was turned up to indicate that the disturbed poor were the rejects from other classes. There are some exceptions to this rule: alcoholics . . . often tend to fall from a high position into the bitterest poverty. Still, current research points to a direct relationship between the experience of poverty and emotional disturbance.

And yet, an ironic point turned up in the Midtown research. It was discovered that a certain kind of neurosis was useful to a minority of poor people. The obsessive-compulsive neurotic often got ahead: his very sickness was a means of advancement out of the other America and into the great world. And yet, this might only prepare for a later crisis. On the lower and middle rungs of business society, hard work, attention to detail, and the like are enough to guarantee individual progress. But if such a person moves across the line, and is placed in a position where he must make decisions, there is the very real possibility of breakdown. . . .

The feelings, the emotions, the attitudes of the poor are different. But different from what? In this question there is an important problem of dealing with the chaotic in the world of poverty. . . .

Take the gangs. They are violent, and by middle-class standards they are antisocial and disturbed. But within a slum, violence and disturbance are often norms, everyday facts of life. From the inside of the other America, joining a "bopping" gang may well not seem like deviant behavior. It could be a necessity for dealing with a hostile world. (Once, in a slum school in St. Louis, a teacher stopped a fight between two little girls. "Nice girls don't fight," she told them. "Yeah," one of them replied, "you should have seen my old lady at the tavern last night.")

Indeed, one of the most depressing pieces of research I have ever read touches on this point. H. Warren Dunham carefully studied forty catatonic schizophrenics in Chicago in the early forties. He found that none of them had belonged to gangs or had engaged in the kind of activity the middle class regards as abnormal. They had, as a matter of fact, tried to live up to the standards of the larger society, rather than conforming to the values of the slum. "The catatonic young man can be described as a good boy and one who has all the desirable traits which all the social agencies would like to inculcate in the young men of the community."

The middle class does not understand the narrowness of its judgments. And worse, it acts upon them as if they were universal and accepted by everyone. In New Haven, Hollingshead and Redlich found two girls with an almost identical problem. Both of them were extremely promiscuous, so much so that they eventually had a run-in with the police. When the girl from Class I was arrested, she was provided with bail at once, newspaper stories were quashed, and she was taken care of through private psychotherapy. The girl from Class V was sentenced to reform school. She was paroled in two years, but was soon arrested again and sent to the state reformatory.

James Baldwin made a brilliant and perceptive application of this point to the problem of the Negro in a speech I heard not long ago. The white, he said, cannot imagine what it is like to be Negro: the danger, the lack of horizon, the necessity of always being on guard and watching. For that matter, Baldwin went on, the Negro problem is really the white problem. It is not the Negro who sets dark skin and kinky hair aside as something fearful, but the white. And the resolution of the racial agony in America requires a deep introspection on the part of the whites. They must discover themselves even more than the Negro.

This is true of all the juvenile delinquents, all the disturbed people, in the other America. One can put it baldly: their sickness is often a means of relating to a diseased environment. Until this is understood, the emotionally disturbed poor person will probably go on hurting himself until he becomes a police case. When he is finally given treatment, it will be at public expense, and it will be inferior to that given the rich. (In New Haven, according to Hollingshead and Redlich, the poor are five times more likely to get organic therapy—including shock treatment—rather than protracted, individual professional care.)

For that matter, some of the researchers in the field believe that sheer ignorance is one of the main causes of the high rate of disturbance among the poor. In the slum, conduct that would shock a middle-class neighborhood and lead to treatment is often considered normal. Even if someone is constantly and violently drunk, or beats his wife brutally, people will say of such a person, "Well, he's a little odd." Higher up on the class scale an individual with such a problem would probably realize that something was wrong (or his family would). He will have the knowledge and the money to get help.

One of the researchers in the field who puts great stress on the "basic universals" of the Freudian pattern (mother figure, father figure, siblings) looks upon this factor of ignorance as crucial. He is Dr. Lawrence Kubie. For Dr. Kubie, the fundamental determinants of mental health and illness are the same in every social class. But culture and income and education account for whether the individual will handle his problem; whether he understands himself as sick; whether he seeks help, and so on. This theory leaves the basic assumptions of traditional psychoanalysis intact, but, like any attempt to deal with the poor, it recognizes that something is different.

For the rich, then, and perhaps even for the better-paid worker, breakdowns, neurosis, and psychosis appear as illness and are increasingly treated as such. But the poor do not simply suffer these disturbances; they suffer them blindly. To them it does not appear that they are mentally sick; to them it appears that they are trapped in a fate. . . .

Out of all this, the research more and more suggests, there emerges the personality of poverty, the "typical citizen" of the other America.

This is how the Midtown researchers described the "low social economic status individual": they are "rigid, suspicious and have a fatalistic outlook on life. They do not plan ahead, a characteristic associated with their fatalism. They are prone to depression, have feelings of futility, lack of belongingness, friendliness, and a lack of trust in others." Translated into the statistics of the Midtown study, this means that the bottom of the society is three times more emotionally depressed than the top (36.2 percent for the low, 11.1 percent for the high).

A small point: America has a self-image of itself as a nation of joiners and doers. There are social clubs, charities, community drives, and the like. Churches have always played an important social role, often marking off the status of individuals. And yet this entire structure is a phenomenon of the middle class. Some time ago, a study in Franklin, Indiana, reported that the percentage of people in the bottom class who were without affiliations of any kind was eight times as great as the percentage in the high-income class.

Paradoxically, one of the factors that intensifies the social isolation of the poor is that America thinks of itself as a nation without social classes. As a result, there are few social or civic organizations that are separated on the basis of income and class. The "working-class culture" that sociologists have described in a country like England does not exist here, or at least it is much less of a reality. The poor person who might want to join an organization is afraid. Because he or she will have less education, less money, less competence to articulate ideas than anyone else in the group, they stay away.

Thus, studies of civilian-defense organizations during World War II showed that almost all the members were white-collar people. Indeed, though one might think that the poor would have more friends because they are packed densely together, there are studies that indicate that they are deprived in this regard, too. In one report, 47 percent of the lower-class women said that they had no friend or no intimate friend.

Such a life is lonely; it is also insecure. In New Haven, Hollingshead and Redlich could find only 19 percent of the people in the bottom class who thought that their jobs were safe. The Yale group described 45 percent of the poor as "inured," and found that their motto was "We take what the tide brings in."

This fatalism is not, however, confined to personal experience alone, to expectations about job and family. It literally permeates every aspect of an individual's life; it is a way of seeing reality. In a poll the Gallup organization did for *Look* magazine in 1959 (a projection of what people anticipated in the sixties), the relationship between social class and political pessimism was striking. The bottom group was much more likely to think that World War III was coming, that a recession was around the corner, that they would not take a vacation in the coming year. As one went up the income scale, the opinion of the world tended to brighten.

This pessimism is involved in a basic attitude of the poor: the fact that they do not postpone satisfactions, that they do not save. When pleasure is available, they tend to take it immediately. The smug theorist of the middle class would probably deplore this as showing a lack of traditional American virtues. Actually, it is the logical and natural pattern of behavior for one living in a part of American life without a future. It is, sad to say, a piece of realism, not of vice.

Related to this pattern of immediate gratification is a tendency on the part of the poor to "act out," to be less inhibited, and sometimes violent. There are some superficial observers who give this aspect of slum life a Rousseauistic twist. They find it a proof of the vitality, of the naturalness of the poor who are not constrained by the conventions of polite society. It would be hard to imagine a more wrongheaded impression. In the first place, this violence is the creature of that most artificial environment the slum. It is a product of human density and misery. And far from being an aspect of personality that is symptomatic of health, it is one more way in which the poor are driven to hurt themselves.

If one turns to the family life of the other America, there is an almost summary case of the dislocation and strains at the bottom of society.

In New Haven, for instance, Hollingshead and Redlich found that in Class V (the poor) some 41 percent of the children under seventeen lived in homes that had been disrupted by death, desertion, separation, or divorce. This, of course, has profound consequences for the personalities of the young people involved. (This would be an instance in which the traditional Freudian account of mental illness would be relevant to the other America. An unstable family structure, with a father or mother figure absent, would predict devastating personal consequences.)

Then, the types of family structure the Yale researchers found among the poor are important. Some 44 percent of the children lived in "nuclear families," which unite father, mother, and children. But 23 percent grew up in a "generation stem family," where different generations are thrown together, usually with a broken marriage or two. Under such circumstances there is the possibility of endless domestic conflict between the different generations (and this is exacerbated when the old people are immigrants with a foreign code). Another 18 percent came from broken homes where one or the other parent was absent. And 11 percent had experienced the death of a parent.

Another aspect of this family pattern is sexual. In New Haven the researchers found that it was fairly common for young girls in the slums to be pregnant before they were married. I saw a similar pattern in St. Louis. There, children had a sort of sophisticated ignorance about sexual matters at an early age. Jammed together in miserable housing, they knew the facts of sex from firsthand observation (though often what they saw was a brutalized and drunken form of sex). In this sense, they were much more sophisticated than the children in middle-class neighborhoods.

But the poor are never that really well informed. As noted before, along with a cynical version of the facts of life there went an enormous amount of misinformation. For instance, young girls were given systematic miseducation on the menstrual period. They were often frightened and guilt ridden about sex at the same time that they were sophisticated.

And finally, the family of the poor lives cheek and jowl with other families of the poor. The sounds of all the quarreling and fights of every other family are always present if there happens to be a moment of peace in one household. The radio and the television choices of the rest of the block are regularly in evidence. Life is lived in common, but not in community.

So it is that the adolescents roam the streets. For the young, there is no reason to stay around the house. The street is a moment of relief, relaxation, and excitement. The family, which should be a bulwark against the sheer physical misery of the poor, is overwhelmed by the environment. . . .

The emotional turmoil of the poor is . . . a form of protection against the turmoil of the society, a way of getting some attention and care in an uncaring world. Given this kind of "defense," it requires an enormous effort for these people to cross over into the great society.

Indeed, emotional upset is one of the main forms of the vicious circle of impoverishment. The structure of the society is hostile to these people: they do not have the right education or the right jobs, or perhaps there are no jobs to be had at all. Because of this, in a realistic adaptation to a socially perverse situation, the poor tend to become pessimistic and depressed; they seek immediate gratification instead of saving; they act out.

Once this mood, this unarticulated philosophy becomes a fact, society can change, the recession can end, and yet there is no motive for movement. The depression has become internalized. The middle class looks upon this process and sees "lazy" people who "just don't want to get ahead." People who are much too sensitive to demand of cripples that they run races ask of the poor that they get up and act just like everyone else in society.

The poor are not like everyone else. They are a different kind of people. They think and feel differently; they look upon a different America than the middle class looks upon. They, and not the quietly desperate clerk or the harried executive, are the main victims of this society's tension and conflict.

The Significance of
the Frontier in
American History

Frederick Jackson Turner

In a recent bulletin of the Superintendent of the Census for 1890 appear these significant words: "Up to and including 1880 the country had a frontier of settlement, but at present the unsettled area has been so broken into by isolated bodies of settlement that there can hardly be said to be a frontier line. In the discussion of its extent, its westward movement, etc., it can not, therefore, any longer have a place in the census reports." This brief official statement marks the closing of a great historic movement. Up to our own day American history has been in a large degree the history of the colonization of the Great West. The existence of an area of free land, its continuous recession, and the advance of American settlement westward, explain American development.

Behind institutions, behind constitutional forms and modifications, lie the vital forces that call these organs into life and shape them to meet changing conditions. The peculiarity of American institutions is, the fact that they have been compelled to adapt themselves to the changes of an expanding people—to the changes involved in crossing a continent, in winning a wilderness, and in developing at each area of this progress out of the primitive economic and political conditions of the frontier into the complexity of city life. Said Calhoun in 1817, "We are great, and rapidly—I was about to say fearfully—growing!" So saying, he touched the distinguishing feature of American life. All peoples show development; the germ theory

From *American Historical Association, Annual Report*, 1893 (Washington, D.C., 1894) pp. 199–227. Reprinted by permission of the American Historical Association.

of politics has been sufficiently emphasized. In the case of most nations, however, the development has occurred in a limited area; and if the nation has expanded, it has met other growing peoples whom it has conquered. But in the case of the United States we have a different phenomenon. Limiting our attention to the Atlantic coast, we have the familiar phenomenon of the evolution of institutions in a limited area, such as the rise of representative government; the differentiation of simple colonial governments into complex organs; the progress from primitive industrial society, without division of labor, up to manufacturing civilization. But we have in addition to this a recurrence of the process of evolution in each western area reached in the process of expansion. Thus American development has exhibited not merely advance along a single line, but a return to primitive conditions on a continually advancing frontier line, and a new development for that area. American social development has been continually beginning over again on the frontier. This perennial rebirth, this fluidity of American life, this expansion westward with its new opportunities, its continuous touch with the simplicity of primitive society, furnish the forces dominating American character. The true point of view in the history of this nation is not the Atlantic coast, it is the Great West. Even the slavery struggle, which is made so exclusive an object of attention by writers like Professor von Holst, occupies its important place in American history because of its relation to westward expansion.

In this advance, the frontier is the outer edge of the wave—the meeting point between savagery and civilization. Much has been written about the frontier from the point of view of border warfare and the chase, but as a field for the serious study of the economist and the historian it has been neglected.

The American frontier is sharply distinguished from the European frontier—a fortified boundary line running through dense populations. The most significant thing about the American frontier is, that it lies at the hither edge of free land. In the census reports it is treated as the margin of that settlement which has a density of two or more to the square mile. The term is an elastic one, and for our purposes does not need sharp definition. We shall consider the whole frontier belt, including the Indian country and the outer margin of the "settled area" of the census reports. This paper will make no attempt to treat the subject exhaustively; its aim is simply to call attention to the frontier as a fertile field for investigation, and to suggest some of the problems which arise in connection with it.

In the settlement of America we have to observe how European life entered the continent, and how America modified and developed that life and reacted on Europe. Our early history is the study of European germs developing in an American environment. Too exclusive attention has been paid by institutional students to the Germanic origins, too little to the American factors. The frontier is the line of most rapid and effective Americanization. The wilderness masters the colonist. It finds him a European in dress, industries, tools, modes of travel, and thought. It takes him from the railroad car and puts him in the birch canoe. It strips off the garments of civilization and arrays him in the hunting shirt and the moccasin. It puts him in the log cabin of the Cherokee and Iroquois and runs an Indian palisade around him. Before long he has gone to planting Indian corn and plowing with a sharp stick; he shouts the war cry and takes the scalp in orthodox Indian fashion. In short, at the frontier the environment is at first too strong for the man. He must accept the conditions which it furnishes, or perish, and so he fits himself into the Indian clearings and follows the Indian trails. Little by little he transforms the wilderness, but the outcome is not the old Europe, not simply the development of Germanic germs, any more than the first phenomenon was a case of reversion to the Germanic mark. The fact is, that here is a new product that is American. At first, the frontier was the Atlantic coast. It was the frontier of Europe in a very real sense. Moving westward, the frontier became more and more American. As successive terminal moraines result from successive glaciations, so each frontier leaves its traces behind it, and when it becomes a settled area the region still partakes of the frontier characteristics. Thus the advance of the frontier has meant a steady movement away from the influence of Europe, a steady growth of independence on American lines. And to study this advance, the men who grew up under these conditions, and the political, economic, and social results of it, is to study the really American part of our history.

In the course of the seventeenth century the frontier was advanced up the Atlantic river courses, just beyond the "fall line," and the tidewater region became the settled area. In the first half of the eighteenth century another advance occurred. Traders followed the Delaware and Shawnese Indians to the Ohio as early as the end of the first quarter of the century. Gov. Spotswood, of Virginia, made an expedition in 1714 across the Blue Ridge. The end of the first quarter of the century saw the advance of the Scotch-Irish and the Palatine Germans up the Shenandoah Valley into the western part of Virginia, and along the Piedmont region of the Carolinas. The Germans in New York pushed the frontier of settlement up the Mohawk to German Flats. In Pennsylvania the town of Bedford indicates the line of settlement. Settlements soon began on the New River, or the Great Kanawha, and on the sources of the Yadkin and French Broad. The King attempted to arrest the advance by his proclamation of 1763, forbidding settlements beyond the sources of the rivers flowing into the Atlantic; but in vain. In the period of the Revolution the frontier crossed the Alleghanies into Kentucky and Tennessee, and the upper waters of the Ohio were settled. When the first census was taken in 1790, the continuous settled area was bounded by a line which ran near the coast of Maine, and included New England except a portion of Vermont and New Hampshire, New York along the Hudson and up the Mohawk about Schenectady, eastern and southern Pennsylvania, Virginia well across the Shenandoah Valley, and

the Carolinas and eastern Georgia. Beyond this region of continuous settlement were the small settled areas of Kentucky and Tennessee, and the Ohio,
with the mountains intervening between them and the Atlantic area, thus
giving a new and important character to the frontier. The isolation of the
region increased its peculiarly American tendencies, and the need of transportation facilities to connect it with the East called out important schemes
of internal improvement, which will be noted farther on. The "West," as a
self-conscious section, began to evolve.

From decade to decade distinct advances of the frontier occurred. By
the census of 1820 the settled area included Ohio, southern Indiana and
Illinois, southeastern Missouri, and about one-half of Louisiana. This settled
area had surrounded Indian areas, and the management of these tribes became an object of political concern. The frontier region of the time lay along
the Great Lakes, where Astor's American Fur Company operated in the
Indian trade, and beyond the Mississippi, where Indian traders extended
their activity even to the Rocky Mountains; Florida also furnished frontier
conditions. The Mississippi River region was the scene of typical frontier
settlements.

The rising steam navigation on western waters, the opening of the Erie
Canal, and the westward extension of cotton culture added five frontier
states to the Union in this period. Grund, writing in 1836, declares:

It appears then that the universal disposition of Americans to emigrate to the
western wilderness, in order to enlarge their dominion over inanimate nature, is
the actual result of an expansive power which is inherent in them, and which by
continually agitating all classes of society is constantly throwing a large portion
of the whole population on the extreme confines of the State, in order to gain
space for its development. Hardly is a new State or Territory formed before the
same principle manifests itself again and gives rise to a further emigration; and so
is it destined to go on until a physical barrier must finally obstruct its progress.

In the middle of this century the line indicated by the present eastern
boundary of Indian Territory, Nebraska, and Kansas marked the frontier of
the Indian country. Minnesota and Wisconsin still exhibited frontier conditions, but the distinctive frontier of the period is found in California, where
the gold discoveries had sent a sudden tide of adventurous miners, and in
Oregon, and the settlements in Utah. As the frontier had leaped over the
Alleghanies, so now it skipped the Great Plains and the Rocky Mountains;
and in the same way that the advance of the frontiersmen beyond the
Alleghanies had caused the rise of important questions of transportation and
internal improvement, so now the settlers beyond the Rocky Mountains
needed means of communication with the East, and in the furnishing
of these arose the settlement of the Great Plains and the development of
still another kind of frontier life. Railroads, fostered by land grants, sent an
increasing tide of immigrants into the Far West. The United States Army

fought a series of Indian wars in Minnesota, Dakota, and the Indian Territory.

By 1880 the settled area had been pushed into northern Michigan, Wisconsin, and Minnesota, along Dakota rivers, and in the Black Hills region, and was ascending the rivers of Kansas and Nebraska. The development of mines in Colorado had drawn isolated frontier settlements into that region, and Montana and Idaho were receiving settlers. The frontier was found in these mining camps and the ranches of the Great Plains. The superintendent of the census for 1890 reports, as previously stated, that the settlements of the West lie so scattered over the region that there can no longer be said to be a frontier line.

In these successive frontiers we find natural boundary lines which have served to mark and to affect the characteristics of the frontiers, namely: the "fall line"; the Alleghany Mountains; the Mississippi; the Missouri where its direction approximates north and south; the line of the arid lands, approximately the ninety-ninth meridian; and the Rocky Mountains. The fall line marked the frontier of the seventeenth century; the Alleghanies that of the eighteenth; the Mississippi that of the first quarter of the nineteenth; the Missouri that of the middle of this century (omitting the California movement); and the belt of the Rocky Mountains and the arid tract, the present frontier. Each was won by a series of Indian wars.

At the Atlantic frontier one can study the germs of processes repeated at each successive frontier. We have the complex European life sharply precipitated by the wilderness into the simplicity of primitive conditions. The first frontier had to meet its Indian question, its question of the disposition of the public domain, of the means of intercourse with older settlements, of the extension of political organization, of religious and educational activity. And the settlement of these and similar questions for one frontier served as a guide for the next. The American student needs not to go to the "prim little townships of Sleswick" for illustrations of the law of continuity and development. For example, he may study the origin of our land policies in the colonial land policy; he may see how the system grew by adapting the statutes to the customs of the successive frontiers. He may see how the mining experience in the lead regions of Wisconsin, Illinois, and Iowa was applied to the mining laws of the Sierras, and how our Indian policy has been a series of experimentations on successive frontiers. Each tier of new States has found in the older ones material for its constitutions. Each frontier has made similar contributions to American character, as will be discussed farther on.

But with all these similarities there are essential differences, due to the place element and the time element. It is evident that the farming frontier of the Mississippi Valley presents different conditions from the mining frontier of the Rocky Mountains. The frontier reached by the Pacific Railroad, surveyed into rectangles, guarded by the United States Army, and recruited by the daily immigrant ship, moves forward at a swifter pace and in a different way than the frontier reached by the birch canoe or the pack horse. The geologist traces patiently the shores of ancient seas, maps their areas, and compares the older and the newer. It would be a work worth the historian's labors to mark these various frontiers and in detail compare one with another. Not only would there result a more adequate conception of American development and characteristics, but invaluable additions would be made to the history of society.

Loria, the Italian economist, has urged the study of colonial life as an aid in understanding the stages of European development, affirming that colonial settlement is for economic science what the mountain is for geology, bringing to light primitive stratifications. "America," he says, "has the key to the historical enigma which Europe has sought for centuries in vain, and the land which has no history reveals luminously the course of universal history." There is much truth in this. The United States lies like a huge page in the history of society. Line by line as we read this continental page from West to East we find the record of social evolution. It begins with the Indian and the hunter; it goes on to tell of the disintegration of savagery by the entrance of the trader, the pathfinder of civilization; we read the annals of the pastoral stage in ranch life; the exploitation of the soil by the raising of unrotated crops of corn and wheat in sparsely settled farming communities; the intensive culture of the denser farm settlement; and finally the manufacturing organization with city and factory system. This page is familiar to the student of census statistics, but how little of it has been used by our historians. Particularly in eastern States this page is a palimpsest. What is now a manufacturing State was in an earlier decade an area of intensive farming. Earlier yet it had been a wheat area, and still earlier the "range" had attracted the cattle-herder. Thus Wisconsin, now developing manufacture, is a State with varied agricultural interests. But earlier it was given over to almost exclusive grain-raising, like North Dakota at the present time.

Each of these areas has had an influence in our economic and political history; the evolution of each into a higher stage has worked political transformations. But what constitutional historian has made any adequate attempt to interpret political facts by the light of these social areas and changes?

The Atlantic frontier was compounded of fisherman, fur-trader, miner, cattle-raiser, and farmer. Excepting the fisherman, each type of industry was on the march toward the West, impelled by an irresistible attraction. Each passed in successive waves across the continent. Stand at Cumberland Gap and watch the procession of civilization, marching single file—the buffalo following the trail to the salt springs, the Indian, the fur-trader and hunter, the cattle-raiser, the pioneer farmer—and the frontier has passed by. Stand at South Pass in the Rockies a century later and see the same procession with wider intervals between. The unequal rate of advance compels us to distinguish the frontier into the trader's frontier, the rancher's frontier, or the miner's frontier, and the farmer's frontier. When the mines and the cow pens were still near the fall line the traders' pack trains were tinkling across the Alleghanies, and the French on the Great Lakes were fortifying their posts, alarmed by the British trader's birch canoe. When the trappers scaled the Rockies, the farmer was still near the mouth of the Missouri.

Why was it that the Indian trader passed so rapidly across the continent? What effects followed from the trader's frontier? The trade was coeval with American discovery. The Norsemen, Vespuccius, Verrazano, Hudson, John Smith, all trafficked for furs. The Plymouth pilgrims settled in Indian cornfields, and their first return cargo was of beaver and lumber. The records of the various New England colonies show how steadily exploration was carried into the wilderness by this trade. What is true for New England is, as would be expected, even plainer for the rest of the colonies. All along the coast from Maine to Georgia the Indian trade opened up the river courses. Steadily the trader passed westward, utilizing the older lines of French trade. The Ohio, the Great Lakes, the Mississippi, the Missouri, and the Platte, the lines of western advance, were ascended by traders. They found the passes in the Rocky Mountains and guided Lewis and Clark, Frémont, and Bidwell. The explanation of the rapidity of this advance is connected with the effects of the trader on the Indian. The trading post left the unarmed tribes at the mercy of those that had purchased fire-arms—a truth which the Iroquois Indians wrote in blood, and so the remote and unvisited tribes gave eager welcome to the trader. "The savages," wrote La Salle, "take better care of us French than of their own children; from us only can they get guns and goods." This accounts for the trader's power and the rapidity of his advance. Thus the disintegrating forces of civilization entered the wilderness. Every river valley and Indian trail became a fissure in Indian society, and so that society became honeycombed. Long before the pioneer farmer appeared on the scene, primitive Indian life had passed away. The farmers met Indians armed with guns. The trading frontier, while steadily undermining Indian power by making the tribes ultimately dependent on the whites, yet, through its sale of guns, gave to the Indian increased power of resistance to the farming frontier. French colonization was dominated by its trading frontier; English colonization by its farming frontier. There was an antagonism between the two frontiers as between the two nations. Said Duquesne to the Iroquois,

Are you ignorant of the difference between the king of England and the king of France? Go see the forts that our king has established and you will see that you can still hunt under their very walls. They have been placed for your advantage in places which you frequent. The English, on the contrary, are no sooner in possession of a place than the game is driven away. The forest falls before them as they advance, and the soil is laid bare so that you can scarce find the wherewithal to erect a shelter for the night.

And yet, in spite of this opposition of the interests of the trader and the farmer, the Indian trade pioneered the way for civilization. The buffalo trail became the Indian trail, and this became the trader's "trace"; the trails widened into roads, and the roads into turnpikes, and these in turn were transformed into railroads. The same origin can be shown for the railroads of the South, the Far West, and the Dominion of Canada. The trading posts reached by these trails were on the sites of Indian villages which had been placed in positions suggested by nature; and these trading posts, situated so as to command the water systems of the country, have grown into such cities as Albany, Pittsburgh, Detroit, Chicago, St. Louis, Council Bluffs, and Kansas City. Thus civilization in America has followed the arteries made by geology, pouring an ever richer tide through them, until at last the slender paths of aboriginal intercourse have been broadened and interwoven into the complex mazes of modern commercial lines; the wilderness has been interpenetrated by lines of civilization growing ever more numerous. It is like the steady growth of a complex nervous system for the originally simple, inert continent. If one would understand why we are to-day one nation, rather than a collection of isolated states, he must study this economic and social consolidation of the country. In this progress from savage conditions lie topics for the evolutionist.

The effect of the Indian frontier as a consolidating agent in our history is important. From the close of the seventeenth century various intercolonial congresses have been called to treat with Indians and establish common measures of defense. Particularism was strongest in colonies with no Indian frontier. This frontier stretched along the western border like a cord of union. The Indian was a common danger, demanding united action. Most celebrated of these conferences was the Albany congress of 1754, called to treat with the Six Nations, and to consider plans of union. Even a cursory reading of the plan proposed by the congress reveals the importance of the frontier. The powers of the general council and the officers were, chiefly, the determination of peace and war with the Indians, the regulation of Indian trade, the purchase of Indian lands, and the creation and government of new settlements as a security against the Indians. It is evident that the unifying tendencies of the Revolutionary period were facilitated by the previous coöperation in the regulation of the frontier. In this connection may be mentioned the importance of the frontier, from that day to this, as a military training school, keeping alive the power of resistance to aggression, and developing the stalwart and rugged qualities of the frontiersman.

It would not be possible in the limits of this paper to trace the other frontiers across the continent. Travelers of the eighteenth century found the "cowpens" among the canebrakes and peavine pastures of the South, and the "cow drivers" took their droves to Charleston, Philadelphia, and New York. Travelers at the close of the War of 1812 met droves of more than a thousand cattle and swine from the interior of Ohio going to Pennsylvania to fatten for the Philadelphia market. The ranges of the Great Plains, with ranch and cowboy and nomadic life, are things of yesterday and of to-day. The experience of the Carolina cowpens guided the ranchers of Texas. One element favoring the rapid extension of the rancher's frontier is the fact that in a remote country lacking transportation facilities the product must be in small bulk, or must be able to transport itself, and the cattle raiser could easily drive his product to market. The effect of these great ranches on the subsequent agrarian history of the localities in which they existed should be studied.

The maps of the census reports show an uneven advance of the farmer's frontier, with tongues of settlement pushed forward and with indentations of wilderness. In part this is due to Indian resistance, in part to the location of river valleys and passes, in part to the unequal force of the centers of frontier attraction. Among the important centers of attraction may be mentioned the following: fertile and favorably situated soils, salt springs, mines, and army posts.

The frontier army post, serving to protect the settlers from the Indians, has also acted as a wedge to open the Indian country, and has been a nucleus for settlement. In this connection mention should also be made of the government military and exploring expeditions in determining the lines of settlement. But all the more important expeditions were greatly indebted to the earliest pathmakers, the Indian guides, the traders and trappers, and the French voyageurs, who were inevitable parts of governmental expeditions from the days of Lewis and Clark. Each expedition was an epitome of the previous factors in western advance.

In an interesting monograph, Victor Hehn has traced the effect of salt upon early European development, and has pointed out how it affected the lines of settlement and the form of administration. A similar study might be made for the salt springs of the United States. The early settlers were tied to the coast by the need of salt, without which they could not preserve their meats or live in comfort. Writing in 1752, Bishop Spangenburg says of a colony for which he was seeking lands in North Carolina,

They will require salt & other necessaries which they can neither manufacture nor raise. Either they must go to Charleston, which is 300 miles distant . . . . Or else they must go to Boling's Point in Va. on a branch of the James & is also 300 miles from here . . . . Or else they must go down the Roanoke—I know not how many miles—where salt is brought up from the Cape Fear.

This may serve as a typical illustration. An annual pilgrimage to the coast for salt thus became essential. Taking flocks or furs and ginseng root, the early settlers sent their pack trains after seeding time each year to the coast. This proved to be an important educational influence, since it was almost the only way in which the pioneer learned what was going on in the East. But when discovery was made of the salt springs of the Kanawha, and the

Holston, and Kentucky, and central New York, the West began to be freed from dependence on the coast. It was in part the effect of finding these salt springs that enabled settlement to cross the mountains.

From the time the mountains rose between the pioneer and the sea-board, a new order of Americanism arose. The West and the East began to get out of touch of each other. The settlements from the sea to the mountains kept connection with the rear and had a certain solidarity. But the over-mountain men grew more and more independent. The East took a narrow view of American advance, and nearly lost these men. Kentucky and Tennessee history bears abundant witness to the truth of this statement. The East began to try to hedge and limit westward expansion. Though Webster could declare that there were no Alleghanies in his politics, yet in politics in general they were a very solid factor.

The exploitation of the beasts took hunter and trader to the west, the exploitation of the grasses took the rancher west, and the exploitation of the virgin soil of the river valleys and prairies attracted the farmer. Good soils have been the most continuous attraction to the farmer's frontier. The land hunger of the Virginians drew them down the rivers into Carolina, in early colonial days; the search for soils took the Massachusetts men to Pennsylvania and to New York. As the eastern lands were taken up migration flowed across them to the west. Daniel Boone, the great backwoodsman, who combined the occupations of hunter, trader, cattle-raiser, farmer, and surveyor—learning, probably from the traders, of the fertility of the lands of the upper Yadkin, where the traders were wont to rest as they took their way to the Indians, left his Pennsylvania home with his father, and passed down the Great Valley road to that stream. Learning from a trader of the game and rich pastures of Kentucky, he pioneered the way for the farmers to that region. Thence he passed to the frontier of Missouri, where his settlement was long a landmark on the frontier. Here again he helped to open the way for civilization, finding salt licks, and trails, and land. His son was among the earliest trappers in the passes of the Rocky Mountains, and his party are said to have been the first to camp on the present site of Denver. His grandson, Col. A. J. Boone, of Colorado, was a power among the Indians of the Rocky Mountains, and was appointed an agent by the government. Kit Carson's mother was a Boone. Thus this family epitomizes the back-woodsman's advance across the continent.

The farmer's advance came in a distinct series of waves. In Peck's New Guide to the West, published in Boston in 1837, occurs this suggestive passage:

Generally, in all the western settlements, three classes, like the waves of the ocean, have rolled one after the other. First comes the pioneer, who depends for the subsistence of his family chiefly upon the natural growth of vegetation, called the "range," and the proceeds of hunting. His implements of agriculture are rude, chiefly of his own make, and his efforts directed mainly in a crop of corn and a "truck patch." The last is a rude garden for growing cabbage, beans, corn for roasting ears, cucumbers, and potatoes. A log cabin and, occasionally, a stable and corn-crib, and a field of a dozen acres, the timber girdled or "deadened," and fenced, are enough for his occupancy. It is quite immaterial whether he ever becomes the owner of the soil. He is the occupant for the time being, pays no rent, and feels as independent as the "lord of the manor." With a horse, cow, and one or two breeders of swine, he strikes into the woods with his family, and becomes the founder of a new county, or perhaps state. He builds his cabin, gathers around him a few other families of similar tastes and habits, and occupies till the range is somewhat subdued, and hunting a little precarious, or, which is more frequently the case, till the neighbors crowd around, roads, bridges, and fields annoy him, and he lacks elbow room. The preëmption law enables him to dispose of his cabin and cornfield to the next class of emigrants; and, to employ his own figures, he "breaks for the high timber," "clears out for the New Purchase," or migrates to Arkansas or Texas, to work the same process over.

The next class of emigrants purchase the lands, add field to field, clear out the roads, throw rough bridges over the streams, put up hewn log houses with glass windows and brick or stone chimneys, occasionally plant orchards, build mills, schoolhouses, court-houses, etc., and exhibit the picture and forms of plain, frugal, civilized life.

Another wave rolls on. The men of capital and enterprise come. The settler is ready to sell out and take the advantage of the rise in property, push farther into the interior and become, himself, a man of capital and enterprise in turn. The small village rises to a spacious town or city; substantial edifices of brick, extensive fields, orchards, gardens, colleges, and churches are seen. Broadcloths, silks, leghorns, crapes, and all the refinements, luxuries, elegancies, frivolities, and fashions are in vogue. Thus wave after wave is rolling westward; the real Eldorado is still farther on.

A portion of the two first classes remain stationary amidst the general movement, improve their habits and condition, and rise in the scale of society.

The writer has traveled much amongst the first class, the real pioneers. He has lived many years in connection with the second grade; and now the third wave is sweeping over large districts of Indiana, Illinois, and Missouri. Migration has become almost a habit in the West. Hundreds of men can be found, not over 50 years of age, who have settled for the fourth, fifth, or sixth time on a new spot. To sell out and remove only a few hundred miles makes up a portion of the variety of backwoods life and manners.

Omitting those of the pioneer farmers who move from the love of adventure, the advance of the more steady farmer is easy to understand. Obviously the immigrant was attracted by the cheap lands of the frontier, and even the native farmer felt their influence strongly. Year by year the farmers who lived on soil whose returns were diminished by unrotated crops were offered the virgin soil of the frontier at nominal prices. Their growing families demanded more lands, and these were dear. The competition of the unexhausted, cheap, and easily tilled prairie lands compelled the farmer either to go west and continue the exhaustion of the soil on a new frontier, or to adopt intensive culture. Thus the census of 1890 shows, in the Northwest, many counties in which there is an absolute or a relative decrease of population. These States have been sending farmers to advance the frontier on the plains, and have themselves begun to turn to intensive farming and to manufacture. A decade before this, Ohio had shown the same transition stage. Thus the demand for land and the love of wilderness freedom drew the frontier ever onward.

Having now roughly outlined the various kinds of frontiers, and their modes of advance, chiefly from the point of view of the frontier itself, we may next inquire what were the influences on the East and on the Old World. A rapid enumeration of some of the more noteworthy effects is all that I have time for.

First, we note that the frontier promoted the formation of a composite nationality for the American people. The coast was preponderantly English, but the later tides of continental immigration flowed across to the free lands. This was the case from the early colonial days. The Scotch-Irish and the Palatine Germans, or "Pennsylvania Dutch," furnished the dominant element in the stock of the colonial frontier. With these peoples were also the freed indented servants, or redemptioners, who at the expiration of their time of service passed to the frontier. Governor Spotswood of Virginia writes in 1717, "The inhabitants of our frontiers are composed generally of such as have been transported hither as servants, and, being out of their time, settle themselves where land is to be taken up and that will produce the necessarys of life with little labour." Very generally these redemptioners were of non-English stock. In the crucible of the frontier the immigrants were Americanized, liberated, and fused into a mixed race, English in neither nationality nor characteristics. The process has gone on from the early days to our own. Burke and other writers in the middle of the eighteenth century believed that Pennsylvania was "threatened with the danger of being wholly foreign in language, manners, and perhaps even inclinations." The German and Scotch-Irish elements in the frontier of the South were only less great. In the middle of the present century the German element in Wisconsin was already so considerable that leading publicists looked to the creation of a German state out of the commonwealth by concentrating their colonization. Such examples teach us to beware of misinterpreting the fact that there is a common English speech in America into a belief that the stock is also English.

In another way the advance of the frontier decreased our dependence on England. The coast, particularly of the South, lacked diversified industries, and was dependent on England for the bulk of its supplies. In the South there was even a dependence on the Northern colonies for articles of food. Governor Glenn, of South Carolina, writes in the middle of the eighteenth century: "Our trade with New York and Philadelphia was of this sort, draining us of all the little money and bills we could gather from other places for their bread, flour, beer, hams, bacon, and other things of their produce, all which, except beer, our new townships begin to supply us with, which are settled with very industrious and thriving Germans. This no doubt diminishes the number of shipping and the appearance of our trade, but it is far from being a detriment to us." Before long the frontier created a demand for merchants. As it retreated from the coast it became less and less possible for England to bring her supplies directly to the consumer's wharfs, and carry away staple crops, and staple crops began to give way to diversified agriculture for a time. The effect of this phase of the frontier action upon the northern section is perceived when we realize how the advance of the frontier aroused seaboard cities like Boston, New York, and Baltimore, to engage in rivalry for what Washington called "the extensive and valuable trade of a rising empire."

The legislation which most developed the powers of the national government, and played the largest part in its activity, was conditioned on the frontier. Writers have discussed the subjects of tariff, land, and internal improvement, as subsidiary to the slavery question. But when American history comes to be rightly viewed it will be seen that the slavery question is an incident. In the period from the end of the first half of the present century to the close of the Civil War slavery rose to primary, but far from exclusive, importance. But this does not justify Dr. von Holst (to take an example) in treating our constitutional history in its formative period down to 1828 in a single volume, giving six volumes chiefly to the history of slavery from 1828 to 1861, under the title "Constitutional History of the United States." The growth of nationalism and the evolution of American political institutions were dependent on the advance of the frontier. Even so recent a writer as Rhodes, in his "History of the United States since the Compromise of 1850," has treated the legislation called out by the western advance as incidental to the slavery struggle.

This is a wrong perspective. The pioneer needed the goods of the coast, and so the grand series of internal improvement and railroad legislation began, with potent nationalizing effects. Over internal improvements occurred great debates, in which grave constitutional questions were discussed. Sectional groupings appear in the votes, profoundly significant for the historian. Loose construction increased as the nation marched westward. But the West was not content with bringing the farm to the factory. Under the lead of Clay—"Harry of the West"—protective tariffs were passed, with the cry of bringing the factory to the farm. The disposition of the public lands was a third important subject of national legislation influenced by the frontier.

The public domain has been a force of profound importance in the nationalization and development of the government. The effects of the struggle of the landed and the landless States, and of the Ordinance of 1787, need no discussion. Administratively the frontier called out some of the highest and most vitalizing activities of the general government. The purchase of Louisiana was perhaps the constitutional turning point in the history of the Republic, inasmuch as it afforded both a new area for national legislation and the occasion of the downfall of the policy of strict construction. But the purchase of Louisiana was called out by frontier needs and demands. As frontier States accrued to the Union the national power grew. In a speech on the dedication of the Calhoun monument Mr. Lamar explained: "In 1789 the States were the creators of the Federal Government; in 1861 the Federal Government was the creator of a large majority of the States."

When we consider the public domain from the point of view of the sale and disposal of the public lands we are again brought face to face with the frontier. The policy of the United States in dealing with its lands is in sharp contrast with the European system of scientific administration. Efforts to make this domain a source of revenue, and to withhold it from emigrants in order that settlement might be compact, were in vain. The jealousy and the fears of the East were powerless in the face of the demands of the frontiersmen. John Quincy Adams was obliged to confess: "My own system of administration, which was to make the national domain the inexhaustible fund for progressive and unceasing internal improvement, has failed." The reason is obvious; a system of administration was not what the West demanded; it wanted land. Adams states the situation as follows:

The slaveholders of the South have bought the coöperation of the western country by the bribe of the western lands, abandoning to the new Western States their own proportion of the public property and aiding them in the design of grasping all the lands into their own hands. Thomas H. Benton was the author of this system, which he brought forward as a substitute for the American system of Mr. Clay, and to supplant him as the leading statesman of the West. Mr. Clay, by his tariff compromise with Mr. Calhoun, abandoned his own American system. At the same time he brought forward a plan for distributing among all the States of the Union the proceeds of the sales of the public lands. His bill for that purpose passed both Houses of Congress, but was vetoed by President Jackson, who, in his annual message of December, 1832, formally recommended that all public lands should be gratuitously given away to individual adventurers and to the States in which the lands are situated.

"No subject," said Henry Clay, "which has presented itself to the present, or perhaps any preceding, Congress, is of greater magnitude than that of the public lands." When we consider the far-reaching effects of the government's land policy upon political, economic, and social aspects of American life, we are disposed to agree with him. But this legislation was framed under frontier influences, and under the lead of Western statesmen like Benton and Jackson. Said Senator Scott of Indiana in 1841: "I consider the preëmption law merely declaratory of the custom or common law of the settlers."

It is safe to say that the legislation with regard to land, tariff, and internal improvements—the American system of the nationalizing Whig party—was conditioned on frontier ideas and needs. But it was not merely in legislative action that the frontier worked against the sectionalism of the coast. The economic and social characteristics of the frontier worked against sectionalism. The men of the frontier had closer resemblances to the Middle region than to either of the other sections. Pennsylvania had been the seed-plot of frontier emigration, and, although she passed on her settlers along the Great Valley into the west of Virginia and the Carolinas, yet the industrial society of these Southern frontiersmen was always more like that of the Middle region than like that of the tide-water portion of the South, which later came to spread its industrial type throughout the South.

The Middle region, entered by New York harbor, was an open door to all Europe. The tide-water part of the South represented typical Englishmen, modified by a warm climate and servile labor, and living in baronial fashion on great plantations; New England stood for a special English movement—Puritanism. The Middle region was less English than the other sections. It had a wide mixture of nationalities, a varied society, the mixed town and county system of local government, a varied economic life, many religious sects. In short, it was a region mediating between New England and the South, and the East and the West. It represented that composite nationality which the contemporary United States exhibits, that juxtaposition of non-English groups, occupying a valley or a little settlement, and presenting reflections of the map of Europe in their variety. It was democratic and nonsectional, if not national; "easy, tolerant, and contented"; rooted strongly in material prosperity. It was typical of the modern United States. It was least sectional, not only because it lay between North and South, but also because with no barriers to shut out its frontiers from its settled region, and with a system of connecting waterways, the Middle region mediated between East and West as well as between North and South. Thus it became the typically American region. Even the New Englander, who was shut out from the frontier by the Middle region, tarrying in New York or Pennsylvania on his westward march, lost the acuteness of his sectionalism on the way.

The spread of cotton culture into the interior of the South finally broke down the contrast between the "tide-water" region and the rest of the State, and based Southern interests on slavery. Before this process revealed its results the western portion of the South, which was akin to Pennsylvania in stock, society, and industry, showed tendencies to fall away from the faith of the fathers into internal improvement legislation and nationalism. In the Virginia convention of 1829–30, called to revise the constitution, Mr. Leigh, of Chesterfield, one of the tide-water counties, declared:

One of the main causes of discontent which led to this convention, that which had the strongest influence in overcoming our veneration for the work of our fathers, which taught us to contemn the sentiments of Henry and Mason and Pendleton, which weaned us from our reverence for the constituted authorities of the State, was an overweening passion for internal improvement. I say this with perfect knowledge, for it has been avowed to me by gentlemen from the West over and over again. And let me tell the gentleman from Albemarle (Mr. Gordon) that it has been another principal object of those who set this ball of revolution in motion, to overturn the doctrine of State rights, of which Virginia has been the very pillar, and to remove the barrier she has interposed to the interference of the Federal Government in that same work of internal improvement, by so reorganizing the legislature that Virginia, too, may be hitched to the Federal car.

It was this nationalizing tendency of the West that transformed the democracy of Jefferson into the national republicanism of Monroe and the democracy of Andrew Jackson. The West of the War of 1812, the West of Clay, and Benton and Harrison, and Andrew Jackson, shut off by the Middle States and the mountains from the coast sections, had a solidarity of its own with national tendencies. On the tide of the Father of Waters, North and South met and mingled into a nation. Interstate migration went steadily on —a process of cross-fertilization of ideas and institutions. The fierce struggle of the sections over slavery on the western frontier does not diminish the truth of this statement; it proves the truth of it. Slavery was a sectional trait that would not down, but in the West it could not remain sectional. It was the greatest of frontiersmen who declared: "I believe this Government can not endure permanently half slave and half free. It will become all of one thing or all of the other." Nothing works for nationalism like intercourse within the nation. Mobility of population is death to localism, and the western frontier worked irresistibly in unsettling population. The effect reached back from the frontier and affected profoundly the Atlantic coast and even the Old World.

But the most important effect of the frontier has been in the promotion of democracy here and in Europe. As has been indicated, the frontier is productive of individualism. Complex society is precipitated by the wilderness into a kind of primitive organization based on the family. The tendency is anti-social. It produces antipathy to control, and particularly to any direct control. The tax-gatherer is viewed as a representative of oppression. Prof. Osgood, in an able article, has pointed out that the frontier conditions prevalent in the colonies are important factors in the explanation of the American Revolution, where individual liberty was sometimes confused with absence of all effective government. The same conditions aid in explaining the difficulty of instituting a strong government in the period of the confederacy. The frontier individualism has from the beginning promoted democracy.

The frontier States that came into the Union in the first quarter of a century of its existence came in with democratic suffrage provisions, and had reactive effects of the highest importance upon the older States whose peoples were being attracted there. An extension of the franchise became essential. It was *western* New York that forced an extension of suffrage in the constitutional convention of that State in 1821; and it was *western* Virginia that compelled the tide-water region to put a more liberal suffrage provision in the constitution framed in 1830, and to give to the frontier region a more nearly proportionate representation with the tide-water aristocracy. The rise of democracy as an effective force in the nation came in with western preponderance under Jackson and William Henry Harrison, and it meant the triumph of the frontier—with all of its good and with all of its evil elements. An interesting illustration of the tone of frontier democracy in 1830 comes from the same debates in the Virginia convention already referred to. A representative from western Virginia declared:

> But, sir, it is not the increase of population in the West which this gentleman ought to fear. It is the energy which the mountain breeze and western habits impart to those emigrants. They are regenerated, politically I mean, sir. They soon become working politicians; and the difference, sir, between a talking and a working politician is immense. The Old Dominion has long been celebrated for producing great orators; the ablest metaphysicians in policy; men that can split hairs in all abstruse questions of political economy. But at home, or when they return from Congress, they have negroes to fan them asleep. But a Pennsylvania, a New York, an Ohio, or a western Virginia statesman, though far inferior in logic, metaphysics, and rhetoric to an old Virginia statesman, has this advantage, that when he returns home he takes off his coat and takes hold of the plow. This gives him bone and muscle, sir, and preserves his republican principles pure and uncontaminated.

So long as free land exists, the opportunity for a competency exists, and economic power secures political power. But the democracy born of free land, strong in selfishness and individualism, intolerant of administrative experience and education, and pressing individual liberty beyond its proper bounds, has its dangers as well as its benefits. Individualism in America has allowed a laxity in regard to governmental affairs which has rendered possible the spoils system and all the manifest evils that follow from the lack of a highly developed civic spirit. In this connection may be noted also the influence of frontier conditions in permitting lax business honor, inflated paper currency and wild-cat banking. The colonial and revolutionary frontier was the region whence emanated many of the worst forms of an evil currency. The West in the War of 1812 repeated the phenomenon on the frontier of that day, while the speculation and wild-cat banking of the period of the crisis of 1837 occurred on the new frontier belt of the next tier of States. Thus each one of the periods of lax financial integrity coincides with periods when a new set of frontier communities had arisen, and coincides in area with these successive frontiers, for the most part. The recent Populist agitation is a case in point. Many a State that now declines any connection with the tenets of the Populists, itself adhered to such ideas in an earlier stage of the development of the State. A primitive society can hardly be expected to show the intelligent appreciation of the complexity of business interests in a developed society. The continual recurrence of these areas of paper-money agitation is another evidence that the frontier can be isolated and studied as a factor in American history of the highest importance.

The East has always feared the result of an unregulated advance of the frontier, and has tried to check and guide it. The English authorities would have checked settlement at the headwaters of the Atlantic tributaries and allowed the "savages to enjoy their deserts in quiet lest the peltry trade should decrease." This called out Burke's splendid protest:

> If you stopped your grants, what would be the consequence? The people would occupy without grants. They have already so occupied in many places. You can not station garrisons in every part of these deserts. If you drive the people from one place, they will carry on their annual tillage and remove with their flocks and herds to another. Many of the people in the back settlements are already little attached to particular situations. Already they have topped the Appalachian Mountains. From thence they behold before them an immense plain, one vast, rich, level meadow; a square of five hundred miles. Over this they would wander without a possibility of restraint; they would change their manners with their habits of life; would soon forget a government by which they were disowned; would become hordes of English Tartars; and, pouring down upon your unfortified frontiers a fierce and irresistible cavalry, become masters of your governors and your counselers, your collectors and comptrollers, and of all the slaves that adhered to them. Such would, and in no long time must, be the effect of attempting to forbid as a crime and to suppress as an evil the command and blessing of Providence, "Increase and multiply." Such would be the happy result of an endeavor to keep as a lair of wild beasts that earth which God, by an express charter, has given to the children of men.

But the English Government was not alone in its desire to limit the advance of the frontier and guide its destinies. Tidewater Virginia and South Carolina gerrymandered those colonies to insure the dominance of the coast in their legislatures. Washington desired to settle a State at a time in the Northwest; Jefferson would reserve from settlement the territory of his Louisiana Purchase north of the thirty-second parallel, in order to offer it to the Indians in exchange for their settlements east of the Mississippi. "When we shall be full on this side," he writes, "we may lay off a range of States on the western bank from the head to the mouth, and so range after range, advancing compactly as we multiply." Madison went so far as to argue to the French minister that the United States had no interest in seeing population extend itself on the right bank of the Mississippi, but should rather fear it. When the Oregon question was under debate, in 1824, Smyth, of Virginia, would draw an unchangeable line for the limits of the United States at the outer limit of two tiers of States beyond the Mississippi, complaining that the seaboard States were being drained of the flower of their population by the bringing of too much land into market. Even Thomas Benton, the man of widest views of the destiny of the West, at this stage of his career declared that along the ridge of the rocky mountains "the western limits of the Republic should be drawn, and the statue of the fabled god Terminus should be raised upon its highest peak, never to be thrown down." But the attempts to limit the boundaries, to restrict land sales and settlement, and to deprive the West of its share of political power were all in vain. Steadily the frontier of settlement advanced and carried with it individualism, democracy, and nationalism, and powerfully affected the East and the Old World.

The most effective efforts of the East to regulate the frontier came through its educational and religious activity, exerted by interstate migration and by organized societies. Speaking in 1835, Dr. Lyman Beecher declared: "It is equally plain that the religious and political destiny of our nation is to be decided in the West," and he pointed out that the population of the West

is assembled from all the States of the Union and from all the nations of Europe, and is rushing in like the waters of the flood, demanding for its moral preservation the immediate and universal action of those institutions which discipline the mind and arm the conscience and the heart. And so various are the opinions and habits, and so recent and imperfect is the acquaintance, and so sparse are the settlements of the West, that no homogeneous public sentiment can be formed to legislate immediately into being the requisite institutions. And yet they are all needed immediately in their utmost perfection and power. A nation is being "born in a day." . . . But what will become of the West if her prosperity rushes up to such a majesty of power, while those great institutions linger which are necessary to form the mind and the conscience and the heart of that vast world. It must not be permitted. . . . Let no man at the East quiet himself and dream of liberty, whatever may become of the West. . . . Her destiny is our destiny.

With the appeal to the conscience of New England, he adds appeals to her fears lest other religious sects anticipate her own. The New England preacher and school-teacher left their mark on the West. The dread of Western emancipation from New England's political and economic control was paralleled by her fears lest the West cut loose from her religion. Commenting in 1850 on reports that settlement was rapidly extending northward in Wisconsin, the editor of the *Home Missionary* writes: "We scarcely know whether to rejoice or mourn over this extension of our settlements. While we sympathize in whatever tends to increase the physical resources and prosperity of our country, we can not forget that with all these dispersions into remote and still remoter corners of the land the supply of the means of grace is becoming relatively less and less." Acting in accordance with such ideas, home missions were established and Western colleges were erected. As seaboard cities like Philadelphia, New York, and Baltimore strove for the mastery of Western trade, so the various denominations strove for the possession of the West. Thus an intellectual stream from New England sources fertilized the West. Other sections sent their missionaries; but the real struggle was between sects. The contest for power and the expansive tendency furnished to the various sects by the existence of a moving frontier must have had important results on the character of religious organization in the United States. The multiplication of rival churches in the little frontier towns had deep and lasting social effects. The religious aspects of the frontier make a chapter in our history which needs study.

From the conditions of frontier life came intellectual traits of profound importance. The works of travelers along each frontier from colonial days onward describe certain common traits, and these traits have, while softening down, still persisted as survivals in the place of their origin, even when a higher social organization succeeded. The result is that to the frontier the American intellect owes its striking characteristics. That coarseness and strength combined with acuteness and inquisitiveness; that practical, inventive turn of mind, quick to find expedients; that masterful grasp of material things, lacking in the artistic but powerful to effect great ends; that restless, nervous energy; that dominant individualism, working for good and for evil, and withal that buoyancy and exuberance which comes with freedom—these are traits of the frontier, or traits called out elsewhere because of the existence of the frontier. Since the days when the fleet of Columbus sailed into the waters of the New World, America has been another name for opportunity, and the people of the United States have taken their tone from the incessant expansion which has not only been open but has even been forced upon them. He would be a rash prophet who should assert that the expansive character of American life has now entirely ceased. Movement has been its dominant fact, and, unless this training has no effect upon a people, the American energy will continually demand a wider field for its exercise. But never again will such gifts of free land offer themselves. For a moment, at the frontier, the bonds of custom are broken and unrestraint is triumphant. There is not *tabula rasa*. The stubborn American environment is there with its imperious summons to accept its conditions; the inherited ways of doing things are also there; and yet, in spite of environment, and in spite of custom, each frontier did indeed furnish a new field of opportunity, a gate of escape from the bondage of the past; and freshness, and confidence, and scorn of older society, impatience of its restraints and its ideas, and indifference to its lessons, have accompanied the frontier. What the Mediterranean Sea was to the Greeks, breaking the bond of custom, offering new experiences, calling out new institutions and activities, that, and more, the ever retreating frontier has been to the United States directly, and to the nations of Europe more remotely. And now, four centuries from the discovery of America, at the end of a hundred years of life under the Constitution, the frontier has gone, and with its going has closed the first period of American history.

From Morality to Morale

David Riesman

It is a difficult problem to attempt as in this series of lectures to link the psychological understanding of people to specific political and other social phenomena. In his paper Professor Parsons tried to show how individuals play roles in a society and how these roles within a social system may harness various types of personalities. To put it more specifically, you can get the same kind of political behavior, for instance, out of quite different human types. Although the behavior has different meanings for these people, the understanding of their differences and those different meanings may be quite irrelevant to their political and public role.

Nevertheless, and this is the topic of my discourse, it seems to me that personality does influence political behavior if we look at it in a sufficiently long-run historical view. Its influence is felt not in terms of specific behavior —in terms of explaining why somebody votes for Truman or Dewey or Wallace—but only in terms of what I like to call political style, the kind of attitude a person has towards the political cosmos: how he reacts to it, how he feels it reacting to him. If one is to speak as more than a spot-news analyst of political crisis, then he must be concerned with these long-run developments both in politics and personality.

In fact, I think there is a danger for the social scientist if he allows such a phrase as political crisis to make him try to be particularly relevant in talking about spot news, the atom bomb, or what not. Because curiously enough if the social scientist is any good he can't help being relevant. He lives in our society as a participant-observer and it is no problem for him to be relevant—he can't help it. If he isn't any good, and hence irrelevant, he is sometimes likely to compensate by grandiose ambitions; and when he tries to communicate about politics—to solve present crises—he is likely to say more about his own personality than he says about politics, ironically just because he is trying too hard to talk about politics.

That is at least my prologue for taking an excursion in this paper which will go back 100 years in American history. In this way we can take a look at the changes in American character and American political style as developing from the nineteenth century to the present. I know what I have to say is difficult, and I hope that in the discussion period the unanswered ambiguities in what I say can be brought up and threshed out.

Let me first present my dramatis personae. There are two types of character in the cast: one I call the inner-directed type and the other I call the other-directed type. And they orient themselves to the world in two political styles. I call the first, the style of the moralizers, and the second, the style of the inside-dopesters. And the scene on which these moralizers and inside-dopesters play their parts is in the changing power configurations of this country in the last decades. Naturally, the broad outlines of such a drama as this must be tentative, must be experimental.

Let me begin by describing what kind of people the inner-directeds are. In framing my character types, in trying to work with character types which have psychoanalytic depth and also historical relevance, I have focused on the problem of how conformity is assured; what these people conform to; what their society or their group in society expects of them. This, it seems to me, changes over historical time. In the nineteenth century—and still to a great extent in this century—it seems to me that conformity was assured by a mechanism which I call inner-direction, in which a person was socialized in an authoritative family group by impressive and often oppressive parents and in which he internalized his image of these parents. Freud's picture of the superego is a magnificent picture of this type. This was the typical American of the middle class of the last century, the parents and grandparents of most of us today. Some of us could still be called inner-directed.

Now, the inner-directed person is oriented early in childhood towards very clear goals in life. It may be money, fame, power, goodness, or any blend of these. And he is headed for these by the kind of intimate family socialization characteristic of his age. I like to use a metaphor to describe this mechanism. I speak of these people as gyroscopically-steered. The parents install a gyroscope in them and it stabilizes them all their life. They are less independent than they seem because the gyroscope keeps them on the course for which their parents headed them.

What is the kind of society in which such types will live and work? Theirs is a world in which the opening frontiers are the frontiers of production, discovery, science. We might call it the job-minded society—a society in which people are very much aware and interested in the malleability of the physical environment, the organizational environment, and in their social mobility, their ambitions. Their preoccupation is to harness themselves to fulfilling the tasks of the expanding society which needs a large physical plant, extensive social organization, extensive military preparation. In this kind of a job-minded society people are protected from too close resonance with each other by their concentration on these necessary and rewarding tasks.

It does not follow from this that the inner-directed man, concentrated on these tasks, is not concerned with people. People may be means to the ends of his gyroscopically-installed goal—people as voters, workers, soldiers. And he may be a pretty good manipulator of them for these ends. The point that is decisive in distinguishing him from the other-directed man is that he does not need anything from these peoples as ends in themselves. He does not look to them for approval. He does not look to them for warmth. He looks to them for usefulness and in other more specific and more tangible ways.

Obviously I am speaking in terms of contrast, and in order to do so I create what those who have sociological training would recognize as an ideal type—ideal not in the sense of noble, but ideal in the sense of abstract. There is no pure inner-directed man. Most of us are blends. We can make a judgment of the emphasis of these tendencies within given individuals or given social epochs.

In this job-minded society in which people oriented themselves early towards clearly defined goals, young people had clear models to follow. They might be very ambitious and hitch themselves to some star in the ancestral firmament. If they were going to be scientists, they might want to imitate Pasteur; or if painters, they might want to imitate Renoir. They thought in terms of great men. Maybe they thought their parents were great men; and they headed for that. They modeled themselves on these people. This was possible because the personal star developed in this way did not become obsolete but was good for a lifetime. In the case of the personality market, the market on which people sell themselves, there was a fair amount of stability so that a person who decided, when he was very young, that he wanted to be like, let us say, Henry Ford or Abraham Lincoln was not likely to find people calling him quaint by the time he was fifty—because others had gyroscopes too, spinning at about the same pace, moving in the same direction. People who had this type of character found themselves on the whole rewarded, found their lives unproblematical in the sense of concern with whether they fitted or not. To put the matter more generally, there was a certain fit between social structure and character structure.

Having said this, I think I have to stop at once and suggest that one should not get nostalgic about "life with father." As a play it may be amusing; but if he is your father, if he has hurt you, that may be a different matter. I think this nostalgia is actually an important social and political force in our time, and I want to come back to it later on.

Let me now introduce the next person in the dramatis personae, the other-directed. A new source of conformity is required, it seems to me, for the urban upper middle class in our big cities, a conformity for which gyroscopic adaption is not sufficiently flexible, not sufficiently resonant with other people. And for this new source of conformity I like to use the metaphor of the radar set. The other-directed child has a radar set installed, by which he can understand the interpersonal environment and see its signals around him. He is oriented very early in life, not to his ancestors, not to his parents or to his image of their exalted selves, but to his peers; that is, the other kids on the block, the other kids at school, the people who will do a great deal of the job of socializing him. In fact, those who are familiar with the work of Harry Stack Sullivan can see that he has become in a sense the analyst of this age because he was the person above all others who called attention to the importance of the peer group in the process of socialization.

One can see that the parents play a hand in this by their concern with whether the child is popular, how he is getting along with the other kids. One can see that the school also is concerned today more with morale than with morality—concerned with the social atmosphere. I speak now obviously of the progressive schools in the suburban and urban areas where the other-directed as a character type is emerging. The school puts a youngster in with the five-year-olds to see if he fits with the five-year-olds, not in terms of how much he knows, but in terms of how he gets along. And the parents are anxious and judge their success with their children by how the children get along, how popular they are; the parents act as chauffeurs and managers for the continuous stage performance of their children in the peer group.

It is important to see what the radar brings to the other-directed child. It brings direction; it brings a sense of what is worth having in life, what is worth experiencing, what is worth talking about, thinking about. And the goals obviously change with what the radar senses rather than being set for a lifetime as in the earlier epoch. Obviously I don't mean to imply that parents set about consciously to create little paragons who will fit into the society of 1950 or 1960 or 1970. They aren't that calculating, even if they would like to be. It is a long and complicated story and one, I am sure, many social investigators have worked on and thought about: how it happens that the parents, without actually being consciously aware of their role in this process, produce the children whom the next society makes use of. It is a story I cannot go into here. But I want to remark on just one of the changes from inner-direction to other-direction which might be called the change from bringing up children to bringing up father, for children may bring up parents in the other-directed society.

I think one might recognize, if he is interested in historical questions, that this does not sound so new. Perhaps the other-directed American is in a way the American as he appeared to the eyes of 150 years of European observation. The European always thought that the American was a person who cared more for what his fellows thought than anything else, that the American was more concerned with indiscriminate approval and with warmth, more dependent on his neighbors than the European was—or at least more than the European who came to America to look around. And certainly there is very much in the way of social change and so on which helps to explain why it is we have a comic strip called "Bringing Up Father" in which the daughter as well as the mother cooperates.

Now, what is the kind of society in which the other-directed person moves? For him the frontiers are not the frontiers of production but the frontiers of consumption, the frontiers of much more abundant leisure and consumer goods. He moves in a society where—at least in his picture of it —the main productive job is done. The steel mills are built, the railroads are built, the mines are dug, the government organizations are set up. And his concern is to live as a consumer. Those who may be economists can recognize the touch of Keynesian economics in that. But I want to make clear that I am not talking about conspicuous consumption—I am not talking about keeping up with the Joneses. That is an older, perhaps a traditional pattern. As long as one is concerned only with what goods he is getting out of the society, out of its physical productiveness, he is still inner-directed. A person is other-directed only when his interest is not in the goods—he takes those for granted. After all, the middle-class family can have a car, a mink coat, good food, and so on. Consumption itself is no issue for most of these people. The problem for the other-directed person is not the goods themselves, but the right attitudes about the goods. Is he having the right experiences vis-à-vis the wine he drinks, the car he drives, the girl he sleeps with, and so on? That is the problem. And he looks to others for guidance as to whether he is experiencing the right experiences on the frontiers of consumption. He takes more or less for granted that he has the wherewithal, the ability to pay unremittingly to provide himself with the goods themselves.

This is another way of saying that in America we have moved from a job-minded society to a people-minded society in which one's concern is no longer with the malleability of the materiel but with the malleability of the personnel. It is a society in which people are no longer protected from each other by the objectivity of their workaday tasks and in which response from others becomes an end in life as well as a means.

In fact, I think it is quite interesting to look at specific individuals and see to what extent they may rationalize their need for warmth, their need for approval from others, in terms of, let us say, some sensible and easily rationalized goal such as money or security.

Think of Willy Loman, in the play, *Death of a Salesman*, as a man who looked to selling, not primarily for money—that too—but as a source of affection, a means of justifying himself, a *Weltanschauung*—all these things wrapped up in the job of the salesman. Incidentally, the play seemed quite incomprehensible to Londoners. They couldn't understand why anybody was that interested in selling and why people responded in terms other than cash. The English response showed that they didn't understand Americans. Obviously in such a society the old clear goals of ambition, the old stars of the heavenly firmament by which the inner-directed man guided himself no longer guide people.

Let me give an illustration. There was an interview with a thirteen-year-old girl about her comic-reading habits. She was asked what comics she preferred and she said Superman. Then she was asked why. "Oh, Superman can fly," she said, "and flying is very important." "Would you like to be able to fly?" the interviewer asked. "Oh, no, that would be kind of conspicuous," the girl said. Here one sees the fear of being conspicuous, the fear of being too ambitious, the fear somebody might say, "So you think you're big—so you think you're something." These are the fears which make it hard for people brought up in other-directed circles to have the same kind of sometimes fanatical and crushing ambition which was a characteristic of the middle-class man of an earlier epoch, a characteristic which still hangs on in this country because—obviously I am talking about trends—there are still men like Henry Ford.

I am talking about something that the investigator finds more among the young than the old, more in the upper middle class in the very large metropolitan areas than in the smaller cities and smaller towns. And this seems to me to be connected in subtle ways with the alteration of mobility channels. One no longer gets ahead in the society by making a better mousetrap but by packaging an old mousetrap in a new way and selling it by selling one's self first.

Those who know Erich Fromm's book *Man for Himself* will recognize the similarity of his marketing orientation to what I call the other-directed man. The man of the marketing orientation is concerned with how he is doing on the personality market of the large corporate enterprises, private, public, academic, and what not, of our society. And in order to succeed on the personality market he must be different but not too different; as different as Ford from Chevrolet—maybe as far different as Studebaker from Ford. And so he must always use his radar to find out: "Am I different enough to be recognized—to have a brand name, so to speak, for my personality—but not so different that I will be priced out of the market as an eccentric?" But even eccentricity can be made to pay in the right professions. Success comes in our society increasingly, it seems to me, through a person's ability to be malleable enough to fit into a cooperative network.

Adam Smith used the phrase "the invisible hand" to describe the economic organization of the free market. I think we have moved from the invisible hand to the glad hand and that today people in industry and the professions—particularly in medicine—are engaged in a cooperative network in which the esteem of colleagues is decisive for one's fate and in which to be known as a rate-buster would exclude one from the system. To be sure, there are survivals of the older age, but I am talking of the social character that seems to me to be emerging.

Let me now turn to the question of the political styles which seem to me in a rather indeterminate way to spring from these respective types of character. Yet first of all it must be recognized that the majority of Americans have no distinctive political style at all. There is very little traceable connection, it seems to me, between their character and their politics. Their politics depends on their situation, as I said at the outset, and not on their personality. Let me give an illustration.

If one takes a look at the book called *Southern Politics*, he will see that Professor Key interprets southern politics in America today as being dominated by what he calls the black-belt whites, the whites who live in the counties of large Negro predominance, and that their influence is, to a degree, based on the southern electoral systems as these have been inherited in several southern states. Now here is a situation in which—in order to understand this kind of southern politics—it would do very little good to interpret in idiosyncratic terms the character structure of the black-belt whites. To be sure, the fact that they are black-belt whites will reveal something about their character structure. But the situation and the electoral machinery in which the populace is caught matters much more than their character. Consequently, when I speak of style, I speak here only of those people in whom one can trace a connection between politics and character, and this limits me to those who are politically active either as political leaders and operators or as avid consumers of the political news of the day.

The first style I shall describe is the style of the moralizer—the political manifestation of inner-direction. However, not all inner-directed people are involved in politics; and they are not inevitably moralizers. Rather, this is the style which is politically compatible with their character. Their character gives them a slight push in the direction of being moralizers.

The moralizer is a person who views politics as a field of work and not primarily as a field of entertainment or consumption. To be sure, in the nineteenth century when the moralizer was in his heyday, there were torchlight parades, and politics was not entirely unamusing and unsportive. But on the whole politics was a field of work or, as many businessmen thought, interference with work. It was judged from the standpoint of work, from the standpoint of the harnessing of the resources of the society. The moralizer would never have attended a lecture with a title of *Personality and Political Crisis*. He would not have known what it meant, because for him politics stayed in its limited place. He thought of it in terms of government institutions, electoral machinery, and so on. Because he defined politics in a limited way, it helped him to view politics as a manageable domain—small, encompassable, not too complicated. And correlatively his own relation to it was uncomplicated because he knew what he wanted. Because his goals were clear, he could decide where in politics his interests lay, either in terms of self-interest, or the interest of his group, his nation, or his god. The moralizer, by defining politics in a limited way, by defining his relationship to it in terms of a clear picture of his self-interest—often mistaken, but clear—did not feel overwhelmed. So many people today feel overwhelmed by politics, but to the moralizer, politics was masterable, was graspable. One had a vision—if one were inner-directed and a moralizer—of what was good work, what was a good political performance, and what was a bad political performance; and one could relate politics to these definitions.

The term moralizer is a little misleading in this connection. I don't mean that the moralizer was necessarily a moral man in the sense of having high morality or ethics. Rather, he was a person who clearly defined his relation to the political world, and since the discourse in this country in the nineteenth century was largely moralistic, he didn't have too much trouble in defending, let us say, a log-rolling job in moral terms.

But we must also think of the nineteenth century as a period in which enormous moralizing energies were harnessed in the political scene. To expand the school system, to do something about prisons and the insane, to free the slaves—all these issues provided a moralistic frame of reference in which people could take clear positions and feel relatively unfloundering in a narrowly-defined political ocean.

But this statement is an oversimplification of the nineteenth century. How much of an oversimplification? We can remind ourselves if we take a look at a very, as I think, exciting passage from Tocqueville who came over and took an unequalled brilliant look at this country in the 1830's. He wrote:

> It is difficult to say what place is taken up in the life of an inhabitant of the United States by his concern for politics. To take a hand in the regulation of society and to discuss it is his biggest concern and, so to speak, the only pleasure an American knows. In some countries the inhabitants seem unwilling to avail themselves of the political privileges which the law gives them. It would seem that they set too high a value on their time to spend it on the interests of the community. But if an American were condemned to confine his activities to his own affairs, he would be robbed of one half of his existence. He would feel an immense void in the life he is accustomed to lead. His wretchedness would be unbearable.

One can see by this quotation some of the ambiguities of the use of politics as an agenda, as a way to get through the day, as a way to harness one's self in the nineteenth century.

It is awfully hard to say where the nineteenth-century American stood. Think of the people up in the State of Vermont who thought the country was engulfed in a masonic conspiracy. Think of the people who thought that Phi Beta Kappa was a subversive organization. But on the whole the moralizer's picture of the world was a pretty clear picture, and the Know-Nothing and so on of that day was rather the forerunner of what I like to call the bewildered moralizer of today—the person whose world has vanished and who turns into a curdled indignant when he contemplates the political scene. He no longer understands it—politics refuses to fit into its narrow compartments. Much of the outcry against the welfare state and so on comes from people who say, "Politics ought to stay where I put it." And it won't stay. Then the self-interest of a person no longer seems clear.

What way does self-interest lie today in politics? What way does morality lie?

While the conflict between public and private moralities is an old one, the network of publics to be considered makes the discussion of moral issues today ever more complicated, ambiguous, and equivocal. The bewildered moralizer, the curdled indignant, reacts negatively to this. The world doesn't make sense to him. And one thing that facilitates this development is the fact that he lives in a society increasingly other-directed, in which the mass media of communication bombard him with messages which he can't understand.

What is the small-town curdled indignant to make of Billy Rose's accounts of love and life at Lindy's? What is he to do about network radio, about the sophisticated pace of A-budget movies? He can't follow them. But there is one place where he can follow. He can follow politics because he can make politics obey him. The editoral writer, the political campaigner appeal to the curdled indignant with an old familiar tune. They tell him that after all his world would make sense if only a few bad people, these smooth city slickers, these other-directed men, were to be thrown out. Then the world would go back to where it could be run by the invisible hand.

This brings me to the inside-dopester, the political manifestation of the other-directed. He is socialized in a setting where he can't be too conspicuous, where he learns to hold his emotional fire, and where he learns to bring certain skills to bear which are chiefly skills of consumption, skills of the consumer.

A short time ago I was talking with some friends of mine who have two children, aged four and five. They told me the children could look at the cars in the street and tell which is a '50 Pontiac and which is a '49 Oldsmobile. As very young children they have become members of the consumers' union. And when they become a little bit older, they bring this consumers'-union skill to bear on politics. They may bring it to bear in one of two ways. First, the inside-dopester may try to manipulate others, in which case he will interpret politics as a problem of being able to get the right man on the telephone. But if he is less close to the switchboard, if he is less close to the politically-operative group, then he is likely not to be able to manipulate others. In this case he will choose the second way: he will harness his manipulative energies solely to himself, in order to make sure that he has the right reactions to the political news.

Many people have doubtless observed, if they have been in government service—or indeed anywhere—that politics is a form of office gossip in which to have the right reaction is all that is required of one. The goal of the inside-dopester is never to be taken in by any person, cause, or event; that is, to be a sharp member of the consumers' union. It is interesting to trace these developments, even in radical left-wing politics. A generation ago the young Communist, for instance, had to have a working knowledge of Marxism, had to be able to handle the dialectic, had to make noises like a Marxist. Today all he has to do is know how to get Marcantonio elected. It is no longer necessary for him to be able to have a stance on principle, at least in the political scene.

I think one can say in general that the inside-dopester sees politics as a field of mood engineering. Sometimes the only moods he can engineer are his own and those of his small peerage. At other times he can try to engineer the mood of a nation. This is his way of coping with the growing complexity of politics, the complexity which no longer submits to the simplifications of the moralizer.

One other way of tracing this development is to ask one's self: In any social setting, who are the people who make a living by scaring businessmen or government officials? In the nineteenth century the people who made the best living in this way were lawyers, and they frightened businessmen and government officials about their standing with two very limited publics—judges and legislators. The scare was not great because often the judges and legislators could be managed for cash on the barrelhead. In this rather simple picture the businessman might be a little frightened by the pictures his lawyer drew for him, but after all he knew what the lawyer was describing; and the lawyer himself was a fellow who knew the institutional structure, knew how to talk to judges and legislators.

Today it is my impression that the dependence of the lawyer has lessened and it is the contact man who frightens businessmen and government officials about a whole range of publics which are as likely to disappear on inspection as did the Cheshire cat. These are all those publics who may say nasty things about the businessman, if, for instance, he does not do the right thing or make the right public-relations move. In this amorphous sea of contacts the businessman no longer knows what his interests are and he has to ask his public-relations advisor not only what publics to propitiate but what interest he has in propitiating them. Of course, this work may still be done by lawyers—that is, members of the bar who have not had this attitude trained out of them by their education.

It may be said, in fact, that whereas the moralizer's gullibility about politics was often based on limiting his definition of politics, the inside-dopester's gullibility about politics is often based on the delusion, basic to his whole character and basic to his attitude, that there is somebody somewhere—maybe Kiplinger, maybe the people who write the Newsweek "Periscope," maybe a private eye of some sort—who sees all and knows all. But actually—and this is part of the ambiguous development of our society—the inside-dopester *does* know more than the moralizer. He is better informed; his range is wider; he is able to see both sides. There are very few innocents left to go fight city hall.

Another facet in this development which has moved us from morality to morale is the necessity of the political consumer today to be ready for rapid changes of line. His political attitude, his political style might be obsolete in a moment if he did not have his radar set in good working order. And this is part of the increasingly fast pace with which our society makes obsolete automobiles, people, and ideas. One interesting way of tracing this empirically —of course in a very tentative way—is to study public opinion polls. And there we see, interestingly enough, that the middle class—that is, the group in which these tendencies are far more manifest than in the working class— shifts its political attitudes much more rapidly and readily. It is true about their opinion on the last war and on Russia.

I have been struck by Machiavelli's observation—contrary to all the political observers of his day and many since—that the masses are far less fickle than the rulers. And I think public opinion polls show this to be true. "Fickle" may be the wrong word, too biased a word, because the readiness of the middle class for rapid changes of line is connected with the actual changes in the situation; with the greater reality-orientation vis-à-vis politics which many inside-dopesters have.

The problem is that the inside-dopester's motive for political consumption, for political operation, is not to secure a reality-orientation. For him politics is a means of group conformity, if he lives in a group where it is fashionable to be up on the political news of the day. In other groups (and, to a degree, in the same group) one might be up on the sporting news.

These are the compelling motivations that keep the inside-dopester political in spite of the evaporation of his political emotions. It is an interesting problem: the inside-dopester is a person who is not committed, who does not bring to politics a clear notion of his own self-interest or clear principles—yet he follows politics. I think he follows politics because he lives in a group which follows politics. Then one might ask, why does the group follow politics? This is a question that I cannot get into here. I would just mention one paradox. Where the group to which the inside-dopester belongs is a moralizing group, he will look like a moralizer, sound like a moralizer, feel himself to be a moralizer.

I want to get into a more fundamental paradox; namely, the fact that the word "morale" conceals a moral judgment. I think we in the Western society have changed our style in hypocrisy. The Victorian hypocrite was a person who concealed bad actions under the high-sounding cloak of good ones. But ever since Freud and a number of other people, the hypocrite has concealed his good actions under the cloak of solid self-interest. This hypocrisy makes it possible to disguise, under such a term as morale, one's morality.

A student working with me has been doing a number of interviews in the community outside Chicago called Park Forest, a newly-developing suburb which has been built by the American Community Builders, a large real estate operation. This student went out there in the early days of this development and he asked people what they thought about the American Community Builders, what they thought about their community, and what their political attitudes were. Many had grievances about their homes, lawns, roads, and so on. But from many of those people with grievances he got this answer: "The American Community Builders has bad public relations." They emphasized no grievance as much as that. What does that mean if you try to analyze it for latent meaning? The respondent seems to be saying: "The trouble with the stupid people who run this town is that they haven't made me like it." Or he might not even be saying that. He may be saying: "They haven't made those other fellows like it." He conceals any judgment based on principle, on his own experience, on his own life, under the cover of the bad mechanics, the poor mood engineering on the part of the operators.

I will cite another illustration. Some of my associates and I did some interviews before the last election. We asked people about the candidates. And we found many people who said, "Well, Truman is sincere and Dewey is insincere." We tried to think what that meant. Why did they use this word? And I was reminded of the fact that in doing interviews on popular music a student came across the same expression. He played a record for people and then asked, "Well, did you like the record?" "Oh, yes, I like Dinah Shore. She's so sincere." Or, "I like Frank Sinatra. He's so sincere." What does this judgment mean? I don't know all the answers to that question. I think we would understand a lot if we knew. I have some hunches about it. I think for one thing this judgment on the basis of sincerity is a moral judgment; that is, "This man can manipulate me because he involves himself in his performance. He sends me. And I allow him to send me because he is sending himself too." But there is more to it than that. This is a judgment in terms of personality—at least in the field of politics and I think also in the field of popular music—and it is not one of personality only. Using the criterion of sincerity may be an avoidance of the judgment of performance. Is Dinah Shore a good singer? Has she got the right vocal equipment? Is the political candidate able to deliver? Judgment on the basis of answers to these questions is ducked by focusing on an issue of mood which in many political situations is of little importance. If the moralizer thought that he wanted a government of laws and not of men, the inside-dopester thinks he wants a government of men and not of laws. Both have unattainable ideals.

I have said that there were concealed moral judgments—repressed morality—in the reaction of the inside-dopester. The psychiatrist knows, I think, that people often end up being what they play at being. And since the inside-dopester has given up trying to find out what he wants in politics, he is more and more apt to tolerate what is wanted of him, provided it is put in a nice way.

I want to turn now to the stage on which these characters play, and ask what are the changes in the political configuration of this country that may evoke and reward either inner-directed or other-directed tendencies within people—thus, in turn, encouraging or repressing one or another political style. In my opinion it is of decisive importance both for political style and for character that we no longer have a clear social-class hierarchy in America.

Let me put the problem this way. Who runs the country? This was a relatively easy question to answer in 1896. The people like Morgan were at the top of the prestige ladder; they were models for ambitious youth, whether in the Horatio Alger stories or in the *Saturday Evening Post*. They were the focus of attention. These were the captains of industry, and they dominated the country fifty years ago.

Who runs the country today? It's a hard question. Who ranks whom at a dinner party? Is an Army colonel superior to a doctor at the Washington School of Psychiatry? How about a college professor, the head of an oil company, the head of a big advertising agency, Jack Benny? Which way is up? Who are the models for youth? The answer to these questions as stated in the mass media—see the brilliant study made by Leo Lowenthal of the popular magazines, *Saturday Evening Post* and *Colliers*—is that the focus of attention is no longer on the captains of industry but on what I like to call the captains of nonindustry: a Hollywood star, a golf pro, a cafe-society boy. Take a look at the men-of-distinction ads and tell me who runs the country!

It seems to me that what we have today is a situation in which the older hierarchy has crumbled and has been replaced by a lot of smaller hierarchies which I like to call the veto groups; that is, the lobbies. And whereas the political leader in 1896 had a clear relationship to his public, the political leader today is found within the lobby, within the Farm Bureau, the trade associations, the American Jewish Congress, the American Medical Association, and so on, endlessly. They are veto groups because they have a much better opportunity to stop action than to start it. Their concern is chiefly with prevention. But with this change in hierarchy comes a change in the type of attitude one has to have to operate in politics and understand politics. The lobbyist within one of these veto groups is concerned with the veto subgroups within his own group down to the last veto group of one. It may be a recalcitrant farmer who will not conform with the Farm Bureau's policies. It may be a recalcitrant who holds out on the union leader. And when the lobbyist is operating with other co-equals who are heads of other veto groups his concern is that each of them has a "reasonable" and just slightly expanding cut of the political pie. In today's politics there are a great many ins and very few outs. And the leader, therefore, in the older sense is virtually disappearing. What we see instead as the so-called leader is either the man who can placate the veto groups and operate within this framework of coalitions—as Roosevelt did so capably—or the man who tries to deal with the few unorganized wretches who have not yet invented their group. But obviously this leads to a situation in which there is a constant elaboration of the publics with which leaders are concerned. The need to see and propitiate these publics can be rationalized in terms of public relations.

One sees a very interesting thing in the discussion of the atom bomb and the hydrogen bomb today which I might put in terms of the old cartoon "Who's excited?" Everybody is concerned with everybody else's mood and asking that question in regard to all these various publics, whether or not these publics have any actual power to affect the course of events. In fact, actual ignorance of who has power is in some ways an asset if one is to be a veto-group leader because it permits one to propitiate still other publics in terms of the fact that they might have power. Let me give an illustration: If a college professor writes a book attacking business, he makes a lot of jobs for his students in the business world, for business must answer him. The businessmen want to be told that there are some people who don't like them and whom they need to propitiate, whether or not the professor's book sells any copies or has any weight.

In this situation of complex and tenuous interpersonal webs within the lobbies and among the lobbies, obviously it takes a man with the gifts and the social skills more nearly like those of the inside-dopester to get along rather than those skills associated with the moralizer. Thus the skills of the inside-dopester are in demand.

Of course, many people still assume we have a ruling class in this country. But I think one of the reasons they assume this is that they need to justify their own propitiation. They can't tell themselves that they need to be liked; therefore they have to assume somebody has power. I think another reason, perhaps more basic, is the feeling of discomfort if there is nobody in charge. Everyone likes to think that there is someone in charge, even if the person in charge does not represent him.

Plainly, these emotional ideas of the inside-dopester are not the only ones current in politics. I have left aside for a moment the curdled indignant —the bewildered moralizer who feels that the world doesn't make sense to him. Mood engineering on the part of the inside-dopester is a red flag to the curdled indignant. What the latter responds to is the appearance of impiety, violence, on the part of a Pegler or the *New York Daily News* or Branch Rickey; that is, the very mood engineering which the inside-dopester attempts as a way of propitiating publics may be just the thing which makes the curdled indignant feel most bewildered and most angry. So he falls back, as I indicated earlier, to a more familiar style, a style of the *political* indignant, of the leader who is able to say: "There are a few bad men around and all we have to do is get rid of them." But even the other-directed man, just because he doesn't know what he wants, just because of his concern with the plethora of publics, has a tendency to call on older types when the going gets rough. When the glad hand is rebuffed, the inside-dopester may even wish *not* to reach an agreement, whereas earlier he would have given anything for someone to say: "Let's agree to disagree." So it is that the inside-dopester is in some ways unfit for conflict. In fact, "conflict" is a word he avoids. He prefers the words "tension," "low morale," or "poor communications."

All this may delay the triumph of morale over morality. But little hope lies in that delay. I think it should be clear, from what I have said, that neither the style of the moralizer nor the style of the inside-dopester is adequate to politics. The former sees politics in too limited a context. And the latter fails to bring to politics the very humanity which would let him react as a human being; as a result, he often fails to see the potentialities which lie underneath the "reality" to which he is so passionately attached.

Now we might ask, What changes in American political structure and what changes in American character structure might bring new motives into play in the political arena and thus reward the development of a more mature political style?

People today are asked to participate and involve themselves in politics for motives that seem to me inadequate. They are asked to involve themselves by appeals to self-interest—as if we were still living in the days of the moralizers when everyone knew what his interests were. They are asked to involve themselves by appeals to group conformity—often snob appeals to be active politically and belong to the PTA or the DAR or what not. Or they are appealed to on behalf of a Sincere Candidate who will decide all the questions for them.

It is probably not possible to decide how to appeal to other motivations and get results. But at least it is necessary to raise the question of whether the trouble lies always with the people, or whether it might not be found in the politics. Is the American political scene so dull or uninteresting that there is no reason why people should be interested for good motives? Might it not make more sense to improve the political wares that are offered to the American people, rather than to spend energy on asking Americans to participate in, to be concerned about, to be less apathetic about politics? Are there not other political packages that Americans can buy?

I think that a beginning can be made on this problem by concentrating on evoking more political imagination. Why not indicate more alternatives to the American people, especially in the domestic scene? For instance, it might be pointed out that there is a wider range of choice in the kinds of lives people might lead, if they wished. But this is only possible if in such an attempt a more experimental attitude is assumed: Americans need not always be satisfied with denouncing the political show, as curdled indignants;

or with trying to alter the mood of the show or their own mood towards it, as inside-dopesters.

SUGGESTIONS FOR FURTHER READING

David Riesman's evidence for a changing American character may be followed in more detail in his *The Lonely Crowd (New Haven, 1961). Henry Steele Commager finds a significant change in the American character in his *The American Mind (New Haven, 1950). Vance Packard argues that the American character is changing because of our great wealth in *The Waste Makers (New York, 1963).

Alexis de Tocqueville studied Americans during his visit in 1831–32. His report, *Democracy in America (in numerous editions), described an American character which seems very much up to date today. As Turner found the westward movement, and Potter, the availability of wealth, to be experiences which all Americans shared, de Tocqueville found the democratic experience to be that which Americans shared and which consequently shaped their character. Numerous other visitors to our shores attempted to describe the American they met. A convenient collection is Henry Steele Commager, *America in Perspective (New York, 1947).

A valuable study reviewing the evidence relating to the question of a changing American character is Clyde Kluckhohn, "Have There Been Discernible Shifts in American Values during the Past Generation?" in Elting E. Morrison, ed., The American Style (New York, 1958), pp. 145–217. Michael McGiffert has brought together a collection of readings on the question of American character and has also assembled a full bibliography in *The Character of Americans (Homewood, Ill., 1964).

On the question of violence in American life, see Richard Hofstadter and Michael Wallace, eds., *American Violence: A Documentary History (New York, 1970); Thomas Rose, ed., *Violence in America (New York, 1969); Hugh Davis Graham and Ted Robert Gurr, *The History of Violence in America (The Report to the National Commission on the Causes and Prevention of Violence) (New York, 1969).

* Available in paperback edition.